中国林业学术论坛

•

森林经理研究文库

森林可持续经营研究

2011

中国林学会森林经理分会 编

中国林业出版社

图书在版编目（CIP）数据

森林可持续经营研究. 2011/中国林学会森林经理分会编 . —北京：中国林业出版社，2012. 9

ISBN 978-7-5038-6658-6

Ⅰ. ①森… Ⅱ. ①中… Ⅲ. ①森林经营 - 可持续发展 - 中国 - 文集 Ⅳ. ①F326. 2-53 ②S750-53

中国版本图书馆 CIP 数据核字（2012）第 144376 号

出版 中国林业出版社（100009 北京西城区刘海胡同 7 号）
E-mail forestbook@163. com 电话 010 - 83222880
网址 http：//lycb. forestry. gov. cn
发行 中国林业出版社
印刷 北京北林印刷厂
版次 2012 年 9 月第 1 版
印次 2012 年 9 月第 1 次
开本 787mm × 1092mm 1/16
印张 30
字数 717 千字
印数 1 ~ 1000 册
定价 89. 00 元

《森林可持续经营研究（2011）》

编　委　会

前　言

2011 年 10 月 9 日，由中国林学会森林经理分会和北京林业大学主办，由国家林业局调查规划设计院、北京林业大学森林经营管理学科、北京林业大学教育基金会和《行动 CSR》杂志社（融创传播机构）共同承办的全国森林可持续经营学术研讨会暨董乃钧林人奖励基金成立大会在北京隆重召开。全国政协副主席罗富和发来贺电。原林业部副部长、中国林学会森林分会名誉理事长刘于鹤研究员，中国科学院院士、中国林科院首席科学家唐守正研究员，北京林业大学校长宋维明教授，国家林业局森林资源管理司巡视员、中国林学会森林经理分会理事长李忠平教授，国家林业局森林资源管理司副司长徐济德同志等专家领导出席大会并致辞。董乃钧先生家属代表、董乃钧林人奖励基金发起方出席会议并发表感言。全国林业系统 50 多个教学、科研、生产单位的专家领导代表 100 多人，人民日报（海外版）、新华社、中国绿色时报等 20 多家媒体代表参加了大会。本次会议共有 17 名学者专家做了关于促进我国森林可持续经营的高水平学术报告和纪念董乃钧先生的报告。

全国政协副主席罗富和在贺信中指出：董乃钧先生是我国著名林学家、林业教育家，是中国森林经理学科的主要开拓者，也是我国林业信息化事业的重要创始人，培养了大批优秀的林业事业建设者和接班人。他毕生致力于建设有中国特色的森林可持续经营管理体系，在推动我国林业走向现代化、信息化等方面做出了巨大贡献。我国林业和森林资源经营管理事业的发展，是千万个像董乃钧先生那样勤奋工作的林业人努力的结果，需要后有来人。“董乃钧林人奖励基金”的成立，将会激励我国的广大林业工作者扎根基层，努力工作与学习，用实际行动把董乃钧先生未尽的林业事业不断推向前进，促进我国林业早日实现信息化、现代化，进入世界发达林业国家行列，为促进林农致富、应对气候变化、维护国家生态安全等做出更大的贡献！

原林业部副部长、中国林学会森林经理分会名誉理事长刘于鹤在致辞中表示，成立"董乃钧林人奖励基金"和举办"全国森林可持续经营学术研讨会"是我们缅怀著名林学家董先生、继承董先生遗志的好方式。今天设立的"董乃钧林人奖励基金"是我国森林可持续经营管理事业的一个崭新的里程碑，这将激励我国广大林业工作者爱岗敬业，开拓进取，开创我国林业事业的新局面，为国家社会经济可持续发展和应对全球气候变化做出新的贡献。

中国科学院院士、中国林学会森林经理分会名誉理事长唐守正指出：森林经营是林业永恒的主题，森林经营管理学科是森林经营的龙头学科，董乃钧先生为森林可持续经营和学科建设做出了重大贡献，作为他的学生和同事，我们要缅怀董乃钧先生，为中国森林可持续经营努力奋斗。

北京林业大学校长宋维明指出：今天我们相聚北京，举办森林可持续经营学术研讨会，成立董乃钧林人奖励基金，共同缅怀我们的良师益友董乃钧先生。董先生是全国著名林学家，是我国德高望重的林业教育大师，是北京林业大学的杰出代表。董先生的逝世，是我国林业界的巨大损失，更是北京林业大学的重大损失。我们全校师生要化悲痛为力量，发扬董先生开拓创新、为人师表的精神，继承董先生的遗愿，加强学风和校风建设，努力把北京林业大学建成国内一流、国际知名的研究型大学。

中国林学会森林经理分会理事长李忠平和国家林业局资源司副司长徐济德指出：董乃钧先生是我国森林经营管理领域的领军人物，他为我国森林经营管理及林业建设事业培养了大批优秀人才。我们今天在此隆重集会，就是为了更好地发扬董先生的精神，继承董先生的遗愿，切实推进我国森林经营管理工作，提高森林经营的综合效益，逐步把我国林业事业推向国际领先行列。

北京林业大学教育基金会秘书长王平指出：成立“董乃钧林人奖励基金”的目的是，要奖励继承董乃钧先生遗志、在我国森林可持续经营管理及林业建设中做出突出贡献的优秀林业工作者和优秀林业大学生，激励广大林人努力拼搏，切实推进我国的森林可持续经营管理工作，促进林业可持续发展，造福中华民族和世界人民。为使“董乃钧林人奖励基金”的资金得到安全、合法的管理，保证基金的可持续发展，促进基金规模的不断壮大，该基金将由北京林业大学教育基金会按照国务院《基金会管理条例》和北京林业大学教育基金会相关管理办法进行规范管理，并接受各方监督和相关部门审计，确保资金监管到位，捐款利用高效，综合效益显著。

董先生之女董小捷发表了感言：父亲是好丈夫，父亲是好父亲，父亲是好老师，父亲是好学者。父亲以其洁身自好、淡薄名利，勤俭节省、多才多艺，刻苦好学、诲人不倦，平易近人、先人后己的高贵品行，赢得了业内人士的公认，被誉为德高望重的一代宗师。纵观父亲一生，是勤奋的一生，是多彩的一生，是我们家人的楷模，更是我们家族的骄傲。父亲是多么希望国家林业行业有朝一日能够遥遥领先于世界，为此他奉献了一生，留给我们不可多得的宝贵财富，更留下了我们对他深深的怀念！

董乃钧林人奖励基金由北京林业大学森林经营管理学科、山东东营三明林业发展股份有限公司、四川博源生态林业开发有限公司、北京地林伟业信息技术有限责任公司四家单位联合发起设立。该基金已获得三家企业捐资人民币460万元。

董乃钧先生是我国杰出的林业战略家和林业教育家，是我国森林经营管理事业的主要开拓者和林业信息化事业的重要创始人，他为学科的建设和林业教育事业奉献了毕生的心血并做出了巨大的贡献。他翻译出版了《森林计测学》，参与编写了《森林调查手册》，提出建立全国森林资源连续清查体系和森林分层抽样等调查技术，牵头编写并审定了全国林业院校林学专业主干课程《森林资源经营管理学》教材，为全国林业系统培养了一大批业务骨干。董乃钧先生凭着开拓创新、锐意进取的精神，善于用系统科学进行战略思考，在森林可持续经营管理、林业跨越式发展、林权制度改革、林业政策等诸多方面取得了一系列有影响力的重大成果，为国家现代林业建设做出了积极的贡献。直到生命的尽头，董先生还惦记着学科的建设，提出许多有关学科建设的宝贵建议。董先生是我们做人、做事、做学问的楷模。森林经理分会为有董先生这样的大师而自豪！我们将继承董先生遗愿，把董先生未尽的森林可持续经营事业不断推向新的水平。

本次研讨会共征集论文和纪念文章66篇，为交流和共享学术成果，进一步推进我国森林可持续经营工作，现将这次研讨会论文编辑成册，正式出版，以飨读者。疏漏之处，敬请批评指正。

中国林学会森林经理分会
北京林业大学
2012年5月3日

目　录

一、应用研究

Monitoring and Forecasting the Forest Dynamic Evolution Based on GIS Technology
…… Gu Li　Zheng Xiao-xian　Gong Zhi-wen (3)
Aboveground Forest Biomass Estimation using ICESat/GLAS and Optical Remote Sensing Data in Yunnan Province, China
…… HUANG Ke-biao　PANG Yong　SHU Qing-tai (9)
森林经理学理论研究之我见 …… 张昂和 (20)
兼顾碳贮量和木材生产目标的森林经营规划研究
…… 戎建涛　雷相东　张会儒　冯启祥 (34)
天然商品林生态效益补偿的 Logistic 模型分析 …… 马志波　黄清麟　Ma Hwan OK (48)
同心圆样地抽样方法在天然阔叶林调查中的应用研究
…… 黄清麟　戎建涛　张晓红　马志波 (58)
江西省杉木大径材经营模式研究 …… 杨馥宁　郑小贤 (63)
广义 Brink 干形方程的适应性扩展 …… 聂秀琴　李　昀　陆道调 (70)
不同立地条件下白桦生长规律的研究 … 刘相兵　王典娜　闫　菁　原民龙　黄选瑞 (77)
高光谱遥感竹资源专题信息提取技术研究 …… 刘　健　余坤勇　缪丽娟　游浩辰 (86)
北京市长城地区森林资源信息系统 …… 沈　林　杨　华　邓华锋 (96)
金沟岭林场杨桦次生林演替与天然更新研究
…… 赵　娜　刘东兰　郑小贤　高　祥　徐　光 (102)
北京市延庆县集体林分地上部分生物量的研究 …… 张晓璇 (109)
不同坡位华北落叶松人工林生长规律研究
…… 闫　菁　姜　涛　原民龙　于树峰　黄选瑞 (116)
长沙市城市森林社会功能与城市梯度相关分析 …… 周晓芳　吕　勇 (124)

桂林后龙山风水林文化现状及承传研究 …………………… 刘代汉 何新凤 蒋家安（132）
巨尾桉纸浆原料林资产评估技术研究 …………… 吕 勇 何 龙 张 震 边更战（138）
磨盘山天然次生林群落早春植物多样性研究 ………………………………………… 于 健（148）
森林生物量估算方法及模型研究 …………………………………………………… 张静菲（154）
森林消防站网点空间布局研究 …………………………… 肖化顺 曾思齐 蒋倩仪（164）
数字式高差测量仪的研制与试验 ……………………………………… 鄢前飞 刘发林（169）
退化林地遥感判定技术研究 ……………………………… 余坤勇 刘 健 许章华（175）
修枝高度与华北落叶松生长的关系
…………………………… 孙海静 原民龙 姜 涛 刘广营 杨 飞 马长明（186）
叶山林场常绿阔叶混交林林分空间结构研究
………………………………… 李 杰 宗 雪 高 祥 徐 光 郑小贤（191）
北京市元宝枫生物量模型的研建 …………………………………………………… 杨 丽（197）
长白山主要阔叶树种子园建园技术的研究 …………………………… 李兴东 顾东杰（207）
黑龙江省次生林的初步探讨 ………………………………………………………… 张玉波（213）
华中地区退耕还林工程开展情况调查分析 ……… 徐 定 彭道黎 谢 晨 黄 东（217）
吉林森林生态系统定位观测研究网络建设 …………… 汪兆洋 姚晨光 孙宏刚（223）
吉林省林业地理信息系统建设方案的探讨 ………………………………… 王君海（228）
吉林省林木生物质能源开发与利用探讨 ……………………………… 谷万祥 马晓龙（233）
吉林省重点国有林区森林认证与森林可持续经营的探讨 …………… 谷万祥 马晓龙（237）
建立我国森林生态效益补偿制度的构想 ……………………………… 曹小玉 吕 勇（240）
金山屯林业局野生花卉栽培技术 …………… 田德君 郑在军 彭立新 潘 宇（245）
开展中幼龄林抚育几点体会 ………………… 田德君 郑在军 于春友 潘 宇（255）
林木产品网络销售平台建设的探讨 …………………………………… 李海波 孙守意（257）
平顶山市森林生态系统服务功能评价初探 ……… 周君璞 郑小贤 高 祥 徐 光（260）
强强融合创新——推进林业信息化的新理念 ……………………………………… 陈谋询（268）
人工红松林镶嵌自然带天然更新阔叶树营造技术
…………………………… 倪柏春 倪 薇 郑在军 田德君 于春友 刘立华（272）
三种枸杞快速繁殖技术研究…………………………………… 刘 思 蔡 超 安文娟（277）
浅析森林认证机制及其与森林可持续经营的关系 …………………………… 陶立超（284）
完善生态补偿制度与强化森林科学经营之技术和政策研究
…………………………… 何美成 易正树 闫顺利 李建军 席明星 等（289）
小陇山林区油松中幼林龄抚育效果评价
……………………………… 潘德乾 赵文杰 刘文桢 张宋智 郭小龙（312）

小叶锦鸡儿人工林黄土高原丘陵区土壤改善过程的研究 …… 温晓林　何振仲（322）
新形势下平原绿化由“线”到“面”的思考 …… 刘安兴　徐　军　杜　群（326）
樱草蔷薇种实性状的观察与测定 …… 王　云（332）

二、文献综述

我国森林经营的有关问题探讨 …… 张会儒（337）
森林蓄积量遥感估测研究进展 …… 涂云燕　彭道黎（343）
森林植被遥感分类技术及方法概述 …… 孙　聃（349）
森林资源动态监测研究综述 …… 莫　可（355）
森林景观分类方法研究进展及发展趋势 …… 岳　刚（361）
遥感影像在林业二类调查中应用的几点建议 …… 栾忠平（372）
澳大利亚森林可持续森林经营现状及启示 …… 邓　广　张　旭　陈　艳（375）
森林生态系统稳定性分析、问题和建议 …… 孙丽萍　牛　纯（380）
可持续发展的森林资源综合管理 …… 涂云燕　彭道黎（387）
我国森林公园的规划设计、现状及发展趋势 …… 陈　英　杨　华（392）

三、学科建设

森林经理：森林的可持续经营与适应性管理 …… 徐国祯（403）
中国森林经理再探讨——森林经理学科滑坡诊断 …… 詹昭宁（412）
教材建设、科学研究、人才培养——谈森林经理学科建设 …… 李明阳　刘　敏　刘米兰（420）
森林经营方案实施不力的主要原因及解决的对策 …… 苏世河（427）
森林经营方案编制与实施探讨 …… 段　河（431）
中国林业信息化方略——内涵与发展、战略重点与规划方法 …… 浙江省林业信息化规划组（434）

四、缅怀董乃钧先生

我国森林资源监测工作的回顾与展望——缅怀董乃钧教授 …… 周昌祥（457）
缅怀林业教育事业的勤奋耕耘人：董乃钧教授 …… 陈谋询（461）
不知疲倦的人　　怀念恩师董乃钧先生 …… 赵天忠（464）
怀念董乃钧先生 …… 宋新民（466）

一、应用研究

Monitoring and Forecasting the Forest Dynamic Evolution Based on GIS Technology

Gu Li[1]　Zheng Xiao-xian[1]*　Gong Zhi-wen[2]

(1. Key Laboratory for Silviculture and Conservation of Ministry of Education College of Forestry, Beijing Forestry University, Beijing 100083, P. R. China; 2. College of Economics and Management, Northwest Agriculture & Forestry University, Yangling 712100)

Abstract: Based on the landscape ecology theory and the application of GIS, this paper studies the forest landscape quantitative classification of the Jingouling forest farm, Changbai Mountains, in the province of Jilin, China, obtains the forest landscape spatial distribution. The author used the forest Resource Inventory data in 1997 and in 2007, through the graphics overlay, to get into the data landscape in this region, and With the Markov model to simulate the dynamic process of forest landscape pattern. This study presents a practical technology and methods for rapid extraction and provides technical reference; the result is reasonable zoning type of forest management and provides a theoretical basis for the program.

Keywords: wetland resource; landscape pattern; dynamic evolution; Markov model; forest management

1 Introduction

Landscape is composed of a series of different land units or ecosystems mosaic structure, with the geographical entities of obvious visual features (Forman and Godron, 1986), and landscape pattern is also spatial patterns, which is plaque and other component units of the type, number, spatial distribution and configuration (Paul, 2000), and the dynamic changes of landscape pattern, including the composition of landscape structure, diversity, shape and spatial changes (LUCC, 1999). The landscape essential factor is refers to land ecology essential factor or unit set which is relative the basic, relatively homogeneous ecological elements. forest landscape is the Polymer of various ecosystems which the forest cover plant type as main body forest cover plant type as main body, and the a-

Received Date: 2011. 09

Fund: financial assistance from Protection (20090014110013)

Author: Guli, Doctor, Engaging remote sensing applications in the environment resource.

Tel: 010 – 62338133 Email: guli_ bj@126. com

* Corresponding author: Zheng Xiao – xian, Tel: 0086 – 10 – 62338133 Email: zheng8355@bjfu. edu. cn

nalysis aim is to reveal the basic laws and master control means, And implementing landscape ecological protection, restoration, construction and management through scientific planning and design (Sun, et al, 2003; Guo, 2011). In this paper, Jingouling Experimental Forest Farm, Wangqing Forestry Bureau, and Jilin Province was as the location example, the author used the data in 1997 and 2007, analysis the forest landscape pattern, dynamics changes and forest management activities on it, the results will be helpful for the evaluation the ecological environment and development trend, and the analysis will provides a very effective means for regional ecological planning and construction (Fu et al, 2001; Wu, 2001, Jiang, 2003).

2 Study Area

The study area is located at the Jingouling Experimental Forest Farm, Wangqing Forestry Bureau, and Jilin Province, situated on the middle lower hill region of Changbai Mountain in northeastern China. Elevation ranges from 550 m to 1100 m and with an annual rainfall from 600 mm to 700 mm. The average annual temperature is 4.8℃, average monthly maximum and minimum temperatures range between 22 and −32.8℃, respectively. Soil type is dark brown forest soil, and the original vegetation type is mixed broad – leaved Korean Pine forest. Most primary forests, however, have been altered to form other forest types such as Spruce – Fir dominated mixed coniferous forests, Polar – Birch mixed broadleaved forests and plantations consisting of Larch, Spruce, Fir and Pine, for example, after long – term management practices and disturbances. Stands used in this study were originally natural forests. The dominant tree species in our study stand are Spruce, Fir, Aspen and Birch. Other tree species composed the stands are Korean Pine, Linden, Elm, Maple, Ash, Corktree and Changbai Larch. The shrub is Lonicera Japonica, Manchurian Lilac, Euonymus Alatus, and Hazelnut et al. The herb species is False Spiraea, Spiraea, Sedges and so on.

3 Materials and Methods

3.1 Basic data

In this paper, the forest map of 1: 5 million and topographic map in 1997 on jingouling forest farm, and the corresponding sixth (in 2007) and the Fifth (in 1997) forest inventory data were used. With the aid of the GIS software, The author layered vector for forest map, then first digitized the field scope, small class and compartment to generate the surface shape graph of topological relation, and corresponding with geography code. The survey data for small class including the number, compartment small number, area, land category, site type, dominant species, origin, species composition, age group, per hectare accumulation, business type, tree species, soil type, soil texture, soil thickness, Slope, aspect, ownership, elevation, solar radiation intensity of more than 20 property items.

3.2 forest landscape classification

In this study, According to the principles of landscape classification and naming, the author used the land category to carry on a forest landscape second – level classification, on the two scales of forest farm and compartment, and divided into 7 categories in Jingouling forest farm, which were the forest land, brush land, the land have not grown forest establishment afforestation, nursery land, slash land, farmland, marshland and others. At the same time, the forest land was divided in to 13 types of forest landscape according to the dominant species, namely Korean pine forest, spruce forest, Pinus sylvestris var. Mon – golica forest, larch forest, Symplocarpus foetidus forest, Ulmus pumila forests, mono maple forest, Betula platyphylla forest, Populus forest, spinney forest, Mixed coniferous forest、mixed forest、broadleaved mixed forest. The author further divided into 5 forest landscape types: coniferous pure forest, Mixed coniferous forest, mixed forest, broadleaved pure forest, broadleaved mixed forest.

3.3 Introduction of Markov process model

Markov process model is a special random movement process model (Shu et al, 2006), which is called "no after effect" According to the study of original transfer probability at different status and it's between status, the change trend of system status is confirmed. The model is a reflection of a given time that a series transfer process from time T to time T + 1 in a sub – stable status. And the model needs only the status of time T + 1 related with times T (Forman and Godron, 1986). According Markov random process theory, we can use the original status probability matrix to model various area proportions which is the landscape pattern, from one of the original phases or the next years to the stability phases (Ning, et al, 2004). The Markov can quantify the changed area of forest to other kinds of forest and described the dynamic evolvement process of forest landscape pattern, the basic equation and mathematical expression are as follows:

$$P_{ij}^{n} = \sum_{k=0}^{n-1} P_{ik} P_{kj}^{n-1} \longrightarrow P_{ij} \begin{Bmatrix} P_{11} & P_{12} & \cdots & P_{1n} \\ P_{21} & P_{22} & \cdots & P_{2n} \\ \cdots & \cdots & \cdots & \cdots \\ P_{n1} & P_{n2} & \cdots & P_{nn} \end{Bmatrix}$$

Where P_{ij} is the area that the landscape i transfer into the landscape j , which is a non – negative. In this paper, the author added the forest landscape type in 2007 to the forest landscape type in 1997, and using the soft ware of ArcGIS's statistical functions, to analysis the forest landscape type transformed situation from 1997 to 2007, and then obtained the transition probability matrix of forest landscape change, and carried on the predictions.

4 Results and Discussion

4.1 Composition proportion of land type

The area of the land type plays a key role in the ecosystem functioning, and the degree and frequency of its variation affect the living and reproduction of rare or endangered species. During 1997 – 2007, the variation of land types was shown in table 1.

In the eight land types from 1997 to 2007, forest land is the most, which area decreased by 16031.9167 hm^2 to 15976.6163hm^2; proportions decline from 98.87% to 97.71%, the share of non – forest land was a very small proportion, less than 3%. This shows that the forest cover is very high in this field, and has obvious importance forest in the control action of landscape, and the study area can be used as the matrix within the landscape

Tab. 1 The statistics of land type areas from 1997 to 2007

Land type	In1997		In2007	
	area /hm^2	percentage /%	area /hm^2	percentage /%
forest land	16031. 9167	98. 87	15976. 6163	97. 91
brush land	38. 7299	0. 24	93. 8623	0. 58
not grown forest	10. 3787	0. 06	30. 8357	0. 19
nursery land	31. 2902	0. 19	31. 2902	0. 19
slash land	17. 9107	0. 11	17. 9107	0. 11
farmland	1. 9746	0. 01	41. 0761	0. 25
marshland	45. 8186	0. 28	41. 3302	0. 25
others	37. 3745	0. 23	84. 5354	0. 52

4. 2 the analysis of forest landscape type

During 1997 – 2007, the area variation of forest landscape types was shown in table 2. In the five forest landscape type divided in this paper, the area proportion of broadleaved forest was more than coniferous forest, especially the broadleaved mixed forest, which more than 40% either in 1997 or in 2007. The area proportion of coniferous forest is small in this field.

Tab. 2 The statistics of forest landscape areas from 1997 to 2007

Forest landscape	In1997		In2007	
	area /hm^2	percentage /%	area /hm^2	percentage /%
coniferous pure forest	2838. 1694	17. 70	1356. 2455	8. 49
Mixed coniferous forest	3355. 8100	20. 93	4394. 0772	27. 50
mixed forest	702. 6264	4. 38	331. 3152	2. 07
broadleaved pure forest	2414. 8628	15. 06	2763. 2028	17. 30
broadleaved mixed forest	6720. 4503	41. 92	7131. 7756	44. 64

4. 3 Analysis of forest landscape transfer matrix

In order to analysis the temporal and spatial evolvement process offorest landscape, we established the transfer matrix model from 1997 to 2007 (Forman and Godron, 1986), which were listed in table 3. We can conclude the evolvement process of every type:

From table 3, we can see the transferred situation of every forest landscape type: (1) Coniferous pure forest was transferred Coniferous pure forest and mixed coniferous forest, and small part was mixed forest. (2) Broadleaved pure forest was transferred Broadleaved pure forest and mixed Broadleaved forest, and small part was mixed forest. (3) Other forest landscape type consist of Mixed coniferous forest, Mixed forest and Broadleaved mixed forest, the proportion of transferred area of which was a little.

4. 4 Dynamic model of forest landscape type

Original transfer probability was determined by the data from 1997 to 2007. According the area of transferred forest landscape (Table 3), we can account the annual average transfer area (hm^2/

a), annual mean transfer probability matrix of forest landscape utilization style (step length once year) and the original transfer probability (Table 4).

Tab. 3 The area change of forest landscape types from 1997 to 2007

In 1997	In 2007				
	Coniferous pure forest	Mixed coniferous forest	Mixed forest	Broadleaved pure forest	Broadleaved mixed forest
Coniferous pure forest	1265. 7573	1173. 5128	363. 3159	0. 0000	6. 1564
Mixed coniferous forest	38. 1718	2931. 1522	267. 5892	33. 8397	44. 0345
Mixed forest	23. 8740	274. 5231	6352. 5396	0. 0000	43. 1726
Broadleaved pure forest	0. 0000	3. 3714	64. 2365	293. 1928	339. 3962
Broadleaved mixed forest	8. 0120	0. 0000	82. 0350	0. 0000	2324. 1072

Tab. 4 The transferred rates of forest landscape types in the beginning state (n = 1)

In 1997	In 2007				
	Coniferous pure forest	Mixed coniferous forest	Mixed forest	Broadleaved pure forest	Broadleaved mixed forest
Coniferous pure forest	0. 4460	0. 4135	0. 1280	0. 0000	0. 0022
Mixed coniferous forest	0. 0114	0. 8735	0. 0797	0. 0101	0. 0131
Mixed forest	0. 0036	0. 0408	0. 9453	0. 0000	0. 0064
Broadleaved pure forest	0. 0000	0. 0048	0. 0914	0. 4173	0. 4830
Broadleaved mixed forest	0. 0033	0. 0000	0. 0340	0. 0000	0. 9624

5 Conclusions

The scientific and reasonable division of forest resources is one of important means to realize forest sustainable management. Due to using unreasonable cutting methods and human destruction, forest resources are being deficient and ecological environment have gotten degenerated gradually. Therefore, the purpose of the paper is to find a way of coordinating the relationship between cutting and environment conservation.

The paper is based on the forest management survey data, using the software of Arc GIS 9. 2, picking up the forest landscape, and generating the forest classification special topic picture, analysis the forest landscape pattern in this field by using the theory and method of landscape ecology. At the present, the forest quantity and quality were improvement in this field, but in the species construction, the Broadleaved was also occupying the dominant species. From 1997 to 2007, the land type has not obvious changed; also the forest land was taken up the dominant, and corresponding with brush land, farmland marshland and so on.

Using Markov transfer matrix model to prediction is not consider the effect of other else factor, but in fact, the change of forest landscape will not be the stable process, it will be a changed process according with the time change[12]. In the social mode of resource consumption and economic increasing, human activity would be the most active factor which affected the land resource[14]. The change of forest landscape will drive by the population policy and economic policy. In order to avoid the forest resource deteriorating in this field, we should perfect forest resource monitor system, constitute scientific decision – making management, achieve the forest sustainable development.

6 Acknowledgements

This project was supported by financial assistance from Protection (20090014110013)". Author thanked all those who provided helpful suggestions and comments on this manuscript.

References

[1]Forman R T T, Godron. Landscape Ecology. New York: Wiley & Sons, 1986, pp. 188 – 210.

[2] Paul A K. Wetland Ecology Principles and Conservation. Cambridge: Cambridge University Press, 2000, 124 – 238.

[3]Land-Use and Land-Cover Change (LUCC) Implementation Strategy. IGBP Report 48. IHDP Report, 1999, 10: 10 – 26.

[4]Sun Y J, Wang X J, Zang Zhi, et al. GIS-Based forest landscape quantitative classification. Acta Ecologica Sinica. 2003, 23(12): 2540 – 2544.

[5]Guo J P. Forest Landscape Ecology [M]. Beijing, Beijing University Publishing house, 2001.

[6]Fu B J, Chen L D, Ma K M, et al. Landscape Ecology Principles and Applications [M]. Beijing, Science Press, 2001: 59 – 65.

[7]Wu J G. Landscape Ecology-Pattern, Process, Scale and Hierarchy [M]. Beijing: Higher Education Press, 2001: 16 – 34.

[8]Jiang X W, Zhou Zh L, Li K R, et al. Application of Landscape Ecology Principle in Watershed Planning [J]. Journal of Northwest Forestry University, 2003, 18(2): 112 – 115.

[9]Shu Q T, Lu Y Ch, Hong L X. Studies on Landscape Pattern Changes Based on Markov Model in Over cutting Forest Region, Northeast China. Journal of Southwest Forestry College, 2006, 26(5): 16 – 20.

[10]Ning L M, Wang X, Hu W. Simulation and forecast of wetland landscapes development with Markov process in Wuhan City [J]. Journal of Central China Normal University (Nat. Sci.), 38(2), 2004, pp. 2555 – 258.

[11]Qiu P F, Wu N, Luo P, et al. Analysis of dynamics and driving factors of wetland landscape in Zoige, Eastern Qinghai-Tibetan Plateau. Journal of Mountain Science, 2009, 6 (1): 42 – 55.

Aboveground Forest Biomass Estimation using ICESat/GLAS and Optical Remote Sensing Data in Yunnan Province, China

HUANG Ke-biao[1,2] **PANG Yong**[2] **SHU Qing-tai**[1 *]

(1. College of Forestry, Southwest Forestry University, Kunming, 650224

2. Institute of Forest Resource Information Techniques, Chinese Academy of Forestry, Beijing, 100091)

Abstract: Forest is a significant part of terrestrial ecosystems. Accurate estimates of forest above ground biomass (AGB) could reduce uncertainties in the characterization of terrestrial carbon fluxes. LiDAR (Light Detection and Ranging) provides an accurate measurement of canopy height and vertical structure and information for estimation of aboveground biomass of vegetation. Spaceborne large footprint LiDAR (ICESat/GLAS) acquired over 250 million observations over forest regions globally and has been used successfully for forest height and biomass estimation in various sites. In this paper, airborne LiDAR and ICESat/GLAS data were used to estimate aboveground biomass of forest at footprint level in Yunnan, China. Vegetation products from EOS MODIS and ENVISAT MERIS were used to expand these discrete estimations from GLAS data to a wall – to – wall map. The R^2 between ICESat/GLAS waveform parameters and airborne LiDAR estimated forest AGB is 0.52 after training with 260 footprints. Results show that the total forest AGB in Yunnan Province was 1272 million ton and the average was 94 Mg/ha. The amount and distribution of predicted aboveground biomass were in good agreement with the reference data. The results showed that the predict model using GLAS data could be used to estimate regional forest aboveground biomass successfully.

Key words: aboveground biomass estimation; LiDAR; ICESat/GLAS; optical data

INTRODUCTION

Forest is an existing biomass stocks in the terrestrial ecosystems and is considered as a carbon sink in the earth system (Anaya et al., 2009). The world's forests sequester and conserve more carbon than all other terrestrial ecosystems and account for 90% of the annual carbon flux between the atmosphere and the Earth's land surface (Winjum et al., 1993).

Forest biomass represents the amount of carbon stocks in forest ecosystems, and has been listed as one of the most important monitoring parameters by International Union of Forest Research Organizations (IUFRO) (Zhao et al., 2005). The role of the forest in reducing atmospheric levels of CO_2 has been recognized in a number of international agreements (e. g. United Nations Framework Convention on Climate Change, Kyoto Protocol) which specifically require countries to quantify their carbon stocks and changes (Hese et al., 2005).

Regional forest biomass estimation is a complicated work. Traditional method of building algometric relationship between ground inventories and forest metrics is tough and impracticable in regional scale (Boudreau et al., 2008). Thus, Applying remote sensing techniques in combination with terrestrial surveys may be a feasible way to guarantee accurate monitoring of activities and impacts during a project's lifetime (Streck et al., 2006) and the method have been proved by many studies. Dong et al (2003) analyzed relationship between forest biomass from 167 provinces and states in six countries and satellite greenness data and found remote sensing data could used to estimate forest biomass; Foody et al (2003) estimated tropical forest biomass from Landsat TM data between sites in Brazil, Malaysia and Thailand and results showed that for each test site, the vegetation indices of Landsat TM data most strongly related to the biomass of the training data. Muukkonen et al (2007) used forest inventory data and MODIS data to estimate forest biomass and compared the results with National Forest Inventory data found the relative RMSE was 9.9%. Researches above showed that optical remote sensing can be used to build empirical relationships between the forest biomass and spectral reflectance, especially at regional scale where field data is scarce (Lim et al., 2003). However, optical sensors are ultimately constrained by the inability to make physical measurements of the vertical structure of forest canopies and their usefulness were limited in dense forest with high biomass (Hyde et al., 2006).

Light Detection and Ranging (LiDAR) is one of the most promising technologies for retrieval of various forest biophysical properties (Nillson 1996; Lefsky et al., 1999; 2005). Studies of Naesset et al (2004) and Means et al (2000) demonstrated that the 80th and 90th percentiles of the heights measured by airborne discrete LiDAR were useful for aboveground biomass and forest volume estimation. Although airborne LiDAR can estimate tree height with sub – meter vertical accuracy and spatial resolution but its utility is limited in large area for its high cost (Boudreau et al. 2008). The first spaceborne large footprint LiDAR sensor (ICESat/GLAS) acquired over 250 million LiDAR observations over forest regions globally and has been used successfully for forest height and biomass estimation in various sites (Lefsky et al., 2007; Boudreau et al. 2008; Duncanson et al., 2010). Lefsky et al (2005) used ICESat/GLAS and SRTM data to estimate forest height and aboveground biomass and demonstrated that GLAS data were able to predict forest heights successfully over a wide range of canopy height and aboveground biomass. (Nelson et al., 2009) used optical data from the MODIS and waveform data from ICESat/GLAS to estimate timber volume in Central Siberia. The encouraging result showed that GLAS and MODIS data can be used to develop accurate regional estimates of timber volume. In this paper, airborne LiDAR and ICESat/GLAS data were used to estimate forest aboveground biomass at footprint level in Yunnan Province of China and a continue forest biomass map was generated by combined optical data and LiDAR estimated biomass samples.

1 STUDY SITE AND DATA

1.1 Study site

The study site of the Yunnan Province in the southwest of China extends from 97°19 ′E to 106° 07 ′E and 21°04 ′N to 29°09 ′N, bordered by Myanmar, Laos, and Vietnam (Fig. 1).

Yunnan is situated in a mountainous area, with highest elevations in the northwest reaching more than 5, 000 m and lowest elevations of 76.4 m in the southeast. Average annual rainfall ranges from 600 mm to 2, 300 mm. It is rich in natural resources and has the largest diversity of plant life in China. The dominant tree species are coniferous (*Pinus yunnanensis* , *Pinus kesiya var. langbianensis* , *Pinus armandii* , *Picea asperata Mast* and *Keteleeria evelyniana*). There are also some broadleaf forests, primarily in regenerated forests (*Alnus nepalensis* , *Hevea brasiliensis* , *Quercus variabilis* and *Quercus cautísima*).

The pilot area is located at the XishanForest Farm and Hongta Forest Farm in the central part of the study area with range of N 24° 09 ′to N 25° 28 ′, E 102° 23 ′to E 102° 36 ′as shown with yellow rectangles in Fig. 1. It is characterized by hilly terrain, with an annual precipitation of 935 mm concentrated from June to August. It is a typical sub – tropical forest region with abundant tree species and a variety of forest types.

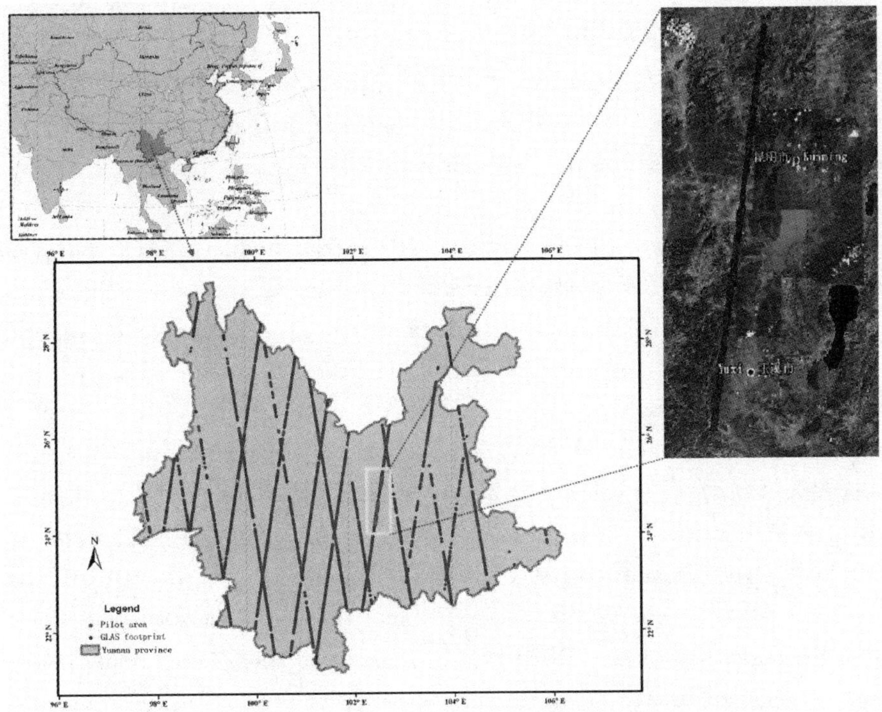

Fig. 1 Study area in Yunnan, China (blue points represent GLAS shots in Yunnan and the zoom in map of yellow rectangle are pilot sites covered by airborne LiDAR data in Kunming and Yuxi)

1.2 Airborne LiDAR data

Airborne LiDAR waveform data was collected using the LiteMapper 5600 system flown an orbit of ICESat/GLAS in December of 2007. The Riegl LMS – Q560 laser was used. This system has a wavelength of 1550 nm, with a 0.5 mrad beam divergence and 3 ns pulse length. It operated at a 50 kHz pulse rate at 650 m relative flight height. The resulting footprint size was 35 cm with a point density of approximately 2 points/m^2.

1.3 ICESat/GLAS Data

The Geoscience Laser Altimeter System (GLAS) board on ICESat (Ice, Cloud, and land Elevation Satellite) launched on Jan. 12, 2003, is the benchmark Earth Observing System mission for measuring ice sheet mass balance, cloud and aerosol heights, as well as land topography and vegetation characteristics. GLAS system has three laser sensors, which emit a laser pulse with an approximate footprint diameter of 70 m and spaced 172 m apart at a time (Boudreau et al. 2008).

GLASLevel - 1A altimetry data (GLA01), level - 1B waveform parameterization data (GLA05) and level -2 land altimetry product (GLA14) were used to estimate forest height and biomass. The GLA01 data include the transmitted and received wavefom from the altimeter. The GLA05 data contain waveform - based range corrections and surface characteristics. The GLA14 data contain the land elevation and land elevation distribution data. A dataset of 20, 317 GLAS full waveforms with cloud - free profiles during period L3E (Feb. 22 to Mar. 27, 2006) over the study area was downloaded from the National Snow and Ice Data Center (NSIDC) (http: //nsidc. org/data/icesat/). There were 185 filtered GLAS shots from L3E period within the coverage of the airborne LiDAR over pilot sites used to link with airborne LiDAR data.

1.4 MODIS data

MODIS Vegetation Continuous Field (VCF) (MOD44B) product of 2005 was used forextending the GLAS estimates. The VCF product shows the coverage of vegetation such as "forest" or "grassland" exists in each pixel. The product is derived from all seven bands of was estimated from MODIS 1 -7 bands using supervised regression tree algorithm (Matthew C. Hansen 2003).

1.5 MERIS Land Cover data

Globcover Land Cover product of ENVISAT MERIS is produced in an automatic, repeatable and global way as a global land cover map at 300 m resolution with a legend defined and documented using the UN Land Cover Classification System (LCCS). The product has 22 different land cover classes at the global level (Defourny et al., 2006). Class ID for 40, 50, 60, 70, 100, 110 and 120 were defined as forest covers in this study (Table 1). The GlobCover Land Cover product of central Asia for the period from Dec., 2004 to Jun., 2006 and GlobCover Annual MERIS FR mosaic product which computed by averaging the surface reflectance values of these bimonthly products generated over the year 2005 were used in this study.

Tab. 1 Forest Classes used in Globcover Product

Class ID	Globcover legend
40	Closed to open (>15%) broadleaved evergreen or semi -deciduous forest (>5m)
50	Closed (>40%) broadleaved deciduous forest (>5m)
60	Open (15% -40%) broadleaved deciduous forest/woodland (>5m)
70	Closed (>40%) needleleaved evergreen forest (>5m)
100	Closed to open (>15%) mixed broadleaved and needleleaved forest (>5m)
110	Mosaic forest or shrubland (50% -70%) / grassland (20% -50%)
120	Mosaic grassland (50% -70%) / forest or shrubland (20% -50%)

1.6 Forest inventory data

Field data were collected from Xishan Forest Farm of Kunming and Hongta Forest Farm of Yuxi from Jul. 16 to Aug. 4, 2008 in Yunnan Province. A total number of 78 circular plots were set and surveyed with radius of 7.5 m or 15 m within the coverage of airborne LiDAR. The centers of the plots were positioned by Trimble GEOXT GPS. Trees with a DBH of 5 cm and larger were measured within those plots. For each plot, biophysical parameters such as species of dominant trees, DBH and height of trees were calculated. DBH was measured by diameter tape, tree heights were measured by Impulse - 200 laser altimeter.

2 DATA PROCESSING METHOD

2.1 GLAS data processing

NSIDC provided IDL tools to read and processing binary data of GLA01, GLA05 and GLA14. GLAS waveforms contain lots of noise. In our work, the threshold was set to the background noise plus 4.5 times the standard deviation (Lefsky et al. 2005). We exclude abnormal data that with low signal to noise ratio or influenced by cloud (e.g., maximum intensity value of waveform under 80).

Early studies (Lefsky et al. 2007; Nelson et al. 2009) demonstrated that some GLAS waveform indices have relation with vertical structure of forest. Three variables of GLAS waveform by Lefsky et al (2005) were used in our study which including width, trailing edge and leading edge. Width, i.e., the extent of waveform, is defined as the distance between signal beginning and signal end; Trailing edge, reflects the vary of ground surface to a certain extent, is calculated from the waveform as the height difference between the lowest elevation at which the signal strength of the waveform is half of the maximum signal above the background noise value, and the elevation of the signal end; Leading edge, reflects the vary of uppermost foliage, is determined as the height difference between the elevation of the signal start and the first elevation at which the waveform is half of the maximum signal above the background noise value (Lefsky et al. 2007).

2.2 Forest biomass estimation from airborne LiDAR

Above ground biomasses of 40 sample plots were calculated from field measurement using species specific algometric equations.

Discrete airborne LiDAR data were classified as ground points, vegetation points and other points by processing first returns and last returns. First returns were selected to retrieve parameters of forest because they appeared more stable compared with other returns (Næsset et al., 2008). Points with 2 m height and lager were defined as vegetation objects that we interested and canopy height and crown density were calculated from these points. Digital Elevation Model (DEM) was created by linear interpolation using ground points, and Canopy Height Model (CHM) could be calculated through vegetation points. Percentiles of airborne discrete LiDAR measured heights were used to develop regression equations with field measurements and model of aboveground biomass was developed (Fu et al., In press).

2.3 Forest biomass estimation from ICESat/GLAS

It is difficult to build estimation models using GLAS and field data with enough training data at 70 m scale, especially in forest area of topographic relief region like Yunnan. Using biomass estimates from accurate airborne LiDAR data as training data to develop GLAS biomass estimates seems to be a more feasible method (Boudreau et al. 2008).

Airborne LiDAR systemwas flight along the orbits of ICESat/GLAS data. Coincidence airborne LiDAR data with GLAS elliptical footprints were extracted. The GLAS footprint size varies with laser operating periods. In the research of (Pang et al., 2008), the azimuth angle, major axis radius and eccentricity fields in the ICESat/GLAS GLA05 product were used to extract Airborne discrete LiDAR data within ICESat/GLAS footprint (Equation 1):

$$\frac{((x_i * \cos(azimuth) - y_i * \sin(azimuth))^2}{ellipse\_a^2} + \frac{((x_i * \sin(azimuth)) - y_i * \cos(azimuth))^2}{ellipse\_b^2} \leqslant 1 \quad (1)$$

where x_i and y_i are the central coordinates of airborne discrete LiDAR point i, and ellipse_ a and ellipse_ b can be calculated by equation 2 using the records of GLA05 data:

$$\begin{aligned} ellipse\_a &= (i\_tpmajoraxis * sqrt(1 - i\_tpeccentricity^2))/2 \\ ellipse\_b &= i\_tpmajoraxis/2 \\ azimuth &= i\_beam\_azimuth \end{aligned} \quad (2)$$

where i_ tpmajoraxis and i_ tpeccentricity are the major axis and eccentricity of GLAS shot; azimuth represent the vector from the ground to the spacecraft.

Forest biomass within GLAS footprints were estimated by airborne LiDAR. Then we developed a predictive regress model between airborne LiDAR estimated biomass and GLAS waveform parameters.

2.4 Extrapolating the biomass estimates to the study area

Models between GLAS waveform parameters and airborne LiDAR estimates of biomass were developed and applied to 20, 317 quality - filtered GLAS footprints of L3E period in the study area to estimate the biomass. The biomass within GLAS footprints of the study area provided basic data which were used to fusion with optical data.

MODIS VCF product and MERIS Globcover product were used toextrapolate GLAS sampling biomass to the entire study area. MERIS Globcover product includes 22 land cover classes which were defined by the LCCS. According to the actual situation of the study area, we utilized 7 land cover classes as vegetation classes (Table 1). MODIS VCF and MERIS NDVI product, which closely related with the vegetation, were classified into 5 levels i. e., the values of VCF (0 to 100) and NDVI (0 to 1) were evenly divided into 5 steps. There were 175 forest classes (7 forest classes, 5 VCF levels, 5 NDVI levels) theoretically. Each forest class was given the mean biomass value of GLAS footprints which falling in it. Then the regional continuous biomass map was generated.

3 RESULTS

3.1 Accuracy of airborne LiDAR estimated forest biomass

A dataset of 40 sample plots were used to develop biomass estimation models from airborne LiDAR. The stepwise regression analysis method was used to select airborne LiDAR variables which contribute biomass estimates. The regression equation show in Equation 3:

$$W_{a\_air} = e^{2.278} h_{30}^{1.17} d_0^{0.991} \quad (3)$$

Where W_{a_air} represents the aboveground biomass estimated by airborne LiDAR; e represents the base of the natural system of logarithms, having a numerical value of approximately 2.7183; h_{30} represents the 30th percentile of airborne discrete LiDAR (i. e., height below which 30% of the discrete LiDAR points); d_0 represents crown density which defined as the ratio of number of canopy hits to total number of pulses. The results showed that forest AGB could be well estimated by airborne LiDAR with an R^2 of 0.68. The RMSE of the regression was 1.54 Mg/ha (2.5% of average value).

3.2 Airborne LiDAR biomass estimation to GLAS observations

A dataset of 260 GLAS shots in L3E period which covered by airborne LiDAR scans were extracted for developing regression equations of forest AGB. Three parameters of GLAS waveform including width, trailing edge, leading edge and some transformations of these three basic waveform parameters were used to develop regression equations with airborne LiDAR estimates (Equation 4).

$$w_a = -48.67 + 7.22 * width - 44.31 * \sqrt{trail} + 2133.08 * \frac{trail}{width^2} \quad (4)$$

where w_a is aboveground biomass; width is GLAS waveform extent; trail and lead represent Trailing edge and Leading edge respectively which mentioned in 1.7. Results showed that the regression equation of biomass has an R^2 of 0.52 and RMSE of 30.96 Mg/ha (Fig 2).

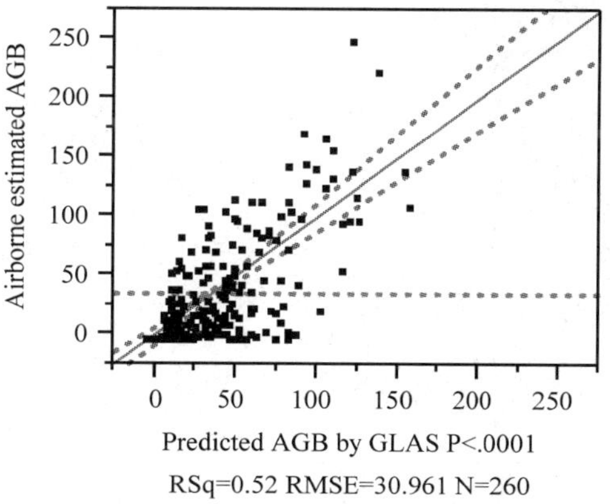

Fig. 2 Forest aboveground biomass estimated using GLAS – airborne LiDAR equations.

Result showed that maximum forest AGB of 427 Mg/ha was estimated by GLAS. High level forest AGB were located in northwest and south of Yunnan.

3.3 GLAS biomass estimates fusion with optical data in the study area

A continuous forest aboveground biomass map was generated using the basic estimates by ICE-Sat/GLAS (total footprints of 20, 317) and extrapolated by MODIS and MERIS products in study area (Fig. 3). Result showed that high AGB levels were distributed in northwest and center southern of the study area. This spatial pattern is reasonable since most of the nature reserves are located in these regions. For example, there are several forest nature reserves located in northwest of Yunan such as Yulong Snow Mountain, Baima Snow Mountain, Haba Snow Mountain and Bita Lake. In southern central of Yunnan, there are nature reserves of Wuliangshan, Ailaoshan, Xishuangbanna and Daweishan which were all rich in forest resource.

The mean and total AGB estimated by GLAS in study area were 94 Mg/ha and 1272 million tons respectively. Forest AGB of broadleaved evergreen forest, broadleaved deciduous forest, needle-leaf evergreen forest and mixed forest account for 31%, 13%, 44% and 12% of the total biomass, respectively. As show in Fig. 4, our estimation is comparable with the early research of Li et al (2010) which reported that total forest biomass (including underground biomass) of Yunnan was 1735 million tons and mean forest biomass was 112 Mg/ha (Based on data of The 7th National Forest Inventory during 2004 - 2008). Zeng (2005) used the biomass expansion factors to estimate forest biomass by use of the data of continues forest inventory of Yunan Province in 2002. In his study, the total forest biomass of Yunan was 1226.22 million tons and mean forest biomass was 87.54 Mg/ha. It should be noted that forest biomass from the two early researches include both of aboveground and underground biomass.

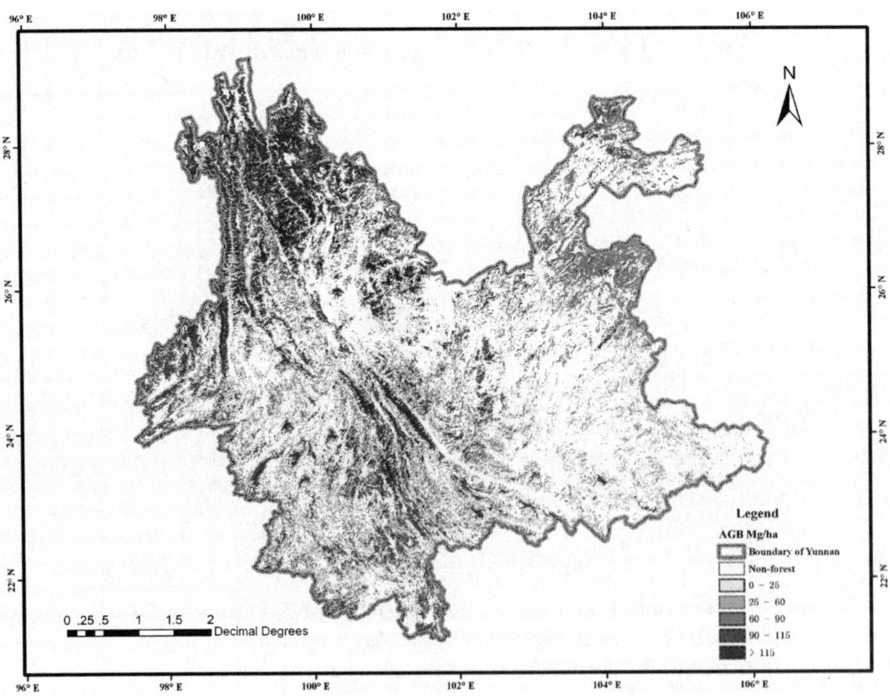

Fig. 3 Estimated forest aboveground biomass of Yunnan Province

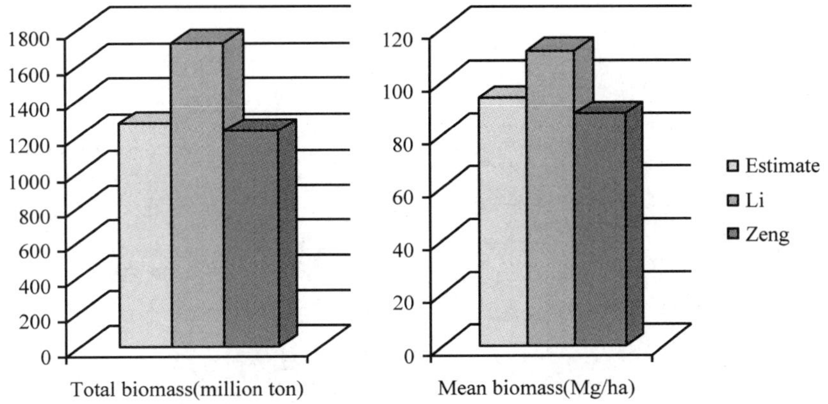

Fig. 4 Total biomass comparison with previous results

4 DISCUSSION AND CONCLUSIONS

A first forest aboveground biomass map of Yunnan from remote sensing data was generated using airborne LiDAR and ICESat/GLAS. Prediction model of forest AGB was developed by linking a dataset of 260 airborne LiDAR estimates to GLAS in the pilot area. Results showed that using accurate airborne LiDAR estimates to training GLAS data for forest AGB estimation was feasible. The forest AGB model using airborne LiDAR explained 83% of field data and biomass estimation model of GLAS data explained 73% of airborne LiDAR estimated AGB. It should be noted that forest coverage data which used in Li et al (2010), Zeng (2005) were different from this study. It resulted in the differences of the total biomass. But, as the result showed in Fig. 4 the average of GLAS estimates AGB was 18 Mg/ha lower than research of Li et al (2010) and 6. 5 Mg/ha higher than research of Zeng (2005). It showed that the results were acceptable in regional scale. In order to compare these data in a uniform standard, we'd better to convent the estimated forest AGB to total biomass (both above & below ground). According to the root – shoot ratios which suggested by IPCC, we used 0. 32 as the root – shoot ratio considering the forest composition in the study area. Figure 5 shows the compared results which include below – ground biomass. Though the compare was not strict enough, but we think these results is acceptable and reasonable in regional scale.

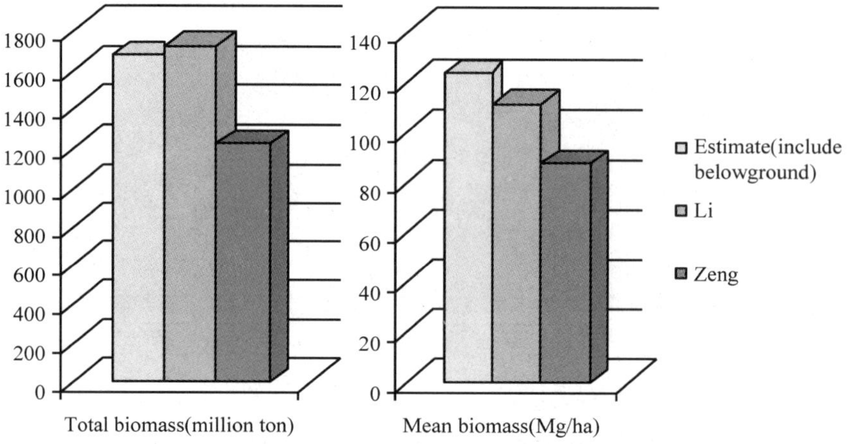

Fig. 5 Mean biomass comparison with previous results (include below – ground biomass)

Regional forest biomass was estimated by combining airborne LiDAR, spaceborne LiDAR of ICESat/GLAS and optical remote sensing data. To conclude, the result of this study is encouraging that ICESat/GLAS can estimate forest above ground biomass successfully in regional scale which described the amount and distribution of forest AGB well in the study area. It makes a significant sense in regional forest biomass estimates and global carbon research.

REFERENCES

Anaya J A, Chuvieco E, Palacios-Orueta A. 2009. Aboveground biomass assessment inColombia: A remote sensing approach. *Forest Ecology and Management* 257(4): 1237 – 1246.

Boudreau J, Nelson R F, Margolis H A, et al. 2008. Regional aboveground forest biomass using airborne and spaceborne LiDAR in Québec. *Remote Sensing of Environment* 112(10): 3876 – 3890.

Defourny P, Vancutsem C, Bicheron P, Brockmann C, Nino F, Schouten L and Leroy M (2006). GLOBCOVER: a300 m global land cover product for 2005 using Envisat MERIS time series. Proceedings of the ISPRS Commission VII mid – term symposium, Remote sensing: from pixels to processes. Enschede, the Netherlands, ISPRS: 59 – 62.

Dong J, Kaufmann R K, Myneni R B, et al. 2003. Remote sensing estimates of boreal and temperate forest woody biomass: carbon pools, sources, and sinks. *Remote Sensing of Environment* 84(3): 393 – 410.

Duncanson L I, Niemann K O , Wulder M A. 2010. Estimating forest canopy height and terrain relief from GLAS waveform metrics. *Remote Sensing of Environment* 114(1): 138 – 154.

Foody G M, Boyd D S, Cutler M E J. 2003. Predictive relations of tropical forest biomass from Landsat TM data and their transferability between regions. *Remote Sensing of Environment* 85(4): 463 – 474.

Fu T, Pang Y, Huang Q, Liu Q, et al. In press. Prediction of SubtropicalForest Parameters Using Airborne Laser Scanner. *Journal of Remote Sensing* .

Hese S, Lucht W, Schmullius C, Barnsley M, et al. Riedel T and Schröter K. 2005. Global biomass mapping for an improved understanding of the CO_2 balance – – the Earth observation mission Carbon – 3D. *Remote Sensing of Environment* 94(1): 94 – 104.

Hyde P, Dubayah R, Walker W, et al. 2006. Mapping forest structure for wildlife habitat analysis using multi – sensor (LiDAR, SAR/InSAR, ETM +, Quickbird) synergy. *Remote Sensing of Environment* 102(1 – 2): 63

–73.

Lefsky M A, Cohen W B, Acker S A, et al. 1999. Lidar remote sensing of the canopy structure and biophysical properties of Douglas – Fir Western Hemlock Forests. New York, NY, ETATS – UNIS, Elsevier.

Lefsky M A. 2010. A global forest canopy height map from the Moderate Resolution Imaging Spectroradiometer and the Geoscience Laser Altimeter System. *Geophys. Res. Lett.* 37(15): L15401.

Lefsky M A, Harding D J, Keller M, et al. 2005. Estimates of forest canopy height and aboveground biomass using ICESat. *Geophys. Res. Lett.* 32(22): L22S02.

Lefsky M A, Keller M, Yong P, et al. 2007. Revised method for forest canopy height estimation from Geoscience Laser Altimeter System waveforms. *Journal of Applied Remote Sensing* 1: 0133537.

Lefsky M A, Turner D P, Guzy M and Cohen W B. 2005. Combining lidar estimates of aboveground biomass and Landsat estimates of stand age for spatially extensive validation of modeled forest productivity. *Remote Sensing of Environment* 95(4): 549 –558.

Li H and Lei Y 2010. Estimation and evaluation of forest biomass crabon storage inChina. Beijing, China, Chinese Forestry Press.

Lim K, Treitz P, Baldwin K, Morrison L, et al. 2003. LiDAR remote sensing of biophysical properties of tolerant northern hardwood forests. *Canadian Journal of Remote Sensing* 29(5): 658 –678.

Matthew C, Hansen R S D, John R G, et al. 2003. The MODIS 500 meter Global Vegetation Continuous Field products. *Analysis of Multi – temporal Remote Sensing Images* : 295 –301.

Means, Joseph E, Acker, Steven A, Fitt, Brandon J, et al. 2000. Predicting forest stand characteristics with airborne scanning lidar. Bethesda, MD, ETATS – UNIS, American Society for Photogrammetry and Remote Sensing.

Muukkonen P, Heiskanen J. 2007. Biomass estimation over a large area based on standwise forest inventory data and ASTER and MODIS satellite data: A possibility to verify carbon inventories. *Remote Sensing of Environment* 107 (4): 617 –624.

Næsset E, Gobakken T. 2008. Estimation of above – and below – ground biomass across regions of the boreal forest zone using airborne laser. *Remote Sensing of Environment* 112(6): 3079 –3090.

Naesset , Erik. 2004. Practical large – scale forest stand inventory using a small – footprint airborne scanning laser. Basingstoke, ROYAUME – UNI, Taylor & Francis.

Nelson R, Ranson K J, Sun G, et al. 2009. Estimating Siberian timber volume using MODIS and ICESat/ GLAS. *Remote Sensing of Environment* 113(3): 691 –701.

Nillson M. 1996. Estimation ofTree Heights and Stand Volume Using an Airborne Lidar System. *Remote Sensing of Environment* 56: 1 –7.

Pang Y, Lefsky M A, Andersen H, et al. 2008. Validation of the ICEsat vegetation product using crown – area-weighted mean height derived using crown delineation with discrete return lidar data. *Canadian Journal of Remote Sensing* 34: S471 –S484.

Streck C, Scholz S. 2006. The role of forests in global climate change: whence we come and where we go. *International Affairs* 82(5): 861 –879.

Winjum J K, Dixon R K, Schroeder P E. 1993. Forest management and carbon storage: An analysis of 12 key forest nations. *Water, Air, & Soil pollution* : 239 257.

Zeng W. 2005. Research on Forest Biomass and Productivity inYunnan. *Central south forest inventory and planning* 24(4).

Zhao M, Zhou G – S. 2005. Estimation of biomass and net primary productivity of major planted forests inChina based on forest inventory data. *Forest Ecology and Management* 207(3): 295 –313.

森林经理学理论研究之我见

张昂和*

林业是个复杂的系统工程。要认清林业的特点，按照客观规律办事。森林经理是按照林业客观规律组织森林经营的科学保证。森林经理学作为一门科学，有其特性与共性。早期森林经理学创始者们认为以森林永续利用和法正林理论为代表的森林经理学是林学的“屋脊”。过去苏联专家来我国讲学说森林经理学是“综合性的上层科学”[1]。我国学术界曾把森林经理学摆在林学的“龙头”地位。可是，由于近年来求快逐新的浮躁心态，一时掩盖了森林经理学科的特点与属性及其在林业发展中的作用，以致造成森林经理学学科性质不明、概念不清、内涵混淆，甚至遭到被取消的命运。而且，当前学术界存在对森林经理学不同的见解：如认为森林经理学属于“技术学科”无需讨论理论问题；同时又有属于《市场经济学》科的森林经理创新理论“提出”；此外还有其他森林经理学论述存在；其学科观点与内涵各不相同、莫衷一是。《老子》讲：“静胜躁”！厘清森林经理学的性质与内涵，应是森林经理学研究的当务之急。现在是所谓信息时代，各种新事物层出不穷，人们总想找点新东西来装饰自己，可是今天时髦的热点，明天可能就会落伍或被淘汰。因此牢牢掌握森林经理学科的本质就显得特别重要。现仅就个人拙见，以：“林、时、续、轮、量、价、法、律、权、组、策、划、管、理、经、正、道、本，”十八字，分三段陈述之。

一、森林经理学研究内容的几点商榷

(1)林：欲了解森林经理，需先了解森林和林业。然而森林和林业是一种不容易被人们所认识和理解的事物，也是常常容易被忽视或轻视的事情。当前信息发达，“秀才不出门便知天下事”。偶尔到了林区，也会“只见树木不见森林”，不了解整体性。有时想到要重视，由于不理解其深邃的内涵和长远的变化，也只触及皮毛不明就里。即使知道了一些，林业生产是以多年生木本植物为主体的森林为对象，森林是一种复杂的生物群体，和具有多种功能的可再生资源，由于它的特点而需要独特的经营方式和方法等。但在实际做的时候往往会简单地对待。如把林业当做采掘工业，所谓“开发森林资源”会立即获得经济利益。或者把林

[注]：张昂和，北京林业大学五四级校友，留校任森林经理学助教，1957年第一届森林经理学研究生毕业，任西北农林科技大学讲师，内蒙古农业大学森林经理学讲师、教研室主任，中国林业科学研究院森林经理课题组组长，副研究员，中国林学会1978年年会科技组长，中国林学会1980年“森林合理经营永续利用学术讨论会”秘书长、中国林学会森林经理学会分创建人之一，第一届常务理事兼秘书长。美国威斯康辛大学访问学者，伯克莱加州大学农业专家客座教授，综合生物资源中心研究员中国(交流)项目主任斯刊编委。北京师范大学客座教授。现退休侨居美国。

2010年12月，八十岁时，返校与森林经理研究生座谈，交流学术观点，发方由全锋、王春红同学根据灵童整理，经本人局部修改补充，为纪念老一辈森林经理学家和追思同窗老友董乃钧教授，呈中国林学会森林经理分会和北京林业大学2011年森林经理学术研讨会。

业当做粗放农业，认为“刨坑栽树”扩大森林面积一时也容易见到“业绩”。对于不易立见成效的长期森林经营工作往往被忽视。或许因为那是“子孙后代”的事，与我何干？因此对于经营森林所需要的森林经理也就可有可无了！

(2)时：两千多年前，孟子讲：“斧斤以‘时’入山林，材木不可胜用也”[2]。“时”反映林业的关键特征“长期性”。一个“时”字起到森林经理学原理的点“睛”作用，是森林经理科学的起点和着眼点。但它常常容易被忽视。人们忽视了长期性这个特点，就会只顾采伐和造林等短期效益而轻予长期的经营管理。“经济再生产过程与自然再生产过程相交织”[3]，这一点在林业当中更为突出。由于自然再生产的过程漫长，容易造成经济再生产中断。因此林业生产时时要考虑时间特点！当然“我们也要与‘时’共进！”用育林技术缩短树木成熟期。但是如果急于求成，像工农业一样短期见效，那就不属于林业的经营范畴了。有些林业工作者不愿意遵从林业的特点和规律的制约，例如所谓森林经理“新《理论》”的提出[注]，主张“商品林经营活动应等同于企业的商品生产活动”，“实行弹性采伐，缩短轮伐期获高回报率”[4]，就把林业和一般工农业等同起来。然而“没有特性就没有共性”。否定林业的特性就等于否定林业本身。缩短森林生长期，只能是相对的。林业的长期性特点，总体上不会改变。因此，森林经理就是必要的！

(3)续：由于森林再生产的过程漫长，林业生产容易中断，因而需要永续(连续)作业。在孟子的那句话里已有了体现。贾思勰《齐民要术》讲种杨树时说：“周而复始，永世不绝”[5]的做法，依次组织森林经营就体现了森林经理的作用。但是在近代，森林永续利用原则在我国长期被否定或忽视。20世纪50年代照搬苏联“林业扩大再生产原则”[1]，提出“大砍大造”等口号和做法，按经济计划对木材的需要采伐森林，脱离林业特点和违背永续利用原则，造成资源、经济和生态危机！现在又提出林业市场化经营按市场需求自由采伐森林[4]，会进一步加深危机！1980年中国林学会全国“森林合理经营永续利用学术讨论会”拨乱反正，重新提起按照林业特点和规律经营森林，贯彻森林永续利用原则[19]。20世纪90年代后又出现森林可持续经营的讨论，然而二者是一致的。保持森林效益能够持久稳定发挥是林业的基本任务。因此森林永续利用或森林可持续经营是森林经理的基本原则，不能任意取消或改变。

(4)轮：轮伐期，又称森林经营周期，是森林物质和经营活动在一定的时空范畴运动周转的过程。使森林经营系统能够持久“有序”地循环运行是森林经理的要务。有序才能有效。早年，轮伐期在苏联被批判，一位前俄国老森林经理学家说过：“没有轮伐期，就没有森林经理！”现在，我们进一步说，“没有森林经理就没有林业！”因为有人指出：“林业搞不好是由于没有做好森林经营，森林经营没做好是因为忽视森林经理。”反推过去：“没有森林经理就没有科学的森林经营，没有科学的森林经营，就没有林业的科学发展”。轮伐期是林业经营重要措施，轮伐期长短影响森林经营过程和结果，轮伐期应依据生物、林学、生态、社会、经济等多因素综合来确定。不应只由单一因素如“经济利益最大”等来简单地确定[4]。一旦确定要保持相对稳定，不宜随意变更。缩短轮伐期在一定时期可以获得较多的经济利

注：《林木市场成熟“理论”的提出与探讨》一书的序言、前言及书介等处均提到该书提出了森林经理“创新理论”，或被称作森林经营(经理)新概念、新理论。以下简称此书为“新《理论》”，《理论》代表这本书，“新”字是形容词，和其他理论书区别，有助理解。见参考文献[4]

益，但长远看对生态环境和林业生产力可能不利。有人主张以市场供求关系和市场价格来确定轮伐期，并随市场的变化而变化。这样的轮伐期等于没有轮伐期。科学正确地确定轮伐期是森林经理的要务。

(5)量：森林蓄积量、生长量、采伐量三者关系是森林经营系统重要的量化关系。从前有位林业部长出国考察向国外介绍中国林业时被质疑。部长回国后做报告建议“要重视研究森林经理。过去关于(森林)采伐量不要超过生长量的提法不科学!”[6](“不科学”，恐怕是我国林业的根本问题，并没有从根本上正视!)因为采伐量是在一定森林时空结构情况下变化发展的，在没有合理森林结构调整前提下会造成不合理采伐。如中幼龄林比重大生长量会很大，而可采蓄积量则很少，按照这一原则确定采伐量，会大量消耗中龄林后备资源！所以采伐量应该不要超过森林经理科学计算的允许采伐量。这种采伐量是根据森林资源结构、林况、森林生长量、经营目标和永续利用，以及对森林的多功能长期稳定的需求等多因素综合计算求出。而不是仅仅按照“市场当前需求”来确定。新《理论》主张以市场价格和需求来确定森林采伐量[4]，取消限制，就等于取消森林经理。部长说要重视研究的森林经理，不但没有重视研究，反而“森林经理学”作为重点学科被取消了！森林经理学的产生与发展是从采伐量的调整与控制开始的。时空要有“序”，量价要有“度”。有序才能有效，适度方可固本。当代量化关系进一步发展，对森林的生物量、价值量、径流量、野生动植物数量以及森林碳汇等均需量化，数量反映森林物质运动、林业生产力和生产关系变化。“研究森林采伐量的理论和技术，历来是森林经理学的核心问题之一”[7]。

(6)价：我国自古就有森林买卖。至明清时代，南方杉木林区已经广泛使用“龙泉码价”进行 森林和木材交易。当年有估青山师傅为交易双方计算林木价值。记得其中有一种“飞码”，即遇到特殊材，如一株可用做帆船桅杆的大树其价值可比一般价码翻几番。有一定科学性。后来学习德日的森林较利，没有实践。学苏联用计划价格的林价，不能反映森林经营成本和效益。现代森林经理中的森林评价，内容扩大包括多种效益等[9,10]。而率是相对值。森林生长率与利率分别反映物质与经济消长变化。林业投资收益率受内外部多方面影响(包括风险因素、税收等)，综合而不是唯一市场经济因素评估投资效益。量价有度方可固本。调节森林物质生产、经济生产、生态效益和社会效益的价值关系是森林经理的任务之一。

(7)法：作业法系统种类很多。常用的同龄林与异龄林的经营措施内容大不相同，早年工业化发展时期，木材工业为获取最大利润多采用皆伐作业经营同龄林。当前随着生态环境和可持续经营的需要逐渐依森林状况采用异龄林经营。哈尔滨市郊区三个林场今年所进行的近自然森林作业是利用欧洲流行的作业法。作业法构成森林经营的技术经济体系，决定着森林的结构、功能和变化。要维护森林生态系统平衡，维护生物多样性，发挥森林多功能效益，不宜只发展单一树种和单一作业法(如杨树同龄纯林)[4]，森林采伐和更新方式是森林作业法系统的重要内容，也是森林经营的重要措施。森林经理学要研究作业法的选择与构成森林经营措施的体系。

(8)律：研究森林经理的基本原则或规律为林业法律法规提供相关的理论依据。如前述森林永续利用原则、轮伐期、作业法、采伐量与生长量关系等林业法律法规多是依据森林经理理论研究的内容。一旦形成法律，森林经理工作就要依照法律法规制定森林经营决策规划方案。森林经理不能违反国家法规，如新《理论》取消森林采伐量限额管理，实行“造采自由”等[4]。

(9)权：森林经理工作是要实现森林所有者的意愿和目的，还要符合社会利益。马克思认为森林具有长期性，需要面积大才能周转，因此林业不适合私人(分散)经营[3]。国有林按照国家法律和规定管理，经营要符合国家和公共利益。我国森林经理如何适应所有制与经营权的变化，是值得研究的问题，如国有林中的经营者获取最大经济利益的分配和资源承载问题等？把国有林交给 私人经营者自由采伐获利，不符合社会主义所有制原则，分林到户不符合国有林经营原则。森林所有制是森林经理工作的经济基础。

(10)组：早期森林经理与森林组织是同义语，或称组织森林经营实现永续利用。为此要调查研究森林和土地类型，以自然和社会因素与森林经营需要等指标划分异质单元，将同质的地段组合为组织经营单位，制定相同的经营方针和措施，这里的森林和土地分类不是指大范围森林种类(如商品林等)，而是一个经营单位内具体森林地块或小班，如林分组、龄级组，立地类型组，水土流失地段，珍稀动植物栖息地等[9]。对其进行调查、测绘，获得森林和林地资源信息与编制地图和统计数表。范围小而简单的林地可用一般测算技术进行调查、测绘。大范围森林应用地理信息系统提高效率，如分层级加空间信息高级土地分类法等(要建专业数据库成本高)[10]。调查测绘方法以及所谓“3S”技术都只是森林经理工作的手段，不能用其取代森林经理学本身的研究内容！因为这些技术方法是属于其他专门学科(如地学、空间科学、测算技术等)研究的对象与范畴。森林经理学研究的对象应是森林组织经营本身的技术经济指标和措施体系。因此“现代森林经理就是3S”说法是错误的。

(11) 策：森林经营决策与调整是森林经理工作的核心。“林业经营具有长期性复杂性，一旦决策失误，改之不易，影响深远。”建议加强“森林资源发展战略决策”的研究(张昂和，《森林资源管理决策与林农复合系统管理》[8]，1986年由科协主席钱学森院士推荐给国务院总理、副总理传阅，万里副总理批示：“此意见很值得重视，”林业“要有百年”战略考虑，原文存国务院档案室。二十五年前建议时引用古人语“人无远虑，必有近忧”，今日重温，依然有用。“我国林业发展由于忽视森林经营和森林经理的长远战略考量”，而出现“两危”(林区资源和经济危机)。只有经过策划与谋略做出科学的长远战略决策和定期调整安排方可解林区之危。

在前述森林资源的特点与变化，对其各方面经营要素做技术经济分析评估策划，在一定约束条件下进行森林经营决策。森林经理一般是为一个森林经营单位如一个林业企业或森林类型进行决策。它上承国家方针政策法律法规的贯彻，向下指导日常具体的森林经营活动或管理行为决策。森林经理是面向未来，经过策划与谋略为达到经营目标和途径而进行长远的综合战略性决策，其内容如：可选择的森林类型、结构与多样性、森林评价、作业法选择、经营单位空间布局与扩展、轮伐期长短与林龄结构、森林收获全程水平与过程(如全轮伐期综合效益最高)，经营措施的选择与时空配置(如采伐、更新、抚育、森林保护与健康的策略和措施等)[9]。森林经理主要是适应森林生长长期性、功能多样性等特征进行综合调整与策划。由于社会发展，人类对森林效益的需求越来越多，各种利益矛盾凸显，需要多目标多层次动态地长期综合平衡寻找解决之道。例如：有一块小面积成熟林的林主要决定其采伐销售木材和更新森林，决策简易；但若此林同时属于木材企业范围，它会被纳入公司轮伐期的木材永续利用计划中做决定；如果此林也坐落在集水区，它的采伐决定要考虑水土流失、水质变化与鱼类生存；若此林也处于旅游观光或社区活动地域附近，则不仅要考虑地区行政管理和社会团体需求，还要考虑景观美学与就业等社会文化问题；而对森林生态系统健康和野生动物保护而言则决策影响范围就更加宽广。以上一块森林的决策由小而简单的情况，变成为大范围、多层次、多目标、多标准、多效益、多维、多参与者等复杂的综合决策情况。面对复杂多变量的森林经营决策可以通过系统策划、综合谋略、用运筹学方法如线性规划、目标规划、非线性、动态规划、和各种启发式方法等[9,10]。系统分析与数学规划方法是常用于解决森林经理中的森林经营规划决策问题方法。但是，数学和计算方法也只是手段，是用来解决森林经营规划中的实际问题[11]，而不是为了显示数学的深奥。运筹帷幄决策“百年大计”并适时加以动态调整是森林经理学研究的中心任务。

(12)划：森林经营计划(或称施业案、经营方案)是森林经营决策体系的具体化。森林经理是为实现森林经营单位的经营目的，而编制森林经营的长远规划与中短期计划，可分等级或层次，如战略、战术方案等。前面讨论的各种森林经营原则、原理、方式、方法、时空结构的设计等都将纳入森林经营方案中。现代森林经理学可用最优化方法提供经营者可选择的多方案和最佳(最适)方案。森林经营规划方案是森林经理工作的重要成果。

(13)管：森林经理是森林经营管理工作的一部分而不是全部。森林经理不是“大管家”(误解)，更不能是林业部门的“总管”(误会)。森林经理编制计划方案属于经营管理工作性质，但是它不能够管理全部森林经营所有的事务。现在实际的森林经营管理工作内容复杂繁重，森林经理不能都管。森林经营管理好比“作战”，森林经理有如“参谋部”，它是负责制订“作战”(经营)计划的谋略，提供指挥官(林场主)决策应用，但具体实施还要靠很多部门，如前方战斗(营林员)，后方支援(后勤部)等部门去实行，就不能都由参谋部(森林经理)包揽。现在的森林经营计划更延伸到短期计划、森林验证和供应链管理等工作[10]。森林经理为验证森林经营是否可持续、验证碳汇量和产业供应链等确定技术经济指标而策划。由于经营过程的变更与不确定因素的发生，依照长期战略规划和战术计划指导，应用“适应性管理”方法，在短期作业计划中予以调整，及时反馈修正，使其与计划施行及检查修订过程衔接起来。而日常具体事务则应由营林监管人员去做。森林经理工作范围应与其分清不致什么都管而造成脱序失衡。

二、森林经理学理论研究的必要性

(14)理：研究一门科学或者做一件事情，应思考三方面问题：一是什么？二是为什么？三是怎么办？即首先，要交代清楚这门科学的概念；其次，是说明它的道理；然后告诉人们怎么办的方法。对于研究森林经理学来说也是如此。尤其我国森林经理长期忽视自己的经验，学习外国又没有弄清道理，就生搬硬套地照办(干)起来，走了弯路。而现代国内外相关学科发展迅速，也影响着森林经理学概念混淆，学科性质不明。在这种情况下，就应该首先加以研究讨论把概念弄清楚。对于一些“新概念”引进来以后，更要把这些概念本身的含义搞清楚，分辨是否正确与适用。而不能没有弄清之前就去把这些概念“变成实际的东西”[14]，或先要告诉大家怎么干的技术问题。对森林经理学的理论更要深入探讨，有了科学的理论指导才能有林业的科学发展。森林经理要贯彻国家的方针和政策，而国家制定林业方针政策也要参照森林经理及其他林业科学的理论，如森林永续利用和可持续经营，森林采伐量的依据和调节，森林轮伐期和作业法的内涵，森林评价与决策，森林的分类、结构、布局，组织、规划与调整等，都是有关林业政策与经济的理论问题，而不是单纯技术。过去片面提出“大砍大造”等口号和单纯提出“森林采伐量不得超过森林生长量”政策[6]，实践证明违反了森林经理学原理。因此，不弄清楚森林经理学概念，不研究理论，只搞实际技术，简单告诉大家怎么干，就会脱离森林经理学的研究方向而钻到其他技术学科的牛角尖里去！这样的森林经理学就不能再是林业科学的“龙头”学科了。

森林经理学的定义：“它应是一门依照林业发展特点研究森林可持续经营长期战略决策和规划调整理论与方法的综合性技术经济管理科学。”这一概念看来冗长，是由于它的特殊复杂性所决定，又要适应现代科学发展而必需有一个综合全面的概括，以便于了解其性质和内容。类似提法有些森林经理学家也已提出过，如美国森林经理学家 K. Davis 曾经提出：“它(森林经理学)是综合性显著，对技术经济问题进行分析与抉择(decisions)的管理科学”[12]。同异之处是根据我国情况和理解做调整补充，如“综合性”、“技术经济”、“决策”是共同的，“管理科学”是美国创立的，“技术经济学”是中国创立的，后者属于前者的分支与发展，并不矛盾。前面冠以常被忽略的林业特点与长期战略[8,13]，显示决策的特殊性与宏观政策性，规划调整包括战略战术决策与微观技术性管理层面，最后加上管理科学以提高学科层次的上层科学属性[1]。这个定义可以体现特殊而完整的学科性质与内涵，说明森林经理学不是单纯的技术学科，也不是简单的技术加经济，而是森林经营决策规划与调整的特殊经济与技术交叉学科。它虽然应用了许多相关学科的理论和方法，但不等于这些学科的简单相加，而是发挥综合的加乘效应，即整体效应大于各项效应之和。森林经理学的思维首先是林业长远战略观念。它的理论不是简单的应用基础理论，不是单纯的技术和工艺[14]，而是融入林业特殊科学性体系的综合与提高。“成功的森林经理是有效整合的艺术”[12]。森林经理学不是“大拼盘”、“大杂烩”或无规则的“群体”，它是一个独特的高层级完整独立的科学体系，是其他学科所无法替代的，是林业要科学发展所必须的综合而又特殊的林学上层科学。

森林经理学研究的对象也不是森林经理工作的全部，不能把森林经理工作中所有技术细节全都放到森林经理学里去研究。它主要是研究森林经营的长期发展战略和规划调整的理论和方法。森林经理学科面拓展的太宽，不能相对集中，也会脱序失衡，影响学科发展。森林经理学科发展需要界定它的范畴，不能把别的相关学科都拉进来作为自己的研究对象，搞所谓“大经理”或群龙无首的“学科群”[14]，这样像似壮大自己，实际是削弱了学科本身！随着时代和科学的发展，与森林经理有关的新事物新观点会不断出现，只要把有用而必要的理论方法吸纳即可，不必为了紧跟时髦，什么新东西都照搬进来。森林经理学本身的名词术语、概念定义、技术方法已经难以搞清，现在又要把别的学科的新名词新概念拿来“改造”原有森林经理学，实际是制造混乱。前述所谓新《理论》[4]提出并受到奖励。过去曾经认为森林经理学只是技术学科，不必研究理论政策，现在转为称赞新《理论》与政策。认为“传统”理论已经过时，需要创新“现代”新理论。我们搞现代化，往往把现代和传统割裂开来。森林是一种历史地理现象[13]，它本身就是历史传承的，森林是长时期在动态平衡中变化发展着，是相对稳定的缓慢的运动，它不同于静止的矿山和迅速运动的工农业。森林经理学要在实践中提炼成理论也不是一时之功。我们要强调总结历史经验，不可轻易否定或忽视传统，并不排斥对其他学科新发展的借鉴和应用。美国农林工作中，往往一方面新科技迅速增加，一方面从整体效应出发，有些传统技术还继续应用。那种机械划分割裂传统与现代的做法在农业问题上已经吃了亏，我国由于否定自己有机循环的传统农业优点，片面学习美国等现代工业化农业弊端，出现食物安全危机。而美国近年学习中国等国传统可持续有机农业的优点，降低食品毒素。这种传统与现代置换的现象，值得我们林业界为鉴。森林经理的“理论与实践紧密不可分”[12]。但在缺乏正确理论指导时，强调重视研究理论就显得突出重要。希望经过深入研究认真讨论，首先把森林经理学的理论概念和学科性质搞清楚。否则，概念不清，道理不明，森林经理学作为林学的“龙头学科”[14]，也就“有头无脑”，带动不了林业科学发展了！

(15)经：重温古典与现代经典森林经理学理论的形成与发展可得到启发借鉴。不应认为“经典理论已经过时”(新《理论》一书》序言)，就任意否定。对于森林经理学理论的“森林永续利用”和“法正林”(包括恒续林)学说[15]，尽管不断有人批判它，反对它，否定它，禁止它，认为它是阻碍按市场需求自由采伐森林的“枷锁”是站不住脚的，它依然存在世界各国森林经理理论中，被看作森林经营原则和“理想森林结构模型”的基础[17,10]，要把它作为一种森林经营理念和森林经理学的理论抽象来理解，而不是简单地当作具体技术去生搬硬套，它会是永恒的科学真理。森林永续利用原则和法正林学说是森林经理学的经典核心理论。我们注意学习和继承传统理论，同时也要注重发展和创新森林经理学理论。但是，森林经理学理论往往产生于长期的科学实验，又经过长期实践考验，才能够确立，不可一蹴而就，一天推翻一个旧理论，一天创新一个新理论。关于继承和发展森林经理学，欧美各国已有先例。早年欧洲顾尔诺和毕奥莱继洪德斯哈根法正林学说之后，用四十余年实验研究“法正异龄林理论与检查法”[16,17]是如此，在欧洲各国如瑞士可见到这种理论仍然在营林实践中纯熟地应用着。近现代美国森林经理学家戴维斯父子两代传承发展森林经理学，自老戴维斯(K. Davis，曾任耶鲁大学教授和美国林学会主席)1954 年出版《美国森林经理学》(第 1 版)[18]，到 2001 年由其子小戴维斯(L. Davis，伯克莱加州大学荣誉教授)等人出版《森林经理学》(第 4 版)[9]也经历四十余年。戴维斯父子与其他学者一起前后编写出版了四本森林经理学著作。第 1 版和第 2 版继传统“法正林”学说基础上，结合美国森林实际提出“完全调整林”理论和方法，[12]曾受到我国著名森林经理学家范济洲教授的推崇。1987 年小戴维斯与约翰森合编森林经理学第 3 版[19]提出森林经营多效益目标决策及大型计算机规划模型。此后，美国林学界出现了几方面变化，一是森林可持续经营与森林永续利用理论的争论，二是环境保护与木材经济的矛盾和森林生态系统管理理论的出现，三是社会参与和林业政策发展。2001 年以小戴维斯为首的四位森林经理学家为适应新情况，编写出版的《森林经理学——可持续生态、经济与社会效益》(第 4 版)[9]。此书首先把森林永续利用与可持续经营原则统一起来，认为二者是继承和发展的关系并不矛盾，从而厘清森林经理的理论基础。然后把森林生态系统管理、以木材生产为主的经济管理系统及公众参与的社会文化系统等多目标多层面的三个不同系统整合成为一个综合大系统，用新方法建立森林经营战略决策与规划模型。这是美国森林经理学理论的又一次发展。林学中将这三大体系的综合论述形成完整森林经理学理论与方法体系的学术专著应属创新之举，是近半世纪父子继承而来，是作者们集体创造并结合前人研究成果得来的经典之作。

三、森林经理学的道德伦理观

(16)正：林业要走上正轨，森林经理首先要导正方向。“道德观”始于我国的古代哲学思想，而“伦理学”则出自欧洲古希腊哲学体系，至十九世纪二者擦出火花，出现“道德伦理观”。随着人与自然关系的变化，产生现代“生态伦理学”(或“生态道德”、“环境道德”)。

进一步阐述人与自然及社会发展的关系，“‘生态伦理’不仅要求人类将其道德关怀从社会延伸到非人的自然存在物或自然环境，而且呼吁人类把人与自然的关系确立为一种道德关系”[18]。道德伦理应成为森林经理学的强音！由于现代化发展所带来的环境破坏、生态危机、社会道德衰落！波及整个林业系统，森林经理更是首当其冲。因此，为导正森林经理，从“道德伦理”关系出发，先以正反两面举例说明。

国家要稳定不折腾，林业也要稳定不能折腾，因为林业周期长，不能随意变更其内容与途径。应理顺林业、经营、经理关系，林业要抓“中间”带“两头”才是正道。“中间”这段很长的森林经营贯穿了林业的整个过程，不确定因素多难控制。“两头”的采伐和造林，时间短较易控制。抓住中间的经营，带动采伐和造林(采和造两者同时也是重要的森林经营环节)林业就可顺利发展。我国人工林面积虽大由于不注重经营管理不能发挥应有效用。因此重视保护和经营管理好现有森林[21]仍然是林业发展的正途。黄中立先生曾说过，森林经理就是森林的“经理”，它的任务是“经理”好森林。不管哪个人当“经理”都要依施业案经营管理好森林。施业案制定后要有法律效力，可以定期检查调整修订，但是经过认真论证依法确定的长远战略目标和安排不能随意变更。例如森林类型、主要树种、轮伐期、作业法和采伐量等经营方向的变更都要慎重。不能一个经理上台要保护，换一个要砍伐；一个要经营天然混交林搞择伐作业，另一个要皆伐搞人工速生林；一个要坚持长轮伐期发挥森林生态和多种效益，另一个要改为短轮伐期发挥经济效益，[4]等等。森林经营要严守科学和道德。否则，一人一个样，一天一个样，没有准则，林业是永远搞不好的。林业管理应该换人不换“案”，因为森林施业期或森林生长周期往往会超越人的工作期甚至生命期。

目前，我国短轮伐期和超短轮伐期的“速生林业”正适应“市场”需要，以所谓森林经理新《理论》[4]指导而方兴未艾。但是在天然原始林区以杨树速生人工林取代天然林的做法长远来看会造成生态灾难，近期也不会收到想象的结果。发展速生丰产林的妙方由来已久，早在上世纪“大跃进”时代就已风行。改革开放以来更加大力推广，所谓“杨家将”、“杉家浜”名扬海内外。记得20世纪80年代，我国有位林业界人士在美国林业杂志发表文章说：中国大力发展速生树种杨树等丰产林，不需很久(大约10年)木材自己用不完(用很多统计数字证明)，还可以大量出口占据国际市场！此论一出外国林业界哗然，害怕这个竞争对手出现！可是30年过去了，未见中国木材大量出口占领市场(据报道，中国杨树纯林连栽病虫害多发，国外将杨树害虫光肩星天牛等列入检疫对象)。改革开放以来，我国造林面积世界第一，估计杨树约占1/3以上，其中新品种速生丰产林应不会少于10%，如按前述计算木材产量应该相当可观，然而至今木材危机不但没有减缓反而愈演愈烈。虽然新《理论》讲“现阶段”(不知未来)主要针对“商品林中的用材林”，“鼓励”将一部分天然林改造为速生丰产林？但在上面大力倡导和舆论宣扬推广起来形成政策举国跟进，把希望寄托在新《理论》计算的速生丰产林上即可解决林区或林业危机！无异画饼充饥。速生林如果经营不当，不但木材不会大增，而且会造成生态灾害，如南方杉木原产地纯林连栽生产力减退，“甚至大雨中造成大面积泥石流，整片整片的林子因林地溜滑倒掉”[22]，即是例证。

新《理论》还说：“林木市场成熟理论”的重要意义，还在于将天然林改造为速生丰产林，“有利于森工企业走出困境”[4]。这里需要先了解森工企业的困境由何而来？它是由于20世纪初中期，苏联林学界否定“森林永续利用原则”、“取消轮伐期改用采伐年龄”，够需要就可以采。紧接着苏联工业化时期木材需要量大增，森林开发由西部向乌拉尔以东原始林区进展，那里森林资源丰富可以扩大采伐，森工企业可以充分利用，做法是每建一个森工企业设定经营年限(如一般30年)集中采伐采完搬家，投入成本低，短期即可以获利。实践证明这种做法弊多利少！于是20世纪70年代后期苏联又重新恢复了森林永续利用原则。然而这种掠夺式开发经验搬到我国东北西南原始林区照办，很快造成资源枯竭。我国资源少，人口多，森工企业无处可搬，大量人口滞留林区，无钱无力搞不易见效的营林工作，于是驾轻就熟扩大或增设各种木材加工和深加工产业，挣钱养人。这样“一增一减”企业进一步走入“困境”。于是新《理论》采取“削足适履”办法，扩大采伐天然林，营造杨树速生林，[4]欲解燃眉之急。但是因此加深资源危机，企业走入更深困境！恶性循环会使东北原始林区如长白山(三江之源)的森林水库作用减低，使东北平原粮仓的天然防护屏障丧失，后果难以想象！正确的做法应该是“改履适足”，即改产或停产那些大量消耗木材的大型加工企业，或者外迁(有报道称，当前俄国表示欢迎外国森工企业合作或投资开发远东森林资源？我们剩余森工生产力可以考虑参与合作对双方都有利。)这里只保留适合当地森林自然生产力的低耗高效先进小型林产工业，使之有利于保护和发展森林，成为名副其实的“绿色企业”。减少采伐，严格控制采伐量，用天然或结合人工方法恢复发展多功能综合效益强的森林，如长白山特有的针阔混交林等。按综合(不是只按市场)的有区别的轮伐期生产，施行严格的永续作业，以维护我国东北森林最后的防线。把过去森工企业赚的钱和全国各木材消耗单位获利赚走的钱，用税收等方法无偿地返回或投入林业再生产。对林区从业人员进行严格科学培训，加强管理，实行真正的科学森林经营。我国各地区为保护环境而改造、关闭或迁移高污染工厂即是先例；美国西部森林为保护斑点猫头鹰而减少森林采伐和改变经营方式；为保护本国森林而从国外进口木材，都是适合的例子。

短伐期如薪炭林(能源)、杨、柳、白蜡条等(1~5年生)在我国作为农、副业经营已有悠久历史。美国的短伐期“木本作物”和“圣诞树”的经营已经纳入农业经营范畴，并未用来取代天然林经营。在德国正实行的“近自然林经营”与我国新《理论》要把“天然林”改为“人工林”[4]的做法相反；那里即使是土地肥沃的平原农区的森林依然保持一二百年的长轮伐期不变，同时获得经济收益和更多生态、社会效益。关键在于森林经理的合理安排和经营措施得当。而不是以短线经济利益为导向去牺牲长远利益和改变林业经营性质。大范围机械地划分商品林任意采伐是不科学的，森林的多功能效益不应以这种森林分类而分割。前述瑞士阿尔卑斯山林区所见，外貌看去是大片原始森林风景如画和青山绿水的旅游胜地，同时又是源源不断的木材生产基地，却见不到采伐迹地，走进林内才能够发现分布有序的大经伐桩与天然或人工更新的幼树和错落有致的分解剩余物。一座小型木材加工厂和堆满原木的贮木场坐落林缘附近，不仅未破坏生态景观，反而成为一道不可缺的风景线。把生态、观光、体育(有雪山和滑雪场)、营林、采伐、加工巧妙地融为一体和谐共存，这种经营水平令人叹为观止！原来那里正是森林经理学前辈毕奥莱(H. Biolley)的家乡，很值得学习思考。森林经营要导向正轨，森林经理必须先走上“正道”。

(17)道：老子《道德经》讲：“人法地，地法天，天法道，道法自然。”[23]“道”即“自然规律”。揭示人与自然，精神与物质辩证关系。人们要按客观规律办事，不能违反客观规律。现代森林经理学开章明义，说明人与自然的关系：是违反规律去征服自然，还是顺应自然或者与自然和谐相处？首先摒弃征服自然的“人定胜天”理论，而以“人与自然和谐共存”为指导森林经理理论路线的出发点[9]，与《生态伦理》一致。恩格斯说：人类征服自然的每一次胜利，都遭受到大自然的报复![24]人们把森林经理研究提升到哲学层面，认为森林经理是一种文化的体现，各国森林经理具有不同文化的内涵。我们祖先讲“天人合一”，早已把人与自然的辩证关系以及森林物质运动变化规律做了说明，而我们却只顾照搬西方的机械唯物论和形而上学的实用主义。当前知识界强调“怎么干的唯技术主义”就是这种表现[25]。有人认为我国森林经理学是1952年设立的，[14]只有短短几十年历史，而忽略了我国千年以上森林经营历史中的森林经理内涵。如果说欧洲的森林经营管理是从中世纪皇室园林管理开始的，那么中国皇室林园包括陵园，如黄帝陵林园管理已有五千年以上的历史。从有记载的用材林经营管理原理，到实际的唐松、汉柏，都在一二千年以上。而著名的杉木用材林经营历史至少在一千年以上，能够永续经营至今，就是探索着森林经营的客观规律，具有森林经理的道理与方法存在。只不过与西方森林经理表现的方式不同而已。然而都要遵循林业特殊的自然和经济规律之道。所不同的基础是东西方文化的差异。外国森林经理学有时还讲到中国的森林经营管理历史，而我们自己却是民族虚无主义地忽略自己的传统。森林经理如果离开了文化传统的依托，那么它的发展就会像一个断了线的风筝，不知飘向何处去了！美国森林经理一百年来从无到有(我国是从有到无被取消了)表面看来发展很快，有各种新技术武装，新理论层出不穷，又结合美国本土特色，不断添枝加叶，但本质上没有脱离欧美传统文化的依托。我们如果隔断历史脱离自己文化的特点与传承，只学几样不断变化着的新技术或照搬市场经济模式，就会感到格格不入地走向迷雾中的泥潭。各国的森林经理都有自己文化的反映。中国传统森林经理更具有东方文明的“神秘”色彩。它们不一定留下完整的学术专著(有些理论方法散记在典籍或地方志中)，然而口耳相传延续千年的实践就是科学(如传统医学、传统农学，古建筑学等都有此现象存在)。杉木林经营的综合作业法、依据地力的多重轮伐期、移动法正林结构、“龙泉码价”估价方法和采伐量调整、小面积皆伐或择伐方式、乔林和矮林相间、不同范围适合自然生产力的伐期龄、长短结合的混农作业、中期的三耕土与近自然经营的阔叶林或针阔叶混交林交互演替恢复地力，然后再进行1~2次中循环。大约三四百年周期在一定范围(如一个小流域)地力尚未衰竭之前与相邻林区交替转换进入一次较大循环。经过多次轮回周转生生不息地再生产(包括复杂的社会生产关系再生产)，永续作业，千年不衰！体现人与自然和谐共存。直到1979和1992年曾在湖南会同、江华和福建溪后等林区，仍可见到稠密茁壮长势喜人的参天大经杉木林，而且龄级结构均匀如同法正林。这是一部鲜活实际的中国森林经理学。知名林学家万晋教授曾说过“杉木是我国的国宝，经验受到外国重视!”国外有识之士认为我国传统农林业是可以借鉴的已经实现的可持续经营，而我们自己却弃之如敝屣！老子讲：“合抱之木生于毫末”，林业的经验与成果得来不易，对现有森林和历史成就都应十分珍惜。根基打好，不可急于求成。

森林经理需要科学实践以探索经营森林的规律。记得20世纪50~80年代，响应毛主席关于大办农林场的指示，曾参与和主持数个教学和科学试验林场的创建。其中1958、1961年建立的秦岭火地塘教学实验林场的生态环境、生物多样性、林分类型多样与典型性世间罕见，我们对其进行一级森林经理调查和用先进的小班经理法编制施业案，并实地进行各种森林经营实验，但遗憾的是不久全部可贵的森林被森工局采伐殆尽，全部原始资料包括调查簿、航空相片，森林模型等丢失损毁。而用日本落叶松人工林取代原有天然林，生态被破坏！其后，在大兴安岭原始林调查样板林场森林经理研究，以及“文革”后在湖南会同集体林办实验林场，均无疾而终！反观国外，如美国加州大学实验林场经营近百年，各种科学试验包括森林经理固定样地连续系统抽样调查、经营与试验档案、遥感图片地理信息系统、森林生态、采伐更新、造林抚育、防火用火、病虫害防治，森林气象，森林碳汇管理、野生动物，等等，持续不断，出了很多高水平科研教学成果。其他各大学和研究单位也多如此。森林经理科学不可能建立在破坏森林的废墟上。森林经理是用客观规律和实践经验，为森林经营策划长远战略决策并付诸实施的科学，即科学经营森林的谋略的理念与方法。其本身要理正道明!

(18)本："君子务本，本立而道生"[26]。孔子讲"以仁为本"。国家"以人为本"。而森林经理则应以"德"为本。即森林生态道德伦理所阐述的人与人、人与社会及人与自然的正确关系。森林经理是由人来做的。森林经理人不仅要有知识和技能，还要讲道德。森林经理学著作都指出森林经理不仅为当前利益考量，而更要从子孙后代和社会的长远利益出发。不讲道德不讲公德，黑心地拿祖宗留下的大木头赚大钱，只顾眼前，不顾子孙后代和长远社会利益，是搞不好森林经理的。在先进国家，真正搞森林经营管理的人是既懂知识又很讲道德的，比如说择伐或抚育间伐时，有两棵树，砍哪棵留哪棵，经过比较，如果另一棵还在长，而有病或弯曲的这一棵就应是砍的对象，不会砍好留坏。从大的方面看，众所周知，许多高科技都会是一柄"双刃剑"，可以有利或有害于人类与环境，如何应用是由人的知识与道德来决定的。例如运用新科技调查所得的森林资源数据可以用来科学经营森林，也可以用于掠夺和破坏森林。过去森林经理和资源清查一度成了"只要立方米，不要经营管理"和"大木头挂帅"的开路先锋！有了资源"信息"就可以去"拔大毛"(粗放择伐)，"剃光头"(大面积皆伐)搞"只要木头不要森林"式的掠夺性林业。而新《理论》的提出，也正是要为新一轮的掠套式经营鸣锣开道!

当前，新《理论》的"提出"与"社会主义市场经济"即"有计划的市场经济"或"有计划的商品经济"[27]理论相抵触。该新《理论》"序"言说"我国由'计划经济'向'市场经济'转变，""在计划经济条件下形成的"森林经理理论"已经很不适应当前我国已经采用的市场经济模式"[4]。从而否定原有的森林成熟理论(森林成熟理论并非计划经济体制下的产物)。该新《理论》以"实现经济利益最大化"为目标，从而背离了社会主义生产"是为了满足社会需要"的目的。新《理论》的实质是主张在林业中推行"自由化市场经济"。这是行不通的。社会主义生产目的首先是为了满足社会需要(共同富裕)，而不是单纯为了追求最大利润(经济利益)。我们应该看到"市场"的缺陷，"市场追求的常常是眼前利益最大化，而不是长远利益最大化"，与森林经营主要考虑长远利益的目标背道而驰。因此就要求发挥"计划"的作用，以校正市场的短视行为。"计划与市场不是划分社会制度的标志，而是社会主义和资本主义都可以利用的配置资源的手段，其各有优点与缺陷"[28]。"市场并不是万能的。有几件大事不能完全交给市场、交给价值规律去管：一是经济总量的平衡；二是大的经济结构的及时调整；三是竞争导致垄断问题；四是生态环境问题；五是社会公平问题。[29]"(刘国光"有计划，是社会主义市场经济的强板"，2009. 3. 17)林业要加入经济总量的平衡，林业自身要平衡；林业要参与经济结构调整，林业本身要调整；参与竞争防止垄断，林业也不例外；森林是生态环境重要组成部分，要维护生态平衡，林业自身先要保持平衡；要维护社会多种利益和需要的公平，也是林业的首要任务。所有这些都不是"市场"能够完全解决的了的。因此，林业更为适合的是计划经济，而较为不适合市场化经济。就是在资本主义林业中也需要有计划。森林经理实际上就是一种林业经营"计划"[10]。在某些方面甚至资本主义搞得比社会主义还好。“现代新自由主义或市场原教旨主义，在西方横行了30年贫者愈贫，富者愈富，以至于经济要靠借债消费和金融投机来支撑，最后是金融海啸和空前的全球经济危机爆发而不可收拾。资本主义无法克服社会化大生产与生产资料的私人占有之间的矛盾，引起了各部门之间的比例失衡，总供给和总需求之间的失衡，‘虚拟经济’和‘实体经济’的失衡，目前的危机就是这些失衡的表现。长期以来好多人对此不屑一顾，现在没有几个人敢继续怀疑了。对市场的迷信，在西方资本主义国家已经降温了[10]”，我们的“市场迷”们还在死抱不放，要在林业范围里无限扩张。最终是要损害林业和国家利益。

新《理论》说：“林木市场成熟的概念，即在林木生长发育过程中，目的产品的市场价格和市场需求量达到最大时的状态为林木市场成熟。并用市场价格和需求量来确定‘采伐期’、采伐量以及树种和规格等。”[4]（第95页）“任何林种的林木市场成熟龄不是固定不变的，而是随市场的变化而变化”（第97页），“根据木材价格动态及时调整轮伐期以便使内部收益率最大”[4]（第146页）。新《理论》根据众多森林成熟方法中选择带有缺陷的内部收益率和净现值法，以偏概全偷换概念衍生出原有经济（金融）成熟中已有的市场因素作为“单一”的因素用来确定森林成熟，推导出要去适合“错综复杂的动态市场”[4]（第97页）随时随地“变化”的林木市场成熟理论，是对森林经理科学的一种扭曲，与森林长期经营永续利用和可持续经营原则相违背[30]，与保持林业长期稳定发展和生态效益持续发挥的需要相悖。森林生长至成熟是以自然因素为主导的，森林成熟与轮伐期的确定也以自然和工艺为基础，依据多方面因素决定，而不能只依靠那只随时改变捉摸不定“看不见的手（市场）”。该《理论》前面对天然林讲‘采伐期’[4]（第95～102页），对后面杨树人工林用的是‘轮伐期’[4]（第103～165页），其中并没有‘经营周期’的含义，都是随市场的千变万化而变化。随时可变的不确定和不可知的（是不可能准确预测的，金融危机就是证明）。新《理论》说：“林木市场成熟龄理论的应用必将把‘单一性’转化为多样性森林经营，从而提高了森林经营的‘稳定性’和‘适应性’”[4]（第97页）。一下子这种单一性因素的林木市场成熟又成了“万能药”转化成了多样性森林经营。然而必须随着市场变化的“森林经营”又如何能“稳定和适应”，是自相矛盾的。相反，现代的森林成熟或轮伐期都需要依照森林经营多样化因素来综合确定。那种只根据某种单因素确定和随时可变化的万能成熟龄与轮伐期，就是没有成熟的“森林成熟龄”和没有轮伐期的“轮伐期”。它们实际是“市场衍生品”的“虚拟”产物。这种脱离森林多种功能实际价值体系的理论是虚假的、不科学的。更有甚者，新《理论》指出：“应该‘取消’对商品林经营的严格‘限制’，根据林产品价格和市场需求决定林木采伐时间和采伐量，实行弹性采伐，造采自由”[4]（第100页），就是说可以“只采不造”或“自由”地“乱砍滥伐”了，取消“限制（控制）”就是取消森林经理，因为森林经理是为防止市场无限制的需求而控制森林采伐时间和采伐量而产生的。新《理论》还说：“商品林经营活动应等同于企业的商品生产活动”[4]（第98页）和“像农民经营耕地一样，自主耕种”[4]（第100页）。这种说法即是把林业“等同”一般工矿企业和农业，也就是改变林业的“特性”。总之，就是等于没有轮伐期、取消森林经理、不要森林经营，和改变“林业”性质。因此“林木市场成熟”是一种自由市场“虚拟经济”的表现。“这种‘虚拟经济’会破坏‘实体经济’”[31]，在林业中起到破坏森林经营实体的作用。该《理论》认为“林业的最终目的不一定是生产更多木材，而是获得最大的经济回报”[4]（第114页），是“以追求经济利益最大化”[4]（第97页）为目标，是赤裸裸的“金钱挂帅”。它的提出与施行好像似一场“赌博”，下的赌注是祖宗留下的“天然林”，得到的是不知何时兑现的人工丰产林和未来生态环境的破坏！这就违背了森林经理学伦理道德观。由此，森林经理学也从有人提倡的纯“技术学科”，一夕之间变成了纯“经济学科”！然而“此理论构成了对于森林采伐要顾及生态效果的全球性潮流的逆动”![32]。“企图使‘利益最大化’原则在法律、道德上合理合法，折射出社会生活中的一些‘道德’景象”[33]。但是，此论一出立即上下欢迎，上面认为是“理论创新”可以推动林业“快速”发展，基层经营者可为迅速销售“产品”得到依据，有人说卖小苗都能快赚钱，自由买卖不必等那么多年了！变本加厉不择手段，大小都要“老少通吃”，比“大木头挂帅”对林业的损害更有过之而无不及，不需太久天然林消失地力衰退生态危机不日可期。然而违背科学、违背历史、违背道德，只顾眼前经济利益，不顾子孙后代和社会长远利益，不是森林经理科学的作为，更谈不上学术创新。

当然任何人与事物都应有道德精神，然而森林经理的道德观念可以说是与生俱来，无论古代孟子“斧斤以时入山林，材木不可胜用”，或是近现代实现森林永续利用和可持续经营本身即是德就是“本”。森林经理从维护社会长远利益出发，为实现森林可持续经营制定战略决策和科学规划调整措施并认真实行，就是立德之行，就是务本。德立而道生(“道”是指方法、道路)，各种相应有益的方法与技术就会应运而生。本固而枝繁。否则，不明哲理，不讲道德，不抓根本，不仅森林经理学科不能正确发展，还可能导向森林资源与生态环境遭受破坏的歧途。从这个角度来看森林经理学应是阐述和解决林业发展中矛盾对立统一，综合平衡，遵法重道，维护森林可持续经营长期健康发展的道德良心学。

用中国哲理总结自己经验，吸收外国合理的理论和方法，发展中国特色的森林经理学。一万年太久只争朝夕。要早出成果，应掌握森林经理学及相关学科基本理论，拥有较深入的林业科学实践经验，选择好适当课题，运用有效方法，创立符合实际的决策规划并施行验证，可以较快获得成果。然后逐步沿着正确道路发展创建新的理论和科学的森林经理学体系。结合外国的经验又保持我们自己好的传统发展自己的理论与方法即是创新。在森林经理学范畴里发扬中华文化，温故知新而创新！传统中孕育着新事物。预祝大家早日创造出具有中国特色的现代森林经理科学。

参考文献

[1]B. B. 马姆菲洛夫. 森林经理学. 北京：中国林业出版社，1957.

[2]《孟子·梁惠王上》

[3]马克思. 资本论(第二卷). 北京：人民出版社.

[4]柏广新. 林木市场成熟理论的提出与探讨. 北京：中国林业出版社，2009 年 7 月.

[5]贾思勰. 齐民要求(卷五)

[6]詹昭宁. 中国森林经理探讨. 林业经济问题，2007，27(1).

[7]于政中. 森林经理学(第二版). 北京：中国林业出版社，1991.

[8]张昂和. 森林资源管理决策与森农复合系统管理. 人民日报(海外版)，1987 年 2 月 2 日.

[9]Davis S L，Johnsos K，Bettinger P，et al. Forest Management. McGraw-Hill，Inc，2001.

[10]Bettinger P，et al. Forest Management and Planning . Academic Press，2009.

[11]Buongiorno J，Gilless J K，Decision Methods for Forest Resource Mnanagement. Academic Press，2004.

[12]Davis K P. Forest Management：Regulation and Valuation. McGraw-Hill Book Company. New York，1966.

[13]张昂和，陆兆苏，王松龄，等. 从林业再生产的特点分析我国森林永续利用的基本途径，林业资源管理，1980(2).

[14]森林经理重点学科建设高级研讨班．材料汇编，2008 年 10 月．
[15]Hundeshagen J C. Die Forstabschatzung auf neuen wissenshaftlichen grundlagen. Tubingen，1826.
[16] Biolley H E. The Planning of Managed Forests by the Experimental Method and Especially the Check Method. Trans. M. L. Anderson(1954). The Scrivener Press，Oxford，1920.
[17]陆兆苏，张昂和．试论标准林．林业资源管理，1980(1).
[18]Davis K P. American Forest Management. MCgraw-Hill Book Company，INC. New York，1954.
[19]Davis S L，Johnson K N. Forest Management. McGraw-Hill，Inc. New York，1987.
[20]余谋昌．生态伦理学．北京：首都师范大学出版社，1999 年 3 月．
[21]张昂和，林龙卓，詹昭宁，等．重视保护和经营管理好现有森林．森林合理经营永续利用．北京：中国林业出版社，1982.
[22]张建国．关于改和森林经营的认识．南方森林经理理论与实践，2010 年 12 月．
[23]老子·道德经(第二十五章)
[24]恩格斯．自然辩证法．北京：人民出版社，1984.
[25]张鸣．学界的技术主义的泥潭．新浪博客，2010 年 9 月 30 日．
[26]孔子．论语·学而篇
[27]江泽民文选(第一卷)．北京：人民出版社，2006 年．
[28]邓小平文选(第三卷)．北京：人民出版社，1993 年．
[29]刘国光．有计划，是社会主义市场经济的强板．光明日报，2009 年 3 月 17 日．
[30]徐国祯．对《林木市场成熟理论》提出的探讨与商榷．林业经济问题，2010(2).
[31]詹昭宁．“林木市场成熟”理论的缺陷．中国生态服务网，2010 年 2 月 2 日．
[32]侯元汾．在詹昭宁《‘林木市场成熟’理论的缺陷》一文中的补充．中国生态服务网，2010 年 2 月 2 日．
[33]金翠仙．透视拍广告新现象——林学界讨论“林木市场成熟理论”．中国生态服务网，2010 年 5 月 3 日．

兼顾碳贮量和木材生产目标的森林经营规划研究

戎建涛[1]　雷相东[1*]　张会儒[1]　冯启祥[2]

（1. 中国林业科学研究院资源信息研究所，北京，100091；

2. 吉林省汪清林业局，汪清，133200）

摘要：本研究以吉林省汪清林业局金沟岭林场为对象，基于小班调查数据，以木材生产和碳增量净现值最大为规划目标，考虑采伐量不大于生长量、均衡采伐、生长模型等约束，建立了的多目标规划模型。通过 LINGO 软件求解，得到了 50 年规划期的最优经营方案，并进行了灵敏度分析。结果表明：各个森林类型在不同分期间伐强度在 1%~15%，择伐强度在 1%~35%。规划期木材总采伐量为 182.33 万 m^3，规划期末地上碳贮增量为 47.92 万 t；规划期总收益为 95434.40 万元，其中木材净现值 91895.50 万元，碳贮增量净现值 3539.30 万元。多目标经营方案可以同时满足对木材生产和碳贮增量的需求，是一个折中的方案。与木材生产经营方案（方案 3）相比，多目标经营方案（方案 1）和碳贮增量经营方案（方案 2）在规划期内的木材净现值分别减少 2.67%、45.43%，但地上碳贮增量净现值分别增加 29.88%、50.42%。因此增加碳贮增量要以减少木材采伐量为代价。分析了低、中、高三种碳价格对多目标经营方案的影响，表明整个规划期内木材采伐量随着碳价格的增加而减少，而碳贮增量随着碳价格的增加而增加。本研究为考虑择伐方式和碳贮存的多目标经营规划研究提供了研究方法和参照。

关键词：木材生产；地上碳贮量；净现值；多目标规划

Forest Management Planning Incorporating Values of Timber and Carbon

RONG Jian-tao　LEI Xiang-dong　ZHANG Hui-ru　FENG Qi-xiang

（1. Institute of Forest Resource Information Techniques, Chinese Academy of Forestry, Beijing, 100091

Wangqing Forestry Bureau, Jilin Province, Wangqing, 133200）

Abstract: Multi-objective harvest programming model was developed based on subcompartment data in Jingouling forest farm of Wangqing Forestry Bureau, Jilin Province. The model set the combination of net present value (NPV) of timber production and above - ground carbon storage change as object function, and included restrictions of harvesting less than incre-

---

基金项目：国家"十一五"科技支撑课题（2006BAD03A0802）的部分内容。

戎建涛，男，在读博士生。主要研究方向：森林可持续经营。Email：jiantaorong@163.com。

＊通讯作者：雷相东，研究员。主要研究方向：森林生长模型与模拟，Email：xdlei@caf.ac.cn。

ment, even flow of timber production, and volume growth models. Optimal solution in 50 years planning horizon was attained by LINGO software. The results showed that: The thinning intensity by volume was from 1% to 15%, and the selective cutting intensity varied from 1% to 35%. The total timber harvest was 1, 823, 300m^3. Above - ground carbon stock change during 50 years was 479, 200tons. The total NPV was 954, 344, 000Yuan including 918, 955, 000 Yuan for timber and 35, 393, 000yuan for carbon. The management planning scenario was a compromise which could meet both timber production and carbon storage. Comparing scenarios of timber production (Scenario 1) with multipurpose forest management (Scenario 2) and carbon stock change management (Scenario 3), results presented that the NPVs of timber harvest for scenarios 1 and 2 were 2.67% and 45.43% lower than that of scenario 3; and the NPVs of aboveground carbon stock were 29.88% and 50.42% larger than that of scenario 3. Therefore, there was a compromise between timber harvest and aboveground carbon stock change. We analyzed the effects of carbon price on scenarios of multipurpose forest management. It showed that timber harvest decreased with the increased carbon price, but carbon storage change was on the contrary. The study provided methodology and reference for multiple objective forest management planning with the consideration of selective cutting regime and carbon storage.

Key words: timber production; aboveground carbon stock change; net present value; multi - objective programming

森林由于可以吸收固定大量二氧化碳而在应对气候变化中有特殊的作用，因此，除了生产木材外，增加森林碳汇也已成为森林经营的一个重要目标。但这两个目标常常是相互冲突的。在森林经营中，如何长期实现生产木材和增加碳汇的平衡，成为一个亟待解决的问题。由于林业生产的长周期性，通过多目标规划方法来制定森林采伐方案是一个主流方法。国外已经有一些针对森林碳目标的多目森林经营规划的研究，如 Hoen 等[1]通过建立木材生产和碳吸存的规划模型来研究未来 30 年森林经营单位的经营措施规划；Meng 等[2]和 Bourque 等[3]将碳吸存作为目标纳入景观层次的森林经营规划，比较了不同目标方案下的采伐规划；Baskent 等[4]建立了以木材生产、碳贮量和氧气价值为目标的线性规划模型，并同单一木材生产目标下的经营方案进行了比较；Baskent 等[5]以土耳其阿尔特温林区为研究对象，在森林规划模型中以水源价值、木材价值为经营目标，通过建立多目标规划模型分析各个目标之间的关系。Yousefpour 等[6]将生长模拟和优化相结合，考虑木材、碳和多样性价值，进行挪威云杉林的改造规划。但以上研究中建立的规划模型，多按皆伐将采伐面积作为决策变量，不能满足择伐收获规划的需要。在国内，虽然有不少关于多目标经营规划的研究[7~8]，但明确将森林碳贮量作为一个经营目标的研究还未见报道。同样大部分采伐规划仍基于皆伐体制，以面积作为决策变量，无法满足目前我国天然林区尤其是东北林区择伐规划的需要。本研究以我国东北过伐林区吉林省汪清林业局金沟林场为对象，研究以木材生产和地上碳贮增量为经营目标的森林景观多目标经营规划技术，为天然林区的气候变化下的多目标森林经营规划提供方法和决策依据。

1 研究地区概况

研究地点为吉林省汪清县林业局金沟岭林场。所处的地理坐标为130°05′~130°19′E，43°17′~43°25′N。地貌属低山丘陵，海拔300~1200m，坡度一般在5°~25°。属季风型气候，全年平均气温为3.9℃左右，年平均降水量600~700 mm。其中5~9月的降水量为438mm，占全年总降水量的80%。土壤主要是玄武岩中低山灰化土灰棕壤类型，平均厚度在40cm左右。该区植被属长白山植物区系，主要针叶树种有红松（*Pinus koraiensis*）、冷杉（*Abies* sp.）、云杉[*Picea jezoensis* var. *icrosperma*（Lindl.）Cheng et L. K. Fu]、长白落叶松(*Larix olgensis* Henry)等。阔叶树种主要有白桦(*Betula platyphylla* Suk.)、杨树(*Populus* sp.)、榆树（*Carpinus* sp.）、水曲柳（*Fraxinus mandshurica* Rupr.）、柞树(*Quercus mongolica*)、椴树（*Tilia* sp.）、色木(*Acer* sp.)、枫桦（*Betula costata*）和其他杂木。

2 数据与方法

2.1 基础数据

基础数据为金沟岭林场2007年二类调查数据，共计1174个小班。按吉林省森林资源规划设计调查规定[10]，划分金沟岭林场主要森林类型和相应的龄组，据此组合为规划的基本单元。共划分为6种森林类型，包括白桦林、天然阔叶林、天然针阔混交林、人工落叶松林和人工混交林。

2.2 生长模型

各森林类型生长模型[11]如下：

白桦林 $$V = 193.135(1 - e^{-0.060A})^{7.799} \quad (1)$$

阔叶混交林 $$V = \frac{152.200}{1 + 145.684e^{0.123A}} \quad (2)$$

人工落叶松林 $$V = \frac{206.548}{1 + 337.348e^{-0.193A}} \quad (3)$$

人工混交林 $$V = 213.749(1 - e^{-0.713A})^{195.889} \quad (4)$$

天然针阔混交林 $$V = 158.399(1 - e^{-0.099A})^{36.5} \quad (5)$$

天然针叶混交林 $$V = \frac{179.145}{1 + 265.230e^{-0.096A}} \quad (6)$$

其中：A为小班年龄(年)，V为小班每公顷蓄积量(m^3/hm^2)。

2.3 多目标规划模型

由于碳贮量不能重复累计，本研究将木材产量和地上碳贮量的增加量作为经营的目标。在建立多目标规划模型时，需要考虑规划期、规划分期、采伐方式、采伐周期，并定义目标函数和约束条件。参照吉林省汪清林业局森林资源2008年调查报告[9]，抚育间伐采伐周期为6~10年，采育择伐周期为10~15年。为了方便模型构建，取10年作为间伐、择伐周期。模型中采用期末采伐。其中每种森林的幼龄林、中龄林采用间伐，近熟林、成熟林、过熟林采用择伐。规划期为50年，每10年作为一个分期。目标是规划期内的木材产量及地上贮量增量的净现值最大。

2.3.1 木材生产效益

采用规划期采伐木材的收入减去采伐和管护等成本之后的净现值来表示。木材收入由各树种每立方米木材价格(表1)乘以对应的出材量而得到，其中价格采用1999～2009年间的平均价格，出材量则是通过各个森林类型蓄积生长模型获得的蓄积量乘以出材率得出，阔叶材出材率取0.65，针叶材出材率取0.75。成本费用主要包括更新造林整地费用、更新造林费用、幼林抚育费用、森林采伐费用、经营管护费用等。本研究中只考虑森林采伐费用和经营管护费用。其中采伐费用为60元/m³，管护费用为30元/亩。贴现率取值3.6%[12]。

表1 不同森林类型木材价格

Tab. 1 Timber value of different forest types (元/m³)

类型	白桦林	阔叶混交林	人工落叶松林	人工混交林	天然针阔混交林	天然针叶混交林
间伐材	850	740	620	510	850	1050
择伐材	930	800	820	620	1020	1100

2.3.2 地上碳贮量增量效益

本研究仅考虑树木地上部分的碳贮增量。以小班为单位，首先计算出每个分期木材蓄积量，通过生物量转化方程[13]，得到每个分期的生物量，乘以碳含量(取0.5)得到碳贮量。碳价格取135.60元/t[4]。

主要森林类型的生物量估计模型形式为 $B = aV^b$，B 为林分生物量(t/hm²)，V 为林分蓄积量(m³/ hm²)。各类型参数见表2。

表2 各种森林类型的生物量估计模型参数

Tab. 2 Prediction parameters of biomass model for various forest types

生物量模型参数	白桦林	阔叶混交林	人工落叶松林	人工混交林	天然针阔混交林	天然针叶混交林
a	0.75	0.553	0.454	0.227	0.207	0.006
b	1.026	1.098	1.107	1.274	1.198	1.746

2.3.3 多目标经营规划模型及求解

本研究取50年作为规划期，每10年作为一个分期，共5个分期内考虑木材生产和碳贮增量两个目标，以规划期内六种森林类型的木材生产和地上碳贮增量的净现值最大为目标函数，以不同森林类型在每个经营分期内的间伐强度和择伐强度作为决策变量，考虑采伐量不大于生长量、每个分期均衡采伐、蓄积生长模型等约束，建立多目标规划模型。利用LINGO软件[14]求解。

目标函数为：

$$\text{Maximize } Z = \mathrm{NPV}^{\text{timber}} + \mathrm{NPV}^{\text{carbon}} \tag{7}$$

约束条件包括：

$$\sum_{i=1}^{6}\sum_{j=1}^{6}\left(\mathrm{npv}_i^{\text{t-timber}} j + \mathrm{npv}_{ij}^{\text{s-timber}}\right) = NPV^{timber} \tag{8}$$

$$\mathrm{npv}_{ij}^{\text{t-timber}} = \frac{v_{tij} s_{tij} x_{ij} d_i p_{tij}}{(1 + p_0)^{n_j}} \tag{9}$$

$$\mathrm{npv}_{ij}^{\text{s-timber}} = \frac{v_{sij} s_{sij} y_{ij} d_i p_{sij}}{(1 + p_0)^{n_j}} \tag{10}$$

$$\sum_{i=1}^{6}\sum_{j=1}^{6}(\mathrm{npv}_{ij}^{\mathrm{t-carbon}}+\mathrm{npv}_{ij}^{\mathrm{s-carbon}})=\mathrm{NPV}^{\mathrm{carbon}} \tag{11}$$

$$\mathrm{npv}_{ij}^{\mathrm{t-carbon}}=\frac{mB[V_{ij}^{t}-V_{i(j-1)}^{t}-H_{ij}^{t}]p_c}{(1+p_0)^{n_j}} \tag{12}$$

$$\mathrm{npv}_{ij}^{\mathrm{s-carbon}}=\frac{mB[v_{ij}^{s}-V_{i(j-1)}^{s}-H_{ij}^{s}]p_c}{(1+p_0)^{n_j}} \tag{13}$$

$$B=av^{b} \tag{14}$$

$$\sum_{i=1}^{6}(V_{ij}^{t}x_{ij}+V_{ij}^{s}y_{ij})=H_j \tag{15}$$

$$-5\%\leqslant\frac{H_{j+1}-H_j}{H_j}\leqslant 5\%\quad j=1,2,3,4,5 \tag{16}$$

$$\sum_{j=1}^{6}H_j\leqslant H^{*} \tag{17}$$

$$0.01\leqslant x_{ij}\leqslant 0.15 \tag{18}$$

$$0.01\leqslant y_{ij}\leqslant 0.35 \tag{19}$$

其中：(18)、(19)间伐择伐强度约束是根据汪清林业局森林资源 2008 年调查报告中采伐要求设定的。目的是能够保持持续采伐和防止过量采伐。

同时为了有利于水土保持，剔除坡度大于 30°的小班数据。每个表达式的含义及各变量含义分别见表 3 和表 4。

表 3 表达式的含义

Tab. 3 Implication of each equation

表达式	含义
7	木材采伐量和碳贮量增量各分期净现值的和
8	各分期内木材效益净现值
9 和 10	间伐和择伐木材效益净现值
11	各分期内在有采伐的情况下碳净现值
12	间伐时碳净现值
13	择伐时碳净现值
14	生物量转化方程
15 和 16	均衡采伐约束
17	生长量大于等于采伐量约束
18 和 19	间伐强度和择伐强度约束

表 4 表达式中符号含义

Tab. 4 Implication of each symbol in equations

符号	含义
i	森林类型数
j	规划分期数
x_{ij}和 y_{ij}	第 i 种森林类型第 j 分期内的间伐强度和择伐强度
$\mathrm{npv}_{ij}^{\mathrm{t-timber}}$	第 i 种森林类型第 j 分期内的间伐木材净现值
v_{tij}	可间伐的第 i 种森林类型第 j 分期内的每公顷蓄积量
s_{tij}	可间伐的第 i 种森林类型第 j 分期内的小班面积
d_i	第 i 种森林类型的出材率

（续）

符号	含义
P_{tij}	第 i 种森林类型第 j 分期时的木材价格（当有采伐进行时，需减去采伐和管理费用，没有采伐进行时，只需减去管理费用）
p_0	贴现率
n_j	第 j 分期末的年度
$npv_{ij}^{s-timber}$	第 i 种森林类型第 j 分期内的择伐的木材净现值
$v\ sij$	可择伐的第 i 种森林类型第 j 分期内的每公顷蓄积量
s_{sij}	可择伐的第 i 种森林类型第 j 分期内的小班面积
$npv_{ij}^{t-carbon}$	第 i 种森林类型第 j 分期内的择伐（采伐对象是近熟、成熟、过熟林）的木材净现值
H_{ij}^{t}	第 i 种森林类型第 j 分期间伐采伐的蓄积
m	含碳率，取 0.5
H_{ij}^{s}	第 i 种森林类型第 j 分期择伐采伐的蓄积
p_c	每吨碳的价格
$npv_{ij}^{s-carbon}$	第 i 种森林类型第 j 分期择伐后碳的净现值
V_{ij}^{t}	第 i 种森林类型第 j 分期间伐的蓄积量
V_{ij}^{s}	第 i 种森林类型第 j 分期择伐的蓄积量
H_j	第 j 个分期内各个森林类型采伐量之和
H^*	每个分期末时各个森林类型的森林蓄积生长量之和

3 结果与分析

3.1 木材收获与碳贮量增量分析

表 5、表 6 和表 7 分别列出了五个规划分期各种森林类型的采伐强度、采伐量和碳贮增量值。可以看出，在五个规划分期，各个森林类型的间伐强度在 10%~15%，择伐强度在 10%~35%。整个规划期内，天然针阔混交林和天然针叶混交林的采伐量最大，人工落叶松、人工混交林次之，阔叶混交林、白桦林采伐量最小。这是因为金沟岭林场天然针阔混交林、针叶混交林面积和蓄积都占总量的比重最大。其中第一分期的间伐蓄积最大，说明此时森林幼中龄林比较多，可采取一定间伐促进林分生长。而除了第一分期外，其他每个分期的择伐蓄积量相差不大，说明在第二、三、四、五分期内森林生长稳定。

表 5 多目标函数采伐强度规划解

Tab. 5 Cutting intensity solution of multi-objective function （%）

分期	采伐蓄积	白桦林	阔叶混交林	人工落叶松林	人工混交林	天然针阔混交林	天然针叶混交林	小计	总计
1	间伐蓄积	0.01	0.05	0.03	0.27	4.57	0.44	5.38	36.52
	择伐蓄积	0.03	0.31	0.13	0.32	15.41	14.95	31.14	
2	间伐蓄积	0.01	0.05	0.00	0.64	2.55	0.34	3.59	36.94
	择伐蓄积	0.04	7.55	2.52	0.26	0.88	22.09	33.35	
3	间伐蓄积	0.00	0.03	0.00	0.10	0.59	0.12	0.84	35.70
	择伐蓄积	0.92	0.37	8.05	0.32	0.94	24.26	34.86	
4	间伐蓄积	0.00	0.13	0.00	0.00	0.19	0.00	0.33	36.75
	择伐蓄积	0.05	0.39	2.76	11.29	21.30	0.63	36.42	

(续)

分期	采伐蓄积	白桦林	阔叶混交林	人工落叶松林	人工混交林	天然针阔混交林	天然针叶混交林	小计	总计
5	间伐蓄积	0.00	0.00	0.00	0.00	0.16	0.07	0.23	36.43
	择伐蓄积	0.05	0.40	9.11	6.35	19.62	0.67	36.20	
合计		1.11	9.28	22.60	19.55	65.20	64.58	182.33	182.33

表 6 多目标函数采伐蓄积规划解

Tab. 6 Volume solution of multi-objective function (万 m^3)

森林类型	第一分期		第二分期		第三分期		第四分期		第五分期	
	间伐强度	择伐强度	间伐强度	择伐强度	间伐强度	择伐强度	间伐强度	择伐强度	间伐强度	择伐强度
白桦林	0.01	0.01	0.01	0.01	0.01	0.33	0.01	0.01	0.01	0.01
阔叶混交林	0.01	0.01	0.01	0.22	0.01	0.01	0.15	0.01	0.01	0.01
人工落叶松林	0.01	0.01	0.01	0.14	0.01	0.35	0.01	0.17	0.01	0.35
人工混交林	0.15	0.01	0.15	0.01	0.15	0.01	0.01	0.35	0.01	0.22
天然针阔混交林	0.15	0.13	0.15	0.01	0.15	0.01	0.15	0.16	0.15	0.19
天然针叶混交林	0.15	0.35	0.15	0.35	0.15	0.35	0.01	0.01	0.15	0.01

表 7 目标函数碳贮增量规划解

Tab. 7 Carbon stock change solution of multi – objective function (万 t)

分期	固碳量	白桦林	阔叶混交林	人工落叶松林	人工混交林	天然针阔混交林	天然针叶混交林	小计	总计
1	间伐	0.16	0.78	0.66	0.13	0.05	0.09	1.87	9.41
	择伐	0.10	0.50	1.02	1.63	2.30	1.99	7.54	
2	间伐	0.15	0.36	0.42	1.30	0.04	0.01	2.28	11.13
	择伐	0.10	0.80	2.17	2.59	0.38	2.81	8.85	
3	间伐	0.00	0.38	0.00	0.05	1.28	3.19	4.90	9.82
	择伐	0.51	0.61	0.50	1.26	0.92	1.12	4.92	
4	间伐	0.10	0.03	0.00	0.00	1.68	0.00	1.81	8.60
	择伐	0.07	0.78	0.59	0.02	1.61	3.72	6.79	
5	间伐	0.00	0.01	0.00	0.00	0.00	0.00	0.01	8.96
	择伐	0.07	0.71	0.80	0.78	1.71	4.88	8.95	
总计		1.26	4.96	6.16	7.76	9.97	17.81	47.92	47.92

整个规划期内，天然针叶混交林和天然针阔混交林碳贮增量最大，这与它们所占森林面积和林木生长率有关，人工混交林、人工落叶松林次之，阔叶混交林和白桦林碳贮增量最小。五个分期内各种森林类型木材采伐蓄积和碳贮增量分布如图 1。

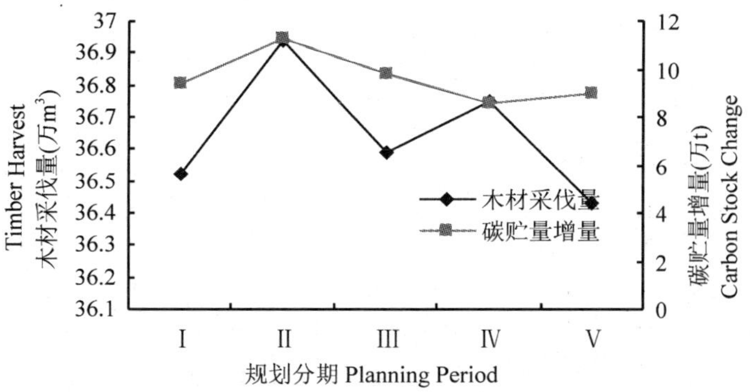

图 1 每个分期内木材采伐量和碳贮量增量

Fig. 1 Timber volume and carbon stock change of different forest types in each period

3.2 木材生产与碳增量净现值分析

五个规划分期的木材和碳贮增量的净现值分别见表8、表9。

表 8 多目标经营五个分期的木材净现值

Tab. 8 Net present value of timber for multi – objective management in five periods （万元）

分期	净现值 NPV	白桦林	阔叶混交林	人工落叶松林	人工混交林	天然针阔混交林	天然针叶混交林	小计	总计
1	间伐	1.92	13.37	25.96	455.09	2020.37	925.49	3442.20	20107.83
	择伐	5.48	92.57	180.55	316.99	3336.50	12733.54	16665.63	
2	间伐	1.25	9.73	0.84	1092.59	672.83	101.60	1878.84	18857.70
	择伐	5.39	1721.31	3414.65	185.70	2252.05	9399.76	16978.86	
3	间伐	0.02	4.90	0.00	250.16	56.96	93.11	405.15	18307.53
	择伐	1914.70	61.99	9873.42	198.73	290.77	5562.75	17902.38	
4	间伐	0.02	15.42	0.00	0.00	41.27	5.98	62.69	17736.54
	择伐	4.84	50.09	5952.18	6900.28	4434.43	2132.04	17673.86	
5	间伐	0.00	0.08	0.00	0.00	52.31	86.01	138.40	16885.51
	择伐	5.12	37.37	7465.11	4048.16	4869.03	322.32	16747.11	
合计		1938.74	2006.83	26912.71	13447.7	18026.52	31362.6	91895.10	91895.10

表 9 多目标经营五个分期的碳贮增量净现值

Tab. 9 NPV of carbon stock change for multi-objective management in five periods （万元）

分期	净现值 NPV	白桦林	阔叶混交林	人工落叶松林	人工混交林	天然针阔混交林	天然针叶混交林	小计	总计
1	间伐	15.38	52.53	44.16	8.71	3.18	6.02	129.98	901.73
	择伐	9.81	33.73	68.16	225.11	152.76	282.18	771.75	
2	间伐	14.03	50.04	36.67	82.87	2.49	0.92	187.02	803.91
	择伐	9.15	53.94	144.73	334.42	25.55	54.04	616.89	

(续)

分期	净现值 NPV	白桦林	阔叶混交林	人工落叶松林	人工混交林	天然针阔混交林	天然针叶混交林	小计	总计
3	间伐	0.32	25.35	0.00	3.55	65.26	280.16	317.03	735.99
	择伐	49.22	40.93	33.09	190.44	52.41	52.87	418.96	
4	间伐	9.68	2.27	0.00	0.00	105.19	0.00	117.14	598.54
	择伐	7.18	52.61	39.34	1.02	99.40	281.85	481.40	
5	间伐	0.00	0.51	0.00	0.00	0.30	0.00	0.81	499.13
	择伐	6.50	47.75	53.42	47.47	80.05	263.13	498.32	
合计		121.27	359.66	419.57	893.59	586.59	1221.17	3539.30	3539.30

五个分期内各种森林类型木材净现值和碳贮增量净现值分布如图 2 所示。

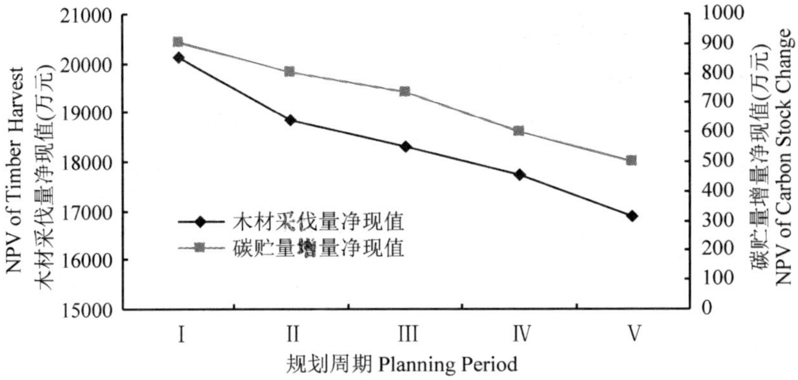

图 2　每个分期内木材采伐和碳贮增量净现值

Fig. 2　NPV for Timber volume and carbon stock change of different forest types in each period

经分析，多目标函数的目标值 Z 为 95434.40 万元，其中木材净现值 91895.10 万元，碳贮增量净现值 3539.30 万元。木材净现值大小按森林类型排序依次是天然针叶混交林、人工落叶松林、天然针阔混交林、人工混交林、阔叶混交林、白桦林。碳贮增量净现值按森林类型排序依次是天然针叶混交林、人工混交林、天然针阔混交林、人工落叶松林、阔叶混交林、白桦林。

3.3　灵敏度分析

3.3.1　目标函数权重

上述规划模型的目标函数(式 7)中木材生产和碳贮量的权重相同。为了检验目标函数中权重变化对采伐方案的影响，设计了另外两种方案(表 10)：即不考虑碳贮量目标以木材采伐量为最大的方案，及不考虑木材生不以碳贮增量为最大的方案。

表 10　目标函数的权重变化方案

Tab. 10　Planning scenarios with different weights

经营方案	目标
方案 1	max（$NPV^{timber}+NPV^{carbon}$）
方案 2	max NPV^{carbon}
方案 3	max NPV^{timber}

通过 LINGO 软件求解获得各种经营方案的木材采伐蓄积量和碳贮增量(表 11)。显然，木材生产单目标经营方案(方案 3)比方案 1 和方案 2 获得更多木材收获。与方案 3 相比，50 年规划期内，方案 1 和方案 2 木材收获分别减少 2.25% 和 34.28%(图 3)，但碳贮增量分别增加 33.71% 和 52.68%(图 4)。

表 11　各种方案的木材采伐量和碳贮量增量

Tab. 11　Timber volume and carbon stock changes produced by various planning scenarios

分期	木材采伐量(万 m^3)			碳贮量增量(万 t)		
	方案 1	方案 2	方案 3	方案 1	方案 2	方案 3
1	36.52	24.57	38.40	9.41	12.15	9.30
2	36.94	24.33	36.10	11.13	12.19	7.41
3	35.70	24.09	37.62	9.82	11.38	7.06
4	36.75	25.01	36.88	8.60	10.78	6.96
5	36.43	24.59	37.52	8.96	8.22	5.11
总和	182.33	122.59	186.52	47.92	54.72	35.84

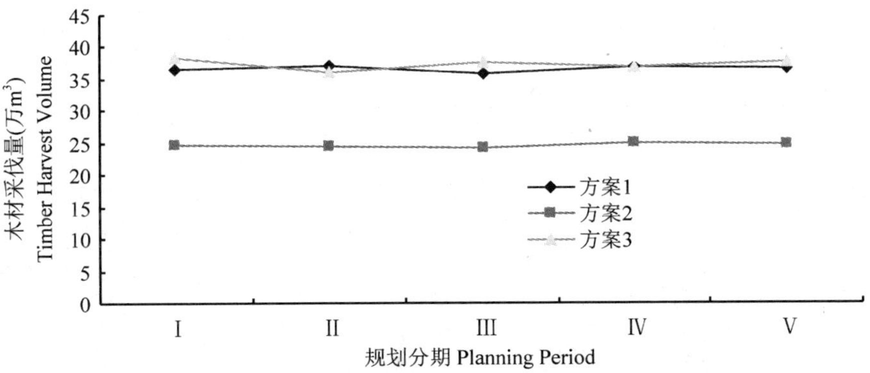

图 3　各种经营方案的每个分期木材收获量

Fig. 3　Timber harvest per period of various management Scenarios

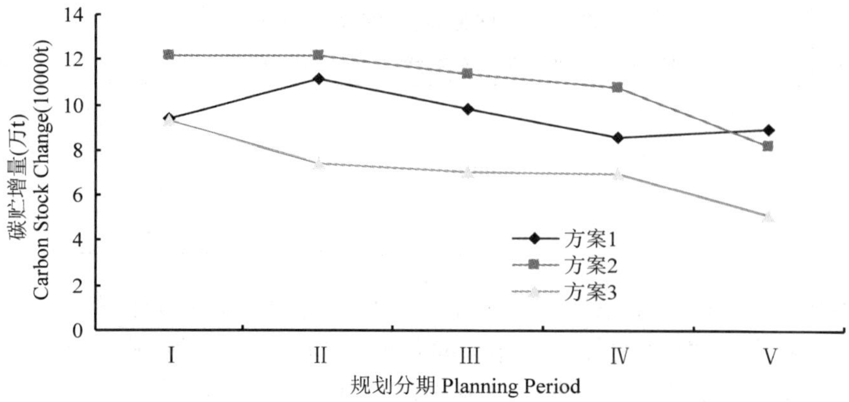

图 4　各种经营方案的每个分期碳贮增量

Fig. 4　Carbon stock change per period of various management scenarios

净现值也有类似的结果(表 12)。相比方案 3，方案 1 和方案 2 木材净现值分别减少了减少 2.67%、45.43%。但碳净现值分别增加 29.88%、50.42%。多目标经营方案 1 净现值总和比木材经营方案 3 净现值总和少 1.76%，但多目标经营方案 1 净现值总和比碳贮增量经营方案 2 净现值总和多 41.72%(图 5)。

表 12　各种经营方案的木材、碳贮增量净现值(万元)

Tab. 12　NPV of timber and carbon stock change produced by various planning scenarios

分期	木材净现值(万元)			碳贮量增量净现值(万元)		
	方案 1	方案 2	方案 3	方案 1	方案 2	方案 3
1	18107.83	13048.78	19432.19	901.73	1164.39	891.31
2	16857.70	8095.49	19253.01	803.91	519.32	535.33
3	22307.53	10628.56	21379.19	735.99	927.98	529.25
4	17736.54	6313.18	18292.21	598.54	1029.26	484.40
5	16885.51	13437.84	16064.13	499.13	458.01	284.67
总和	91895.10	51523.85	94420.74	3539.30	4098.95	2724.96

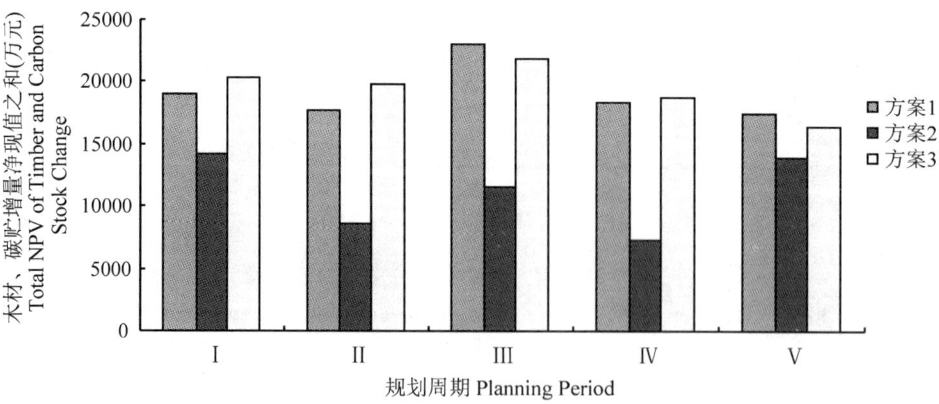

图 5　各种经营方案的木材、碳贮增量净现值之和

Fig. 5　Total NPV of timber and carbon stock change of various planning scenarios

3.3.2 碳价格

根据国际市场上碳汇交易的价格，采用低(67.80 元/t)、中(101.70 元/t)、高(135.60 元/t)三种碳价格[15]分析对多目标经营方案 1(木材生产和碳贮量增量取相同权重)结果的影响。

表 13 不同碳价格下的木材采伐量和碳贮增量

Tab. 13 Timber volume and carbon stock change produced by different carbon price

分期	木材采伐量(万 m^3)			碳贮量增量(万 t)		
	67.80 元/t	101.70 元/t	135.60 元/t	67.80 元/t	101.70 元/t	135.60 元/t
1	38.44	37.27	36.52	8.95	9.08	9.41
2	38.83	36.81	36.94	12.64	12.64	11.13
3	38.23	37.42	35.70	7.03	7.03	9.82
4	38.31	37.19	36.75	6.25	6.28	8.60
5	39.27	38.92	36.43	3.65	6.51	8.96
总和	193.08	187.61	182.33	38.52	41.55	47.92

表 14 不同碳价格在规划期内木材和碳贮增量净现值

Tab. 14 NPV of timber and carbon stock change in planning period by different carbon prices

(万元)

分期	木材净现值			碳贮量增量净现值		
	67.80 元/t	101.70 元/t	135.60 元/t	67.80 元/t	101.70 元/t	135.60 元/t
1	18967.11	18353.76	18107.83	438.55	657.82	901.73
2	17003.19	16980.43	16857.70	518.85	778.27	803.91
3	21500.82	21495.59	22307.53	457.83	686.75	735.99
4	18211.13	18183.41	17736.54	400.73	601.09	598.54
5	17798.07	17357.80	16885.51	417.66	626.50	499.13
总和	93480.31	92370.99	91895.10	2233.61	3350.43	3539.30

当取低、中、高三种碳价格时，整个规划期内木材采伐蓄积变化趋势为随着碳价格的增加而减少，其中低价格和中价格(与高价格比较)的减少值百分比为 2.83% 和 5.57%；整个规划期内碳贮增量变化趋势为随着碳价格的增加而增加，其中低价格和中价格(与高价格比较)增加值百分比为 19.61% 和 13.29%。木材净现值变化趋势为随着碳价格的增加而减少，其中低价格和中价格(与高价格比较)的减少值百分比为 1.19% 和 1.70%；整个规划期内碳贮增量净现值变化趋势为随着碳价格的增加而增加，其中低价格和中价格(与高价格比较)增加值百分比为 36.89% 和 5.34%；价格 1、价格 2、价格 3 净现值和则相差不大，其中价格 1 净现值和最大，价格 2 净现值和次之，价格 3 净现值和最小，价格 2 和价格 3(与价格 1 比较)净现值和增加百分比仅为 0.00007% 和 0.29%。

4 结论与讨论

4.1 讨 论

(1)本研究将小班年龄作为蓄积生长模型的自变量，未来小班的年龄是随规划分期机械增加。这种方法并不能准确地表达由于间伐和择伐引起的林分年龄变化。此外模型未考虑采伐对于蓄积生长量的影响。需要在下一步的研究中建立更准确和灵活的生长模型作为约束。

(2)规划中把间伐周期和择伐周期设为 10 年，这种处理虽然将问题简单化了，但结果也反映了经营方案的差异。下一步的研究中可将采伐周期设为变量，使模型及规划更加灵活。

(3)更新是长期规划中的一个重要过程，限于数据，本研究没有考虑更新。

(4)林木在采伐变为林产品后，产品依旧储存一定的碳，产品碳的分解和释放是一个缓慢的过程。下一步可在规划模型中考虑加入产品碳释放计算。

(5)利用规划技术研究森林经营规划模型对于可持续经营决策有重要作用。其中多目标森林经营规划越来越受到人们的关注和发展。森林管理者和决策者可以依据定量模型分析解决越来越复杂的森林经营问题，比如包括水土保持、生物多样性保护、娱乐休闲价值、为野生动物提供栖息所等一系列生态、经济、社会问题。上述所说的各种问题都可以作为经营目标在经营规划模型中进行研究。

4.2 结 论

本研究首次将木材收获和地上碳贮增量作为经营目标，建立关于木材产量和地上碳增加量净现值的多目标经营规划模型。在设定决策变量时，不是采用传统皆伐体制下的小班面积，而采用异龄林经营下的间伐强度和择伐强度。在均衡采伐和采伐量小于生长量等约束下，通过 LINGO 软件求解，得到了间伐强度在 1%~15%，择伐强度在 1%~35%。50 年规划期中，木材总采伐量为 182.33 万 m^3，规划期末地上碳贮增量为 47.92 万 t；规划期总收益为 95434.40 万元，其中木材净现值 91895.50 万元，碳净现值 3539.30 万元。多目标经营方案可以同时满足对木材生产和碳贮量增量的需求，是一个最优的方案。研究结果为为择伐体制下考虑碳目标的多目标森林经营规划提供了方法和依据。

(2)对多目标森林经营方案(方案 1)和单目标碳贮增量经营方案(方案 2)和单目标木材生产经营方案(方案 3)进行了比较：结果表明：方案 1，方案 2 与方案 3 相比，木材净现值减少，碳贮增量净现值增加。因此，碳贮增量的增加要以减少采伐量为代价。同时考虑木材生产和碳目标时，需要进行折中。

(3)碳的价格对采伐方案有显著影响。当取低、中、高三种碳价格时，整个规划期内木材采伐量随着碳价格的增加而减少，其中低、中价格比高价格下降减少 2.83% 和 5.57%；整个规划期内碳贮量增量随着碳价格的增加而增加，其中低、中价格与高价格相比增加值百分比为 19.61% 和 13.29%。但三种价格得到的净现值和则相差不大，中、高价格(与低价格比较)净现值和增加百分比为 0.00007% 和 0.29%。

参考文献

[1] Hoen H F, Solberg B. Potential and economic efficiency of carbon sequestration in forest biomass through silvicultural management [J]. Forest Science, 1994, 40, 429 ~ 451.

[2]MengF - R, Bourque CP - A, Oldford S P, Swift D E, Smith H C. Combining carbon sequestration objectives with timber management planning [J]. Mitigation and Adaptation Strategies for Global Change, 2003, 8: 371 ~ 403.

[3]Bourque C. P - A, Nielson E T, Gruenwald C, Perrin S F, Hiltz J C, Blin Y A, Horsman G V, Parker M S, Thorburn C B, Corey M M, Meng F, Swift D E. Optimizing carbon sequestration in commercial forests by integrating carbon management objectives in wood supply modeling[J]. Mitigation and Adaptation Strategies for Global Change, 2007, 12(7): 1253 ~ 1275.

[4]Baskent E Z, Sedat K, Yolasigmaz H A. Comparing multipurpose forest management with timber management, incorporating timber, carbon and oxygen values: A case study [J]. Scandinavian Journal of Forest Research, 2008, 23: 105 ~ 120.

[5]Baskent E Z, Sedat K. Development alternative forest management planning strategies incorporating timber, water and carbon value: an examination of their interactions [J]. Environmental Modeling and Assessment, 2009, 14 (4): 467 ~ 480.

[6]Yousefpour R, Hanewinkel M. Modeling of forest conversion planning with an adaptive simulation - optimization approach and simultaneous consideration of the values of timber, carbon and biodiversity [J]. Ecological Economics. 2009, 68: 1711 ~ 1722.

[7]徐文科，曲智林，王文龙．带岭林业局森林生态系统经营多目标规划决策[J]．东北林业大学学报，2004，32(2)：22 ~ 26.

[8]Xu W K, Qu Z L, Wang W L. Multi - target layout and decision making of the management of forest ecosystem for Dailing forestry bureau[J]. Journal of Northeast Forestry University. 2004, 32(2): 22 ~ 26.

[9]陈增丰．目标规划和线性规划两步优化法在森林收获调整中的应用[J]．福建林学院学报，1994，14 (4)：329 ~ 338.

[10]Chen Z F. Application of objective planning and linear planning in forestharvest [J]. Journal of Fu Jian Forestry University. 1994, 14(4): 329 ~ 338.

[11]吉林省林业勘察设计研究院．吉林省汪清林业局森林资源调查报告[R]．2008，1 ~ 39.

[12]吉林省林业厅．森林资源规划设计调查技术细则[R]．2004，1 ~ 92.

[13]戎建涛，刘殿仁，林召忠，等．东北过伐林区主要森林类型林分蓄积量生长模型[J]．林业科技开发，2011，25(1)：30 ~ 34.

[14]Rong J T, Liu D R, Lin Z Z*et*, *al.* Volume growth models of main forest types in over - logged forest region, North China[J]. China Forestry Science and Technology. 2011, 25(1): 30 ~ 34.

[15]Baskent E Z, Sedat K, Yolasigmaz H A. Comparing multipurpose forest management with timber management, incorporating timber, carbon and oxygen values: A case study [J]. Scandinavian Journal of Forest Research, 2008, 23: 107.

[16]曾翀．基于潜在植被的近自然森林景观规划研究[D]．中国林业科学研究院硕士学位论文．2009：39 ~ 40.

[17]Zeng C. Close - to - nature forest landscape planning based on potential natural vegetation [D]. Dissertation of Graduate in Forestry Academy of China. 2009: 39 ~ 40.

[18]谢金星，薛毅．优化建模与 LINGO/LINDO 软件[M]．北京：清华大学出版社．2005，174 ~ 179.

[19]Kossoy A, Ambrosi P. State and trends of the carbon market 2010[M]. The Word Express, inc. 2010, 12 ~ 15.

天然商品林生态效益补偿的 Logistic 模型分析

马志波[1,2]　黄清麟[1]　Ma Hwan OK[3]

（1. 中国林业科学研究院资源信息研究所，国家林业局林业遥感与信息技术重点实验室，北京，100091；2. 廊坊市农林科学院，廊坊，065000；3. 国际热带木材组织，日本横滨，220－0012）

摘要：本文简要分析了造成取得天然商品林林权证的农民自主经营权、受益权等权益落实困难的原因，提出通过生态效益补偿解决公共生态效益诉求与个人经济利益追求之间的矛盾。进一步，采用 Logistic 模型分析了基于条件价值法取得的示范点数据资料，结果表明农户接受按照当地公益林生态效益补偿标准对其占有的天然商品林进行补偿的概率与种植业收入占家庭收入的比例呈负相关关系，预测正确率达到 67.9%。说明降低当地农民对种植业的依赖，有助于天然商品林生态效益补偿政策的实施，实现保护天然林资源、促进当地环境与经济的可持续发展。

关键词：天然商品林；生态效益补偿；受偿意愿；概率；模型分析

Modeling theprobabilityofwillingness to accept the compensation for natural commercial forest ecosystem services

MA Zhi-bo[1,2]　HUANG Qing-lin[1]　Ma Hwan OK[3]

(1. Institute of Forest Resource Information Techniques, Chinese Academy of Forestry, Beijing, 100091, P. R. China; 2. Langfang Acadamy of Forestry and Agriculture, Langfang, 065000, Hebei, P. R. China; 3. International Tropical Timber Organization, Yokohama, 220－0012, Japan)

Abstract: Natural forests in China have been rehabilitated well in quantity and quality since the banning deforestation policy for natural forests official issued in 1990s. Substantial opinion regards cutting natural forests, especially clear－cutting them, as one that imposes risks to ecological resilience and human well－being. Now these risks could recur because natural forests using rights were distributed to the villagers after *Reform of Collective Forest Using Rights System* (RCFURS)

基金项目：国家林业局林业公益性行业科研专项：《南方集体林区天然阔叶用材林可持续经营技术试验示范》(编号：200704010)，国际热带木材组织(ITTO)项目：Development and demonstration on scheme of payment for environmental services (PES) derived from degraded and secondary tropical production forests in Hainan province, China[编号：ITTO RED－SPD 020/09 Rev. 1(F)]

第一作者：马志波，在读博士，助理研究员。研究方向：森林可持续经营。电话：010－62889060
Email：populus@163.com

责任作者：黄清麟，研究员，博士，博士生导师，主要研究方向：森林可持续经营理论与技术。
电话：010－62888889　E-mail：huangql@caf.ac.cn

done in south China recently. As 'rational people', villagers could cut natural forests they owned and alter them to plantation (to plant Rubber tree, Eucalyptus etc.) to maximize economic benefits. As there risks are real in south China, a policy suggestion was raised in that paper that public should pay for the ecological services (PES) provided by owners of 'private public goods'. A logistic regression model was also built in that paper to test the probability that villagers could accept the PES programme, based on data gained by using contingent valuation method in Dagan Demonstration Area, and to analysis the correlation of the socio - economic factors might effect on willingness to accept the ecological benefits compensation (WTA). The results showed that there were negative correlations between the proportion of planting income of total family income with the probability of local people to accept the programme. So the key issue to protect the natural commercial forests from changing to artificial forests was to reduce the dependency on farming of livelihood of local people.

Key words: natural commercial forests; PES; WTA; probability; logistic regression model

我国于2008年全面推进了集体林权制度改革(以下简称"林改")，核心是国家把集体林地承包经营权和林木所有权作为财产分给农民，由此确立农民的经营主体地位。林改对解放和发展农村生产力具有重要推动作用，随着林改的逐步落实，配套政策研究引起了广泛关注，成为新的研究热点，主要涉及产权交易、资源资产评估、资产抵押贷款等方面[1~3]。

但是，随着林权转移产生的另一新问题尚未得到充分关注，即天然商品林保护与利用间的冲突，表现为农户取得天然商品林(天然商品林就是天然起源的、按照用途划分为商品林属性的、经由地方政府和林业主管部门界定并发放林权证的一类森林)林权后自主经营权等权益落实困难，原因如下：

林权所有者依法享有林地承包经营权和林木所有权、处置权、受益权等权益。作为"理性人"，他们通常选择把天然商品林转为经济效益更高的森林类型(比如人工纯林，包括用材林和经济林)，在经营中采取成本更低的经营技术(比如皆伐)[4]。但是我国天然林资源因历史原因已严重萎缩，从公共利益出发，各地林业主管部门通常要求采取可持续的方式经营天然林商品林，比如近自然经营、生态采伐等理论和方法[4~6]，采伐技术以择伐为主。分布在重要水源保护区、水土流失易发区、生物多样性热点区域的，则采取严格的保育措施，主要用于发挥生态效益而非经济效益。由于公共利益的约束，目前农户分得的天然商品林事实上成为"私有公共物品"，类似于发挥生态功能的公益林。然而我国目前实施的森林生态效益补偿基金制度不补偿商品林，意味着天然商品林林权所有者既不能以追求经济效益为目标经营森林，也得不到任何补偿，势必引起消极管护，使森林质量下降、功能退化，增大潜在的生态风险。所以，如何保障生态效益持续发挥、促进区域可持续发展，同时不对天然商品林林权所有者的合法权益造成损害，是林改后急需解决的问题。

解决环境资源保护与利用的矛盾，主要有法律法规、政策引导、经济刺激和教育途径。其中，生态效益补偿(即国外的 payments for environmental/ecological services, PES)是目前广受欢迎的一种经济刺激方法[7~9]，可以把具有外部性的、非市场化的生态系统服务价值转换成真正的货币，从而激励人们供应这些服务。森林生态效益补偿是较早开展研究和取得较多实践经验的重要领域。在国外，PES 一般针对生产性私有土地(用途类似于我国的商品林)[7, 10~12]。在我国，随着产权的转移，保护与利用矛盾的凸显，有必要针对具有重要生态价值的商品林，尤其是划归农户的天然商品林，建立准入和补偿机制，通过经济激励防止集体天然林分配到户后转变为人工纯林，达到保护天然林资源，促进生态系统服务持续供应的最终目的。

补偿标准是补偿机制的关键和核心，因为它直接作用于生态系统服务提供者和购买者，很大程度上决定着补偿机制能否实施和最终效果。根据生态效益补偿的概念和内涵，笔者认为在理论上有 2 种途径研制补偿标准：①评估提供的生态系统服务的价值和持续供应所需成本，据此制定补偿标准；②按照由于供应某种(或某些)生态系统服务而使提供者丧失的机会成本制定补偿标准。但是在国内外实践中，补偿标准通常低于上述任意一种途径的研究结果，说明现实可行的补偿标准还受其他因素(例如权益人的受偿意愿、当地的经济发展水平)的影响[9, 13,14]。

条件价值法(Contingent Valuation Method, CVM)在国内外环境/生态经济学问题研究中经常用到[15~20]，其一般步骤是：①通过问卷调查受访者对某个环保行动构想的最大支付意愿(Willingness To Pay, WTP)或者最低受偿意愿(Willingness To Accept, WTA)，同时收集受访者的年龄、性别、收入、受教育程度、生态意识等社会经济背景信息；②建立模型分析社会经济因素与受访者 WTP(或 WTA)之间的相关关系，并根据模型估计平均 WTP(或 WTA)值作为受访者真实意愿的趋近值和资源环境的总经济价值。

CVM 问卷调查取得的数据资料通常既包括数值变量(例如收入、年龄)，也包括分类变量(例如受教育程度、生态环保意识)，因此可以用广义 logistic 回归模型(LRM)进行相关分析[16]、预测平均 WTP(或 WTA)值[18~20]，但是预测的平均值往往偏大[18]，对实践的指示意义不大。此外，LRM 本身具有预测概率功能，但是尚未得到重视和应用。本文从实际出发，参照中国农村选举超过半数可以通过的思路，建立模型分析示范点农户收入、受教育程度等因素与农户接受天然商品林生态效益补偿构想的相关关系，预测农户接受预设的天然商品林生态效益补偿标准的概率，并对预测效果进行评价，目的是为制定切实可行的天然商品林生态效益补偿标准提供参考。

1 示范点概况

1.1 自然地理概况

示范点设在大干村，位于海南省陵水黎族自治县群英乡。地处北纬 18°34°35"，东经 109°51°05"，海拔 30~340 m，面积约 399.48 hm^2。属热带季风岛屿性气候，多年平均气温 24.7℃，1 月份平均最低气温 19.8℃，7 月份平均最高气温 30℃。历史最高气温 37℃，历史最低气温 5.6℃。年降雨量 1500~2500mm。干、湿季分明，11 月份至翌年 4 月份为旱季，5 至 10 月份为雨季，占全年降水量的 85% 以上。季风明显，夏半年盛行西南季风，冬半年盛行东北季风，每年平均遭受 3~5 次台风袭击。研究区北接陵水河，西临走装水库，水资源丰富。地貌以丘陵为主，土壤以棕色黄壤为主。

1.2 社会经济发展

当地是典型的黎族聚居区，包括芬优、芬界和大干三个村民小组。截至 2010 年底，全村约有 140 户、600 人，种植业和外出务工是村民的主要收入来源。栽培物种以橡胶、槟榔、芒果、荔枝、木薯等为主。外出务工者多从事周边地区的瓜菜种植，也有一部分在岛内其他地市和广东省等附近地区就业。

1.3 森林资源状况

根据本项目组调查，大干村总土地面积为 399.48hm^2，现有天然商品林占总面积的 22.43%，由于向人工林的转变，天然林比 1990 年减少了 32.14%。当地天然植被以低地雨林为主，受经济因素刺激，原生植被受人为干扰严重，珍稀、名贵的热带乡土树种降香黄檀(*Dalbergia odorifera*)、无翼坡垒(*Hopeawxalata*)、青皮(*Vatica mangachapoi*)、野生荔枝(*Litchi chinensis*)等已变得极为罕见，常见的水石梓(*Sarcosperma laurinum*)、海南红豆(*Ormosia pinnata*)、万宁柯(*Lithocarpus elmerrillii*)、猫尾木(*Dolichandron ecauda -felina*)、丛花厚壳桂(*Cryptocarya densiflora*)、黄杞(*Engelhardtia roxburghiana*)、海南哥纳香(*Goniothalamus howii*)等也变得少见。

1.4 已有研究情况

在本次调查之前，已经有研究者采用参与式调查等方法在该示范点开展了森林景观恢复研究[20]，当地居民对访谈和问卷调查已经有所了解，对森林的生态功能可能也有一定的认识。国家和海南省重点公益林在该村有分布，在 2010 年完成了划界和护林员招聘工作，因此认为当地居民对森林生态效益补偿机制也有初步认识。

2 研究方法

2.1 问卷调查

根据 Carson(2000)[15]、张志强等(2003)[22]、赵军和杨凯(2006)[23]对 CVM 应用原则、方法的总结，制定问卷主要内容和实施步骤：①根据当地自然环境特征，向受访者介绍天然林的主要生态功能、天然林转为人工林或者遭破坏的后果，介绍实施天然商品林生态效益补偿的构想。②调查受访者家庭成员基本情况，包括成员性别、年龄、文化程度、收入来源、年收入水平、家庭种植业发展计划，等等。③调查受访者对森林生态系统服务的认识，对我国以及海南省森林生态效益补偿相关政策的了解。④介绍目前国家制定的关于森林生态效益补偿的政策，以及海南省公益林生态效益补偿相关文件(琼审农[2009]257 号，琼府[2008]71 号)中关于补偿标准的规定。⑤调查受访者在接受一定生态效益补偿的前提下，是否可以保证不将天然林转为人工植被，从而保障天然林生态系统服务的持续供应。如果同意此构想，是否同意参照政府文件规定的标准执行补偿，或者提出个人认为合理的补偿标准；如果不同意此构想，进一步询问不同意的原因。

为保证访谈数据资料的全面性和可靠性，①聘请了当地居住年限较长、农村生产生活经验较丰富的群众做向导，同时解决语言不通问题；②选择户主在场时进行访谈；③记录家庭成员信息时验证了户口簿；④记录了受访家庭的联系电话，便于后续资料检验。

2.2 LRM 简介

参考 Johnson(2005)[16]、Kutner 等(2004)[17]，简述 LRM 如下：

对于一个二分类(dichotomous)的名义变量，可以用 0 和 1 代表不同的状态，比如城市和乡村，男性和女性。在一定数据资料支持下可以进行 logistic 回归分析。用 $E(y/x)$表示因变量之于自变量的条件平均数(conditional mean)。若因变量不是连续的数值变量，而是用 0 和 1 表示的数值变量，则其条件平均值必然落在 0 ~ 1 之间，即：

$$0 \leqslant E(y/x) \leqslant 1$$

对于普通的多元线性回归函数，有：

$$\hat{y} = E\left(\frac{y}{x}\right) = a + \sum_{j=1}^{m} b_j x_j \quad (1)$$

对于二分类名义变量的条件平均数，属于广义的 logistic 函数，有：

$$f(x) = \frac{1}{He^{-(a+\sum_{j=1}^{m} b_j x_j)}} \quad (2)$$

由于函数值在 0 ～ 1 之间,至少在形式上等同于概率累计分布,因此可以将(2) 式视为因变量的条件概率分布,记为 p(y),有：

$$P(y) = \frac{1}{1 + e^{-(a+\sum_{j=1}^{m} b_j x_j)}} \quad (3)$$

若定义“成功的概率与失败的概率之比” 为胜负比(*odds*),即某一事件出现的概率相应于不出现的概率的倍数,并定义“对胜负比取对数即为 *logit* 变换”[16],则有：

$$\text{odds} = \frac{p(y)}{1 - p(y)} = e^{a+\sum_{j=1}^{m} b_j x_j} \quad (4)$$

两边取自然对数，有：

$$g(x) = \ln odds = a + \sum_{j=1}^{m} b_j x_j \quad (5)$$

(5)式建立了自变量与概率 p 之间的非线性关系，这种关系就是 logistic 关系，基于这种关系开展的回归分析就是 logistic 回归分析。

2.3 建模工具和预测效果检验

本文使用 R 软件(版本号 2.13.0)完成模型建设、检验和预测分析。主要调用 glm( )、step( )、wald.test( )等函数。随机选取 70% 的调查数据用于建模，剩余数据用于检验预测效果。用预测正确率(CR)检查预测效果，公式如下：

$$CR = \frac{A + D}{A + B + C + D} \times 100\% \quad (6)$$

对于选定的某个临界值(一般取 0.5)，可把大于临界值的预测值全部表示为 1，小于的计为 0，此时预测结果可以分为 0 或 1 两类。预测值与观测值之间的关系可以分为 4 类，用(6)式中的 A、B、C、D 代表，其中：A 代表观测值 =1，预测值近似为 1 的情形；B 代表观测值 =1，预测值近似为 0；C 代表观测值 =0，预测值近似为 1；D 代表观测值 =0，预测值近似为 0。

3 结果分析

3.1 社会经济因素分析

示范点内有部分居民长期外出经商、务工，可以采访的家庭数为 106 户，其中 8 户明确表示拒绝接受访谈，实际完成 98 个家庭的入户访谈，占当地总家庭数的 70.0%（占可采访家庭数的 90.7%），访谈中登记家庭成员信息覆盖 488 人，占该村总人口数的 81.3%。根据访谈数据，分析示范点社会经济情况如下。

3.1.1 收入水平和收入结构

在 2010 年，大干平均家庭年总收入为 26338 元(变动区间 1280 ~ 85000 元)。人均收入为 5289 元。以人均收入为标准，低于标准的家庭占调查家庭总数的 37.8%。

调查种植业收入情况知，目前该村种植业收入占家庭总收入的比例平均值为 32.3%。进一步调查知，其余收入主要来源于外出务工和经商(以营销农牧产品，和日用品、自酿米酒等为主)。

橡胶和槟榔是当前栽培面积最大的经济植物，但超过60%是最近10年内栽植，处于幼树、幼苗期，个别达到初产期。受价格上涨刺激，以及黎族群众嚼食槟榔的传统，有约90%的受访者最近3年内调整了种植结构，通过缩减果树林和农作物(主要是木薯)扩大了橡胶和槟榔种植面积；有75%的农户表示，如果有土地，将继续扩大家庭橡胶和槟榔种植面积。

3.1.2　家庭劳动力资源

根据入户调查资料计算，平均每个家庭有人口约5.0人，其中：务农劳动力(18~50岁)2.2人，外出务工的1.0人，其他人员1.8人。18岁以上务农人口约占60.1%。

3.1.3　教育水平和对森林生态系统服务的认知

家庭成员(不包括在校生和学前儿童)平均受教育年限为8.4年(变动区间为4.5~11.0年)，登记98个家庭中成年人受教育年限满9年义务教育及以上的有265人，占54.3%；有大学生2人，占0.4%。98位户主中，有8人是高中学历，小学学历10人，其余80人为初中学历。在主要家庭成员(主要是配偶和父母)在场可提示的情况下，98位户主中有14位可以说出3项以上的森林生态功能，43位可以说出1~3项，有41位说出0项。说明约有58.2%的家庭至少了解1项森林生态系统服务，有41.8%的家庭对森林生态系统服务缺乏了解。

3.1.4　小　结

根据上述分析可以初步判断：当地种植业发展势头较强，在缺乏土地的情况下，把天然林转变为人工林的可能性较大。原因是：①当地家庭之间收入差距较大，广大群众发展经济、提高收入、降低收入差距的愿望强烈。②种植业，尤其是橡胶和槟榔的种植可能是目前最重要和最有前景的致富门路。当地具有种植橡胶、槟榔传统和气候土壤优势，示范点所在乡镇近期被县政府确定为扩大橡胶种植规模的重点乡镇，受市场需求和价格上涨因素的刺激，当地群众调整家庭种植结构的行动已经开展，扩大种植规模的意愿也较强。③当地群众受教育程度普遍不高，劳动力主要分布在种植业，这种现状在短期内较难改变。

3.2　模型建立与分析预测

3.2.1　变量选择与回归分析

基于3.1小节的分析，优先选择种植业收入占家庭的比重作为预测变量。为分析其他社会经济因素对WTA的影响，同时选择受访者年龄、家庭年总收入、家庭务农人口等作为预测变量。各个变量的描述、简记符号、取值范围等见表1。调查中94.9%受访者家庭表示同意在接受一定的生态效益补偿前提下，不把其占有的天然林转变为人工植被，从而保证天然林生态系统服务的持续供应和质量的提高。这一比例较高，因此本研究以“是否同意按有关政府文件规定的公益林生态效益补偿标准补偿”为因变量。

表1　变量的取值范围与描述

Tab.1　description of the variables in LRM

变量名称 name of the variable	描述 description	简记 logogram	取值范围 range
年龄，age	数值变量，自变量	age	0~100
家庭务农人数，labor force in agriculture	数值变量，自变量	agrilab	0~10

变量名称 name of the variable	描述 description	简记 logogram	取值范围 range
种植业占总收入的比例， planting income/total income	数值变量，自变量	perpla	0.00～1.00
受教育程度，education grade	分类变量，自变量	edugra	0：初中及以下；1：高中及以上
能说出的生态功能项数分级， ecological awareness grade	分类变量，自变量	ecogra	0：0项；1：1～3项；2：>3项
是否同意按公益林生态效益补偿标准补偿＊？ willingness to accept compensation of governmental std.	二分类变量，因变量	wta	1：同意，0：不同意

注：＊海南省政府(琼府[2008]71号)制定了5年规划逐步提高公益林生态效益补偿标准至20元/(亩·年)

Hainan governmental std. of ecological compensation for non－commercial forest is RMB20/(mu·a), mu is an Chinese unit for area, 15mu＝1ha

本文主要采用逐步回归的方法进行建模。为便于比较，同时给出了全变量模型 logit01 和逐步回归得到的模型 steplogit01，参数估计和检验结果等列于表2和表3(表中的 intercept 即截距)。由表2知，表1所列变量全部进入模型时，通过检验的只有 agrilab 与 perpla(显著水平分别为 $a = 0.1$ 和 $a = 0.05$)，说明这两个变量对受访农户的 wta 影响显著，而年龄、受教育程度、生态意识对 wta 影响不显著。此时有必要对变量做进一步筛选。

采用逐步回归法筛选变量，最终得到模型 steplogit01。steplogit01 中通过显著性检验的只有 perpla($a = 0.05$)，agrilab 和截距的 p 值不能通过检验(具体结果见表3)。因此需要再次对变量做出取舍。考虑到变量 agrilab 与 perpla 可能存在共线性，或者说存在 perpla 中已经包含 agrilab 信息的可能性，因此尝试在逐步回归结果 steplogit01 基础上剔除 agrilab，拟合结果见表4。新拟合模型(logit02)的截距和系数均通过了检验，整体拟合效果较为满意。检查三次拟合所得变量 perpla 的系数(具体值见表2至表4)可知其均为负值且变幅较小，在一定程度上说明自变量 perpla 对因变量 wta 的解释力较为可靠。

表2　全变量模型拟合结果

Tab. 2　Parameter estimates results for model*logit*01

变量 variable	变量系数 variable coefficient	标准误差 standard errors	z 统计量 z－statistic	p 值 $Pr > \|z\|$
intercept	－1.11624	1.22870	－0.908	0.3636
age	0.03113	0.02279	1.366	0.1719
agrilab	0.38378	0.23098	1.662	0.0966
perpla	－1.51101	0.68749	－2.198	0.0280＊
as. factor(edugra)1	－0.25412	0.80314	－0.316	0.7517
as. factor(ecogra)1	0.14375	0.48484	0.296	0.7669
as. factor(ecogra)2	－0.60607	0.70301	－0.862	0.3886

注："·"表示通过显著水平 $a = 0.1$ 检验，"＊"表示通过显著水平 $a = 0.05$ 检验

Signif. codes：'＊' 0.05；'·' 0.1

表 3 逐步回归的拟合结果

Tab. 3 Parameter estimates results by stepwise regression method

变量 variable	变量系数 variable coefficient	标准误差 standard errors	z 统计量 z - statistic	p 值 Pr > | z |
intercept	0.3701	0.5618	0.659	0.510
agrilab	0.3296	0.2118	1.557	0.120
perpla	-1.6642	0.6546	-2.542	0.011 *

注：· 表示通过显著水平 $a = 0.1$ 检验，* 表示通过显著水平 $a = 0.05$ 检验

Signif. codes：'*' 0.05；'·' 0.1

进一步，对 perpla 进入模型(即 logit02)和只保留截距的情形(称为 Null model，Null 模型)做 χ^2 检验，p 值 $=0.01334976 < a = 0.05$，说明 logit02 的整体拟合效果显著优于 Null 模型，也就是说变量 perpla 进入模型具有实际意义。logit02 的形式如下：

$$logit02 = lnodds = \ln\left(\frac{p}{1-p}\right) = 1.0733 + 1.5519i \tag{7}$$

表 4 剔除变量 agrilab 后的拟合结果

Tab. 4 Results of model fit after *agrilab* eliminated from *steplogit*01

系数 coefficients	系数估计值 estimate	标准误差 standard errors	z 统计量 z - statistic	p 值 Pr > | z |
intercept	1.0733	0.3501	3.066	0.00217 **
perpla	-1.5519	0.6411	-2.421	0.01548 *

注："**"表示通过显著水平 $a = 0.01$ 检验，"*"表示通过显著水平 $a = 0.05$ 检验

Signif. codes：'**' 0.01；'*' 0.05

3.2.2 预测效果检验

根据公式(6)、模型(7)和用于检验预测的 28 个样本，计算得到预测正确率为 67.9%，具体的 wta 值及其对应的预测值 wta * 列于表 5。根据 2.3 节所定义的分类方法，以及表 5 给出的预测值，计算 A 类结果占检验样本的比例为 53.6%(剔除 B、C 两类预测失误的计数)，即预测接受 wta 的农户所占比例超过半数，说明通过天然商品林生态效益补偿的途径保护当地的天然林具有可行性。目前直接应用预测正确率检验预测效果的实例较少。缪柏其等(2008)用超过 1000 个样本建模，用 1 和 0.5 为标准分析 24 个样本的预测误差，其中预测相对误差 <0.5 的占 54%，参照该应用案例[25]，认为本研究预测效果可以接受。

表 5 观测值与预测值

Tab. 5 observation values (wta) and prediction results(wta *)

wta	1	1	1	0	1	1	1	1	1	1	1	1	1	1
wta *	0.682	0.466	0.647	0.692	0.427	0.745	0.593	0.574	0.383	0.682	0.658	0.383	0.619	0.589
wta	1	0	1	0	1	1	0	0	0	1	1	1	0	0
wta *	0.665	0.383	0.589	0.705	0.637	0.675	0.559	0.383	0.383	0.685	0.633	0.447	0.383	0.689

4 结论与讨论

4.1 结 论

林改赋予了农户林地承包经营权和林木所有权、处置权、受益权等合法权益，但是受国

家和地方天然林保护政策的约束，分配给农户的天然商品林成为“私人公共物品”，适宜采用生态效益补偿途径解决天然商品林保护与利用中的利益冲突。

从决策者角度出发，沿用现有制度对天然商品林进行补偿，成本较低，便于被其他人群接受，从而有利于进入决策程序、最终转变为决策实践，解决当前的突出矛盾。

种植业收入占总家庭收入的比例(自变量 perpla)与村民接受天然商品林受偿建议的意愿呈负相关关系，结合本文社会经济调查结果，可以认为通过改善教育状况、增加就业技能培训、拓宽家庭经济收入渠道，降低群众对种植业的依赖性，是缓解天然商品林转为人工林压力的有效途径。

建立用于预测林权所有者受偿意愿的 logit 模型只包括截距和一个自变量 perpla，形式简单，预测正确率达到67.9%。预测接受 wta 的农户超过半数，参考我国农村选举中超过半数可以通过的原则，可以认为按当地现有公益林生态补偿标准对天然商品林实施生态效益补偿具有可行性。

4.2 讨 论

(1)当数据等离散或者过离散时，用零膨胀泊松模型(ZIP)或者零膨胀负二项分布模型(ZINB)分析可以取得更好的效果[24]，ZIP 和 ZINB 已经在医学和生物学领域得到了大量应用[24~26]，但是在环境/生态经济学研究中尚未得到关注。ZIP 和 ZINB 要求大样本[24-27]，但是最低要求多少样本不得而知，目前所见最小样本数来自加利福尼亚大学洛杉矶分校(UCLA)学术技术服务网站给出的应用案例，其样本数超过 200[27]。由于示范点总户数低于200，无法满足 ZIP 或 ZINB 建模要求，因此，本研究仍使用 LRM 描述和分析调查数据，从模型检验和预测正确率分析看，logit02 可以接受，尽管 LRM 可能不是最适合的模型。

(2)产权转移后，天然商品林生态效益补偿的实施无疑需要林权所有者的认可。本文采用了常用的 CVM 途径获得调查数据，建立模型分析当地政府现有公益林补偿标准被群众接受的概率，从而为尽快解决林权落实中的利益冲突提供决策依据。这种思路能否在其他类似决策行动中加以利用还有待进一步的实践检验。

参考文献

[1]景谦平，侯元兆．森林资源资产评估管理[J]．世界林业研究，2009，22(3)：5~7

[2]陈瑶．森林资源资产价值的综合评估方法[J]．东北林业大学学报，2009，37(6)：89~99

[3]王富炜，王自力．森林资源资产评估的价值类型及其估值[J]．北京林业大学学报(社会科学版)，2009，8(4)：83~86

[4] STONE R. Nursing China's ailing forests back to health[J]. Science, 2009, 325(5940): 556~558

[5]陆元昌．近自然森林经营的理论与实践[M]．北京：科学出版社，2006

[6]张会儒，唐守正．森林生态采伐理论[J]．林业科学，2008，44(10)：127~131

[7] LANDELL - MILLS N, PORRAS TI. Silver bullet or fools' gold?: A global review of markets for forest environmental services and their impact on the poor[EB/OL]. (2002 - 3) http://www.cbd.int/doc/external/iied/iied - silver - report - 2002 - en.pdf

[8] WUNDER S. Payments for environmental services: Some nuts and bolts[R]. Bogor, Indonesia: CIFOR, 2005

[9]李文华，李芬，李世东，等．森林生态效益补偿的研究现状与展望[J]．自然资源学报，2006，21(5)：676~688

[10]ZBINDEN S, LEE DR. Paying for environmental services: an analysis of participation in Costa Rica's PSA pro-

gram[J]. World development, 2005, 33(2): 255 ~272

[11] ENGEL S, PAGIOLA S, WUNDER S. Designing payments for environmental services in theory and practice: an overview of the issues[J]. Ecological economics, 2008, 65(4): 663 ~674

[12] Muñoz – Piña C, GUEVARA A, TORRES JM, *et al.* Paying for the hydrological services of Mexico's forests: Analysis, negotiations and results[J]. Ecological economics, 2008, 65(4): 725 ~736

[13] ASQUITH NM, VARGAS MT, WUNDER S. Selling two environmental services: In – kind payments for bird habitat and watershed protection in Los Negros, Bolivia[J]. Ecological economics, 2008, 65(4): 675 ~684

[14] TURPIE JK, MARAIS C, BLIGNAUT JN. The working for water programme: evolution of a payments for ecosystem services mechanism that addresses both poverty and ecosystem service delivery in South Africa[J]. Ecological economics, 2008, 65(4): 788 ~798

[15] CARSON RT. Contingent valuation: A user's guide[J]. Environmental science & technology, 2000, 34(8): 1413 ~1418

[16] JOHNSON DE. 应用多元统计分析方法[M]. 北京：高等教育出版社，2005

[17] KUTNER MH, NACHTSHEIM CJ, NETER J. 应用线性回归模型(第 4 版)[M]. 北京：高等教育出版，2004

[18] KOTCHEN MJ, REILING SD. Environmental attitudes, motivations, and contingent valuation of nonuse values: a case study involving endangered species[J]. Ecological economics, 2000, 32(1): 93 ~107

[19] LOOMIS J, KENT P, STRANGE L, *et al.* Measuring the total economic value of restoring ecosystem services in an impaired river basin: results from a contingent valuation survey[J]. Ecological economics, 2000, 33(1): 103 ~117

[20] MACMILLAN D, DUFF E, ELSTION D. Modelling the non – market environmental costs and benefits of biodiversity projects using contingent valuation data[M]. Environmental and resource economics, 2001, 18(4): 391 ~410

[21]张晓红，黄清麟．森林景观恢复研究[M]. 北京：中国林业出版社，2011

[22]张志强，徐中民，程国栋．条件价值评估发的发展与应用[J]. 地球科学进展，2003，18(6)：454 ~463

[23]赵军，杨凯．自然资源与环境价值评估：条件价值法及应用原则探讨[J]. 自然资源学报，2006，21(9)：834 ~843

[24] HALL DB. Zero – inflated Poisson and binomial regression with random effects: a case study[J]. Biometerics, 2000, 56(4): 1030 ~1039

[25]缪柏其，韦剑，宋卫国，等．林火数据的 logistic 和零膨胀 poisson(ZIP)回归模型[J]. 火灾科学，2008，17(3)：143 ~149

[26]郭福涛，胡海清，金森，等．基于负二项和零膨胀负二项回归模型的大兴安岭地区雷击火与气象因素的关系[J]. 植物生态学报，2010，34(50)：571 ~577

[27] UCLA Academic technology services. R data analysis examples[EB/OL]. (2011) http://www.ats.ucla.edu/stat/r/dae/.

同心圆样地抽样方法在天然阔叶林调查中的应用研究

黄清麟　戎建涛　张晓红　马志波

（中国林业科学研究院资源信息研究所，国家林业局林业遥感与信息技术重点实验室，北京，100091）

摘要：以福建省永安市麻岭天然阔叶林为试验研究对象，应用 100m×100m 和 100m×200m 的抽样密度，分别采用 6m 半径和 12m 半径的同心圆样地抽样方法探讨主要测树因子的抽样估计结果。结果表明：在 100m×100m 抽样密下，采用 12m 半径样圆抽估计林分的平均胸径、平均树高、平均密度、平均单位面积蓄积量和任何胸径级的株数是完全合适的和可靠的。即使在 100m×100m 抽样密下，也不宜采用 6m 半径样圆抽估计林分的平均胸径、平均树高、平均密度、平均单位面积蓄积量和任何胸径级的株数。

关键词：天然阔叶林；同心圆样地；抽样调查

中图分类号：S758.5；S718.542　文献标识码：A

Study on the application of concentric sampling method on natural broad-leaved forest

HUANG Qing-lin　RONG Jian-tao　ZHANG Xiao-hong　MA Zhi-bo

(Institute of Forest Resource Information Techniques, Chinese Academy of Forestry, Key Laboratory of Forestry Remote Sensing and Information Technology, State Forestry Administration, Beijing, 100091)

Abstract: Took the natural broad-leaved forest at Maling in Yong'an City of Fujian Province as a case study. Concentric sampling method of 100m×100m and 100m×200m density was applied in the natural broad-leaved forest. Plots with radius 6m and radius 12m respectively in concentric sampling were used to evaluate the impact of inventory on main mensuration factors of the natural broad - leaved forest. The results showed that sampling density of 100m×100m and radius of 12m

---

基金项目：国家林业局引进国际先进农业科学技术(948)项目(2006-4-23)和国家林业局林业公益性行业科研专项(200704010)。

作者简介(Biography)：黄清麟(1967~)，男(汉族)，福建莆田人，博士、研究员、博士生导师，主要从事森林可持续经营理论与技术研究。E-mail：huangql@caf.ac.cn.

had best estimation for main mensuration factors and tree number of different diameter group.

Key words: natural broad – leaved forest; concentric sampling plots; sampling inventory

抽样调查是森林调查中的重要方法，在林业中应用极为广泛。我国的抽样调查样地多采用方形样地，在德国多采用同心圆样地进行森林经营单位水平森林资源的调查[1~4]。而我国关于同心圆调查样地调查的文章报道较少。本文以福建省永安市麻岭天然阔叶林为试验研究对象，应用 100m × 100m 和 100m × 200m 的抽样密度，分别采用 6m 半径和 12m 半径的同心圆样地抽样方法探讨主要测树因子的调查效果，以期为我国森林经营单位水平和林分水平的森林资源调查提供借鉴。

1 试验林分概况

试验天然阔叶林位于福建省永安市燕东街道办事处麻岭村 3 林班 17 大班 1 小班和 2 小班，面积 $23hm^2$，地处海拔 400 ~ 600 m，平均坡度 30°，主要土壤类型为红壤，立地类型为 II 类地，为成熟林。2008 年 7 月进行第一次调查、2009 年 7 月和 2010 年 7 月分别进行第一次和第二次复查。林分平均胸径、树高、密度和单位面积蓄积量分别为 25.44 cm、16.51 m、799 N/hm^2 和 286.20 m^3/hm^2。

2 研究方法

2.1 调查方法

按照系统抽样的原则，以 100m × 100m 和 100m × 200m 两种抽样密度在试验天然阔叶林分别设置了 24 个和 14 个同心圆样地(半径分别为 3m、6m 和 12m)，对半径为 3m 样圆内胸径 DBH < 5cm 的所有林木和植物(含乔木幼树、乔木幼苗、灌木和草本植物)进行调查，测定其物种、高度和株数；对半径为 6m 的样圆内的胸径 DBH ≥ 5cm 的所有林木进行每木检尺，测定其树种、胸径、树高、枝下高和冠幅；对处于 6m 半径样圆外和 12m 半径样圆内的胸径 DBH ≥ 25cm 的所有林木进行每木检尺，测定其树种、胸径、树高、枝下高和冠幅。

2.2 抽样估计值与抽样精度计算

$$\bar{y} = \frac{1}{n}\sum_{i=1}^{n} y_i$$

$$S_y^2 = \frac{1}{n-1}\left[\sum_{i=1}^{n} y_i^2 - \frac{1}{n}\left(\sum_{i=1}^{n} y_i\right)^2\right]$$

$$S_{\bar{y}} = \frac{S_{\bar{y}}^2}{n}$$

$$\Delta \bar{y} = tS_{\bar{y}}$$

$$P = \frac{\Delta\bar{y}}{\bar{y}} \quad E = 100(1-P)$$

式中：n 表示样本总量，t 表示置信系数，$\bar{y}$ 表示观测样地均值，S_y^2 表示方差估计值，$S_{\bar{y}}$表示标准误，$\Delta\bar{y}$ 表示估计误差，P 表示相对误差，E 表示估计精度。

3 结果与分析

3.1 不同直径组林木株数的估计结果

将林木胸径分为三个胸径级，Ⅰ级为胸径 5 ~ 14.9cm 的林木，Ⅱ级为胸径 15 ~ 24.9cm 的林木，Ⅲ级为胸径 ≥25cm 的林木。同样分别利用 100m × 100m(24 个同心圆样地)与 100m × 200m(14 个同心圆样地)2 种抽样密度和半径为 6m 与 12m 的 2 种样圆估计三个胸径级的林木株数，结果见表 1。

表 1 不同半径样圆的不同胸径级株数预估值与精度

Tab. 1 Estimation value and accuracy of tree number for different diameter group in different radius sampling plots

抽样密度	样圆半径(m)	总株数		Ⅰ级株数		Ⅱ级株数		Ⅲ级株数	
		估计值(N/hm²)	预估精度(%)	估计值(N/hm²)	预估精度(%)	估计值(N/hm²)	预估精度(%)	估计值(N/hm²)	预估精度(%)
100m × 100m	6m	779	86.40	445	87.89	218	85.70	116	76.95
	12m	799	91.27	381	94.25	210	88.65	208	94.69
100m × 200m	6m	714	84.72	417	79.32	202	78.50	113	61.77
	12m	748	90.19	365	83.45	180	82.21	216	82.13

利用 100m × 200m 抽样密度估计中，6m 半径样圆抽样估计的三个胸径级株数估计精度分别为 79.32%、78.50% 和 61.77%，估计精度均不高，25cm 以上林木株数估计精度最低，且估计值明显过低。12m 半径样圆各个胸径级估计精度分别为 83.45%、82.21% 和 82.13%，总株数的估计精度达 90.19%。因此，对试验天然阔叶林，在 100m × 200m 抽样密下，不宜采用 6m 和 12m 半径样圆来估计任何胸径级的株数，只可以考虑采用 12m 半径样圆来估计林木总株数。

利用 100m × 100m 抽样密度估计中，6m 半径样圆抽样估计的三个胸径级株数分别为 445、218 和 116N/hm²，其中Ⅲ级株数预估精度不高，仅为 76.95%，即对 25cm 以上林木株数估计过低。在林分中大径阶林木株数估算更为重要，因为它们不仅是林分蓄积的主要组成部分和林分经营的重点对象，而且它们还发挥着重要的生态和经济作用。12m 半径样圆估计的三个胸径级株数分别为 381、210 和 208N/hm²，且三个胸径级预估精度都较高，分别为 91.27%、94.25% 和 94.69%，其中 25cm 以上林木株数估计最为准确，预估精度最高。因此，对试验天然阔叶林，在 100m × 100m 抽样密度下，采用 12m 半径样圆来估计任何胸径级的株数是完全合适的和可靠的。

3.2 林分平均胸径、平均高、密度和单位面积蓄积量的估计结果

分别利用 100m × 100m(24 个同心圆样地)与 100m × 200m(14 个同心圆样地)抽样密度和半径为 6m 与 12m 的样圆估计林分平均胸径、平均高、平均密度和单位面积蓄积量，结果见表 2。

表 2 不同半径样圆的主要测树因子预估值与精度

Tab. 2 Estimation value and accuracy of main mensuration factors in different radius sampling plots

抽样密度	样圆半径(m)	平均胸径		平均树高		平均密度		平均单位面积蓄积量	
		估计值(cm)	预估精度(%)	估计值(m)	预估精度(%)	估计值(N/hm^2)	预估精度(%)	估计值(m^3/hm^2)	预估精度(%)
100m×100m	6m	18.19	93.66	12.25	93.55	779	86.40	168.92	91.18
	12m	25.44	94.59	16.51	97.39	799	91.27	286.20	96.30
100m×200m	6m	18.08	89.61	12.15	84.97	714	84.72	146.74	88.79
	12m	26.41	92.08	15.68	90.26	748	90.19	277.83	90.52

利用100m×100m抽样密度估计中，6m半径样圆得到的平均胸径、平均树高和平均单位面积蓄积量的预估精度都在90%以上，但其估计值都明显偏低，特别是平均单位面积蓄积量；其原因是6m半径样圆偏小，不足以反映大胸径级林木情况，对大胸径级林木的估计严重不足的结果。因此，对试验天然阔叶林，在100m×100m抽样密度下，不宜采用6m半径样圆抽估计林分的平均胸径、平均树高、平均密度和平均单位面积蓄积量。12m半径样圆得到的平均胸径、平均树高、平均密度和平均单位面积蓄积量的预估精度分别为94.59%、97.39%、91.27%和96.30%，估计精度都很高，特别是平均单位面积蓄积量的预估精度在95%以上，因此，对试验天然阔叶林，在100m×100m抽样密度下，采用12m半径样圆抽估计林分的平均胸径、平均树高、平均密度和平均单位面积蓄积量是完全合适的和可靠的。

利用100m×200m抽样密度估计中，无论是6m半径还是12m半径样圆数据，估计精度都比对应100m×100m估计精度低。其中半径为6m样圆的各种主要测树因子估计精度都在90%以下，且对应各种主要测树因子估计值都明显偏低，特别是平均单位面积蓄积量的估计。半径为12m样圆的各主要测树因子估计精度都在90%以上，且对应各种测树因子估计值与100m×100m抽样密度估计值接近，在实际应用中可考虑采用。因此，对试验天然阔叶林，在100m×200m抽样密度下，不宜采用6m半径样圆来估计任何主要测树因子，只可考虑采用12m半径样圆来估计主要测树因子。

4 结 论

对试验天然阔叶林，在100m×200m抽样密度下，不宜采用6m和12m半径样圆来估计任何胸径级的株数，只可以考虑采用12m半径样圆来估计林木总株数；在100m×100m抽样密下，采用12m半径样圆来估计任何胸径级的株数是完全合适的和可靠的。

对试验天然阔叶林，在100m×200m抽样密度下，不宜采用6m半径样圆来估计任何主要测树因子，只可考虑采用12m半径样圆来估计主要测树因子。

对试验天然阔叶林，在100m×100m抽样密度下，不宜采用6m半径样圆抽估计林分的平均胸径、平均树高、平均密度和平均单位面积蓄积量；在100m×100m抽样密度下，采用半径12m样圆抽估计林分的平均胸径、平均树高、平均密度和平均单位面积蓄积量是完全合适的和可靠的。

参考文献

[1]孟宪宇．测树学[M]. 北京：中国林业出版社，1996，45～65.

[2]王伯荪，余世孝，彭少麟，等．植物群落学实验手册[M]. 广州：广东高等教育出版社，1996，1～22，100～106.

[3]Annika Kangas，Matti Maltamo. Forest Inventory Methodology and Application. Springer，2006.

[4]黄清麟．浅谈德国的"近自然森林经营"[J]. 世界林业研究，2005，18(3)：73～77.

江西省杉木大径材经营模式研究

杨馥宁[1]　郑小贤[2]

（1. 江西省南昌市林业局，南昌，330038；2. 北京林业大学林学院，北京，100083）

摘要： 以靖安县为研究对象，提出了建设杉木大径材的经营目标及经营技术，首次从作业级层次提出了杉木大径材的经营模式，在现有18地位指数以上的杉木林地选取目标树，然后通过合理的抚育间伐、林地施肥等后期集约经营管理措施，不断调整林分密度，使目标树保留密度为1200株/hm^2左右，最终培育成大径材。这对于指导南方集体林区县级开展森林经营，促进区域森林持续经营水平的提高具有指导意义。

关键词： 作业级；杉木；大径材；经营模式；江西省

Study on sustainable management pattern of Chinese Fir for big-diameter timber in Jiangxi Province

YANG Fu-ning[1], ZHENG Xiao-xian[2]

(1. Bureau of Nanchang Forest, Jiangxi Province, Nanchang, 330038; 2. College of Forestry, Beijing Forestry University, Beijing, 100083)

Abstract: Based on Jing'an County, This paper put forward the management goal and technique and sustainable management pattern of Chinese Fir for big - diameter timber in a level of management class for the first time. It is available to select goal tree of Chinese Fir in the forest land with site index 18 and through some measures such as reasonable tending thinning and forest fertilization. Adjusting stand density continuously so as to keep 1200 individual plant per hectare and can finally reach the goal of cultivating big - diameter timber. Among them, improved varieties are basis, density control is key measure. This paper provided guidance for instructing forest management and improving the level of forest management in collective forest regions in south of China.

Key words: management class; Chinese Fir; big-diameter timber; management model; Jiangxi Province

---

资助项目：国家林业局森林认证试点项目（S2007003）。

通讯作者简介：杨馥宁（1969～）男，博士，林业高级工程师，从事林业管理，森林文化可持续经营研究。电话：079－83686577，传真：0791－83586591，E-mail：fred72169@yahoo.com.cn

大径级材是指小头径在24cm以上、长4m以上的原木，为建筑、装修、家具制造等特殊用途的材种。杉木是我国南方的主要用材树种，生长快，干形直，材质好，用途广。根据近10a来江西木材市场分析结果看，杉木中、小径材出现供过于求，而大径材出现严重短缺[1]，培育杉木大径材极富市场竞争力。目前，对杉木大径材经营的研究并不多，探讨杉木大径材的经营模式将为南方集体林区森林可持续经营的实践提供一种思路和借鉴，不仅具有重要的科学意义，也具有一定的生产实践价值。

1 研究区概况

江西是我国南方的杉木重要产区省之一，而靖安县是江西省重点林业县，该县位于江西省西北部，属中亚热带湿润季风气候区，光照充足，热量丰富，雨水充沛，常年平均日照数为1799h，常年平均气温13.7～17.0℃，常年平均无霜期240～260d，常年平均降水量1644～1759mm。该县是我国南方集体林区重点林业县，森林资源丰富，多年来向国家提供了大量的商品材，为当地的经济发展作出了较大的贡献。林业用地面积117119.6hm^2，占全县国土面积的85.02%，其中，商品林地面积55319.6 hm^2，占47.2%。在商品林中，用材林面积39744.4 hm^2，其中杉木林面积24627.0 hm^2，占61.96%[2]。

2 杉木大径材经营模式

2.1 杉木大径材经营模式理论

2.1.1 杉木大径材可持续经营概念的提出

从森林经营思想演变过程不难看出，森林经营思想总是围绕和制约着森林经营目标和任务。当前已步入生态社会，可持续发展战略已经为全球社会的广泛认同和接受。而森林可持续经营与林业可持续发展是整个经济、社会可持续发展的基础，森林资源的消长变化直接影响和反映着生态环境的改善与恶化，直接关系到林产品的供给和林业经济发展的水平，迅速增加森林资源是改善生态环境和保障林产品供给最根本的途径。

法正林提出了用材林经营实行同龄纯林，按一定轮伐期进行皆伐，在经营类型(作业级)内追求“法正龄级结构、法正林分排列、法正生长量、法正蓄积量”，采用生长量控制采伐量，实现均衡的木材永续利用(于政中，1991)。至今仍然指导着我国森林经营管理实践，并将其列入我国的《森林法》。

近年来，由于木材比较效益偏低等多方面原因，用材林培育特别是大径材的发展已经成为林业生产的短腿，因而培育大径材是解决木材供需矛盾的必然举措，是满足社会木材需求而有效保护生态公益林、加强生态环境建设的迫切需要，是提高山地综合效益、促进林业跨越式发展的良好举措。目前国内所产的杉木大径材极少，那么，如何保证可持续地向市场提供大径材，使杉木大径材经营在理论的指导下得到持续、健康发展是必须解决的理论问题。为此，本研究提出了杉木大径材可持续经营的概念，并在此概念基础上构建杉木作业级水平大径材可持续经营的理论模式。杉木大径材可持续经营是指人类为了满足社会日益增长的木材需求，缓和大径材的供需矛盾，采用良种化、集约化、经营过程流程化、短周期经营的方式，在兼顾生态效益的同时追求经济效益最大化的森林经营方式。其基本内涵包括三个方面：①森林经营目标专业化，即专门为特定的工业部门生产符合工艺要求的木材；②是经营技术和经营手段的集约化，即经营技术上高度集约，按现代企业的管理模式进行经营管理；

③在效益上追求林地投入产出经济效益的最大化。其中追求林地投入产出经济效益最大化是大径材可持续经营最显著的特征。

2.1.2 杉木大径材经营的框架和原则

正如大径材可持续经营概念所指出那样，大径材可持续经营理念和思想基础是以产业思想来经营森林，充分利用各种融资渠道，高度重视采用良种化和先进技术，用更少的林地生产更多的木材，从而腾出更多的林地经营生态公益林，以达到生态建设与保护环境的目的。

培育杉木大径材是建设现代林业、增加单位面积产量、优化林产品材种结构、提高经济效益和增强林业发展后劲的重要举措，应遵循以下原则：

①大径材基地布局与林产工业的布局相协调。

②适当引进优良品种，优化树种结构，提高林分质量。

③改造和新造林相结合，建设大径材基地。

④在较高立地质量的林地上区划，基地相对集中连片，造林地选择以宜林荒山荒地、采伐迹地，疏林地为主，积极稳妥改造低质灌木林，形成规模经营。

⑤在单层林中改皆伐为择伐，杉木人工林大多是相对同龄林，通过人工干涉，可以使其成为多层林。在采伐时采用中等强度的择伐，在择伐中每公顷保留胸径 26cm 以上长势良好的杉木林林木 100~200 株，以保证下次择伐时(一般 10~15 年后)有大径木可伐。择伐应进行孔状择伐，使林地内有较大的保留林窗以促进阔叶林的更新，形成镶嵌状针阔混交林。

2.1.3 杉木大径材经营的目标体系

由于靖安县现有的杉木用材林面积大，达 24627hm^2，为此，除了在新造林之前就规划培育大径材外，也可挑选其中符合条件的现有杉木林通过有目的的改造经营培育成大径材，本文中提到的大径材经营是指后者。根据靖安县目前的状况，设计出杉木大径材经营目标体系。通过对现有林分改造培育和新造林的途径，在立地条件较好的区域建设大径材基地。2020 年建成以杉木为主的大径材基地面积 2600hm^2，从现在开始，每年建设 200 hm^2。

杉木大径材经营模式的总目标是：通过科学经营，维持杉木人工林林地长期生产力，提供优质、高产值、可再生的大径木材资源，实现经济效益最大化，同时兼顾生态效益，维持林分景观多样性、遗传多样性和生物多样性，最终实现杉木人工林的可持续经营。总目标分解为四个子目标：

(1)资源经营目标。该目标是林木资源的产出效益目标，要求长期保持或提高单位面积的木材产量。

(2)经济效益目标。在现有经营条件下，追求投入产出比的最大化，充分体现资源的经济效益。本经营目的就是选择地位指数 18 以上的林地培育大径材，杉木大径材的轮伐期为 32~36 年，主伐时林分平均胸径 28cm 以上，蓄积量为 450m^3/hm^{2}以上，出材量 300m^3/hm^{2}以上(表 1)。

(3)地力维持目标。长期保持林地土壤的养分，维持林地土壤良好的物理结构，使林地不退化。

(4)生态功能目标。维持和提高林分景观多样性、遗传多样性和生物多样性，提高杉木人工林生态系统的稳定性。

表1　杉木大径材培育目标、技术措施

项	分项	措施
选地及造林	立地选择	Ⅰ、Ⅱ立地级
	造林密度(株/667m^2)	70~150
	造林材料	良种(二代)Ⅰ级苗
	整地规格(cm)	60×40×40
	抚育次数	2~2~2
间　伐	起始期(年)	5~7年
	次数	1~3
	间隔期(年)	3~5年
	强度(%)	20~30
	最后保留株数(株/667m^2)	30~60
深　翻	林龄(年)	10~15
	深度(cm)	15~25
	林龄(年)	5~15
	次数	2
施　肥	方法	沟施、撒施、翻埋
	肥种	复合肥
	肥量(g/株)	200~400
	开始期	第4年
修　枝	间隔期	3年
	强度(冠高比)	1:2
	主伐年龄	32~36
培育目标(生长指标)	D(cm)	≥26
	蓄积量(m^3/667m^2)	30
	出材量(m^3/667m^2)	20

2.2 杉木大径材作业级水平经营模式

2.2.1 作业级水平森林经营模式的概念及基本内涵

所谓模式，就是实现某种目标的途径。作业级(经营类型)水平的森林经营模式，从层次上划分属于森林经营类型(作业级)层次[3]。作业级水平森林经营模式的概念是指森林经营思想、目标、技术标准及经营措施(作业法)相一致的森林经营标准格局和典型样板。其基本内涵应包括如下4个方面：①经营目标一致，即作业级有特定的经营目标，如经营目标是大径材或短周期工业原料林等，具有特定的培育目的，能采取统一林学技术体系；②具经营利用价值和经营前景的小班，即具有明显的经济、生态和社会功能；③具有科学的经营技术体系，作业措施可行和具有普遍推广价值的林分；④是结构相似及相对稳定、生长规律一致、能维持林地长期生产力的小班。

2.2.2 作业级水平大径材森林经营模式

靖安县杉木大径材作业级水平森林经营模式的经营目标是培育杉木大径材，可弥补杉木木材市场材种单一的不足，同时大径材培育周期较长，可克服短轮伐期经营林地养分消耗速度过快的缺陷。缺点是资金周转速度慢，较难实现资本投入产出效益的最大化。

(1)选择适当的小班：一般来说，经营杉木人工林，12 地位指数级以下的林地，只宜培育小径材；14~16 地位指数级的林地，可培育中径材；18 指数级以上的林地方可培育大径材[4]。将全县所有的大于等于 18 地位指数级，良种(或优良无性系)造林的杉木林分视为经营对象(作业级)，同一山场(或同一作业小班)划定中下部为培育对象。

(2)间伐确定目标树：目标树是在第一次疏伐时作为培育对象挑选的最终采伐利用的树木，目标树应干形端直粗壮，树冠发育良好，生长势旺盛，无节无疤，无病虫害，处于地利优势和竞争优势。目标树选择的原则[5]是：

①生长力。在林分中处于优势地位或者绝对优势的树木生长旺盛，相对冠长大约在 1/2~1/3 之间。

②质量。干形通直，生长良好，经济价值较高，树干无损伤，生长健康。

③分布。目标树应尽可能均匀地分布在林分中。例如 2 株杉木目标树之间的最小距离应保持 3m，目标树选出后应及时做好标记，以利于确定间伐木和得到保护。

(3)间伐的技术要求：

①间伐时间。杉木对空间的要求与它达到的高度有关，因此，杉木大径材间伐时间的确定，应根据林分密度和优势高，无需确定林分的年龄和立地质量。

按照林分优势高的生长量确定间伐周期，而不再根据年龄来确定，这种方式的间伐能够更好地发挥树高的生长潜力，例如，以 3m 优势高生长量为一个间伐周期。在幼龄林中间伐间隔比在大龄林中短，这是因为在大龄林中树高的生长减弱了。

根据我们在靖安县所作的调查，不同密度的杉木林，其第一次间伐时间不一样，造林密度为 1800~2505 株/hm^2，其第一次间伐时间在 10~12 年，而密度更大一些的造林地，其第一次间伐时间选择 8~10 年为宜。

②间伐方式。开始是对准目标树的判读疏伐，在没有目标树的地方一般进行下层疏伐，在靠近目标树的周围伐去影响目标树生长的林木，保证目标树有足够的生长空间，随后逐步过渡到下层疏伐。

③间伐强度。根据叶功富[6](2005)等学者的研究，不同的间伐强度将导致不同的大径材培育结果，强度间伐(保留 600 株/hm^2)管理方式有利于单株材积生长，提高林分总出材率，但密度减少使规格材产量降低。弱度间伐(保留 1620 株/hm^2)管理方式因密度较大，有利于提高单位面积规格材和木材总产量，但大径材出材率较低。相对而言，中度间伐(间伐强度达 52.1%)是最好的，间伐后林分密度控制在 1200 株/hm^2，既能提高规格材和木材总产量，又能维持较高的目标树(大径材)出材率，增加单位面积的目标树(大径材)出材量。因而，对于定向培育杉木大径材，目标树保留密度以 1200 株/hm^2左右较为适宜(表 2)。

间伐保留密度按可及度大小确定，山场偏僻，采伐难度大的小班间伐保留密度 600~900 株/hm^2；郁闭度在 0.5 左右，紧靠公路边采伐容易的小班，间伐保留密度 900~1200 株/ hm^2。对 10 年生左右林分间伐保留密度 1200~1500 株/hm^2，以备进行第 2 次间伐。

表 2 不同密度管理方式对 32 年生杉木出材量的影响

地位指数	造林密度（株/hm^2）	保留密度（株/hm^2）	每公顷总蓄积（m^3/hm^2）	每公顷规格材(m^3/hm^2)				每公顷间伐出材量(m^3)
				大径材	中径材	小径材	合计	
20	630	600	535.67	352.36	60.63	4.06	417.05	
	2505	600	502.93	307.42	64.71	7.24	379.37	67.84
	2505	1200	662.49	401.81	113.83	16.71	532.35	50.17
	2505	1620	648.32	231.48	214.90	40.64	509.06	34.25
18	630	600	490.53	287.82	82.49	6.37	376.68	
	2505	600	463.78	254.74	83.16	9.02	346.92	58.26
	2505	1200	604.75	330.87	130.65	20.16	481.68	41.98
	2505	1620	587.16	198.61	207.57	48.75	454.93	28.59

(4)调整：由于杉木大径材的周期很长，在大径材经营类型内实行目标树经营。对选定的培育对象(小班)通过间伐等调整措施，改变目前所用的大砍大造的杉木人工林的单层林皆伐方式，采用用材林结构调整的方法进行调整。采取乔林择伐作业，采用人工干涉的方式，将人工单层林改造调整成以杉木为主的复层异龄林，通过对其进行改造，降低林分的密度，辅以劈杂施肥等营林措施促进其直径的生长并培育成大径材资源，使之形成稳定的法正林模式，每年均能提供一定数量的大径材。该经营类型具有：

①法正龄级分配。具备 1 年生到轮伐期 u 年生的杉木林分，并且各龄级的面积相等。每年采伐 u 年生的林分，每 2 年又补植造林形成 1 年生林分，其他林分都长 1 年。即每年持续收获定量木材，又保持龄级结构不变。

②法正林分排列。林分的排列有利于森林更新、保护和作业。

③法正蓄积量。各林分有与年龄相应的正常生长量。如果满足了以上 2 个条件，可以假设各林分每年的生长量相同，分别记为 $Z_1, Z_2, Z_3, \cdots, Z_{u-1}, Z_u$，各林分的蓄积量分别为 m_1，$m_2, m_3, \cdots, m_{u-1}, m_u$。则：$Z_1 = m_1, u \times Z = \sum Z_i = m$

也就是每年采伐最老的林分(32～36 年的杉木)，即每年收获总生长量，并且每年收获相等，又不破坏法正状态。

④法正生长量。各林分有与年龄相应的正常蓄积量。各林分的蓄积等于生长量之和，各林分的蓄积之和为法正蓄积量，即法正蓄积量 $V_n = \sum m^i$

(5)轮伐期及采伐

根据相关研究[7～8]，经营杉木人工林，12 地位指数级以下的林地，只宜培育小径材；14～16 地位指数级的林地，可培育中径材；18 指数级以上的林地方可培育大径材[8]。为此，将靖安县杉木大径材的轮伐期定为 32～36 年。

对于杉木大径材，一般采用小块状或小片皆伐作业。伐区面积一般不超过 5hm^2，最多不超过 10 hm^2。并且，伐区间应留有一定的间隔，不宜集中连片，防止由于大面积皆伐连片造成林地生态条件的严重破坏。采伐后，迹地要及时更新。更新方法主要包括栽苗(或插条)造林或萌芽更新二种。实行萌芽更新的杉木林，采伐季节最好在休眠期进行。此时林木养分转移到根部，伐后翌春萌条多而健壮，利于萌条生长，早日恢复成林。

3 结 语

（1）首次从作业级层次提出了杉木大径材的可持续经营模式，大径级杉木并不一定非要通过新造林培育途径，可通过在现有18地位指数以上的杉木林地选取目标树，然后通过合理的抚育间伐、林地施肥等后期集约经营管理措施，不断调整林分密度，使目标树保留密度为1200株/hm^2左右，改良树木生长环境，保证杉木林整个群体能充分利用地力和光能，最终培育成大径材。

（2）培育长周期经营的大径材已是社会所急需，建设大径材基地，良种选择是基础，密度控制是关键措施，必须将造林学原理与现代营林科技手断有机结合起来，通过“立地控制、遗传控制、密度控制”，来发挥杉木增长潜力，从而获得最大量化的经济效益，达到青山常在，永续利用的目标。

（3）抓好大径材森林经营方案的编制和实施。森林经营方案是科学、依法经营的依据，是指导经营单位提高经营水平的保证[9]。为培育杉木大径材，必须以森林可持续经营理论为指导，因地制宜，分析国民经济和社会发展对大径材的需求，紧密结合经营单位的实际情况，单独编制森林经营方案，经依法批准后执行。在经营方案编制过程中，将大径材的经营措施落实到山头地块，引导经营者科学经营。

参考文献：

[1]曾志光，黄晓春，杨先锋．发展商品林 首选红心杉[J]．江西林业科技，2003(4)：33～43.

[2]靖安县林业局．靖安县2004年森林资源二类调查成果[R]．江西省靖安县林业局，1993.

[3] 于政中．森林经理学[M]．北京：中国林业出版社，1993.

[4] 张志云，蔡学林．杉木人工林主伐年龄研究[J]．江西农业大学学报，1991，13(4)：336～343.

[5] 马爱国．目标经营——介绍一种森林经营方法[J]．世界林业研究，1992，5(3)：50～55.

[6] 叶功富，涂育合，林瑞荣，等．杉木人工林不同密度管理定向培育大径材[J]．北华大学学报，2005，6(6)：544～549.

[7] 杨馥宁．江西省靖安县森林经营模式研究[D]．北京：北京林业大学，2008.

[8] 盛炜彤，惠刚盈，罗云伍．大岗山杉木人工林主伐年龄的研究[J]．林业科学研究，1991，4(3)：113～121.

[9] Victoria Government Department of Sustainability and Environment. Forest management plan for the Gippsland [R]. Melbourne：Gill Miller Press，2004.

广义 Brink 干形方程的适应性扩展

聂秀琴[1]　李　昀[1]　陆道调[2]

（1. 北京林业大学信息学院，北京，100083；

2. 广西大学林学院，南宁，530004）

摘要：广义的 Brink 干形方程在描述林木干形的研究中起着非常重要的作用，但是该方程将林分平均直径作为其中的一个变量，这一点使得应用其进行干形描述和后期造材设计时存在较大的局限性，即当干形数据中不包含或无法计算出林分平均直径时，这样 Brink 干形方程将不能够对相应干形进行描述。为了突破这一限制，本文通过分析林分平均直径在广义的 Brink 干形方程中的作用，提出化简该自变量的方法，并且通过非线性回归分析，考虑决定系数、均方误差、残差等对其结果进行了分析，从统计学意义上验证了改进后 Brink 干形方程的预测效果是可靠的。

关键词：Brink 干形方程；林分平均直径；均方误差；决定系数

The adapted extensions of general Brink stem profile function

NIE Xiu-qin[1]　LI Yun[1]　LU Dao-diao[2]

(1. Information College, Beijing Forestry University, Beijing, 10083

2. Forestry College, Guangxi University, Nanning, 530004)

Abstract: Generalized Brink stem profile function plays a very important part in the research of describing stems profile, but using quadratic mean diameter (Dg) as a variable in such method limits its ability to describe stem form and cross – cutting later, which means, the quadratic mean diameter is not contained in the data or cannot be calculated, then the generalized Brink function will not able to describe certain stem form . To breakthrough such restriction, a method to simplify the quadratic mean diameter is proposed by studying its role in Brink stem profile function. This improved Brink stem profile function is proved reliable and statistically significant by non – linear regression analysis considering the coefficient of determination, mean square error, residual, etc.

Key words: Brink stem profile function; quadratic mean diameter; mean square error; determination coefficient

---

作者：聂秀琴，北京林业大学信息学院硕士研究生。北京市海淀区北京林业大学 827 信箱，邮编：100083；E-mail：xiuqinluoyang@163.com

李昀，北京林业大学信息学院副教授，E-mail：liyuu@bjfu.edu.cn

引 言

干曲线方程用来描述林木树干各部位直径随树干高度的变化过程，对确定林木干形、材积、出材量等方面具有重要意义。干形方程的发展经历了很长的阶段，最早期是利用测得的原木数据，构造适当的数学模型，通过回归分析等方法进行模拟、辨别该模型的适用性和预测精度，近代根据其参数具有生物学意义的生长曲线的适用性和特点，利用计算木的有效信息和系统推导，最终确定能够准确描述干形的削度模型。

树干曲线的研究始于20世纪初，最早为 Hoger(1903)提出并建立了树干削度曲线。随后有很多的干形方程随之提出，其中最为广泛流行的是孔兹曲线(Kunze)，孔兹曲线的优势在于其形状指数不同，可以描述多种旋转体，但是孔兹曲线仅树干的某一部分描述是准确的，对于树干整体来说，预测效果并不理想。20 世纪 80 年代中，Hradetzky 利用样条函数进行干形模拟，Sloboda(1984)构造了新的林分干曲线模型，虽然这些方法对特定树木的干形或对单个林分的各个树木的干形能够进行精确的模拟，但由于该类模型中的参数多而难以实现树木干形的普遍化，从而也就无法确定营林措施对干形的影响。

由于林木干曲线随林木的大小和林分环境的不同而有所不同，所以为了建立能够描述不同林分环境条件下林木干形变化的广义的干曲线方程是非常必要的。广义干曲线的提出和发展能够描述不同林分的林木树干各部位直径随树干高度的变化程度，并且对来源于不同环境的同种林木的干形描述有很好的作用和明显的效果，即用来描述不同立地、不同密度和不同年龄林分的林木树干任意高度处直径的变化，因此广义干形曲线得到了广泛的应用。

对于干形模型，当模型过于简单时，不能够精确地表示干形，当模型过于复杂和具体时，其适用范围将会受到制约，不能用于一般的造材环境等不同的干形。这样构造一个合适的含有有限元参数的干形方程显得非常重要(Gadow et al，2001)，C. Brink and K. von Gadow (1986)最早提出了 Brink 干形方程，Riemer 等(1995)在此基础上对其修正构造了少参数的 Brink 干形方程，基于 Brink 函数的干曲线方程的建立使得不同立地、不同密度和不同年龄林分的林木树干任意高度直径的变化可通过此类方程得到描述，实现了树干干形的广义模拟，并且替代仅适合于单株树木的单株干曲线方程和适合模拟单一林分的林分干曲线方程成为研究的主流，这具有很好的现实意义。后来 Brink 干形方程被广泛地应用于不同的树种和年龄的原木造材中，并且达到了较满意的效果(Hui and Gadow，1997)，佟金权等将 Brink 干形方程在修正基础上建立了杉木人工林广义干曲线模型(佟金权，盛炜彤，2000)。

广义的 Brink 干形方程能够用于描述不同立地、不同密度和不同年龄林分的林木干曲线的变化，其中林分平均直径是一个非常重要的变量，在为专门进行某一特定林分干形研究而采集的数据中，林分平均直径是一个已知量，或可以通过计算得出。但是在实际工作中，有时会遇到数据集中不包含林分平均直径，同时也无法间接获得的情况，这使得利用广义 Brink 干形方程描述其干形时则受到限制。本研究的主要目的是根据林分平均直径这一变量在广义 Brink 函数中的作用，将其看作一个新的参数进行估计，从而去除广义 Brink 干形方程中林分平均直径作为变量之一的条件限制，利用广西马占相思木的数据信息验证其化简后的拟合效果。

1 问题的提出

1.1 Brink 干形方程及其发展

Brink 干形方程最早是由 Brink(1986)依据干形上下两部分的结构特征，采用两个经典的衰减函数构造得到的，其含有 i , p 和 q 三个参数，其中 p 和 q 分别与树干形下半部分和树梢部分相关的，i 与干形拐点处的半径相关。其形式为：

$$r(h) = i - \frac{pi}{p+q}e^{q(h-H)} + (r_0 - i + \frac{pi}{p+q}e^{-qH})e^{-ph} \tag{1-1}$$

Brink 干形方程是以指数型函数作为基函数构成的，其简单的结构使得方程中的参数 i ，p 和 q 的值很容易通过回归分析得到，但是在使用该干形方程时，首先必须要已知地径 r_0 ，并且 Brink 干形方程不能够严格地通过点 $(H,0)$ 和 (h_b,r_b) ，其中 H 为全树高，r_b 为胸高 h_b 处的半径，$h_b = 1.35$ 。

由于胸径在林业研究上起着非常重要的作用，Brink 考虑将 r_b 代替地径 r_0 作为初值，将式(1-1)改进使其能严格地通过点 (h_b,r_b) 。

$$r(h) = i + (r_b - i) - \frac{pi}{p+q}[e^{q(h-H)} - e^{q(h-H)+p(b-h)}] \tag{1-2}$$

Riemer 等(1995)在式(1-2)的基础上进行了修正，而且根据林学研究上对胸高的定义，将式(1-2)中的 h_b 修正为式 1-3，使得修正后的 Brink 干形方程能够严格地通过点 $(H,0)$ 和 (h_b,r_b) ，其中 $h_b = 1.3$ 。

$$r(h') = u + v \cdot e^{-ph'} - w \cdot e^{qh'} \tag{1-3}$$

这里：$u = \dfrac{i}{1-e^{q(1.3-h)}} + (r_{1.3} - i)(1 - \dfrac{1}{1-e^{p(1.3-h)}})$

$$v = \frac{(r_{1.3} - i)\cdot e^{p\cdot 1.3}}{1-e^{p(1.3-h)}}$$

$$w = \frac{i\cdot e^{-qh}}{1-e^{q(1.3-h)}}$$

其中：$r(h')$ ——在树高 h'(m)处对应的半径(cm)；

h ——全树高(m)；

$r_{1.3}$ ——胸径(cm)；

i ——参数(统一渐近线)；

p ——参数(描述干形底部向外弯曲的程度)；

q ——参数(描述干形顶部向内弯曲的程度)。

修正的 Brink 干形方程被成功地应用于不同种类和不同年龄的树种(Riemer et al.，1995；Trincado，1996；Trincado and Gadow，1996；Hui and Gadow，1997；Van Laar and AKca，1997)，其拟合实测的不同树种和大小的干形效果很好。但是由于其参数 i 、p 和 q 与树种等有较强的联系，这样修正的干形方程的使用将受到一定的限制，为了其能使用范围更广泛，将其推广到广义的干形方程。

1.2 广义的 Brink 干形方程

惠刚盈和 Gadow(1997)将修正的 Brink 干形方程推广到广义的干形方程，使其适用范围变得更广，即可对不同立地环境条件下的林木干形进行较精确的描述。其形式为：

$$r(h') = u + v \cdot e^{-ph'} - w \cdot e^{qh'}$$

这里：$u = \dfrac{i}{1 - e^{q(1.3-h)}} + (r_{1.3} - i)(1 - \dfrac{1}{1 - e^{p(1.3-h)}})$

$$v = \frac{(r_{1.3} - i) \cdot e^{p \cdot 1.3}}{1 - e^{p(1.3-h)}}$$

$$w = \frac{i \cdot e^{-qh}}{1 - e^{q(1.3-h)}}$$

其中：$i = k_1 d^{k_2}$——(统一渐近线)；

$p = e^{\frac{k_3}{D_g}}$——表示树干下部向外弯曲的程度；

$q = k_5 e^{\frac{k_6}{D_g}} h^{k_4}$——表示树干上部向内弯曲的程度；

$k_1, k_2, \cdots, k_6$——参数；

d——胸径；

D_g——林分平均胸(直)径。

且等式满足：$r(h') = 0$ 当 $h' = h$ 时；$r(h') = r_{1.3}$ 当 $h' = 1.3$。

广义的 Brink 干形方程能够描述不同林分的林木树干各部位直径随树干高度的变化程度，并且对来源于不同环境的同种原木的干形描述有明显的效果，即用来描述不同立地、不同密度和不同年龄林分的林木树干直径随树高变化的曲线。但是在其参数 p 和 q 中均含有林分平均直径 D_g 这一项，当数据集缺少林分平均直径 D_g 时，将不能使用广义的 Brink 干形方程对立木干形进行绘制，从林分平均直径均 D_g 在参数方程 p 和 q 中出现的位置，可以考虑通过简化消除这一限制，并且利用实际数据进行实验分析验证。

2 广义 Brink 干形方程的改进

2.1 实验设计

广义 Brink 干形方程形式的灵活性使其可以描述不同立地环境、不同林分的立木干形，但是由 1.2 可知 p 和 q 中均含有林分平均直径 D_g 项，而且对于 p，D_g 仅影响参数 k_3，对于 q，D_g 仅影响参数 k_5 和 k_6，这样当林分平均直径 D_g 不可知时，可以把 D_g 看作新的参数，保证不改变 p 和 q 结构的前提下对其进行改进；由于 D_g 仅与林木的胸径相关，这样也可以考虑利用胸径代替 D_g，对 p 和 q 进行化简。即采用以下两种方法对广义干形方程进行改进，并利用数据检验改进后的广义 Brink 干形方程的拟合效果。

(1)将林分平均直径信息看作新的参数，则对应 $p = e^{k_3}$，$q = e^{k_6} h^{k_4}$，对改进后的 Brink 干形方程进行参数估计，并且对拟合效果进行分析；

(2)利用 $p = \exp(k_3/\mathrm{DBH})$，$q = k_5 e^{\frac{k_6}{\mathrm{DBH}}} h^{k_4}$，其中 DBH 为样本的胸径，并且对拟合效果进行分析。

利用 SAS 中 NLIN 过程，对其模型进行非线性参数估计，并且根据得到结果进行分析，判断将广义 Brink 干形方程进行简化的方法的可靠性。

2.2 数据来源

本研究采用了 101 株马占相思不同高度的皮外直径数据共 1635 个样本测量数据。这些样木来自于广西壮族自治区南部的南宁市、钦州市和玉林市，三市形成近似三角形的三点，相距200～300km。地理位置在北纬23°30′以南。南宁市的调查数据主要在高峰林场；钦州市的数据来自钦廉林场；玉林市的数据则来自陆川县的所属林场。

马占相思林作为我国南方新的森林类型，其木材可用做纸浆，锯材，木片和薪材，已成为工业木材原料生产的新主力。虽然大规模的同龄纯林种植使马占相思林的林分结构有一定的单纯性，但其仍然存在自身独特的结构规律性，研究马占相思木的直径随树高的变化过程，能够准备计算马占相思木的材积，为确定合理的木材采伐年龄、研制经营模型及优化栽培模式提供依据。

这些样本数据包括胸径、地面直径以及从距地面高度1m开始至树梢间，以1m为间距各个高度对应的直径。1635个样本数据中胸径变化范围从6.1～22.2cm，树高最小值为6.9m，最大值18.5m。树高与胸径对应关系的散点图见图1，树高分布情况见图2，胸径的分布情况见图3。

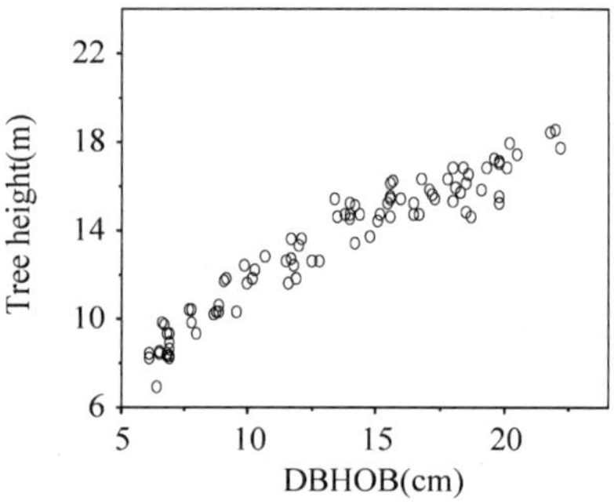

图1　树高－胸径关系图

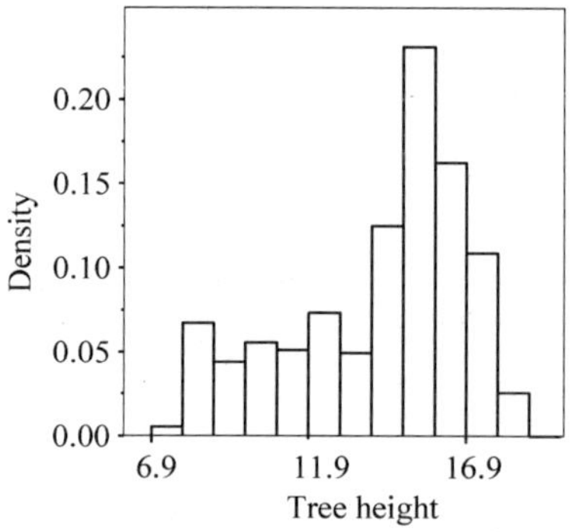

图2　树高分布图

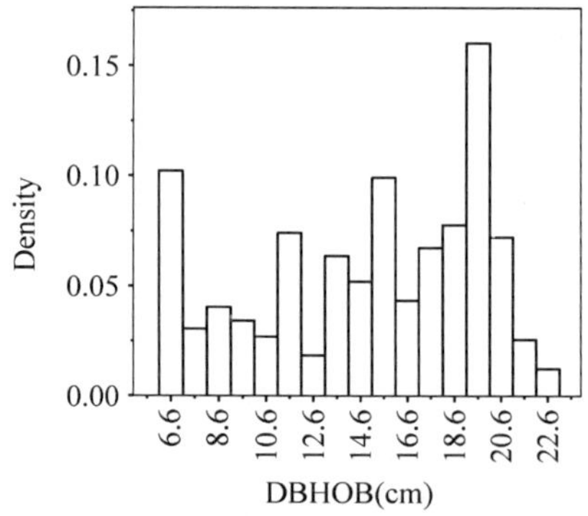

图3　胸径分布图

2.3　结果分析

对模型进行非线性最小二乘回归分析评价主要考虑因素为：①模型的拟合统计量：决定系数R^2、均方误差(MSE)、残差(Residual)和绝对残差(Bias)；②残差分布等(Myers, 1990)。

其中决定系数R^2反映了模型回归分析的拟合效果，其中$0 \le R^2 \le 1$，当R^2越接近于上确界时，说明模型的预测效果越好，当$R^2 = 1$时，说明模型的回归分析拟合效果是完美的。当均方误差MSE越小时，则说明拟合过程中偏离的点越少，模型的拟合效果越好。

表 1　方法 a 与方法 b 对应广义干形方程中参数的估计值

Parameter	Coefficients	Approx Std Error	Parameter	Coefficients	Approx Std Error
K1	0.4617	0.0111	K1	0.4653	0.0177
K2	1.0085	0.00781	K2	1.0056	0.0118
K3	0.0589	0.0456	K3	0.8653	0.0353
K4	-2.7936	0.0067	K4	-1.6250	0.3178
			K5	4.0558	0.0595
K6	5.1294	0.0803	K6	8.6305	0.2489

表 2　方法 a 对应的残差的矩统计量

矩统计量			
N	1635	权重总和	1635
均值	0.0689	总和	112.6635
标准偏差	0.4409	方差	0.1944
偏度	-0.5628	峰度	4.8116
未校平方和(USS)	325.4305	校平方和(CSS)	317.6672
变异系数	639.8746	标准误差	0.0109

由表 2 计算残差可以计算出模型非线性回归分析的决定系数 $R^2 = 0.975$，由决定系数可发现回归分析部分可以解释的 Brink 干形方程的部分达到了很好的程度。

表 3　方法 b 对应的残差的矩统计量

矩统计量			
N	1635	权重总和	1635
均值	0.0649	总和	106.0714
标准偏差	0.4393	方差	0.1930
偏度	-0.5517	峰度	5.0440
未校平方和(USS)	322.2604	校平方和(CSS)	315.3789
变异系数	677.1885	标准误差	0.0109

由表 3 计算残差可以计算出模型非线性回归分析的决定系数 $R^2 = 0.979$，由决定系数可发现回归分析部分可以解释的 Brink 干形方程的部分达到了很好的程度。

残差的平方 $(y_i - y_i)^2$ 对应的距统计量结果，可以得到该回归分析的均方误差，$MSE = 0.5660$。

通过对决定系数 R^2、均方误差(MSE)及残差 - 预测值的散点图的分析，及决定系数的值，可以得出两种方法都是可靠的，其中方法 2 的拟合效果更好，其采用方法 2 将广义的 Brink 干形改进后进行参数估计是可靠和可行的。

3 结　论

广义的 Brink 干形方程对干形的描述和材积的计算起着非常重要的作用，而且其精确度高，但是其自身的特点也决定了其适应范围，尤其是当林木林分平均直径 D_g 不能够得到时，则便不能够使用广义的 Brink 干形方程，为了能够更广泛地使用广义的 Brink 干形方程，通过研究 D_g 在广义的 Brink 干形方程的位置，发现其存在于 p 和 q 中，这样考虑对 p 和 q 进行化简，而且不改变 p 和 q 的结构，通过实验数据验证改进后干形方程对干形的估计结果，进而从统计学角度对结果进行分析，从而发现其改进是可行的，这样对广义 Brink 干形方程适应性进行了扩展，使其使用范围变得更广泛。

参考文献

[1]克劳斯．冯佳多，惠刚盈．森林生长与干扰模拟．Germany：CUVILLIER VERLAG，Goettingen. 1998，89 ~ 93.

[2] 佟金权，盛炜彤．杉木人工林广义干形模型的研究[J]．林业科学研究．2000，13(3)：239 ~ 248.

[3] 曾翀，雷相东，刘宪钊，等．落叶松云冷杉林单木树高曲线的研究[J]．林业科学研究，2009，22(2)：182 ~ 189.

[4] Brink C，von Gadowk K V. On the use of growth and decay functions formodeling stem profiles. EDV in Medizin und Biologie. 1986，17(1/2)：20 ~ 27.

[5] Hradetzky J. Spline – Funktionen und ihre Anwendung in der Forstlichen Forschung. Forstwiss. Centralblatt 1981(1)45 ~ 49.

[6] Hui G Y，Gadow K V. Entwicklung und Erprobungeines Einheitsschaftmodells fur die Baumart Cunninghamia lanceolata. Forstw. Cb1. 116(5)：325 ~ 321. 1997.

[7] Gadow K V. Modeling growth in managed forests – realism and limits of lumping[J]. The Science of the Total Enviornment. 1997，183：167 ~ 177.

[8] Gribko L S，Wiant Jr H V. A SAS template program for the accuracy test[J]. Compiler，1992，10：48 ~ 51.

[9] Klaus von Gadow，Gangying Hui. Modelling Forest Development[M]. KLUWER ACADEMIC PUBLISHERS：97 – 102，2001.

[10] Myers R H. Classical and modern regression with applications. PWSKENT，Boston. 1990.

[11] Renolds M R. Estimating the error in model predictions [J]. For Sci，1984，30：454 ~ 469.

[12] Riemer Th，Gadow K V，Sloboda B. Ein Modell Zur Berchreibung von Baumschaften. Allg. Forest – und J. – Ztg. 1995，166(7)：144 ~ 147.

[13] SHONGMING Huang，STEPHEN J. TITUS. Comparison of nonlinear height – diameter functions for major Alberta tree species. Department of Forest Science，Unversity of Alberta，Edmonton，Alta.，Canada T6G 2HI. 1992.

[14] Sloboda B. Bestandesindividuelles biometrisches Schaftformmodell zur Darstellung und zum Vergleich von Formogkeit und Sortimentausbeute sowie Inventur. Tagungsbericht d. Sektion Ertragskunde，Neustadt，1984.

[15] Trincado G，Gadow K V. Zur Sortimentschatzung srehender Laubbaume. Zentralblatt fur das gesamte Forstw. 1996，113(1)：27 ~ 38.

[16] Trincado G. Modellierung der Schaftform von Fichten (Picea abies) und Buchen (Fagus sylvatica). Wissenschaftliche Arbeit zur Erlangung des Grades Magister der tropischen Forstwirtschaft der Grorg – August – Unversitat，Gottingen. 1996.

[17] Van Laar A，AKca A. Forest Mensuration. Cuvillier，Gottingen. 1997，418.

不同立地条件下白桦生长规律的研究

刘相兵[1]　王典娜[1,2]　闫　菁[1]　原民龙[2]　黄选瑞[1]

（1. 河北农业大学 林学院，河北 保定 071000；
2. 河北省木兰围场国有林场管理局，河北 围场 068450）

摘要：本文采用树干解析的方法，对比分析承德孟滦林场和赤城黑龙山林场白桦的生长规律，研究结果表明：孟滦林场直径平均生长量15a左右达到一个高峰，连年生长量在10a左右达到一个高峰。黑龙山林场直径平均生长量没有达到一个高峰，但连年生长量在20a达到了一个高峰；树高平均生长量在两个地区生长达到10a左右都出现了最大值，但孟滦林场白桦生长较快，树高连年生长量在两个地区白桦生长到10a左右都出现最大值，但黑龙山林场白桦树高连年生长量在生长20a后还会出现一个高峰；白桦在孟滦林场材积总生长量较大，平均生长量和连年生长量比黑龙山林场白桦生长较快。生长过程中，两个地区材积生长量均没有达到一个顶峰，所以白桦没有到达数量成熟期。并用现有模型进行拟合，其两个地区的最优生长模型为查理德模型。

关键词：树干解析；白桦；生长规律；生长模型

Under different site conditions of growth of *Betula*

LIU Xiang-bing　WANG Dian-na　YAN Jing　YUAN Min-long　HUANG Xuan-rui

(Forestry College of Agricultural University of Hebei, Baoding, 071000;
Mulanweichang State Forest Farm Administration, Weichang, 068450)

Abstract: In this paper, using the stem analysis method, comparative analysised the growth rhythm *White Birch* in Chengde MengLuan Forest Farm and Chicheng Black Dragon Hill Forest Farm. The results of the study show that: diameter average increment come up to summit about 15 years, meanwhile current annual increment about 10 years in MengLuan Forest Farm. But in Black Dragon Hill Forest Farm, diameter average increment did not achieve a summit, while current annual increment at 20 years has a summit. Both average increment height come up to the summit about 10 years, but *White Birch* in MengLuan Forest Farm growth faster than the other Forest Farm. Current annual increment of height in different farm appear summit a-

---

基金项目：国家公益专项(20100400205)资助。

作者简介：刘相兵(1987～　)，男，河北承德人，在读硕士生，研究方向：森林资源管理理论与方法。

通讯作者：黄选瑞(1962～　)，男，内蒙古人，教授，主要从事森林经营理论与技术研究。通讯地址：071000　保定市河北农业大学西校区林学院。

bout 10 years, but after 20 years height current annual increment of *White Birch* also can appear a peak in Black Dragon Hill Forest Farm. In MengLuan Forest Farm total growth volume of *White Birch* is bigger, both average increment and current annual increment are more than Black Dragon Hill Forest Farm. Growth process, two areas volume growth are not summit, so *White Birch* did't arrive at the quantity maturity. And the existing model fitting, the two areas where the optimal growth model is Charilie DE Model.

Key words: trunk analysis; birch; growth rhythm; growth model

白桦(*Betula platyphylla* Suk.)为桦木科(Betulaceae)桦木属(*Betula* L.)乔木，树皮白色，纸质薄片剥落[1]。白桦为阳性树种，常在干扰后形成的迹地上天然更新成林，是落叶松林、红松林云冷杉林的伴生树种。能耐－50℃极端低温对霜冻、日灼等的抗性也很强。白桦适应的生态幅度较宽、适应性较广、生长快、结实量大，在分布区内的各种立地和土壤类型上均有天然分布[2]。

白桦次生林多在自然和人为大规模破坏或反复破坏原始林分后形成[3]。天然次生林生长规律的研究是森林经营中基础工作之一，目的是使森林经营活动能够按生长规律进行并提供可靠的理论基础。树木的生长规律主要是分析树木的生长过程，分析林木生长过程是森林经理学的经典内容，常见的乔木种，甚至连灌木都有详细的生长过程[4]。在分析树木的生长过程中，分析的项目主要有树高、胸径、材积、生物量以及形数等，分析的指标主要有总生长量、平均生长量、连年生长量以及生长率等。在一定间隔期内树木各种调查因子所发生的变化称为生长，变化的量称为生长量。树木自种植开始至调查时整个期间累积生长的总量为总生长量；树木在某一时期的平均生长速度称为平均生长量；树木某一年的实际生长速度称为连年生长量[5]。

林木的生长受立地条件、林分密度、营林措施、林种结构等影响较大，同一树种在不同地域的生长不尽相同，所以，掌握林木的生长规律对于确定间伐抚育期，促进林分生长、提高造林的经济效益等具有很强的指导意义[6]。本文通过对不同地区白桦天然次生林生长规律的研究，掌握白桦的生长过程，为今后的经营提供理论依据。

1 研究区概况

黑龙山林场位于赤城县东北部，地理坐标为东经116°00′37″～116°11′30″，北纬41°17′04″～41°22′14″。所辖面积18.8万亩，其中有林地面积16.8万亩，森林覆盖率90%，是黑龙山林区的核心区。东与丰宁满族自治县邓栅子林场接壤，北靠丰宁满族自治县大滩镇，西接沽源县老掌沟林场，南连白草镇及三道川乡。境内海拔1330～2292m，7月平均最高气温18.1℃，1月平均最低气温－16.2℃，年平均气温1.9℃，年降水量560mm，无霜期95d左右。林区内有天然分布的主要树种有白桦树、落叶松(*Larix principis-rupprechtii* Mayr.)、油松(*Pinue tabulaeformis* Carr.)、柞树(*Quercus* L.)等。

孟滦林场位于河北省围场满族蒙古自治县境内，地处浑善达克沙地南缘的滦河上游地区，属阴山、大兴安岭、燕山余脉的汇接地带，北纬41°35′～42°40′，东经116°32′～117°14′，海拔高度750～1998 m。这一地区属半干旱向半湿润过度、寒温带向中温带过度、大陆性季风型山地气候，无霜期67～128 d，年平均气温－1.4～4.7℃，极端最高气温38.9℃，

极端最低气温 -42.9℃，年均降水量380~560 mm，主要集中在7~9月。林区由于地形复杂，土壤种类多，因此植物资源丰富，属华北植物区系，是落叶林区，天然分布的阔叶乔木主要是白桦树、山杨(*Pobulus davidiana* Dode)、柞树等。天然分布的针叶乔木主要有华北落叶松、云杉(*Picea asperata* Mast.)、油松等。人工林主要有落叶松(*Larix gmelini* Rupr.)、油松，少量云杉、樟子松(*Pinue sylvescris* var. *mongolica* Litv.)。主要灌木有榛子(*Corylus heterophylla* Fisch. ex Bess. *Corylus heterophylla* Fisch. ExBess. var)、胡枝子(*Lespedeza bicolor* Turcz.)、沙棘(*Hippophae rhamnoides* L.)、绣线菊(*Spiraeasalicif olia*)等。

2 研究方法

2.1 解析木数据采集

在每个地区，根据平均胸径分别选取5株平均木，打去枝丫，在全树干上标明北向。伐倒后，先测定由根颈位置至第一个死枝和活枝在树干上的高度，然后测量树的全高和全高的1/4、1/2以及3/4处的带皮和去皮直径。截取圆盘时，从根颈起，在胸径处截断，再从胸径处向上1.3m再将树干截断，以后每2m作为一个区分段截断，最后所余不足一个区分段长度的树干为梢木头。在每个圆盘的非工作面上详细地记录树干的南北向，标注地号，解析木号，圆盘号和断面高度。根颈处为0号圆盘，加注采伐地点和时间。截取圆盘带回留作内业分析。

查定各圆盘上的年轮个数时，首先将圆盘工作面刨光，并通过髓心划出东西、南北两条直径线，0号圆盘由髓心向外按每个龄阶为5年标出各龄阶的位置，其余圆盘要由外侧向髓心查数。

测定解析木各项因子，然后统计出各解析木在每个龄阶的胸径、树高、材积的总生长量、连年生长量和平均生长量的变化情况，进一步分析出白桦在不同生长年龄时的生长变化过程，并模拟出白桦胸径、树高、材积的生长曲线。为充分说明白桦的生长特性，并且在不同地区之间进行对比分析其生长规律的差异。

2.2 白桦树高、直径、材积生长模型的建立

以年龄为自变量，林木直径、树高、材积为因变量，研究选择了4种模型进行生长模拟。这四种模型分别为：理查德曲线、Logistic生长曲线、Levakovic2曲线和对数线性生长模型。并在这四种模型中选择最优生长模型。

3 结果分析

3.1 白桦天然林生长规律

研究林木的年龄与树高、胸径、材积之间的相关性，对于掌握该树种在本地区的生长动态，制定有效的经营措施，提高森林资源的质量和数量有着重要的现实意义。将白桦平均木进行树干解析后，分别计算各株样木的树高、胸径、材积的总生长量、连年生长量、平均生长量，其中孟滦林场白桦生长过程和黑龙山林场白桦生长过程分别见表1、表2。

表1 孟滦林场白桦生长过程

Tab. 1 Growth course of Betula platyphylla Suk of MengLuan forest farm

龄阶	直径(cm)			树高(m)			材积(m^3)		
	总生长量	平均生长量	连年生长量	总生产量	平均生长量	连年生长量	总生长量	平均生长量	连年生长量
5	1.6	0.32	0	3.277794	0.655559	0	0.000746	0.000149	0
10	4.8	0.48	0.64	7.537658	0.753766	0.851973	0.007258	0.000726	0.001302
15	7.5	0.5	0.54	9.918713	0.661248	0.476211	0.023856	0.00159	0.00332
20	10.3	0.515	0.56	11.82222	0.591111	0.380702	0.048472	0.002424	0.004923
25	12.4	0.496	0.42	12.7	0.5288	0.279556	0.077211	0.003088	0.005743
27	13.2	0.488889	0.4	13.22	0.47037	0.26	0.088119	0.003264	0.005454

表2 黑龙山林场白桦生长过程

Tab. 1 Growth course of Betula platyphylla Suk of HeiLongshan forest farm

龄阶	直径(cm)			树高(m)			材积(m^3)		
	总生长量	平均生长量	连年生长量	总生长量	平均生长量	连年生长量	总生长量	平均生长量	连年生长量
5	0	0	0	1.352288	0.270458	0	0.000299	0.00006	0
10	0.8	0.08	0.46	4.7871	0.47871	0.686962	0.001763	0.000176	0.000293
15	4.7	0.313333	0.78	7.244362	0.482957	0.491452	0.007064	0.000471	0.00106
20	9.85	0.4925	1.03	9.046532	0.452327	0.360434	0.014357	0.000718	0.001459
25	13.4	0.536	0.71	11.57058	0.462824	0.504811	0.023976	0.000959	0.001924
27	16.4	0.607407	1.5	12.8	0.474074	0.614706	0.030215	0.001119	0.003119

3.1.1 直径生长过程

树木直径生长反映了林木的横向动态变化，其白桦直径生长量如图1所示。其中图1-a为白桦总生长量，从中可以看出，白桦直径生长随年龄增加而增大，在生长的22a中，白桦在孟滦林场直径生长较快，同一个龄阶总生长量较大，生长在22~27a时，白桦在黑龙山林场总生长量较大。生长到达27a时，白桦在孟滦林场直径总生长量为13.2cm，而在黑龙山林场27a生白桦直径总生长量为16.4cm。

图1-b为白桦平均生长量，在生长的22a中，同一龄阶孟滦林场比黑龙山林场白桦平均生长量较大，生长在22~27a时，白桦在黑龙山林场平均生长量较大。孟滦林场白桦生长到15a的时候其平均生长量达到一个最大值，而黑龙山林场中的白桦平均生长量还在继续增大，在生长的27a中没有达到一个顶峰。

图1-c为白桦直径的连年生长量，从总体趋势来看，孟滦林场白桦的连年生长量在10a左右的时候出现了一个生长高峰期，之后的生长呈下降的趋势。而黑龙山林场白桦生长在20a左右达到了一个顶峰，而生长到24~25a以后其直径连年生长量又开始加大，在以后的生长中还会出现一个连年生长量高峰期。在孟滦林场中的白桦在5~10a年连年生长量增长幅度较大，而黑龙山地区的白桦相对较小些。所以在前10a期间白桦林分对水、热等条件要求较高，在此期间应注重林分经营管理，提高林木的快速生长。

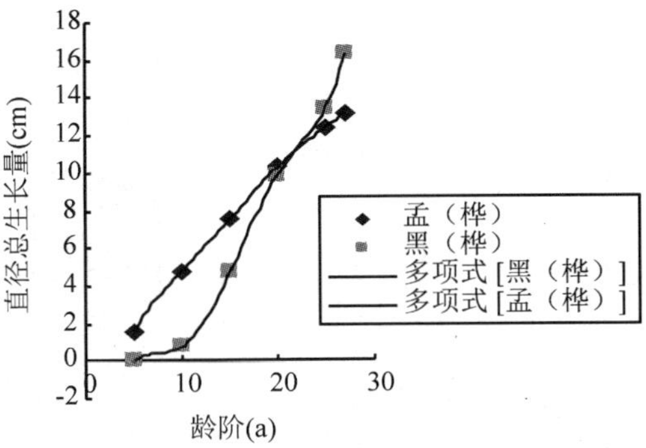

图1-a

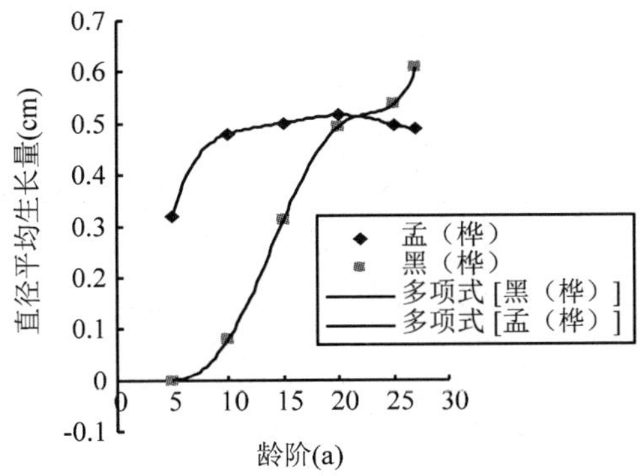

图1-b

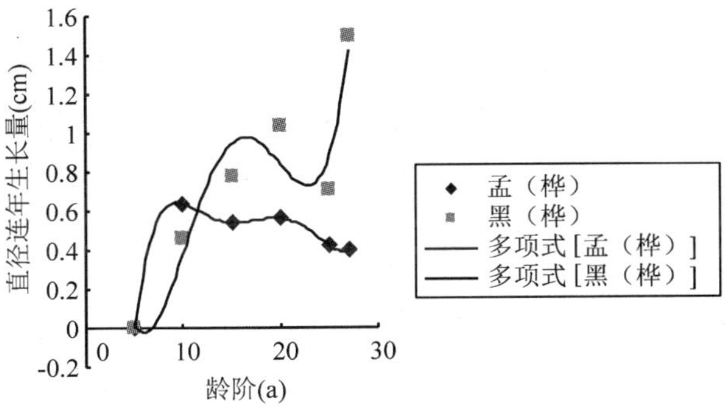

图1-c

图 1　白桦直径生长过程

Fig. 1　DBH increment curve of Betula platyphylla Suk

3. 1. 2　树高生长过程

树高生长反映了林木纵向的动态变化，不同地区白桦生长过程如图 2 所示。其中图 2-a 为白桦树高总生长量，从中可看出，在白桦生长的 27a 中树高与年龄呈正相关，树高随年龄增加而增大。且从图中可以看出孟滦林场白桦树高生长较快。

图 2-b 为白桦树高平均生长量，从中可看出白桦平均生长量在 10a 左右出现了最大值，且在前 10a 中生长较快，10a 后树高平均生长量呈下降趋势。孟滦林场白桦在不同龄阶比黑龙山林场白桦平均生长量较高。

图 2-c 为白桦树高连年生长量，从中可看出孟滦林场白桦连年生长量在 10a 左右出现一个高峰期，10a 后呈下降趋势。黑龙山林场白桦在 10a 左右同样出现了一个高峰，但在生长的 20a 后连年生长量又开始增大，在以后的生长中还会出现一个高峰。

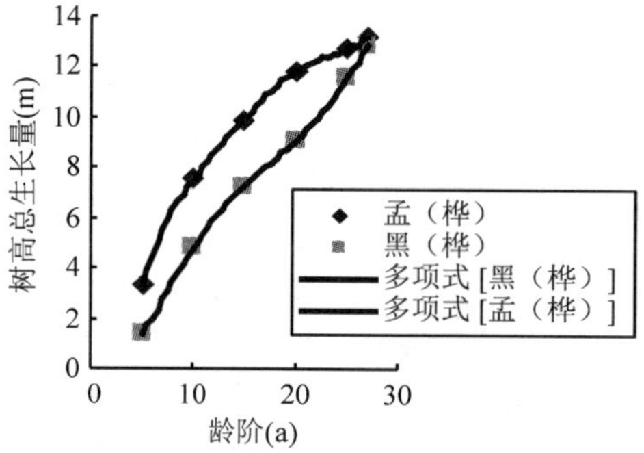

图2-a

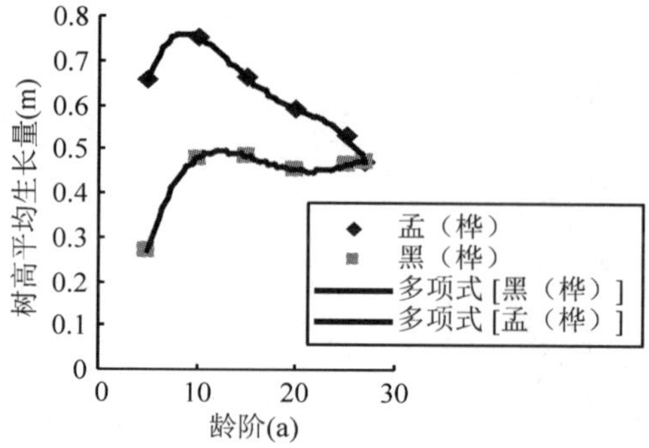

图2-b

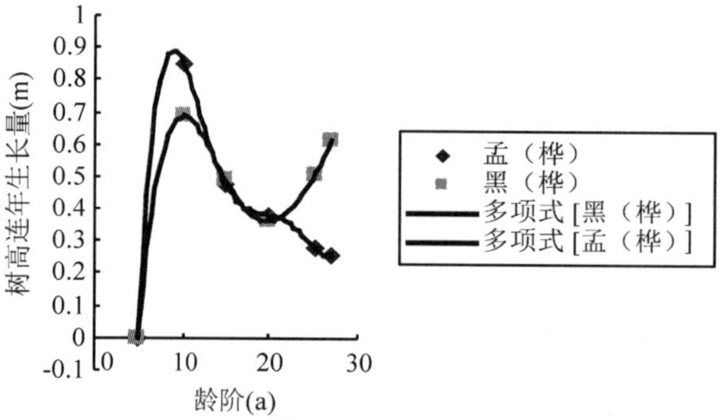

图2-c

图 2　白桦树高生长过程

Fig. 2　Height growth curve of Betula platyphylla Suk

3.1.3　材积生长过程

材积的生长过程如图 3 所示，由图 3-a 可看出，白桦材积总生长量在 27a 内随年龄的增加而增大，但在孟滦林场白桦 27a 材积总生长量较大，材积总生长量为 0.088119m^3，而黑龙山林场白桦 27a 材积总生长量相对较小，其材积总生长量为 0.030215m^3。

由图 3 – b 中也能看出，白桦平均生长量也随年龄的增加大，特别是孟滦林场，其白桦材积平均生长量较大。

由图 3 – c 中可以看出白桦材积连年生长量也随年龄的增加而增大，生长到 27a 没有到达顶峰。由此材积生长过程可以看出，两个地区的白桦材积生长没有达到一个顶盛时期，所以，白桦没有到达数量成熟时期。

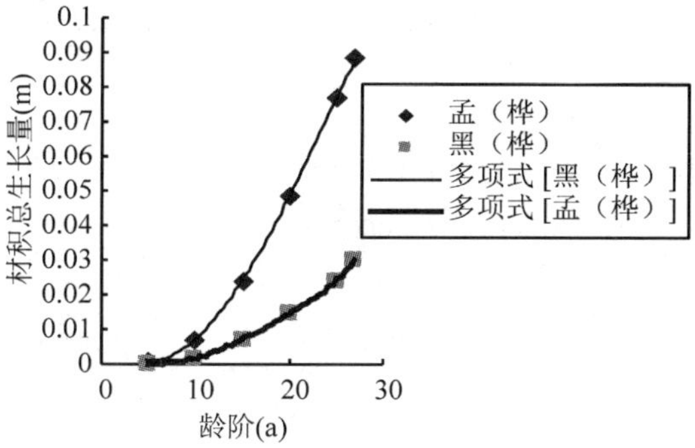

图3-a

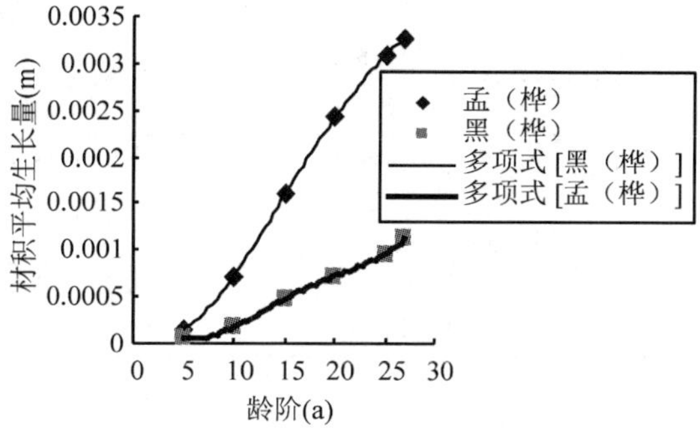

图3-b

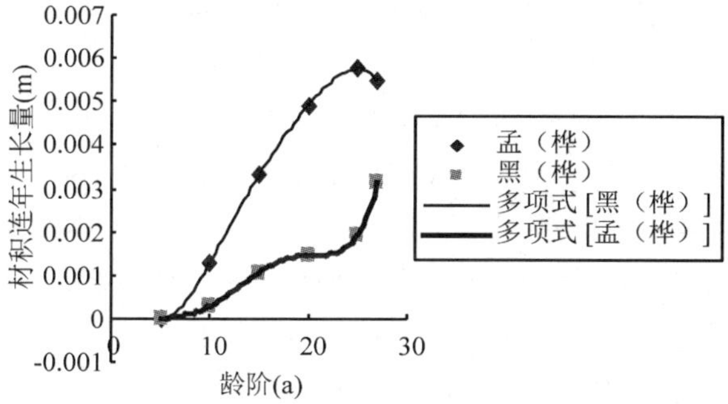

图3-c

图 3　白桦材积生长过程

Fig. 3　Volume increment curve of Betula platyphylla Suk

3.2　白桦直径、树高和材积生长曲线拟合

对白桦直径、树高和材积进行现有模型的拟合，本文采取四种模型进行拟合，包括：理查德曲线、Logistic 生长曲线、Levakovic2 曲线和对数线性生长曲线。其结果如表 3 和表 4 所示，其中表 3 为孟滦林场白桦直径、树高和材积生长过程曲线；表 4 为黑龙山林场白桦直径、树高和材积生长曲线。

表 3　孟滦林场白桦生长模型的拟合

Tab. 3　Growth model of Betula platyphylla Suk of MengLuan forest farm

指标	模型类型	回归模型	R^2
直径	理查德	$D = 17.9409 \times [1 - Exp(-0.0711 \times A)]$^1.9973	0.9997
	Logistic	$D = 12.6331/[1 + 23.0791 \times Exp(-0.2509 \times A)]$	0.9783
	Levakovic 2	$D = 21.8234 \times [A/(1.9999 + A)]$^7.9019	0.9969
	对数线性	$D = -15.1584 + 8.2705 \times Log(A + 1.9999)$	0.9914
树高	理查德	$H = 13.9062 \times [1 - Exp(-0.125 \times A)]$^1.8801	0.9995
	Logistic	$H = 12.7921/[1 + 10.4439 \times Exp(-0.26 \times A)]$	0.9903
	Levakovic 2	$H = 18.6405 \times [A/(1.0729 + A)]$^8.9379	0.9992

续表

指标	模型类型	回归模型	R^2
树高	对数线性	$H = -6.1255 + 5.9035 \times Log(A + 0.001)$	0.9991
材积	理查德	$V = 0.2731 \times [(1 - Exp(-0.0524 * A)]^{\wedge} 4.0251$	0.9999
	Logistic	$V = 0.0728/[1 + 609.5637 \times Exp(-0.4002 \times A)]$	0.9186
	Levakovic 2	$V = 0.2668 \times [A/(1.9999 + A)]^{\wedge} 17.9717$	0.9935
	对数线性	$V = -0.1347 + 0.06194 \times Log(A + 1.9999)$	0.9229

表 4 黑龙山林场白桦生长模型的拟合

Tab. 4 Growth model of Betula platyphylla Suk of HengLongshan forest farm

指标	模型类型	回归模型	R^2
直径	理查德	$D = 10.0804 \times [(1 - Exp(-1.1208 \times A)]^{\wedge} 187234.7424$	0.9999
	Logistic	$D = 10.0453/[1 + 1643.1138 \times Exp(-0.4935 \times A)]$	0.5687
	Levakovic 2	$D = 6.3125 \times [A/(1.00002 + A)]^{\wedge} 4678.0626$	0.9229
	对数线性	$D = -25.3281 + 11.5828 \times Log(A + 1.9999)$	0.9303
树高	理查德	$H = 14.7562 \times [1 - Exp(-0.0933 * A)]^{\wedge} 2.4024$	0.9974
	Logistic	$H = 11.3005/[1 + 30.2057 \times Exp(-0.2930 \times A)]$	0.9515
	Levakovic 2	$H = 21.3188 \times [A/(1.9999 + A)]^{\wedge} 8.2342$	0.9894
	对数线性	$H = -14.337 + 7.8047 \times Log(A + 1.9999)$	0.9991
材积	理查德	$V = 4.4313 \times [1 - Exp(-0.00736 \times A)]^{\wedge} 2.9045$	0.9987
	Logistic	$V = 2.7291/[1 + 449.1151 \times Exp(-0.3347 \times A)]$	0.9622
	Levakovic 2	$V = 0.0749 \times [A/(1.9999 + A)]^{\wedge} 17.2711$	0.9800
	对数线性	$V = -0.0444 + 0.0202 \times Log(A + 1.9999)$	0.9015

从表 3 中可以看出，孟滦林场白桦拟合的 4 种直径生长模型，其中树高、直径和材积的生长模型中，相关系数最大的都为理查德模型，相关系数分别为：0.9997；0.9995；0.9999。所以，在孟滦林场中，白桦直径、树高和材积的最优生长模型分别为：$D = 17.9409 \times [1 - Exp(-0.0711 \times A)]^{\wedge} 1.9973$；$H = 13.9062 \times [1 - Exp(-0.125 \times A)]^{\wedge} 1.8801$；$V = 0.2731 \times [1 - Exp(-0.0524 \times A)]^{\wedge} 4.0251$。同样可以从表 4 中可以得出黑龙山林场白桦直径、树高和材积的最优生长模型为查理德模型，其生长方程分别为：$D = 10.0804 \times [1 - Exp(-1.1208 \times A)]^{\wedge} 187234.7424$；$H = 14.7562 \times [1 - Exp(-0.0933 \times A)]^{\wedge} 2.4024$；$R^2 = 0.9987$。

4 结论与讨论

白桦在孟滦林场生长 27a 直径总生长量较小，为 13.2cm；平均生长量较快，生长到达 15a 时达到一个高峰；连年生长量在生长到达 10a 左右达到一个高峰，之后呈下降趋势。所以白桦直径、树高生长较快时期是在幼龄林阶段。在黑龙山林场白桦直径总生长量为 16.4cm；平均生长量相对生长较慢，在生长的 27a 内没有达到一个高峰；连年生长量在 20a

左右达到了一个高峰，而 25a 后连年生长量又开始增加，在以后的生长中还会达到一个高峰期。

白桦树高生长在随年龄增加而增大，但在孟滦林场白桦树高生长较快；平均生长量在两个地区 10a 左右都出现了最大值，但孟滦林场白桦生长量较大；树高连年生长量在孟滦林场 10a 左右出现一个高峰期，10a 后呈下降趋势，而在黑龙山林场在 10a 左右也出现了一个高峰期，但生长 20a 后连年生长量又开始增大，还会出现一个高峰期。

白桦在孟滦林场材积总生长量较大，平均生长量和连年生长量比黑龙山林场白桦生长较快。在 27 年的生长过程中，两个地区材积生长量均没有达到一个顶峰，所以白桦没有到达数量成熟期。

通过对现有模型的拟合，选出不同地区白桦的最优生长模型，在孟滦林场中，白桦直径、树高和材积的最优生长模型分别为：$D = 17.9409 \times [1 - Exp(-0.0711 \times A)]^{\wedge} 1.9973$；$H = 18.6405 \times [A/(1.0729 + A)]^{\wedge} 8.9379$；$V = 0.2731 \times [1 - Exp(-0.0524 \times A)]^{\wedge} 4.0251$。同样可以从表 4 中可以得出黑龙山林场白桦直径、树高和材积的最优生长模型分别为：$D = 10.0804 \times [1 - Exp(-1.1208 \times A)]^{\wedge} 187234.7424$；$H = 14.7562 \times [1 - Exp(-0.0933 \times A)]^{\wedge} 2.4024$；$R^2 = 0.9987$。

从白桦生长过程来看，其树高、胸径和材积生长在不同立地条件下有所差异，利用单株解析木生长性状平均值以及与不同单株生长过程的差异，以了解白桦生长过程及其规律，这对于白桦天然次生林的经营具有十分重要的指导意义。但要全面了解白桦随立地条件、林分条件以及气候因素的影响程度，还需要取得相应的解析样木。因此，研究结果具有较大的局限性。

参考文献

[1]郑万钧．中国树木志(第二卷)[M]．北京：中国林业出版社，1985. 2124 ~2131.
[2]徐化成．森林生态与生态系统经营[M]．北京：化学工业出版社，2004.
[3]柴一新．天然白桦林的特点与经营[J]．东北林业大学学报，2000，28(5)：31 ~34.
[4]张远彬，王开运，胡庭兴，等．扁刺栲在两种类型林分中的生长过程分析[J]．应用与环境生物学报，2003，9(4)：336 ~340.
[5]孟宪宇．测树学[M]．北京：中国林业出版社．1996.
[6]梁有祥，秦武明，等．桂东南地区火力楠人工林生长规律研究[J]．西北林学院学报．2011，26(2)：150 ~154.

高光谱遥感竹资源专题信息提取技术研究

刘　健[1,2,3]　余坤勇[1,2]　缪丽娟[1,2]　游浩辰[1,2]

（1. 福建农林大学3S技术应用研究所，福州，350002；2. 福建农林大学林学院，福州，350002；3. 三明学院，三明，365004）

摘要：以Hyperion遥感影像为数据源，采用主成分分析法对光谱分类特征进行降维处理，提取光谱特征差异信息进行片层分割，再融合均值、角二阶距和对比度的最佳纹理特征量信息，实现高光谱竹资源专题信息的提取。研究表明，单纯依靠不同地物的光谱特征差异进行竹资源专题信息提取，精度仅为75%。而利用“基于光谱片层－面向纹理类”的信息提取技术，分类精度达到84.78%。该方法能够解决地形因素引起的阴影问题，是提升高光谱影像山区竹林信息提取精度的一种有效方法。

关键词：高光谱遥感；竹资源；专题信息；光谱片层；纹理

Study on Bamboo Resources Thematic Information Extraction Based on Hyperspectral Image

LIU Jian[1,2,3]　YU Kun－yong[1,2]　MIAO Li－juan[1,2]　YOU Hao－chen[1,2]

(1. Institute of Geomatics Application of Fujian Agriculture and Forestry University, Fuzhou, Fujian 350002;
2. Forestry College of Fujian Agriculture and Forestry University, Fuzhou, Fujian 350002;
3. Sanming University, Sanming, Fujian 365004)

Abstract: Based on hyperspectral remote sensing data, the principal component analysis was used in different spectrum classification features in order to reduce dimension and carved up the spectrum film, then it combined with texture feature of mean value、ASM and contrast to extract the bamboo resources thematic information. The results showed that extraction accuracy reaches 75% only by means of spectral signature, but it's increased to 84.78% based on spectrum film－Texture oriented. This method can solve the shadow problem caused by geomorphic factors, and effectively improve the extraction accuracy of bamboo information in mountainous areas.

Key words: Hyperspectral Image; Bamboo Resources; Bamboo Resources; Spectrum film; Texture

1 引　言

竹资源是一类特殊的非木质资源，在区域经济发展和生态环境保护中发挥着举足轻重的作用。我国竹资源分布在山区和边远丘陵地带，监测和管理手段较为落后，竹资源基础资料

基金项目：国家自然科学基金(40971043)。

不详尽，缺乏有效的决策指导。竹资源调查周期比其他森林更短，现有调查周期无法及时反映资源的动态变化。遥感作为一种准确、及时的信息获取手段，在森林资源专题信息的提取和动态监测中得到广泛的重视和应用。但目前国内外在竹资源监测研究方面的信息源主要采用航空相片和中等空间分辨率影像[1~2]，对于高分辨率和高光谱信息源的研究较少。TM、ETM、ALOS 等遥感影像的光谱分辨率相对于南方复杂的地形因子来说，成像覆盖仍会有大量混合像元存在，是造成树种识别精度不高的原因之一，制约了遥感技术在林业调查、监测方面的应用。光谱分辨率的提高高光谱遥感迅速兴起并成为遥感发展的主导趋势之一。高光谱数据的波段宽度达到纳米量级，能够充分反映地物光谱的细微特征[3~7]。但目前尚未有针对性地建立可为竹资源分类提供重要理论依据的光谱数据库。将光谱特征、纹理特征与多源地学辅助数据结合进行竹资源专题信息提取的研究尚未报道。为此，以 Hyperion 遥感影像为数据源，采用基于“光谱片层 - 面向纹理类”的方法，对福建省顺昌县竹资源信息进行提取和精度评价，进一步探求竹资源信息提取的最佳方法。

2 研究区概况与资料收集

2.1 研究区概况

福建省顺昌县位于西北部隶属于南平市，南与沙县相邻，北与建阳市交界，属中亚热带海洋季风气候，地形以低山丘陵为主。顺昌县竹类资源丰富，主要分布有 11 属 100 多种珍贵竹种，是重点林业县和省毛竹生产基地县，也是国家林业局命名的“中国竹子之乡”之一。

2.2 资料收集

研究采用的卫星遥感影像为顺昌县 2007 年 Hyperion 遥感影像，空间分辨率为 30 m。其他辅助数据包括顺昌县 1: 50000 地形图及资源分布图。同时，实地调查共获得研究区各典型地物点 490 个，同时采集野外光谱数据。其中林地点 385 个（包括竹林、杉木林、马尾松林、阔叶林、经济林及混交林样地点）、非林地点 105 个（包括水域、耕地、居民地及工矿用地、道路等样地点），将这些样地点导入研究区 Hyperion 影像图，转换为感兴趣区域。

3 研究方法

3.1 高光谱遥感影像预处理

Hyperion 遥感数据共 242 个波段，数据经坏线修复、反射率反演、垂直条纹去除、大气校正及几何精校正之后，达到应用要求。其中垂直条纹去除采用逐波段检查的方法（朱珂，2009），即用各波段所有像元均值 D_n（$n = 1, 2, \cdots, 144$）替代云的像元值，然后再使用全局去条纹法去除条纹噪音。大气校正对比分析了辐射传输理论模型、QUAC 以及简化黑暗像元法三种模型校正后的图像光谱曲线后，发现大气辐射传输理论模型的校正效果较优，校正后光谱曲线更符合植被的光谱特性（图 1），因此研究选择该方法进行大气校正。从理论上讲，一旦 Levell 数据集生成，理应不再有坏像元或条纹等误差存在。但是，实际上仍有许多质量差的波段或像元存在，统称为“非正常的像元”。在进行图像应用之前，必须将非正常的像元识别出来并加以纠正，使图像得以恢复。去除未定标及受水汽影响波段后，初步通过筛选排除部分响应小、信息量低的波段，最终对剩余 122 个波段（1 ~ 122）进行研究。

3.2 竹资源光谱特征分析

由实验区野外地物光谱曲线（图 2）可知，竹资源的光谱反射曲线处于杉阔混交林、竹阔混交林、竹针混交林、阔叶树、马尾松与杉木之间，在一些波长位置上，还与其他林种存在交错的可能性，这也再次论证了长期以来竹资源遥感识别与监测的精度普遍较低的现实。从各主要林种看，杉木的反射率最高，阔叶树的反射率最低，马尾松的反射率与竹林的反射率最为接近。相对来说，在绿光波段上，各植被的反射率小高峰特征明显，竹林与其他林种尤其是杉木的光谱特征差异较为明显。野外实测分析而得的竹资源与其他主要林种的差异特征可作为最佳波段选择的一个重要参考依据。

根据遥感图像各波段包含的信息量来选择波段是进行波段选择的第一步。其中，标准差是衡量图像信息量的重要指标，反映了灰度偏离灰度均值的程度，标准差越大，则灰度级分布越分散，图像中所有灰度级出现概率越趋于相等，则包含的信息量越趋于最大，地物之间就越容易区分。由图3可以看出，波段1~30、51~53、69~74、90~93标准差较小，所以这些波段子集包含的信息量就少，在选择波段时可以不予考虑；而波段31~50、54~68、75~89、94~122的标准差较大；波段119~122的标准差很大，其中波段122的标准差最大，为最优波段，这些波段子集包含的信息量就较多，是理想的候选波段子集。观测五种主要植被在Hyperion影像上122个波段的光谱(DN值)曲线变化趋势(图4)，以DN值重叠少、差异大为原则有针对地选择波段。研究发现在1~25波段、31~50波段、58~66波段、74~85波段、92~122波段，竹林、杉木、阔叶林、经济林的DN值差异较明显，是理想的波段子集；在80~85波段，经济林、竹林和阔叶林的DN值差异较其他波段显著，所以这几种植被在这些波段子集上可分性要好一些。而具有重叠现象的26~30波段、51~57波段、67~73波段、86~91波段并非不适合，而要结合其他因子来考虑是否选择。

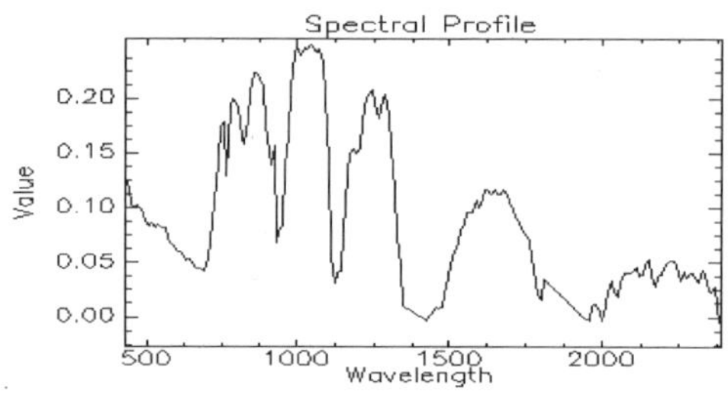

图1 大气校正后的图像光谱曲线

Fig. 1 Spectrum curve after atmosphere correction

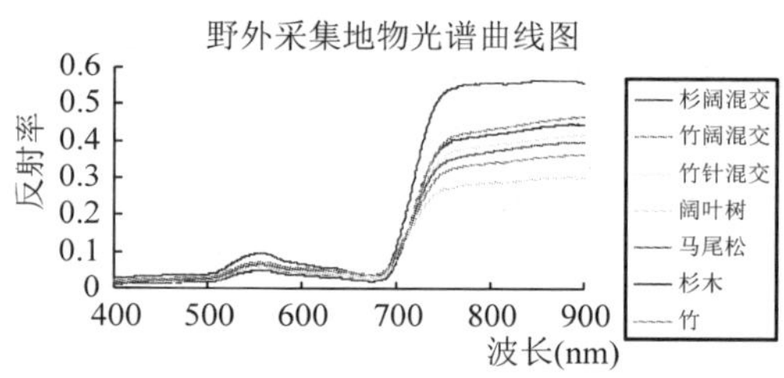

图2 野外采集地物光谱曲线图

Fig. 2 Spectral curve by field acquisition

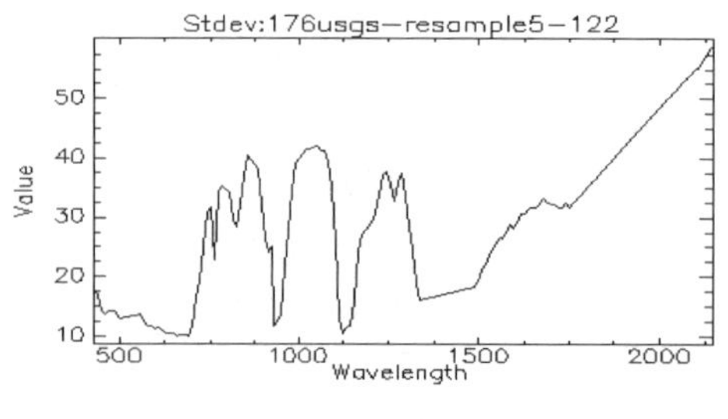

图3 各波段的标准差曲线图

Fig. 3 Standard deviation curve of each band

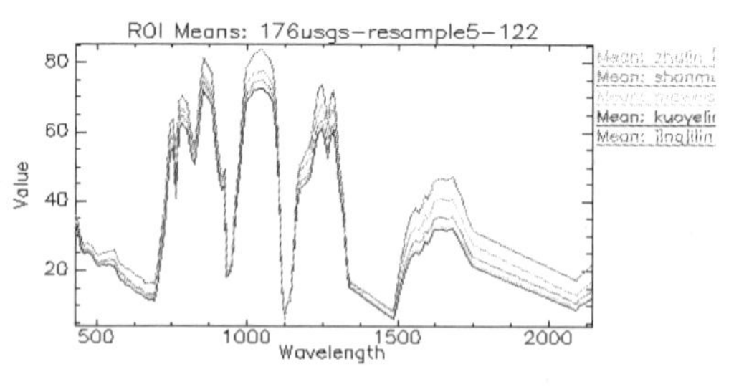

图4 五种地物的高光谱特性

Fig. 4 High spectral features of five planting types

3.3 竹资源高光谱有效特征量分析

遥感图像的信息量主要取决于两个因素，一是图像的灰度等级或量化等级的数目，另一是瞬时视场或像元的大小。前者主要影响波谱信息量，而后者主要影响空间信息量。在高光谱数据中，由于波段宽度窄的特点决定了其信息冗余度要比多光谱数据大得多，因此波段选择显得尤为重要。研究用到的五种波段选择方法包括波段指数法、自适应波段选择法、均值标准距离法、OIF 指数法以及主成分分析法(表 1)进行有效特征量的提取。具体的特征量分析结果见表 5。

表 1 五种高光谱有效特征量分析方法

Tab. 1 Five analytical methods of hyperspectral effective characteristic quantities

光谱特征量选择方法	波段指数法	自适应波段选择法	均值标准距离法	OIF 指数法	主成分分析法
主要公式	$P_i = \frac{S_i}{R_i}$	$I_i = \frac{\sigma_i}{(R_{i-1,i} + R_{i,i+1})/2}$	$d = \frac{\vert u_1 - u_2 \vert}{\sigma_1 + \sigma_2}$	$OIF = \sum_{i=1}^{3} S_i / \sum_{j=1}^{3} \vert r_{ij} \vert$	$(\sum_{i=1}^{m} \lambda i)/(\sum_{i=1}^{p} \lambda_i) \geq 85\%$

4 结果与分析

4.1 基于“光谱片层－面向纹理类”的高光谱遥感数据竹资源信息提取

4.1.2 基于光谱的竹资源光谱片层分割

研究利用主成分分析法，得到光谱信息的分类特征。并以监督分类为基础，在明亮区和阴影区各取 30 个样地点，将明亮区和阴影区的林地片层分割开来。采用最大似然法将阴影区和明亮区的竹资源片层挖掘出来(图 5 至图 8)。对预处理后波段数为 122 个的 Hyperion 影像进行掩膜，根据明亮区和阴影区竹资源信息所对应的影像图，建立了具有相似像元灰度值的光谱片层(图 9)。

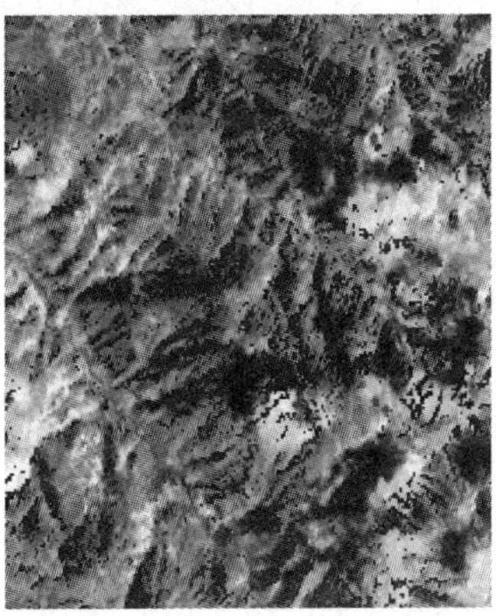

图 5 明亮区林地

Fig. 5 Bright forest land

图 6 明亮区竹资源光谱片层

Fig. 6 Spectrum film of bamboo resources in bright forest land

图 7 阴影区林地

Fig. 7 Shadow forest land

4.1.3 面向纹理类的竹资源专题信息提取

4.1.3.1 主成分变换

研究采用 ENVI4.3 软件对 Hyperion 影像(竹林片层)进行主成分变换，所得出各主成分的贡献值，并依次求出贡献率。由表 2 靠前的几个主成分可以看出，第一主成分贡献率达到 99.93%，能较充分地代表原始影像数据的信息(图 10)。

表 2 主成分变换分析表

Tab. 2 Analytical statement of principal component transform

主成分序号	1	2	3	4	5	6	7	8	9
贡献值	12168.8860	5.6095	1.5389	0.5935	0.3239	0.2291	0.1754	0.1486	0.1188
贡献率%	99.9283	0.0461	0.0126	0.0049	0.0027	0.0019	0.0014	0.0012	0.0010

4.1.3.2 基于灰度共生矩阵的纹理信息提取

窗口大小的选择方法与多光谱研究中类似。研究分别设置不同的窗口大小，分析均值和熵两种纹理的特征与窗口大小的联系，纹理均值随着窗口大小的变化无明显改变，纹理熵随着窗口的变大而增大。当窗口大小设为 13×13 以上时，熵值趋于稳定。研究发现 5×5 大小的窗口纹理紧密适中，目视效果也较好(图 11)，而步长不宜选取过大，因此最终将步长选择设为(1，1)。

为提高面向类的竹林信息提取效率，选择最佳的纹理量组合，研究中引入香农信息熵、

图 8 阴影区竹资源光谱片层

Fig. 8 Spectrum film of bamboo resources in shadow forest land

图 9 竹资源光谱片层

Fig. 9 Spectrum film of bamboo resource

图 10 第一主成分

Fig. 10 The first principal component

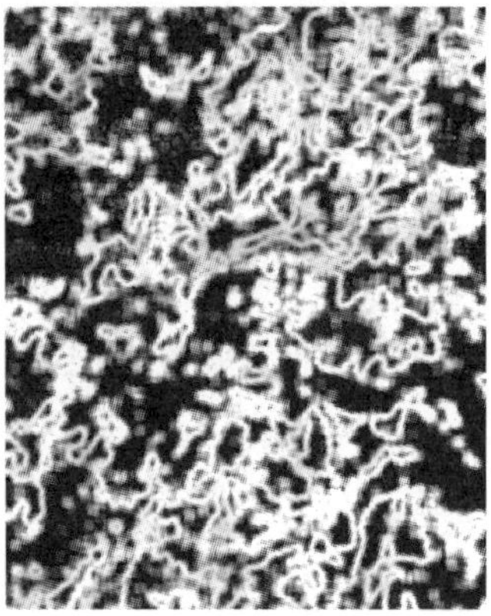

图 11 5×5 and (1，1) variance

Fig. 11 5×5 and (1，1) variance

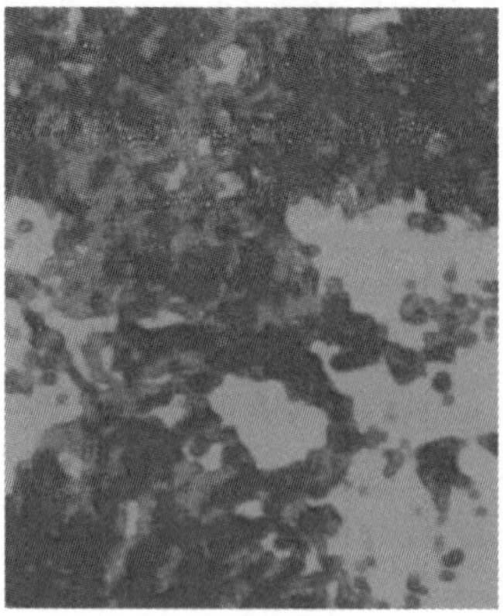

图 12 最佳纹理量组合

Fig. 12 Optimum combination of texture quantity

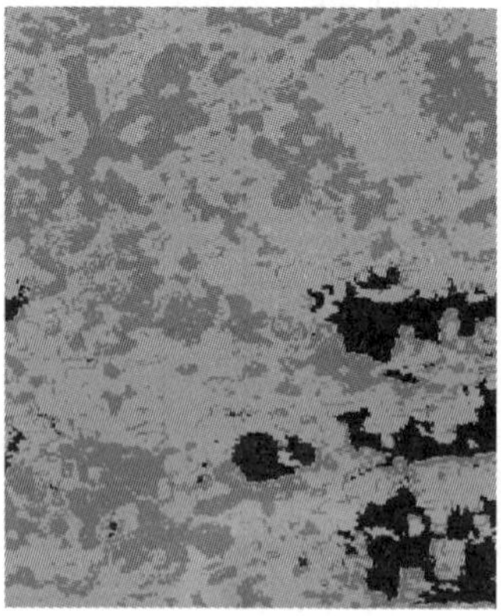

图 13 竹资源信息提取结果

Fig. 13 Extraction results of bamboo resources information

相关系数两项指标加以分析。香农信息熵可表征一幅图像信息量的多少，而信息量也是最佳波段选择的一个衡量指标。综合分析8个纹理量的香农信息熵(表3)。协同性、熵和相关性三个纹理子图像的信息熵与其他纹理子图像的信息熵具有较大差异，而其图像的目视效果也较差，予以剔除。

表3　各纹理子图像信息熵

Tab. 3　Texture comentropy of each sub image

纹理量	均值	方差	协同性	对比度	相异性	熵	角二阶矩	相关性
信息熵	0.97370	0.96399	1.06556	1.00647	1.00929	1.05666	0.98399	0.00990

上述八种纹理量都是基于灰度共生矩阵计算而得，因而各纹理量之间必定存在相关性。在分类中，分类特征的相关性越小越有利于分类。研究利用相关系数指标进行分析，剔除冗余信息，这样既保证了优选波段的有效性，同时也减少工作量。计算出各纹理子图像信息熵的相关系数矩阵，见表4。

表4　各纹理子图像信息熵的相关系数矩阵

Tab. 4　Correlation matrix on texture comentropy of each sub image

纹理量	均值	方差	协同性	对比度	相异性	熵	角二阶矩	相关性
均值	1.00000							
方差	-0.58180	1.00000						
协同性	0.91641	-0.77930	1.00000					
对比度	-0.56338	0.93754	-0.80050	1.00000				
相异性	-0.59158	0.93886	-0.81969	0.99799	1.00000			
熵	-0.85779	0.82551	-0.89324	0.81352	0.83798	1.00000		
角二阶矩	0.92540	-0.81805	0.97251	-0.80570	-0.82700	-0.95511	1.00000	
相关性	0.15349	0.01413	0.09313	0.01354	0.00514	-0.12640	0.11001	1.00000

相异性与对比度、方差的相关性很大，说明信息存在较多的重叠和冗余。对比各纹理图像的目视效果与香农信息熵的分析结果，最终确定均值、角二阶距、对比度作为最佳纹理量组合(图12)，并采用支持向量机法(SVM)分类[8]。SVM是建立在VC维理论和结构风险最小化原则之上的机器学习方法，它根据有限样本信息在模型复杂性和无错误地识别任意样本的能力之间寻求最佳折中，以期获得最好的推广能力。它的一个重要的优点是可以处理线性不可分情况下的分类问题，通过投影转换，将低维特征空间转换为高维特征空间，并在高维特征空间中寻找一个超平面作为分类面，将样本分类。研究采用ENVI 4.5嵌入的支持向量机，发现其对林地与非林地的分类效果很好，实现竹资源专题信息的提取(图13)。

4.2　精度评价

利用精度评估方法评价竹资源专题信息提取结果。从精度评估结果(表5)可以看出，竹林信息提取总精度为84.78%。115个竹林样点中有98个被正确划分，另有17个被误分；115个非竹林样点中，有97个被正确划分，剩余18个被误分为竹林，竹林信息提取总体精度为84.78%。

研究进一步比较了五种基于单一光谱特征的分类法在竹资源信息的提取中的结果(图14)，不同光谱特征量的选择[9~11]下分别运用决策树和支持向量机二大分类法进行竹资源信息的提取，分类结果见表6。

通过表5、表6综合可以看出，横向比较于五种基于光谱单特征的分类方法，基于“光谱片层-面向纹理类”的方法分类精度较高。虽然Hyperion遥感影像光谱分辨率高，但空间分辨率也只为30m。受信息载荷量影响，南方地区多丘陵地带，局部地区反而存在更为严重的光谱混淆现象。五种基于光谱单特征的信息提取方法中，只有均值标准距离和主成分分析法的提取精度达到80%以上。但均值标准距离法比较复杂，且该方法主要是一维特征空间的一种度量，不适于进行多变量的研究。其他3种分类特征的分类结果都不理想，波段指数法的分类效果最差，其次是自适应波段选择法和OIF指数法。波段指数和自适应波段选择均受波段均方差控制，容易出现波段组合间的高相关性，不利于植被分类；而OIF指数虽说考虑了波段的信息量和独立性，但由于高光谱数据量庞大，该方法的计算量大，用普通的方法无法现实(研究采用了C++编程)。综合考虑，OIF指数方法也不适用于Hyperion高光谱数据。纵向对比决策树法与支持向量机法的分类结果，可以发现二者总体精度相差不大，决策树法的分类结果图呈一定程度的椒盐状，其影像连续性与目视效果较SVM法有所欠缺。可见对于Hyperion高光谱数据，选用SVM分类器为最优。

表5　竹资源信息提取误差矩阵

Tab. 5　Error matrix on bamboo resources information extraction

样点数	竹林	非竹林	合计
竹林	98	17	115
非竹林	18	97	115
总计	116	114	230
分类总精度=84.78%　Kappa总系数=0.7142			

表6　不同分类特征分类结果精度比较

Tab. 6　Comparison on extraction results of different classification feature

分类方法		决策树		SVM	
光谱特征量选择方法	选择波段	总分类精度	Kappa系数	总分类精度	Kappa系数
波段指数法	122、63、36	72.61%	0.4522	63.91%	0.2783
自适应波段选择法	122、63、111	75.65%	0.5130	72.17%	0.4435
均值标准距离法	122、97、6	80.87%	0.6174	80.43%	0.6104
OIF指数法	122、82、44	72.61%	0.4522	77.83%	0.5365
主成分分析法	可见光、近红外和短波红外波段组的第一和第二主成分	81.30%	0.6261	83.04%	0.6609

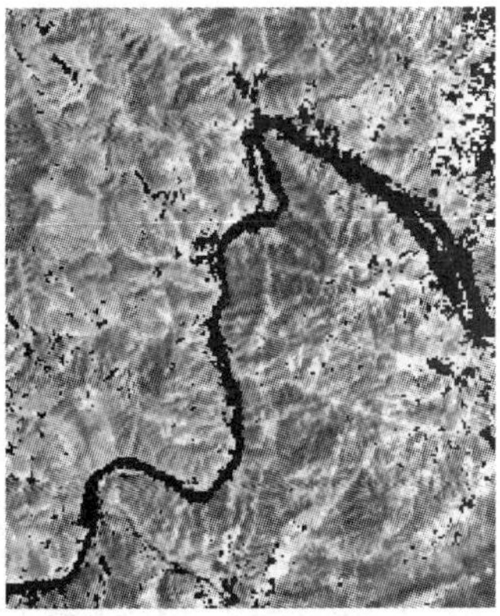

波段指数法最佳波段组合
Optimum band combination

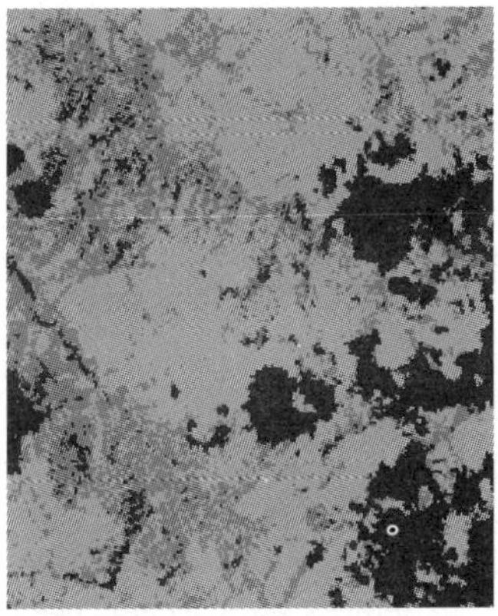

波段指数法决策树分类
Band index method with

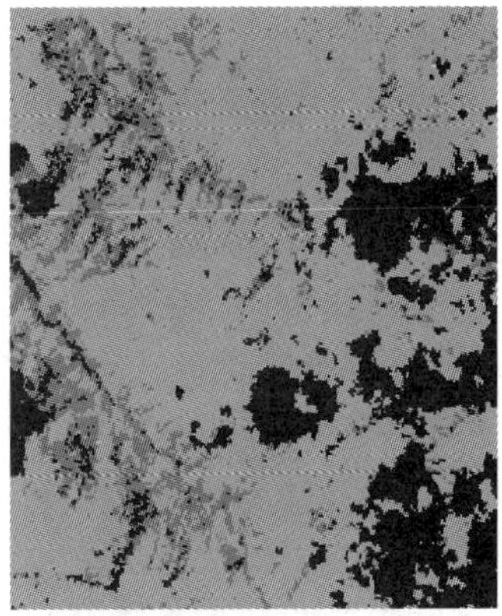

波段指数法 SVM 分类
Band index method

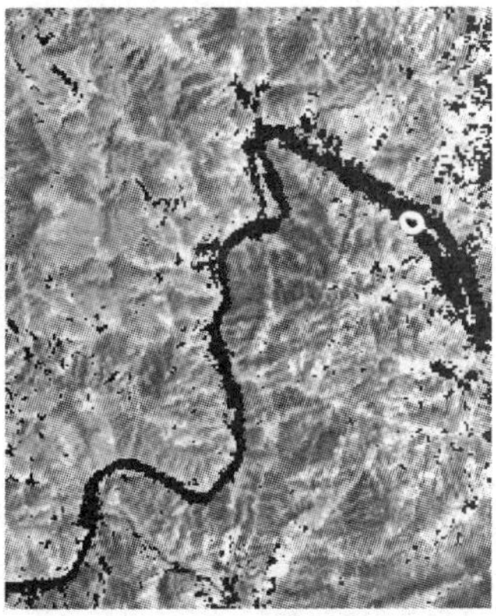

适应波段选择法最佳波段组合
Optimum band combination on ABS method

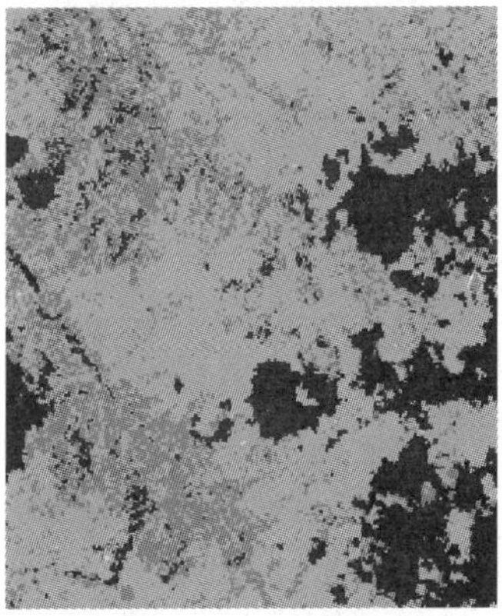

自适应波段选择法决策树分类
ABS method with decision tree classifier

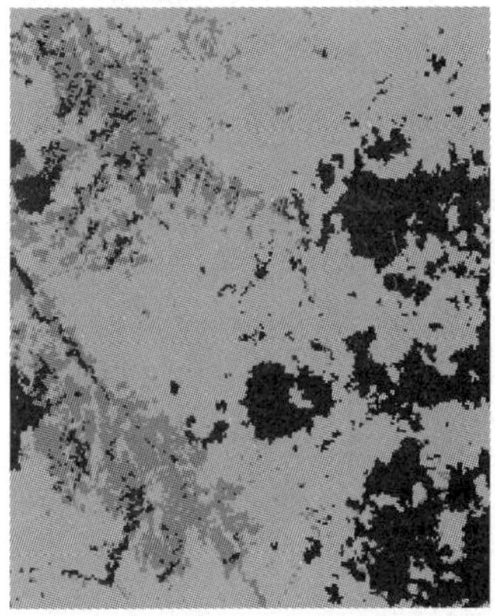

自适应波段选择法 SVM 分类
BS method with SVM classifier

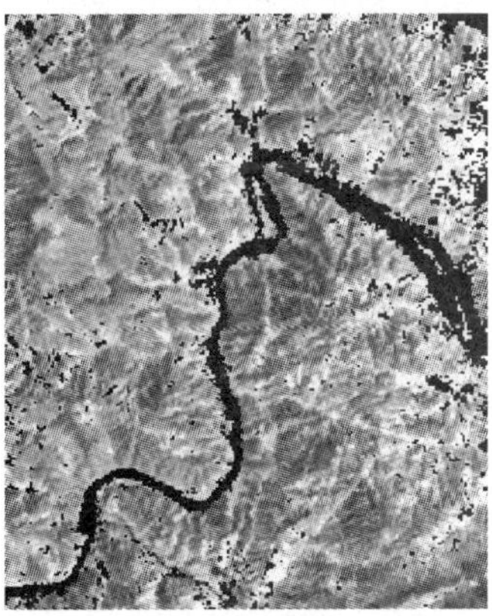

均值标准距离法最件波段组合
Optimum band combination on mean distance standard method

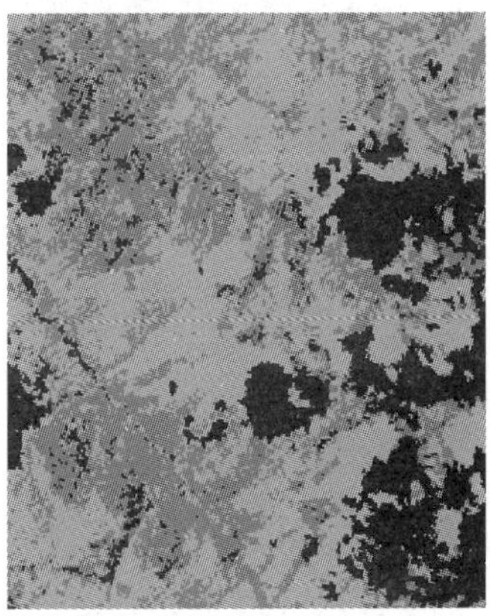

均值标准距离法决策树分类
Mean distance standard method with decision tree classifier

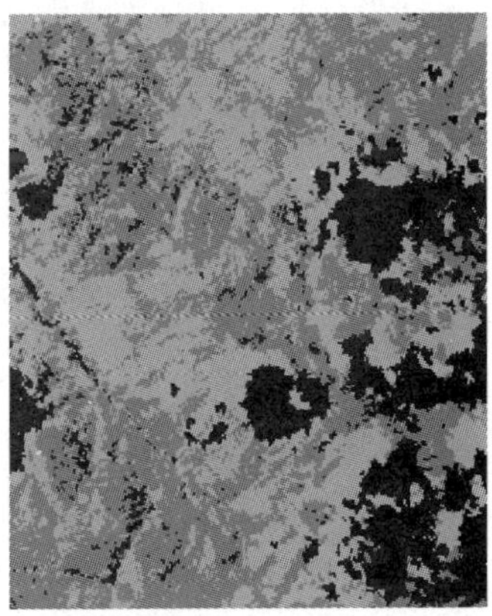

均值标准距离法 SVM 分类
Mean distance standard method with SVM classifier

图 14　不同分类特征最佳波段组合及分类结果比较(一)

Fig. 14　Optimum band combination and results by different classification feature(Ⅰ)

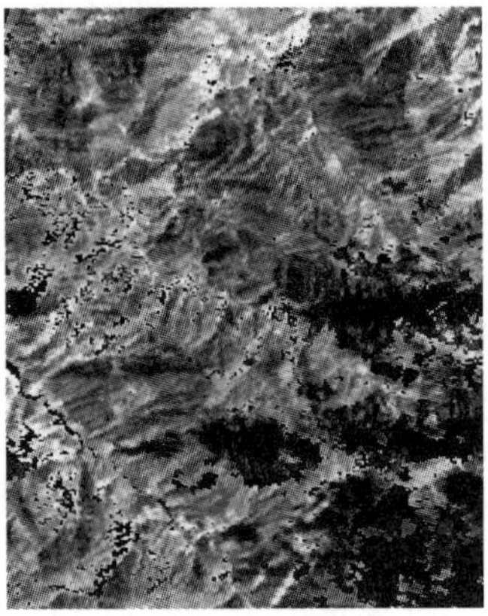

OIF 指数法最佳波段组合
Optimum band combination on OIF method

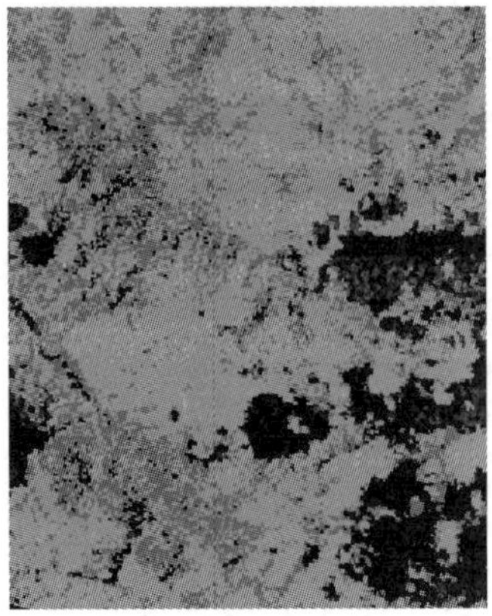

OIF 指数法决策树分类
OIF method with decision tree classifier

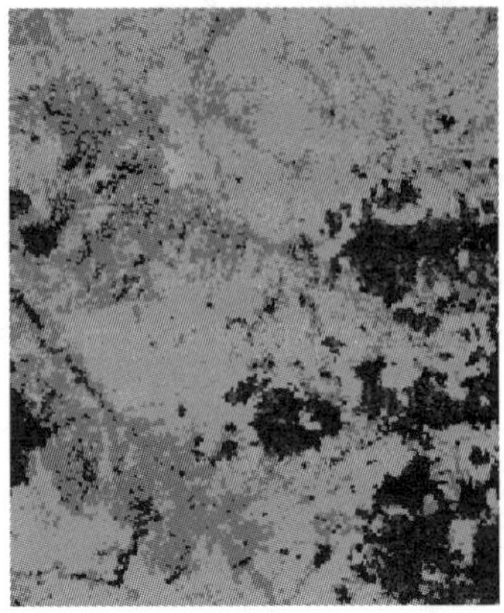

OIF 指数法 SVM 分类
OIF method with SVM classifier

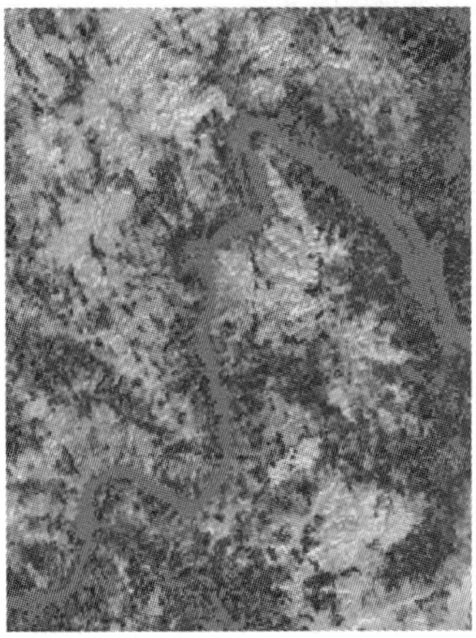

主成分分析法最佳波段组合
Optimum band combination on PCA method

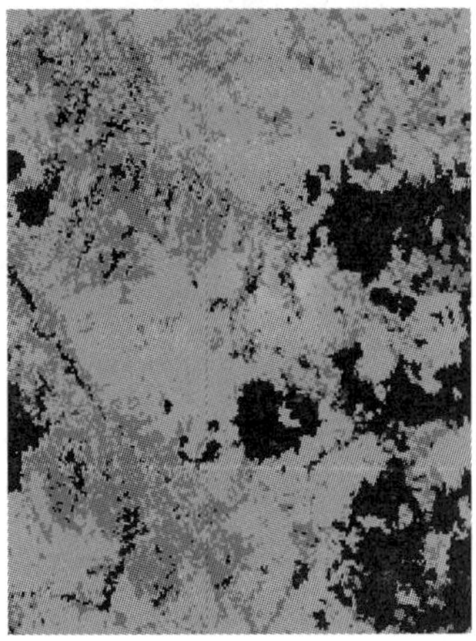

主成分分析法决策树分类
PCA method with decision tree classifier

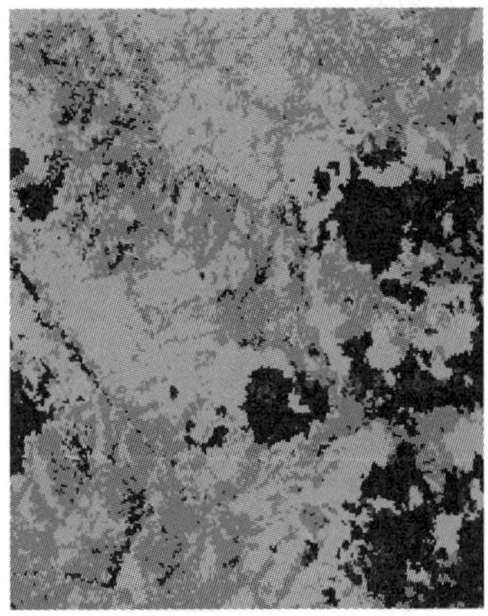

主成分分析法 SVM 分类
PCA method with SVM classifier

图 14 不同分类特征最佳波段组合及分类结果比较(二)
Fig. 14 Optimum band combination and results by different classification feature(Ⅱ)

5 总 结

与常规遥感不同，高光谱遥感影像提供了几乎连续的地物波谱曲线，降低了分类过程中因为波谱信息不足而造成的错分率，大大地改善对地物的识别与分类精度。但南方地区竹子多与马尾松或杉木等针叶林混交，仅仅利用光谱特征信息量单薄，对于竹资源信息提取难度较大，很容易出现错分现象。而基于“光谱片层－面向纹理类”方法充分考虑竹类植被特有的光谱与纹理特征，综合信息量丰富，具有更高的信息提取精度。以主成分分析法对光谱分类特征进行降维处理，提取光谱特征差异信息进行片层分割，同时融合均值、角二阶距和对比度的最佳纹理特征量信息，利用支持向量机分类器实现高光谱竹资源专题信息的提取。该方法可为高光谱竹资源分类依据提供技术参考，也为南方混交生长的竹资源专题信息的提取提供重要的基础数据。

参考文献

[1]杜华强，周国模，葛宏立，等．基于 TM 数据提取竹林遥感信息的方法．东北林业大学学报，2008，36(3)：35 ~ 38.

[2]Bharadwaj S P，Siva – Subramanian，Sudhakar – Manda，et al. Bamboo livelihood development planning，monitoring and analysis through GIS and remote sensing. Journal – of – Bamboo – and – Rattan. 2003；2(4)：453 ~ 461.

[3]浦瑞良，宫鹏．高光谱遥感及其应用[M]．北京：高等教育出版社，2000.

[4]温兴平，胡光道，杨晓峰．从高光谱遥感影像提取植被信息[J]．测绘科学，2008，33(3)：66 ~ 68.

[5]颜梅春，张友静，鲍艳松．基于灰度共生矩阵法的 IKONOS 影像中竹林信息提取．遥感信息，2004，(2)：31 ~ 34.

[6]吴昊．高光谱遥感图像数据分类技术研究[D]．北京：国防科学技术大学，2004.

[7] Dura D B，Hiura H. Expansion characteristics of bamboo stand and sediment disaster in South Western Japan (CAB)．Pakistan – Journal – of – Biological – Sciences. 2006；9(4)：622 ~ 631.

[8]蔡华利．基于 SVM 的多源遥感分类的竹林信息提取方法研究——以福建省顺昌县为例[D]．北京林业大学，2009.

[9]程乘旗，马廷，王立明．用于植被冠层分析的高光谱波段的组合方法研究[J]．地理学与国土研究，2002，18(2)：23 ~ 25.

[10]Marin John A，Assessing band selection and image classification techniques on HYDICE hyperspectral data [C]. Proc. Of IEEE Soc. Of SMC，Tokyo，Japan，2000.

[11]杨可明，郭达志．植被高光谱特征分析及其病害信息提取研究[J]．地理与地理信息科学，2006，22(4)：31 ~ 34.

北京市长城地区森林资源信息系统

沈　林　杨　华　邓华锋

（省部共建森林培育与保护教育部重点实验室，北京林业大学，北京，100083）

摘要：本文介绍了 ArcGIS Server 的基本概念和体系结构，阐述了分布式 ArcGIS Server 系统的管理机制。分析了服务器端配置和管理方法、数据库管理技术以及开发 Web 应用相关问题，并结合北京市长城地区高保护价值森林，采用 ArcGIS Server ADF 开发了一个北京市长城地区森林资源信息系统。

关键词：ArcGIS Server ；分布式系统；北京市长城森林资源信息系统

Information System of Beijing Great Wall's Forest Resource

Abstract: In this paper, the basic concept and system structure of ArcGIS Server are introduced and the management mechanism of the distributed ArcGIS Server is stated. The configure and management of the server-side, management of database and problems of Web development have been analyzed. Using the ArcGIS Server ADF and combined with high conservation value forest resources in the area of Beijing Great Wall, we develop an information system for Beijing Great Wall's forest resource

Key words: ArcGIS Server; distributed system; Beijing Great Wall's forests resource information system

引　言

森林的自然服务功能对人类不可或缺，森林对地方社会的文化认同以及文化价值的维持也同样重要。森林状况的变化可能会潜在的引起当地社会或者社会在文化价值难以恢复的改变，因此维持这些价值，正确经营周围的森林，将有助于保护地方社区以及整体社会的文化价值与传统，有利于维持文化整合。

北京地区长城历史悠久，现存长城多为明长城，绝大多数地段属自然状态的“野长城”，存在很多未被保护和管理遭到破坏的地段，甚至一些地段毁坏现象极为严重，对保持自然状态下长城景观的保存工作造成极大的威胁。长城遗址周围的森林植被保护、恢复和经营成为北京市生态林公益林管护体系中重要组成部分，如何对长城高保护价值森林进行现代管理成为了亟需解决的问题。本文基于 ArcGIS Server 开发 Web 应用程序，在 Windows 平台的 .NET ADF 框架下开发了一个以沿线区县为主导、统一管理与分散管理相结合的北京市长城地区高保护森林植被信息管理系统，使长城森林植被的保护和经营建设实现信息化、系统化和科学化。

1 ESRI 的 WebGIS 平台 ArcGIS 简介

1.1 ArcGIS Server

网络地理信息系统，又称 WebGIS，是 Internet 技术应用于 GIS 开发的产物，具有传统 GIS 软件的功能和 Internet 优势的特有功能，用户通过客户端或者浏览器向 GIS 服务器提交请求和接受结果，大大扩展了用户的使用范围，实现了高度综合，为多源空间数据、非空间数据的集成和共享提供了技术保障，在各领域都得到了广泛的应用。ArcGIS Server 是 ESRI 发布的提供面向 Web 控件数据服务的一个企业级 GIS 软件平台，提供创建和配置 GIS 应用程序和服务的框架，并实现空间数据管理、空间可视化、空间分析的功能，ArcGIS Server 提供的服务包括 Map Services、Globe Services、Geocode Services 等[1]。

1.2 ArcGIS Server 的组成

ArcGIS Server 包含两个主要部分：GIS 服务器和 .NET 框架及 Java 的 Web 应用开发框架（ADF）。其中 GIS 服务器支持 ArcObjects，用于网络、企业和桌面应用程序，它包含了 ArcObjects 中心函数库；ADF 包含一个软件开发工具包，其中有网络控件、网络应用模板、开发者帮助和源代码范例[2]。ADF 在 GIS 服务器中运行时调用 ArcObjects 创建和配置 .NET 框架或者 Java 的桌面和网络应用。

2 分布式 ArcGIS Server 构建

ArcGIS Server 是一个由多个可以分布于多台机器的组件构成的分布式系统[3]。ArcGIS Server 系统的每个组件都在各自扮演者特定的角色，诸如进程管理、激活、解除活动以及平衡分配到给定服务器对象或服务器对象组的资源等[4]。如图 1 所示，ArcGIS Server 的组件可以概括为 GIS Server、Web 服务器和客户端 3 类。

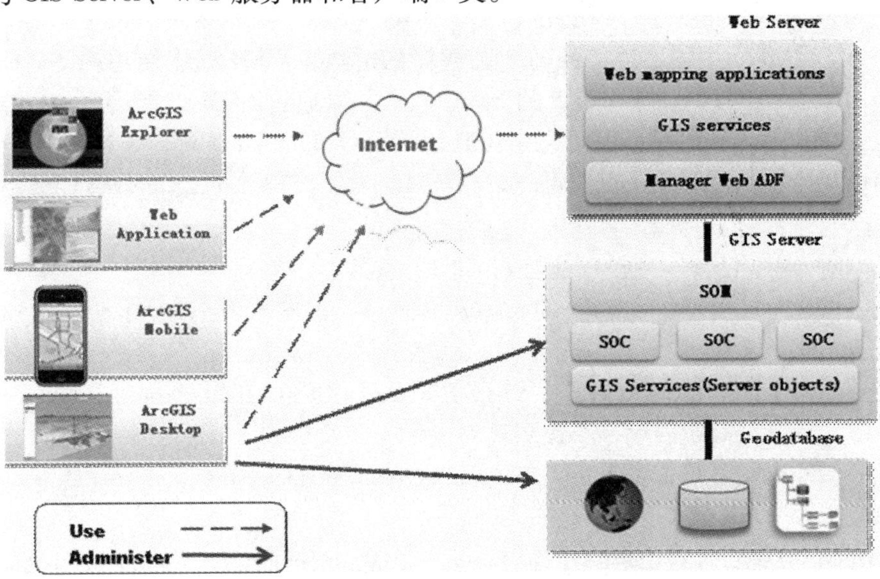

图 1 ArcGIS Server 体系结构

Fig1 Architecture of the ArcGIS Server System

2.1 GIS Server

GIS 服务器宿主和运行服务器对象，例如 Maps、Globes、Address Locators，并封装为服务提供给客户端应用。GIS Server 包括服务器对象管理器(SOM)以及一个或者多个服务对象容器 SOC 组成，即 GIS Server = SOM + n × SOCs，客户端发送请求到 SOM，SOM 将分配的资源提供给客户端，通过 SOM 对所有 SOC 进行调度与管理，实现系统负载均衡

2.2 Web 服务器

Web 服务器包含 Web 应用的部署，以及 Web 服务，它们均使用 GIS Server 上的服务资源。这些 Web 应用和 Web 服务可以通过 ADF 来编程实现。通过 ArcGIS Server 建立的网络服务和网络应用运行在 Web 服务器上，通过 Web 服务器访问 GIS 服务器。

2.3 客户端

客户端是多样化的，主要包括 Web 浏览器和桌面产品两种形式。利用 ArcGIS Server ADF 构建的 Web 应用程序支持的浏览器，比如 Internet Explorer 和 Netscape；Mobile 移动设备；通过 HTTP 连接到 GIS 服务器的 ArcGIS 桌面应用，比如 ArcCatalog 和 ArcGIS Server Manager。

3 关键技术

以 ArcGIS Server 为基础，用 ArcSDE 来管理空间数据库，在 Windows 平台的 .NET ADF 框架下，结合北京市长城沿线高保护价值森林资源，开发了一个北京市长城地区高保护价值森林资源信息查询系统。关键技术详解如下

3.1 服务器对象获取

ArcGIS Server 是一个三层模型，第二层 Web 服务器主要包括通过浏览器访问的 WEB 程序和 WEB 服务，为了让 WEB 服务器上的程序能够通过操作 ArcObjects 组件与 GIS 服务器上的 ArcObjects 组件进行交互，需要在 WEB 服务器上安装 ADF。WEB 程序或 WEB Service 使用的组件是 Server API，这些 API 分为三种：Server API、.NET WebControl 和 Java WebControl[5]。当一个 WEB 应用程序连接到 GIS 服务器的时候，WEB 程序使用的 Server API 将调用一个代理对象去访问远程服务器上的 SOM 对象，并通过 SOM 对象寻找到 SOM 管理的 Server Object。通过 Server Object，可以引用其他相关粒度的 ArcObjects。这个过程大致如下：

```
ESRI.ArcGIS.Server.IGISServerConnection pGISSC = new ESRI.ArcGIS.Server.GISServerConnection-Class();
pGISSC.Connect("maple"); //连接到 GIS 服务器
ESRI.ArcGIS.Server.IServerObjectManager SOM = pGISSC.ServerObjectManager; //找到 GIS Server 上的 SOM
ESRI.ArcGIS.Server.IServerContext pServerContext = SOM.CreateServerContext("maple","MapServer"); //通过 SOM 创建一个服务器对象的上下文
ESRI.ArcGIS.Server.IServerObject pSO = pServerContext.ServerObject; //从上下文对象找到服务器对象
ESRI.ArcGIS.Server.IMapServer pMapServer = (IMapServer)(pSO); //使用 IMapServer 接口来访问服务器对象
……
```

pServerContext. ReleaseContext( ); //释放服务器对象的上下文，即关闭该进程

3.2 数据库服务配置

系统采用 Microsoft SQL Server 2005 空间数据管理平台，ArcSDE 作为空间数据引擎以及 Geodatabase 数据模型的原理管理空间数据库。ArcSDE 是 ArcGIS 与关系数据库之间的 GIS 通道，ArcGIS Server 企业级包含企业级 ArcSDE 技术，允许用户使用关系数据库管理系统存储和管理空间数据，可以将空间数据和属性数据集成在常用的数据库管理系统中，比如 Oracle、SQLServer、Informix，同时所有的 ArcGIS 应用程序都能够应用这些数据[6]。ArcSDE 以层的方式管理空间数据，将具有相同属性的要素存到同一层，在数据库中由一个或多个数据表组成，由 ArcSDE 通过它自建的关联字将多个表关联起来。将北京市林业相关部门提供的原始数据存储到 Microsoft SQL Server 2005 数据库中，空间数据是通过 ArcSDE 数据引擎来管理，属性数据则直接通过 SQL Server 操作。

4 信息系统 Web 界面中基本功能的实现

.NET ADF 包含许多地图操作中需要的基本控件和对应的类，另外可以通过调用 ArcGIS Server 和 ArcObjects 的 API 函数开发更高级的功能。本信息系统的构建用到了以下几种控件：①Map 控件，提供地图显示及平移、缩放等功能；②Table of contents(TOC)控件，用于显示地图的内容列表，用户可以使用这个控件来显示或关闭图层；③Overview map 控件，显示地图的鹰眼图；④Magnifier 控件，与鹰眼对应的放大镜提供多种倍数的放大；⑤Toolbar 控件，即工具栏控件，可增加或删除用户自定义的按钮。本信息系统主要功能如下

4.1 图形基本操作

图形的基本操作是通过 WebMap 控件来实现的，通过它获得了 WebObject 组件提供的其他接口，从而实现了各种功能，包括漫游功能(Pan)、全图功能(Full Extent)、放大(ZoomIn)和缩小(ZoomOut)等。此外提供了测距和任意多边形面积计算的功能，同时可以进行多种单位间的换算。

4.2 查询功能

4.2.1 信息查询功能

查询功能中主要实现了属性到图形查询，图形到属性查询，空间关系查询。例如图形查询属性这个功能的实现，首先要接收用户点击处的坐标，然后遍历当前视图上的所有层，获取靠近点击处一定范围内的要素目标。具体代码如下：

```
Carto. IFeatureLayer pFLayer;
pFLayer = GetFeatureLayerByLayerID ( webmap, layerIDs. Element(i)); //设置查询过滤条件
Geodatabase. ISpatialFilter pSpatFlter = new Geoda -
tabase. SpatialFilter( );
pSpatFlter. Geometry = Ctype (pPoint, Geometry. IGeometry); //获得 FeatureCursor 游标
Geodatabase. IFeatureCursor pFeaCur;
pFeaCur = pFeatureClass. Search ( pSpatFlter, False); //返回查询目标的索引值
Geodatabase. IFields pFields;
pFields = pFeaCur. Fields;
```

index = pFields. FindFieldByAliasName (pField - Name); //用 DataTable 来装载查询结果的 Feature 信息

dataRow(0) = pFeature. Value(index). ToString();

4.2.2 地图搜索功能

用 IQueryFunctionality 接口实现根据指定条件搜索地图相关信息的功能，主要包括三个控件：显示结果的 TreeViewPlus、输入查询条件的 TextBox 和确认执行的 Button。根据输入的条件对指定的图层进行查询，然后结果显示在 TreeViewPlus 中，并在地图上高亮显示。

```
//对指定的图层进行查询，查询的结果保存为 DataTable
datatable = qfunc. Query(null, lids[0], spatialfilter);
TreeViewPlus1. Nodes. Clear();
if (datatable ! = null)
{System. Data. DataSet ds = new System. Data. DataSet();
ds. Tables. Add(datatable);
TreeViewPlus1. ShowClearAllButton = false;
//将结果绑定到 TreeViewPlus 控件上
TreeViewPlus1. BindToDataSet(ds);
TreeViewPlus1. Nodes[0]. Expanded = true;}
//查询结果高亮显示
……
ESRI. ArcGIS. ADF. Web. Display. Graphics. GraphicElement ge = null;
ge = new ESRI. ArcGIS. ADF. Web. Display. Graphics. GraphicElement ( geom, System. Drawing. Color. Yellow);
……
```

4.3 缓冲区分析功能

北京市高保护价值森林标准规定长城 500m 周围内森林及与该范围相交的所有小班的森林均为高保护价值森林[7]，并且对不同距离范围的森林采取各种保护经营措施。根据需求，该系统提供对指定点进行缓冲区查询，用户根据需要选择图层，再输入缓冲距离，利用工具 Buffer Tool 选定中心点就能得到一个相应的圆形缓冲区，并且显示缓冲区内的数据，如图 2。进而识别主体对邻近对象的辐射范围或影响程度，为分析或决策提供依据。

结 语

WebGIS 是一种全新的交互式、分布式和动态的地理信息系统，具有很多优点，并且应用广泛，是今后 GIS 发展的主要趋势之一。WebGIS 对于地域分布广、层次性强的森林资源管理信息系统的建立，具有极其重要的作用。ArcGIS Server 提供了一种基于 ArcGIS Server. NET ADF 和 ArcObjects 组件快速开发 Web 应用的方法

本文利用 ArcGIS Server 技术设计并实现了北京市长城地区高保护森林植被信息管理系统，对所涵盖的大量与森林资源相关的图表、文字和地理空间信息资源进行了有效集成，为用户提供各种林业信息的查询、检索和统计操作以及按不同用户要求输出相应的专题要素，为高保护森林的保护、预测、科学管理以及规划决策提供可靠依据；基于 Web 方式的信息

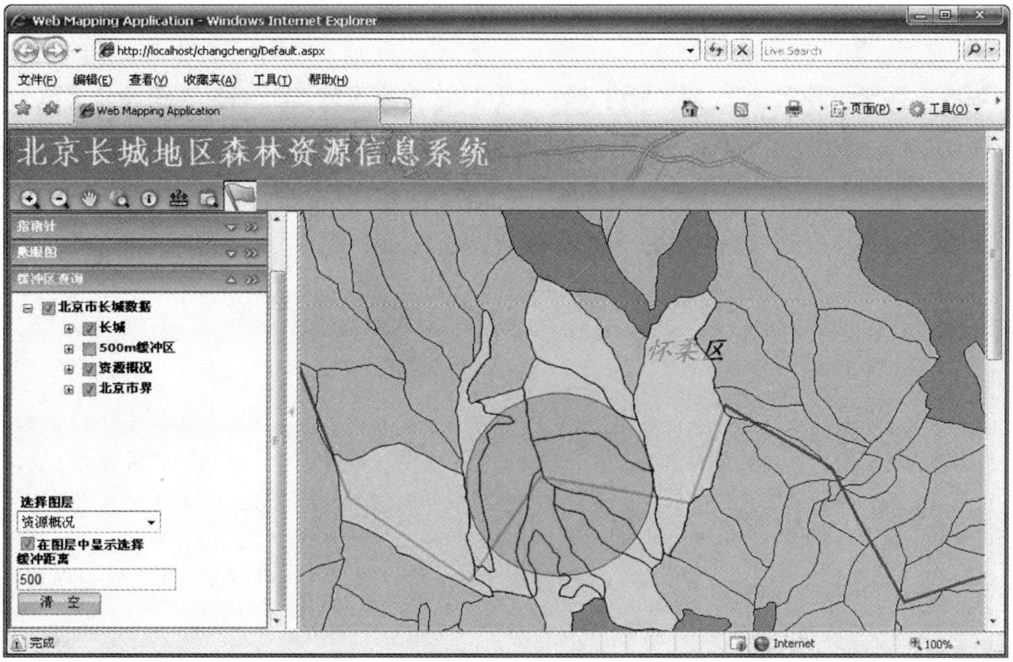

图 2　缓冲区分析

Fig2　Buffer analysis

检索脱离了 C/S 模式下桌面客户端的束缚，使用户对长城周围的高保护价值森林资源信息数据的操作和共享更加方便和快捷。

由于森林资源 WebGIS 的建设是一个庞大的工程，各种专业模型的开发、不同的数据的集成以及各种高级功能的开发，需要投入大量的人力和时间，由于时间和精力优先，本文只对实现的方法和关键技术进行了探讨，如何最大程度的挖掘 ArcGIS Server 的开发潜力，使现有的系统更加完备和方便用户使用是下一步的工作目标。

参考文献

[1]ESRI. ArcGIS9.2 系列产品介绍[M]. 北京：ESRI 中国(北京)有限公司，2006.

[2]朱政．通过．NetADF 开发和部署 ArcGIS Server 应用[R]. 北京，ESR I 中国(北京) 有限公司，中国，2004.

[3]沈百玲．ArcGIS Server 体系结构和开发简介[M]. 北京：ESRI 中国(北京)有限公司，2004.

[4]ArcGIS Server Administrator and Developer Guide[R]. ESRI Corp，2004.

[5]刘光，唐大仕．WebGIS 开发——ArcGIS Server 与．NET[M]. 北京：清华大学出版社．2009.

[6]孙永华，李小娟，尹连旺．基于 ArcSDE 和 SQL Server2000 洪水灾害信息数据库的设计研究[J]. 河北师范大学学报．2007，3(31)：400～402.

[7]邓华锋，王小平等．北京市高保护价值森林经营指南[M]. 北京：科学出版社，2010.

金沟岭林场杨桦次生林演替与天然更新研究

赵　娜[1]　刘东兰[1]　郑小贤[1]　高　祥[2]　徐　光[2]

（1. 北京林业大学省部共建森林培育与保护教育部重点实验室，北京，100083；
2. 吉林省汪清林业局，吉林汪清，133200）

摘要：森林更新是森林演替重要阶段，国内外对于更新的研究多局限于天然更新过程中各因子对于更新的影响及更新对环境产生的影响。本文利用金沟岭林场长期固定样地数据分析杨桦次生林演替和森林天然更新，得到以下结论：以先锋树种、伴生树种和顶级树种所占比例为依据划分演替阶段是一种划分次生林演替阶段可操作的新方法，随演替林分针阔比逐渐趋于7∶3，在演替中后期林分郁闭度为0.7～0.8时天然更新达到良好，建议在杨桦次生林经营过程中要保持适宜的郁闭度以促进林分天然更新。

关键词：金沟岭林场；杨桦次生林；演替；天然更新

Studies on Succession and Natural Regeneration of Secondary Forest in Jingouling forest farm

ZHAO na　LIU dong-lan　ZHENG xiao-xian

（The key Laboratory for Silviculture and Conservation of Ministry of Education，Beijing Forestry University，Beijing，100083）

Abstract：Forest regeneration process is an important research stage of forest succession，scholars of each country limited their study on impact of each factor and the impact on the environment during regeneration. This study use the data of long – term forest permanent plots to analysis and some result are achieved：it is a new way to classify the successional stage by the proportion of pioneer species，associated species and top species，the proportion of coniferous broad – leaved tends to a health level as 7∶3，the number of update is unsatisfactory. In the mid – successional and late successional canopy density were 0.8 and 0.7 update to achieve a good level，so we should promote update by changing forest canopy density.

Key words：Jingouling forest farm；Secondary forest；Succession；Natural regeneration

---

基金资助：林业公益性行业科研专项(20100400203)。

作者简介：赵娜(1989～)，女，河北保定人，在读硕士。E-mail：mandyhappy1989@yahoo.cn

通讯作者：郑小贤(1956～)，男，上海人，教授，研究方向为森林可持续经营。E-mail：zheng8355@bjfu.edu.cn

林分更新是森林经营一个重要过程，是森林生态系统经营研究中的主要领域之华[1~2]。天然更新是充分依靠自然的力量来实现森林生态环境自然恢复，不仅可培育出合乎自然规律的高生物多样性和高生态质量的森林，而且是一种低投入高产出的森林培育方式。[3]天然更新，就是依靠先前林地上的林木或者附近生长起来的林木作为母树，借助于风力和重力作用，自然下落的种子发芽生长恢复成林，或者由伐根萌芽，根系萌蘖来恢复森林[4]。天然林生态系统结构复杂，功能完善。但是由于过去我国一味片面的追求短期的经济效益，我国的天然林一度成为无限制采伐掠夺的对象，致使目前我国天然林中的原始林已经不复存在，留下大部分都是不同程度破坏的过伐林和天然次生林，天然更新对恢复和扩大森林资源与人工更新造林具有同等的效果和作用。有些人提倡以人工林来代替天然林，以解决我国木材供需矛盾，但是，国内外经验和实践都证明人工林是不稳定的，容易导致地力衰退和发生病虫害，而且天然更新范围广、面积大，在某种程度是上不用投资，依靠自然力量达到恢复森林的良好方式，因此，研究次生林的天然更新的研究就变得尤为重要。

关于天然更新，国内外进行过广泛的研究。不少研究是从更新树种的生物学特性、干扰与更新对策等方面进行研究与探索[5]。从 20 世纪 80 年代以来，国内很多学者都对天然林的人工更新进行了研究，但多数侧重于定性研究[6]。林分更新是一个复杂的生态学过程，是群落动态学的研究热点之一，因此也受到了国内外学者的重视，并且取得了很多重大的研究成果。近几十年，国内外生态学者对林分更新有大量的研究报道，研究内容大部分侧重于森林中各因子对于更新的影响及更新对环境产生的影响，其中对于林隙更新及郁闭度对更新影响的研究较多。大部分研究主要集中于利用林分某一阶段的数据进行分析，而利用森林更新的长期固定样地数据的研究分析仍然较少。

本研究通过对金沟岭地区次生林天然更新过程的调查研究，将次生林的更新划分演替阶段，分析数据了解在不同的演替阶段林分更新过程中不同郁闭度下更新数量、更新针阔比、树种组成及更新树种组成的变化，为次生林经营提供理论和方法依据。

1 研究区概况及研究方法

汪清林业局金沟岭林场位于吉林省汪清县境内东部山区，属低山丘陵，平均海拔 500 ~ 800m，平均坡度 10° ~25°左右，个别陡坡在 35°以上。[7]全区四面环山中间为河谷平地，属吉林省东部山区。本区属季风型气候，气温以 1 月份最低，平均在零下 30℃左右，7 月份最高，平均在 32℃左右。年降水量为 600 ~ 700mm，多集中在 7 月份。

本研究数据来自金沟岭林场 19 块长期固定样地，调查时间是 1987 ~ 2003 年，平均每两年调查一次。数据包括：样地的基本情况，如经纬度、海拔、坡度、坡向等；历次每木调查、立木空间位置调查、灌草调查以及天然更新调查等。

2 研究结果与分析

2.1 森林演替阶段的划分

本文以树种组成来划分研究对象的演替阶段，首先计算杨桦林主要乔木种的种间联结值，以此来判定演替过程中的先锋树种、伴生树种和顶级树种，然后依据林分组成中先锋树种、伴生树种和顶级树种所占比例来划分演替阶段。

以先锋树种白桦为参照树种，山杨、存在明显的正联结关系，因此将其确定为先锋树种；枫桦、紫椴、落叶松、水曲柳没有明显的联结关系，属于伴生树种；云杉、冷杉和红松存在明显的负联结关系，属于顶级树种。[8]

依据树种组成来划分演替阶段，先锋树种组成占优势的时期划分为演替初期(A 阶段)，伴生树种组成占优势的时期划分为演替中期(B 阶段)，顶级树种组成占优势的阶段划分为演替后期(C 阶段)。

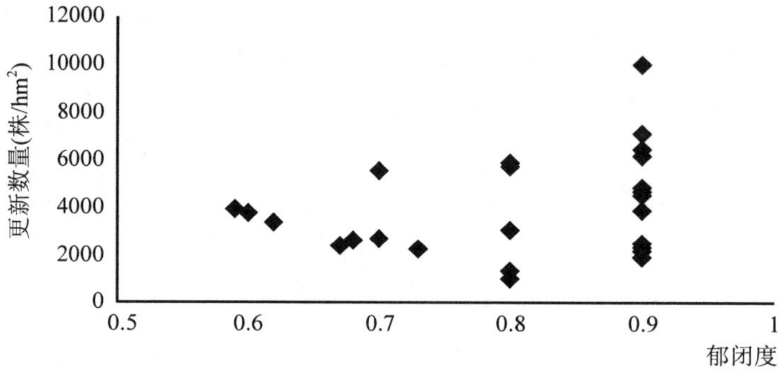

图 1　B 阶段林分更新数量

2.2　更新数量与郁闭度关系

由图 1 可知，更新的 B 阶段，在郁闭度为 0.6 时，林分的更新数量在 2367 ~ 3909 株/hm^2的范围内；在郁闭度为 0.7 时，森林更新数量在 2635 ~ 4525 株/hm^2的范围内；在郁闭度为 0.8 时，林分更新数量处在 938 ~ 5865 株/hm^2的范围内；在郁闭度为 0.9 时，林分更新数量在 1876 ~ 10000 株/hm^2的范围内。

不同的郁闭度下林分的更新数量变动较大，分别计算平均值，可以得到林分更新随着郁闭度的变化趋势，如图 2。

由图 2 可以看出：B 阶段林分更新数量均在 2000 株/hm^2以上。在郁闭度为 0.73 时，更新数量达到最低，郁闭度为 0.8 时，林分更新数达到最大值。

B 阶段的林分更新数量随着郁闭度的变化经历减—增—减—增的变化。

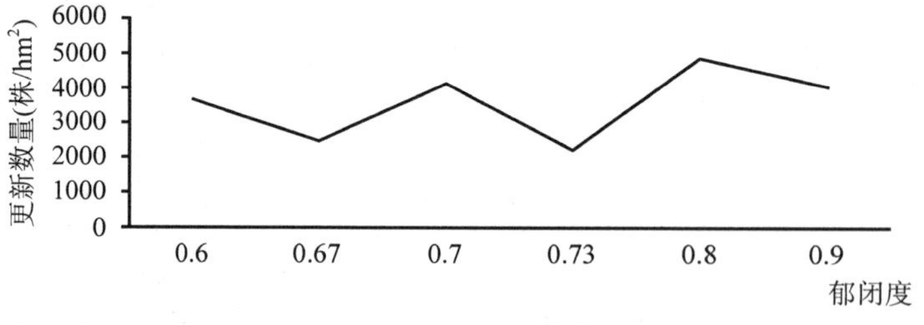

图 2　B 阶段林分更新数量变化

用同样的方法处理 C 阶段林分更新数据，可以得到图 3。

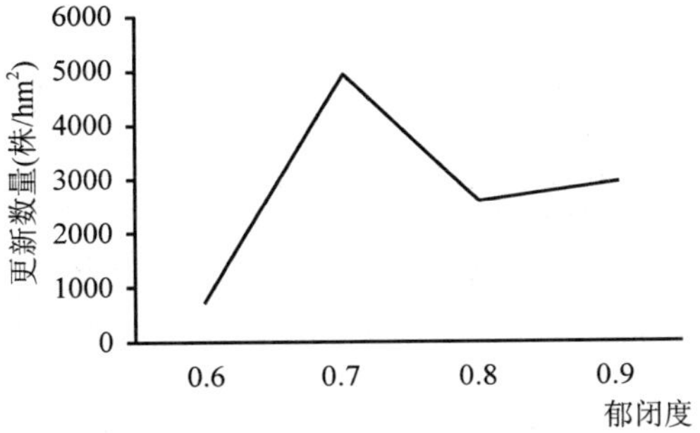

图 3　C 阶段不同郁闭度下更新数量

由图 3 可知，在 C 阶段随着郁闭度的增大林分的更新数量先增多后减少，在郁闭度为 0.7 时，更新数量达到最大值。

2.3　更新针阔比与郁闭度的关系

根据表 1 可以了解到，在 B 阶段的更新过程中，针叶树在更新树木中均占较大比例。在郁闭度 0.6 ~ 0.7 的范围内，针叶树占到了更新树种的 94.02% ~ 96.47%；在郁闭度 0.8 ~ 0.9 的范围内，针叶树在更新树种中所占比例下降为 80% 左右。虽然所占比例有所下降，但是仍然占更新树种中的较大比值。

表 1　B 阶段不同郁闭度下样地更新的针阔比例

郁闭度	针叶树比例(%)	阔叶树比例(%)
0.6	94.02	5.98
0.7	96.47	3.53
0.8	79.02	20.98
0.9	80.56	19.44

由表 2 可知，C 阶段的郁闭度的变化对林分更新针阔比有较大影响。在郁闭度为 0.6 时。针叶树种在更新中所占比例较小，仅为更新数量的 11.5%，而在郁闭度 0.7 ~ 0.9 的范围内，针叶树所占比例有所增加，占到了更新树种的 64% ~ 96%，但是不同郁闭下更新所占比例差别明显。

表 2　C 阶段更新中针叶树所占比例

郁闭度	针叶树比例(%)	阔叶树比例(%)
0.6	11.50	88.50
0.7	96.66	3.34
0.8	64.70	35.30
0.9	84.16	15.84

2.4　林分树种组成与更新树种组成

选择其中立地条件相同的 2 块样地，对不同年份的林分树种组成及更新树种组成进行整理，观察两者的变化。

表 3 中，更新的树种组成中，冷杉在更新树种中所占比例较大，针叶树更新比例随着郁闭度的增大逐渐变小；而林分的树种组成中，随着时间的推移，云杉、红松及冷杉等针叶树随着郁闭度的更加变化较小。

表3 1-1样地在1987、1992、2005年更新树种及林分的树种组成

	1987	1992	2005
郁闭度	0.6	0.7	0.9
更新树种组成(更新株数)	5冷杉+2红松+1云杉+1色木+0.5椴树+0.5枫桦	6冷杉+2红松+2云杉	4冷杉+3红松+1云杉+1椴树+1黄波罗
林分树种组成(断面积)	2云杉+2冷杉+2椴树+1枫桦+1色木+1红松+1杨树	2冷杉+2椴木+2桦木+1红松+1云杉+1色木+1杂木	2红松+2冷杉+2云杉+2椴木+1枫桦+1色木

表4中，更新树种组成中，冷杉作为主要树种，但所占更新比例有递减趋势。而云杉、冷杉及红松等针叶树种所占比例也呈递减趋势；林分的树种组成也有相同规律，随着郁闭度的增大，针叶树所占比例递减，但在林分组成中仍然占较大比例。

表4 1-2样地在1998、2002及2006年更新树种及林分的树种组成

	1998	2002	2006
郁闭度	0.7	0.8	0.9
更新树种组成(更新株数)	7冷杉+2云杉+1红松	6冷杉+2云杉+1红松+1色木	6冷杉+1红松+1云杉+1椴木+1色木
林分树种组成(断面积)	3云杉+3冷杉+2红松+1椴木+1色木	3云杉+3冷杉+1红松+1椴木+1枫桦+1色木	3云杉+3冷杉+1红松+1椴木+1枫桦+1色木

以针阔比作为评断指标。云杉、冷杉和红松作为针叶树种，枫桦、椴树、色木和杨树等是阔叶树种。样地1-1的针阔比变化是5∶5～4∶6～6∶4；样地1-2的针阔比变化为8∶2～7∶3～7∶3。更新树种针阔比的变化，样地1-1为8∶2～10∶0～8∶2；样地1-2为10∶0～9∶1～8∶2。在林分针阔比逐渐趋于稳定的时候，更新树种的针阔比也有一定的变化趋势，针叶树种所占比例逐渐减小。林分针阔混交比逐渐达到7∶3，通过阅读书中指标可以了解到样地所在林地在更新过程中针阔比的更新数量健康且合理。[10]

2.5 林分更新数量特征

图4为研究对象林下幼苗幼树更新情况，由图可知B阶段的更新在2500～4862株/hm^{2}的范围内，在郁闭度为0.8时，更新数量达到最高为4862株/hm^2。C阶段的更新数量处于748～4908株/hm^{2}的范围内，在郁闭度为0.7时，更新数量达到最大为4908株/hm^2。

通过更新数量了解森林的更新现状，可以使用乌吉斯古楞在研究长白山过伐林区云冷杉针叶混交林经营模式研究，依据“森林资源规划设计调查主要技术规定”中规定的天然更新等级标准制定的更新密度等级标准(表5)。

根据表5可以了解到，每公顷更新株数最多的为C阶段郁闭度为0.7时，其更新株数达到4908株/hm^2，更新等级属于中等，其余时期C阶段的更新数量均在中等水平以下，所以C阶段更新的平均水平处于不良。B阶段的更新数量虽然随着郁闭度增加差别较大，但是由图可知B阶段的更新数量大部分仍处于不良阶段，只有在郁闭度为0.8时，更新数量达到4862株/hm^{2}属于更新中等阶段。由此可知，大部分样地更新的平均水平处于不良阶段，应该对样地所在林地的更新施以适当的人工促进措施。

表 5 天然更新等级划分

等级	良 好	中 等	不 良
更新数量(株/hm^2)	>10000	4500 - 10000	<4500

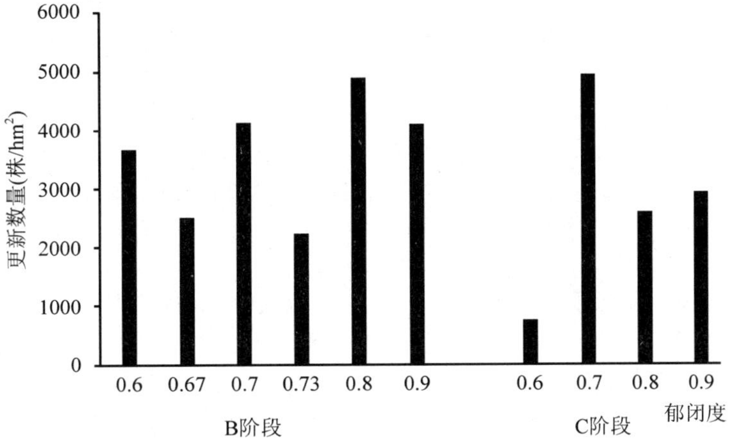

图 4 幼树更新情况

通过对样地数据的分析、汇总，了解到样地内更新数量并不理想，没有达到更新良好的标准，因此建议使用一些人工方法促进林分的天然更新。当下木盖度过大影响更新时，进行割灌。既促进了森林更新，又充分利用了山林副产品，增加药源而其枝干又可充作薪材。加强对幼苗的管护也是人工促进更新的重要措施。加强幼林的看管，防止动物的践踏；在幼木成活率低的情况下适当补植，保证幼林的保存率；适时进行抚育，避免杂草与幼数的水、肥、光的斗争影响幼树的生长。[11]间伐作为人工促进天然更新的最佳手段，在合适的情况下使用。

3 结 论

以金沟岭林场的长期固定样地为研究对象，通过整理 1987 ~ 2003 年的定期调查数据，将林分的更新过程以先锋树种、伴生树种及顶级树种所占比例为依据划分演替阶段，并分演替阶段研究了林分更新过程中郁闭度和针阔比对更新数量及更新针阔比例的影响，并且对更新现状进行评价。

(1)研究为今后森林更新的研究中演替阶段的划分提供了新的思路，通过先锋树种、伴生树种和顶级树种所占比例进行划分。

(2)随着林分天然更新，树种组成逐渐趋于稳定及合理的结构，针阔混交比逐渐达到 7:3，说明样地所在林地在更新过程中针阔比的更新数量合理。

(3)通过研究了解到演替中期(B 阶段)郁闭度为 0.8 时更新状况良好，演替末期(C 阶段)郁闭度为 0.7 时更新状况良好。林分的过疏过密都不利于林分的天然更新，因此应该人工改善林分郁闭度，促进林分天然更新。

参考文献

[1]韩有志，王政权．森林更新与空间异质性[J]．应用生态学报，2002，13(5)：615～619.

[2]金莹杉，翟明普，王超，等．北京西山风景林林下更新种空间分布特征研究[J]．西北林学院学报，2007，22(3) ：11～15.

[3] 任丽华，邹桂霞，李凤鸣．辽西油松林下幼树分布规律及其天然更新研究[J]．防护林科技，2010(1)，11～13.

[4] 李国猷．北方次生林经营[M]．北京：中国林业出版社，1992：120.

[5]韩有志，王政权．森林更新与空间异质性[J]．应用生态学报，2002，13(5)：615～619.

[6]林田苗．长白山云冷杉林生态采伐更新技术研究[D]．北京林业大学，2005.

[7]李婷婷，王俊峰，郑小贤．金沟岭林场主要森林类型林分更新比较研究[J]．林业资源管理，2006(3)，81～84.

[8]宁杨翠．长白山杨桦次生林健康经营模式[D]．北京林业大学，2011.

[9]乌吉斯古楞．长白山过伐林区云冷杉针叶混交林经营模式研究[D]．北京林业大学，2010.

[10]唐守正．东北天然林生态采伐更新技术指南[M]．北京：中国科学技术出版社，2006：43.

[11]胡楠，张恒月．宝天曼自然保护区锐齿栎林更新潜力研究[J]．南阳理工学院学报，2009，1(3)：78～80，113.

北京市延庆县集体林分地上部分生物量的研究

张晓璇

（北京林业大学信息学院，100083）

摘要：本文以北京市延庆县四海镇西沟里村集体林分作为研究对象，对其中5种落叶乔木(包括白桦、楸树、山杨、柞树、落叶松)进行野外调查，基于对标准地中标准木测定的生物量数据，以树木各测树因子为自变量建立了各树种单木生物量的估测模型，通过计算得出单位蓄积下的生物量，用以推算出整个林分乔木层生物量；同时对林下灌木层生物量采用直接收割法进行了测定。研究结果表明，该林分单木各分量生物量的最优模型形式均为CAR模型，各最优模型的变量主要为胸径(D)和树高(H)因子，D2H能够很好地反映树干的干重，胸径和树高能够很好地反映树枝、树叶及全树重的变化；该地区集体林分地上生物量总量为79032.947t。

关键词：北京延庆；四海镇；生物量；生物量估测模型

中图分类号：S757.2+4

Study on the Aboveground Biomass in Yanqing, Beijing

Abstract: In this paper, taking deciduous forest including 5 defoliation trees (White Birch, Catalpa bungei, Aspen, Oak tree, Larix) in Yanqing , Beijing as studying object and survey them and based on the the data of biomass from the sample trees in the plots, biomass predicting models of stem, branch, leaves of a single tree were formulated by using the measurement factors as independent variables. Basing on the biomass per uint accumulation can calculate the aboveground biomass of defoliation forest. , and the understory shrub biomass was be determined. The results showed that: the optimization biomass models of various components were CAR models and the best variables were diameter at breast height (D) and height (H) which indicated the changes of branch, leaves and total weight, and the combination of D and H (D^2H) showed the changes of dry weight of stem. The aboveground biomass is 79032.947t.

Key words: Yanqing, Beijing; biomass; the predicting model

生物量是指一个有机体或群落在一定时间内积累的有机质总量。森林生物量是森林生态系统的最基本数量特征，生物量数据是研究许多林业问题和生态问题的基础，是现代森林生态系统研究中的重要组成部分．对研究生态系统物质和能量的固定．消耗，分配．积累和转化有着重要意义[1]。生物量模型(biomass model)是确定森林生物量的主要方法，是一种有效并且相对准确的调查方法。生物量模型按照研究对象尺度不同分为：单木生物量模型、大尺度森林生物量模型。乔木层的生物量是森林群落生物量的最重要组成，对其的准确测定对于研究森林生长和森林生态系统的生产力具有重要作用[2]。目前测定乔木层生物量的方法很多，如：皆伐实测法、全枝法、随机抽样法、相关曲线法等，不同的方法各有其优缺点。本文主要使用全枝法测定乔木层生物量，直接收割法测定林下灌木层生物量及其相关指标并构建模型，从而推测整个林分的生物量。

1 研究区简介

研究区设在北京市延庆县，延庆县地处北京市西北部，距北京市区 74km，是首都北京的北大门。全县总面积 1992.5 km^2，其中山区占 72.8%，平原占 26.2%，水域占 1%。境内地形地貌多样，包括中低山、丘陵、平原、河谷等。年平均气温 8.5℃；多年平均降水量 470mm，最大年降水量 862 mm(1933 年)，汛期(6 ~ 9 月)，降水量占全年降水量的 70% 以上；相对湿度 57%，全年无霜期 165d，年平均风速 2.1 m/s，主导风向为西北风。土壤主要包括山地草甸土、棕壤、褐土、潮土和水稻土等 5 个土类。公路沿线多为耕地，少量为林地，山区林带较多[3]。

四海镇，平均海拔 700m，森林覆盖率 85%，为全国绿化百强乡镇之一，年降水 550 ~ 600mm，无霜期 150 天左右，属典型的大陆性季风气候。现辖区内有 18 个行政村，6 个自然村，总人口 7025 人，总面积 115.7km^2，其中基本农田面积 7342 亩，山场面积 142866 亩，林地面积 109316 亩，林果面积 21486 亩，村镇占地面积 3480 亩。

2 研究方法

2.1 标准地的选取与生物量的测定

2.1.1 乔木层生物量的测定

在北京市延庆县四海镇西沟里村的集体林分中，选择各树种不同年龄、不同立地和不同密度的林分中有代表性的林分，设置相应半径为 7.98m(注意斜距改算)，面积为 200m^2的圆形标准地 5 块，然后对标准地内的乔木层林木逐一进行每木检尺，测定胸径(精确到 0.1cm)和树高(精确到 1cm)，根据实测结果得出林分平均直径在 12cm 以上，则以 4cm 为一径阶距分径阶，同时计算各径阶的平均胸径、平均树高。在各径阶中，按照径阶中值进行分类，每个径阶范围内采伐 1 株标准木，即对应不同的径阶中值选择一棵标准木进行采伐，一共 15 株。同时采伐之前对树木进行树干以及树枝方向、树号等进行标记。将标准木伐倒后，实测标准木的树高、地径、胸径以及 1/4、1/2、3/4 和每整米处的直径，并测量带叶侧枝重、侧枝的鲜重(到三级)、叶鲜重，然后将所取林木的各器官样品在 85℃恒温下烘干至恒重，根据样品各器官的干重和鲜重，计算出含水率，进而计算出各器官绝干重，将各部分绝干重累积得到标准木单株总生物量。然后建立各器官生物量与其测树因子 D^2H 的回归模型，最后推算乔木层的生物量。标准木调查数据见表 1。

表 1　标准木调查数据

Tab. 1　The data of the sample trees

编号	树种	胸径(cm)	树高(m)	主干长度(m)	地径(cm)	树干 1/2 直径(cm)	树冠基径(cm)	散枝重量(kg)	干重
1	白桦	7.80	9.85	7.75	10.00	5.90	3.00		20.9
2	白桦	16.20	14.63	11.38	19.40	12.40	5.90	8.80	119.3
3	白桦	21.50	17.29	12.69	32.00	18.00	9.48	18.90	256.4
4	落叶松	9.85	11.60	8.97	12.35	8.00	4.10	6.25	38.55
5	落叶松	13.50	13.20	9.40	15.70	11.00	6.40	4.60	70.75
6	落叶松	17.80	13.39	9.65	24.00	13.50	7.00	12.90	123.3
7	楸树	10.65	10.88	7.93	14.65	8.00	5.40	2.85	5
8	楸树	14.65	13.67	9.04	17.70	8.45	6.20		65.65
9	楸树	17.80	15.20	10.20	23.00	16.90	6.30	4.25	143.75
10	山杨	7.95	7.87	5.27	9.40	7.50	4.70	0.40	12.25
11	山杨	14.88	12.20	8.80	16.00	12.00	5.45	2.25	70.05
12	山杨	18.00	13.00	9.00	26.00	17.00	6.20	6.30	126.95
13	柞树	7.40	7.10	4.10	10.00	6.80	4.00	1.55	11.85
14	柞树	10.89	9.47	7.22	14.20	9.10	5.42	2.80	46.2
15	柞树	18.50	9.67	7.37	23.50	15.80	7.40	6.50	123.3

2.2.2　林下灌木层生物量的测定

灌木生物量是灌木群落和生态系统研究的一个重要指标，到目前为止，灌木生物量的测定仍主要采用直接收割法，我们此次研究也是采用对样地内灌木样方进行全部割灌，进而测定重量等相关指标。

在选定各个树种的标准地内，使用罗盘仪设 3m × 3m 的样方各 4 个(分为密、中、疏、极疏四个等级)，共 20 块，分别测量每个样方内灌木丛数、每丛株数、东西冠幅、南北冠幅、丛高度等相关因子。待测量工作完成之后，对样方内的灌木进行全部割灌、装袋，在标记好后，称重存放，将样品烘干求得含水率，并计算干重。测量出样地灌木生物量，然后拟合灌木生物量模型，推算单位体积以及单位面积灌木生物量。

2.2　模型的建立

2.2.1　白桦，落叶松，楸树，山杨，柞树单木生物量模型

(1)模型的选择。相对生长模型是指用指数或对数关系反映林木各分量之间按比例协调增长的模型[4]。相对生长模型有 2 种：一种为相对生长系数为常量的模型(CAR 模型)，另一种为相对生长系数为变量的模型(VAR 模型)：

CAR(Constant Allometric Ratio)模型：$Y = aX^b$ 或 $\ln Y = \ln a + b\ln X$

VAR(Constant Allometric Ratio)模型：$Y = aX^b e^{cX}$ 或 $\ln Y = \ln a + b\ln X + cX$

这两种模型可用于林木各分量和总量的估计，自变量根据各分量的特点可选用不同的变量[5~7]。通过对模型参数的稳定性和模型的预估能力进行分析，CAR 模型不仅参数估计值稳定，而且预估能力强，考虑到实际可行性，本研究采用回归法的 CAR 模型进行拟合。

树干：

CAR(Constant Allometric Ratio)模型：$W_i = b_0 (D_i^2 H_i)^{b_1} + \varepsilon_i$

树枝、树叶：

CAR(Constant Allometric Ratio)模型：$W_i = b_0 (D_i)^{b_1} + \varepsilon_i$

上式中，W 为树干、树枝或树叶的重量；D 为胸径(1.3m 处直径)；H 为树高；ε 为误差；i = 第 1、2、3…n 株；e 为指数函数；b_0、b_1 为参数。

(2) 变量的设定和选取。关于立木生物量模型的建立，模型自变量可选用不同的变量，例如：D^2、D^2H、冠下径、冠幅、树冠体积、树冠表面积等。由于林分在生长过程中存在种内竞争，树冠对树叶、树枝生物量有一定的影响，其反映指标如冠幅、冠长在建立模型过程中有一定的贡献率，尤其在对树枝和树叶生物量的估计上，冠长的相关性要高于树高。但在实际建模过程中，经过多次的拟合和试验，胸径 D、树高 H 仍是生物量建模最主要的测树因子，对于 5 种树种来说也同样如此。因此，本研究以 D^2H 作为基本因子对生物量进行估测，采用 Spss 统计软件拟合出各树种单木生物量的最优估测模型。

2.2.2 林下灌木生物量模型

(1)模型的选择。根据国内外以往对生物量模型的研究来看，一般使用线性方程和非线性方程中的幂函数作为拟合模型的函数[8]，经比较 5 种林下灌木同样采用 CAR 模型。

灌木树枝、树叶生物量的最优模型为：$W = b_0 + b_1(D^2H) + b_2(D^2H)^2 + b_3(D^2H)^3$

(W 为树枝或树叶的重量；D 为冠幅直径；H 为树高；b_0、b_1、b_2、b_3为参数。)

根据实际测量的标准地中灌木的各项数据，采用 Spss 统计软件拟合出灌木生物量模型。

(2)变量的选择。对于模型变量的选择一般从 2 个方面考虑：一是易于测量，二是与因变量有紧密的相关关系为增强模型的实用性，应该实行简便为主的原则，尽量减少模型中的自变量。刘琪璟[9]在对灌木生物量的研究中发现，用单个测树因子来模拟生物量回归方程是不理想的，只有各个测树因子的适当组合才能比较准确地估算灌木生物量。D^2H、DH 以及 CH 组合建立的模型精度较高。这些因子组合的物理意义可近似认为：对 DH 可理解为树干纵断面周长，对 CH 可以理解为投影纵断面积，对 D^2H 可近似地理解为树干纵断面积。在影响灌木生物量的诸多因素中，冠幅直径 D 和高度 H 易于准确测量，是表达生物量的理想指标，因此也采用 D^2H 作为基本因子对林下灌木生物量进行估测。

3 结果与分析

3.1 5 种落叶乔木的单木生物量模型

本研究以胸径 D 和树高 H 的组合 D^2H 作为基本因子对生物量进行估测，采用 Spss 统计软件拟合出各树种单木生物量的最优估测模型，经不同模型的拟合和各指标的评价得出各树种各分量生物量最优估测模型见表 2。

表 2 各树种各分量生物量回归方程的拟合结果

Tab. 2 Biomass models of five kinds of trees

树种	生物量	模型	R^2(相关系数)	b_0的 Sig(标准误差)	b_1 的 Sig(标准误差)
白桦	树干	$W=0.218(D^2H)^{0.778}$	0.881	0.413	0.005
	树枝、叶	$W=0.027(D)^{2.776}$	0.905	0.443	0.004
落叶松	树干	$W=2.158(D^2H)^{0.455}$	0.949	0.065	0.001
	树枝、叶	$W=0.474(D)^{1.629}$	0.858	0.304	0.008
楸树	树干	$W=0.0053(D^2H)^{0.895}$	0.931	0.343	0.002
	树枝、叶	$W=0.018(D)^{3.037}$	0.824	0.612	0.012
山杨	树干	$W=0.09(D^2H)^{0.874}$	0.941	0.349	0.001
	树枝、叶	$W=0.001(D)^{3.927}$	0.925	0.520	0.002
柞树	树干	$W=0.038(D^2H)^{1.02}$	0.854	0.540	0.008
	树枝、叶	$W=0.018(D)^{2.955}$	0.921	0.403	0.002

利用各标准地随机抽取出的检验数据，对各树种各分量的生物量模型进行了模型预测效果的检验，经相关系数检验均达显著，可用方程估测林分的乔木层生物量。

3.2 林下灌木生物量模型

本研究以灌木高度 H，冠幅直径 D 的组合 D^2H 作为基本因子对林下灌木生物量进行估测，采用 Spss 统计软件拟合出各树种林下灌木生物量的最优估测模型见表 3。

表 3 各树种林下灌木生物量回归方程的拟合结果

Tab. 3 Biomass models of underground shrub

各树种林下灌木	模型	R^2(相关系数)	Sig(标准误差)
白桦	$W=2.22+2.137(D^2H)-0.571(D^2H)^2$	0.997	0.000
落叶松	$W=-1.657+9.999(D^2H)-3.501(D^2H)^2$	0.996	0.000
楸树	$W=-7.877+23.118(D^2H)-9.485(D^2H)^2$	0.978	0.003
山杨	$W=-2.319+11.062(D^2H)-2.785(D^2H)^2$	0.996	0.000
柞树	$W=-4.266+11.554(D^2H)-3.007(D^2H)^2$	0.998	0.000

利用各标准地随机抽取出的检验数据，对各树种灌木的生物量模型进行了模型预测效果的检验，可知总体上拟合率很高，平均相对误差也很低。该回归模型可以用于灌木生物量的估算。

3.3 生物量与蓄积间的关系

3.3.1 标准地蓄积的计算

依据外业调查获取的相关信息，标准地蓄积的计算采用平均断面积法以及中央断面积法计算得出，这是一种常用的有效的计算方法，采用两种方法计算将减小测量中的误差。首先用平均断面积法以及中央断面积法算出各标准木材积，然后通过公式 $f=\frac{V_{实测}}{g_{1.3}H}$ 求出相应形数，通过标准地实测数据求得各标准地蓄积。其中形数 f_1，蓄积 V_1 是用平均断面积法求出的，形数 f_2，蓄积 V_2 是用中央断面积法求出的(表 4)。

表 4 样地蓄积求算表

Tab. 4 The accumulation of five kinds of trees

树种	形数 f_1	形数 f_2	形数平均值	蓄积 V_1	蓄积 V_2	蓄积平均值
白桦	0. 530423	0. 478712	0. 504567	2. 50838	2. 27539	2. 38611
落叶松	0. 618445	0. 590481	0. 604463	1. 74268	1. 82521	1. 78394
楸树	0. 620595	0. 591336	0. 605966	3. 09583	2. 94987	3. 02285
山杨	1. 086199	1. 060926	1. 073563	5. 70641	5. 57363	5. 64002
柞树	0. 851962	0. 767295	0. 809628	3. 76625	3. 39196	3. 57911

3. 3. 2 乔木层生物量与蓄积间的关系

将标准地测得的 142 株树的胸径，树高数据分别带入各树种的生物量最优估测模型中得到该标准地生物总量，再结合算得的各标准地蓄积，最终求得生物量与蓄积、面积的关系(表 5)。

表 5 乔木层生物量与蓄积关系表

Tab. 5 The correlation between the biomass and the accumulation

树种	标准地面积 (m^2)	标准地蓄积 (m^3)	生物量 (kg)	每公顷重量 (kg/hm^2)	每公顷蓄积 (m^3/hm^2)	每立方米重量 (kg/m^3)
白桦	199. 9565	2. 38611	3292. 5699	164664. 3095	119. 3314822	1379. 88992
落叶松	199. 9565	1. 78394	2103. 7594	105210. 8534	89. 21658533	1179. 274604
楸树	199. 9565	3. 02285	1804. 64146	90251. 70275	151. 1755092	596. 9994957
山杨	199. 9565	5. 64002	3801. 51534	190117. 1175	282. 0623459	674. 0251588
柞树	199. 9565	3. 57911	3791. 6972	189626. 1037	178. 994303	1059. 397425

3. 3. 3 灌木层生物量与蓄积间的关系

将 20 块标准地测得的灌木东西冠幅 a、南北冠幅 b、从高度 c 分别代入公式 $V = \frac{1}{6 \times 3.14 \times a \times b \times c}$ 以椭球方式求出灌木体积，进而推算出单位面积和单位体积灌木生物量(表 6)。

表 6 灌木层生物量与蓄积关系表

Tab. 6 The correlation between the biomass and the accumulation

树种	标准地面积 (m^2)	标准地灌木体积 (m^3)	生物量 (kg)	每公顷重量 (kg/hm^2)	每立方米重量 (kg/m^3)
白桦林下灌木	9	4. 8332	2. 25	2500	0. 465529
落叶松林下灌木	9	4. 0129	2. 35025	2611. 389	0. 585679
楸树林下灌木	9	3. 2133	2. 8625	3180. 556	0. 89084
山杨林下灌木	9	5. 82313	3. 975	4416. 667	0. 682623
柞树林下灌木	9	4. 6530	2. 45025	2722. 5	0. 526592

4 结 论

由乔木层生物量与蓄积关系表5中的各树种每立方米重量乘以延庆县四海镇集体林分各树种的蓄积量即得出该地区各树种乔木生物量总量为：70912.104t；由灌木层生物量与蓄积关系表6中各树种林下灌木每公顷重量乘以延庆县四海镇集体林林分各树种林下灌木的面积即得到该地区各树种林下灌木层生物量总量为：8120.843t。该地区生物量总量为：79032.947t。

综合考虑白桦、落叶松、楸树、山杨、柞树各测树因子与林木各分量干重之间的回归方程拟合结果表明，延庆县四海镇地上部分总生物量树干、树枝、树叶生物量与胸径、树高之间存在密切线性相关，各最优模型的变量主要为胸径和树高因子，其他因子如冠长、冠幅等也可描述各分量生物量模型，但拟合效果不如以胸径和树高作为参数的模型，D^2H 能够很好地反映树干的干重、树枝、树叶及全树重的变化。在综合考虑各种评价指标的前提下，各分量所建立的最优模型形式均为CAR模型。

参考文献

[1]薛立，杨鹏．森林生物量研究综述[J]．福建林学院学报，2004，24(3)：283～288.

[2]胥辉，张会儒．林木生物量模型研究[M]．昆明：云南科技出版社，2002：1～2.

[3]陈敬贤．延庆山区公路边坡植物群落物种多样性特征[J]．中国水土保持，2010，(2)：3～5.

[4]张世利，刘健，余坤勇．基于SPSS相容性林分生物量非线性模型研究[J]．福建农林大学学报，2008，9：496～500.

[5]陈美高．不同年龄马尾松人工林生物量结构特征[J]．福建林学院学报，2006，26(4)：332～335.

[6] Schroeder P, Brown S, Mo J, et al. Biomass estimation for temperate broadleaf forests of the US using inventory data [J]. For. Sci., 1997, (43): 424～434.

[7] Cramer W, Kicklighter D W. Comparing global models of terres2 trial net primary productivity (NPP): overvlew and key results[J]. Global Change Biology, 1999, 5 (51): 1～15.

[8] Haase R. Haase P Above－ground biomass estimates for invasive trees and shrubs in the Pantanal of Mato Grosso, Brazil 1995.

[9]曾珍英，刘琪璟，曾慧卿．江西千烟洲几种灌木生物量模型的研究[J]．福建林业科技，2005(4).

不同坡位华北落叶松人工林生长规律研究

闫　菁　姜　涛[2]　原民龙[2]　于树峰[2]　黄选瑞[1]
（1. 河北农业大学 林学院，河北　保定　071000；
2. 河北省木兰围场国有林场管理局，河北 围场 068450）

摘要： 系统的了解和掌握林木生长规律，是科学合理经营森林的重要依据。本研究以河北省木兰围场国有林场管理局下属的孟滦林场的华北落叶松（*Larix principis – rupprechtii* Mayr.）为研究对象，采用空间代替时间的方法，借助 Excel 和 ForStat 统计分析软件，分析不同坡位华北落叶松树高、胸径以及材积变化规律，以掌握树木个体生长的基本规律。研究结果显示：华北落叶松各生长因子在生长过程中都会出现二次生长，树高和胸径的连年生长量在 10 年达最大值，而材积连年生长量在 20 年达最大值，在 25 年各因子同时出现二次生长。华北落叶松平均树高生长量最大为 0.7m，平均胸径生长量最大为 0.78cm，平均材积生长量为 0.00629m^3。

关键词： 华北落叶松；人工林；生长规律；坡位

Study on the Growth Laws of *Larix principis-rupprechtii* Mayr. Plantation about Different Location

YAN Jing　JIANG Tao　YUAN Ming-long　YU Shu-feng　HUANG Xuan – rui
（Forestry College of Agricultural University of Hebei, Baoding 071000, China;
Mu Lan State-owned Forest Farm in Hebei Province Authority, Weichang 068450, China）

Abstract: It is very important for scientific forestry management to understand and grasp the forest growth systematically. In this study, to research the *Larix principis-rupprechtii* Mayr. of MengLuan Forest Farm State – owned Forest Farm Bureau in HeiBei Province, use space instead of time method, with Excel and Forstat statistical analysis software analysis of the variation rule law of *Larix principis-rupprechtii* Mayr. height、DBH and stem volume under different slope, so as to master the basic law of growth of individual trees. The results of the study showed that: *Larix principis-rupprechtii* Mayr. growth factor in the growth process will be a secondary growth. Current annual increment of height and DBH reaches the maximum at 10 years, current annual increment of stem volume reaches the maximum at 20 years, at 25 years will be a secondary growth. It's average tree height growth up to 0.70m, the largest average DBH increment is 0.78cm, and average stem volume increment is 0.00629m^3.

Key words: *Larix principis-rupprechtii* Mayr.; plantations; growth rhythm; location

---

基金项目：国家公益专项（200804027）资助。

作者简介：闫菁（1988～），女，陕西宝鸡人，在读硕士研究生，主要从事森林可持续经营方面的研究。
通迅作者：黄选瑞（1962～），男，内蒙古人，教授。主要从事森林经营理论与技术研究。

在林学中，把一定间隔期内树木各种调查因子所发生的变化称为生长，变化的量称为生长量，林木生长规律是指林木生长发育随年龄变化的规律。林木生长量更能直观的反映林木的生长规律，并可以通过对林木现实生长状况的研究来科学预估其资源动态和发展趋势，因此，研究林木生长量不仅对掌握其生长发育规律，而且对制定相应的抚育管理措施有重要的现实意义[1~4]。树木生长主要取决于两个相反的方面，合成代谢(同化作用)及分解代谢(异化作用)。正是由于同化和异化作用的相互影响，是树木生长曲线呈现“S”形，这种“S”形曲线称为生长曲线。早在100多年前，Sacks(1873)就用“S”形曲线来描述树木的生长过程[5]。对树木个体生长进程的分析多沿用传统的树干解析的方法，分析树高、胸径和材积的动态变化过程，并对各测树因子进行预测。

华北落叶松是华北地区森林类型的主要优势树种，具有分布广、生长快、易成活、干形好等特点。也是燕山山地分布最广、蓄积量最大的主要森林生态树种，对燕山山地水源涵养、水土保持，以及林区生态系统的形成与维护发挥着不可代替的作用。近年来，国内对华北落叶松生长规律的研究逐渐增加，但其系统性并不是很高。本文以30年生的华北落叶松为研究对象，深入展开对各生长指标(树高、胸径、材积)之间的变化规律进行分析，比较不同坡位各因子的连生长量和平均生长量之间的差异，揭示其动态生长规律，可以为华北落叶松森林生态系统结构和功能的长期动态监测提供基础数据，可以为森林经营管理技术体系提供理论依据，对揭示森林碳汇和温室气体的关系有重要的意义。

1 研究区概况

研究区位于河北省木兰围场国有林场管理局下属的孟滦林场，地理坐标为116°32′~118°14′E，41°35′~42°40′N，地势西北高，东南低，海拔在820~1850m，冬季多西北风，夏季多东南风，属寒温带大陆性季风气候。年平均降雨量440mm，最低气温-39℃，最高气温35℃，年平均气温3.1℃，大于10℃积温21200℃，无霜期106s，初霜始9月中旬，晚霜终于5月上旬。全林区多为棕色森林土，并覆有10cm厚腐殖质层，主要分布在林分中，植物区系为东北区系、内蒙古区系和华北区系的交汇带，植被类型包括落叶针叶林、常绿针叶林、针阔叶混交林、阔叶林、灌丛或灌草丛、草原与草甸、沼泽及水生群落。乔木树种主要有华北落叶松(*Larix principis-rupprechtii* Mayr.)、油松(*Pinue tabulae formis* Carr.)、云杉(*Picea asperata* Mast.)、白桦(*Betula platyphylla* Suk.)、山杨(*Pobulus davidiana* Dode.)、柞(*Quercus* L.)、榆(*Ulmus pumila* L.)等。

2 研究方法

2.1 样地选择

采用空间代替时间的样地调查方法，于2009年7~8月份，在承德木兰林管局下属的孟滦林场进行调查。样地大小为20 m×30 m，选好样地后，对样地内的林木进行每木检尺，采用望高法测量部分树高。采用等断面积径级法确定标准木[6]；样地内，将林木划分为三级，即优势木、平均木和被压木，对每一级的单株木进行树干解析。而本文只对所选取的平均木进行分析，总共有12块样地，主要对生长在坡上、坡中和坡下的30年华北落叶松进行研究。样地基本情况见表1。

表 1 所选样地基本情况表

Tab. 1 General situation of selective plot

项目 Aspect	年龄(年) Age	郁闭度 Canopy density	密度(株/hm^2) Density	海拔(m) Altitude	胸径(cm) DBH	树高(m) Height	立地条件 Site condition
样地概况	4 ~ 30	0.5 ~ 0.8	675 ~ 5350	1350 ~ 1938	2.40 ~ 16.45	1.90 ~ 15.58	中

2.2 数据处理

采用标准地法与标准木树干解析法，对样地内标准木进行树干解析，按区分段截取圆盘，在室内测定各年轮宽度，以树干解析的内业数据，通过 Forstat[7] 统计之林软件“测树学”中的树干解析功能，分析过程主要有以下三个步骤：第一步是把树干解析内业数据在 Forstat 软件中打开；第二步选择主菜单中的“测树学/树干解析 I，II 型”，系统会弹出“树干解析”对话框，供用户选择需要分析的数据及分析方法；第三步系统给出计算分析的结果，以图表的形式显示在输出窗口。结果包括：总生长量，平均生长量，连年生长量等，并输出树干纵断面图，计算得出树高、胸径及单株材积的总生长量和年生长量。

3 结果分析

通过对孟滦林场不同坡位的 30 年生华北落叶松人工林内所选取的平均木进行树干解析，将解析木的树高、胸径和材积数据分别进行平均处理，并通过 Forstat 统计之林软件“测树学”中的树干解析功能，计算出各自平均木的生长率，得到各自平均木树干生长过程总表(表 2)。

表 2 30 年生树干生长过程表

Tab. 2 The growth process of 30 years stem

坡位 Location 及年龄 and Age		树高 Heigh(m)			胸径 DBH(cm)			材积 volume(m^3)		
		总生长量 Cumulate increment	平均生长量 Mean annual increment	连年生长量 Current annual increment	总生长量 Cumulate increment	平均生长量 Mean annual increment	连年生长量 Current annual increment	总生长量 Cumulate increment	平均生长量 Mean annual increment	连年生长量 Current annual increment
上坡	5	2.51	0.50	0.50	1.40	0.28	0.28	0.00067	0.00013	0.00013
	10	7.43	0.74	0.98	7.10	0.71	1.14	0.01751	0.00175	0.00337
	15	10.76	0.72	0.67	11.45	0.76	0.87	0.06125	0.00408	0.00875
	20	13.26	0.66	0.50	14.15	0.71	0.54	0.11420	0.00571	0.01059
	25	14.27	0.57	0.20	15.55	0.62	0.28	0.15201	0.00608	0.00756
	30	15.58	0.54	0.33	16.45	0.57	0.23	0.18243	0.00629	0.00761
中坡	5	1.81	0.36	0.36	0.40	0.08	0.08	0.00026	0.00005	0.00005
	10	6.62	0.66	0.96	4.15	0.42	0.75	0.00649	0.00065	0.00125
	15	9.26	0.62	0.53	7.10	0.47	0.59	0.02383	0.00159	0.00347
	20	10.97	0.54	0.34	9.45	0.47	0.47	0.04567	0.00228	0.00437
	25	11.85	0.47	0.18	10.70	0.43	0.25	0.06032	0.00241	0.00293
	30	12.93	0.43	0.22	12.45	0.42	0.35	0.08578	0.00286	0.00509
下坡	5	2.35	0.47	0.47	1.35	0.27	0.27	0.00059	0.00012	0.00012
	10	7.04	0.70	0.94	7.35	0.73	1.20	0.01514	0.00151	0.00291
	15	9.48	0.63	0.49	11.70	0.78	0.87	0.04859	0.00324	0.00669
	20	11.77	0.59	0.46	13.90	0.70	0.44	0.09272	0.00464	0.00883
	25	12.72	0.51	0.19	15.20	0.61	0.26	0.11630	0.00465	0.00472
	30	13.60	0.47	0.22	16.05	0.55	0.21	0.13876	0.00479	0.00561

3.1　华北落叶松树高生长规律

3.1.1　树高生长过程分析

由树高生长过程曲线与散点图(图1)可知，华北落叶松在20年间生长迅速，在20年之后高生长稳步上升。不同坡位的树高生长曲线基本一致，没有太大差异，但是坡上由于郁闭度小而且林分采光了能力较强，因此总的树高生长量要大于中坡和下坡的华北落叶松树高生长量。

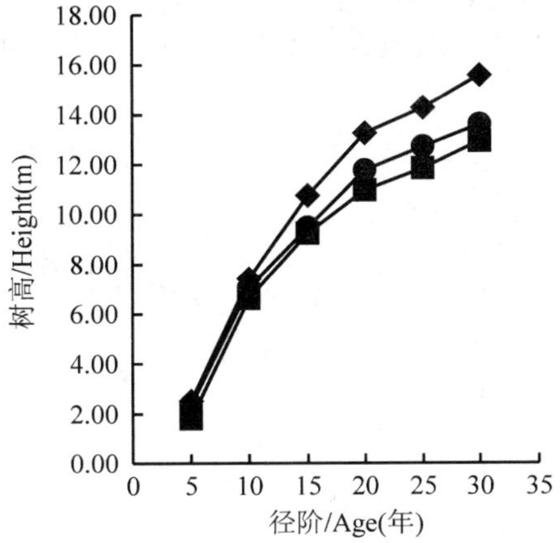

图1　树高生长过程曲线与散点图

Fig. 1　Growth curve and spots of Height

—◆—坡上；—■—坡中；—●—坡下；

—◆—upslope；—■—mesoslope；—●—downslope

3.1.2　树高连年生长与平均生长分析

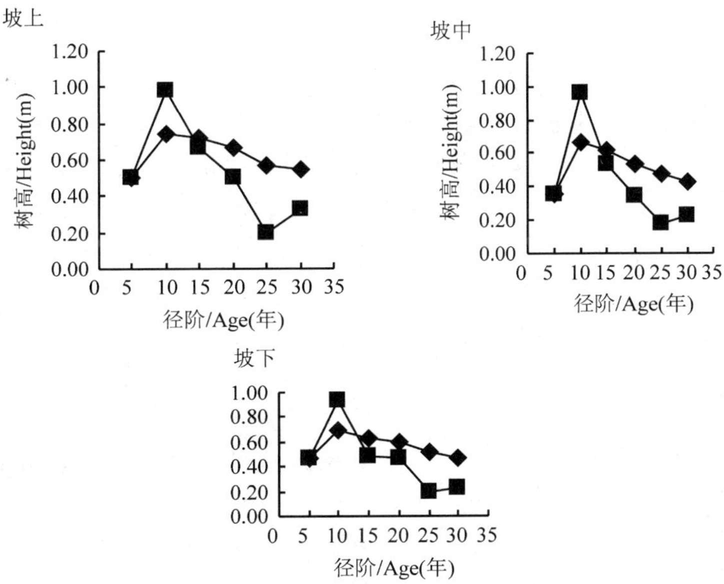

图2　树高连年生长与平均生长曲线

Fig. 2　Current annual height growth curve and mean annual height growth curve

—■—为连年生长量；—◆—为平均生长量；—■—Current annual increment；

—◆—Mean annual increment

图2分别显示出，华北落叶松在不同坡位下的高生长过程，均接近二次曲线，呈偏态分布的增长方式，前期的连年生长量均高于后期。从连年生长量看，三种不同坡位的林木树高生长速生期都出现在5～10年生期间，而在同一时间段内，坡上和坡中的连年生长量要大于坡下的连年生长量，10～25年生期间，坡上和坡中的连年生长量迅速下降，而坡下的比较稳定，呈现出稳定的下降趋势，主要是由于坡下环境条件比较稳定，25年之后连年生长量又都有所增加，但是增长缓慢。连年生长量在15年后总体小于平均生长量，生长速度都有下降。不同坡位平均生长量的变化幅度较连年生长量小一些，进入高生长高峰期的时间也基本一致。

3.2　华北落叶松胸径生长规律

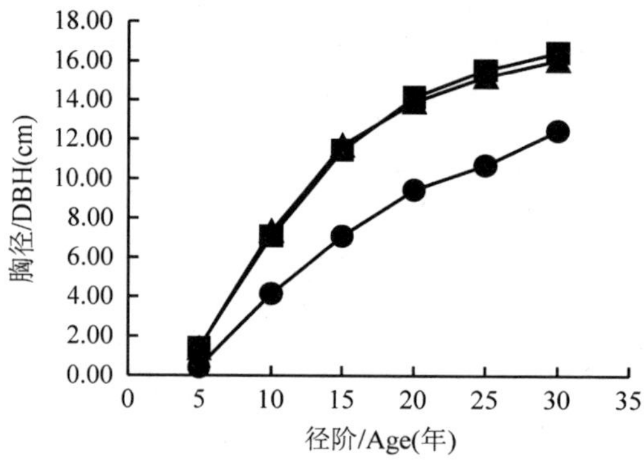

图3　胸径生长过程曲线与散点图

Fig. 3　Growth curve and spots of DBH

—■—坡上；—●—坡中；—▲—坡下；—■—upslope；—●—mesoslope；—▲—downslope

3.2.1　胸径生长过程分析

从图3可以看出，30年生的华北落叶松胸径总生长量达16.45cm。胸径总生长量在幼苗阶段非常缓慢，5年以后胸径总生长量迅速增加，20年慢慢趋于平缓。由图上可以看出，坡上和坡下的胸径总生长量基本一致，而坡中同一时间的胸径生长量都低于坡上和坡下，主要是由于中坡的草本生长比较茂盛，与华北落叶松争夺养分最激烈，华北落叶松生长缓慢。

3.2.2　胸径连年生长和平均生长分析

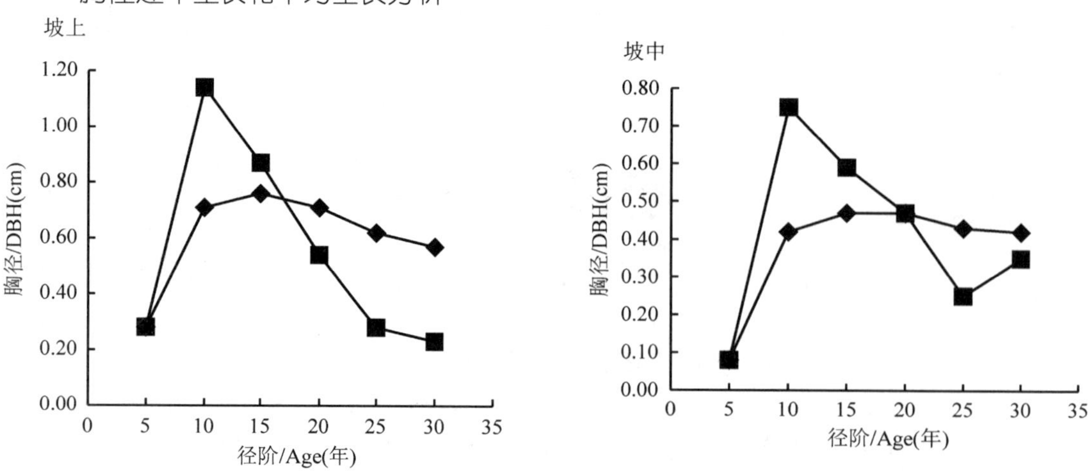

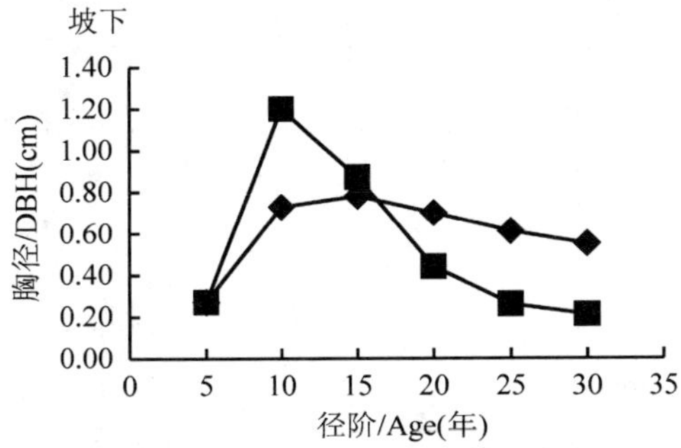

图 4　胸径连年长与平均生长曲线

Fig. 4　Current annual breast diameter growth curve and mean annual redial growth curve

—■—为连年生长量；—◆—为平均生长量；—■—Current annual increment；

—◆—Mean annual increment

由图 4 所示，不同坡位林木的胸径连年生长曲线均接近二次曲线，呈偏正态分布，说明华北落叶松前期的胸径生长逐年加快，后期逐年减缓，10 年胸径生长出现高峰值，之后连年生长量逐年下降。平均生长量曲线较平滑，说明林木的生长环境条件在较长的时期内是较稳定的，而连年生长量表现出较大的波动性，出现这种情况的原因可能是由该地区年际间环境的变化，尤其是水热条件的变化和激烈的种内竞争造成的。降水和温度在年际间的变化，必然会影响到林木的生长量。

从胸径连年生长量和平均生长量来看，坡上和坡下的胸径最高连年生长量都超过了 1.20cm，而坡下的只有 0.7cm，主要是由于林分中水热条件的变化和激烈的种内竞争造成的。研究地区的降水和温度在年际间的变化，必然会影响到华北落叶松的生长量。

3.3　华北落叶松材积生长规律

3.3.1　材积生长过程分析

从图 5 可以看出，不通坡位上的华北落叶松的材积生长曲线基本上都呈“S”曲线，即材

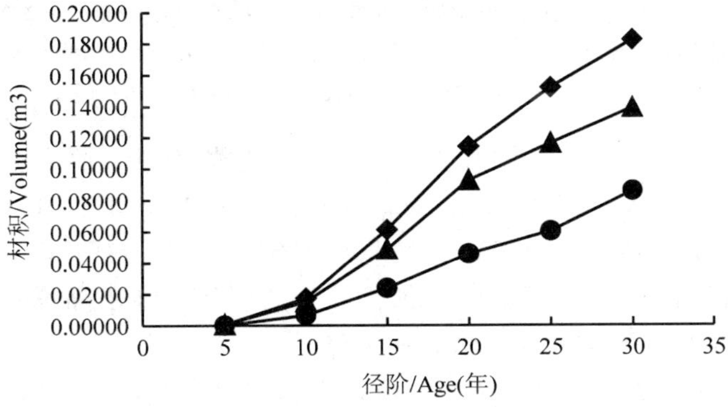

图 5　材积生长过程曲线与散点图

Fig. 5　Growth curve and spots of stem volume

—◆—坡上；—●—坡中；—▲—坡下；；—◆—upslope；

—●—mesoslope；—▲—downslope

积生长为"慢-快-慢"的生长模式。在最初的5~10年材积生长非常缓慢，之后材积迅速增长，随着年龄的增长，材积增长的种内差别较大，这个主要是由于立地条件以及林分的郁闭程度的差异所引起的。总体来说，坡上的材积生长要大于坡下和坡中，主要是由于上坡有有利于华北落叶松生长的光热条件。

3.3.2 材积连年生长量和平均生长量分析

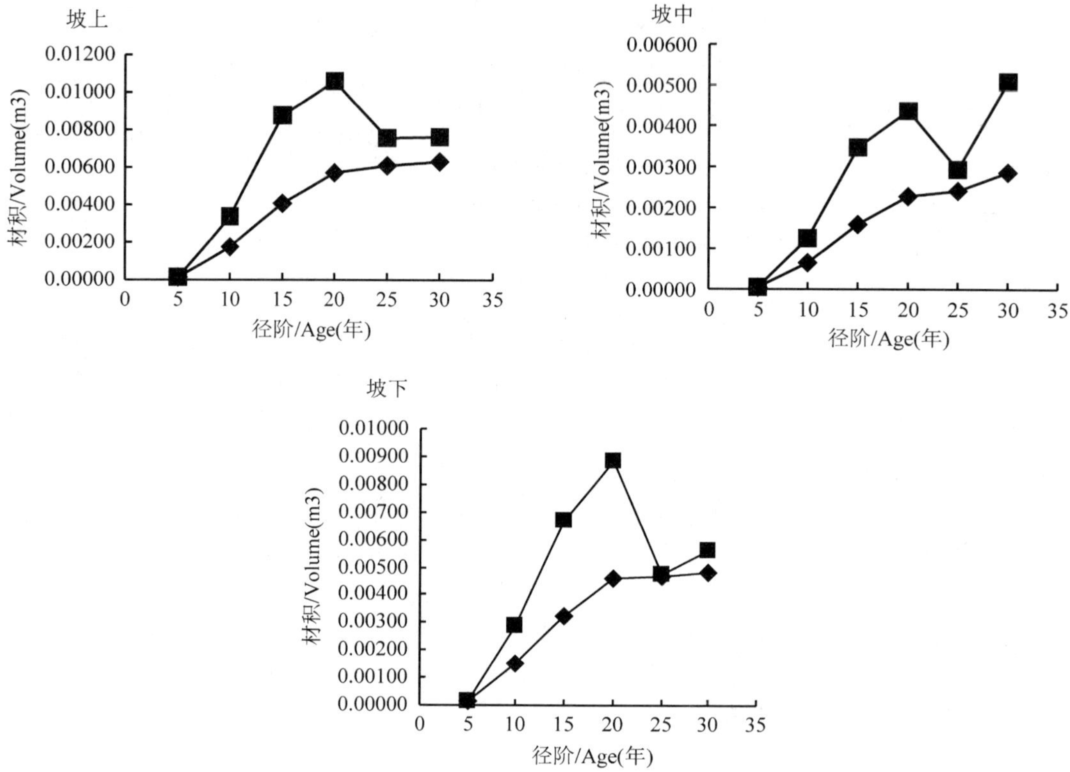

图6 材积连年生长与平均生长曲线

Fig. 6 Current annual stem volume growth curve and mean annual growth curve

—■—为连年生长量；—◆—为平均生长量；—■—Current annual increment；

—◆—Mean annual increment

树木材积连年生长量随树龄的增长而表现出一定的规律性。同一树种在不同的生长地区，其增长规律也不同。从图6可以看出，华北落叶松在20年时连年生长量达到最大，之后逐渐下降，25年之后，坡上华北落叶松的材积连年生长量趋于平稳，而坡中和坡下的材积生长量都有所增加。随着林分年龄的增加，林分的郁闭度在不断增加，种内竞争非常激烈，因此在20~25年材积的连年生长量有所下降。

造成以上这些情况的原因可能是由年际间环境的变化，尤其是水热条件的变化和激烈的种内竞争造成的。调查地区的降水和温度在年际间的变化，必然会影响到华北落叶松的生长量。密度制约学派关于种群调节的理论认为，密度增大，植物种对可利用资源的竞争加剧，会影响到树木树高和直径的生长；密度增加到一定程度后，群落通过自然稀疏来保持群落的合理密度。群落达到郁闭，种内竞争激烈，直径的生长受到抑制，开始出现自然稀疏的现象，此时应及时采取人为稀疏的经营措施，随着密度的降低，华北落叶松的树高、胸径和材积的生长量就又加快，直到出现第二个高峰，树高、胸径和材积的连年生长量的这种波动过程将伴随着华北落叶松的整个生命周期[8]。

4 结论与讨论

(1)本研究的结果表明，华北落叶松人工林的高生长过程均接近二次曲线，呈偏态分布的增长方式，前期连年生长量和平均生长量均高于后期。连年生长量在15年后总体小于平均生长量，生长速度都有下降。不同坡位平均生长量的变化幅度较连年生长量小一些，进入高生长高峰期的时间也基本一致。华北落叶松的平均树高生长量最大为0.7m。

(2)林木胸径生长既受立地条件影响，又与林分密度结构有密切关系。在相同立地条件下，胸径生长节律常常反映出林分密度适宜程度的大小[9]。Schrnitt等[10]曾指出，一个树种在不同立地上的各生长指标之间的变化规律区别可能并不大，除非是立地条件优劣差异很大。本文研究显示：在立地条件基本一致的情况下，坡上和坡下的胸径生长量均大于坡中的，这种结果是由于林分密度过大，以及林分内的光热条件所引起的。

(3)树木材积连年生长量随树龄的增长而表现出一定的规律性。同一树种在不同的生长地区，其增长规律也不同。连年生长量在20年达到最大值，平均材积生长量最大为$0.00629m^3$，材积生长高峰期为18～24年。

(4)华北落叶松的胸径、树高和材积总生生长量随着林龄的增大而持续上升。连年生长量和平均生长量在起始阶段随着林龄的增加而增加，但连年生长量比平均生长量增加速度快，其值大于平均生长量。连年生长量达到最高峰的时间比平均生长量要早，连年生长量达到高峰后逐渐下降与平均生长量相交，相交后，连年生长量总小于平均生长量。胸径的连年生长量高峰比树高连年生长量高峰更为持久。胸径、树高和材积的连年增长量表现出明显的波动性。

参考文献

[1]杨长职．福建青冈天然林生长规律的研究[J]．华东森林经理，2005，19(3)：29～33.

[2]郭文福，蔡道雄，贾宏炎，等．米老排人工林生长规律的研究[J]．林业科学研究，2006，19(5)：585～589.

[3]刘春延．塞罕坝地区华北落叶松人工林土壤水肥变化规律的研究[J]．河北林果研究，2009，24(1)：38～40，50.

[4]杨玉盛．不同栽植代数29年实生杉木生长规律的研究[J]．林业科学，1999，35(1)：52～56.

[5]刘丽华．桦树天然林生长发育规律的研究[D]．保定：河北农业大学，2002.

[6]白云庆，郝文康等．测树学[M]．哈尔滨：东北林业大学出版社，1988.

[7]唐守正，郎奎建，李海奎．统计和生物数学模型计算[M]．北京：科学出版社，2008：291～293.

[8]杜彦超．燕山山地华北落叶松林群落特征及其生产力研究[D]．保定：河北农业大学，2007.

[9]栾士波，范玉清，周希利，等．天然杨桦林生长规律的研究[J]．吉林林业科技，1999(2)：3～8.

[10]Schmitt，M. D. C. Generalized Biomass Estimation Equation For Betula Papyrifera Marsh[J]. Can. J. For. Res.，1981，(11)：837～840.

长沙市城市森林社会功能与城市梯度相关分析

周晓芳　　吕　勇

（中南林业科技大学，长沙，410004）

摘要：构建城市梯度综合指数，对长沙市进行梯度评价。利用城市梯度得分，对长沙市进行梯度分区。选取居民对城市森林的利用、对城市森林和社区的总体满意程度以及对城市森林提供生态服务和社会服务的认知等三个指标构建长沙市城市森林社会功能评价模型。在此基础上，对城市森林社会功能总体水平以及各指标因子与城市梯度进行相关分析。

关键词：城市森林；社会功能；城市梯度；相关分析

Correlation Analysis between Social Function of the Urban Forest and Urban Gradient in Changsha

Abstract: A composite urban gradient was created to analyze the city Changsha. The gradient intervals were divided on the basis of the gradient score. Direct use, general satisfaction with forests and the neighborhood, and the perceived role of the forest in providing ecological and social services were selected to estimate the social functionality of urban forests. correlation analyses between the general social function and every determinant and urban gradient were conducted.

Key words: urban forest; social function; urban gradient; correlation analysis

随着城市化进程的不断发展，人们逐渐认识到环境、经济和社会之间的复杂关系，并对自然环境的多功能作用，如城市保健、公共福利和生活质量等产生了更深刻的理解。城市森林是这种自然环境的重要组成部分，这种功能性绿色基础设施能够提供许多不同的社会效益并为社会各个层面服务[1]。同时，人们对城市林地和其他绿地在促进个人发展、健康生活、社会凝聚力和创造可持续社区等方面的重要性也日益达成共识[2]。

对城市森林而言将其社会功能放在首位是必要的，良好的城市森林是支撑城市生活的基础，能够使城市发展成为适宜人们生活、工作、休闲的可持续的场所[3]。通过向人们在附近提供丰富而又高质量的生存空间，创造一种能让城市社会中不同阶层的人们共享的社会价

作者简介：周晓芳(1974～)，女，湖南常德人，在读博士生，讲师，主要城市林业规划与管理的教学与科研工作。e－mail：mtrzeng@163.com；电话：13975884635

吕勇(1965～)，男，湖北崇阳人，教授、博士生导师，主要从事森林资源经营管理的教学和科研工作。

值。然而，同一城市中不同梯度位置的城市森林所能提供的社会效益存在差异，同时，人们对城市森林社会效益的需求也不同。分析不同城市梯度的社会效益，对城市森林及绿地的规划与管理具有现实的意义。

1 研究背景与研究方法

1.1 自然概况

长沙市位于长江以南地区，湖南省的东部偏北。地处洞庭湖平原南端向湘中丘陵盆地过渡地带。总面积为 11819km^2。天然林为常绿阔叶林，但破坏严重。人工林以国外松、马尾松、杉木、油茶为主，生长较好，总体上绿化水平较高[4]。2011 年，长沙市国土总面积为 11819km^2，其中林业用地 62.06 万 hm^2，占土地总面积的 52.47%，非林业用地 56.22 万 hm^2，占土地总面积的 47.53%，森林覆盖率为 53.25%。城市建成区绿化覆盖率为 42.21%，人均公共绿地面积为 18.8m^2。

1.2 研究区域与调查样点的选择

由于影响城市森林社会功能的因素，不仅包括城市森林等自然因子，还包括人口密度等社会因子，因此，本文选择长沙市主城区范围内的芙蓉区、雨花区、天心区、开福区、岳麓区与周边的星沙、暮云及望城等为研究区域。在研究区域中，按照随机性、独立性、连续性代表性、正确性等原则进行抽样，样点共计 1659 个。

1.3 梯度分析方法

1.3.1 数据来源

城市梯度的分析是以 2007 年长沙市卫星遥感影像图为底图，利用 ArcGIS 软件，将调查样点标注在相应的位置，可以获得离样点最近林地的距离，以及该林地的规模。研究区域内最大的林地面积大于 50km^2，本文没有将最大林地的数据计算在内，而是将这个林地的有效面积调整为 10km^2，这是研究区域范围内第二大林地面积的两倍，目的是为了合理调整梯度中不同规模林地的分布。因为城镇化程度较高地区的林地规模往往较小，如将较大林地的数据计算在内将掩盖小规模林地。除了计算最近林地的距离和规模外，还需计算距指定点 500m 范围内的森林覆盖率和人口密度，以评估当地社区的环境特征。森林覆盖率的计算采用底图中森林资源数据，而人口密度的计算采用 2010 年长沙市统计数据。

1.3.2 梯度分析模型的构建与参数估计

梯度分析常用来描述不同事物发展水平的差异。它可以提供一些简单参数来描述不同区域发展水平的差异[5]。本文的主要目的是了解长沙市城市森林社会功能效益的梯度变化以及可能的影响因子，所以选取了最近林地的规模，最近林地的距离，500m 范围内的森林覆盖率以及 500m 范围内的人口密度等四个指标，以构建一个城市梯度综合指数。即：

$$GS = a_0 + a_1 S + a_2 D + a_3 F + a_4 P + \varepsilon$$

式中，GS 为城市梯度向量；S 为最近林地的规模矩阵；D 为最近林地的距离矩阵；F 为 500m 范围内的森林覆盖率矩阵；P 为 500m 范围内的人口密度矩阵；a_0，为常数；a_1，a_2，a_3 与 a_4 为回归系数矩阵；ε 为误差项向量。

对上述四个梯度评价指标进行主成分分析以建立一个复合的城市梯度评分指标。其相关系数矩阵 R 的特征值和累积贡献率及各梯度变量在各主成分上的载荷见表 1，表 2。由表 1 可知，第一，第二主成分的累计贡献率已达 90.52%，故只需求出第一，第二主成分 z_1，z_2

即可。由此可得到长沙市城市梯度模型，即：

$$CS = 0.377S - 0.378D + 0.457F - 0.447P$$

表 1 特征值及方差贡献率和累计贡献率

Tab. 1 Total variance explained

主成分 Components	特征值 Eigenvalues	贡献率/Variance(%)	累计贡献率 Cumulative(%)
1	6.522	67.23	67.23
2	2.259	23.29	90.52
3	0.626	6.45	96.97
4	0.293	3.03	100.00

表 2 主成分 z_1，z_2 载荷矩阵

Tab. 2 Component matrix

变量 Variances	z_1	z_2
S	0.75	−0.36
D	0.43	−0.93
F	0.91	−0.11
P	−0.89	0.17

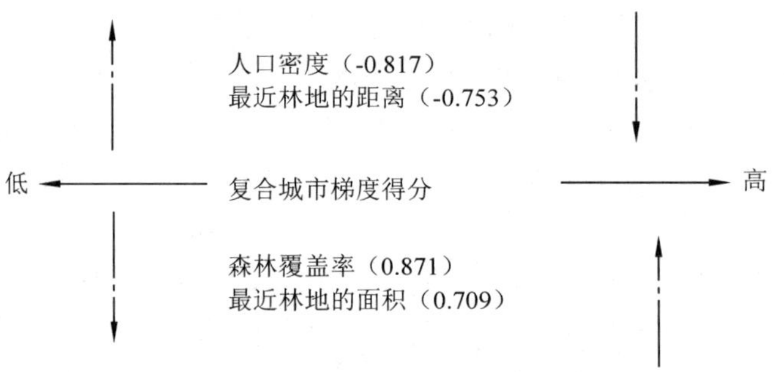

图 1 城市梯度构成

Fig. 1 The Composite Urban Gradient Score

1.4 城市森林社会功能的评价方法

1.4.1 城市森林的社会功能

城市森林的主要社会功能之一是它提供的休闲机会。户外休闲是许多现代社会城市居民参与的活动方式。在城市森林中漫步成为最普遍的休闲活动。其他的休闲活动还有骑车兜风、慢跑、野餐以及采摘浆果和蘑菇。但不同区域存在较大的差异，这些差异与某一环境中最近森林用来休闲的可能性和森林的可接近性相关，只有在附近容易找到森林才能利用森林环境进行日常锻炼[6]。

绿地尤其是森林能够促进邻里之间产生积极的社会联系，增强居民对社区的认同感和归属感，并有利于降低盗窃和暴力犯罪率[7]。

健康方面的效益主要表现为积极利用绿色空间进行体育活动或休闲活动；由于较高的森

林覆盖率所带来的空气质量的改善以及接触自然有利于康复等方面。

同时，环境知识的培养能够增强居民保护城市森林与自然环境的意识，并帮助他们鉴赏城市的花草和动物。

总之，城市森林的社会功能可视为一种多样性的产品，它可以为当地不同的家庭、个人以及其他团体提供不同的服务。

1.4.2 城市森林社会效益的评价方法

1.4.2.1 评价指标的选择与模型的构建

本文选取居民对城市森林的利用、对城市森林和社区的总体满意程度以及对城市森林提供生态服务和社会服务的认知等三个指标构建城市森林社会效益评价模型。即：

$$SE = b_0 + b_1U + b_2S + b_3R + \delta$$

式中，SE 为城市森林的社会效益矩阵；U 为居民对城市森林利用矩阵；S 为居民对城市森林和社区的总体满意程度矩阵；R 为居民对城市森林提供生态服务和社会服务的认知矩阵；b_0为常数；b_1，b_2与 b_3为回归系数矩阵；δ 为误差项向量。

1.4.2.2 数据来源

2011 年 3 月，我们对研究区域内的 1659 个样点内的 4000 位居民进行了调查。为了确保调查资料能代表城市梯度的整体水平，调查范围的选择以长沙市城市梯度划分为基础，调查样点从各个梯度中分别抽取，再在各样点中随机抽取不同类型的调查对象。

调查函的第一部分是要求调查对象归纳出自己社区的特征，然后确定其中最重要的三个。

调查函的第二部分是一份标准的问卷，包括一系列 Likert - scale 问题，要求调查对象对他们利用林地的方式、对城市森林和社区的总体满意程度以及对城市森林提供生态服务和社会服务的认知等方面的重要性进行打分。关于林地利用方式的问题包括主动的利用(如散步、体育运动)和被动的利用(如野餐、与邻居闲聊)[8]。对社区满意的问题包括住户接近开敞空间的机会、自然景观、邻里关系以及安全保障等[9]。关于对林地的生态和社会服务认知的问题包括水土保持，改善水质，提供休闲空间，提供自然景观，增强社区的特征以及提供私密空间。有些问题与居民本身有关，如受教育程度、年龄、从事何种职业与工作年限等。

1.4.2.3 模型参数的估计

在调查函的第一部分中，被调查对象提到的位于前三位的特征将用于分析当中。在调查函的第二部分，利用 Likert - scale 的排序资料进行分析，可得到对城市森林的利用、对城市森林和社区的总体满意程度以及对城市森林提供生态服务和社会服务的认知等城市森林社会效益三部分的得分。

运用统计分析软件 SPSS14 对调查数据进行主成分分析，其相关系数矩阵 R 的特征值、累积贡献率与各主成分载荷矩阵，见表 3、表 4。第 1 个特征值的贡献率为 85.79%，超过 85%，故选择第一主成分即可。由此，可得到长沙市城市森林社会功能模型。即

$$SE = 1.226 + 0.754U + 0.512S + 0.211R$$

表 3 特征值及方差贡献率和累计贡献率

Tab. 3 Total variance explained

主成分 Components	特征值 Eigenvalues	贡献率 Variance(%)	累计贡献率 Cumulative(%)
1	5.953	85.79	85.79
2	0.772	11.13	86.92
3	0.214	3.08	100

表 4 主成分 z_1，z_2载荷矩阵

Tab. 4 component matrix

变量 Variances	z_1
U	0.623
S	0.728
R	0.637

2 结果分析

2.1 长沙市城市梯度的划分

在长沙市城市梯度评价中，每一个梯度变量载荷相对均衡（图 1）。这意味着这个复合的梯度评分能较好的描述这些成分。梯度评分较低的区域，往往人口密度大，森林覆盖率低，并且林地的规模小，远离居住区的质心或调查点，而且城镇化水平较高（图 1）。而梯度评分较高的区域，人口密度较低，森林覆盖率较高，林地的规模更大，距离也更近，这些特点在开发程度低的区域很明显。利用城市梯度得分，将研究区域分为“城区”、“近郊”、“远郊”和“野地”等四个城市梯度(表5)。具体分区如图 2。由于文中所讨论的城市森林社会效益重视人的活动与参与，所以本文只对前三个梯度的数据相关分析，而对还没有开发的“野地”这个梯度暂不考虑。

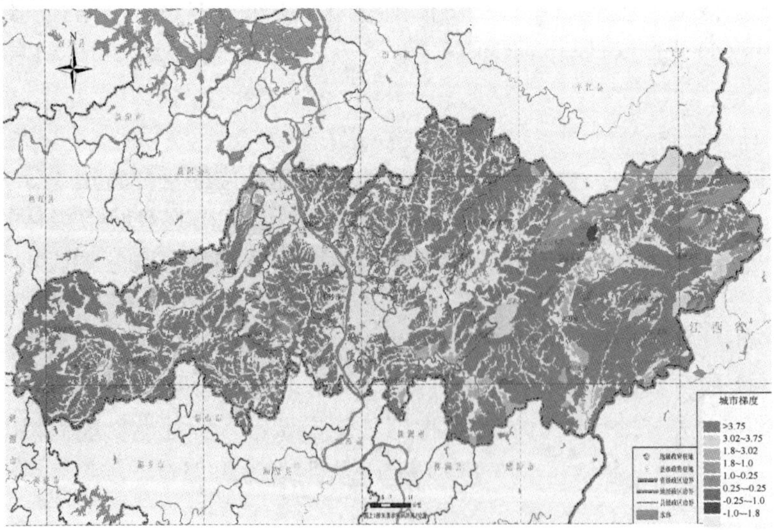

图 2 长沙市城市梯度分区

Fig. 2 Study area and urban gradient

表 5 长沙市城市梯度分区

Tab. 5 Urban gradient score interval in Changsha

梯度分区	城区	近郊	远郊	野地
梯度得分区间	< -1.80	-0.25 ~ 0.25	1.8 ~ 3.02	>3.75

2.2 长沙市城市森林社会功能的梯度分析

2.2.1 城市森林社会功能梯度特征分析

分析调查问卷的第一部分数据可知，有 8 个特征的返回率超过了 10%：购物的便利性、商业机会、交通便利性、友善、安静、邻近公园、邻近森林、近水。其中，邻近公园、临近森林与友善等社区特征直接涉及我们的研究内容：对森林的认知、自然环境以及社区的品质（地方感，社区凝聚力）。

调查对象认为靠近公园是重要社区特征的概率与梯度得分成逆相关（model $\chi^2 = 4.329$，$P = 0.024$，图 3）。最有可能将靠近公园作为最重要社区特征的调查对象居住地离林地最远，森林覆盖率最低。调查结果表明，与居住在森林覆盖率高于 40% 区域的调查对象相比，居住在森林覆盖率低于 20% 的调查对象认为靠近公园是重要社区特征的比例超过 50%。同样，居住地离林地距离大于 1km 的调查对象与居住地离林地距离小于 0.5km 的调查对象相比，认为靠近公园是重要社区特征的比例要高 5%。这意味着人们已经明确地认识到这种独特的自然环境在高人口密度区是珍贵的，因此会得到更广泛的认识和珍惜。与城市居民认为靠近公园是重要社区特征的高比例相比较，居住在远郊的人们认为靠近森林很重要。（$x^2 = 31.671$，$P < 0.001$）。

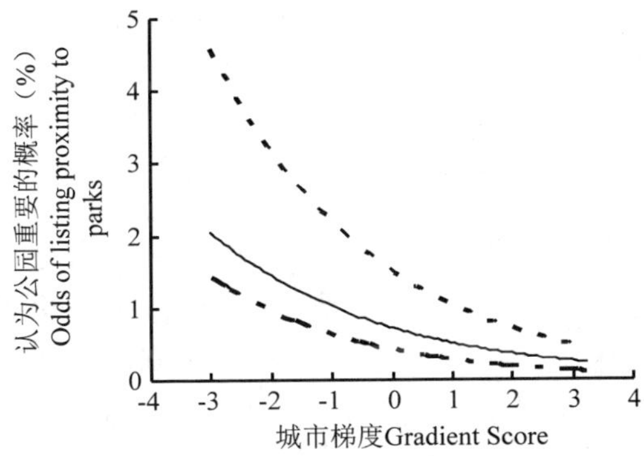

图 3 认为靠近公分离器重要的概率与城市梯度关系

Fig. 3 Odds of listing parks as one of three top attributes of their neighborhood

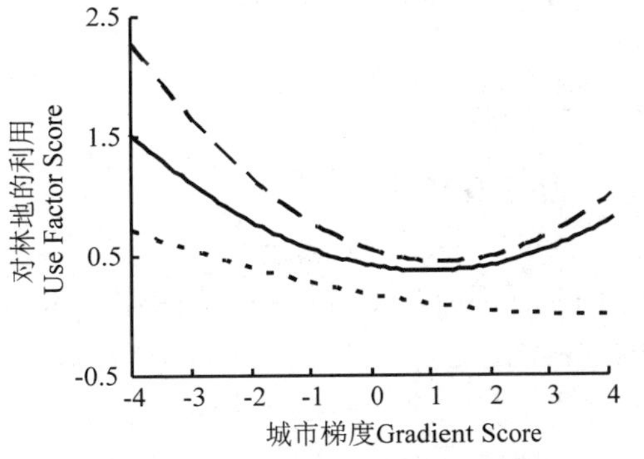

图 4 林地利用与城市梯度关系

Fig. 4 Use of forest patches

2.2.2 长沙市城市森林社会功能影响因子的梯度分析

利用调查问卷的第二部分数据对城市森林社会效益影响最大的三个因子即对林地的利用，总体上对森林和社区的满意度，社区森林提供的生态和社会服务进行梯度相关分析。

（1）对林地的利用：关于对林地利用问题的分值占总分的 30%。得分最多的利用方式是主动的利用（散步、慢跑、体育运动以及骑自行车）。得分越高反映了利用林地进行各种活动越多。对林地的利用与梯度得分的相关性较弱（adj. $R^2 = 0.053$，$P < 0.001$）。城镇化水平

高的居民利用社区林地的程度高于低城镇化水平的居民（图4）。也就是说，与近郊和远郊的居民相比，城区居民对附近公园和林地的利用率更高 。大多数被调查者认为，自然环境作为休闲场地比高楼林立的地方更有吸引力，而且森林被认为是更具魅力的休闲自然区域。

(2)对社区的满意度：与居民对其社区属性满意度相关的问题的分值占总分的40%。所有问题的得分相对均衡，其中较重要的特征为宁静、卫生、自然景观。是否有体育设施的重要性最低。在远郊地区，接近开敞空间的机会、自然景观、安全、卫生和宁静等特征增加了居民对社区的总体满意度(adj. $R^2=0.148$, $P<0.001$)（图5）。城镇化水平最高的区域，对社区的满意度得分最低。

(3)对地方林地功能的认知：这部分问题的分值占总分的30%。对城市森林不同功能认知的得分比重相对比较均衡，所以分数越高说明对城市森林作用的认识越多。对森林功能的总体认知与梯度得分的相关性较弱（adj. $R^2=0.082$, $P<0.001$）（图6）。

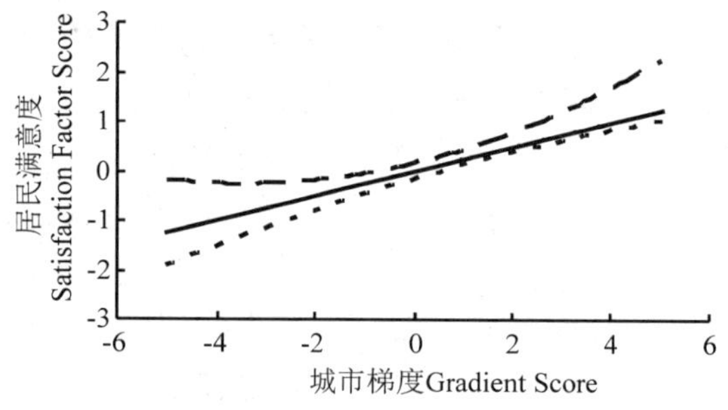

图5 满意度与城市梯度关系

Fig. 5 Satisfaction with neighborhood

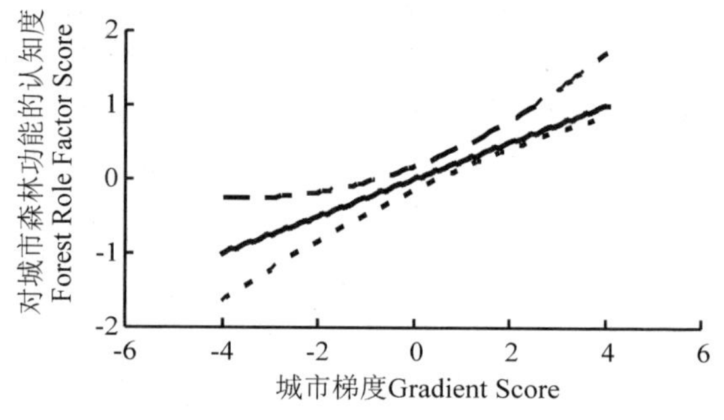

图6 对城市森林功能的认知与城市梯度关系

Fig. 6 Perceived role of forests

3 结 论

3.1 城区森林功能

城区的梯度得分为 −2.25 ~ −1.80 之间，城镇化水平最高，周边的森林覆盖率最低小于10%，现有的森林面积都较小，平均面积为$0.01km^2$，最近林地距离较远，平均距离大于2500m，人口密度较高，为8480 人/km^2。这个区域的居民更有可能认为友好的邻里关系是重要的社区因子，但这并不意味着他们总体上对社区满意[10]。该区域的人们更有可能将公园视为社区的重要特征，这说明他们已经明确地认识到这样一种独特的自然环境在高人口密度区是珍贵的，因此会得到更广泛的认识和珍惜。此外，与近郊和远郊的居民相比，城区居民对附近公园和林地的利用率更高（图4）。

3.2 近郊森林的功能

典型近郊社区的梯度得分在 −0.25 ~ 0.25 之间，该区域的森林覆盖率相对较低，平均值为27.3%，在1000m 的步行距离内林地的规模中等，平均值约$1.24km^2$，平均人口密度为2513 人/ km^2。功能得分都处于中间水平，没有出现峰值。这种处于中等状态的区域居住的人口较多，与处于极值状态的城区与远郊比较，它代表了长沙市的大部分区域。这个地区森林社会功能实际上处于中间水平，大多数的森林由于稀缺而受到重视，但森林作为环境特征是不够的。居住在这类区域的人们也认为森林是社区重要的部分，但还有其他的因素更重要，如住房价格、社区管理等。

3.3 远郊森林的功能

最近林地面积大、最近林地距离近、人口密度低是远郊社区的特征，该区域的城镇化程度最低，梯度得分为1.8～3.02，森林覆盖率最高，平均值为68%。该区域森林的社会功能有较大变化，这是由于社会功能的本质特征本来就是复杂的、多方面的。人们常常会对那些在区域调查中提到社区特征更满意，其中很多都与森林、自然景观以及安静等特征有关。相反，该区域的居民认为公园和邻里友好等特征是最不重要的，在该区域的梯度得分中也是最低的。满意度得分与居民对森林的认知有关，林地在远郊能更长久的生存这个事实可以解释这样的结果。

参考文献

[1]塞西尔 C. 科奈恩德克等. 城市森林与树木[M]. 李志勇，等，译. 北京：科学出版社，2009.

[2]Frumkin H，Frank L，Jackson R. The public health impacts of sprawl. Island Press[J]. Washington DC，2004.

[3]叶功富，洪志猛. 城市森林学[M]. 厦门：厦门大学出版社，2006.

[4]陈彩虹，肖默. 长株潭城市群城市森林生态系统服务功能的价值评估[J]. 中南林业科技大学学报，2011，31(2)：50～54.

[5] 郭泺，夏北成等. 城市化进程中广州市景观格局的时空变化与梯度分异[J]. 应用生态学报，2006，17(9)：1671～1676.

[6]梅燕。城市森林游憩的开发研究－以成都市为例. 安徽农业科学，2009，37(28)：13827～13828，13833.

[7]Kweon BS，Sullivan WC. Wiley AR. Green common spaces and the social integration of inner－city older adults[J]. Environ Behav，1998，30(6)：832～858.

[8]肖亮，张立明，王剑. 武汉市居民城市森林游憩需求特征调查. 林业调查规划，2007，32 (1)：124～127.

[9]Kaplan R，Kaplan S. The experience of nature：a psychological perspective[J]. Cambridge University Press，New York. 1989.

[10]Gobster PH，Westphal LM. The human dimensions of urban greenways：planning for recreation and related experiences[J]. Landsc Urban Plan，2004，68(2～3)：147～165.

桂林后龙山风水林文化现状及承传研究*

刘代汉　何新凤　蒋家安

（桂林师范高等专科学校，桂林，541001）

摘要：风水林是中国人认为对一人一家、一族一姓、一村一镇乃至一国的现在及将来具有吉凶影响的人工培植或天然生长并严加保护的林木。它是中国传统风水文化的产物。本文通过田野调查，了解了当代桂林人对后龙山风水林文化的认同状况，探索风水林文化的承传方式，提出了通过学校教育，正确认识风水林文化，弘扬优秀传统文化，构建森林保护法律法规及村规民约相结合的风水林保护体系，加强风水林保护，建设生态文明，以实现中华民族伟大复兴。

关键词：桂林；风水林；后龙山

1　前　言

1.1　风水文化及风水林

“风水”又叫“堪舆”。堪者天也，舆者地也，古人“仰观天象，俯察地理”，是谓之。因此，风水，概括地说，就是古人根据天时的变化和地理形势的不同，选择适合人类生存的最佳环境。作为一种文化形态的风水文化其产生发展历史悠久。风水文化是中国人在长期适应自然生态环境过程中形成的一种传统思想意识，其目的是追求理想的生存环境。中国人认为好的风水能保佑人们人丁兴旺、富裕安康、荣华富贵，坏风水则给人带来灾难。为了趋吉避凶，人们在选择居住地时要尽可能选择好风水之地，并对之严加保护，在天然风水略显不足时，则采用人工补之。

风水林是中国人认为对一人一家、一族一姓、一村一镇乃至一国的现在及将来具有吉凶影响的人工培植或天然生长并严加保护的林木，主要包括村庄风水林、陵墓风水林和寺庙风水林。村庄风水林可分为后龙山林、水口林、垫脚林、宅基林[1]。

风水林是风水文化的产物。

1.2　研究目的及意义

桂林地处岭南，以汉民族为主，有壮、瑶、侗等12个民族聚居。受传统风水文化影响，许多村庄都保留有后龙山风水林，尤其是在漓江两岸岩溶地区，这种后龙山风水林文化特征十分显著，以致你只要看见山上林木繁茂，即可判断山脚必定有一村庄。反之，童山赤岭，则无村庄。这种保护后龙山风水林的思想深深地根植于传统桂林人的血脉中，并形成自律与

---

*项目资助：广西教育厅科研项目（编号：200911MS280），桂林师范高等专科学校资助项目（编号 GLSZ200901）。

作者简介：刘代汉（1956～）桂林师范高等学校教授，博士，研究方向：森林经理及森林文化。

自觉。即使在历经打倒"四旧"，破除"风水"等"文革"运动之后，后龙山风水林依然得以保存。可见，后龙山风水文化对于保护森林资源，维护生态安全发挥着十分重要的作用。但随着我国城市化，农村人口逐步向城市转移，传统文化正经历着深刻的嬗变。因此，了解当代桂林人后龙山风水林文化的认同状况，探索风水林文化的承传方式，对于弘扬优秀传统文化，建设生态文明，构建和谐社会、实现中华民族伟大复兴都具有十分重要的现实和历史意义。

2 研究方法

本研究采用问卷调查与访问调查相结合，定性研究与定量研究相结合的方法。

2.1 调查对象

学校是文化传承的主要场所，青年学生则是传统文化传承的关键。因此，本课题调查对象以大学生和中学生为主，其他人员为辅。调查的学校主要有位于桂林的大专院校：广西师范大学、桂林师范高等专科学校、桂林林校、阳朔职业中等学校、阳朔白沙初中5所学校。此外，还对临桂县、兴安县、荔浦县、阳朔县部分干部、农村居民等进行了调查。调查对象中有3070人居住的村庄或老家村庄后有山，占受调查总人数的91.65%。

2.2 调查方法

采用问卷调查方法。共发放问卷3500份，收回有效问卷3360份，有效率为96%。问卷涉及对风水林的认知、对风水林功能的信仰、对风水林保护与利用的态度等方面。

3 结果与分析

3.1 对后龙山风水林认知程度

对村庄后龙山风水林的认知程度见表1。

表1 对风水林认知程度

项目 \ 认知程度		合计		知道				不知道	
				叫风水林		叫其他林			
		人数	%	人数	%	人数	%	人数	%
合计		3350	100.0	263	7.8	1810	54.0	1277	38.2
性别	男	1491	100.0	101	6.7	1012	67.8	378	25.5
	女	1859	100.0	162	8.6	798	43.0	899	48.4
年龄	30以下	2768	100.0	169	6.1	1458	52.7	124	44.8
	31以上	582	100.0	94	16.1	452	77.7	36	6.2
学历	大专以下	2617	100.0	163	6.2	1284	49.1	1170	44.7
	本科以上	733	100.0	100	13.6	526	71.8	107	14.6
身份	农民	381	100.0	11	2.9	359	94.2	11	2.9
	学生	2678	100.0	162	6.1	1284	47.9	1232	46.0
	干部	82	100.0	11	13.4	61	74.4	10	12.2
	教师	209	100.0	80	38.3	108	51.7	21	10.0

从表 1 可知：

⑴风水林观念在受调查的人群中已很淡漠，只有 7.7% 知道后龙山森林叫风水林，有 38.2% 的人明确表示不知道。

⑵性别对风水林观念认知影响不大有 6.7% 的男性、8.6% 的女性知道后龙山的森林叫风水林。但年龄、学历、身份不同的人群对风水林观念认知存在明显差异。30 岁以下的人知道风水林的人只有6.1%，31 岁以上的人中有 15.5% 知道，后者是前者的2.5 倍；大专学历以下的人知道风水林的人只有 6.5%，本科以上的人中有 12.3% 知道，后者是前者的近 2 倍；农民中有 2.6%、学生中有 6.0%、干部中有 12.5%、教师中有 38.1% 的人知道后龙山的森林叫风水林，认知比为 1∶2.3∶4.8∶14.7。

3.2 对后龙山风水文化接受程度

这里的后龙山风水林文化接受程度是指对后龙山风水林的惩恶佑善功能的信仰。采用两个指标进行调查，一是是否相信后龙山森林能保佑村寨安宁，二是砍伐后龙山森林是否担心遭报应。

两项指标调查结果见表 2。

表 2 接受后龙山风水文化程度

接受程度 / 项目		合计		相信				不相信				不知道			
				能保佑村寨安宁		砍伐会遭难		能保佑村寨安宁		砍伐会遭难		能保佑村寨安宁		砍伐会遭难	
		人	%	人	%	人	%	人	%	人	%	人	%	人	%
合计		3350	100.0	1432	42.7	1405	41.9	1708	51.0	1744	52.1	210	6.3	201	6.0
性别	男	1491	100.0	581	39.0	463	31.1	841	56.4	941	63.1	69	4.6	87	5.8
	女	1859	100.0	851	45.8	942	50.7	867	46.6	803	43.2	141	7.6	114	6.1
年龄	30 岁以下	2768	100.0	1138	41.1	1211	43.8	1432	51.7	1383	50.0	198	7.2	174	6.3
	31 岁以上	582	100.0	294	50.5	194	33.3	276	47.4	361	62.0	12	2.1	27	4.6
学历	大专以下	2617	100.0	1100	42.0	1098	42.0	1307	49.9	1340	51.2	210	8.0	179	6.8
	本科以上	733	100.0	332	45.3	307	41.9	401	54.7	404	55.1	0	0.0	22	3.0
身份	农民	381	100.0	158	41.5	111	29.1	197	51.7	261	68.5	26	6.8	9	2.4
	学生	2678	100.0	1106	41.3	1191	44.5	1388	51.8	1306	48.8	184	6.9	181	6.8
	干部	82	100.0	42	51.2	0	0.0	40	48.8	78	95.1	0	0.0	4	4.9
	教师	209	100.0	126	60.3	103	49.3	83	39.7	99	47.4	0	0.0	7	3.3

从表 2 可以看出：

⑴目前桂林人接受后龙山风水文化的人约占 4 成，有 5 成的人不接受，近 1 成的人将信将疑。

⑵从性别上看，不同性别的人们的后龙山文化观念不同。39% 的男性相信后龙山能保佑村寨安宁，31% 的人相信破坏后龙山林会遭报应，而女性的比例则分别为 46% 和 51%。两者差距较明显，对后龙山风水林心存敬畏的女性明显比男性多。

⑶不同年龄段的人对后龙山风水林持有的观念不一样。总体上年长者，比年幼者更接受后龙山风水林文化。

(4)不同学历教育的人群对后龙山风水林接受程度基本上没有差异，说明近60年来风水文化的传承不是依赖学校教育。

(5)不同身份(职业)的人，对后龙山风水林文化的接受程度差异较大。授受后龙山风水林能保佑村寨安宁观念的农民和学生比例基本相同，约为41%，干部则51%，教师则为60%。

3.3 对后龙山风水林保护意识

对后龙山风水林的保护意识从两个方面去测定，一是自律意识，即自我控制不去破坏的意识，二是律他意识，在此是指当别人破坏自己村后龙山时采取行动的意识。

3.3.1 自律意识

自律就是自我约束，没有外力作用时的自我控制。约束自己不去破坏后龙山森林，即使家中无薪柴时，仍能坚持不去砍伐后龙山风水林，这种自律意识对于后龙山风水林保护起着十分重要的作用。目前保留下来的风水林就是这种自律的结果。当代桂林人对后龙山风水林保护的自律程度见表3。

表3 风水林保护自律程度

项目＼自律程度		合计		当无柴烧时是否敢去砍伐后龙山林木				不知道	
				敢		不敢			
		人数	%	人数	%	人数	%	人数	%
合计		3350	100.0	941	28.1	2262	67.5	147	4.4
性别	男	1491	100.0	321	21.5	1111	74.5	58	3.9
	女	1859	100.0	620	33.4	1151	61.9	89	4.8
年龄	30以下	2768	100.0	862	31.1	1773	64.1	138	5.0
	31以上	582	100.0	78	13.4	489	84.0	9	1.5
学历	大专以下	2617	100.0	704	26.9	1772	67.7	147	5.6
	本科以上	733	100.0	236	32.2	490	66.8	0	0.0
身份	农民	381	100.0	78	20.5	288	75.6	11	2.9
	学生	2678	100.0	852	31.8	1691	63.1	136	5.1
	干部	82	100.0	0	0.0	82	100.0	0	0.0
	教师	209	100.0	10	4.8	201	96.2	0	0.0

从表3可以看出：

(1)2/3的人(67.5%)能够自律不去砍伐后龙山风水林，即便是家中无柴，仍能自律。这其中有41.9%(表2所示)的人是因担心砍伐会引来灾难而自律，尚有25.6%的人是由于其他原因而自律；另有四分之一强(28.1%)的人不受后龙山风水林文化左右，当个人需要与风水林保护冲突时，会采取破坏后龙山风水林的行动。

(2)在保护后龙山风水林方面无论男女，多数人都能自律，但男性似乎比女性更自律些，男性有74.5%的人能够自律，而女性只有61.9%，相差12.6个百分点。

(3)不同年龄的人群自律程度不同，30岁以下的人中有64.1%的人能够自律，而31岁以上的人群中这一比例高达84.0%。

(4)接受大专以下学历教育与接受本科以上学历教育的人群中都是67%左右的人有自律

保护意识。这从另一侧面说明了后龙山风水林文化传承主要依靠社会教育和家庭教育，学校教育在这一文化领域似乎不起什么作用。

(5)不同身份的人，在自律程度上差别较大：从低到高，依次为学生63.1%、农民75.6%、教师96.2%、干部100%。

3.3.2 律他意识

这里的律他是指当发现别人对本村后龙山林木进行砍伐时，是否去制止的行动。在这一问题上，绝大多数人会采取制止行动，比例高达94.9%，只有5.1%人采取听之任之的态度。

3.4 对后龙山风水林的利用观

对后龙山如何开发利用的问题，调查结果见表4。

表4 对后龙山开发利用的态度

利用方式/人数	合计	将后龙山改成公园			将后龙山改成果园		
		同意	不同意	犹豫不定	同意	不同意	犹豫不定
人数	3350	1201	1742	407	1782	1411	157
%	100.0	35.9	52.0	12.1	53.2	42.1.1	4.7

从表4可以看出，对如何利用后龙山的观点上存在着不同的观点。有53.2%的人同意将其改建成果园，有35.9%的人同意改建成森林公园，不同意改建成森林公园的人数多达52%。说明当代桂林人中多数人对后龙山的利用还是以获取经济利益为主要目的。

3.5 后龙山风水林保护的传承方式

在3350个调查对象中有3066人村庄后有山，占91.5%，其中山上有林木的有2593人，占村庄后有山的调查对象的84.6%，没有林木的473人，占15.4%。在后龙山有林木的调查对象中，有50.2%是有村规民约保护后龙山森林的，有46.3%是依靠老一辈言传身教；既有村规民约，又有言传身教的有占28.2%。

4 结论与讨论

4.1 结 论

(1)后龙山风水林文化传承面临着十分严峻的挑战。当代桂林人“后龙山风水林”观念已十分模糊，能清楚说出后龙山森林叫后龙山风水林的人已不多，不足一成。这是近现代，尤其是“文化大革命”期间。中华民族的一些传统文化精华与糟粕一同被革了命，学校是不可能开设“风水”此类的课程的，就是家庭中、社会上也不敢公开宣传。

(2)多数人对传统后龙山风水林文化存疑，甚至不相信。随着科学知识的普及，那种依靠“神诫”或“赐福”来恫吓、引导人们相信后龙山风水林能赐福祛灾，扬善惩恶，进而实现保护后山森林的文化传承方式已不适应时代潮流，后龙山文化传承方式需要创新。

(3)后龙山风水林的保护、开发利用面临抉择。承着社会主义市场经济体制的确立，人们追求经济发展，利用一切可利用的资源获取经济利益已成为潮流。人们需要在经济发展与环境保护、短期利益与长远利益，局部利益与整体利益的博弈中审视后龙山风水林。

4.2 讨论

4.2.1 正确认识后龙山风水林

传统的后龙山风水林文化，是我们先人的智慧结晶。在绝大多数人是文盲的时代，要想通过长篇巨论，花费许多时间来教育人们了解人与森林关系显然是难以做到。为保护后山的森林，让子孙后代能安居乐业，古人智者，利用人们敬畏神灵的心理、用通俗易懂的言语，将蜿蜒起伏的山脉比作龙，将山岭上的森林比作龙之毛发，将后山称之为后龙山，将后山的林木称之为后龙山风水林，辅之以风水林能赐福祛灾，破坏则会带来灾难等传说，要求子孙后代严加保护，有其合理性与科学性[3]。然而，长期以来，风水观念被阴阳家、道士、风水先生所利用，作为欺骗群众、诈取钱财的工具，使风水观念中的唯心主义宿命论、迷信思想成分大大超过其合理内涵，产生很大的消极影响。但风水文化注重林木景观、推崇绿化环境的风水思想，倡导植树的风水绿化思想和禁止毁林的风水护林思想是值得我们继承的传统文化精华[2]。我们不能因为风水林带有迷信色彩而将后龙山风水林这一优秀传统文化的精华和糟粕一同抛弃，将婴儿与洗澡水一块倒掉。

4.2.2 弘扬后龙山风水林文化。

文化传承方式主要是家庭教育、学校教育和社会教育三种。当前，风水林文化传承主要依靠家庭教育和社会教育，学校教育处于缺失状态。因此，建议在中小学“自然”课程中增补风水林内容。把后龙山森林的经济价值、环境价值、科学价值、文化价值讲透，把人类与森林、人类与自然的关系说明白。让具有鲜明中国特色的“风水林文化”光明正大地走进学校，走进课堂，溶化在中华民族的血脉里。

4.2.3 切实保护好后龙山风水林。

风水林不仅具有重要的文化价值，还具有重要的科研价值，值得切实加强保护。要保护好后龙山风水林，首先要摸清其现状。目前在森林资源调查有关技术规程中，“风水林”仅作为风景林进行调查，与其他森林公园的森林合在一起统计，无法准确了解风水林的状况。因此，建议将风水林作为特种用途林下的一个二级林种(亚林种)单独列出，反映在调查统计表上，以便在制定森林经营方案及其他规划时做到科学的保护、开发和利用。

其次，完善森林保护法律、法规。修建村规民约和现有森林法规，明确后龙山风水林的地位，将代代言传身教、口耳相传与村规民约、法律法规建设结合进来，实现他律与自觉自律相结合，构建后龙山风水林完整保护体系。

参考文献

[1]陈名实．传统风水观念与水土保持[J]．福建水土保持，2000，02.

[2] 关传友．中国古代风水林探析 [J]．农业考古，2002，03.

[3] 祝功武．整理村落与“风水林” 建设绿色新农村[J]．中国城市林业，2007，06.

巨尾桉纸浆原料林资产评估技术研究

吕　勇[1]　　何　龙[2]　　张　震[2]　　边更战[3]

（1. 中南林业科技大学 林学院，长沙，410004；

2. 四川省林业调查规划院 营林调查队，成都，610081；

3. 南方林业产权交易所，南昌，330000）

摘要：纸浆原料林是短轮伐期工业原料用材林的一种，特指以生产为目的按照工程项目管理、采取集约经营、定向培育的森林和林木。文章通过编制广东省河源市巨尾桉纸浆原料林标准表和构建其主伐年龄模型来解决在评估该地巨尾桉林木资产时所出现的部分问题，得到了广东省河源市巨尾桉纸浆原料林标准表并求出了其主伐年龄为5.7年。

关键词：巨尾桉；纸浆原料林；资产评估；技术；模型

Abstract: Pulpwood, one of the industrial timber stand with short rotation age, is especially defined as: forests or trees that is operated intensively and cultured in directed form in accordance with project management and under the purpose of producing paper fiber material. In this paper, Eucalyptus is set as an example to elaborate some solutions needed during the process of asset evaluation of pulpwood.

Key words: pulpwood; eucalyptus; asset Evaluation; technology; model

纸浆原料林在国外起步较早，但其迅速发展却在近40年，在这个阶段，世界上许多国家都营建了相当规模的高质量纸浆原料林，促进了本国造纸工业的发展，取得了极大的生态、社会和经济效益。[1]

我国纸浆原料林的发展始于速生丰产林，早在20世纪60年代我国就开始进行林纸一体化的探索。进入新世纪以来，国家林业总局根据林业发展的需要，确立了林业分类经营的思想，将森林划分为生态公益林和商品林。[2,3]

随着纸浆原料林的快速发展，涉及纸浆原料林资产的转让、置换、租赁经营、抵押贷款、担保或偿还债务、资产诉讼、资产占有等情形时，需要进行资产评估。[4~8]中共中央、国务院有文件指出："发展森林资源资产评估机构，促进林木合理流转，调动经营者投资开发的积极性。"(《关于加快林业发展的决定》，2003年)；"加快林地、林木流转制度建设，建立健全产权交易平台，加强流转管理，依法规范流转，保障公平交易，防止农民失山失地。加强森林资源资产评估管理，加快建立森林资源资产评估师制度和评估制度，规范评估行为，维护交易各方合法权益。"(《关于全面推进集体林权制度改革的意见》，2008年)。

目前，用于纸浆原料林资产评估的方法和经济技术指标仍然沿用一般用材林的，没有体现出纸浆原料林与传统的用材林在速生丰产性上的显著差异，国内外还没有学者针对这方面做过系统的研究，本文将对纸浆原料林资产评估关键技术做相对详尽的分析、研究，以期为纸浆原料林资产评估工作中的方法、指标选择提供参考。

1 研究区域概况与数据来源

研究的数据来自于广东省河源市，在该地区的紫金县、连平县、和平县、龙川县、东源县布设241块巨尾桉标准地，分别于2008年10月和2009年10月对标准地进行调查，因此这241块标准地的两次调查共得到482块标准地的数据。调查因子包括空间位置、立地因子和林分因子，涉及的地类、林种、树种、密度、造林规格、起源、郁闭度、造林年度、立木胸径、林分平均树高、海拔、坡度、土壤等。这些标准地分布于不同年龄、不同立地、不同密度的巨尾桉人工林中，林分郁闭度在0.4以上且生长正常，每块标准地面积400~600m^2。在标准地内进行每木调查，采用巨尾桉人工林的单株木二元材积公式计算标准地的蓄积量。每100m^2测一株最高树木的树高确定标准地的优势木平均高，标准地其他有关的测树因子按常规方法测算。

用随机抽样的方法抽取80株样木，样木分布在不同立地、密度、年龄的林分中。样木伐倒后，量测树干长度、胸径，并以区分段测定各区分段中央带皮直径。根据样木资料建立削度方程。

该地区巨尾桉基本种植于每年的3~5月，到调查日止，标准地的巨尾桉年龄存在1.5、2.5、3.5、4.5、5.5、6.5、7.5年，共7个年龄层。以下分析未考虑采伐限额政策问题，假设条件为林木可无限、随时采伐。

2 巨尾桉纸浆原料林资产评估技术

2.1 构建巨尾桉林木主伐年龄模型

2.1.1 计算数量成熟年龄

数量成熟是指林木的材积平均生长量达到最大时的状态，这时的年龄称作数量成熟龄，在此年龄主伐能保证在单位时间单位面积上获得最高的木材产量，数量成熟年龄应作为确定主伐年龄的基础考虑。

计算各年龄层的平均胸径、平均树高，用广东二元材积公式计算材积平均生长量、连年生长量(表1)，并绘制材积平均生长量、连年生长量曲线，分析数量成熟年龄。

表1 各年龄层巨尾桉材积统计表

Tab.1 Timber volume statistics of eucalyptus in different ages

年龄	1.5	2.5	3.5	4.5	5.5	6.5	7.5
平均胸径	3.2	6.1	9.7	12.8	14.8	15.6	16.2
平均树高	3.5	7.4	12.1	14.4	16.2	17.7	18.3
单株木材积	0.0021	0.0132	0.0472	0.0923	0.1337	0.1583	0.1747
平均生长量	0.0014	0.0053	0.0135	0.0205	0.0243	0.0244	0.0233
连年生长量	0.002	0.0111	0.034	0.0451	0.0414	0.0246	0.0164

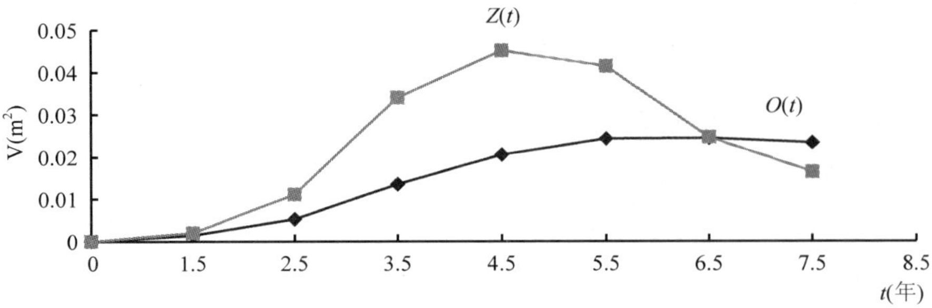

图 1　桉树材积连年生长量(Z)与平均生长量(θ)关系

Fig. 1　The relationship between the current annual increment and the average increment of eucalyptus

由图 1 可知，单株木巨尾桉材积年平均生长量在极接近第 6.5 年时达到最大，此时连年生长量与总平均生长量相等，因此确定 6.5 年为调查区巨尾桉的数量成熟年龄。

2.1.2　计算净现值最大时的年龄

净现值是指投资方案所产生的现金净流量以资金成本为贴现率折现之后与原始投资额现值的差额。因此，净现值越大说明产生的经济效益也越大，投资的收益就越大，此时的年龄是理论化的经济收益最大时的年龄。

与传统林业相比，发展短轮伐期人工林更关注其经济效益的大小，要确定某种人工林是否可作为短轮伐期林进行投资，需要引进财务分析的手段，通过计算净现值(NPV)和内部收益率(IRR)来评价投资方案。

本研究中巨尾桉的 NPV、IRR 指标计算结果见表 2。

表 2　财务分析结果

Tab. 2　The result of financial analysis

主伐年龄	1.5	2.5	3.5	4.5	5.5	6.5	7.5
NPV			-6487.53	-1144.34	2698.51	2272.18	300.57
IRR			-30%	4%	13%	9%	8%

上表基础数据(包括营造林成本、各项经济技术指标)来源于 2009 年 10 月广东省河源市的平均水平。

由表 2 可以看出，本研究中巨尾桉在 5.5 年时 NPV、IRR 均达到最大值，因此从财务角度分析其成熟龄在 5.5 年。

2.1.3　确定工艺成熟年龄

桉树人工林主要用在纸浆、木材、纤维板、改性材、单宁、清油、蜂蜜、芦丁、燃料、饲料等方面，各个用途对桉树主伐年龄的要求也不尽一致，因此必须充分考虑其在工艺上的成熟年龄。

本研究中巨尾桉主要用途为制造纤维板，桉树纤维长宽比变化不大，随着桉树年龄的增加，桉树纤维平均长宽比越大，2 年以后渐趋于平衡，5 年达到成熟期，此时按树的纤维长宽比可达到稳定值。因此，本例中桉树的工艺成熟年龄确定为 5 年。

2.1.4　判断市场需求情况

市场对于桉树木材，或者桉树某种规格的木材的需求情况是一个动态的变化过程，必须随时把握市场信息，才能根据市场情况决定是否采伐木材，只有这样才能取得最大的经济效益。

2.1.5 建立主伐年龄动态模型

通过以上各种对林木主伐年龄影响因素的相关关系分析，构造判断矩阵，得到各种因素确定的主伐年龄所占的权重，构建林木主伐年龄模型。

(1)构造判断矩阵并进行一致性检验：

判断矩阵表示本层次有关因素之间相对于上一层某因素的相对重要性的比较。采用 A. L Saaty“1 -9 比率标度法”进行量化比较，得到每一层次两两比较的判断矩阵，由判断矩阵求其非零最大特征根 λ_{max}，检查其一致性，计算一致性指标 CI，$CI = \frac{\lambda_{max} - n}{n - 1}$，然后用 CI 与平均一致性指标 RI 比较，当 CI/RI < 0.1 时则判断矩阵取得满意的一致性，否则重新调整判断矩阵的取值，使之具有满意的一致性。

本研究中巨尾桉的主伐年龄主要由数量成熟年龄、经济成熟年龄、工艺成熟年龄、市场成熟年龄影响，设各年龄对应为 x_1、x_2、x_3、x_4，在各指标比较的过程中采用头脑风暴法。

在指标的重要性比较过程中，邀请相关专家 9 人，运用头脑风暴法对各指标进行重要性表态，指标间的比较结果必须要有 70% 以上的专家认可，经统计、分析、整理，用 A. L Saaty“1 -9 比率标度法”进行标注，得到表 3。

表 3 各指标重要性比较表

Tab. 3 Comparison of the importance of indexes

指标	x_1	x_2	x_3	x_4
x_1	1	3	7	5
x_2	1/3	1	5	3
x_3	1/7	1/5	1	1/5
x_4	1/5	1/3	5	1

由表 3 得到判断矩阵 A：

$$A = \begin{pmatrix} 1 & 3 & 7 & 5 \\ 1/3 & 1 & 5 & 3 \\ 1/7 & 1/5 & 1 & 1/5 \\ 1/5 & 1/3 & 5 & 1 \end{pmatrix}$$

对以上矩阵用 Mathematica 计算得到其最大特征值 $\lambda(A) = 4.24$，$CI = \frac{\lambda(A) - 4}{4 - 1} = \frac{4.24 - 4}{4 - 1} = 0.08$，查 RI = 0.9，则 $CR = \frac{CI}{RI} = \frac{0.08}{0.9} = 0.089 < 0.1$，这说明 A 不是一致阵，但 A 具有满意的一致性，A 的不一致程度是可接受的。

计算得到 A 的权向量 $\omega(X) = (0.48, 0.28, 0.05, 0.20)^T$ (2 -1)

(2)构建巨尾桉主伐年龄模型：

设巨尾桉主伐年龄模型为：

$$y = a_0 + a_1x_1 + a_2x_2 + a_3x_3 + a_4x_4$$

在理论上，巨尾桉自种植以后即可采伐，因此，a_0值取0，将2.1.5(1)中计算得到的各种年龄的权向量代入式(2－1)，得到：

$$y = 0.48x_1 + 0.28x_2 + 0.05x_3 + 0.20x_4 \quad (2-2)$$

式2－2即为巨尾桉主伐年龄模型，将本研究中的各年龄代入式2－2，得到主伐年龄

$$y = 0.48 \times 6.5 + 0.28 \times 5.5 + 0.05 \times 5 + 0.20 \times 4 = 5.7 \text{ 年}$$

由此，本研究区巨尾桉主伐年龄应确定为5.7年。

2.2 编制评估所需标准表

2.2.1 标准表的编制步骤

将收集的482块标准地资料其中的400块进行数据整理后按特烈其亚柯夫提出的方法编制标准表，剩下的82块用于检验精度。

2.2.1.1 断面积的确定

根据全部编表的标准地材料，选用以下林分每公顷总断面积与林分平均高的相关方程拟合现实林分每公顷断面积的经验方程作为提升标准断面积的依据。常用的方程有：

$$G = a_0H + a_1 \quad (2-3)$$

$$HG = a_0H + a_1 \quad (2-4)$$

$$G = a_0\lg H + a_1 \quad (2-5)$$

$$G = H/(a_0H + a_1) \quad (2-6)$$

$$G = a_0\lg H + a_1H + a_2 \quad (2-7)$$

$$G = a_0 + a_1H + A_2H^2 \quad (2-8)$$

式中：a_0 a_1 a_2——参数；

G——每公顷胸高总断面积；

H——林分平均高。

将400块标准地资料录入SPSS统计软件，通过计算得到结果见表4。

表4 林分每公顷断面积模型拟合结果

Tab.4 The result of model fitting of stand basal area per hectare

方程	a_0	a_1	a_2	R^2
2.3	-3.105	0.218		0.872
2.4	9.608	-14.072		0.792
2.5	-6.469	6.67		0.707
2.6	-3.256	0.743		0.834
2.7	-3.212	2.342	1.674	0.868
2.8	-0.065	0.198	0.056	0.902

从表4可以看出，式(2－8)的判决系数最大，林分每公顷断面积用式(2－8)进行拟合比较理想，式(2－8)的拟合图如图2。

因此选择式(2－8)作为适用方程，拟合的经验式为：

$$G = -0.065 + 0.198H + 0.056H^2 \quad (2-9)$$

为了评价此模型的好坏，对模型进行适用性检验。对于模型的适用性检验，关键是看模型是否存在趋势性系统误差，可对实测值与模型预测理论值进行成对数据的T检验。统计

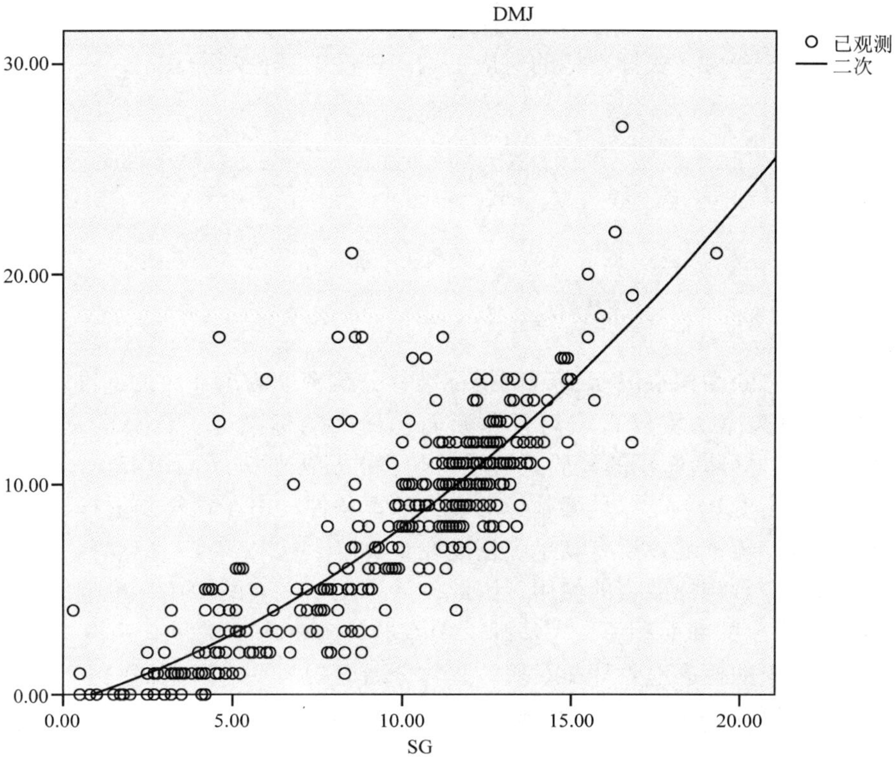

图 2　林分每公顷断面积模型拟合图

Fig. 2　The chart of model fitting of stand basal area per hectare

量 t 可由以下几式计算得到：

$$x_i = G_0 - G_i$$

$$x_0 = (x_1 + x_2 + ... + x_n)/n$$

$$s^2 = [(x_1 - x_0)^2 + (x_2 - x_0)^2 + ... + (x_n - x_0)^2]/n$$

$$t = x_0 (n-1)^{0.5}/s$$

其中：G_0表示每公顷断面积实际值，G_i为用式(2－9)计算出来的每公顷断面积理论值，n 为标准地个数，查表求 t 的临界值 $t_{0.05}(n-1)$，在95%的可靠性下，当 $|t| > t_{0.05}(n-1)$ 则说明模型预测值与实测值之间存在着显著性差异，该模型存在系统偏差。当 $|t| \leq t_{0.05}(n-1)$，则说明模型预测值与实测值之间不存在显著性差异，模型不存在系统偏差。进行95%置信区间的 T 检验，通过对检验样本数据进行计算，可得 $t=1.812$，小于 $t_{0.05}(399)=1.96$，从而说明模型预测值与实测值之间不存在显著性差异，该模型不存在系统误差。

将经验式展开，求得对应各林分平均高的总断面积的理论值 G_0。G_0是制表样本平均疏密度时的总断面积，编制标准表必须将平均断面积线提升到疏密度为1.0时的总断面积。

最大断面积线提高的依据，是从各树高阶中选几块总断面积最大且年龄分布

均匀的标准地，求算平均提升系数 q_0。

则

$$q_i = \frac{G_{i1} - G_{i2}}{G_{i1}} \quad (2-10)$$

式中：G_{i1}——第 i 块标准地的实际断面积；

G_{i2}——第 i 块标准地的对应平均疏密度的理论断面积。

令：

$$q = \frac{\sum_{i=1}^{n} q_i}{n} \tag{2-11}$$

则提升系数为：

$$q_0 = \frac{1}{1-q} \tag{2-12}$$

将各树高阶的总断面积乘以 q_0值，则得标准林分疏密度为 1.0 时的标准断面积 $G_{1.0}$。

在本次研究中选择 5 块分布均匀且总断面积最大的标准地，计算的提升系数为 $q_0 = 1.299$，由平均高和林分断面积的经验式可求得初步的标准林分断面积 $G_{1.0} = q_0 \times G$。

原始标准地疏密度 0.7 以上是编制标准表的基本条件。由于在初步选择编表材料时，其中有一部分标准地的疏密度并没有满足疏密度在 0.7 以上这一条件，标准林分的断面积与蓄积量被人为地降低，影响标准表的使用。因此，计算用于编表的原始标准地的实际疏密度必须式 $G_{1.0} = q_0 \times G$ 求出的断面积 $G_{1.0}$为基础，剔除那些疏密度不满足 0.7 以上的标准地。经测算，满足编表要求的标准地共计 246 块，其林分断面积与平均高的回归方程为：

$G = 1.947 - 0.156H + 0.071H^2$，此模型的拟合图如图 3。

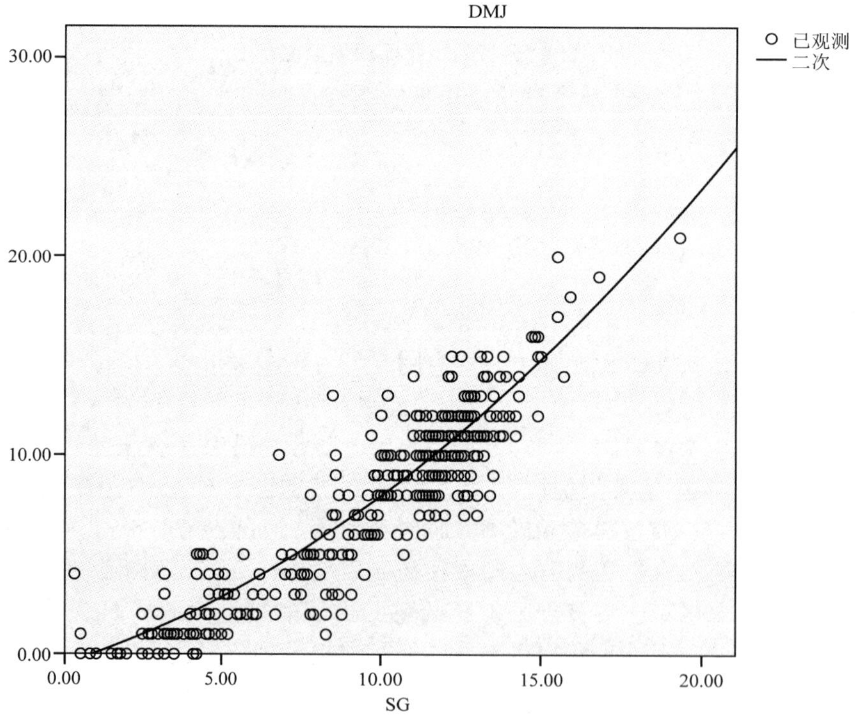

图 3 林分每公顷断面积模型拟合图

Fig. 3 The chart of model fitting of stand basal area per hectare

仍按前述方法，重新选择 5 块断面积最大的标准地，求得提升系数 $q = 1.103$。据此，最终确定的巨尾桉人工林疏密度为 1.0 时的标准林分断面积模型为：

$$G_{1.0} = 1.103(1.947 - 0.156H + 0.071H^2)$$
$$= 2.147541 - 0.172068H + 0.078313\ H^2$$

2.2.1.2 形高的确定

根据全部编表的标准地资料，分别用下式求算每块标准地的形高值：

$$(HF)_i = M_I/G_i \quad (2-13)$$

再拟合求得形数模型：

$$HF = a_0H + a_1 \quad (2-14)$$

本研究经拟合得到的形高模型为：

$$HF = 0.2806H + 2.625 \quad (2-15)$$

2.2.1.3 蓄积量的确定

依据林分蓄积量与形高乘积的关系，按下式计算出标准蓄积，即

$$M_{标} = G_{标}(HF) \quad (2-16)$$

最后，将不同树高阶的 $G_{标}$ 和 $M_{标}$ 列成表即为标准表(表 5)。

表 5 桉树人工林标准表

Tab. 5 Standard table of eucalyptus plantation

平均高	断面积	蓄积量
5	3. 245	13. 07086
6	3. 9344	16. 95176
7	4. 7804	21. 93821
8	5. 783	28. 16205
9	6. 9423	35. 75562
10	8. 2582	44. 85028
11	9. 7307	55. 57787
12	11. 3598	68. 07019
13	13. 1456	82. 45972
14	15. 0879	98. 87704
15	17. 1869	117. 4553
16	19. 4426	138. 3263
17	21. 8548	161. 6206
18	24. 4237	187. 4714
19	27. 1492	216. 0099
20	30. 0314	247. 3686

2.2.2 标准表适用性检验

在编表范围内，随机布设足够数量的标准地计算出平均高、每公顷断面积和蓄积量，与标准表求得的蓄积量进行比较确定其适用程度。一般要求系统误差和标准差不大于 ±5%，

标准误差不大于 ±2%。

为说明标准表的使用精度，用未参加编表的82块标准地按标准表计算蓄积量，与实际蓄积量作差异显著性 F 检验，并计算平均系统误差及精度。检验结果 $F = 1.87 < F_{0.05}(2, 80) = 3.13$，平均系统误差为2.51%，精度为95.32%，表明巨尾桉人工林标准表适用，精度较高。

2.3 选择评估方法

目前，巨尾桉纸浆原料林资产评估按《森林资源资产评估技术规范(试行)》执行。《森林资源资产评估技术规范(试行)》第三十条提到幼龄林的评估主要选用重置成本法和序列需工数法，也可以选用现行市价法。中龄林评估通常选用现行市价法 和收获现值法。但是，能反映当地生产过程的生长过程表或收获表在收获现值法的使用中至关重要。如果没有这些数表，只能取得预测值，方法是通过利用当地的调查材料拟合当地的林木平均生长过程。市场价倒算法用在近、成、过熟林的评估中。各龄组评估值之间的衔接在用材林林木资产评估时必须要特别留意。

根据《森林资源资产评估技术规范(试行)》规定，用材林资产评估必须分龄组进行，但短轮伐期巨尾桉人工林生长迅速，在一个龄组期限内树高、蓄积等会有很大差别，那么一年中不同月份的巨尾桉用同一个参照林分标准会对评估结果产生很大误差，比如只有一个月树龄的巨尾桉用的则是一年的参照树高和存活率，这显然是不合理的，评估结果肯定会偏小。另外，幼、中龄林生长很快，如果评估方法采用不一样，评估值将不能得到很好的衔接。在以下的研究中，将针对评估方法的选择等问题作一定的研究。

2.3.1 改变评估期

巨尾桉纸浆原料林不适合按照《森林资源资产评估技术规范(试行)》分龄组划分进行评估，一方面桉树各地主伐年龄不明确、不一致，如果按照龄组划分进行评估，则没有很好的参照林分，另一方面各年度蓄积量差别太大，方法选择不当容易出现中龄林前期评估价值比幼龄林评估价值小的情况。因此按照各年度具体情况采取不同方法更能接近其真实价值。

2.3.2 确定经济技术指标

按照评估方法要求，需要调查了解相应经济技术指标，具体指标见表6。

表6 各种评估方法所需经济技术指标

Tab. 6 Economic and technical indicators required by different assessment methods

方法	市场法	剩余法	收益法	成本法
所需技术参数	林分质量调整系数	价格	价格	林分质量调整系数
	物价指数调整系数	蓄积量	蓄积量	折现率
	参照物单位蓄积量的交易价格	木材经营成本(包括采运成本、销售费用、管理费用、财务费用及有关税费)	生长量	每年的生产成本，主要包括各年投入的工资、物质消耗、地租等
	被估林木资产的蓄积量	木材经营合理利润	营林生产成本	林分年龄
		林木资源的再生价值	经营期	
			资本化率	

2.3.3 选择评估方法

对于不同林木年龄，各种方法适用程度不一样，通过比较各方法用于不同年龄时，收集经济技术指标难易、准确度等方面，筛选出各年龄短轮伐期巨尾桉人工林最适合采用的评估方法。

市场法是通过以相同或类似林木资产的现行市价作为比较基础的，因此，寻找市场上的同类林木参照物是关键。各地的巨尾桉纸浆原料林发展水平不一致，大部分地区的交易市场还不够成熟，此方法只能根据具体情况使用。

剩余法即市场价倒算法，评估时需要林木采伐后所得的木材的蓄积量，因此，此方法仅适用于主伐年龄以后的林木。

收益法即收益净现值法，此方法需要每年的净收益，对于巨尾桉纸浆原料林而言，只存在皆伐一种采伐方式，只有一次收益。收益法的关键是预测主伐时的蓄积量，因此，年龄越小，预测难度越大，准确度越低。

成本法的主要思想是将所用成本折现，此方法在使用时应加入一定的利润，否则只是将成本折现不匹配林木的真实价值，利润可由林业行业的基本利润率结合林分质量调整系数测算。

3 结 论

在本研究前期，分别于2008年与2009年两次对广东省河源市的241块巨尾桉人工林标准地进行了资源调查。通过对这些数据的统计分析得到如下几点结论：

(1)通过对桉树人工林的各种主伐年龄进行分析，得到巨尾桉人工林主伐年龄模型 $y = 0.48x^1 + 0.28x^2 + 0.05x^3 + 0.20x^4$，通过此模型计算得到巨尾桉人工林主伐年龄为5.7年左右；

(2)通过调查的标准地资料编制了巨尾桉人工林标准表，通过此表可以简易查出巨尾桉人工林的标准蓄积，这为收获现值法中的调整系数求算提供了参考依据。

(3)本研究通过深入研究巨尾桉生长特点与评估方法，采用缩短评估期的办法合理解决了各种评估方法用于巨尾桉评估时所出现的相关问题。

参考文献

[1]吴福骞．加强林业建设增加造纸用材[J]．中国造纸，2000，(2)：46～50.

[2]李遨夫．抓住机遇加快发展庭湖区林纸产业[J]．湖南林业科技，2003：30(1)：4～8.

[3]Peter J Ince，Irene Durbak，2002，Pulp wood Supply and demand：Development in the south little growth elsewhere. Journal of Forestry. 2002，(100)：20.

[4]任诚．资产评估[M]．北京：中国财政经济出版社，2002. 1～2.

[5]姜楠．资产评估[M]．大连：东北财经大学出版社，2007. 1.

[6]张志云．关于森林资源资产评估问题[J]．江西农业大学学报，1995(3)：258～262.

[7]Turner J，Thompson C H，Turvey N D，et al. 1990. A soil technical classification system for Pinus radiata plantaions. I. Development. Aust. J. Soil Res. 28，797～811.

[8] Burrough P A.，1989. Fuzzy mathematical methods for soil survey and land evaluation. J. Soil Sci. 40，477～492.

磨盘山天然次生林群落早春植物多样性研究

于　健

（北京林业大学林学院，北京，100083）

摘要：本文以磨盘山次生林为研究对象，简要叙述了国内外关于生物多样性的研究进展，以及有关早春植物研究的现状。并运用野外定位调查法对次生林恢复过程中其早春植物的种类及多样性变化进行研究。因此研究早春植物的多样性及其动态变化规律无论在理论上，还是在实践生产上都具有重要意义

关键词：早春植物；生物多样性；物种组成；次生林

物种多样的生物资源是人类生存的基础。当今世界面临着人口、资源、环境、粮食和能源五大危机，这些问题均与生物多样性的变化有着密切的联系。由于人类活动范围的扩大和活动强度的加剧，以及因此而造成的环境恶化，生物多样性正受到前所未有的威胁。有人估计，目前的世界，每天有一个种正在消灭，热带地区每天有 100 个种正在灭绝。如果人类的消费模式和破坏作用仍不改变的话，到 2008 年，地球上所有物种的 15% ~20% 写将会消失。在自然情况下，物种一方面在进化，一方面也在自然灭绝，但由于人类破坏的干扰，物种灭绝的速率是自然灭绝速率的 1000 倍。按估计，世界上现有 1000 万个物种（有人估计有 3000 万种），但已为人们定名的仅 140 万种。很多物种在连名都未定下来，用途更不知道的情况下正在不断地从地球上消失。一个物种一旦消失，不可能在地球上再出现，这对人类本身来说，是多么悲惨的现实[1]！

目前，生物多样性的问题已不仅仅被科学家所关心，它已引起了国际社会的广泛关注，生物多样性的保护和持续利用已成为人类可持续发展的中心议题[2]。

综上所述，保护生物多样性的重要性已是不言而喻。所以，在巴西召开的举世瞩目的联合国环境与发展大会（UNCED）上，生物多样性成为会议的主要议题之一。

1.1　生物多样性概念的形成及内涵

生物多样性是生物学、生态学，环境科学以及农、林、牧、渔等应用学科，甚至社会科学等交叉的领域[3]。这一术语及其内涵在 20 世纪 80 年代后期才开始逐步为人们所认识和理解。迄今为止，至少有 85 种有关生物多样性的定义。根据 1992 年巴西联合国环境与发展大会通过的《生物多样性公约》中，生物多样性的定义是：“生物多样性是指所有来源的形形色色的生物体，这些来源包括陆地，海洋和其他水生生态系统的及其所构成的生态综合体；这包括物种内部，物种之间和生态系统的多样性。”陈灵芝也对生物多样性下了一个定义，她认为生物多样性是所有生物种类，种内遗传变异和它们生存环境的总称，包括所有不同种类的动物、植物和微生物以及它们拥有的基因，它们与生存环境所组成的生态系统[4]。McNeely 等将生物多样性简单地表述为：“生物之间的多样性和变异性及物种生境的生态复杂

性[5]。"综上，生物多样性(Biological diversity)是生物及其与环境形成的生态复合体以及与此相关的各种生态过程的总和，它包括数以百万种的动物、植物、微生物和它们所拥有的基因以及它们与生存环境形成的复杂的生态系统。因此，生物多样性是一个内涵十分广泛的概念，包括多个层次或水平，其中研究较多、意义重大的主要有遗传多样性、生态系统多样性和物种多样性。

物种多样性是指地球上活有机个体(物种)变异的一个概念，它是一定空间范围内物种的丰富性及其优势与均匀性来衡量的，用测定种的不均匀性来划分种的优势或均匀性所得出的指数表达。物种是生态系统的重要组成部分，又是遗传物质的载体。物体的生物学、生态学和行为学特征的多样性，既是生物遗传性状的具体表现，又是生态系统过程的重要因素，因此物种的保护与研究是生物多样性保护与研究的基础和核心。

1.2 生物多样性的研究

1.2.1 生物多样性现状

生物多样性的保护与持续利用研究已受到国际社会的普遍关注，成为当今人类环境与发展领域的中心议题之一。特别是引起了各国政府和有关国际组织的高度重视，在进行生物多样性保护实践的同时，开展了大量的基础工作，为生物多样性的有效保护奠定了基础。

1.2.2 国外对生物多样性的研究

有关生物多样性的研究，国外开始的较早。自20世纪60年代以来，国际上出现了关心人类环境的热潮。1962年Rachacl Carson的《寂静的春天》的出版，标志着这一阶段的开始。联合国于1972年召开了第一次人类环境会议，对人类面临的环境问题包括生物多样性的保护，形成了一系列决议。Wilson[6]发表了"世界上平均每天有一个物种消失，到2000年地球上15%～20%的物种将会消失，物种灭绝速率是自然灭绝速率的1000倍"这样的评述，使人们对生物多样性有了新的认识。特别是在1992年6月举行的联合国环境与发展大会上，包括中国在内的153个国家在《生物多样性公约》上签了字，保护生物多样性从而成为世界范围内的联合行动[7]。1994年1月，IUCK在阿根廷布宜诺斯艾利斯召开第十九届大会，主题是"关系地球及其居住者"，这是继1992年联合国环发大会后的又一次讨论保护自然和人类环境的重要会议。目前，有关的国际组织或机构以及许多国家政府都纷纷致力于生物多样性的保护事业，开展各种研究项目，举行各种学术会议，建立全球或区域性的监测网络等。

对于生物多样性的研究主要集中在物种多样性的现状、物种多样性的形成、演化及维持机制、种群生存力分析、物种的濒危状况、灭绝速率及原因、珍稀、濒危和衰退物种的就地保护和移地保护的方法与可持续利用以及物种多样性编目等工作。关于生物多样性形成即变化的机制已成为国外生态学家们研究的一个热点问题。如Abrams[8]关于生物多样性与生产力及竞争原理的讨论；Rosenzweig和Sandlin[9]关于物种多样性与纬度的关系及面积效应的研究；Caley等[10]对局部特有现象及其与局部和区域多样性关系的研究；Hoagland和Collins[11]对梯度与植物群落等级结构关系的分析；Prach[12]等对物种特性随演替梯度变化的机制研究等都对生物多样性的研究做出了巨大的贡献。此外，Rosenzweig[13]在其专著《时间和空间的物种多样性》(Species Diversity In Space And Time)中分别从时间、空间及无维度(Dimensionless)梯度几个方面研究论述了生物多样性的格局机制，其时间尺度包括生态时间尺度和进化时间尺度两个方面，空间尺度则是指面积与物种多样性、纬度与物种多样性及生产力与物种多样性的关系等。而无维度梯度则是包括物种多样性随个体大小及食物等的变化规律。特别针对热带雨林的生物多样性动态问题，Sheil[14]和Phillips[15]等人，在OIKOS上展开了激烈的讨论，Rohde[16]和Rosenzweig也就面积与物种多样性纬度梯度问题展开了争论。

1.2.3 我国对生物多样性的研究现状

中国作为世界上生物多样性特别丰富的国家之一，积极开展生物多样性保护活动，是少数几个最早制定国家级生物多样性保护行动计划的国家之一，并在生物多样性的研究方面取得了一定成就。

从20世纪80年代开始，我国就陆续开展了有关濒危植物的解剖、生理、生殖、遗传和生态研究。1993年实施的国家自然科学基金重大项目——中国主要濒危植物的保护生物学研究，对10种具代表性的濒危植物同时进行生态学、生殖生物学、遗传多样性的研究，这是我国对濒危植物研究的开始，也是对生物多样性重视的开始。中国科学院生物多样性委员会主编的《生物多样性研究的原理与方法》，对相关类型的生物多样性保护和退化生境的恢复重建有一定的指导意义。具体对于生物多样性的研究是多方面的。在生物多样性形成机制方面，有一些综述论及了生物多样性的梯度变化与生物多样性的格局机制等。如黄建辉对物种多样性的形成机制作了探讨[17]。贺金生等对近年来陆地植物群落物种多样性的梯度变化特征的研究作了概括[18]。2002年，在海岛生物多样性研究大会上，蒋有绪等探讨了海南岛的生物多样性格局及其形成机制。对与植物物种多样性的垂直分布格局，唐志尧、方精云[19]也有一些综述。我国以往有关植物群落物种多样性的研究较多，如高贤明[20]对秦岭太白山弃耕地植物群落演替过程中不同群落的物种多样性变化进行了分析，也对北京山区辽东栎群落物种多样性及其演替规律进行了探讨。谢晋阳等[21]研究了暖温带落叶阔叶林的物种多样性特征。余世孝等[22]研究了海南岛霸王岭热带植被物种多样性的特征，并对其进行了空间分析。在应用生物多样性评判林分抗虫性方面的研究也有一些，如李孟楼等早在1995年已开始了应用生物多样性评判林分抗虫性的分析和研究，并利用生物多样指数，探索性地研究了秦岭落叶松林昆虫群落结构的多样性与稳定性，秦岭南坡半翅目昆虫的多样性等，并取得一定成果[23]。

我国从事生物多样性研究主要是中科院各研究所，现有30多个所从事有关生物多样性的研究工作，已建立了一支生物学各分支学科的强大研究队伍。科技人员1000多名，除少部分从事以保存遗传多样性为目的的细胞和其他基础研究外，大部分从事分类学、生态学、生物资源学的研究工作，并保存大量标本。近年来，在国家环保局和国家林业局支持下，中科院会同有关部门专家编写了《中国濒危动植物红皮书》，提出了国家重点保护动植物名单。《中国植被》及《中国1/400万植被图》以及各省区的植被类型的特点和分布，为生态系统多样性的研究打下了坚实的基础。

1.3 早春植物概述

早春植物主要指一年生短命植物和多年生类短命植物，也包括少数非短命植物(蒋瑞芬等，1992)。在早春当大多数植物刚刚萌发，早春植物便充分利用这一有利时机进行有效的光合积累，至春末夏初迅速完成从种子萌发到成熟的生活史，是高效利用环境资源的独特类群。早春植物延长了森林群落的生长期，对提高生态系统生产力具有重要意义[24]。

早春植物对光照特别敏感，即不能适应强烈的直射光照条件，也不能忍受过度庇荫。在樟子松和落叶松人工林下，由于郁闭度大，光照不足，早春植物不能生长；在柞木林中，由于郁闭度小，光照过强，早春植物生长不良，分布频率低；而在光照中等的桦木林及杂木林下，则生长旺盛。可见早春植物是光照中性植物。光照是早春植物生境中的主导因子。

早春植物具有较强的抗寒能力。在土壤温度处在零下时，有些草本植物已经萌发，甚至已进入花盛期，如顶冰花等。在3～4月间，地面平均最低气温为－14.7～3.4℃，植物体内结冰的情况下仍能保持旺盛的生命力[25]。

1.3.1 早春植物的类型及生态作用

根据早春植物季节变化的动态规律，可将其分为3种类型：①在乔灌木树种处于休眠状态的早春时期已经开始生长，在林分郁闭前已经完成开花、结果等各个生活阶段，林分郁闭后，这些植物生长结束，进入休眠期。这类植物称为早春生长植物；②生长、开花、结果在早春，但林分郁闭后继续生长，这类植物称为早春开花植物；③生长在早春，开花、结果在林分郁闭后，这类植物称为早春展叶植物[26]。

早春植物是较原始的残遗植物。落叶阔叶林下特有环境条件长期作用使它们形成了相应的适应方式和途径它们同属地下芽植物，以球茎、根茎或多年生根的形式度过不良环境。早春植物对落叶阔叶林有较大的依附性，二者的生活节律相互合拍，融为一体。早春植物的个体较小，但群体密度极大，所以其生物量较大，在森林的初级生产中占有一定的比例。早春植物体内含水量较高，枯死后易于在微生物的作用下迅速分解，加速了生态系统的物质循环和能量流动。同时作为初级生产者的重要组成部分，它增加了生态系统的能量和物质输入，提高其能量水平，从而增加了系统的稳定性。早春植物在垂直结构上占据了30cm以下的空间，对土壤有较强的固持作用和覆盖作用，并能够提高土壤的肥力，保持土壤的温湿度，为上层林木种子的萌发。幼苗的生长及林木本身的生长创造了条件。另外早春草本层植物多为药用植物和食用植物，同时又多为比较鲜艳的观赏植物，经济价值大，是非常有必要研究如何保护、开发和利用的植物资源[27]。

1.4 早春植物多样性的研究现状研究

我国学者曾对早春植物进行大量研究，涉及生态习性、群落特征（中国科学院新疆综合考察队，1979；李世英，1961；陈昌笃等，1983；胡适之，1962），形态解剖（于喜凤等，1987；庄重等，1990）和固氮特性（关桂兰等，1990）等范围。亦曾就其根系形态划分生活型（张立运，1983，1985）。

近些年人们对早春植物的研究越来越多，主要研究内容有对择伐后阔叶红松林早春草本植物进行的研究，有对原始阔叶红松林草本植物的研究，还有对不同林型下早春植物的研究。郭忠玲等对红松阔叶林择伐后早春植物物种及多样性变化研究发现，红松阔叶林经择伐后，与对照林分相比，不仅早春优势植物种类及其在群落中的地位有一定的改变，物种种类组成也发生了较大的变化[28]。赵秀海等通过对长白山西部20世纪50年代择伐过的阔叶红松林早春阶段草本植物的调查，结果表明其分布是均匀的，没有明显的优势种，生态优势度较低。Shannon Wiener多样指数、种数及个体总数明显与坡向、坡位有关[29]。郝占庆等通过对长白山原始阔叶红松林草本植物早春（5月5～20日）、夏季（6月20日～7月10日）和秋季（8月20日～9月10日）的三次调查，结果表明其物种多样性是很丰富的，同时其季节变化也比较明显[30]。叶万辉等对不同林型下早春植物层片的组成和多样性进行了分析并得出不同林型下早春植物的分布特点。于凤英、郝占庆等研究了长白山阔叶红松林内早春植物群落特征，为进一步深入研究其在森林生态系统内物质循环和能量流动等生态功能奠定基础[31]。

1.5 研究的目的及意义

生物多样性能源作为一种可再生能源是人类生活的基础。但目前，生物多样性正以空前的速度消失，在消失的物种中，存有许多人类还没有命名的，对于它们的用途更无从了解。在一些人类没有研究过的植物中，可能含有对抗人类疾病的成分，包括大部分早春植物，这些物种如果绝迹，将是人类的重大损失。

早春植物因其独特的个体和生态学特性而具有多种资源价值，诸如饲用、药用、观赏和育种等方面。因此，研究早春植物的种类及多样性，能够为开发利用适应性强、具有一定观赏及经济价值的早春植物资源提供理论依据，对开展林业多种经营、天然林保护工程的顺利实施有着重要的理论及现实意义，同时研究早春植物，也为确定落叶阔叶林的分布、特征、经营利用技术提供了一定的理论基础。因此，研究早春植物的多样性及其动态变化规律无论在理论上，还是在实践生产上都具有重要意义。

参考文献

[1]钱迎倩. 生物多样性的保护和永续利用[J]. 广西科学院学报，1994，10(1)：5~6.

[2]Orians G H，Dirzo R，Cushman J H. Biodiversity and ecosystem processes in tropical forests[J]. *Springer*，*Ecological studies*，1996，Vol. 122.

[3]臧润国等. 天然林生物多样性保育与恢复[M]. 北京：中国科学技术出版社，2005.

[4]陈灵芝. 生物多样性保护现状及对策[M]. 北京：中国科学技术出版社，1994

[5]Mcneely J A，Miller K，et al. Conserving the World's Biological Diversity[M]. Gland，Switzerland，1990.

[6]Wilson E O，et al The Current State of Biological Diversity. E. Wilson，E. O(ed.) Biodiversity[M]. Washington，DC：National Academy of Sciences Press，1998.

[7]马克平，钱迎倩. 生物多样性的研究现状与发展趋势//中国科学院生物多样性委员会. 生物多样性研究的原理与方法[M]. 北京：中国科学技术出版社，1994.

[8]Abrams P A. Monotonic or unimodal diversity – productivity gradients：What does competition theory predict[J]. *Ecology*，1995，76(7)：2007~2019.

[9]Rosenzweig M L，Sandlin E A. Species diversity and latitudes：listening to arer's signal[J]. *OIKOS*，1997，80：172~176.

[10]Caley M J，Schiluterr D. The relationship between local and regional diversity[J]. *Ecology*，1997，78(1)：70~80.

[11]Hoagland B W，Collins S L. Gradient models，gradient analysis，and hierarchical structure in plant communities[J]*OIKOS*，1997，78 (1)：23~30.

[12]Prach K，et al. Changes in species traits during succession：a search for pattern[J]*KOS*，1997，79 (1)：201~205.

[13]Rosenzweig M L. Species diversity in space and time[M]. New York：*Cambridge University press*，1995.

[14]Sheil D. Further notes on species richness，tropical forest dynamics and samping[J]. *OIKOS*，1997，79 (1)：188~190.

[15]Phillips O，et al. Species richness，tropical forest dynamics，and sampling：response to Sheil[J]. *OIKOS*，1997，79 (1)：183~187.

[16]Rohde K. The larger area of the tropics does not explain latitudinal gradients in species diversity[J]. *OIKOS*, 1997, 79 (1): 169 ~ 172.

[17]黄建辉. 物种多样性的空间格局及其形成机制初探[J]. 生物多样性, 1994, (2): 103 ~ 107.

[18]贺金生, 陈伟烈. 陆地植物群落物种多样性的梯度变化[J]. 生态学报, 1997, 17(1): 91 ~ 99.

[19]唐志尧, 方精云. 植物物种多样性的垂直分布格局[J]. 生物多样性, 2004, 12(1): 20 ~ 28.

[20]高贤明, 马克平, 陈灵芝, 等. 暖温带若干落叶阔叶林群落物种多样性及其与群落动态的关系[J]. 植物生态学报, 2001, 25(3): 283 ~ 290.

[21]谢晋阳, 陈灵芝. 暖温带落叶阔叶林的物种多样性特征[J]. 生态学报, 1994, 14(4): 337 ~ 344.

[22]余世孝, 臧润国, 蒋有绪, 等. 海南岛霸王岭垂直带热带植物物种多样性的空间分析[J]. 生态学报, 2001, 21(9): 1438 ~ 1443.

[23]李孟楼, 刘朝斌. 秦岭南坡火地塘林区落叶松人工林的昆虫群落及其结构[J]. 西北林学院学报, 1995, 10(1): 68 ~ 73.

[24]叶万辉, 国庆喜, 高嵩, 等. 早春植物层片的物种组成及多样性分析研究. 齐齐哈尔师范学院学报(自然科学版), 1994, 14(1): 34 ~ 37.

[25]刘晓春. 早春植物及其生态学特性初探. 林业勘察设计, 2003, (1): 28 ~ 29.

[26]吴刚, 尹若波, 周永斌, 等. 长白山红松阔叶林林隙动态变化对早春草本植物的响. 生态学报, 1999, 19(5): 660 ~ 663.

[27]邵国凡, 刘琪璟. 长白山阔叶红松林早春草本层生物量初报[J]. 森林生态研究, 1992, (6): 24 ~ 30.

[28]郭忠玲, 杜凤国, 郑焰峰, 等. 马元旦红松阔叶林择伐后早春植物物种及多样性变化研究. 北华大学学报(自然科学版), 2003, 4(4): 337 ~ 341.

[29]赵秀海, 戚继忠, 孙广仁, 等. 长白山阔叶红松林早春草本层植物的数量特征[J]. 吉林林学院学报, 1997, 13(1): 5 ~ 9.

[30]郝占庆, 陶大立, 赵士洞, 等. 长白山北坡阔叶红松林草本植物物种多样性及其季节动态 [J]. 生物多样性, 1994, 2(3): 125 ~ 132.

[31]于凤英, 周永斌, 安云全, 等. 长白山阔叶红松林早春植物群落特征研究[J]. 沈阳农业大学学报, 2003, 34(6): 430 ~ 432.

森林生物量估算方法及模型研究

张静菲

（北京林业大学信息学院）

摘要：总结分析目前国内外的森林生物量和生长量模型(包括相对生长关系和生物量－蓄积量模型)的研究状况，提出今后我国在森林生物量估算领域的研究重点：①整合经验相对生长方程；②系统研究生物量估算参数的规律性及其不确定性。

关键词：生物量；模型；综述

Study on Forestry Biomass Model and Oriental Arborvitae Biomass Model

ZHANG Jing-Fei

（Beijing Forestry University，Beijing，100083）

Abstract：This paper analysis the forestry biomass and volume models（including the relationship between relative growth and biomass－growing stock model）current domestic and international，studies the situation ，made in China in the future to estimate forest biomass research focus areas：①integration experience relative growth equation；②systematic study of the regularity of biomass estimation parameters and their uncertainties.

Key words：biomass；mode；summary

1 研究的目的和意义

森林生物量约占全球陆地植被生物量的90%以上，是森林固碳能力的重要保证，是研究很多林业问题和生态问题的基础。因此，准确测定森林生物量无论在生产上还是理论研究上都具有十分重要的意义。

森林生物量是森林生态系统最基本的数量特征，它既表明森林的经营水平和开发利用的价值，同时又反映森林与环境在物质循环和能量流动上的复杂关系。生态系统的能量和营养循环的研究首先依赖于生物量和生产力的数据。森林生物量便成为生态学和全球变化研究的重要内容之一，同时还可为系统研究中国森林植被碳库及其变化提供基础数据。森林群落的生物量是森林生态系统生产力的最好的指标，是森林生态系统结构优劣和功能高低的最直接的表现，是森林生态系统环境质量的综合体现。

森林生物量测定非常困难，而且耗时费力，因此确定一种行之有效而又准确的调查方法是十分重要的。生物量模型估计法是目前比较流行的方法，它是利用林木易测因子来推算难于测定的林木生物量，从而减少测定生物量的外业工作。虽然在建模过程中，需要测定一定数量样木生物量的数据，但一旦模型建立，在同类的林分中就可以利用森林资源清查资料来估计整个林分的生物量，而且有一定的精度保证。特别是在大范围的森林生物量调查中。利用生物量模型能大大减小调查工作量。

要准确测定森林生物量数据，关键在于林木生物量的准确测定与估计。目前世界上最常用的是生物量模型估测方法。该方法是利用林木易测因子来推算难于测定的林木生物量，从而减少测定生物量的外业工作。

2 国内外研究现状

森林生物量是森林生态系统最基本的数量特征。近几十年来其提供了大量可靠的基础数据用以研究森林生态系统的生产能力以及揭示森林生态系统能量平衡和养分循环等功能过程的变化规律。森林生物量已成为度量森林结构和功能变化的重要指标，并为生态系统的碳汇和碳素循环研究提供关键数据，在碳循环、全球气候变化研究中起到重要作用。目前国际林联在《国际森林资源监测大纲》中已将森林生物量列为最主要的监测项目之一[1]。

2.1 国外生物量研究

最早的有关生物量的研究是 Ebermeryer 于 1876 年在德国进行的几种森林的树枝落叶量和木材重量的测定[2]，后 Boysen Jensen 在研究森林自然稀疏问题时，研究了森林的初级生产量[3]。1929 ~ 1953 年，Burger 研究了树叶生物量和木材生产的关系[4]。1944 年，Kittredge 利用叶重和胸径的拟合关系，成功拟合了预测白松等树种叶量的对数回归方程[5]。20 世纪 50 年代以来，世界上开始重视对森林生物量研究，日本、美国相继开展了对森林生产力的研究，其中包括大量对生物量的调查，此后在 IBP(国际生物学计划)和 MAB(人力生物圈)的推动下，生物量的研究发展迅速，有关学者研究了地球上主要森林植被类型的生物量和生产力，估算了地球生物圈的总生物量，研究方法变得多样多，精确度也显著提高。

2.2 国内生物量研究

我国的植物生物量研究起步较晚，但经过近几十年的研究，已经对森林生态系统中的乔木、林下植物 、根系等生物量进行了大量研究，并在森林类型、不同气候带与区域尺度生物量等研究领域有所开拓。目前，我国森林生物量已经有大量分散资料的积累，这些研究极大地推进了我国森林生物量及相关的生态系统和全球变化研究的开展，也为系统研究我国的森林植被碳库及其变化打下了基础。

随着计算机技术和各种统计分析软件的广泛应用，在直接收获法的基础上衍生出了回归模型估测法，根据相对生长理论以胸径(D)、树高(H)等变量配置回归方程建立统计关系进行宏观拓展以此来获得某一树种或者某一林型的生物量状况。该种方法具有较高的可信度，在局部森林生物量估测中被广泛采用。平均生物量法结合了大量调查数据和单株测树因子建模，也是比较常用的方法。近几十年来，各地学者结合直接收获法和回归模型对我国的主要树种的生物量进行了深入研究。在乔木单株木生物量研究方面，温远光等按径级标准木法测定了尾叶桉干、皮、枝等器官生物量，建立了相对生长方程推算尾叶桉林分的生物量和生产力[20]。李燕燕等通过分级取样测定法对马尾松纯林、格氏栲混交林生物量进行了分析，发现混交林生物量明显大于纯林生物量[21]。在乔木生物量与林分因子、群落关系研究方面，段爱国等总结前人资料并结合杉木人工林固定样地长期观测材料的基础上研究了杉木人工林在不同林岭、立地条件喝林分密度下的生物量变化规律[23]。刘申等根据鼎湖山多种植被类型乔木生物量的研究结果得到群落生物量递减、倒钟形和递增种径级分配规律认为山区常绿阔叶林生物量发展潜力巨大[23]。目前，我国主要树种以及一些主要森林类型的生物量都已经得到测定，并提出了许多较为成熟的估算模型。但是，树冠等因子与乔木生物量关系的研究尚处于起步阶段。如何规范生物量计量参数并解决总量与各维量模型间的相容性也是目前困扰生物量研究的主要问题。

在区域尺度生物量估测领域，平均生物量法、平均换算因子法及换算因子连续函数法是比较常用的几种方法，平均生物量法、平均换算因子法及换算因子连续函数法基于系统抽样进行样地调查或建立在森林资源清查资料基础上，是估算区域尺度森林生物量较常用的方法。平均生物量法对于大量不同的森林类型和树种构建模型并不容易实现。平均换算因子法和换算因子连续函数法分别通过固定和随材积变化的生物量转换因子，再根据蓄积计算得到生物量。冯宗炜等率先总结了全国不同森林类型的生物量及其分布状况[14]。罗天祥、李文华等进一步建立了我国主要生物生产力优化模型系列，以此估算我国森林总生物量[24]。

2.3 森林生物量研究

生物量的传统研究方法有二氧化碳平衡法(气体交换法)、微气场法(昼夜曲线法)和直接收获法。二氧化碳平衡法是将森林生态系统的叶、枝、干和土壤等组分封闭在不同的气室内，根据气室内 CO_2浓度变化计算各个组分的光合速率和呼吸速率，进一步推算出该生态系统 CO_2的流动和平衡量[6]。由于林冠的叶光合特性的时空异质性，用叶片 CO_2气体交换量推算林冠光合量有一个复杂的尺度转换过程。微气场法则与风向、风速和温度等因子测定相结合，通过测定从地表到林冠上层 CO_2浓度的垂直梯度变化来估算生态系统 CO_2的输入量和输出量。

直接收获法是全球普遍采用的研究方法，也是对陆地群落和森林最实用的方法。潘维俦等针对人工林的特点和大量的样地数据提出了分级分层测定法[7]，胥辉通过增加形状变量如冠长、冠幅和体积等改进了相对生长方程[8]。直接收获法可以大致分为皆伐法、平均木法和相对生长法[9]。

皆伐法是将一定单位面积上的林木全部伐倒后测定各部分的鲜重并换算成干重，加和后即为单株木的生物量。该法精度高，但是耗费大量人力和时间，一般较少采用。李意德等在对我国海南岛尖峰岭热带山地雨林生物量的调查中曾结合森林采伐运用了此方法[10]。

平均木法是根据样地每木调查的资料计算出全部立木的平均胸高断面积，选出代表该样地最接近这个平均值的数株标准木，伐倒后求出平均木的生物量，再乘以该林分单位面积上的株数，得到单位面积上林分乔木层的生物量。这种方法比较适用于林木大小具有小的或者中等里三度的正态频率分布的林分，例如人工林[11]。平均木法是很粗略的计算方法，因为根据不同的测树因子(胸径、树高、断面积和树干材积)选取的平均木是不一样的，由此可以得出不同的林分生物量[12]。

相对生长法是在样地每木调查基础上，按照径阶选取标准木，一般在株数较多的中央径级选取 2～3 株，其他径级各选取 1～2 株，对两端的径级特别是最大的径级至少要选一株标准木，按照标准木调查方法测定其单株木的各部分生物量，再根据林木的各种生物量与某一测树学指标之间存在的相关关系，；利用数理统计配置回归方程[13]。在森林群落里，胸径是最容易测定的因子，一般都尽量利用这个因子作自变量来推算其他因子[15]。

方精云等提出用树干材积推算生物量的方法[16]。他认为，树干与总生物量和其他器官之间存在相关关系，因此以树干材积推算总生物量是可行的。用这种方法计算的生物量称作材积得出的生物量。统计表明，林分蓄积量与生物量之间存在良好的相关关系，因为林分蓄积量包含了森林类型、年龄、立地条件和林分密度等诸多因素，利用它与林分生物量之间的关系推算生物量就消除了这些因素的影响。

通过遥感技术(RS)和地理信息系统(GIS)等先进手段可以测定从林分到区域等不同空间尺度的森林生物量。光合作用是植被生产力形成的重要生理生态过程，树冠层的叶面积指数和生物化学成分是森林碳获得量的决定因素，植物对太阳辐射的吸收、反射、投射及其辐射，会在林冠和大气中产生传递，这种传递信息和影响植被生产力的生态因子与卫星接受的信息之间可以建立一定的解析式，可利用这些解析式来测定林分生物量。遥感可以氛围光学和近红外遥感及微波遥感。光学和近红外光谱只对绿叶产生反应，而微波可以穿透林冠，不仅能作用于叶，也能作用于树干，因此可以利用微波遥感对森林生物量进行全面和准确的估测[17]。郭志华、彭少麟等借助于全球定位系统(GPS)为调查样方准确定位，通过样方调查获取森林蓄积，根据 Landsat TM 数据 7 个波段信息及其线性与非线性的组合，应用逐步回归技术分别建立估算针叶林和阔叶林蓄积的最优光谱模型，进而确定了粤西及附近地区的森林生物量[17]。陈利军等用遥感技术对中国陆地植被的生物量做了估测[18~19]。

2.4 森林生物量模型概况

生物量模型是确定森林生物量的一种有效并且相对准确的方法，也是确定生物量的主要方法，可根据研究对象的不同分为大尺度生物量模型和单木生物量模型两种。

2.4.1 大尺度生物量模型

大尺度森林生物量测定的测定对象是一片森林，通过基于材积转化比的生物量模型或基于遥感技术的生物量模型来测定森林生物量，是推算森林生物量的一种简易方法。通常人们认为生物量与材积有一定的比例关系，许多研究中都将这一比值看作常数。当这一常数确定时，就可以根据森林资源调查数据中的森林蓄积量来估计森林生物量。基于遥感技术的生物量模型的原理是根据植被遥感图像信息中的不同反射光谱曲线得到植被的叶绿素含量，再依据叶绿素含量与叶生物量、叶生物量与群落生物量之间的相互关系逐步估算森林植被生物量。

大尺度森林生物量的估算方法一直是人们关注的焦点，自 20 世纪 70 年代起很多学者就开始对全球范围内的生物量进行估测，包括基于材积转化的生物量模型和基于遥感技术的生物量模型。

(1)基于材积转化的生物量模型：

随着全球各地有关生物量实测资料的大量增加，对提高森林生物量估算的精度变得更加可能，并由此提出一系列研究方法，其中主要有生物量转换因子法、生物量转换因子连续函数法。

①生物量转换因子法(Biomass Expansion Factor，BEF)是利用林分生物量与木材材积比值的平均值，乘以该森林类型的总蓄积量，得到该类型森林的总生物量[8,27]。

李意德等对海南岛热带山地雨林林分生物量的研究表明，生物量转换因子法估算的生物量较皆伐法高出 20%~40%[40]，而基于实测资料建立的生物量回归模型的估计值与皆伐法非常接近，相对误差在10%以内[10]。这是由于林分生物量和蓄积量与森林类型、年龄、立地条件和林分密度等诸多因素有关。

对郁闭度较大的森林生物量，该方法估测误差较大，原因是该方法将生物量转化因子看作常数，因此未能准确估计郁闭森林的林下部分。但是对非郁闭森林的估测结果较好。

②生物量转换因子连续函数法是为克服生物量转换因子法将生物量与蓄积量比值作为常数的不足而提出的。因此，换算因子连续函数法将单一不变的平均换算因子改为分龄级的换算因子，以更准确地估算国家或地区尺度的森林生物量。林分材积综合反映了林龄、立地、个体密度和林分状况等因素的变化，因此，可以作为换算因子的函数，以表示BEF的连续变化。

但是，目前该模型仅对兴安岭落叶松进行了研究。是否适用于其他类型森林有待进一步研究[26]。

(2)基于遥感技术的生物量模型：

遥感图像信息是由其反射光谱特征决定的，植物的光合作用表现为对红光和蓝紫光的强烈吸收而使其反射光谱曲线在该部分波段呈波谷形态。所以，植物的反射光谱特征反映了植物的叶绿素含量和生长状况。而叶绿素含量与叶生物量相关，叶生物量又与群落生物量相关，所以，利用遥感数据来估算森林植被生物量，首先需要分析森林植被生物量估测的遥感模型机理，从光合作用即森林植被生产力形成的生理生态过程出发，以及森林植被对太阳辐射的吸收、反射、透射及其辐射在植被冠层内及大气中的传输，结合植被生产力的生态影响因子，在卫星接收到的信息与实测生物量之间建立完整的数学模型及其解析式，进而利用这些解析式来估算森林生物量。

基于遥感技术的生物量模型主要包括经验模型、基于植被二向反射的特性的物理模型、半经验模型和机理模型(或过程模型)这几种。与传统的生物量估算方法比较，遥感方法可快速、无损、相对准确的对生物量进行估算，对生态系统进行宏观监测。研究者可以利用遥感的多时相特点定位分析同一样地一段时间后的干扰变化，使传统方法难以解决的问题变得轻而易举，使动态监测成为可能。

2.4.2 单木生物量模型

单木生物量模型是由模拟林分内每株树木的干、枝、叶、皮根等分量的干物质重量为基础的一类模型。单木生物量模型是能够反映和表达树木各分量干重和其他测树因子之间的内在联系的一个或一组数学表达式，通过样本观测值建立树木各分量干重与胸径(D)、树高(H)等其他测树因子的函数关系，从而达到利用树木易测因子来估测森林生物量的目的。在模型的建立过程中需要测定一定量样木作为基础数据，而模型建立之后就可以利用森林资源清查数据来估计同类的林分中的林分生物量，而且具有一定的精度。因此，单木生物量的研究工作一直是研究的热点。

林木生物量模型比较常用的有线性模型、非线性模型和多项式模型三种。在这三种模型中，非线性模型应用最广泛，其中以相对生长模型最具有代表性，是所有模型中应用最普遍的一种模型[27]。

相对生长模型是用指数或对数关系描述林木各分量之间按比例协调增长的模型。作为比例变化协调增长的这些指数或对数关系被称为相对生长。相对生长早期研究是在生物体上[28]。

$$Y = aX^b \tag{2-1}$$

$$\ln Y = \ln a + b\ln X \tag{2-2}$$

假设：X 和 Y 的生长率成比例，即$\frac{\mathrm{d}Y}{Y\mathrm{d}t} = b\ \frac{\mathrm{d}X}{X\mathrm{d}t}$，其中 b 称为相对生长系数，两边积分结果为：

$$\ln Y + k_1 = b\ln X + k_2(k_1、k_2\text{为积分常数}) \tag{2-3}$$

$$Y = e^{e^{k_2-k_1}}X^b \tag{2-4}$$

$$\text{令 } a = e^{k_2-k_1}\text{，则得到：}Y = aX^b \tag{2-5}$$

公式(2-1) 中 b 为相对生长系数，英文原意 Constant Allometric Ratio ，因此该模型简称为 CAR 模型。当 $b>1$ 时，Y 与 X 表示为正的相对生长关系 Y 的生长快于 X 生长；当 $b<1$ 时，则表示为负的相对生长关系，Y 的生长慢于 X 生长；当 $b\ =1$ 时，为等速生长。Kittredgt 首次将相对生长模型引入到树木上。并成功地估计了叶的重量[29]。随后许多研究者纷纷应用该模型估计林木其他器官的重量。直到 Ruark[30]等人对该模型提出了不同见解，他们认为林木各分量之间相对生长率随林木大小的变化有可能不是一个常数。提出 X 和 Y 的生长率与 X 大小呈线性关系。

$$\frac{\mathrm{d}Y}{Y\mathrm{d}t} = (b + cX)\frac{\mathrm{d}Y}{X\mathrm{d}t} \tag{2-6}$$

两边积分得：$\ln Y + k_1 = b\ln X + cX + k_2$

$$Y = e^{k_2-k_1}X^b e^{cX}\text{令 } a = e^{k_2-k_1}\text{，则：}Y = aX^b e^{cX} \tag{2-7}$$

公式(2-7)中 X 和 Y 的生长率变化关系并不是一个固定常数，而是与 X 大小有关。这种关系英文称作 Variable Allometric Ratio，简称 VAR 模型。

在生物量模型研究与应用中，CAR 模型和 VAR 模型是最常用的形式，它们是非线性模型，两种模型具体形式如下：

(1) 树干：

CAR 模型：$W_i = b_0(D_i^2H)^{b_1} + \varepsilon_i$

VAR 模型：$W_i = b_0(D_i^2H_i)^{b_1}e^{b_2(D_i^2H_i)} + \varepsilon_i$

(2)树枝、树叶：

CAR 模型：$W_i = b_0(D_i)^{b_1} + \varepsilon_i$

VAR 模型：$W_i = b_0(D_i)^{b_1}e^{b_2D_i} + \varepsilon_i$

式中：W 是树干、树枝或树叶的重量；D 是 1.3m 处直径；H 为树高；ε 为误差；i = 第 1、2、3…n 株；e 为指数函数；b_0、b_1、b_2 为参数。

2.4.3 模型变量的选择

模型确定之后，要测定单木生物量的下一项工作就是要确定模型的参数。首先可以确定不同树种之间，即使采用相同的生长量模型，其参数也是不同的。除此之外，还有其他一些因子对生长量模型有影响，比如树龄、树木长势、海拔、坡向等。这些因子或多或少都对模型有影响。

模型变量的选择一般遵循两个原则：一是容易测量，二是与因变量有紧密的相关关系。而自变量的个数，要具体情况具体分析。在生物量模型中，不宜采用过多的自变量，使得模型较为复杂，造成变量间的相互抵触[31]。

在具有代表性、未经过间伐、生长正常林分中设置标准地。选取了5~8块具有典型特征的标准地，逐株测定林木各调查因子，每块标准地按等断面积径级法选取4~5株标准木，并进行树干解析及生物量测定(包括枝，叶、树干与全树重)等。对外业采得的样木的生物量的拟合数据进行整理，通过它与林分调查因子间的简单相关关系的分析，选择相关系数较大的变量，对所获得的样本数据进行拟合，根据模型方程配置回归模型，或者采用最小二乘法求解。

变量的确定一般从两个方面考虑，一是易于测定，二是与因变量有紧密的相关关系。

(1)树干模型变量：因变量是树干干物质重量，自变量选用胸径(D)、树高(H)、或组合变量(D^2H)。在自变量中加入H后，能消除同一树种不同林分间的差异，对于树皮、木材模型同树干模型一样。

(2)树冠模型可分解为树枝模型和树叶模型。树冠受到许多外界因素的影响，叶片受到当年环境变化的影响，也同时随季节变化而波动，是生物量模型研究中最困难的环节，可选用的自变量较多，常用的有胸径(D)、树高(H)、冠长(L)、冠幅(Cw)或这些变量的组合变量。

采用SYSTAT软件对各种形式的公式进行回归估计，观察其相关系数、参差平方和最小的作为进一步选型的模型，观察与比较模型中的变异系数，找出变异系数最大的对应的变量，去掉此变量后得到一个新的模型，再进行回归估计，比较相关系数和残差平方和。按照这种方法可以选出最优模型。这样选型的优点在于能充分考虑各变量的组合形式，不会漏选，还可以减少方程拟合的次数使工作量减少到最低程度。

2.4.4 模型参数估计

在线性回归模型中，最常用的参数估计方法是最小二乘法。对于相对生长两模型，通常的参数估计方法是将模型线性化，再利用线性回归的参数估计方法求解其参数。如果非线性强度很强，则这样线性近似时产生的模型误差将会很大(王新州，2002)。这样的对数线性化方法并不满足标准线性回归中误差项的方差为常数的基本假设，存在异方差性。王仲峰(王仲峰，2006)比较了对数法与非线性最小二乘法这两种参数估计方法，他认为非线性最小二乘法的残差平方和最小，更能满足最小二乘法的条件。

回归模型存在基本假设。如果基本假设不成立，用最小二乘法就不能得到回归参数的最优无偏估计量。等方差，即误差项的方差为常数，就是一个基本假设。然而如材积模型、生物量模型、生长率模型等众多林业上涉及的模型中都存在异方差(骆期邦，1992；曾伟生，1992；曾伟生，1996)。在数理统计上克服模型异方差的方法主要有三种：加权最小二乘法、对原模型变换的方法和模型的对数变换法，其中加权最小二乘法最为常用。加权最小二乘估计的关键在于权函数的选择，曾伟生等人(曾伟生，1998；曾伟生，1999；张会儒，1999；胥辉，1999)提出以原函数本身的变换作为权函数能够使新模型满足等方差的要求，并且对任意多个变量形式的回归模型都很容易实现。

2.4.5 相容性生物量模型

目前的生物量模型通常按照林木各分量(干、枝、叶、根)分别建立选型，模型建立后根据各分量实际观测数据对各个模型分别拟合求其参数，因而造成总量、树冠、树干与其对应的各分量之和之间存在着误差，即各维量模型间不相容，且随着直径、树高和分量方程个数的增大误差也逐步增大(唐守正，2000)。解决生物量模型的相容性的传统方法是平差法，即按比例进行平差。这种方法虽然可以解决相容性问题，但效果并不理想(梁长秀，2001)。唐守正等人(唐守正，2000；张会儒，1999:)将各维量独立模型联合估计，进一步修正模型和参数得到较比例平差法更优化的结果，由此引出了非线性模型联合估计法，并使模型预估精度贺适用性有了显著提高，这样解决了生物量模型的不相容问题。

2.4.6 模型误差分析

长久以来，在林业上人们总是习惯于从已直接观测到的数据的拟合情况来选择生物量数学模型、讨论模型的精度，而缺乏对生物量数据本身的误差分析，因而很容易导致生物量数学模型在参数估计上产生偏差。在误差测定理论中误差主要分为数据测定误差和数学模型误差。在单木生物量测定中存在的误差主要就是生物量的测定误差和生物量的模型误差[34]。

根据误差来源分析，郭清文等认为各径阶树生物量的量测是不等权的，其权重与该样本树的鲜重成反比[35]。

通过生物量测算误差分析和生物量模型 $W=a(D^2H)^b$ 模型误差分析，得出结论，回归误差中包括生物量的测算累积误差和所选的生物量模型误差，直接利用回归拟合中误差来评价生物量模型精度是不符合实际情况的[36]。

在确定参数时比较常用的是赫尔默特(Helment)法和稳健估计法。赫尔默特法常用于不同类观测值定权。稳健估计也称为抗差估计，通过预平差的方法估计各观测值的方差因子，再对各观测值赋予不同的权值，以削弱或剔除粗差带来的影响[37]。

稳健估计不像最小二乘法估计那样，追求参数估计在绝对意义上的最优，而是在抗粗差前提下的最优或接近最优。所以，稳健估计的特点对于单木生物量数学模型是非常有利的。首先，在野外采集大量的数据中出现少量粗差一般是不可避免的，相比于最小二乘估计，稳健估计能使得估计的参数仍接近最优；其次，对于任何单木生物量计算模型，包括模型 $W=a(D^2H)^b$，它们本身也都是在前人回归统计分析的基础上所得到的一种较优的近似模型，与实际模型仍存在一定的偏差；另外，对于单木生物量的估算，不同径阶的树木的影响因子以及分径阶标准木选择的偏差将会使得对各径阶生物量的拟合产生很大影响[38]。

郭清文等认为：

(1)稳健估计回归方程非常稳定，而且稳健估计样本的总体估值也最为稳定。所以稳健估计有更好的抗差性，估计结果不因粗差而含有大的波动性。

(2)两种最小二乘估计之间，平均相对误差和平均相对误差绝对值，鲜重倒数加权回归均优于未加权即等权回归。

(3)由于两种最小二乘随机模型过于强调残差平方和最小的缘故，曲线拟合受到那些具有较大离差观测值的影响很大，使得回归曲线不精确[39]；而稳健估计使那些偏差大的样本在解算中所占的权重减小，这不仅有利于减弱粗差的影响，而且也有利于降低模型误差的影响。所以相比之下稳健估计是一种值得在林业生物量模型建立等数据处理中普遍推广应用的方法。

3 结 论

生物量模型研建要涉及的数据类型很多，范围广，如何获取并将这些数据很好的整合与统一是首先要解决的问题。如何建立更加精确有效的生物量模型是今后森林生物量模型研究的关键所在。在前人的基础上需要进一步研究如何减小生物量模型估测的误差值。此外，在模型建立之后，对模型进行评价、优化也将是森林生物量模型需要解决的重要问题。

参考文献

[1]马炜，孙玉军．我国的森林生物量研究[J]．世界林业研究，2009，05.

[2] Ebermeyr, E. Die gesmte Lehre der Waldstreu mit Rucksicht auf die chenische static des Waldbaues[M]. Belin: J. Speinger, 1876. 116.

[3] Boysen Jensen P. Studier over skovtraernes forhold til lyset Tidsskr[J]. F. Skorvassen, 1910, 22: 11 ~ 16.

[4] Burger H. Hold, Blattmenge, Zuwachs. 12 Fichten im Plenterwald Mitteil, Schweiz, Anst. Forttl[J]. Versuchsw, 1952, 28: 109 ~ 156.

[5] Kitterge, J. Estimation of amount of foliage of trees and shrubs[J]. J. Forest, 1944, 42: 905 ~ 912.

[6] Botkin, D. B., Woodwell, G. M. Tempel, N. Forest productivity estimated from carbon dioxide uptake[J]. Ecology, 1970, 51: 1057 ~ 1060.

[7] 潘维俦，田大伦．森林生态系统第一性生产量的测定技术与方法[J]．湖南林业科学，1981，2：1 ~ 12.

[8]胥辉．一种生物量模型构建的新方法[J]．西北农林科技大学学报(自然科学版)，2001，29(3)：35 ~ 40.

[9]佐藤大七郎，堤利夫．陆地植物群落的物质生产[M]．北京：科学出版社，1986.

[10]李意德，曾庆波，吴仲民．尖峰岭热带山地雨林生物量的初步研究[J]．植物生态与地植物学报，1992，16(4)：293 ~ 300.

[11] Ovinhton, J. D. Th form, weights and productivity of trees species grown in closestands[J]. Nes Phytol, 1956, 55: 289 ~ 304.

[12] Baskerville, G. L. Estimation og dry weight og tree components and total standing crop in conifer stands[J]. Eclolgy, 1965, 46: 867 ~ 869.

[13]杨忠，张建平，王道杰，等．元谋干热河谷桉树人工林生物量初步研究[J]．山地学报，2001，19(2)：503 ~ 510.

[14]冯宗炜，王效科，吴刚．中国森林生态系统的生物量和生产力[M]．北京：科学出版社，1999. 9.

[15]方精云，刘国华，徐嵩龄．我国的森林植被的生物量和净生产量[J]．生态学报，1996，16(5)：497 ~ 508.

[16]陈尔学．合成孔径雷达森林生物量估测研究进展[J]．世界林业研究，1999，12(6)：18 ~ 23.

[17]郭志华，彭少麟，王伯荪．利用TM数据提取粤西地区的森林生物量[J]．生态学报，2002，22(11)：1832 ~ 1839.

[18] Chen, L - J, Liu, G - H, Feng, X - F. Estimation of net primary productivity of terrestrial vegetation in China by remote sensing[J]. Acta Botanica Sinica, 2001, 43(11): 11191 ~ 1198.

[19]陈利军，刘高焕，厉惠国．中国植被第一性生产力遥感动态监测[J]．遥感学报，2002，6(2)：129 ~ 135.

[20]温远光，陈放，刘世荣，等．广西桉树人工林物种多样性与生物量关系[J]．林业科学，2008，4：14 ~ 19.

[21]李燕燕，樊后保，孙新．马尾松纯林及其混交林生物量的空间结构[J]．福建林学院学报，2005，25(3)：215 ~ 220.

[22]段爱国，张建国，何彩云，等．杉木人工林生物量变化规律的研究[J]．林业科学研究，2005，2：13 ~ 16.

[23]刘申，罗艳，黄钰辉，等．鼎湖山五种植被类型群落生物量及其径级分配特征[J]．生态科学，2007，26(5)：387 ~ 393.

[24]罗天祥，李文华，赵士洞．中国油松林生产力分布格局与模拟[J]．应用生态学报，1999，10(3)：257 ~ 261.

[25]吕晓涛，唐建维，何有才，等．西双版纳热带季节雨林的生物量及其分配特征[J]．植物生态学报，2007，31(1)：11 ~ 22.

[26]张家武，冯宗炜．桃源县丘陵地区杉木造林密度与生物产量的关系[C]．中国科学院林业土壤研究所，

杉木人工林生态学研究论文集，1980：201 ~208.

[27]胥辉．立木生物量模型构建及估计方法的研究．[D]．北京：北京林业大学．1998.

[28] Zeide B. Analysis Growth Equations[J]. For. Sci. 1993，39(3)：594 ~616.

[29] Kitterge J. Estimation of amount of foliage of trees and shrubs. J. Forest，1944(42)：905 ~912.

[30]田奇凡，杜连海，李秀军．洋槐人工林生物量的研究[J]．北京林业大学学报．1997，19(2)：175 ~178.

[31]吕晓涛，唐建维，何有才，等．西双版纳热带季节雨林的生物量及其分配特征[J]．植物生态学报，2007，31(1)：11 ~22.

[32] Leth H，WHITTAKER R H. Primary Productivity of the Biosphere[M]. New York：Springer - Verlag，1975.

[33]刘志刚．华北落叶松人工林生物量及生产力的研究[J]．北京林业大学学报．1992，14(1)：114 ~123.

[34]李文华，邓坤枚，李飞．长白山主要生态系统生物产量的研究[C]//中国科学院长白山森林生态系统定位站．森林生态系统研究第二卷．1981：34 ~50.

[35]刘兴良，刘世荣，宿以明，等．巴郎山川滇高山栎灌丛地上生物量及其对海拔梯度的响应[J]．林业科学，2006，42(2)：1 ~7.

[36] Fang J Y，Chen A P，Peng C H，et a1．Changes in forest biomass carbon storage in China between 1949 and 1998[J]．Science，2001，292：2320 ~2322.

[37] Ruank G A. Comparison of Constant And Variable Allometric Ratios for Estimating Populus Tremuloides Biomass[J]．Forest Science. 1987，33：294 ~300.

[38] 胥辉．林木生物量模型研究评述[J]．林业资源管理．1997，5：33 ~36.

[39]郭清文，冯仲科，张彦林，等．单木生物量误差分析与定权方法探讨[J]．中南林业调查规划．2006：1 ~5.

[40]赵敏，周广胜．基于森林资源清查资料的生物量估算模式及其发展趋势[J]．应用生态学报，2004，15(8)：1468 ~1473.

森林消防站网点空间布局研究

肖化顺　曾思齐　蒋倩仪

（中南林业科技大学森林经理学科，长沙，410004）

摘要：区域森林消防资源的空间分布是影响森林消能力建设的重要因素，其中森林消防站网点的空间布局对于科学进行森林火灾防控具有重要意义。依据区域森林消防要求，根据地形、水源条件、森林资源分布、交通道路、森林火险等级等要素设定备选消防站网点，借助GIS空间分析功能，利用ArcEngine编程进行最短路径功能开发，可以调整备选站点位置或增加备选站点。以广州市西部白云林区为例，在新庄新增一个消防站点，可以基本满足高火险区森林消防要求。

关键词：森林消防站；森林消防资源；空间布局

Study on Forest Firehouse spatial distributing

XIAO Hua-shun，ZENG Si-qi，IANG Qian-yi

（South University of Forestry & Technology，forest college，Changsha，410004）

Abstract：Spatial distribution of regional forest fire prevention resources is the important factor of its' capacity building，the spatial arrangement of forest firehouse's sites play a significant role in doing forest fire prevention and control scientifically. According to the topography，water，forest resource，forest fire risk grade，the preliminary forest fire prevention sites are confirmed to meet the requirements of forest fire. By virtue of GIS's function of spatial analysis，and using ArcEngine module to develop the functions of shortest path，So the results to adjust or to increase the location of alternative sites can be displayed Baiyun town ought to add one or two forest fire prevention sites to meet the requirements of forest fire throughout the region，while focusing on high－grade fire district to meet the needs of the forest fire prevention.

Key words：forest firehouse；fire fighting resources；spatial distributing

森林火灾是危害森林可持续经营的一个重要因素[1~2]，对于区域森林消防而言，必须要有数量一定、质量可靠、结构科学的森林火灾防控资源。森林消防站是重要的一类森林火灾防控资源，目前，有关城市消防站的优化配置及森林火灾扑救的最优路径的研究较多，对于

基金项目：中南林业科技大学博士基金项目（104－0141）。

作者简介：肖化顺（1968～），男，湖南邵阳人，副教授，博士，主要从事森林可持续经营教学与科研。

林区森林消防站网点的空间布局的研究很少[3~9]，本文结合区域森林消防特点与消防要求，以广州市西部白云林区为例，探讨了如何科学地进行森林消防站设置，以发挥森林消防站的最大功能。

1 问题的描述

森林消防站的数量与布局，直接影响消防资源的响应能力。在较大区域范围内，使消防资源既能在规定的时间内达到火灾地点，又尽可能节约成本(尽量少建站点，或同样站点情况下，能尽可能多完成重点消防任务)，描述如下。

(1)由于森林火险区域分布不规则，为了便于分析，将森林火险图划分成 N×N 个网格，按面积占优法确定森林网格火险等级[3]，每个网络对应一个森林节点，同时，消防站点和水源点抽象成节点，见表 1。

表 1　节点要素描述

Tab. 1　Nodes element

节点名称	描述
forest	Ⅰ级：R(red)，Ⅱ级：Y(yellow)，Ⅲ级：O (orange)
station	消防站点：　S (station)
water	可取水的水源点：W(water)

(2)找出消防站点至少经一处水源点到各森林节点的路线，以连线的方式将节点连接起来(两节点之间有路可走即连线反之不连)，构成节点路线网。

(3)根据地理位置，周边环境的植被种类，路面情况等各种因素综合考虑，得出从一个节点到另一个节点需要耗费的时间，其约定见表 2。

(4)两节点之间有线连接的路径所需耗费的时间都算出，这个数据就是这边上的权(时间)。形成了一个带权的拓扑结构图，如图 1。

表 2　道路等级类型与行驶速度

Tab. 2　The level types of road

序号	道路等级	行驶速度(km/min)
0	高速公路	2
1	国道	1
2	省道	1
3	市内主干道	0.5
4	一般市政道路	0.4
5	乡村道、机耕道	0.3
6	可通行的防火线	0.05

2 过程分析

在图 1 中，拟有 3 个点可以建消防站，分别为 S1、S2、S3，运用最短路径算法算出站点到各森林节点所需时间。首先算出从 S1 至少经一处 W 节点到 R、O 或 Y 标示的节点所需的最短时间存放在一个数组中，接下来以同样方法算出从 S2 和 S3 到标示的节点的所需最短时间存放在另外两个数组中，然后根据需要来进行消防站点的调整与增删。

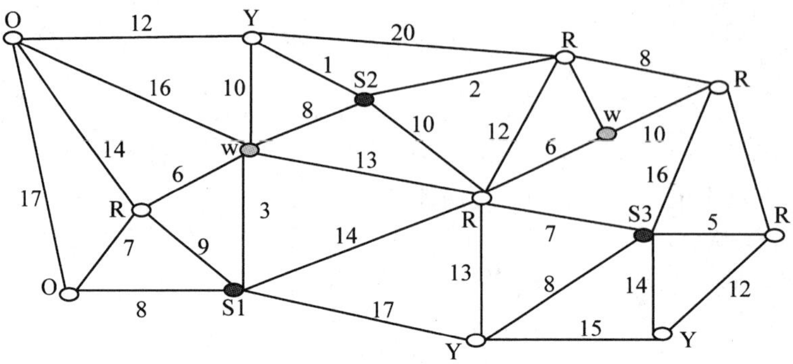

图 1　消防站网点分布拓扑结构

Fig. 1　Fire control stations net Topology structure

假设火灾一旦发生，至少要有一个消防站的消防力量能在 30min 内赶到火灾现场，那么根据计算的从各站点到各森林节点所需最短时间的数组进行选择，判断需要建立几个消防站点既能满足消防最低要求时间要求，又能节约资源。

第一步，假设只需建立一个消防站，那么首先判断对应 S1 节点的数组，是否这个数组中存储的数据都小于或等于 30。如果结果为真(T)代表从 S1 节点到各森林节点所需的最短时间都在要求范围内，也就是说从 S1 节点出发到各森林节点都可以在 30min 内到达。反之结果为假(F)，说明从 S1 节点出发到各森林的时候至少到其中一片森林节点花费的时间超过了 30min，把这样的森林节点都标示出来。用同样的方法判断从 S2 节点或从 S3 节点到各森林节点的时间，只要有一个节点对应的数组满足要求，那么说明建一个站点的方案是可行的，反之说明建一个站不能满足需要，则进行第二步的判断。

第二步，假设建两个站点来判断是否满足需求。第一步中，把从消防站点 S1 到森林节点的最短时间超过 30min 的节点标示出来，然后到对应 S2 节点的数组中去判断，如果在 S1 数组中超时的节点在 S2 数组中不超时，那么我们假设建两个站点的方案是可行的。同理对这三个可建站点的节点两两一组进行判断，只要有一组满足要求，就能得出最低建两个消防站点的结论，反之进入第三步。

第三步，在图 1 中，最多只要建三个消防站并且建三个消防站点是一定能满足森林消防最低要求的，所以不用继续往下判断了。如果在更大的区域中，需要判断三个消防站是否能满足要求，判断过程同第二步类似，如不满足则需继续往下判断，也就是再增加一个站点或调整站点至另一个备选位置。这样依次类推下去，可以在任何范围内根据需要来建立合理的消防站点。

第四步，实际工作中，如果需要建立 N 个消防火站点，但建设能力限，或分年度建设，就要考虑森林火险高低，尽量先行满足高火险等级的消防需要，如图 1。可以考虑先建设 S1、S3，再建设 S2。

3 消防站网点布局

GIS 可以根据交通道路的分布情况，以及消防力量的实际位置和要到达的目的地信息，自动计算出备选消防站点至火场的最佳行进路线、次佳行进路线、并根据表 2 计算达到目的地所需的时间，可确定网点的设定是否满足森林消防指挥的要求。如果不能满足要求则适当调整备选站点位置或增设站点。

最优和次优扑救路线的实现可应用 ESRI 公司推出的组件式开发工具 ArcEngine 实现，也可以用 ArcObject 或是 MapObjcct 组件来实现。研究中，利用 ArcEngine 实现最优路径操作。在 ArcGIS 环境下，用于网络分析的数据存储在网络数据集中，要进行最短路径实现，首先要建立网络数据集，步骤如下：

(1)选择创建网络数据集的工作空间。可以选择在 shapefile 工作空间或 geodatabase 工作空间中创建网络数据集，其区别在于，在 shapefile 工作空间中创建的网络数据集只支持单源数据，而在 geodatabase 工作空间中创建的网络数据集支持多源数据。研究中，选择 geodatabase 工作空间创建数据集。

(2)设置网络数据源。把参与网络分析的数据源设置为网络数据源，即把道路图和火险区划图设置为网络数据源。

(3) 连通性建模。网络数据集连通性通过使用 ArcGIS 连通性模型和高程字段模型共同完成。

(4) 定义网络属性并赋值。道路数据设定，通过时间属性并赋值。可使用 Fieldevaluator 求值程序为网络属性赋值。求值时根据道路长度及行进速度求得，道路长度可通过道路属性得到，行进速度根据道路的具体情况进行分类，见表 2。网络数据集建好后，利用 ArcEngine 中的一些类和接口来实现最短路功能。

使用 ArcEngine 进行最短路径功能开发，涉及 NetworkAnalyst 库中的 NARouteSolver、NAClassFieldMap、NAClassLoader、NaLayer、NAContext、NAClass 等组件类，及 INASolver、INARouteSolver、INASolverSetting、INAClassFieldMap、INAClassLoader、INALayer、INAContext、INAContextEdit 等接口。

具体编程实现主要分为以下六个步骤来：

①打开工作空间并打开加载网络数据集；

②创建 NAContext 网络分析上下文对象和最短路径分析适用的分析决策对象 NASolver；

③从要素类中载入最短路径所要经历的停留点，将其映射到网络拓扑中，并创建最短路径图层；

④设置路径查找决策对象的各参数；

⑤进行最短路径分析；

⑥显示分析结果。

如果不能满足，就在符合消防站点设置要求的地点，拟设站点，直到任一森林节点发生森林火灾，至少有一个站点的扑救力量能够经一处水源点 30min 内到达火灾现场。如果建设力量(资金)暂时不能满足要求，那么应首先考虑满足高火险等级区，或者重点森林消防单位的森林消防要求。如图 2，广州市白云林区在白云区区政府已配置了一个消防站点，由于西北向平缓，警民多，社区居民的火灾防控意识较高，可以利用现代通讯工具进行防控；在东北边新庄和东南边竹树下预设消防站点可以基本满足森林消防要求，如果该区只有建设2站点的能力，结合森林资源分布与森林火险等级划分图，则东北站点可以缓建。

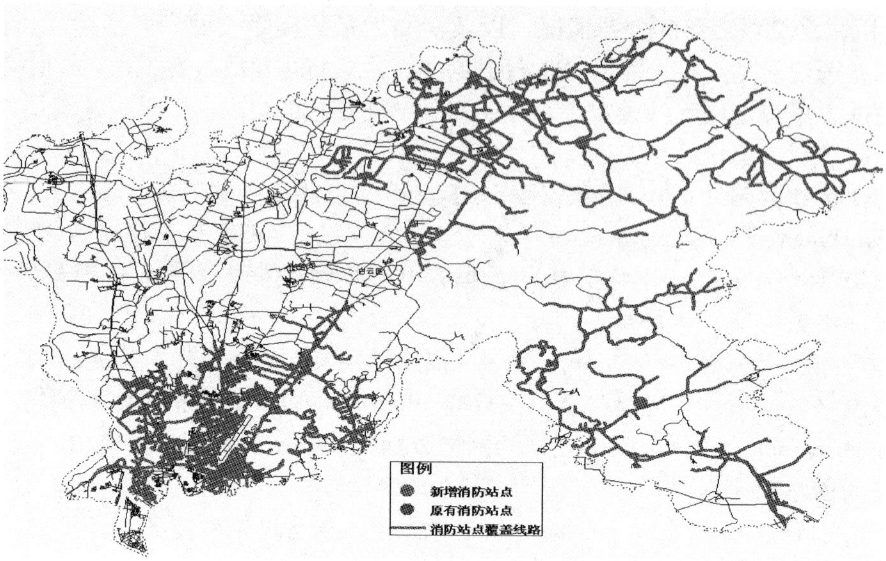

图2　森林消防站网点布局

Fig. 2　Forest fire prevention station distribution

4　结　论

根据交通状况，地形条件、水源分布、火险等级等情况设定备选消防站点位置，运用ArcEngine控件中的相关组件类及接口编程，自动计算从备选站点到火场区域所需的时间是否能满足森林消防指挥的要求(30min)，依据结果调整备选站点位置或增加备选站点，使整个消防站网点能满足森林火灾防控最基本要求，在周边区域消防站点参加分析的情况下，得到白云林区今后相对长期内，建设消防站点的数量与布局结果。为区域森林消防站网点建设提供科学依据。

参考文献

[1]罗盛健. 集体林区林权制度改革后森林“三防”体系建设探索[J]. 防护林科技，2007，81(6)：77~79.

[2]国家林业局科技司. 中国森林灾害减灾成就[J]. 中国减灾，2000，10(4)：18~20.

[3]肖化顺. 森林火灾防控资源结构体系研究[D]. 中南林业科技大学博士论文，2009.

[4]姚树人，文定元. 森林消防管理学. 北京：中国林业出版社，2002. ：150~280

[5] 杨超 北京市西山试验林场防火监测点布局研究[D] 北京林业大学，2006.

[6]杨志高，肖化顺，刘峰. 应用GIS的瞭望台模糊选址[J]. 中南林业科技大学学报，2008，28(2)：121~124.

[7]王国华，肖化顺. 基于MapX的林火扑救最优路径的设计与实现[J]. 中南林业调查规划，2008(3)：35~38.

[8] Peter A. Bissona, Bruce E. Riemanb, Charlie Luceb, et al.. Fire and aquatic ecosystems of the western USA: current knowledge and key questions. forest ecology and management, 2003: 213~229.

[9] Douglas A. D. 1990. Choose route with care to avoid costly mistakes. Canadian Forest Industry, 110(5): 44~46.

数字式高差测量仪的研制与试验

鄢前飞　刘发林

（中南林业科技大学森林经理学科，湖南长沙，410004）

摘要：为了解决复杂森林环境和障碍条件下高差测量问题，利用传感器技术，采用水平转盘旋转角度与角位移传感器旋转角度同步一致以及望远镜旋转角度与倾角传感器旋转角度同步一致的联动方式，设计并开发了数字式高差测量仪，测量两点之间的高差、水平距离和坡度，高差测量误差±0.3%。

关键词：高差；测量；传感器

中图分类号：S758.7　文献标识码：A 文章编号：1000－1298(2011)

Research and Application on Digital Measurer of Height Difference

YAN Qian-fei　LIU Fa-lin

(College of Forestry, Central South University of Forestry &Technology, Changsha, 410004)

Abstract: In order to solve measurements of the height difference problem under complex forest environment and barrier conditions, It used the sensor technology and adopted synchronous interactive way on rotation angle between level turntable and angular displacement sensor, as well as between telescope and tilt sensor. Then we designed and developed digital height difference measuring instrument, it can measure the height difference, horizontal distance and slope between two points, error of height difference is ± 0.3%. Applying this method can improve the efficiency.

Key words: height difference; measurement; sensor

引　言

林区道路测量、林地地形测量和地面点高程测量等经常要先测定两点之间的高差[1]。目前高差测量在林业实际应用中很少使用先进的全站仪、自动安平水准仪、电子水准仪以及精密水准仪[2~4]，其原因主要是森林环境林冠茂密，山高坡陡、灌草丛生，测量过程中只要观察目标前稍有一点树枝树叶与灌丛遮挡物，就可使全站仪等先进仪器无法测量，要对遮挡

湖南省科技厅资助项目(2010FJ4067)。

作者简介：鄢前飞，副教授，硕士，主要从事森林经理和测树仪器等研究。

物进行清除，费时、费力，加上这类仪器价格昂贵和携带不便等多种原因，致使先进仪器在林业工程勘测设计中难以发挥其应有的作用。目前，林业上测高差仍以普通的水准仪配合水准尺来完成，同样，如果林下杂灌丛生，利用水准仪的水平视线读取水准尺的前尺读数和后视读数很困难，要花大量时间清理障碍物，又因水准仪的作业最重要和最基本的条件是视线水平，水准仪的检验与校正、消除视差、精确整平、精确读数等工作要求细致认真，这项工作一般需要熟练的专业测量人员才能完成，尽管如此，专业测量人员在肉眼读数、记录员记数，繁琐的内业整理等诸多过程中难免出错，另外，在实际测量中，不仅要测量两点间的高程，还要测量两点间的水平距离和坡度，而水平距离测量仍使用皮尺，如果地形很陡，皮尺只能测斜距，然后测坡度再进行坡度改正[5~7]，工作麻烦且精度低。因此，开发一款携带方便、精度高、效率高的高差测量仪器具有重要的理论与实践意义。

1 整机结构

数字式高差测量仪包括光学瞄准组件、水平转盘、电控功能单元、显示屏、外部控制部件及三角支架，如图1至图4。光学瞄准组件包括望远镜，通过铰接的支撑架安装于水平转盘上，整体可随水平转盘左右水平旋转，也可绕支撑架与其铰接的固定轴在垂直面上下转动。水平转盘安装在三角支架上，水平转盘上有显示屏与外部控制部件，内部设置有角位移传感器、电控功能单元，角位移传感器的转动轴固定在水平转盘内部的中心旋转轴上；外部控制部件有电源开关、数据查询键、读数制动键、测量一模式选择键、测量二模式选择键、存贮键、删除键等功能键；电控功能单元包括电源模块、中央控制器、倾角传感器、角位移传感器、放大器、存储器及数据通讯接口，电源模块为电控功能单元各功能部件提供工作电源；显示屏及外部控制部件中的功能按键与电控功能单元电连接。水平转盘下部设有水平制动螺旋、旋转中轴和水平微调螺旋。电控功能单元中倾角传感器与角位移传感器通过读数制动键向中央控制器输入角度信号，中央控制器调用专用计算程序运算后，将计算结果送到存储器单元及放大器并驱动显示屏，通过数据通讯接口控制数据的输出。数字式高差测量仪的主要参数见表1。

表1 数字式高差测量仪的主要参数

Tab. 1 Specifications of digital measurer of height difference

参数	数值
外型尺寸(不含支架)(mm)	125×82×125
整机质量(kg)	0.7
测量方位角误差(°)	≤0.5
高差测量误(mm/km)	≤3
水平距离测量范围(m)	1~200
水平距离测量精度(%)	>99.8
高差测量误差(%)	±0.3
工作温度(℃)	-20~+50

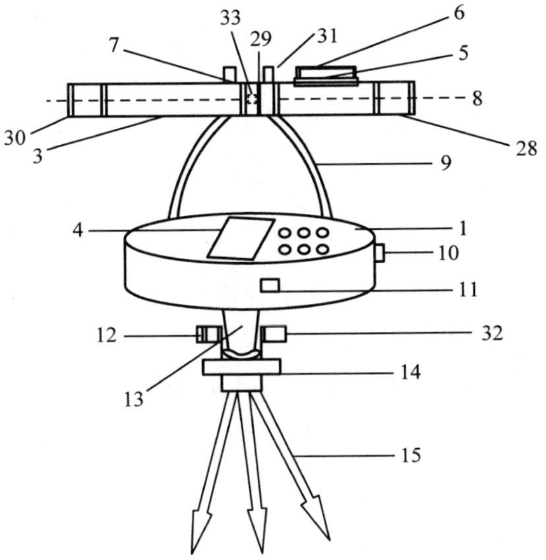

1. 水平转盘
3. 望远镜
4. 显示屏
5. 倾角传感器
6. 倾角传感器箱体
7. 制动螺旋
8. 视中轴线
9. 支撑架
10. 电源开关
11. 数据通讯接口
12. 水平制动螺旋
13. 旋转中轴
14. 三脚支架组件
15. 三脚架
28. 目镜
29. 对光螺旋
30. 物镜
31. 微动螺旋
32. 水平微调螺旋
33. 固定轴

图 1　高差测量仪整体结构图

Fig. 1　Overall structure of digital measurer of height difference

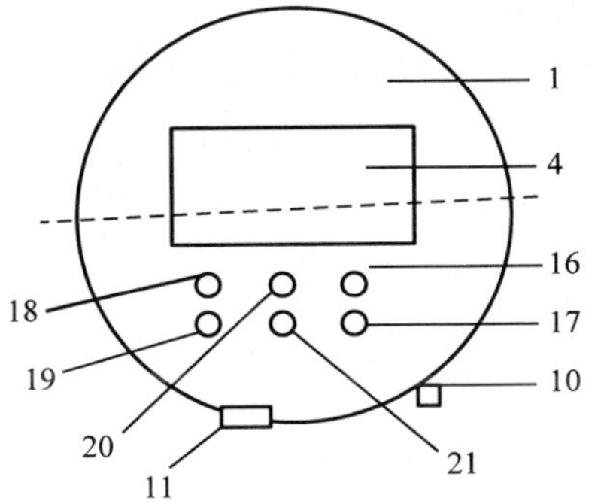

16. 数据查询键
17. 读数制动键
18. 测量一模式选择键
19. 测量二模式选择键
20. 存贮键
21. 删除键

图 2　高差测量仪水平转盘外部结构图

Fig. 2　The external structure on level turntable of digital measurer of height difference

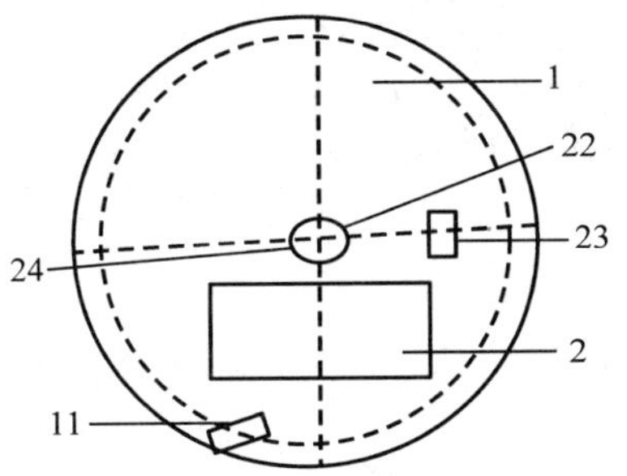

2. 电控功能单元
22. 中心旋转轴
23. 电源模块
24. 角位移传感器

图 3　高差测量仪水平转盘内部结构图

Fig. 3　The internal structure on level turntable of digital measurer of height difference

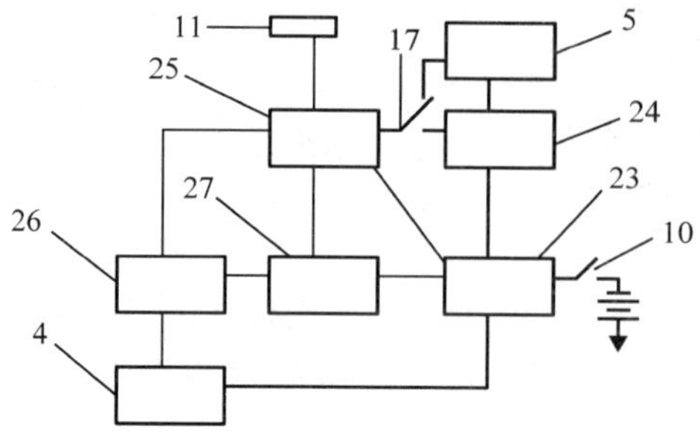

图 4 高差测量仪电控单元功能框图

Fig. 4 Function on electronic control unit of digital measurer of height difference

2 工作原理

测量时，在两目标点之间安置仪器并调平，打开电源开关，进入工作状态。电控功能单元向倾角传感器和角位移传感器发送读数命令并且显示信号。第一，选择测量模式(测量一模式选择键或测量二模式选择键)；第二，对前视标尺两标识点依次瞄准，如图 5A 中的 A 点的 $H_{0.7}$、H_3，打开读数制动键，电控功能单元读取倾角传感器和角位移传感器的角度信号；第三，对后视标尺两标识点重复第二步操作，B 点的 $H_{0.7}$、H_3，四个标识点测量完毕后，电控功能单元自动调用相应程序模块进行计算，求出水平距离和高差数据，输出到显示屏。如果多次测量时，数据可以按顺序存储，测量结束后统一将测量数据输出到外部计算机中进行数据处理和利用。

3 高差测量试验

如图 5A 与图 5B 所示，测量地形 A 点与 B 点的高差 h。

(1)仪器设置在 A 与 B 之间，任意选定一观测点 O。

(2)在 A 与 B 分别竖立一根 3m 长的标尺，标尺上有两个观察标志点，离地面 0.7m 的标志点为基础高记为 $H_{0.7}$，3m 处标志点为固定高记为 H_3。

(3)在 O 点对 A 地形标尺两标志点进行观测，测量基础高点 $H_{0.7}$、固定高点 H_3 的视线倾角 $\theta_{A0.7}$、θ_{A3}。在 O 点对 B 地形测量基础高点 $H_{0.7}$、固定高点 H_3 的视线倾角 $\theta_{B0.7}$、θ_{B3}。

(4)设 A 与 O 两点间的水平距离为 S_{AO}，B 与 O 两点间的水平距离为 S_{BO}，

根据三角函数原理：

标尺上基础高与固定高间距 $\Delta H = H_{固} - H_{基} = 3 - 0.7 = 2.3 = S_{AO}(\mathrm{tg}\theta_{A3} - \mathrm{tg}\theta_{A0.7}) = S_{BO}(\mathrm{tg}\theta_{B3} - \mathrm{tg}\theta_{B0.7})$；

所以，水平距离 $S_{AO} = \Delta H/(\mathrm{tg}\theta_{固} - \mathrm{tg}\theta_{基}) = 2.3/(\mathrm{tg}\theta_{A3} - \mathrm{tg}\theta_{A0.7})$；

水平距离 $S_{BO} = \Delta H/(\mathrm{tg}\theta_{固} - \mathrm{tg}\theta_{基}) = 2.3/(\mathrm{tg}\theta_{B3} - \mathrm{tg}\theta_{B0.7})$；

设 A 点与 B 点两点的高差为 h，高差 h 实际上为同样标尺的固定高或基础高在水平线上的高度值之差，以标尺固定高 3m 为例，在 A 点固定高 3m 的标志在水平线上垂直高等于 $S_{AO} \times \mathrm{tg}\theta_{A3}$，同样，在 B 点固定高 3m 的标志在水平线上垂直高等于 $S_{BO} \times \mathrm{tg}\theta_{B3}$，因此，高差 $h =$

$S_{AO} \times tg\theta_{A3} - S_{BO} \times tg\theta_{B3} = 2.3[tg\theta_{A3}/(tg\theta_{A3} - tg\theta_{A0.7}) - tg\theta_{B3}/(tg\theta_{B3} - tg\theta_{B0.7})]$，同理：$h = S_{AO} \times tg\theta_{A0.7} - S_{BO} \times tg\theta_{B0.7} = 2.3[tg\theta_{A0.7}/(tg\theta_{A3} - tg\theta_{A0.7}) - tg\theta_{B0.7}/(tg\theta_{B3} - tg\theta_{B0.7})]$。

(5)又设 A 点与 B 点两点的间水平距离为 S_{AB}，A、B、O 三点水平投影构成平面三角形的顶角为 $\angle O$，按照余弦定理：则有 $S_{AB} = \sqrt{S_{AO}^2 - 2S_{AO} \times S_{BO} \times COS\angle O + S_{BO}^2}$

而水平距离 $S_{AO} = \Delta H/(tg\theta_{固} - tg\theta_{基}) = 2.3/(tg\theta_{A3} - tg\theta_{A0.7})$；

水平距离 $S_{BO} = \Delta H/(tg\theta_{固} - tg\theta_{基}) = 2.3/(tg\theta_{B3} - tg\theta_{B0.7})$，只需测量出角度 $\angle O$，就可测量出两点间水平距离为 S_{AB}，也就可得出两点间平均坡度即：

平均坡度 $P = arctg(h/S_{AB})$。

公式中凡仰角为正值，俯角为负值，公式具有通用性。

由此可见，只要通过倾角传感器测量出四个倾角值和角位移传感器测量出两点间的水平夹角，即可得出两点地形间的水平距离和高差数据。数字式高差测量仪不需要事先测定测点的高程和测站到各测量目标的水平距。经测验，数字式高差测量仪的效率是传统水准仪的16 倍，测量误差 ±0.3%，满足一般森林资源调查的精度要求。

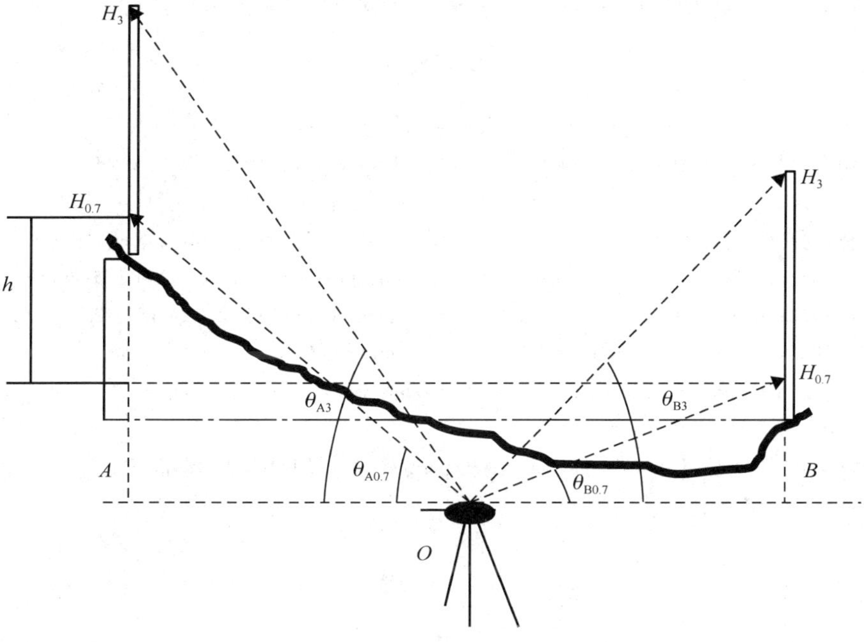

图 5A 高差测量仪测量原理图

Fig. 5A Measuring principle of digital measurer of height difference

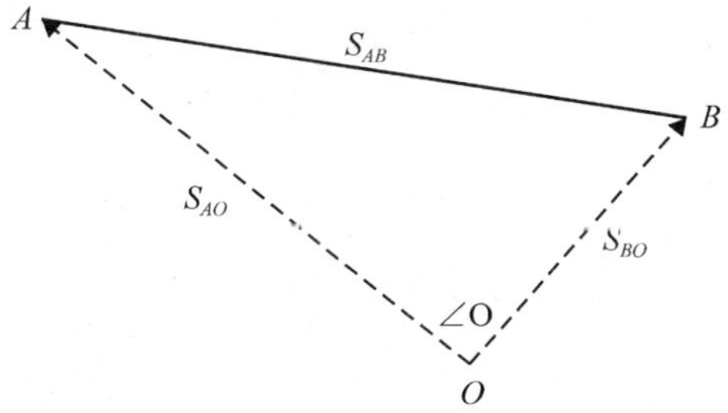

图 5B 高差测量仪测量原理图

4 结束语

(1)在水平转盘旋转轴心上安装角位移传感器，采用水平转盘旋转角度与角位移传感器旋转角度同步一致以及望远镜旋转角度与倾角传感器旋转角度同步一致的联动方式，测量两点之间的高差、水平距离和坡度，测量结果高精度数字化读量，为林业勘测调查提供了高技术测量装备，提高林地高差测量的效率，对环境要求低，特别是解决了两点之间有障碍物情况下高差及水平距的测量问题，设备操作简便，性能稳定。数字式高差测量仪已获得国家专利，专利号为 ZL200920062846.2。

(2)数字式高差测量仪与水准仪方法不同，无需前视后视在标尺读数，也无需视线水平，只需在前后标尺上各测二个标志线的倾角，四个倾角即可自动显示两点高差，同时得两点之间的水平距与坡度。

(3)采用角位移传感器与倾角传感器相结合，开发成本低、结构简单、携带方便，实现了测点快、读数快、信息数字化显示与存贮，经试用，测量高差的效率是水准仪的 16 倍，测量误差 ±0.3%，极大地提高了测量工效和在复杂森林环境中的适应性，效果良好。

参考文献

[1]林业部调查规划院．森林调查手册[M]．北京：中国林业出版社，1984.

[2]王宝钦，赖惟亿．两种测高器的改良使用[J]．福建林学院学报，1992，12(1)：75～82.

[3]董金伟，李承水，卢胜西，等．任意点不量距测高器的功能[J]．山东林业科技，1995，(6)：39.

[4]鄢前飞．林业数字式测高测距仪的研制[J]．中南林业科技大学学报，2007，27(5)：66～70.

[5]Chiesi M, Maselli F, Bindi M, et al. Calibration and application of Forest_ BGC in a Mediterranean area by the use of conventional and re－mote sensing data[J]. Ecological Modelling, 2002, 154: 251～262.

[6]Coops N C, Waring R H, Brown S R, et al. Comparisons of predictions of net primary production and seasonal patterns in water use derived with two forest growth models in Southwestern Oregon[J]. Ecological Modelling, 2001, 142: 61～81.

[7]SHALLOWAY A, TROTT J R. Design patterns explained[M]. XIONG J, tran. Beijing: Tsinghua University Press, 2004: 78～85.

退化林地遥感判定技术研究

余坤勇[1,2]　刘　健[1,2,3]　许章华[1,2]

（1. 福建农林大学3S技术应用研究所，福建福州，350002；2. 福建农林大学林学院，福建福州，350002；3. 三明学院，福建三明，365004）

摘要：快速判定退化林地区域，将为林木的适地适树、营林规划适时调整、林地优化经营措施的制定提供重要依据，具有重要意义。文章以福建省永安市退化林地的判定为研究对象，利用2期遥感数据，从林地的物理、养分及生产力角度出发，选择了林地土壤侵蚀、林地土壤有机质及NPP等指标构建了永安市林地土壤综合指数，参照林木蓄积的生长状况，分析综合土壤综合指数在退化和未退化林地上与土壤侵蚀模数增量、干扰指数、植被覆盖度等因子的相关关系及变化规律，确定0.8500为利用土壤综合指数阈值判定退化林地的有效阈值，并制作了研究区退化林地分布专题图，为森林经营管理提供决策辅助。

关键词：退化林地；立地质量；遥感；综合指数；永安

On the Determination Technology of Degradation Forest Land Based on RS

YU Kun-yong[1,2]　LIU Jian[1,2,3]　XU Zhang-hua[1,2]

(1. Institute of Geomatics Application of Fujian Agriculture and Forestry University, Fuzhou, Fujian, 350002;
2. Forestry College of Fujian Agriculture and Forestry University, Fuzhou, Fujian, 350002;
3. Sanming University, Sanming, Fujian, 365004)

Abstract: Fast determinant of degraded forest land is important significance to matching tree species with site, timely adjusting economic forest planning and instituting measure for forest land optimal management. Taking the determinant of degraded forest land of Fujian, Yongan as study object, using the two period remote data, and choosing some index such as soil erosion, soil organic matter, and NPP to structure soil comprehensive index from the angle of physics, nutrient and productivity, then in the basic of grow status of forest accumulation, analysing the change law and the correlativity between soil comprehensive index and erosion modulus increment, interference in-

---

基金项目：国家自然科学基金(40971043)。

作者简介：余坤勇(1980～)，男，讲师。主要从事资源统计分析及3S技术应用。Email：yuyky@126.com

通迅作者：刘健，男，教授，博士生导师。主要从事林业可持续发展和3S技术应用。

dex, vegetation coverage and other factor in degraded and ono - degraded forest, to determine 0.8500 as degraded forest effective hold value using the soil comprehensive index, make the thematic map of the degraded forest of study area, and provide the decision aiding for forest management.

Key words: degraded forest; site quality; remote sensing; comprehensive index; Yongan

随着人工林的经营和发展，较粗放的人工经营模式对林地土壤质量产生了较大的影响，即林地退化现象。这种林地退化加上粗放的经营水平，直接影响着林分质量，影响着林业的可持续发展，较早地引起了众多学者的重视。国际上，最早开展退化林地研究可追溯到19世纪中叶，德国和瑞士开展的第二代挪威云杉林生产力下降的问题。20世纪初，人工林的土地退化问题引起了许多国家学者的重视。20世纪后期至今，德国、英国、挪威、印度、法国、澳大利亚、南非和俄罗斯等国家都开展了人工林地力衰退和林地生产力下降的研究。我国地力衰退研究相对较迟，自20世纪50年代末，国内众多学者开展了第二代人工经营所引起的地力衰退问题，如但新球(1996)指出林地持续经营是可持续林业的核心，原福建林学院杨元梁等(1997)也针对林业可持续发展已成为国内外讨论热点的现状，对林地可持续经营模式进行了一些评价。随着3S技术的发展，为时空领域林地土壤质量专题信息的获取提供了重要技术(张晓丽，1998；张志，2004；王博文，2006；林晓利，2007；彭佳红，2010；王凌河，2010)。张泱(2004)则从林地的重要性入手，针对我国林地管理存在的主要问题，提出相应措施，其中一项重要措施是依靠3S技术，建立林地资源管理信息系统，进行林地动态监测。目前研究对象主要反映在杉木人工林、马尾松、杨树、长白落叶松和华山松等(刘占锋，2006；许宁，2008)。笔者于2010年构建林地退化评价指标体系，应用层次分析法，探讨了基于RS林地退化监测技术。从当前的研究来看，评价的技术方法多样，林地退化的标准暂未统一认识。我国人工林面积大，约占全国森林面积的20%，针对人工林尤其是近年发展的工业原料林如桉树等大规模的种植，引发了诸多学术界关注问题。罗小荷(2002)指出应在充分认识人工林在林业可持续发展中的重要性的前提上，改进人工林经营方式，搞好人工林林种、树种规划，做到适地适树适生境。王宗海等(2005)从植物地理学的视角针对江西省各地不同区位、不同水热和地理条件，对短周期工业原料林造林进行科学区划，并本着适地适树原则筛选树种。张慧(2005)利用GIS与数学模型集成技术，在建立福建省林地资源基础数据库的基础上，研究主要桉树树种土地适宜性评价的因子体系和技术方法，并结合风险评价，对福建省主要桉树树种用地进行区划。但简单的综合指数阈值并不能揭示出林地退化的内在机理，同时在研究中尚采用的是“空间”代“时间”的方法。而林地是一个受区域范围内的气候、地质、地貌、土壤以及森林生态系统各种生物条件相互联系、相互作用的综合体，在受人工经营干扰影响下，林地土壤肥力的恢复具有较多的不稳定性因素，“空间”代“时间”的相似性受较大影响。因而利用多期遥感影像，反演出不同时期林地的立地质量，探讨林地土壤退化遥感判定标准和判定技术，将为林地适地适树优化经营，提供辅助依据。

1 研究区概况

永安市位于闽中偏西，闽中大谷地南端，沙溪河中上游地段，处武夷山脉与戴云山脉的过渡地带，大约界于北纬25°33′~26°12′，东经116°56′~117°47′，东西宽82km，南北长约

71km，全市土地总面积294110hm²，素有“九山半水半分田”之称，境内群山叠拥，山体多呈北东—南西或北西—南东方向展布。气候温润，四季夏长冬短，年均气温14.3～19.2℃，1月均温4～9℃，7月均温20～21℃，年降雨量1490～2050mm，年平均相对湿度80%以上，土地资源肥沃富饶，具有典型的中亚热带地带性特征，适于常绿阔叶林等亚热带林木生长，植被覆盖好，属亚热带常绿阔叶林区、(湿润)常绿阔叶林亚区、中亚热带常绿阔叶林地带。有木本植物514种、竹类28种，主要植被类型为常绿阔叶林、毛竹林、杉木林、马尾松林和针阔混交林等，其中，马尾松林面积大(达64670hm²)、分布广，占该市现有林面积的1/4以上。

2 资料收集和研究方法

2.1 资料收集

1996年和2008年的永安市二类调查小班数据，经过校正的永安市1999年TM影像、2008年ALOS影像、1999年和2008年林地土壤侵蚀图、土壤有机质图、林地植被净第一生产力分布图[图1至图6，备注，由刘健教授主持的福建省科技计划重点项目(2008N003)提供]。

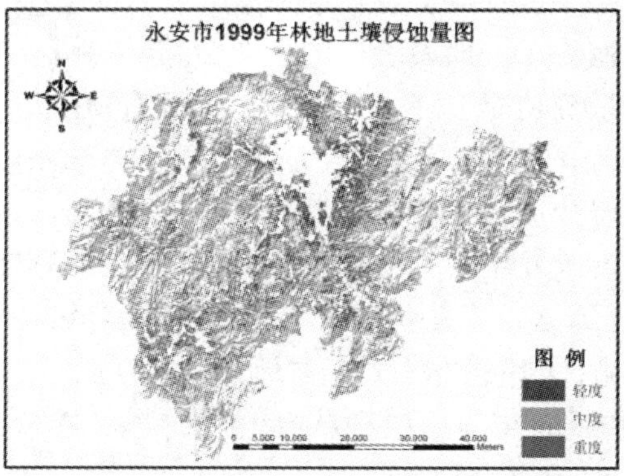

图1 永安市1999年林地土壤侵蚀量图

Fig. 1 Forestland soil erosion of Yong'an County in 1999

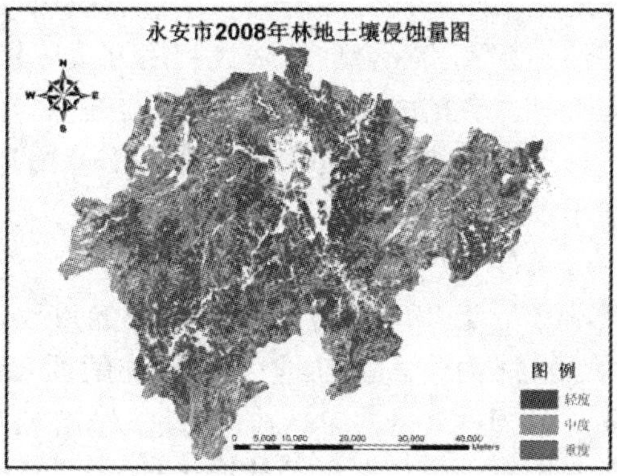

图2 永安市2008年林地土壤侵蚀量图

Fig. 2 Forestland soil erosion of Yong'an County in 2008

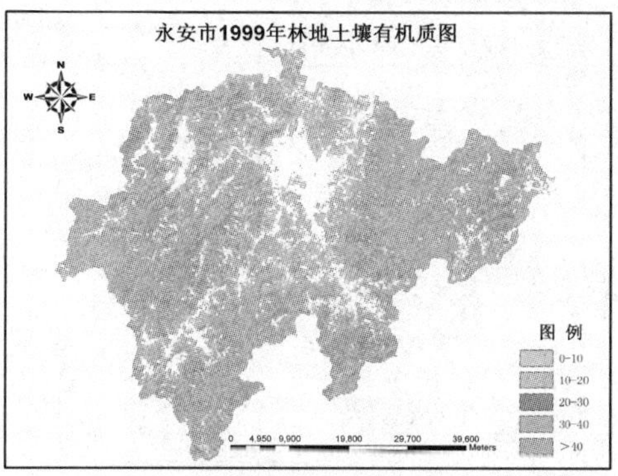

图3 永安市1999年林地土壤有机质图

Fig. 3 Forestland organic matter of Yong'an County in 1999

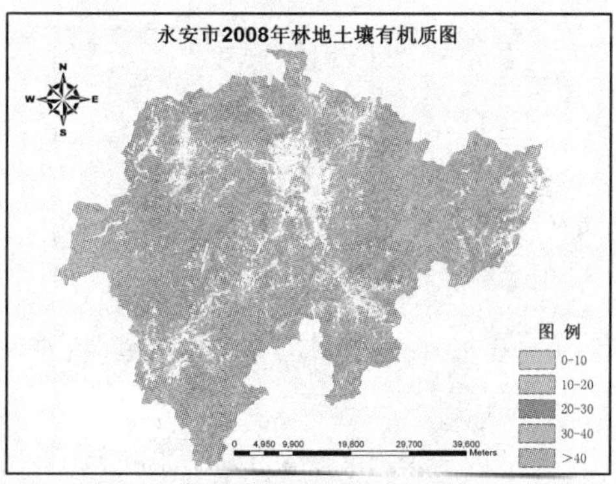

图4 永安市2008年林地土壤有机质图

Fig. 4 Forestland organic matter of Yong'an County in 2008

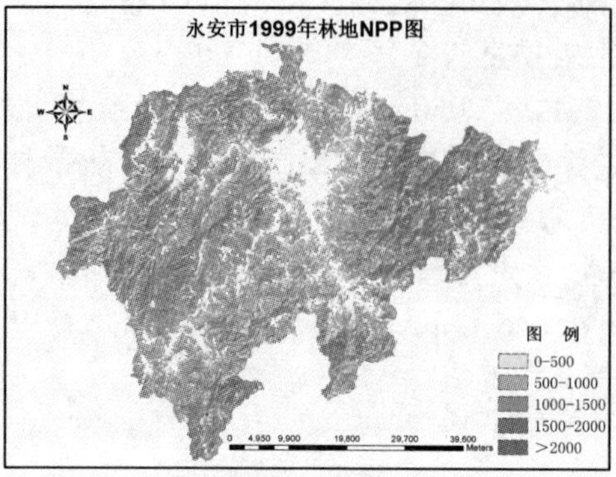

图5 永安市1999年林地NPP图
Fig. 5 Forestland NPP of Yong'an County in 1999

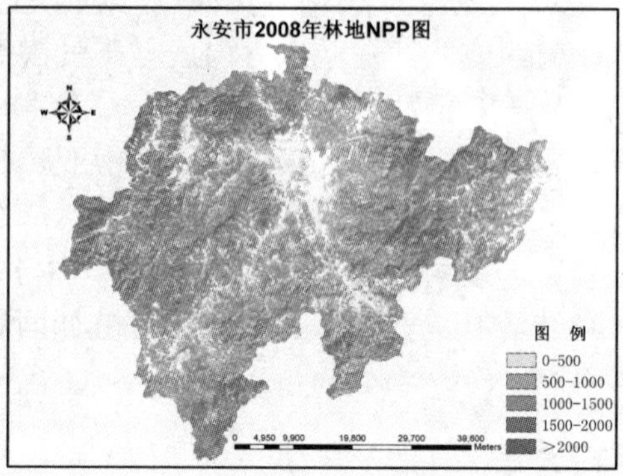

图6 永安市2008年林地NPP图
Fig. 6 Forestland NPP of Yong'an County in 2008

2.2 林地土壤综合指数计算

林地土壤质量评价应遵循科学性、实用性、主导性及可比量化等原则。林地退化主要是整地、幼林抚育和不合理的采伐利用方式等极大地破坏了地表表层的植被覆盖物，以及大量营造人工林造成植物群落多样性降低，进而导致系统功能下降，如炼山后土壤有机质、全N损失，林地8年的水土流失量分别是不炼山造林地的2.64倍和16.81倍；拖拉机集材严重改变了土壤的硬度、土壤孔隙度和通透性，土壤侵蚀加剧，使伐区有机质下降。同时，由于局部气候条件变化差异，可能导致降雨量、温湿度等发生较大变化，直接影响植被净初级生产力(NPP)。而NPP作为地表C循环的重要组成部分，直接反映了植被群落在自然环境条件下的生产能力，表征陆地生态系统的质量状况，同时也是反映林地有机C的重要体现(Liveman D M, et al, 1988)。为此，结合研究区域的实际情况，从林地的物理、养分及生产力角度出发，分别选择了林地土壤侵蚀、林地土壤有机质及NPP作为评价指标。在此基础上，采用笔者(2010)在永安市林地退化研究中所确定的指标权重(物理指标0.3290，养分指标0.2692，生产力指标0.4018)，构建林地土壤质量综合指数Q(图7、图8)。

$$Q = 0.3290A + 0.2692O + 0.4018NPP$$

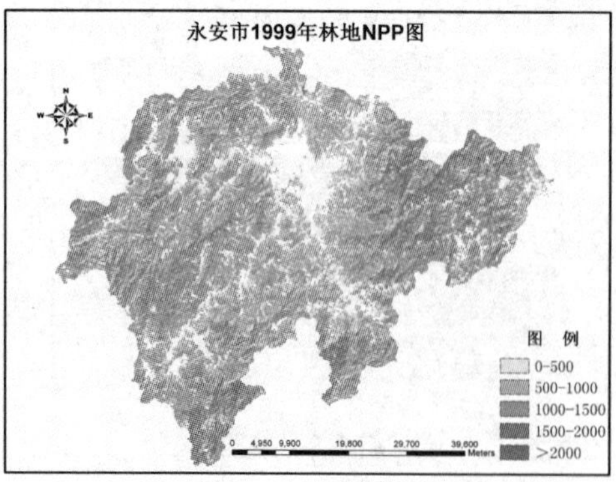

图7 永安市1999年林地土壤综合指数图
Fig. 7 Forestland Soil composite index of Yong'an County in 1999

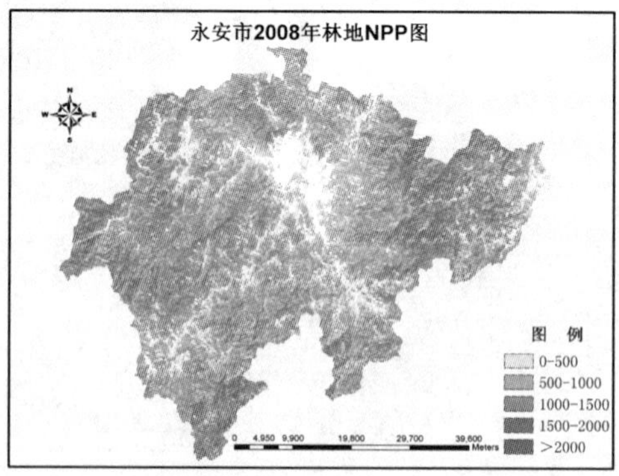

图8 永安市2008年林地土壤综合指数图
Fig. 8 Forestland Soil composite index of Yong'an County in 2008

式中：Q 为林地土壤质量综合指数；A 为林地土壤侵蚀；O 为林地土壤有机质；NPP 为林地净第一生产力。

2.3 基于遥感技术的人工干扰指数专题信息提取

人工干扰指数(图 9、图 10)的计算方法采用 Zurlini 使用的公式：

$$D(x,y) = \frac{[f_{t1}(x,y) - f_{t2}(x,y)] - m}{\sqrt{S_{T1}^2 + S_T^2 2 - 2COV_{T1T2}}}$$

式中:f_{Ti} 是第 i 年的 NDVI,m 是两时相影像像元差异的均值,S_{Ti}^2 是基于一张遥感影像上的所有栅格第 i 年 NDVI 的方差,COV_{T1T2} 是两年 NDVI 的协方差。当 $D(x,y) < 0$ 则说明区域人工干扰处于退化状态。

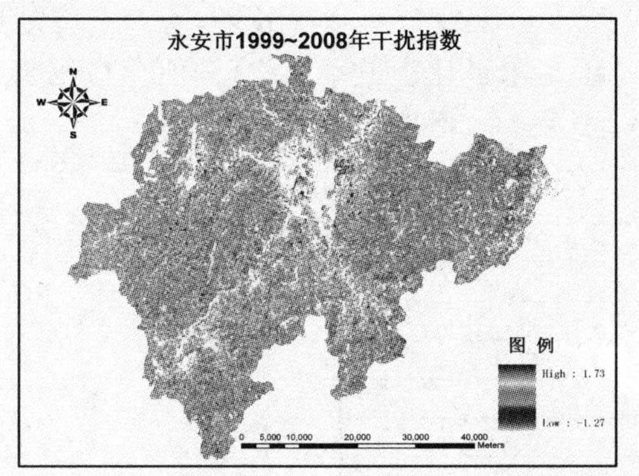

图 9 永安市 1999 ~ 2008 年干扰指数

Fig. 9 Disturbance index of Yong' an County from 1999 to 2008

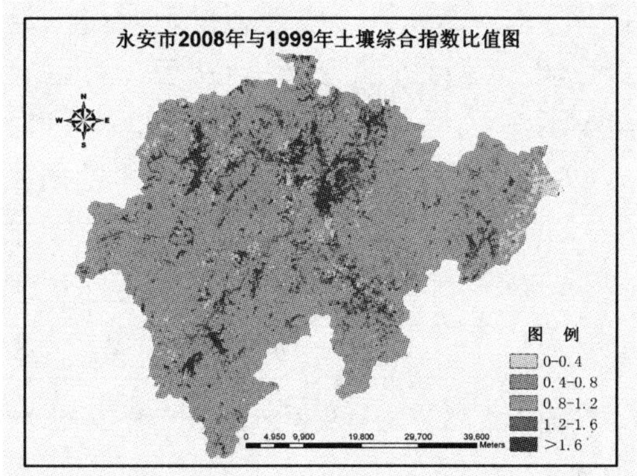

图 10 永安市 2008 年与 1999 年土壤综合指数比值图

Fig. 11 Soil composite index ratio of Yong' an County between 2008 and 1999

2.4 林地土壤退化的判别标准确定方法

理论上，当干扰指数值即 $D(x, y) <0$ 或 2008 年和 1999 年土壤综合指数的比值(Q_{2008}/Q_{1999}) <1，即 2008 年林地土壤综合指数小于 1999 年林地土壤综合指数时，表明林地土壤质量下降，林地发生了退化。然而，林地土壤质量受多种因素的影响，且两期影像受大气等干扰程度不同，即使采用了直方图匹配等辐射校正手段，影像间的差异依然会存在，所以，林地土壤退化仅以 $D(x, y) <0$ 或 $Q_{2008}/Q_{1999} <1$ 为判别标准是较为粗泛的。林木蓄积的生长状况是林地土壤质量的直观表征之一，也是判别林地土壤是否退化的最有效依据，为此文章以 1999 ~ 2008 年的单木蓄积生长量为参照，结合土壤侵蚀模数增量、干扰指数与 Q_{2008}/Q_{1999} 的回归关系，并以国家环境保护总局建议的中国土地退化分类与分级中的植被覆盖度标准为参照，综合判定林地土壤退化的判别标准。单木生长量数据以收集的 1996 年和 2008 年的永安市二类调查小班数据，遵从：①两期树种相同，且均为纯林；②1996 ~ 2008 年内未进行采伐，即两期同属于一个经营周期内 2 个准则，通过 GIS 些随机抽取功能，提取 72 个可比较的样本。

3 结果分析

3.1 林地土壤退化判别标准的确定

3.3.1 基于单木蓄积生长量退化条件的确定

树种与林龄是除林地质量外影响林木生长的主要物质条件，不同的树种单位蓄积生长量不同，同一树种在不同的生长发育阶段蓄积量增长亦存在较大差异。文章在进行单木蓄积生长量比较时，依据树种相同、起始龄组一致的原则，对样本进行分组比较确定不同树种不同龄组条件下的平均单木蓄积生长量($\overline{\Delta C_{ij}}$)(i 为树种，i = 杉木，马尾松，阔叶树；j 为龄组，j = 幼龄林，中龄林，近熟林)。则依此下述两个判定准则，分别得到林地土壤退化与未退化的样本组，见附表 1。

当 $\Delta C_{ij}\Delta C_{ij} < \overline{\Delta C_{ij}}$时，判定该龄组树种的林地土壤发生退化；

当 $\Delta C_{ij} > \overline{\Delta C_{ij}}$时，判定该龄组树种的林地土壤未发生退化。

3.3.2　林地土壤退化判别标准确定

根据提取的 72 个样本数据，通过 GIS 的空间分析功能获取相应的土壤综合指数比值专题图即 Q_{2008}/Q_{1999}，土壤侵蚀模数增量专题图即 2008 年土壤侵蚀模数 - 1999 年土壤侵蚀模数(图 10、图 11 和附表 1)。从表中可以看出，退化组与未退化组的 Q_{2008}/Q_{1999} 值存在较明显的差异性，二者均值分别为 0.8283、0.8822，总体均值为 0.8500。

(1)土壤侵蚀模数增量与林地土壤质量综合指数比值关系分析：

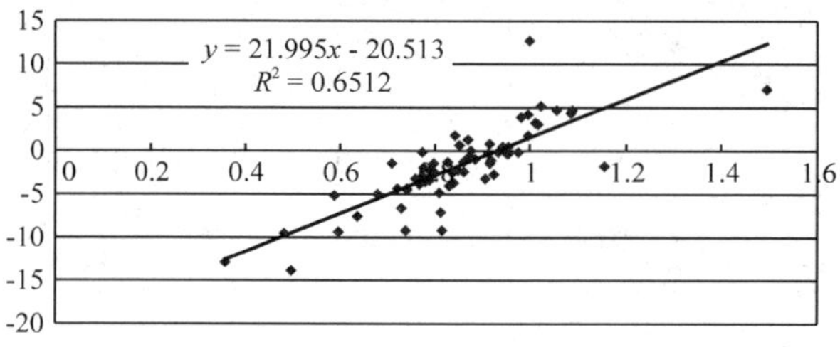

图 11　永安市土壤侵蚀模数比值与综合指数比值的回归关系

ig. 11　Regression relation between soil erosion modulus increment and composite index ratio of Yong' an County

从永安市土壤侵蚀模数增量与林地土壤质量综合指数比值的散点图关系(图 11)和所拟合二者回归关系模型(见式 1)，可以看出永安市土壤侵蚀模数增量与综合指数比值表现出良好的正相关关系，土壤侵蚀模数增量距 0 最近的两个样本点分别是(0.7731，-0.0988)、(0.8725，0.0566)。

$$y = 21.995x - 20.513 \quad (R = 0.807) \tag{1}$$

式中：y 为土壤侵蚀模数增量；x 为综合指数比值。

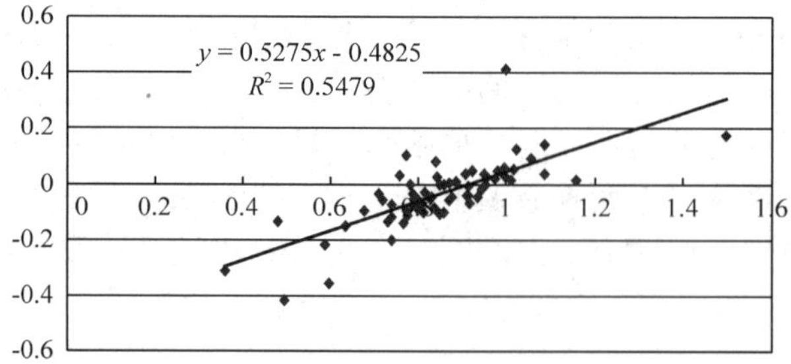

图 12　永安市干扰指数与综合指数比值的回归关系

Fig. 12　Regression relation between disturbance index and composite index ratio of Yong' an County

（2）干扰指数与林地土壤综合指数关系分析：

从所构建的永安干扰指数与林地土壤综合指数比值的散点图关系（图12）和所拟合二者回归关系模型（见式2），可以看出干扰指数与林地土壤综合指数比值同样表现出良好的正相关关系，干扰指数距0最近的4个样本点分别是（0.7817，－0.0015）、（0.9553，－0.0008）、（0.8719，0.0033）、（0.8868，0.0081）。

$$y = 0.5275x - 0.4825 \quad (R = 0.741) \tag{2}$$

式中：y为干扰指数；x为综合指数比值。

（3）植被覆盖度分析：

土地退化类型包括水蚀、风蚀、化学退化和物理退化等，分析永安市林地现状可知，其退化的类型主要是指水蚀和风蚀两种。沈渭寿等建议（2006），水蚀作用下土地退化评价标准中将植被覆盖度因素划分为轻度退化（50%～75%）、中度退化（30%～50%）、强度退化（10%～30%）、极强度退化（＜10%），风蚀作用下土地退化评价标准中将植被覆盖度因素划分为轻度退化（＞50%）、中度退化（30%～50%）、强度退化（10%～30%）、极强度退化（＜10%），依此，可以将植被覆盖度等于75%视为林地土壤退化的临界，样本中，在此附近的4个样本点为（0.9144，0.7469）、（0.7682，0.7481）、（0.9142，0.7515）、（0.7919，0.7516）。

综合分析可知，林地土壤综合指数比值与土壤侵蚀模数增量、干扰指数和植被覆盖度均存在良好的线性关系，当土壤侵蚀模数减少、人为干扰降低、植被覆盖增强时，林地土壤质量向好的方向发展，综合土壤侵蚀模数和人为干扰趋于0以及植被覆盖度等于75%时，林地土壤综合指数比值的取值均在其均值0.8500附近，为此，文章综合确定林地土壤退化的送别标准为$Q_{2008}/Q_{1999} < 0.8500$，依此制作永安市1999～2008年林地土壤退化区域图（图13）。

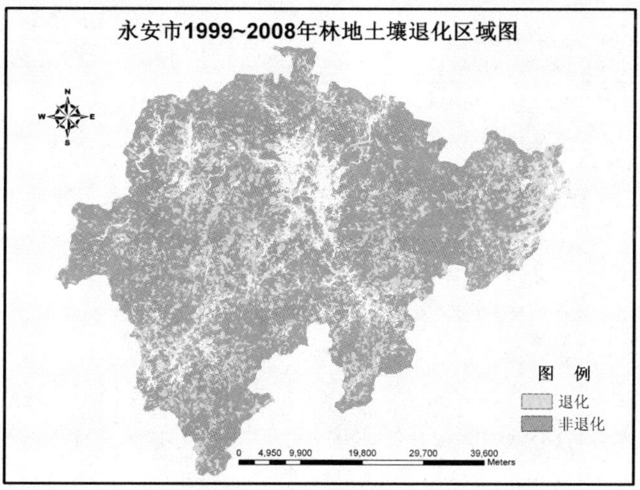

图13　永安市1999～2008年林地土壤退化区域图

Fig. 13　Forestland soil degradation zone of Yong'an County from 1999 to 2008

4 结论与讨论

林地土壤质量受多种因素的影响，且两期影像受大气等干扰程度不同，即使采用了直方图匹配等辐射校正手段，影像间的差异依然会存在，所以，林地土壤退化仅以干扰指数值($\triangle Q$) <0 或土壤综合指数的比值(Q_{2008}/Q_{1999}) <1 为判别标准是较为粗泛的。林木蓄积的生长状况是林地土壤质量的直观表征之一，也是判别林地土壤是否退化的最有效依据，故文章以 1999 ~2008 年的单木蓄积生长量为参照，由此确定林地土壤退化的判别标准。

文章依据退化与未退化组的综合指数比值，确定 Q_{2008}/Q_{1999} 值域为(0.8283，0.8822)。在此基础上，进一步引入土壤侵蚀模数增量、干扰指数、植被覆盖度等指标，综合分析土壤侵蚀模数增量、干扰指数与 Q_{2008}/Q_{1999} 的回归关系，并以前人建议的中国土地退化分类与分级中的植被覆盖度标准为参照，最终确定林地退化与未退化的土壤综合指数阈值为 0.8500，据此提取了研究区退化林地专题信息。

随着林权改革的建设与完善，具有自主经营权的林农对林地的经营也日益重视。但林农经营技术水平总体上相对较弱，急需林业相关部门给予相应林林经营尤其是退化林地上经营技术的指导。但目前退化林地有哪些，如何确定退化林地的分布尚无具体的基础数据。同时，不同退化程度上的林地在恢复林地生产力的经营过程中，受林木生物学特性影响，经营措施存在着较大差异。因而如何在确定退化林地的基础上，实现林地退化程度的定量化测定，对实施科学营林，稳定林地生产力，促进林业可持续发展具有重要意义，将是利用遥感技术应用于促进林业可持续发展的重要方向之一。

附表 1 分析基础数据表

Tab. 1 The analyzed data

序号	1996			2008		单株蓄积差	$\overline{\Delta C_{ij}}$	Q_{2008}/Q_{1999}	土壤侵蚀模数增量	干扰指数	2008 年植被覆盖率
	树种	龄组	单株蓄积	龄组	单株蓄积						
1	马尾松	幼龄林	0.0417	近熟林	0.0583	0.0167	0.0217	0.9435	0.527	-0.0167	0.7948
2	马尾松	幼龄林	0.02	近熟林	0.0467	0.0267		1.0248	5.0891	0.124	0.8299
3	马尾松	中龄林	0.019	成熟林	0.03	0.011	0.0164	0.7201	-4.4102	-0.0592	0.7141
4	马尾松	中龄林	0.0158	中龄林	0.0271	0.0113		0.7874	-3.1914	-0.0829	0.6292
5	马尾松	中龄林	0.0136	成熟林	0.0273	0.0136		0.9246	-2.773	0.0491	0.6399
6	马尾松	中龄林	0.0138	成熟林	0.0275	0.0137		0.7401	-4.4036	-0.1216	0.614
7	马尾松	中龄林	0.0094	近熟林	0.0265	0.0171		1.017	3.0933	0.0514	0.6614
8	马尾松	中龄林	0.0067	中龄林	0.0267	0.02		0.7818	-3.5868	-0.0015	0.6547
9	马尾松	中龄林	0.0043	成熟林	0.0261	0.0217		1.0867	4.3456	0.142	0.6416
10	马尾松	中龄林	0.0045	成熟林	0.0273	0.0227		0.8511	0.6065	-0.002	0.6923
11	马尾松	中龄林	0.01	中龄林	0.0387	0.0287	0.0399	0.8606	-2.3497	-0.0044	0.7327
12	马尾松	中龄林	0.0041	中龄林	0.0386	0.0345		0.4821	-9.5703	-0.1335	0.6573
13	马尾松	中龄林	0.0004	中龄林	0.0389	0.0385		1.1568	-1.8453	0.0123	0.6917
14	马尾松	中龄林	0.002	成熟林	0.06	0.058		0.9506	-0.3065	0.0341	0.5321

（续）

序号	1996 树种	1996 龄组	1996 单株蓄积	2008 龄组	2008 单株蓄积	单株蓄积差	$\overline{\Delta C_{ij}}$	Q_{2008}/Q_{1999}	土壤侵蚀模数增量	干扰指数	2008年植被覆盖率
15	马尾松	近熟林	0.0143	成熟林	0.0286	0.0143	0.0162	0.741	-4.5841	-0.0738	0.4554
16	马尾松	近熟林	0.0091	成熟林	0.0273	0.0182		0.9742	-0.162	0.022	0.5275
17	杉木	幼龄林	0.0048	中龄林	0.0238	0.019	0.057	0.8096	-4.7954	-0.0667	0.4886
18	杉木	幼龄林	0.02	近熟林	0.04	0.02		0.873	-0.6622	-0.0595	0.3888
19	杉木	幼龄林	0.002	近熟林	0.04	0.038		0.843	1.6942	0.0269	0.6493
20	杉木	幼龄林	0.0024	过熟林	0.0476	0.0452		0.5876	-5.1496	-0.2198	0.6477
21	杉木	幼龄林	0.001	成熟林	0.065	0.064		0.843	1.6942	0.0269	0.7141
22	杉木	幼龄林	0.0044	中龄林	0.1091	0.1047		0.4973	-13.9223	-0.4155	0.6565
23	杉木	幼龄林	0.0478	中龄林	0.1556	0.1078		0.7397	-9.1994	-0.2037	0.5165
24	杉木	中龄林	0.0075	近熟林	0.015	0.0075	0.0325	0.7588	-3.2769	0.0287	0.7078
25	杉木	中龄林	0.0068	成熟林	0.0159	0.0091		0.8096	-4.7954	-0.0667	0.477
26	杉木	中龄林	0.0196	近熟林	0.0304	0.0109		0.8124	-7.0217	-0.1044	0.7419
27	杉木	中龄林	0.014	成熟林	0.025	0.011		0.7785	-1.8704	-0.0894	0.6911
28	杉木	中龄林	0.0135	成熟林	0.025	0.0115		0.7682	-3.9509	-0.1384	0.7481
29	杉木	中龄林	0.0375	成熟林	0.05	0.0125		0.9559	0.4467	0.0253	0.6614
30	杉木	中龄林	0.007	中龄林	0.02	0.013		0.8868	-1.0008	0.0081	0.6254
31	杉木	中龄林	0.0114	近熟林	0.025	0.0136		1.495	7.0194	0.1717	0.7092
32	杉木	中龄林	0.0001	近熟林	0.0138	0.0137		0.596	-9.3254	-0.3581	0.4947
33	杉木	中龄林	0.0412	中龄林	0.0559	0.0147		0.3587	-12.8317	-0.3132	0.7183
34	杉木	中龄林	0.0206	成熟林	0.0361	0.0156		0.9178	-1.0775	-0.0671	0.6064
35	杉木	中龄林	0.0136	近熟林	0.0295	0.0159		0.9344	-0.2005	-0.0461	0.6807
36	杉木	中龄林	0.0172	近熟林	0.0333	0.0161		1.0883	4.6587	0.0346	0.7665
37	杉木	中龄林	0.0108	成熟林	0.0271	0.0163		0.6351	-7.5334	-0.1533	0.5986
38	杉木	中龄林	0.0052	成熟林	0.0238	0.0186		0.9115	-0.3451	-0.0411	0.7246
39	杉木	中龄林	0.043	近熟林	0.065	0.022		0.7758	-2.9652	-0.1136	0.5982
40	杉木	中龄林	0.0005	成熟林	0.0238	0.0233		0.9818	3.8581	0.0463	0.7576
41	杉木	中龄林	0.0143	过熟林	0.0381	0.0238		0.7588	-3.2769	0.0287	0.7243
42	杉木	中龄林	0.001	近熟林	0.025	0.024		0.8719	1.2816	0.0033	0.6824
43	杉木	中龄林	0.0108	成熟林	0.0378	0.027		0.7731	-0.0988	0.1046	0.7088
44	杉木	中龄林	0.0017	近熟林	0.0333	0.0316		0.8492	-2.2937	-0.1104	0.6431
45	杉木	中龄林	0.0088	近熟林	0.0412	0.0324		0.8002	-2.6291	-0.0564	0.7628
46	杉木	中龄林	0.0563	成熟林	0.0903	0.034		0.8002	-2.6291	-0.0564	0.7697
47	杉木	中龄林	0.0025	成熟林	0.0376	0.0351		0.9144	-1.4498	-0.0062	0.7469
48	杉木	中龄林	0.0022	近熟林	0.0389	0.0367		0.8314	-3.9743	-0.0443	0.5871
49	杉木	中龄林	0.0011	成熟林	0.0378	0.0367		0.8314	-3.9743	-0.0443	0.6261
50	杉木	中龄林	0.0023	成熟林	0.0435	0.0411		0.8002	-2.6291	-0.0564	0.7086

(续)

序号	1996			2008		单株蓄积差	$\overline{\Delta C_{ij}}$	Q_{2008}/Q_{1999}	土壤侵蚀模数增量	干扰指数	2008 年植被覆盖率
	树种	龄组	单株蓄积	龄组	单株蓄积						
51	杉木	中龄林	0.0016	成熟林	0.0429	0.0413	0.0325	0.9144	-1.4498	-0.0062	0.7423
52	杉木	中龄林	0.0003	近熟林	0.05	0.0497		0.8394	-3.6952	-0.0859	0.6174
53	杉木	中龄林	0.015	近熟林	0.065	0.05		1.0121	3.2107	0.014	0.7641
54	杉木	中龄林	0.015	近熟林	0.065	0.05		0.9559	0.4467	0.0253	0.6932
55	杉木	中龄林	0.036	成熟林	0.09	0.054		0.8773	0.0566	-0.049	0.7546
56	杉木	中龄林	0.0175	成熟林	0.075	0.0575		0.8609	-1.2687	-0.1015	0.4102
57	杉木	中龄林	0.0175	成熟林	0.075	0.0575		0.7099	-1.3767	-0.0373	0.7141
58	杉木	中龄林	0.0015	近熟林	0.065	0.0635		0.9072	-3.1919	0.0347	0.7271
59	杉木	中龄林	0.0036	成熟林	0.09	0.0864		0.6771	-5.0317	-0.0971	0.7284
60	杉木	中龄林	0.0025	成熟林	0.129	0.1266		0.7885	-3.3999	-0.0377	0.6686
61	杉木	近熟林	0.0357	成熟林	0.0524	0.0167	0.0361	0.8163	-9.1811	-0.0306	0.8223
62	杉木	近熟林	0.0143	成熟林	0.0348	0.0204		0.9142	0.8528	-0.0424	0.7515
63	杉木	近熟林	0.0196	近熟林	0.0435	0.0239		0.799	-1.4333	-0.0839	0.5925
64	杉木	近熟林	0.0139	成熟林	0.0389	0.025		0.7919	-2.3727	-0.053	0.7516
65	杉木	近熟林	0.0075	成熟林	0.035	0.0275		0.8402	-2.3708	0.0806	0.7223
66	杉木	近熟林	0.0143	近熟林	0.0429	0.0286		0.998	4.1736	0.0556	0.7952
67	杉木	近熟林	0.001	成熟林	0.0304	0.0294		1.0575	4.6768	0.0911	0.8542
68	杉木	近熟林	0.0019	成熟林	0.0318	0.0299		1	12.7162	0.4111	0.6371
69	杉木	近熟林	0.0014	近熟林	0.0409	0.0395		0.9974	1.797	0.0318	0.7385
70	杉木	近熟林	0.002	近熟林	0.0435	0.0415		0.7307	-6.5536	-0.1338	0.7009
71	杉木	近熟林	0.0011	成熟林	0.0458	0.0448		0.8278	-1.2693	-0.0547	0.7775
72	杉木	近熟林	0.014	成熟林	0.1196	0.1056		0.9553	-0.3747	-0.0008	0.7445

参考文献

[1]Liveman D M, Hanson M E, Bromn B J, et al. Global sustainability: toward measurement[J]. Environmental Management, 1988, 12(2): 133~143.

[2]D G Sullivan, J N Shaw, D Rickman, et al. Using remote sensing data to evaluate surface soil properties in Alabama ultisols[J] Soil Science, 2005, 170(12): 954~968.

[3]但新球. 论林地持续经营[J]. 中南林业调查规划, 1996, 15(2): 43~46.

[4]林晓利. 基于3S技术的流沙河流域土地退化评价研究. 四川农业大学硕士学位论文, 2007.

[5]刘占锋, 傅伯杰, 刘国华. 土壤质量与土壤质量指标及其评价. 生态学报, 2006, 26(3): 901~1003

[6]罗小荷. 人工林与中国林业可持续发展[J]. 福建林业科技, 2002, 29(2): 69~71.

[7]彭佳红. 亚热带区域几种典型人工林生态系统林地土壤质量评价. 土壤通报, 2010, 41(1): 93~99

[8]王博文, 陈立新. 土壤质量评价方法述评[J]. 中国水土保持科学, 2006, 4(2): 120~126

[9]王凌河. 近20年来嫩江流域土壤退化的初步研究. 水土保持通报, 2010, 30(2): 70~74

[10]王宗海，吕聚煜，陈述亮，等．江西短周期工业原料林造林区划与树种筛选[J]．江西林业科技，2005，(5)：23～26，37.

[11]许宁，郭旭东，洪友堂，等．基于文献分析的土地退化评价指标研究．地理科学，2008，28(3)：425～430.

[12]杨元梁，黄祖泰，丁艺，等．林地可持续经营模式评价的研究[J]．林业科技情报，1997，(4)：3～9.

[13]余坤勇，刘健，许章华，等．基于RS退化林地监测技术研究．东北林业大学学报(自然科学版)，2010，38(1)：60～63.

[14]张慧．基于GIS技术的福建省主要桉树树种用地适宜性及风险评价[D]．福州：福建农林大学硕士学位论文，2005.

[15]张晓丽，游先祥．应用"3S"技术进行北京市森林立地分类和立地质量评价的研究[J]．遥感学报，1998，2(4)：292～297.

[16]张泱．维护生态环境的林地管理措施[J]．森林工程，2004，20(3)：1～2.

[17]张志．红松人工林土壤质量演变规律．东北林业大学硕士学位论文，2004.

[18]沈渭寿，曹学章，沈发云．中国土地退化的分类与分级[J]．生态与农村环境学报，2006，22(4)：88～93.

修枝高度与华北落叶松生长的关系

孙海静[1]　原民龙[2]　姜　涛[2]　刘广营[2]　杨　飞[1]　马长明[1]

（1. 河北农业大学林学院，河北保定，071000；2. 河北省木兰围场国有林场管理局，河北围场，068450）

摘要： 修枝是速生丰产林后期经营管理中一项重要的措施。本研究以木兰林管局境内的 14 年生华北落叶松人工林为研究对象，用标准地调查法对其进行每木检尺，然后进行分析和比较。研究发现，人工修枝可以促进华北落叶松的胸径和蓄积的生长，且修枝高度为树高的 1/4 ~ 1/3 时较合理。

关键词： 华北落叶松；修枝高度；胸径生长；蓄积生长

Relationship of Pruning Height and the Growth of the Artificial *larix principis-rupprechtii* Mayr. Forest

SUN Hai-jing　YUAN Yu-min　JIANG Tao　LIU Guang-ying　YANG Fei　MA Chang-ming

（1. College of Forest, Agricultural University of Hebei, Baoding, 071000

2. Mu Lan State-owned Forest Farm in Hebei Province Authority, Chengde, 068450）

Abstract: Pruning is an important measure in later stage management for the fast growing and high yield. The paper studied 14-year-old *larix principis-rupprechtii* Mayr. of Magnolia Forest Management Bureau, with the method of sample plots investigation to tally, and then analyze and compare. The results shows: artificial pruning can promote the growth DBH and accumulation of larch, and pruning height is 1/4 ~ 1/3 of the tree height is more reasonable.

Key words: *Larix principis-rupprechtii* Mayr.; prunes the altitude; DBH; volume growth

修枝是指人为地除去树冠下部的枯枝及部分活枝的抚育措施（又叫人工整枝）。修枝是应对当前所面临的木材质量严峻问题的关键措施之一。人工修枝通过剪除树木根部萌蘖枝和树冠下部竞争枝，减少无价值的水分和养分消耗，保证主干和上部树冠的营养需要，促进主干木材生长。同时，修枝还可以改善林分的通风透光状况，为树木生长发育创造良好条件，加快成林成材，提高造林保存率和成材率，缩短培育周期[1]。华北落叶松（*Larix principis* -

---

基金项目：国家公益专项（20100400205）资助。

作者简介：孙海静（1988 ~ ），女，河北定州市人，硕士在读，研究方向：森林可持续经营。

通讯作者：马长明（1980 ~ ），男，讲师，博士，研究方向：森林培育. E-mail: machangming@126.com *rupprechtii* Mayr.)是我国华北地区的主要造林树种，也是承德市木兰林管局经营的主要目的树种。通过对华北落叶松人工林修枝与其生长的关系进行研究，以找到最适的修枝高度，从而确定相应的营林措施，达到对华北落叶松人工林的科学管理。

1 研究区概况

新丰林场隶属于于河北省围场县木兰林管局，地理坐标为东经116°32′~118°14′，北纬41°35′~42°40′，其属于内蒙古高原和冀北山地的过渡带，海拔在820~1850m，地势西北高，东南低。木兰林管局的气候具有水热同季，冬长夏短、四季分明、昼夜温差大的特征，属于中温带向寒温带过渡、半干旱向半湿润过渡、大陆性季风型高原山地气候。本地日照充足，总的趋势是北部少于南部，其季节分配以春、夏季居多。木兰林管局年平均气温-1.4~4.7℃，极端最高气温38.9℃，极端最低气温-42.9℃，无霜期67~128d。年均降水量380~560mm，主要集中在6~8月，占全年降水量的69%，各月降水量分配特征是两头小，中间大。植物资源十分丰富，在华北北部地区具有典型性和代表性。

本研究以新丰林场境内的14年生华北落叶松人工林为研究对象，2008年选择了4个立地条件基本相同的林分设置作为试验区，并对其中3个试验区进行不同高度修枝，分别为1m、1.5m、2m，并将其修去的枝条放置于地面上，剩余一组作为对照。在这4个试验区中分别设置三块小样地(20m×30m)，作为3个重复，然后进行每木检尺。2010年7月份进行了复测。标准地情况见表1。

表1 标准地基本情况

Tab.1 Characteristics of the sample plots

编号	重复	海拔(km)	坡位	坡度(°)	修枝高度
草帽梁实验区Ⅰ	1	1.28	上坡	20	1m
	2	1.28	中坡	20	1m
	3	1.28	下坡	20	1m
草帽梁实验区Ⅱ	1	1.28	上坡	20	2m
	2	1.28	中坡	20	2m
	3	1.28	下坡	20	2m
草帽梁实验区Ⅲ	1	1.26	上坡	18	1.5m
	2	1.26	中坡	18	1.5m
	3	1.26	下坡	18	1.5m
草帽梁实验区Ⅳ	1	1.25	上坡	14	CK
	2	1.25	中坡	14	CK
	3	1.25	下坡	14	CK

2 数据处理

利用Excel，对所调查的数据进行处理。林分平均胸径是反映林木粗度的数量指标。森林调查，常用平均断面积法求算平均胸径。即通过每木调查取得各径阶的株数，求出各径阶断面积合计和全部林木断面积总和，被总株数除即得平均断面积：

$$\bar{g} = \frac{G}{N} = \frac{g_1n_1 + g_2n_2 + \cdots\cdots + g_n + n_n}{n_1 + n_2 + \cdots + n_n} = \frac{\sum g_i}{N}$$

然后，求出与平均断面积相对应的直径即为林分平均胸径。

$$D_g = \sqrt{\frac{4}{\Pi}\bar{g}} = \sqrt{\frac{4}{\Pi} \cdot \frac{\sum g_i}{N}} = \sqrt{\frac{4}{\Pi} \cdot \frac{\sum d_i^2 \frac{\Pi}{4}}{N}} = \sqrt{\frac{\sum d_i^2}{N}}$$

式中：$\bar{g}$，平均断面积；N，被总株树；G，各径阶合计；D_g，林分平均胸径；d_i，各林木胸径。

利用一元材积表法求算各标准地蓄积。即根据每木检尺的数据，统计各树种每个径阶株数，并由华北落叶松的一元材积表，查出各径阶中值所对应的单株材积，分别乘以该径阶株数得径阶材积，各径阶材积之和即为其蓄积。然后对所求算的数据进行方差分析。

3 结果与分析

3.1 修枝高度对胸径的影响

根据样木实测资料，利用平均断面积法求算出四个试验区的2008和2010年的林分平均胸径，根据2008年所测的胸径和树高，利用Excel作图，即可做出树高曲线，然后利用2008年的林分平均胸径在树高曲线上找到林分平均高，即可知修枝高与树高比。利用Excel，求算出各标准地的胸径年平均生长量。结果见表2。

表2 胸径增长情况

Tab. 2 Situation of DBH growth

编号	修枝高与树高比	各重复胸径年平均生长量(cm)		
		重复1	重复2	重复3
试验区Ⅰ	1/6	0.58	0.71	0.76
试验区Ⅱ	1/3	0.89	0.91	0.71
试验区Ⅲ	1/4	0.77	0.89	0.85
试验区Ⅳ	0	0.71	0.60	0.52

对各试验区的胸径年平均生长量进行差异性分析，结果见表3。

表3 胸径增长差异性分析

Tab. 3 Analysis the differences of diameter growth

处理	均值	5%显著水平	1%极显著水平
处理2	0.83667	a	A
处理3	0.83667	a	A
处理1	0.68333	ab	A
处理4	0.61000	b	A

由表3可知，试验区Ⅱ、Ⅲ与Ⅳ相比差异显著，即可得出修枝可促进华北落叶松胸径的生长，而试验区Ⅱ与Ⅲ没有差异，通过均值比较发现整枝高度为树高的1/4～1/3时更能促

进其胸径生长。

3.2 修枝高度对蓄积的影响

利用一元材积表法求算各标准地的蓄积生长量，结果见表4。

表4 蓄积增长情况

Tab. 4 Situation of volume growth

编号	修枝高与树高比	蓄积年平均生长量(m^3)		
		重复1	重复2	重复3
试验区Ⅰ	1/6	0.80534	0.86934	0.62049
试验区Ⅱ	1/3	0.79933	0.78600	0.80459
试验区Ⅲ	1/4	0.85377	0.99935	0.96000
试验区Ⅳ	0	0.69979	0.61642	0.49609

对各试验区蓄积年平均生长量进行差异性分析，结果见表5所示。

表5 蓄积增长差异性分析

Tab. 5 Analysis the differences of volume growth

处理	均值	5%显著水平	1%极显著水平
处理3	0.93771	a	A
处理2	0.79664	a	AB
处理1	0.76506	ab	AB
处理4	0.60410	b	B

通过上表可知，试验区Ⅲ与Ⅳ相比差异极显著，试验区Ⅱ与Ⅳ相比差异显著，说明修枝可以促进华北落叶松蓄积的生长。试验区Ⅲ与Ⅱ、Ⅰ差异不显著，但试验区Ⅲ蓄积均值高于试验区Ⅱ和试验区Ⅰ。

修枝促进林分生长的原因：修枝增加了林木的生长空间，提高光能利用率，促进光合作用产物的积累；修枝修去了那些下层枝，由于这些枝条光合作用积累的产物满足不了枝条呼吸作用的消耗，因此这些枝条的去除，减少了损耗，从而促进物质向生长旺盛的部位积累；修枝修去的枝条直接回归林地，这些枝条的分解增加了林地土壤的肥力，改善林分的土壤营养，以促进林木生长。

4 结论与讨论

4.1 结　论

(1)不同修枝高度的14年生华北落叶松的胸径、蓄积的年平均生长量均高于未修枝的胸径及蓄积，说明人工整枝可以提高林木生长量。

(2)比较修枝的3个不同处理的胸径生长量，发现试验区Ⅲ、Ⅱ胸径年平均值相同，且大于试验区Ⅰ，可以得出修枝高度占树高的1/4～1/3时较为合理。

(3)蓄积年平均值为试验区Ⅲ＞Ⅱ＞Ⅰ，即修枝高度占树高的1/4～1/3时有利于华北落叶松蓄积生长。

4.2 讨　论

修枝主要是除去枯死枝和树冠下部受光不足的枝条。这些枝条叶量较少，光和作用微弱，其制造的有机物质常不足以供其自身呼吸作用的消耗，而需要消耗其他枝叶产生的营养物，所以及时地将其除去，有利于林木生长。此外，有时还修去一些妨碍主干生长的大侧枝，也有利于主干的高径生长[2]。黄治等[3](2002)研究发现，红松人工林修枝林分的生长速率明显大于未修枝林分。孙志虎等[4](2004)报道，修枝强度对林木的胸径生长产生显著影响，弱度修枝(1/2 树高)利于树木的胸径生长量。肖祥希[5](2005)对 6 年生福建柏林分修枝，胸径得到一定程度增加。这与本研究中的人工整枝可以提高胸径生长量相一致。

材积生长量是林业速生丰产的主要衡量指标，与最终的经济效益密切相关。修枝对材积的影响一直以来都有不同结论，这与树种、修枝强度等有关[6]。一般认为合理修枝不会降低材积的增长。陈森锟[7]等研究表明：杨树修枝的材积增长速率比不修枝高，其中以中度修枝效果最好，而强度修枝和重度修枝效果相对差。程朝阳[8]对杉木修剪枝研究得出适当的修枝有利于蓄积的生长。肖祥希[5]对 6 年生福建柏林分修枝，修枝 4 年后，蓄积得到一定程度增加。本研究得出人工修枝可以促进蓄积生长。

李盼威[2]提出了落叶松第一次修枝时整枝高度应为树高的 1/3。张永光[9]认为对落叶松人工林在整枝高度不超过树高 1/3 的情况下，对林木生长较明显的促进作用。孙时轩[10]提出松树年龄在 11 ~ 15 年时，冠高比应为 3/5。本研究得出修枝高度占树高的 1/4 ~ 1/3 时较为合理，与上述三种研究成果有相似之处，但也有区别。原因可能是本研究中所做的重复较少，且未进行长时间的连续观测，而未能找到最适修枝高度临界值，应该进一步对修枝高度为 1/4 ~ 1/3 的林分进行更深入的调查研究比较，以确定华北落叶松人工林的最适修枝高度。

对用材树种进行修枝是具有较高增值空间的一项有利措施。落叶松作为我国比较重要的工业用材树种，栽植面积较大。其只通过自然整枝的生长量要比进行人工修枝的低。因此，在落叶松培育的过程中，采用标准、系统、科学的修枝技术显得尤为重要。

参考文献

[1]刘球，李志辉，陈少雄．桉树无节材修枝技术研究进展与展望[J]．桉树科技，2009，26(2)：67 ~ 73.

[2]李盼威，胡庆禄．华北落叶松速生丰产林培育技术[M]．北京：中国林业出版社，2003：115.

[3]黄冶，袁玉峰，孔红娃．修枝对红松人工林林木生长和木材力学性质的影响[J]．东北林业大学学报，2002，30 (1)：76 ~ 77.

[4]孙志虎，王庆成，梁淑娟．间伐和修枝对白桦天然林林木生长的影响[J]．东北林业大学学报，2004，32(6)：11 ~ 12.

[5]肖祥希．修枝对福建柏林分生长及无节材形成的影响[J]．林业科学研究．2005，18(1)：22 ~ 26.

[6]张秀秀，曹帮华，张晓文，等．杨树修枝理论和技术研究进展[J]．河北林果研究，2010，9(25)：235 ~ 239.

[7]陈森锟，尹伟伦，刘晓东，等．修枝对欧美 107 杨木材生长量的短期影响[J]．林业科学，2008，44(7)：130 ~ 135.

[8]程朝阳．修枝强度对杉木幼林生长的影响[J]．福建林学院学报，2007，27(1)：70 ~ 73.

[9]张永光，张洪林，陶涛．落叶松人工整枝和生长量的研究[J]．林业勘查设计，2001，1：37.

[10]孙时轩．造林学[M]．北京：中国林业出版社，1990：322.

叶山林场常绿阔叶混交林林分空间结构研究

李 杰[1] 宗 雪[2] 高 祥[3] 徐 光[3] 郑小贤[1]

（1. 北京林业大学省部共建森林培育与保护教育部重点实验室，北京，100083；
2. 国家林业局调查规划设计院，北京，100714；
3. 吉林省汪清林业局，汪清，133200）

摘要：利用混交度(M)、大小比数(U)和角尺度(W)三种结构参数结合树种组成，分析了叶山林场常绿阔叶混交林林分空间结构。结果表明，主要树种麻栎多呈单种聚集，其余树种中强度混交比例达到96%；马尾松在空间大小对比上占有一定的优势，其余树种则分化严重，既有占优势的树种，也有受压的树种；从林木水平分布格局上看，该林分是以团状分布为主。通过叶山林场常绿阔叶混交林空间结构研究，了解其生态特征和动态规律，为天然更新和抚育间伐提供依据。

关键词：常绿阔叶混交林；空间结构；角尺度；混交度；大小比数

Analysis of the Spatial Structure of evergreen Broad Leaved Mixed Forest in yeshan farm

LI Jie[1] ZONG Xue[2] ZHENG Xiao-xian[1]

(1. Ministry of Education Key Laboratory for Silviculture and conservation, Beijing Forestry University, Beijing, 100083; 2. Academy of Forestry Inventory and Planning of State Forestry Administration of China, Beijing, 100714)

Abstract: Stand spatial structure of evergreen broad leaved mixed forest was investigated using three structure parameters (mingling, neighborhood comparison, and uniform angle index-neighboring tree distribution pattern). The results showed that *Quercus acutissima* was the main species in the mixed forest, which exhibited aggregation of single species, and the rest tree species were more or most intensive in mingling. When using neighborhood comparison method to characterize the size differentiation of trees, *P. massoniana* had an advantage over other species which differentiated seriously both in dominant species and suppressed species. Considering tree distribution pattern using

---

基金项目：林业公益性行业科研专项(20100400320)。

作者简介：李杰，女，硕士在读。研究方向：森林可持续经营。Email：lijie_ 6077@ 163. com
地址：100083 北京林业大学林学院。

通讯作者：郑小贤，博士，教授。研究方向：森林可持续经营。Email：zheng8355@ bjfu. edu. cn
地址：100083 北京林业大学学院。

uniform angle index, the stands in this community was found to be a clumped distribution. Through the analysis of the Spatial Structure of evergreen broad leaved mixed forest for natural regeneration, and tending to provide a theoretical model, thinning of understanding ecological characteristics and dynamic rule.

Key words: evergreen broad leaved mixed forest; spatial structure; neighborhood pattern; mingling; neighborhood comparison

林分空间结构是指林木在林地上的分布格局及其属性在空间上的排列方式，也就是林木之间树种、大小、分布等空间关系。林分空间结构决定了树木之间的竞争势及其空间生态位，它在很大程度上决定了林分的稳定性、发展的可能性和经营空间大小[1]。惠刚盈等提出一种新的空间结构参数——角尺度、混交度和大小比数[2,3]，对林分结构具有很好的解析能力，已经在很多森林类型中得到应用[4,5]。本研究以叶山林场常绿阔叶混交林为研究对象，利用这三个林分空间结构参数对林分的空间结构进行研究，分析研究对象的混交、竞争、林分空间格局及其林分的优势组成种，为制定合理的森林经营目标和技术措施提供依据。

1　试验地概况

研究地点位于安徽省铜陵市叶山林场，长江中下游南岸，地理坐标为117°42′00″~118°10′6″E、30°45′12″~31°07′56″N。亚热带湿润季风气候，全年气候温暖湿润，四季分明；年平均气温17.8℃，年平均降水量1370mm，雨量充沛，无霜期年平均为230d；地貌主要为丘陵，主要土壤类型有黄红壤、石灰土，土层厚度80~120cm之间，pH值均在6.8~7.2之间；全年日照2000~2050h，光照充足。叶山林场经营总面积近600hm^2，林场内现存植被保存完好，森林覆盖率93%[6]。森林类型以栎类天然次生林为主，从新中国成立初期开始封育以来至今未进行过大的人为与自然干扰，树种组成丰富，主要组成树种有麻栎(*Quercus acutissima*)、马尾松(*Pinus massoniana*)、苦槠(*Castanopsis sclerophylla*)、青冈栎(*Cyclobalanopsis glauca*)、石栎(*Lithocarpus glaber*)、枫香(*Liquidambar formosana*)、白栎(*Quercus albus*)、黄檀(*Dalbergia hupeana*)等。

2　研究方法

2.1　试验地调查

本研究采用了样地调查法，调查试验地内所有大于起测径阶(5cm)的林木特征值。试验地大小为100m×100m，面积1hm^2。试验地四周设缓冲区，宽度为5m，在余下的90m×90m范围内分割成9个网格，称为调查单元，每个调查单元为30m×30m。以每个调查单元西南角为坐标原点，用全站仪对试验地内每株树木进行定位，得到每株树木坐标(x，y)，x表示东西方向坐标，y表示南北方向坐标。调查并记录每株树木的树名、树高、胸径、平距等因子。

2.2　林分空间结构参数

2.2.1　角尺度

角尺度用来描述相邻树木围绕参照树的均匀性。用其来描述林木个体在水平地面上的分布形式，或者说是种群的空间分布格局[7]。计算公式为：

$$\overline{W} = \frac{1}{n}\sum_{i=1}^{m} W_i$$

式中：n 为林分中所有林木的株数，w_i 为第 i 株林木的角尺度。根据 $\overline{W}$ 的值可以对林分的分布情况进行判别。当 $\overline{W}$ 取值范围属于(0.475，0.517)时，林分为随机分布；当 $\overline{W}>0.517$ 时为团状分布；当 $\overline{W}<0.475$ 时，为均匀分布。

2.2.2　混交度

树种混交度被定义为参照树的 n 株最近相邻木中与参照树不属同种的个体所占的比例，用以描述树种的空间隔离程度，或者说树种种间关系情况[7]，可采用林分混交度分布均值($\overline{M}$)其计算公式为：

$$\overline{M} = \frac{1}{n}\sum_{i=1}^{n} M_i$$

其中，n 林分内所有林木株数，M_i表示第 i 株树的混交度。

2.2.3　大小比数

大小比数是大小分化度的改进，是指胸径大于参照树的相邻木占 n 株最近相邻木的株数比例，用以描述林木个体大小分化程度，或者说是树种的生长优势程度，它能准确地判断出参照树是否比其相邻木大，同时量化了参照树与其相邻木的关系[7]，可采用该树种的大小比数分布均值($\overline{U}_{sp}$)其计算公式为：

$$\overline{U}_{sp} = \frac{1}{l}\sum_{i=1}^{l} U_i$$

式中：l 为林分内该树种(sp)的数量，U_i为该树种的第 i 株树的大小比数值。

3　结果与分析

试验地中符合检尺要求(枯立木、风倒木不计数)的林木共有 837 株。为避免边缘效应，确定试验地内距每条边线 5m 之内为缓冲区，其余部分为核心区，缓冲区内的林木只做相邻木处理，不参与统计，其中参与统计树木 805 株。计算核心区内全部单木的空间结构参数，分析林分的空间结构状况。

3.1　林分空间分布格局

经统计计算，该林分的平均角尺度为 0.5189，其角尺度取值及株数分布如图 1。

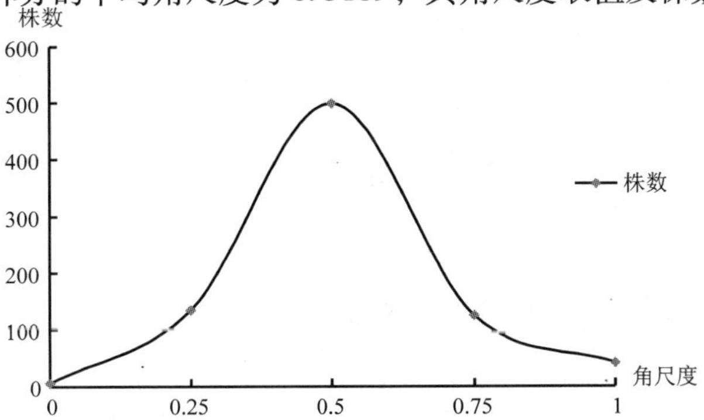

图 1　角尺度株数分布图

如图1所示，叶山林场常绿阔叶混交林中角尺度取值为0和1的频率很低，这说明林分中极少有很均匀和很不均匀的结构单元出现。角尺度的取值为0.5出现的频率最高，达到50%以上。由上图可以看出研究对象的角尺度分布属于正态分布。本研究计算出该林分类型的平均角尺度为0.5189，依照空间分布格局的判定标准，本试验地的林木分布格局为团状分布。

3.2 林分树种组成与空间配置

试验地内主要组成树种有麻栎、马尾松、苦槠 、青冈栎、石栎、枫香、白栎、黄檀等。不同树种混交度的大小和频率见表1。

表1 各树种的混交度及其频率分布

Tab.1 The mingling and its distribution frequencies of species

树种	株数	混交度M值分布					平均混交度
		0	0.25	0.50	0.75	1.0	
麻栎(壳斗科)	573	240	192	98	37	6	0.2282
马尾松(松科)	65	0	7	14	22	22	0.7269
苦槠(壳斗科)	61	5	11	11	22	12	0.6025
青冈栎(壳斗科)	49	0	2	6	22	19	0.7959
石栎(壳斗科)	26	0	4	6	8	8	0.6923
枫香(金缕梅科)	10	0	0	3	0	7	0.8500
油桐(大戟科)	6	0	0	0	3	3	0.8750
白栎(壳斗科)	6	0	0	0	1	5	0.9583
黄檀(豆科)	3	0	0	0	2	1	0.8333
椴树(椴树科)	3	0	0	0	2	1	0.8333
黑枣(柿树科)	2	0	0	0	0	2	1.0000
刺柏(柏科)	1	0	0	0	0	1	1.0000

由表1可以计算出林分平均混角度为0.3718，说明叶山林场常绿阔叶混交林林分混交程度不高，结构单一，趋于不稳定状态。试验地内株数最多树种麻栎平均混交度为0.2282，在零度混交与弱度混交之间，说明麻栎存在聚集现象。其余几种如马尾松、苦槠、青冈栎、石栎、枫香等树种都呈现出强度混交，由于林分中它们株数较少的原因，周围最近的4株相邻木均为不同的树种，即全都呈现出现强度混交。其中有2种树种的混交度达到了1.0000，表现为极强度混交，但是这些树种在试验地内占有量很低，对试验地的总体空间配置影响很小，总的林分依然是结构较单一，趋于不稳定的状态。从表1也可以明显看出混交度为0、0.25、0.5、0.75、1时各树种株数的分布情况，分布情况表明林分结构的情况不佳。

3.3 林木大小分化程度

各树种的胸径大小比数和频率分布见表2。

表 2 试验地各树种直径大小比数及其频率分布

Tab. 2 Value and frequency of the neighborhood comparison based on DBH for different species

树种	大小比数 U 取值分布					平均大小比数
	0	0.25	0.50	0.75	1.00	
麻栎	109	153	114	101	96	0.4660
马尾松	34	16	5	6	4	0.2308
苦槠	5	7	10	20	19	0.6680
青冈栎	4	6	5	17	17	0.6888
石栎	4	1	4	5	12	0.6923
枫香	0	1	1	1	7	0.8500
油桐	0	0	0	1	5	0.9583
白栎	1	1	1	1	2	0.5833
黄檀	0	0	0	1	2	0.9167
椴树	0	0	0	1	2	0.9167
黑枣	0	0	0	0	2	1.0000
刺柏	0	0	1	0	0	0.5000

从表 2 可看出试验地内林分的直径大小比数的总平均值为 0.4936，表明离每一株树最近的 4 株相邻木中几乎有一半是比该参照树的直径小，各树种的平均直径大小比数取值范围为 0.2308 ~ 1.000，反映出该林分内树种空间大小分化存在很大差异。

马尾松的平均大小比数为 0.2308，小于 0.25，说明生长占一定的优势。麻栎的平均大小比数为 0.4660，介于 0.25 ~ 0.50 之间，生长上介于优势和中庸状态之间，生长上也占有优势。白栎、刺柏的平均大小比数在 0.50 左右，生长上处于中庸状态，在由它构造的结构单元中，比它大和比它小的相邻木数量基本一致。苦槠、青冈栎、石栎等树种的平均大小比数大于 0.50，但没有达到 0.75，这几个树种单木在构成结构单元时，两三株相邻木较粗大的情况经常发生，生长上不占优势。像油桐、黄檀、椴树等树种大小比数都在 0.8 ~ 0.9 之间，据此可以判断在由它们构成的结构单元中，它们处于劣势，属于被压木。从上面的分析来看，马尾松空间大小对比上占有一定的优势，麻栎也占有优势但相对马尾松较弱，其余树种则分化严重，既有占优势的树种，也有受压的树种。

4 结论与讨论

叶山林场常绿阔叶混交林的树种零度混交和轻度混交的比例不高，中度混交和强度、极强度混交占很大比例，树种很少呈现单种聚集，多为不同树种混交。树种之间的混交度属性差异很大。树种空间大小分化和大小组合的差异极大，马尾松树种在空间大小对比上占有一定的优势，其余树种则分化严重，既有占优势的树种也有受压的树种。试验地林分平均混交度为 $M = 0.3718$，平均大小比数为 $\bar{U}_{sp} = 0.4936$，结合混交度和直径大小比数分析麻栎、马尾松、苦槠等的空间属性，并辅以实地调查可知，在这种林分中，麻栎多呈单种聚集，并且在生长上占有一定优势；其他树种马尾松、苦槠、青冈栎等多相互混交，呈现出混交程度很高。在大小配置上，麻栎处于优势状态，其余树种有的处于优势，有的处于劣势，分化严重。林分平均角尺度为 $M=0.5189$，结合角尺度的结果分析表明，该混交林的分布格局基本上以团状分布为主。

参考文献

[1]胡艳波，惠刚盈，戚继忠．吉林蛟河天然红松阔叶林的空间结构分析[J]．林业科学研究，2003，16(5)：523~530.

[2]惠刚盈，Von GADOW K，ALBERT M. 角尺度——一个描述林木个体分布格局的结构参数[J]．林业科学，1999，35(1)：37~42.

[3]惠刚盈，Von GADOW K，ALBERT M. 一个新的林分空间结构参数——大小比数[J]．林业科学研究，1999，12(1)：1~6.

[4]安慧君，惠刚盈，郑小贤，等．不同发育阶段阔叶红松林空间结构的初步研究[J]．内蒙古大学学报(自然科学版)，2005，36(6)：714~718.

[5]贾秀红，郑小贤．长白山过伐林区云冷杉针阔混交林空间结构分析[J]．华中农业大学学报，2006，25(4)：436~440.

[6]许剑辉，汪茂林，黄庆丰，等．天然麻栎单木地上生物量模型研究[J]．安徽林业科技，2011，37(4)：3~6.

[7]郑丽凤，周新年，江希钿，等．松阔混交林林分空间结构分析[J]．热带亚热带植物学报 2006，14(4)：275~280.

北京市元宝枫生物量模型的研建

杨　丽

（北京林业大学信息学院，北京，100083）

摘要：本文以北京市元宝枫为研究对象，结合测量数据和统计学软件 SPSS 来拟合元宝枫的生物量模型，通过模型评价指标来选取各器官的最优数学模型。模型共包括五部分，分别是：总量、树干、树冠、树枝和树叶，单位为 kg。结果表明，建立的元宝枫地上总量、树冠、树干和树枝的生物量模型预估精度达到97% 以上；建立的元宝枫树叶的生物量模型预估精度略低一些，不过也达到了91%。最终筛选出总量及各部分生物量模型分别是：总量：$W=0.043(D^2H)^{0.994}$；树干：$W=0.03(D^2H)^{0.977}$；树冠：$W=0.014(D^2H)^{1.02}$；树枝：$W=0.012(D^2H)^{1.015}$；树叶：$W=0.002D^{2.136}H^{0.942}$。由于独立生物量模型具有不相容性，因此本研究采用平差法即以总量按比例分配的方法解决生物量模型相容性问题。

关键词：生物量；指标；模型；相容

The build study of *Acer truncatum* biomass model in beijing

YANG Li

(College of Information, Beijing Forestry University, Beijing, 100083)

Abstract: Taking *Acer truncatum* in Beijing as research object, this paper tries to draw phytomass through measured data and SPSS and selects the most optimized mathmatical model of each part based on model selection criteria. The model includes five parts: gross, trunk, crown, branch and leaf with the unit being kg. The result indicates that the estimated accuracy of the established total, crown, runk, branch models of *Acer truncatum* is more than 97%; the estimated accuracy of the established leaf model of *Acer truncatum* is slightly lower, but also to 91%. The models biomass about total, trunk, crown, branch, leaf are following: $W=0.043(D^2H)^{0.994}$, $W=0.03(D^2H)^{0.977}$, $W=0.014(D^2H)^{1.02}$, $W=0.012(D^2H)^{1.015}$, $W=0.002D^{2.136}H^{0.942}$. Because of the incompatibility of each models, this study employs consummation of errors, that is prorate distribution, to solve this compatibility problem.

Key words: biomass; indicators; model; compatibility

基金项目：北京市园林绿化废弃物资源化再利用关键技术研究及产业化推广示范。

作者简介：杨丽，女，在读硕士。主要研究方向：资源信息管理。电话：13466389077；Email：yangli0457@126.com
地址：北京市海淀区清华东路35号北京林业大学837信箱

在当今生态学研究领域，对森林生物量的研究是一项基础工作，是一个重要的研究方面[1]。森林生物量的估测对于评价森林生产力、碳汇功能等具有重要的作用[2]。元宝枫喜凉润湿肥地，略耐阴，萌芽力强，能够抗烟，在华北地区常见。其在改良土壤和美化环境中占有重要的地位。因此，元宝枫生物量及其结构特征的研究对指导林业科研、生产实践有一定指导意义，同时对于了解我国北方地区森林生态系统的生产规律，提高森林生产力等也都具有十分重要的意义。

1　研究地概况

研究地区需要具备以下几个特点：树木繁多，森林茂密，森林覆盖率高，这样才能为估算北京市元宝枫生物量模型提供有力的数据依据。基于上述要求，本研究区域共有两处，分别位于北京市西山试验林场和北京林业大学试验林场即鹫峰国家森林公园。

西山试验林场位于北京市西郊五环路的外缘，基本涵盖了北京市所有优势树种。隶属于北京市林业局，为生态公益型林场。经营总面积 5931hm^2，森林覆被率 98%，有林地面积 5457hm^2，灌木林地面积 383hm^2，疏林地面积 19.5hm^2，未成林造林地面积 62.7hm^2。

鹫峰国家森林公园位于北京市西北约 30km 的群山怀抱之中，是北京市最近的国家森林公园之一，主峰海拔 465m，公园最高峰可达 1153m。鹫峰数目茂密且多，油松、华山松、山杏、元宝枫、栎树和侧柏是其主要树种。鹫峰林地面积为 832.04hm^2，森林覆被率高达 100%，是绿色植物的天然储藏地。

2　研究方法

2.1　生物量的测定及样品的采集

在研究区域内选择典型地段设置标准地，标准地形状为圆形，标准地面积为 200m^2，相应半径为 7.98m。调查标准地内所有大于起测径阶(4cm)的林木特征，包括胸径和树高，分径阶记录，并计算各径阶平均胸径和平均树高，按照此平均值采伐标准木。测量标准木各部分鲜重，并抽取样品烘至恒重，然后依次计算出树干、树冠、树枝、树叶以及整树的干物质重量。流程图如图 2-1。

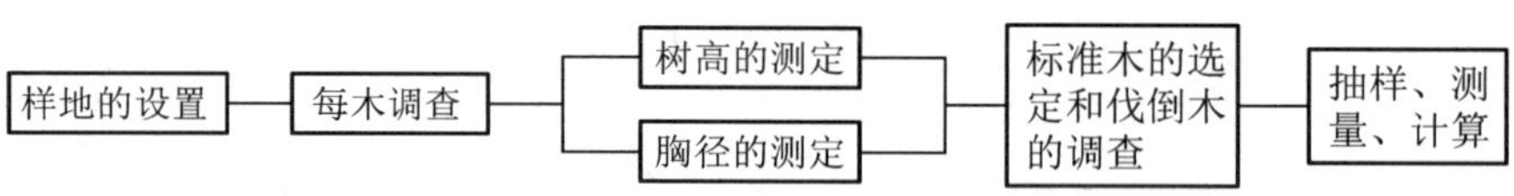

图 2-1　生物量测定流程图

Fig. 2-1　Biomass measurement flow chart

2.2　数据分析与模型选择

生物量模型是确定森林生物量的主要方法，是一种有效并且相对准确的调查方法，按照研究对象尺度不同分为：单木生物量模型、大尺度森林生物量模型[3]，本文主要针对的是前者的研究。生物量模型一旦建立，则可利用树木易测因子的调查，推算树木单株产生的生物量，而且具有一定的精度，省去了全部伐树的麻烦，为日后生物量的计算提供了方便。

本文中独立生物量模型包括 5 部分，其代数关系如图 2-2。

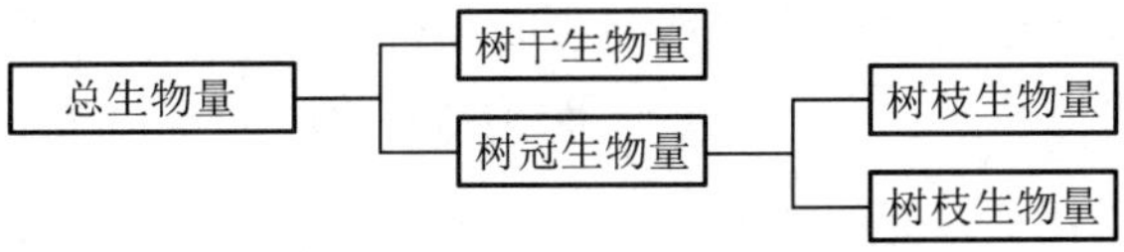

图 2-2　生物量模型代数关系

Fig. 2-2　Algebraic relations of biomass model

利用 SPSS 软件进行模型回归分析，构造线性模型和非线性模型并进行精度比较，对总生物量及各器官生物量进行模型模拟分析，选出拟合度最好、相关最密切的数学模型来估算生物量。本研究采集数据为 85 组，其中 43 组来自鹫峰国家森林公园，42 组来自西山试验林场。按径阶随机抽取 70 组数据用来拟合模型，未使用过的 15 组数据用来对模型进行独立性检验。

综合考虑多种因素并参考以往研究，本研究最终确定以胸径、树高和材积相互之间的组合为解释变量，以总生物量和各器官生物量为因变量[4]，构造出 8 种生物量模型，具体模型形式见表 2-1。

表 2-1　生物量模型形式

Tab. 2-1　Biomass model form

$W = f(X)$	$W = f(X)V$
$W = aD^b$	$W = aD^bV$
$W = a(DH)^b$	$W = a(DH)^bV$
$W = a(D^2H)^b$	$W = a(D^2H)^bV$
$W = aD^bH^c$	$W = aD^bH^cV$

2.3　模型评价

模型的选型以及最优模型的确定，需要一系列指标进行评价。本研究对于模型的评价指标有：剩余标准差(S)，判定系数(R^2)，参数变动系数($C_i\%$)，总相对误差(R_s)，平均相对误差(E_p)，相对均方差(E_r)，预估精度(P)。相关指标计算公式如下：

总相对误差：$$R_s = \frac{\sum(y_i - \hat{y}_i)}{\sum \hat{y}_i} \times 100\% \qquad (2-1)$$

平均相对误差：$$E_p = \frac{1}{n}\sum\left(\frac{y_i - \hat{y}_i}{\hat{y}_i}\right) \times 100\% \qquad (2-2)$$

相对均方差[5]：$$E_r = \sqrt{\frac{1}{n}\sum_{i=1}^{n}\left(\frac{y_i - \hat{y}_i}{y_i}\right)^2} \times 100\% \qquad (2-3)$$

参数变动系数：$$c_i\% = \frac{s_{c_i}}{c_i} \times 100\% \qquad (2-4)$$

预估精度：$$p = \left[- \frac{t_\alpha \cdot \sqrt{\sum(y_i - \hat{y}_i)^2}}{\bar{\hat{y}} \cdot \sqrt{n(n-T)}} \right] \times 100\% \qquad (2-5)$$

在以上公式中，y_i 表示实际测量值，$\hat{y}_i$ 表示模型估计值，n 表示样本容量，c_i 表示在回归模型中，第 i 个参数的估计值，s_{c_i} 表示第 i 个参数的估计值的标准差，表示 t_α 置信水平 α = 0.05 时的 t 分布值，$\bar{y}^{\wedge}$ 为预估平均值，即 $\bar{y}^{\wedge} = \frac{1}{n}\sum \hat{y}_i$，T 表示回归模型参数[6]。在以上指标中，$R_s$ 和 E_p 指标可以反映出回归模型系统偏差的情况，E_r 主要反映模型预测误差的变异即方差情况，预估精度 P 能够反映出回归模型平均预估的能，$C_i\%$ 反映模型参数估计值的稳定性。在模型建立过程中，参数稳定性非常重要。它决定了模型对新数据估计误差，参数变化越小，模型参数估计越准确[7]。

3 结果与分析

3.1 指标对比

根据所计算的各方程的拟合统计量，选择其中判定系数(R^2)最大，剩余标准差(S)、总相对误差(R_s)、平均相对误差(E_p)、相对均方差(E_r)最小，预估精度(P)最大以及参数变动系数($C_i\%$)最小的，作为最佳方程。表 3-1 至表 3-5 为元宝枫各器官 8 种生物量模型的评价指标。

表 3-1 元宝枫总生物量模型评价指标

Tab. 3-1 The evaluation of *Acer truncatum* total biomass model

模型 \ 指标	R^2	S	R_s	$E_p\%$	$E_r\%$	$P\%$	$C_a\%$	$C_b\%$	$C_c\%$
$W = 0.126D^{2.383}$	0.941	0.218	3.93%	5.87%	29.71%	82.63%	16.67%	3.06%	
$W = 0.032(DH)^{1.598}$	0.974	0.143	-3.22%	-1.33%	18.95%	84.49%	12.50%	1.94%	
$W = 0.043(D^2H)^{0.994}$	0.998	0.038	1.47%	0.69%	1.05%	97.94%	2.33%	0.50%	
$W = 0.04D^{1.966}H^{1.057}$	0.994	2.499	0.76%	0.47%	2.14%	97.49%	10.00%	1.22%	3.69%
$W = 774.516D^{0.068}V$	0.989	3.218	-0.40%	1.29%	2.62%	98.01%	8.26%	45.59%	
$W = 792.626(DH)^{0.033}V$	0.989	3.314	-1.15%	0.25%	1.94%	98.34%	11.98%	75.76%	
$W = 769.631(D^2H)^{0.025}V$	0.989	3.282	-0.65%	0.97%	2.42%	98.32%	10.67%	56.00%	
$W = 861.679D^{0.074}H^{-0.057}V$	0.990	3.210	-0.54%	0.56%	2.28%	97.61%	12.36%	41.89%	-85.96%

表 3-2 元宝枫树干生物量模型评价指标

Tab. 3-2 The evaluation of *Acer truncatum* trunk biomass model

模型 \ 指标	R^2	S	R_s	$E_p\%$	$E_r\%$	$P\%$	$C_a\%$	$C_b\%$	$C_c\%$
$W = 0.086D^{2.399}$	0.930	0.234	-9.17%	-4.19%	26.10%	78.43%	17.44%	3.25%	
$W = 0.022(DH)^{1.574}$	0.969	0.156	-2.70%	-1.55%	18.69%	84.53%	13.64%	2.16%	
$W = 0.03(D^2H)^{0.977}$	0.990	0.087	1.51%	-0.05%	1.69%	97.32%	6.67%	1.23%	
$W = 0.027D^{1.873}H^{1.131}$	0.969	3.281	-0.83%	-1.60%	5.17%	95.36%	22.22%	2.72%	7.60%
$W = 569.46D^{-0.003}V$	1.000	0.164	-0.17%	-0.04%	0.78%	99.72%	0.68%	-100.00%	
$W = 575.64(DH)^{-0.004}V$	1.000	0.162	-0.16%	-0.12%	0.72%	99.71%	0.95%	-50.00%	
$W = 573.101(D^2H)^{-0.002}V$	1.000	0.164	-0.14%	-0.08%	0.74%	99.71%	0.86%	-50.00%	
$W = 577.748D^{-0.002}H^{-0.008}V$	1.000	0.161	-0.17%	-0.13%	0.67%	99.72%	1.01%	-150.00%	-50.00%

表 3-3 元宝枫树冠生物量模型评价指标

Tab. 3-3 The evaluation of *Acer truncatum* crown biomass model

模型 \ 指标	R^2	S	R_s	E_p%	E_r%	P%	C_a%	C_b%	C_c%
$W = 0.041D^{2.452}$	0.942	0.223	2.58%	6.61%	30.39%	82.01%	17.07%	3.02%	
$W = 0.01(DH)^{1.637}$	0.966	0.169	-1.20%	1.92%	21.40%	83.63%	20.00%	2.26%	
$W = 0.014(D^2H)^{1.02}$	0.994	0.073	-1.04%	0.27%	2.28%	98.43%	7.14%	0.98%	
$W = 0.015D^{2.094}H^{0.926}$	0.993	1.081	-1.30%	0.17%	2.79%	97.24%	13.33%	1.29%	4.64%
$W = 239.089D^{0.156}V$	0.935	3.230	-0.94%	3.18%	6.40%	95.50%	21.70%	51.28%	
$W = 260.302(DH)^{0.069}V$	0.932	3.315	-2.74%	0.35%	4.29%	96.35%	31.08%	92.75%	
$W = 239.759(D^2H)^{0.055}V$	0.933	3.289	-1.57%	2.19%	5.61%	96.31%	27.86%	67.27%	
$W = 315.162D^{0.171}H^{-0.148}V$	0.936	3.220	-1.38%	1.25%	5.60%	94.39%	31.94%	47.37%	-85.14%

表 3-4 元宝枫树枝生物量模型评价指标

Tab. 3-4 The evaluation of *Acer truncatum* branch biomass model

模型 \ 指标	R^2	S	R_s	E_p%	E_r%	P%	C_a%	C_b%	C_c%
$W = 0.035D^{2.441}$	0.942	0.221	2.41%	6.48%	30.46%	82.58%	8.57%	3.03%	
$W = 0.009(DH)^{1.629}$	0.966	0.169	-5.59%	-1.71%	20.31%	83.95%	11.11%	2.27%	
$W = 0.012(D^2H)^{1.015}$	0.994	0.074	-0.84%	0.41%	2.56%	98.08%	8.33%	0.99%	
$W = 0.011D^{2.116}H^{0.938}$	0.992	0.932	3.19%	4.87%	6.88%	97.47%	9.09%	1.32%	4.80%
$W = 186.658D^{0.178}V$	0.933	2.718	-0.26%	4.73%	8.59%	95.33%	22.15%	46.07%	
$W = 198.16(DH)^{0.087}V$	0.931	2.797	-2.34%	1.75%	6.13%	96.03%	31.81%	75.86%	
$W = 183.511(D^2H)^{0.066}V$	0.932	2.771	-1.22%	3.61%	7.75%	95.88%	28.48%	57.58%	
$W = 241.04D^{0.192}H^{-0.137}V$	0.935	2.751	-0.46%	3.03%	7.30%	94.50%	32.66%	42.71%	-93.43%

表 3-5 元宝枫树叶生物量模型评价指标

Tab. 3-5 The evaluation of *Acer truncatum* leaf biomass model

模型 \ 指标	R^2	S	R_s	E_p%	E_r%	P%	C_a%	C_b%	C_c%
$W = 0.007D^{2.465}$	0.944	0.219	-1.01%	3.59%	29.45%	82.12%	14.29%	2.96%	
$W = 0.002(DH)^{1.642}$	0.964	0.174	-17.84%	-11.84%	22.67%	81.39%	0.00%	2.31%	
$W = 0.002(D^2H)^{1.024}$	0.993	0.075	14.60%	12.60%	14.85%	86.43%	0.00%	0.98%	
$W = 0.002D^{2.136}H^{0.942}$	0.990	0.216	9.92%	10.16%	12.62%	91.72%	0.00%	1.50%	5.41%
$W = 35.897D^{0.2}V$	0.931	0.569	0.79%	5.45%	9.56%	95.81%	22.85%	42.00%	
$W = 37.496(DH)^{0.102}V$	0.927	0.587	-1.13%	2.63%	7.33%	96.45%	32.90%	66.67%	
$W = 34.755(D^2H)^{0.076}V$	0.929	0.580	-0.26%	4.35%	8.85%	96.28%	29.43%	51.32%	
$W = 46.05D^{0.213}H^{-0.132}V$	0.932	0.569	0.44%	3.65%	8.18%	94.99%	33.70%	39.91%	-100.00%

运用上述研究方法，对以上5个表格进行模型筛选，最终得到的各器官最优生物量模型见表3-6。

表3-6　元宝枫各器官生物量最优模型

Tab. 3-6　Optimal biomass model of *Acer truncatumle* organs

器官	模型
总量	$W = 0.043\ (D^2H)^{0.994}$
树干	$W = 0.03\ (D^2H)^{0.977}$
树冠	$W = 0.014\ (D^2H)^{1.02}$
树枝	$W = 0.012\ (D^2H)^{1.015}$
树叶	$W = 0.002D^{2.136}H^{0.942}$

从最优模型指标评价结果中，可以看出，总量、树干、树冠和树枝拟合效果都较好，预估精度能达到97%以上；树叶生物量预估精度略低，但也达到了91%，因此，都能够应用于生物量的估测。

3.2　图形验证

图3-1至图3-5是根据初步筛选出来的最优模型所绘制的图形，包括残差分布图和多线图(分径阶对实际值与模型预估值进行比较)。通过这两种图形来对最优模型进行进一步的验证，从而保证数据的准确性与科学性。

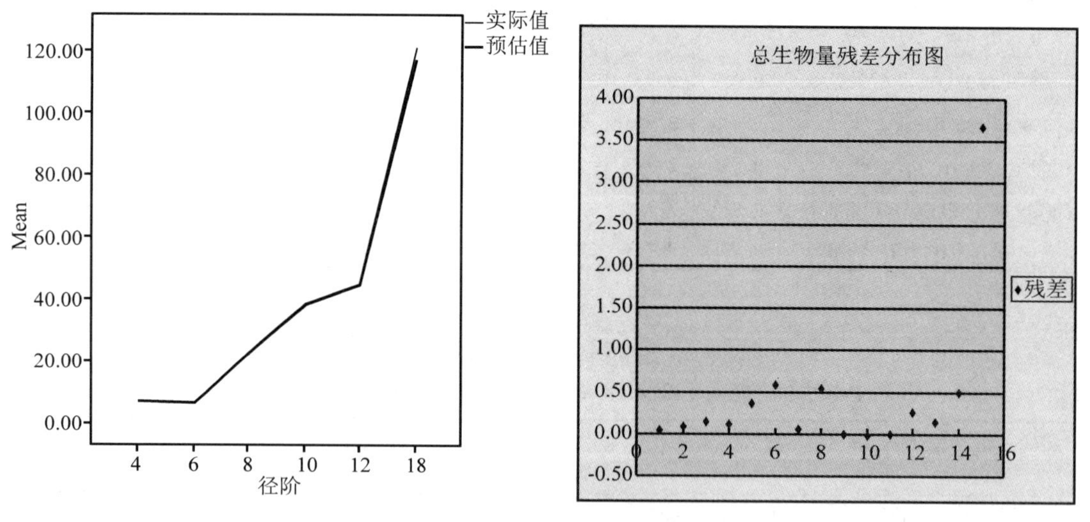

图3-1　总生物量模型图

Fig. 3-1　Total biomass model diagram

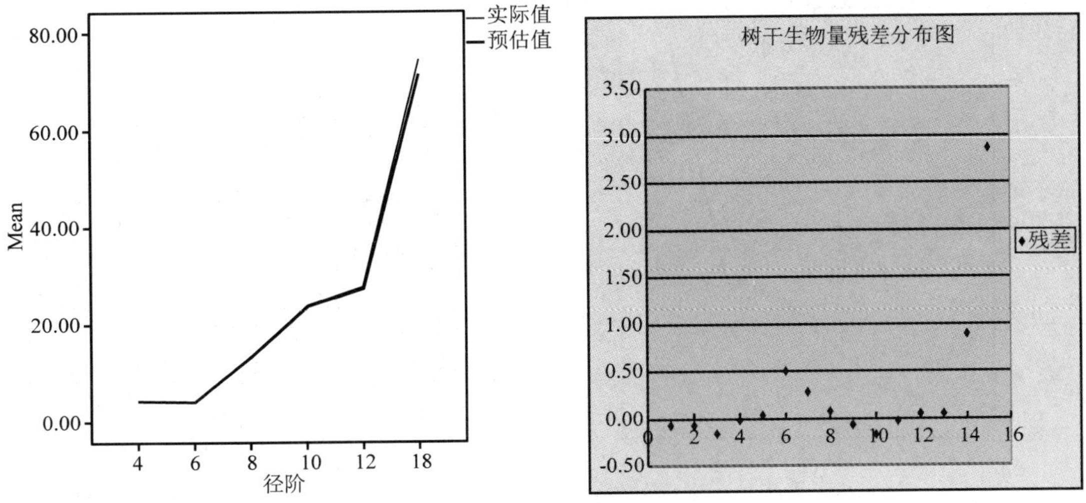

图 3-2　树干生物量模型图

Fig. 3-2　Trunk biomass model diagram

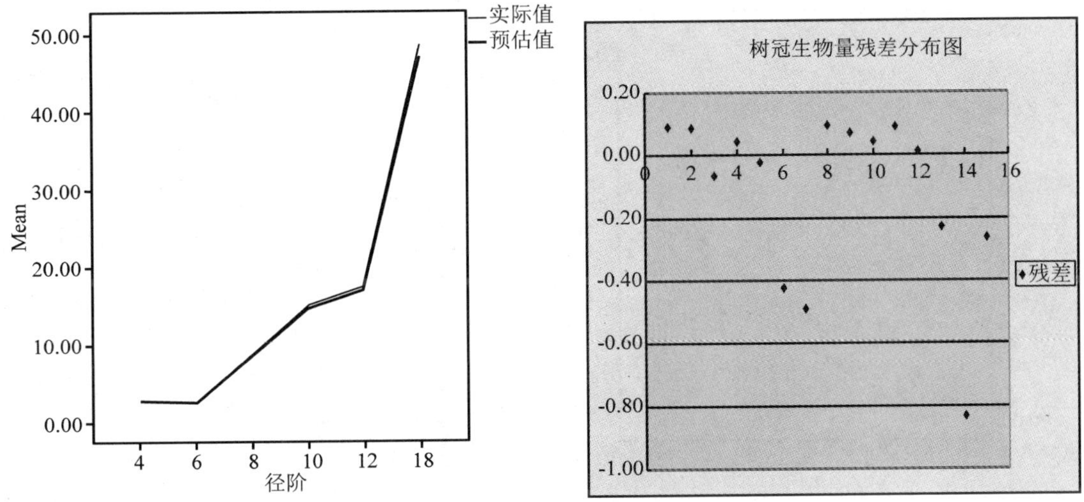

图 3-3　树冠生物量模型图

Fig. 3-3　Crown biomass model diagram

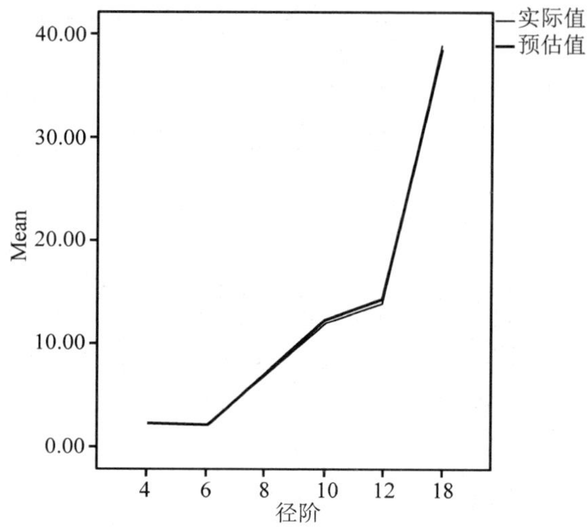

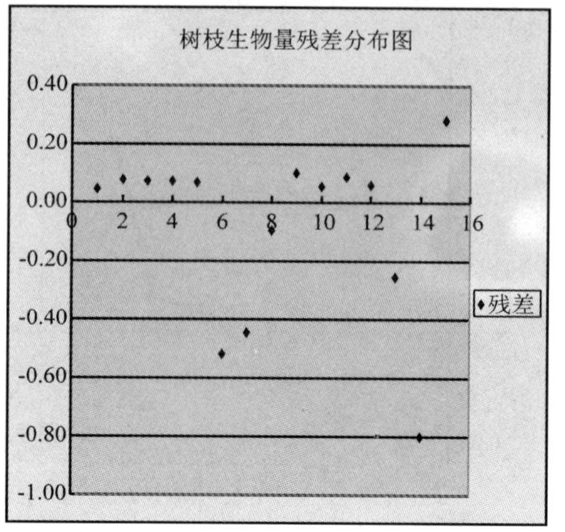

图 3-4 树枝生物量模型图

Fig. 3-4 Branch biomass model diagram

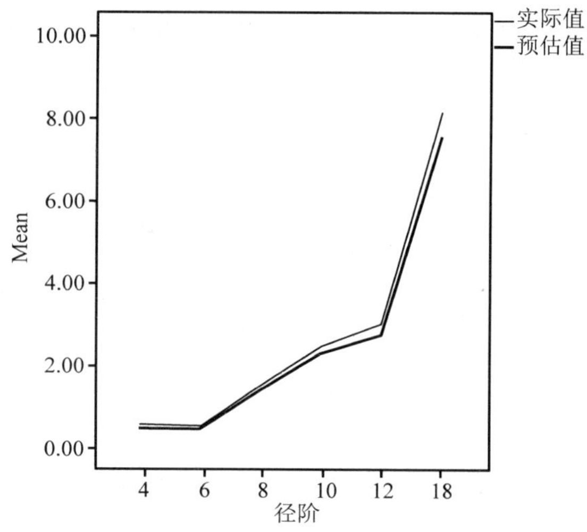

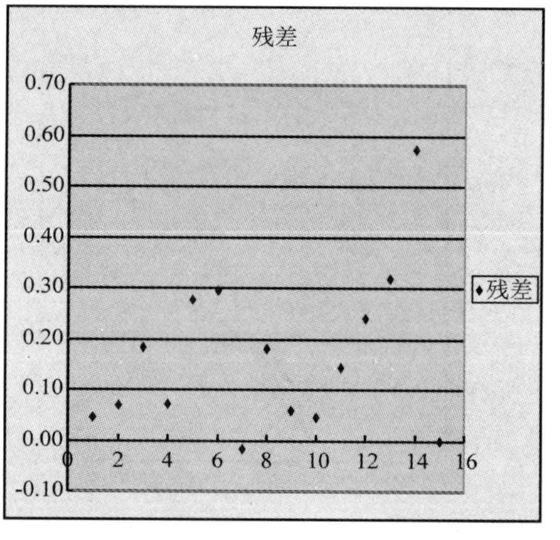

图 3-5 树叶生物量模型图

Fig. 3-5 Leaf biomass model diagram

从实际值与模型预估值图形可以看出，由总量与树干数据所绘制的图形几乎重合，说明估计效果较好；由树冠与树枝数据所绘制的图形在径阶 10～12 这一范围稍有偏离，但总体估计效果仍较好；由树叶数据所绘制的图形在各个径阶上稍有偏离，但是幅度较小，仍然称得上是一个较好的估计，这一结果正好与之前指标评价的结果相对应。从各个器官的残差分布图可以看出，残差分布较集中，在一定范围内上下波动，证明该数学模型在统计学上具有意义。

3.3 模型兼容

生物量各分量模型之间存在着不相容性，已有研究可以建立相容性生物量模型。本文使用平差法解决不兼容问题，平差法是以生物量总量为基础按比例平差。

为了达到各分量占总量比例之和等 1 的目的，第一级控制变量为总量。通过按比例分配使得树干与树冠之和等于总量；第二级控制变量为树干和树冠，在第一级控制基础上，通过第二级比例分配使得树冠等于树枝加树叶[8]。用公式表示为：

一级控制：$$\hat{W}_{干} = \frac{W_{干}}{W_{干} + W_{冠}} \times W_{总} \tag{3-1}$$

$$\hat{W}_{冠} = \frac{W_{冠}}{W_{干} + W_{冠}} \times W_{总} \tag{3-2}$$

二级控制：$$\hat{W}_{枝} = \frac{W_{枝}}{W_{枝} + W_{叶}} \times \hat{W}_{冠} \tag{3-3}$$

$$\hat{W}_{叶} = \frac{W_{叶}}{W_{枝} + W_{叶}} \times \hat{W}_{冠} \tag{3-4}$$

公式简化后分别为：

一级控制：$$\hat{W}_{干} = \frac{W_{总}}{1 + \frac{W_{冠}}{W_{干}}} \tag{3-5}$$

$$\hat{W}_{冠} = \frac{W_{总}}{1 + \frac{W_{干}}{W_{冠}}} \tag{3-6}$$

二级控制：$$\hat{W}_{枝} = \frac{\hat{W}_{冠}}{1 + \frac{W_{叶}}{W_{枝}}} \tag{3-7}$$

$$\hat{W}_{叶} = \frac{\hat{W}_{冠}}{1 + \frac{W_{枝}}{W_{叶}}} \tag{3-8}$$

$W_{总}$、$W_{干}$、W 、$W_{枝}$、$W_{叶}$分别表示根据表 3-6 中的最优模型计算得到的总量、树干、树冠、树枝和树叶的生物量值；而 $\hat{W}_{干}$ 、$\hat{W}$ 、$\hat{W}_{枝}$ 、$\hat{W}_{叶}$ 分别表示根据式(3-5)至(3-8)计算得到的树干、树冠、树枝和树叶的预估值。

公式(3-5)与(3-6)相加有 $\hat{W}_{干} + \hat{W}_{冠} = W_{总}$，同样，公式(3-7)与(3-8)相加有 $\hat{W}_{枝} + \hat{W}_{叶} = \hat{W}_{冠}$ ，即有 $\hat{W}_{干} + \hat{W}_{枝} + \hat{W} = W_{总}$，因此，很好地解决了模型不相容的问题。表3-7 即为采用上述研究方法得到的各器官相容生物量模型，通过此相容性模型计算的生物量数据，能够在一次调查结果中呈现一致性。

表 3-7 元宝枫各器官相容性生物量模型

Tab. 3-7 Compatibility biomass models of *Acer truncatumle* organs

分量	相容性模型
总量	$\hat{W}_{总} = W_{总} = 0.043\ (D^2H)^{0.994}$
树干	$\hat{W}_{干} = \frac{0.043\ (D^2H)^{0.994}}{1 + 0.46667\ (D^2H)^{0.043}}$

(续)

分量	相容性模型
树冠	$\hat{W}_{冠}=\frac{0.043\ (D^2H)^{0.994}}{1+2.14\ (D^2H)^{-0.04}}$
树枝	$\hat{W}_{枝}=\frac{0.043\ (D^2H)^{0.994}}{[1+2.14\ (D^2H)^{-0.04}][1+0.17D^{0.106}H^{-0.073}]}$
树叶	$\hat{W}_{叶}=\frac{0.043\ (D^2H)^{0.994}}{[1+2.14\ (D^2H)^{-0.04}][1+6D^{-0.106}H^{0.103}]}$

4 结 论

通过对北京市鹫峰国家森林公园和西山试验林场元宝枫生物量模型的建立与评价，初步得到总量、树干、树冠、树枝生物量模型以 $W=a(D^2H)^b$ 最好，树叶生物量模型以 $W=aD^bH^c$ 最好。然而初步筛选的最优生物量模型需要进行兼容性处理，从而保证独立生物量之和与总量相等。

参考文献

[1]邵殿坤，李广玉，陈国林，等．长白落叶松生物量模型的初步研究[J]．吉林林业科技，2010，39(5)：32～36.

[2]李建强，菊花，张秋良．白桦天然林生物量模型的研究[J]．内蒙古农业大学学报，2010，31(1)：76～82.

[3]王维枫，王雪峰，赵浩彦．森林生物量模型综述[J]．西北林学院学报，2008，23(2)：58.

[4]许俊利．东折棱河落叶松生物量模型研究及生物量估算[D]．北京林业大学，2009.

[5]钟义山．预测模型精度指标的探讨[J]．西北林学院学报，1990，5(3)：34～40.

[6]彭小勇．闽北杉木人工林地上部分生物量模型的研究[D]．福建农林大学，2007.

[7]胥辉．两种生物量模型的比较[J]．西南林学院学报，2003，23(2)：36～38.

[8]胥辉．相容性生物量模型研究[J]．福建林学院学报，2001，21(1)：18～23.

长白山主要阔叶树种子园建园技术的研究

李兴东　顾东杰

（吉林省林业勘察设计研究院，吉林长春 130022）

摘　要：研究报告总结了长白山林区珍贵阔叶树种—水曲柳、胡桃楸、黄波罗、蒙古栎在长期自然选择过程中，产生具有不同遗传结构的种源和个体，这些优良个体在造林时表现出较大的遗传增益。通过对长白山林区的水、胡、黄、椴、柞天然林、人工林的优势林分的生长状况及立地条件的关系、营造林技术、种子园现状及其他相关资料的分析，并对继往建园技术进行总结，提出了水曲柳、胡桃楸、黄波罗、蒙古栎的建园立地选择，天然林、人工林选优方法，同时对，嫁接苗培育，无性系或家系配置、树体管理、花粉管理、土壤管理，主要病虫鼠害防治等一整套第一代种子园营建技术。该研究对吉林省长白山林区珍贵阔叶树种子园设计营建具有实践性指导意义。

关键词：阔叶树、种子园、营建技术

The Research of Broadleaved Tree Seed Garden Building Technique in Changbai Mountain

LI Xing-Dong　GU Dong-Jie

Abstract: The researching report summarizes that in the long - term natural selection, the valuable broadleaved tree seeds in Changbai Mountain Forest - *Fraxinus mandshurica Rupr.* , *Juglans mandshurica Masim. Phellodendron amurense* Rupr. , *Quercus mongolica* Fisch. , generate the seeds and individuals of different hereditary structure , and these fine individuals show great increasing benefit of heredity in the forest building Through the analysis of the growing condition of natural woods and advancing man - made woods *Fraxinus mandshurica* Rupr. , *Juglans mandshurica* Maxim. , *Phellodendron amurense* Rupr. , *Tilia amurensis* Rupr. , *Quercus mongolica* Fisch . in Changbai Mountain forest and the conditional relationship constructing , woods technique, present condition of seed garden and other relative materials , the report puts forward a whole set of building techniques for seed garden of the first generation, such as the building land selection of *Fraxinus mandshuria* Rupr. , *Juglans mandshurica* Maxim. , *Phellodendron amurense* Rupr. , *Quercus mongolica* Fisch. , the escellent selecting way of natural woods and man - made woods, instant zone, the growing power management, soil management and prevention and cure of main disease, worms and mice defection , This subject research has a pragmatic meaning to guide seed garden designing construction of valuable broadleaved tree in Changbai Mountain Forest District of Jilin Province.

Key words: broadleaved tree; seed garden; building technique

1 研究的目的意义

吉林省中东部山地丘陵分布着大量的珍贵阔叶树种，但多为天然林，人工林很少。随着珍贵阔叶树的不断开发利用，特别是在家具、装饰工艺等行业的兴起，珍贵阔叶树木材在国际、国内市场上需求迅速增加，价格不断攀升，超过了以往珍贵用材——红松。如大径的水曲柳、胡桃楸、蒙古栎、紫椴等树种的木材非常紧缺，珍贵阔叶树种后备资源的培育显得尤为重要。对树种多样化的需求日益增强。因此，长白山林区在完成红松、落叶松、樟子松主要用材针叶树种子园，加快珍贵阔叶树的良种选择，建立良种基地，为营林生产提供速生优质的种子是一项十分紧迫的任务。

长白山林区蕴藏着丰富的针阔叶树种，其中水曲柳、胡桃楸、黄波罗、统称三大珍贵阔叶用材树种，是构成红松针阔叶混交林的重要建群树种。蒙古栎是长白山低山丘陵阔叶林的建群树种之一。分布广、面积大，但是几十年来，天然林过量采伐，资源锐减，有的树种如水曲柳、胡桃楸已列为濒危物种，许多优良树种资源损失严重，特别最近几年家具加工业、装饰业的迅速发展，对材质优良、花纹美观的硬阔叶树种木材需求急剧增加，大径材的水曲柳、蒙古栎国际市场的价格十分昂贵，供不应求。同时，2000 年国家正式启动了天然林保护工程，天然林资源保护工程的实施，开展森林分类经营，实现由采伐利用天然林向采伐利用人工林，培育森林资源的转变。林木良种基地建设是林业生产实现可持续发展的基础工作。水曲柳、胡桃楸、蒙古栎及黄波罗已逐渐成为长白山林区的主要造林树种，建立珍贵阔叶用材树种种子园，保存优良基因，为林业生产提供遗传品质优良的种子是实现林业现代化的主要措施之一。

长白山珍贵阔叶树种子园建园技术在国内外尚无成熟的经验，本研究是借鉴针叶树建园的技术路线，总结近年有关四个树种的研究成果，提出第一代长白山主要阔叶树种子园营建技术。

长白山珍贵阔叶用材树种由于生长周期较长，栽培历史较短，良种的研究开展时间为初级阶段，研究成果和资料较少，此次第一代种子园的建园研究，还是尝试，需要在建园过程中不断改进。

2 研究方法

2.1 长白山主要阔叶树种子园建园的基础材料调查研究

自 20 世纪 80 年代以来东北林区(长白山、小兴安岭)陆续对水曲柳、胡桃楸、黄波罗、蒙古栎等树种进行了人工造林，开展了适宜立地条件，种子采集、育苗技术、造林技术、生态习性及种源、选优的研究，为种子园建园的研究，提供了基础资料。

水曲柳、胡桃楸、黄波罗是东北林区三大珍贵硬阔叶树种。水曲柳(*Fraxinus mandschurica*)天然分布于小兴安岭南坡经完达山到长白山延伸至燕山山地，长白山北坡是中心分布区，是一个喜光、喜肥、喜湿润、耐寒和稍耐盐碱，材质优良、力学强度大、纹理通直、花纹美丽，耐腐耐水湿，是航空用材、胶合板、装修、地板及军械、工业配件等用材树种。20 世纪 80 年代以来东北林业大学已经进行适生立地条件、造林、生长发育规律的研究，吉林省林科院、临江林业局进行了种子处理、育苗及无性繁殖的研究，吉林市林科院对水曲柳历经12年种源研究，从19个种源的种子，8个参试点中进行了多性状综合指数分析，选择出大海林和辉南种源为我省造林及选优的全适性种源，十年生树高遗传增益达46%，为建园选优完成了前期工作。

胡桃楸(*Juglans mandshurica*)分布于小兴安岭、长白山海拔500～800m沟谷两岸，多与红松、沙松、水曲柳、黄波罗、槭类组成混交林，喜生于深厚、肥沃、排水良好的沟谷和山坡中下部，是硬阔叶树种中较速生，木材坚硬，纹理通直，有光泽、花纹美观，易于加工的优良树种。是价值很高的军工、家具、运动器材及乐器制作用料；种仁营养丰富，作食品加工及滋补品；外果皮可提取单宁、制作染料及农药等。吉林省白石山林业局已在播种造林、集约栽培技术上进行了研究，省林科院在良种选择及扦插繁育方面取得了研究成果。东北林业大学在适宜立地条件和混交林营造上进行了调查研究。

黄波罗(*Phellodendron amurense*)主要分布在小兴安岭南坡、长白山山地及燕山山地，在长白山垂直分布在700m以下，常零散分布于河谷两侧，山地中下腹阔叶林或红松阔叶林内，极少形成片林。该树种较耐寒，幼龄阶段易受冻害，随着林龄增加抗寒能力增强。喜光、喜湿润肥沃土壤，在河谷两侧及排水良好山地的中下部生长良好。黄波罗材质坚硬、耐水湿、耐腐，纹理美观，有光泽、易加工，是军械、家具、造船、飞年来，东北林业大学进行分布界限论析，种子处理、人工混交的研究及适地适树的调查，吉林省林科院进行了黄波罗的育苗和造林的研究，吉林市林科院在长白山林区进行个体选优，选出的优树，建立了基因库。

蒙古栎(*Quercus mongolica*)广泛分布于黑龙江、吉林、辽宁的东部山地，向南伸延到华北、华中及陕西、内蒙古等地，国外俄罗斯的远东地区、东西伯利亚、蒙古东部，朝鲜北部和日本也有分布，是长白山天然林中混交树种及中东部山区半山区常见的落叶阔叶森林植物群落之一，也是分布广、面积大的次生林森林类型。具有喜光、喜温凉气候，耐寒、耐干旱，在零下50℃，降水量300～450mm，生长期100天的气候条件下生长发育。其材质坚硬，耐腐性强，纹理美观，是装饰材料、家具、车辆、船舶、细木工、建筑的优良用材。小径木是木炭、培育本耳等食用菌的优质材。

吉林省林业厅自2001年起首先选择对水曲柳、胡桃楸、黄波罗、蒙古栎作为第一批阔叶树建园技术的研究，由省林业设计研究院负责，在较短的时间内，拿出调研技术报告，以便尽快开展工作。

2001年判定了研究工作路线，2001～2002年进行了外业调查研究工作，2003年末根据收集的资料完成了研究报告。

阔叶树建园工作，既往研究较少，在掌握针叶树建园技术程序的基础上，首先收集了有关国内阔叶树建园工作的资料，并深入调查长白山林区四个树种的天然林、人工林优势林分的状况，自2001～2002年先后调查和收集到水曲柳、蒙古栎建园设计资料，胡桃楸、水曲柳、黄波罗阔叶树育苗、营造技术，并调查了敦化、蛟河、露水河、三岔子、辉南等林区的水曲柳、胡桃楸、黄波罗、蒙古栎天然林和人工林优势林分的立地条件及生长状况及营造技术，为建园选地提供了依据，并分别总结了采种、穗条、育苗、嫁接、定植及子代林建园技术等。

通过对省内外有关水曲柳、胡桃楸、黄波罗、蒙古栎天然林、人工林及建园资料的分析总结，提出了四个树种的种子园营建技术报告。总结出四个树种建立种子园的选地、选优标准，并对阔叶树建园的方法及嫁接、无性系配置、定植等技术提出了整套的较详细的经营管理技术，包括土壤管理、树体管理、花粉管理、开花结实规律的观测研究，以及主要病虫鼠害的防治和档案管理的内容和方法，报告完成了合同中规定的水曲柳、胡桃楸两个阔叶树种的建园研究，并增加了黄波罗、蒙古栎的建园技术，圆满完成了合同中要求的各项内容。

吉林市林科院对蒙古栎进行了种子处理、育苗和造林技术的研究，并开展了种源试验，从十一个种源中苗期生长性状方差分析和多性状综合评定，选出松花湖、磐石种源为吉林地区及毗邻地区的优良种源，蛟河县的4[#]个体为优良个体。其中二年生苗高松花湖种源超出其他种源平均值38.9%，磐石种源超出其他种源平均值的44.9%，蛟河4[#]个体超出其他种源平均值31.6%。上述种源及优良个体为蒙古栎种子园建园提供了第一批材料。

吉林市林科院在水曲柳、蒙古栎种源试验地的大海林、长白、辉南、抚松、和龙、临江、白石山等地优良种源区选择出优良林分中的优良个体及黄波罗的优忍受个体优良230株，并在临江、白石山、三岔子林业局建立了15hm^2的基因库及蒙古栎种子林5hm^2，水曲柳种子林2hm^2。

为了建园掌握第一手资料，先后调查了辉南森经局水曲柳、胡桃楸三十年生人工林；白石山林业局的胡桃楸人工林丰产栽培技术，蒙古栎的育苗、造林生长状况；敦化林业局、临江林业局、汪清林业局、黄泥河林业局将要规划的水曲柳等阔叶树种子园；汪清林业局、敦化林业局的红松、落叶松及樟子松种子园，建园布局及管理技术；松江河林业局营造小片的黄波罗人工林经调查已有30年历史，生长良好，为建园提供了素材。近二十年来有关科研单位和生产部门对中东部林区相继进行了4个阔叶树的育苗、造林、培育技术的研究，为建立阔叶种子园提供了实践经验和理论依据。

阔叶树建园内容、程序与针叶树建园相似，总结为以下六个方面：

(1)建园树种选优、嫁接、无性系繁育技术。

(2)进行各树种无性系花期观察，辅助授粉，结实规律，缩短种子园间隔期。

(3)种子园经营管理技术。

(4)建好基因库，拓宽种子园的遗传基础。

(5)搞好子代测定、无性系测定、提供遗传参数。

(6)提供遗传品质得到改良的种子。

2.2 种子园建园用优树的选择

优树是建立种子园最重要的基础材料，优树质量的好坏直接关系到种子园遗传增益的大小，关系到种子园建园的成败。优树选择就是从群体中按育种目标和优树标准进行个体表型选择，选择的优树是树木多层次改良的基本材料之一。因此阔叶树种子园的建立，宜应按选优程序进行。

2.3 优树选择的基本方法

2.3.1 在人工林中选优

对有一定造林史的水曲柳、胡桃楸、蒙古栎，可在人工林中选优，人工林中选优，采用优势木对比法，即候选树中心，在立地条件一致的林分，半径为10～25m的范围内，包括30～40株树木，选出仅次于候选树的3～5株优势木作为对照，按性状(生长量，结实能力、干形、抗性等)逐项比较评定，当候选树超过对比树平均规定标准时方可定为优树。

2.3.2 在天然林中选优

对水曲柳、胡桃楸、黄波罗在一然林中选优，可采用基准线法。方法之一，回归线法：首先按标准实测候选树的生长量如直径树高、材积、年龄，分别不同立地类型，建立回归曲线，候选树、平均木及较差木分别为A、B、C。候选树A在回归线上方，结实及形质指标都符合标准即可入选。方法之二，绝对生长量法：根据生长过程表或立地指数表，分别龄级制定出优树生长量绝对标准，当预选树的生长量达到或超过标准时，结实与形质指标也符合要求，即可入选。

2.3.3 数量化选优

蒙古栎选优采用数量化选优方法，即在天然林群体中布设样地，每块样地选1株候选树，并在候选树周围10~15m范围选出5株大树为对比木。

(1)对优树和对比木，分别实测树高(H)、胸径(D)、冠幅(cd)、冠长(cl)、通直度(S)、冠型(cd/D)、圆满度(R)、侧枝夹角(T)、形数(F)、自然整枝能力(k)、侧枝数(B)、年龄(A)、冠影面积(S')、树皮厚度及胸径近5年净生长量(Δd)等15项指标。

(2)采用逐步回归方法对15个性状进行统计分析，筛选出对主要经济性状显著相关的测树因子。

(3)对筛选后的因子进行数量化综合分析，计算出各性状的权重及其得分值。

(4)根据对比值划分各性状评分等级[对比值 $i\% = (a/b-1)\times 100$]，其中：a，候选树观测值，b，对比树观测平均值。

(5)确定最低分数限 $G(G = G—1.64\delta/\sqrt{n})$，$a = 0.05$，$G$，优树平均得分值，$\delta$，标准差，$n$，样木数，$a$，危险率。

3 研究成果

3.1 建园技术

水曲柳、胡桃楸、黄波罗、蒙古栎阔叶树第一代种子园建园技术主要包括建园地选择，建园方式、嫁接苗培育、无性系或家系配置，移栽定植等。

建园方式有两种方式，一是预先培育嫁接苗法，即按一定标准培育超级苗作为砧木，然后嫁接从优树上采集的接穗，待嫁接苗成活后，按无性系配置图定植到种子园。此法可一次建成种子园，成活率高，接穗整齐一致，便于经营管理。二是预先定植砧木法，即先锋超级苗，按预定的株行距栽植在种子园。砧木培育达到嫁接标准时，一般2年以后，直接在种子园进行嫁接。

3.2 子代测定

子代测定是种子园极其重要的工作，主要任务：①通过对表型选择进行检验，对优树实行再次评选，为种子园去劣或重建提供依据。②为下一代选择生产基本群体，提供营建改良种子园的物质基础。③研究遗传参数，为制定育种策略、改进育种方法，提高育种效率提供依据。子代测定区可与种子园其他部分分开，选择有代表性的、立地条件变化小，坡度均匀，环境条件便于控制地段进行。在初级无性系种了园中子代测定主要进行优树自由授粉子代测定。

3.3 阔叶树种子园经营管理技术

林木种子园的经营目标就是尽快大量生产经过遗传改良的林木种子。因此，除在建园时采用物候期同步的优良遗传型外，还要对种子园的环境采取各种管理措施使之提早结实，保证种子园稳产高产。采取的措施主要有土壤管理、树体管理、花粉管理、主要病虫害防治等。

4 结论与建议

(1)确定出水曲柳、胡桃楸、黄波罗、蒙古栎优树选择的数量指标和形质指标；提出四树种天然林和人工林选优的方法，对蒙古栎天然林采用数量化选优，选优效果较为理想。

(2)提出了水曲柳、胡桃楸、黄波罗、蒙古栎等建园方法、嫁接苗培育、无性系或家系配置、基地清理、整地、移栽定植等阔叶树种第一代种子园营建技术。

(3)确定出阔叶树优树自由授粉子代测定技术，为进一步遗传改良奠定了基础。

(4)提出了树体管理、花粉管理、土壤管理、主要病虫鼠害防治、档案管理等一整套阔叶树第一代种子园经营管理技术。

(5)水曲柳、胡桃楸、黄波罗、蒙古栎在长期自然选择过程中，产生具有不同遗传结构的种源和个体。水曲柳种源选择结果，选择出大海林和辉南种源为吉林省推广造林的全适性优良种源，其遗传增益为16.2%；蒙古栎种源及个体选择结果，选择出松花湖、磐石种源为吉林地区及毗邻地区的优良种源，估算蒙古栎种源及个体的遗传力分别为0.7977和0.79。黄波罗采用优良的松花湖、磐石种源及优良个体造林，树高可分别获得18.4%和12%的遗传增益，为阔叶树种子园建园提供了材料。

(6)建议建立水曲柳、胡桃楸、黄波罗、蒙古栎等树种优良种源采种基地和基因库，为进一步开展长白山珍贵阔叶树种基因收集、保存提供了基础。

(7)黄波罗人工林历史短，天然林中成片极少，选优时只能单株选择；蒙古栎的次生林中多代萌生林较多，选优应在实生天然林中进行。

(8)长白山林区的阔叶用材树种在天然林中以混交方式存在，如黄波罗、紫椴、槭树类，即是水曲柳、胡桃楸表现好的单株，也常在混交林中出现，因此选优工作深入探讨个体选优方法，以防遗漏具有遗传特性的材料。

(9)无性系种子园不同树种、不同单株嫁接不易成活，亲和力差异较大，胡桃楸嫁接成活率极低，黄波罗嫁接口有开裂现象，表明亲和力较差。建园时值得注意，有条件地方可以现有林分建立采种林基地也收到事半功倍的作用。

黑龙江省次生林的初步探讨

张玉波

（牡丹江林业科学研究所，黑龙江牡丹江，157009）

摘要：本文对次生林的研究进行了回顾，总结出了黑龙江次生林的现状，认为黑龙江应用价值较高的次生林有山杨和白桦林，但是需要改造；针对这些现状，本文提出了4种具体的经营方式。

关键词：次生林；现状；经营方式

Discussion about Secondary Forest of Heilongjiang

ZHANG Yu-bo

(Mudanjiang forestry institution, Heilongjiang, Mudanjiang, 157009)

Abstract: In this paper, review of the research about secondary forest is made and the situation of Heilongjiang secondary forest is summarized. 4 management methods pointed to how to manage those secondary forest are given.

Key words: secondary forest; situation; management method

黑龙江省是我国最大的林业省，林木资源居全国之首。掠夺性的采伐使森林结构发生了质的变化，具有较高利用价值的针叶树逐渐减少，同时具有较强萌生能力的阔叶树不断增加，最终导致植被的总体特征发生了变化，次生森林开始形成。建国后随着一系列林业法规的实施，制止了森林的继续破坏，次生林发生了转折性的变化，开始由逆行演替向进展演替的方向发展，由此次生林进入了恢复发展的阶段。黑龙江省次生林分布区域很广、从大小兴安岭到完达山脉皆有大片存在。在全省的森林资源中，天然次生林面积占一半以上，如此分布广大的次生林中蕴藏着丰富的木材和多种林副产品资源，对维持该省的生态平衡起着极其重要的作用。如何经营好现有的次生林，是直接关系到全省林业发展的主要问题。

1 研究现状和主要问题

1.1 次生林概念的界定及其特点

次生林的研究始于对阔叶红松林的研究。次生林问题20世纪50年代末就已经被提出，特别是在1960年天水次生林会议以后，各地林业工作者对次生林进行了广泛深入的研究，对次生林的概念、分类、群落的基本规律以及合理经营管理方式、方法等问题的研究开展很多、已经取得一定的研究成果。

1964年，邵均、周正、孙成璧对次生林的定义进行了经典的界定：原始林经过采伐或破坏而丧失其原始面貌，而在一定条件下，从植生演替过程中再次发生发展起来的新的天然林相。该定义从生态学演替的角度描述了次生林的形成原因和发生起点，要把林相的改变理解为森林生态系统结构的改变，进而理解为功能的改变，后来有的学者对这种结构改变引起的功能改变的质、量进行了进一步的研究。他们认为，次生林是原生(始)林的相对概念，次生林应该和原始林、人工林并列作为森林经营的一个独立对象。

孙洪志等认为次生林是原始林经过大面积的反复破坏后，在次生裸地上经次生演替而形成的次生群落。次生林的显著特征是经过大面积的反复破坏，引起原生群落大面积的消失，失去原始的森林环境。并认为黑龙江东部山地大面积次生林的形成是一次自然竟观的巨变。

次生林的特点：

(1)次生林是原始林发展过程中的一个临时过渡阶段，具有较大可塑性；

(2)次生林的发生是外因动力的结果；

(3)不能完善的反映出林地的自然历史条件；

(4)次生林有地带性

(5)林分结构具有多样性。

2 黑龙江次生林的现状

黑龙江次生林多为幼壮林，常以阔叶树种居优势，林相混杂，乔木、灌木混生，生长率较低，材质不良，利用价值和效能不高。黑龙江省次生林林分价值较高的主要有山杨林、白桦林。但大多数次生林质量不高、效能低，需要人工改造。我省林区经过几十年的过量采伐，原始林所剩无几，可采资源越来越少，森林质量低，生态效能下降，特别是林农交错的浅山区，低效次生林分所占有相当大比重，严重制约了森林资源快速增长和生态效能的发挥。

据黑龙江省森林资源调查统计，次生林龄组结构为：成熟林面积、蓄积仅占10%左右；近熟林占20%左右；中龄林占40%左右；幼龄林占30%左右。由此可见次生林龄组结构极不合理，可用资源和近期可用资源所占比例小，幼中龄林的次生林所占比例大。

黑龙江省次生林区针叶树种仅占次生林面积的6%，蓄积的9%；水曲柳、胡桃楸、黄波罗珍贵树种更少，面积占次生林的1%，蓄积的2%。而所占比例更多的是柞、白、椴、黑、杨等阔叶树种，占次生林面积的90%以上，占蓄积近90%。众所周知，这些阔叶树种材质不佳，利用价值较低。水胡黄及针叶树才是我们经营的理想树种。因此，我们必须不断地调整次生林树种比例，保护好现有的散生成熟的单株珍贵树种，作为天然种源，增加珍贵树种的面积，降低其他利用价值较低的阔叶树种的面积。除组成树种外，现有成林的次生林中普遍存在密度偏低、林分稀疏的现象，据全省二类调查成果统计，现有次生林达到经营密度标准的有60%，这种不合理的林分结构是对林地资源的浪费。所以，我们认为对黑龙江省现有次生林，要在保持其稳定性和生态效益不被破坏的条件下，根据立地条件和植被演替规律，确定合理的改造或冠下补植及抚育方式。

3 次生林分类的和经营方式

3.1 次生林分类

不同学者对如何划分次生林类型有过讨论，有代表性的是1964年，邵均、周正、孙成璧对次生林的分类进行了阐述，他们建议在自然分类的基础上，按照经营的目的和经济要求的不同而建立一种综合分类法。他们建立的三级自然类型划分法为：林分的组成+地貌的坡度+林龄和郁闭度。据他们调查认为：黑龙江次生林可以分为六个大的自然类型：柞树林、杨桦林、硬阔混交林、杂木林、阔叶针叶林和矮木林。地貌按坡度分为：山脊或陡坡(25°以上)、坡地(5~25°)、谷平地(5°以下)；林龄和郁闭度分为幼林、壮林、成林及小、中、大密度各三种类型。作者认为这种三级分类法符合经营的实际需要，因此采用此种方法划分次生林类型。

3.2 次生林经营方式

3.2.1 次生林管护、培育型经营方式

重点生态公益林实施方案明确规定，凡国营林场规划为重点生态公益林的区域，必须按林班及面积落实到具体责任人进行不间断专项管护及定向培育，这一类型主要在立地条件较好，生产力较高，具有一定培育价值的中幼龄次生林中进行。在这种林分中主要是进行抚育间伐，保留有利用价值、生长良好的林木，伐去利用价值低，生长落后的林木，同时对林下更新层也进行抚育，保留有价值的目的树种。伐后上层林木保留株数在800株/hm^2以上为宜，彻底改善林内卫生环境。此抚育方式在黑龙江省宾县万人欢林场实施较为突出。

3.2.2 次生林改造型经营方式

主要在土壤肥力较高，但由于组成林分较差、林分密度较低以及单位生长量较低(阔叶树每年低于$2m^3/hm^2$、针叶树每年低于$1m^3/hm^2$)的次生林中进行。通常可采取先造后抚的技术措施，主要适宜林分密度低，林中空隙多的林分，首先清除林隙中的杂草、灌木，然后栽植耐阴的针叶树，填充林分中的多余空间，使林分达到要求密度。经过若干年后再进行人工调整，伐除抑制针叶树生长的上层阔叶树，并抚育一部分天然更新的阔叶树，保证人工更新层与天然更新层协调发展，使次生林的树种组成达到优化目的。

3.2.3 林—副复合型经营方式

由林木与经济植物、药材以及食用菌等复合而成，根据与林木搭配的经济植物种类的不同，要求的环境条件也不同，要通过在次生林下或在林中引进经济植物、药材以及食用菌等。目前黑龙江省能够利用的经济植物主要有草莓、黑加仑、山葡萄、及各种蕨菜等；能够利用的药用植物主要有五味子、黄芪、人参、西洋参、细辛、平贝等；同时还有很多种类的食用菌均可在次生林内栽培。

林—副复合型经营方式以林为主，兼有多种经营，通过合理搭配后，提高了土地和光能利用率，改善了林木及其他经济植物的生长环境，可以防止水土流失，减少林地病虫害的发生，维护了生态平衡，生态效益显著。同时亦提高了单位面积上有机物质的产量，丰富了林产品的种类，整体经济效益明显。

3.2.4 次生林封育保护型经营方式

主要针对发挥水土保持和水源涵养等生态效益的次生林。这种林分虽然生长量较低，林分结构亦较差和简单，但由于其发挥的生态效益大于经济效益，因此对这种林分应进行封育管护，防止人为破坏造成不良后果。山脊陡坡柞树林即属该类型。

参考文献

[1]孙洪志，屈红军，任青山．黑龙江省次生林研究进展[J]．森林工程．2010.(19)，4：8~9.

[2] 朱洪坤．黑龙江省次生林类型及经营方式的探讨[J]．东北林业大学学报．2010.（20），5：23～24.
[3] 孙洪志，屈红军，郝雨，等．次生林改造的几种模式[J]，东北林业大学学报．2004(3)：18～23.
[4] 王玉琢，王绍斌，张云波，等．黑龙江省尚志县帽儿山地区次生森林植被的初步研究[J]．哈尔滨师范大学自然科学学报．1964(0)：23～25.
[5] 邵均，周正，孙成璧．黑龙江省次生林分类与经营技术问题的探讨[J]．林业科学，1964.9(2)：134～148.

华中地区退耕还林工程开展情况调查分析

徐　定[1]　彭道黎[1]　谢　晨[2]　黄　东[2]

（1. 北京林业大学，北京，100083；2. 国家林业局经济发展研究中心，北京，100714）

摘要：为了解退耕还林工程十年来的开展情况，本研究根据华中地区退耕还林县和调查学生的分布布局，对华中五省575个退耕还林农户进行问卷调查并进行了深入细致的研究分析。结果表明，退耕后生态环境、农户生态意识和生计都有显著改善，退耕还林政策执行顺利，受到农民的一致赞成，农户普遍关注的是补助问题。最后，分析了当前存在农户重视程度不高、农户林业生产经验不足、退耕地的经营状况十分不理想、农村基层村组织执行政策不力等问题，并针对问题提出了政策性建议。

关键词：华中地区；退耕还林；农户调查；政策建议

Implementation investigation analysis on Grain for Green Program in Central China.

XU Ding [1]，PENG Dao-li[1]，XIE Chen[2]，HUANG Dong[2]

(1. Beijing Forestry University, Beijing, 100083;

2. National Forestry Economics and Development Research Center, Beijing, 100714)

Abstract: In order to hold the truth of Grain for Green project implement past 10 years, based on the distribution of Central Forest County and students, selected 575 households of the five provinces in the Central conducting an investigation and interview and carried through research. The results are as follows, the ecological environment, the eco-awareness and livelihoods of households have improved significantly than before, related policies have reached the designated position and supp-orted by the farmers, subsidy issue is a common concern. In the meanwhile, shows the current pro-blems as follows, farmers do not pay attention, lack of experience in forestry production, manage-ment is extensive, policy executive is not strong. Then the paper made policy recommendations aiming at these issues.

Key words: Central China; Grain for Green Program; rural household survey; policy advise

---

“十一五”国家支撑课题：国家林业重点工程监测技术研究(2006BAD23B05)。

作者简介：徐定，硕士研究生，森林资源监测与评价研究；E - mail：110748708@ qq. com。

通信作者：彭道黎，教授，博士生导师，从事森林环境监测与评价研究；E - mail：dlpeng@ bjfu. edu. cn。

改革开放以来，我国社会经济迅速发展，与此同时也带来了一些问题。华中地区农村面临就是大量劳动力外出打工，导致当地农村部分田地荒芜，农村常住人口迅速减少。国家统计局于2009年第三季度对全国31个省(自治区、直辖市)近20万农村劳动力进行了农民工监测调查。结果显示，中部地区外出劳动力达4529万人，高于东部地区的3877万人和西部地区的3802万人[1]。退耕还林工程的实施无疑将对这一状况具有改善作用，农户将荒芜的坡耕地转换为林地，既使土地得到了充分利用，又能改善生态环境、增加生态效益，同时有助于农民增收。

国务院近期对完善退耕还林工作下达通知，以巩固退耕还林成果、解决退耕农户生活困难和长远生计问题[2]。在新的退耕还林工程规划正在筹划之时，为给下一步退耕政策提供坚实的决策信息，国家重点林业工程社会经济效益监测退耕还林工程项目组与北京林业大学合作，组成联合项目组，于2010年寒假组织家有退耕任务的学生以大学生假期社会实践的方式开展退耕还林农户问卷调查。选用我国华中地区(含安徽及河南、湖北、湖南、江西五省)作为调查范围，调查涉及25县81村和575户。问卷内容包括退耕还林农户家庭基本情况、参加退耕还林情况、退耕政策执行情况、退耕成效、退耕成果巩固以及趋势与建议六大板块，共计48道题。本文采取描述性统计分析方法[3]，针对其中退耕还林农户家庭基本情况和参加退耕还林情况进行分析。

1 农户家庭基本情况

1.1 农户基本信息

本次调查受访对象年龄以40~70岁居多，占总调查人数的84.10%，此年龄段多为家中主要劳动力或户主，这使得本次调查所了解的情况具有一定的代表性。少数民族仅占5.06%。受访农户的受教育程度普遍偏低，文化程度以初中居多，约为48.06%；文盲比例占7.77%；大专及以上高等学历者较少，仅占3.53%。受访农户家庭总平均人口数为4.44，其中户均劳动力数为3.22人，外出劳动力总数占总人口数35.21%。这充分体现了华中地区的显著特征——外出务工人员比例较大。

1.2 农户经济状况

调查农户的主要收入来源以务农为主。49.65%的农户收入主要来源于务农，41.93%的农户收入主要来源于务工，主要收入来源是工副业和农家乐的农户比例分别为6.14%、2.28%。在调查林业收入占家庭总收入比重(表1)时，发现林业收入占家庭收入比重在20%以下占绝大多数，从中不难看出林业收入在家庭收入中的作用十分有限。所调查农户认为自家收入在村里处于中等收入水平的占73.59%，好与差的仅各占13.97%和11.76%，其中低保户占6.64%。

表1 林业收入占家庭经济比重分布

林业收入占家庭经济比重	户数
0~10	111
10~20	264
20~30	42
30~40	24
41~50	14
50~60	8
60~70	4
70~80	1
80~90	5
90~100	1

1.3 退耕前后农户基本情况对比

通过退耕还林，农户家庭的耕地、林地面积及林业收入等都发生了显著的变化。退耕前后农户基本情况平均水平对比见表2。

表2 退耕前后农户基本情况平均水平对比

项目	退耕前	2009年
耕地面积(亩)	7.67	4.43
林地面积(亩)	6.74	13.29
牧草地面积(亩)	0.02	0.02
园地面积(亩)	0.19	0.28
年粮食产量(kg)	3204.74	2461.36
外出务工人数(人)	0.80	1.63
现金收入(元)	11357.68	15983.01
林业收入(元)(不包括退耕补助)	384.38	1052.76

退耕后农户耕地面积减少原有42.21%，而粮食产量只减少了23.20%，说明耕地粮食单产水平得到了提高。林地面积增加了将近1倍，林业收入也增长约为之前的3倍。耕地面积的减少，腾出了更多空余的劳动力，农民外出务工人数随之增多，现金收入比以前增加了40.72%。由此可见，退耕还林工程的实施，促使了农村外出务工人员增加，农户的年人均纯收入呈现上涨趋势。

2 调查分析结果

2.1 退耕地基本情况

退耕还林工程于1999年开展试点，之后开始在全国范围内大规模推广，退耕户急剧增多，在2002年和2003年居多(表3)，调查发现各地开始退耕的年份主要与国家和当地政策推广执行政策的时间有关，且同村农户大多是同时开始退耕，这有利于进行统一经营管理。

表3 不同年份农户退耕情况

年份	退耕户比例
2000	2.65%
2001	2.65%
2002	39.75%
2003	27.56%
2004	7.77%
2005	6.71%
2006	9.19%
2007	3.71%
2008	0.00%

退耕地中主要为在册耕地，占总数73.38%。农户所退耕地主要属于陡坡地，占总退耕地面积的44.72%，沙化地占12.85%，其他耕地占42.44%。退耕地单产水平基本上是低产或中产，分别占46.71%和50.62%，极少退耕高产耕地。这反映了退耕还林工程对土地利

用方式的影响，同时也反映出工程将低经济效益的耕地转化为产生生态效益林地的目标。

调查数据显示，农户初次退耕时主要种植的作物为用材林或果树林，分别占68.31%和24.10%，也有部分果木兼用林，占7.60%(表4)。

表4 农户初次退耕主要种植作物

林种	比例
用材林	68.31%
果树林	24.10%
果木兼用林	7.59%

2.2 退耕还林参与情况

进一步调查退耕林地的效果，结果显示：大部分农户认为木材林和果树林生态效果较好，分别占46.69%和30.12%，认为果木兼用林生态效果好的占19.43%(表5)。有86.19%的农户退耕林地上没有更换过树种，只有13.81%的农户表示更换过。更换过树种的农户中，48.00%的表示因为初植树种成活率低，46.00%的认为初植树种产出低。

表5 农户认为生态效果最好的林种

林种	比例
用材林	46.69%
经济林	30.12%
兼用林	19.43%
灌木林	3.16%
草	0.60%

华中地区在退耕还林的同时荒山造林和封山育林也在进行，但范围较小，只有13.56%的农户反映家中有荒山造林任务，16.93%的农户反映家中有封山育林任务，这些农户大部分集中在湖南省。

2.3 政策知晓程度

对退耕政策的了解程度直接影响到农户的退耕积极性和权益保障等。调查中我们发现大部分农户对于退耕政策只是大概了解，占48.08%，还有15.56%的不了解，完全了解的只有36.36%。

而在“退耕延长期补助与原补助是否一样”这个问题上，仍有41.49%的农户不了解政策，认为延长期补助和原补助一样。由此可以看出农户对退耕政策的了解程度还有待提高。

2.4 退耕补助发放

退耕还林工程的顺利开展，在很大程度上得益于国家所提供的优惠补助政策。而农户作为该项政策的直接参与者与政策结果的重要维护者，其收入能否增加直接关系到退耕还林成果的巩固和工程的顺利推进，其在工程期满后的行为选择将直接影响工程本身的可持续性，一旦退耕之后农户无法获得其他较稳定的替代收入来源，则很可能为了维持生计而返耕，而这将影响国家预期政策目标能否顺利实现[4,5]。

国家对退耕还林连续8年实行补助政策：每退1hm^2陡坡耕地，一次性补助苗木费750元，同时每年给农民补助粮食，北方地区1500kg/hm^2，另外还有生活补助每年300元/hm^2。

退耕收入占家庭收入平均比重为12.95%。调查中的55.75%的农户认为退耕补助对自家收入作用重要，25.86%认为作用一般，还有18.39%认为不重要。

调查中78.04%的农户反映足额领取了补助，15.25%的农户反映补助未足额领取，究其原因(表6)：56.76%的农户不清楚其原因，10.81%反映补助被克扣。进一步落实补助的发放，保护农户既得利益是今后工作的重点和难点。

表6 补助未足额领取的原因

原因	比例
缴纳统一管护费	10.81%
被克扣	32.43%
不清楚	56.76%

基层村组织在退耕还林政策执行的透明度上也存在着一定问题，约50.53%的农户反映村委会对退耕还林补助情况不进行公示，比例较高。从中我们可以看出基层村组织在执行政策中还存在着不少让农户存疑的地方，下一步希望相关部门能加大监管力度，保证退耕还林工程在实施过程中尤其是补助的发放中做到公平、公正、公开。

2.5 退耕地管护

退耕地的管护关系到退耕成活率的高低，是影响退耕还林效率的关键因素。在所调查农户中，83.89%的农户知道应对退耕还林地负有管护、补植补造责任，87.32%的农户认为补植补造任务不算重，41.97%的农户认为补植补造效果好，54.74%的农户认为效果一般。

调查中反映出来的退耕地验收和管护工作比较到位，84.63%的农户反映退耕地有人验收，88.45%的农户反映对自己的退耕地进行了管护，所有受访农户认为村中无人管护的退耕地比例平均为8.86%。71.20%的农户主要管护人员是家中的大人即主要劳动力，这在一定程度上有效保证了管护的效用。

多数农户家的退耕成活率在70%以上，其中成活率在90%以上的占51.22%，成活率在70%到90%之间的占37.19%，极少数农户退耕成活率在10%以下，其主要原因是因为所退耕地的自然条件差以及08年雪灾等大规模自然灾害等，但也有人为管理不善的因素存在。

3 存在的问题

尽管退耕还林政策的开展取得了很大成效，76.70%的农户认为退耕还林工程是成功的。但通过此次调查，我们也发现了不少的问题。下一步退耕还林的推进，应是更好的调整政策、以对生态的改善、农户的生计起到更大作用。

一是，农户重视程度不高。由于华中地区自然条件和历史传统所致，长期以来重农轻林，林业收入占家庭收入比重非常小，因此农户对于退耕还林的重视程度尚不够高。

二是，农户林业生产经验不足。华中地区在退耕还林之前从事林业生产的比例相当低，且绝大部分只是从事经济林木的种植和管护，规模大的也比较小。

三是，退耕地的经营状况十分不理想。退耕地产量低、农民对未来是否能增产信心不足；退耕地产品状况一般、销路不稳定；退耕地经营缺技术、缺劳动力以及自然状况频发等原因对退耕还林工程的继续开展及成果巩固造成了不小的困难，这是调查中所发现的最大问题。我国政府最关注的是由于退耕还林带来的土地利用变化及其可持续性。政府要确保当退耕补助终止后，农户不会复耕反弹[6]。

四是，农村基层村组织执行政策不力。调查中有不少农户反映补助被故意克扣，部分地区对于退耕补助情况不进行公示。这严重挫伤了农户的积极性，且容易引发干群矛盾，对此需引起重视。

4 政策建议

第一，扩大宣传力度，重视技术培训。华中地区农户林业收入占家庭经济收入比重较小，林业生产经验不足，导致农户对退耕还林工程的重视度不够高，退耕地成活率低。下一步应该加大宣传和培训力度，提高农户对退耕还林工程的重视程度和林业技术水平[7]。

第二，规范林权管理，保护退耕户权益。受访农户中还有35.19%未给退耕地办理林权证，产权不明势必也对退耕农户的积极性造成影响。下一步可借助集体林权改革的契机，加速林权证的发放，并在此基础之上加强对退耕地的管护责任制，以产生更好的生态经济效益。

第三，调整补助政策，加强监督力度。对于部分环境破坏严重、自然条件恶劣的地区，国家可参照种粮补贴的方式建立长效补助机制；对生态地位比较重要，后续产业和结构调整还需要一段时间才能见效的退耕地，适当延长补助年限，待后续产业发挥效益后，再停止补助[8]。

第四，完善退耕规划。调查中有32.88%的农户提出希望增加退耕造林面积，41.76%的农户反映家中还有坡度在25°以上的耕地，农户对于国家继续安排退耕还林任务有强烈的愿望。为进一步推进退耕还林工程，应做好下一步规划，明确退耕范围和年度任务，并提前做好作业设计等前期工作。

第五，扶持后续产业。缺乏资金是农户反映制约退耕的重要因素。应多渠道增加对退耕还林后续产业发展的资金扶持，通过小额信贷、财政贴息等方式，扶持退耕农户发展后续产业。将退耕还林后续产业开发作为调整农村产业结构、增加农民收入、确保退耕还林稳步推进的主要举措。

参考文献

[1]国家统计局农村司. 2009年第三季度农村劳动力外出务工情况[R]. http://www.stats.gov.cn/tjfx/fxbg/t20100319_402628281.htm, 2010-03-19.

[2] 国务院. 关于完善退耕还林政策的通知[Z]. 国发(2007)25号.

[3] 李桦，姚顺波，郭亚军. 退耕还林对农户经济行为影响分析——以全国退耕还林示范县(吴起县)为例[J]. 中国农村经济，2006，10：37~42.

[4] 朱山涛，张世秋，陶文娣. 影响退耕还林农户返耕决策的因素识别与分析[J]. 中国人口资源与环境，2005，15(5)：108~112.

[5] 王秋菊，王立群. 退耕还林对农户的经济影响[J]. 北京林业大学学报，2009，1：88~92.

[6] 张蕾，戴广翠，谢晨，等. 退耕农户长期生计分析[J]. 林业经济，2006，2：12~19.

[7] 莫显平，杨绍芝. 荔波县退耕还林工程调研分析[J]. 现代农业科技，2010，2：261~263.

[8] 张国明，袁卫国，汪飞跃. 退耕还林工程与“三农”问题[J]. 绿色中国，2005，6：20~22.

吉林森林生态系统定位观测研究网络建设

汪兆洋　姚晨光　孙宏刚

（国家林业局调查规划设计院，北京，100714）

从20世纪90年代开始，随气候变化的进程，生态环境问题越来越受到社会各界的广泛关注，加强生态环境建设，维护生态安全，已经成为21世纪人类面临的共同问题。

吉林省地处我国东北地区中部，属温带气候区。自东向西气候、植被、地形梯度变化明显，景观类型多样。东部天然次生林和人工林分布广阔，是我国重要的林业生产基地和物种基因库；中部地势平坦、土壤肥沃，农田防护林体系健全，环境承载力较强；西部草原辽阔，湿地面积较大，也是湿地与荒漠交错分布区。为减缓生态环境恶化的趋势，从80年代起我省先后实施了"三北防护林工程"、"天然林保护工程"、"西部生态草建设工程"等系列生态工程的建设，生态环境恶化的趋势得到了初步遏制

一、国外发展现状

长期生态定位观测研究始于1843年英国Rothamsted实验站对土壤肥力与肥料效益长期定位试验。随后，世界上其他一些主要国家相继开展了定位研究工作。目前世界上已持续观测60年以上的长期定位试验站有30多个，主要集中在欧洲、前苏联、美国、日本、印度等国家。

国内外著名长期生态研究网络

序号	野外观测网络名称	英文名	简称	所属国家或组织
1	联合国陆地生态系统监测网络	Terrestrial Ecosystem Monitoring site	TEMS	联合国环境规划署
2	美国长期生态学研究网络	United States Long Term Ecological Research Network	USLTER	美国
3	英国环境变化网	United Kingdom Environmental Change Network	ECN	英国
4	加拿大生态监测和评估网络	Ecological Monitoring and Assessment Network	EMN	加拿大
5	哥斯达黎加长期生态学研究网络	Costa Rica Long Term Ecological Research	CRLETR	哥斯达黎加
6	捷克长期生态学研究项目	Czech Republic Long Term Ecological Research Network	CLTER	捷克
7	匈牙利长期生态学研究网络	Hungary Long Term Ecological Research	HLTER	匈牙利
8	波兰长期生态学研究网络	Poland Long Term Ecological Research	PLTER	波兰
9	韩国长期生态学研究网络	Korea Long Term Ecological Research Network	KLTERN	韩国
10	巴西长期生态学研究网络	Brazilian Long – term Ecological Research	BLTER	巴西

(续)

序号	野外观测网络名称	英文名	简称	所属国家或组织
11	墨西哥长期生态学研究网络	Mexico Long Term Ecological Research Network	MLTERN	墨西哥
12	委内瑞拉长期生态学研究网络	Venezuela Long Term Ecological Research Network	VLTERN	委内瑞拉
13	乌拉圭长期生态学研究网络	Uruguay Long Term Ecological Research Network	ULTERN	乌拉圭
14	中国生态系统研究网络	Chinese Ecosystem Research Network	CERN	中国
15	中国森林生态系统研究网络	Chinese Forestry Ecosystem Research Network	CFERN	中国
16	中国台湾长期生态研究网络	Taiwan Ecological Research Network	TERN	中国台湾
17	瑞士森林生态系统观测网络	Swiss Forest Ecosystem Observation	SFERN	瑞士

二、国内发展现状

我国陆地生态系统定位观测研究经历了专项半定位观测研究、生态站长期定位观测以及生态站联网协作三个阶段。

20 世纪 50 年末代至 60 年代初，老一辈科学家借鉴原苏联生物地理群落的理论和方法，开展了专项半定位的观测研究。70 年代后，在上述地区逐步建立了森林生态站，并广泛吸收了欧美的生态系统理论和观测方法，开展了系统水平上的物质循环、能量流动的定位研究，为开展跨站联合观测研究奠定了基础。

截至 2008 年，全国已建立 43 个生态站(其中森林生态站 33 个、湿地生态站 6 个和荒漠生态站 4 个)，初步形成了较为完善的生态站网台站布局，2008 年，国家林业局针对目前生态站网站点布局及数量、经费投入、资源共享等急需解决的问题，出台了《陆地生态系统定位研究网络中长期发展规划》，展示了生态站网的未来发展规模——到 2020 年整个站网的森林生态站数量将发展到 99 个，湿地生态站达到 50 个，荒漠生态站达到 43 个。建成布局合理、功能完备、覆盖全国主要生态区域、力争达到世界先进水平的生态定位观测和研究网络。

三、吉林省生态定位观测发展现状

目前，吉林省长期生态学定位观测研究工作刚刚起步，已建吉林松江源森林生态站(国家林业局森林生态站)、吉林汪清森林生态站(吉林省省级森林生态站)、吉林九台森林生态站(吉林省省级森林生态站)、吉林向海湿地生态站(吉林省省级湿地生态站)，对当地森林水文、土壤、气象和生物开展了初步的观测与研究。但现有的生态站点不能代表整个吉林省的植被气候类型和地带性陆地生态系统类型。为适应林业发展，满足全省生态工程建设对科学技术研究和生态效益观测的要求，吉林省有必要新建一批森林、湿地、荒漠化野外科学观测研究台站，为吉林省林业生态建设提供决策依据和技术保障。

四、建设目标和研究方向

(一)总体目标

吉林省森林生态系统定位观测研究网络建设要在《国家林业局陆地生态系统定位观测研究网络中长期发展规划(2008 ~ 2020)》总体目标下进行，到 2020 年，按照分阶段、分层次建设的目标，建成吉林省布局合理、类型齐全、条件完备、机制完善，能够为林业生态工程建设提供服务，满足林业发展需求，回答生态环境与林业建设过程中重大科学问题的生态站网；培养、吸引和稳定一定数量的基层技术骨干、在本领域具有较大影响和发展潜力的科技人才、国内外具有重要影响的学术带头人；建立起创新能力突出、达到国内领先水平的吉林省陆地生态系统定位研究网络平台。

（二）阶段目标

第一阶段（2010～2012年）：新建3个生态站，包括已建吉林松江源森林生态站（国家林业局）、吉林九台森林生态站（省级）、吉林向海湿地生态站（省级）、汪清森林生态站（省级），生态站总数量达到6个，其中新建国家林业局森林生态站1个（汪清森林生态站（原省级生态站升级））、新建国家林业局湿地生态站1个（莫莫格湿地生态站）、新建省级荒漠生态站1个（通榆荒漠生态站），使吉林省生态站网站点布局基本形成，同时，对现有生态站进行升级改造。稳定人才，逐步建立起年龄结构、学历结构及知识结构合理的人才队伍。初步开展吉林省陆地生态系统服务功能、森林固碳能力以及平原地区林业生态工程建设与可持续经营技术等方面的研究。

第二阶段（2013～2015年）：新建生态站4个，全省生态站总数将达到10个，其中新建省级森林站2个（抚松森林生态站、德惠森林生态站）、新建国家林业局湿地生态站2个（龙湾湿地生态站、查干湖湿地生态站），使生态站网站点布局趋于完善，对现有生态站继续进行升级改造。组建有实力的研究队伍和创新研究团队，培养大批在国内具有一定影响的学术带头人和技术骨干。开展陆地生态系统关键生态要素作用机理与生态过程研究，研究内容能够初步回答林业重大科学问题，为生态建设、生态效益补偿及绿色GDP核算等提供技术支撑和理论依据，产生若干原创性的生态学研究成果。

第三阶段（2016～2020年）：新建4个生态站，全省生态站总数将达到14个。其中新建省级森林站3个（蛟河森林生态站、集安森林生态站、珲春森林生态站），新建荒漠生态站1个（扶余荒漠生态站）。本阶段目标是对现有生态站继续进行升级改造，使生态站网达到国内领先水平，部分已有国家林业局生态站由常规站升级到重点站。随着国家相关政策调整，使吉林省省级生态站逐步纳入国家林业局生态站网规划范围之内。以生态站网为平台，培养和造就出一批与地方需求相适应，能够引导学科潮流的一流拔尖型人才。研究内容瞄准国际长期生态学研究前沿，进行多站联合攻关与技术集成，在生态学基础研究方面取得较重突破的同时，取得一批应用性强、能够解决重大科学问题的应用性成果。

生态站建设布局一览表

站　别	原有生态站	第一阶段（2010～2012）	第二阶段 2013～2015）	第三阶段（2016～2020）	生态站总数
森林生态站	松江源（国家） 汪清（省级） 九台（省级）	汪清（国家）	抚松（省级） 德惠（省级）	蛟河（省级） 集安（省级） 珲春（省级）	8
湿地生态站	向海（省级）	莫莫格（国家）	龙湾（国家）、 查干湖（国家）		4
荒漠生态站		通榆（省级）		扶余（省级）	2
合　计	4	3	4	4	14

注：生态站第一阶段布局“汪清森林生态站”由省级生态站申请建立国家林业局森林生态站。

(三)研究方向

所形成的吉林陆地生态系统定位研究网络能够反映不同尺度范围内森林、湿地、荒漠生态系统结构、功能规律以及对全球变化影响的响应；可充分保证空间气候范围和大气模型的重叠，而且完全能与决策尺度相适应。可为吉林省陆地生态系统研究网络提供基础数据；开展基础及应用基础研究，服务区域及地方生态与经济建设，全面提升吉林省陆地生态系统定位观测研究与评估的科技创新能力，推动当地生态环境的有效保护、恢复与建设。

五、管理体系建设

吉林省生态站网在国家林业局科技司和 CFERN、CWERN 和 CDERN 的直接指导下开展工作，管理体系实行在主管部门领导下的多级管理。参照国家陆地生态系统定位观测研究网络管理办法，在主管部门吉林省林业厅的直接领导下，设立吉林省陆地生态系统野外观测研究管理委员会和吉林省陆地生态系统野外观测研究科学委员会，并设立吉林省陆地生态系统野外观测研究与管理中心。管理中心设在吉林省林业厅，中心下设森林、湿地和荒漠化三个管理分中心，分别负责相应生态站的管理工作。

(一)森林生态站建设

依据国家林业局《陆地生态系统定位研究网络中长期发展规划(2008 ~2020)》对全国森林站点的规划，吉林省生态环境建设和长期定位观测研究的迫切需求，在具有代表性的典型森林生态系统，进行分类投资新建一批生态定位观测研究站，并对现有生态站进行升级改造，从而更加有效地开展长期科学观测与专项研究等工作。

根据新建站点的布局和规划，参照国家林业行业标准《森林生态系统定位研究站建设技术要求》(LY/T 1626—2005)、《森林生态站数字化建设技术规范》(LY/T 1873 —2010)与《森林生态系统定位研究站数据管理规范》(LY/T 1872—2010)的建设规范和技术要求，分阶段、分层次进行建设，逐步建成达到基本观测要求、符合野外工作条件、具备试验研究能力的森林生态站。

对于国家林业局《陆地生态系统定位研究网络中长期发展规划(2008 ~2020 年)》在吉林省规划的两个森林生态站，其建设内容严格按照上述三个规范执行。对于吉林省生态站网规划的六个省级森林生态站，结合吉林省资金投入及观测技术力量等实际情况，其建设内容总体上符合国家林业局森林生态站建设技术要求，具备较为常规的观测仪器设备及基础设施。

(二)湿地生态站建设

根据湿地新建站点的布局和规划，参照国家林业行业标准《湿地生态系统定位研究站建设技术要求》(LY/T 1780—2007)的建设规范和技术要求，分阶段、分层次进行建设，逐步建成达到基本观测要求、符合野外工作条件、具备试验研究能力的湿地生态站。

对于国家林业局《陆地生态系统定位研究网络中长期发展规划(2008 ~2020)》在吉林省规划的两个湿地生态站。对于吉林省生态站网规划的一个省级湿地生态站，结合吉林省资金投入及观测技术力量等实际情况，其建设内容总体上符合国家林业局湿地生态站建设技术要求，具备较为常规的观测仪器设备及基础设施。

(三)荒漠生态站建设

参照国家林业行业标准和《荒漠生态系统观测研究站建设技术要求》(LY/T 1753 —2008)的建设标准和技术要求，对于吉林省生态站网规划的两个省级荒漠化生态站，结合吉林省资金投入及观测技术力量等实际情况，其建设内容总体上符合荒漠生态站建设技术要求，具备较为常规的观测仪器设备及基础设施。

六、保障措施

（一）加强组织领导

吉林省林业厅要加强对生态站建设的领导。充分发挥管理中心和各分中心的组织协调作用，建立协作与沟通机制，研究生态站运行、管理方面的重大问题，确定生态站网的发展规划，组织讨论重大科学问题，组织科研、科普重大活动、学术交流和科技合作，从人力、物力、财力等多方面、多角度、多层面，集成资源、整合力量、协同合作，共同推进生态站网建设。

（二）切实增加投入

生态站网建设是一项长期的公益性事业，其基础设施建设和基本运行要以中央财政投资为主，并采取部门匹配和地方配套等多渠道筹资办法保障生态站网长期稳定的投入。在积极争取上述三种筹资渠道支持的同时，要积极筹措多方资金，鼓励和引导企业、社会资本投入生态站网的建设和科研工作。通过建立拨款、自筹经费相结合的经费投入机制，保障生态站网建设、运行和科研费用投入的可持续性。

（三）强化规范管理

加强生态站网制度建设，完善各项管理制度，保证生态站管理和科研工作的稳定性，维护生态站基础设施和观测仪器的正常运行以保证观测数据的质量，保障生态站资金运用安全、高效；制订吸引国内外优秀的科研人员来生态站开展研究工作的优惠政策，实现生态站开放、流动、竞争、联合的运行机制。

（四）加强队伍建设

加强生态站的组织机构和人才队伍建设。对生态站的专业科技人员和管理人员要开展定期培训，提高综合业务能力和素质；重视学术带头人以及技术骨干队伍的培养与提高，使生态站具有高水平的多学科人才队伍和较强的综合研究能力，并充分发挥生态站在创新人才培养中的重要作用；形成人员梯队合理、结构稳定的高水平的管理与科研队伍，保障生态站的稳定高效运行。

（五）促进交流合作

加强森林、湿地和荒漠生态站网内部及三类站网间的交流合作；促进与国内外、林业行业内外的站点、网络之间的交流合作；积极参加国内外学术会议，参与制订国内外重大科学项目、计划，争取共同开展跨国界、跨区域、跨生态系统的长期生态学研究。通过交流与合作，在消化吸收国际先进技术和方法的基础上实现再创新，全面提升生态站网的建设研究水平。

吉林省林业地理信息系统建设方案的探讨

王君海
（吉林省林业勘察设计研究院，长春，130022）

摘　要： 林业资源信息量大、属性复杂，虽然已形成了比较完备的森林资源规划设计调查体系，但因没有建立统一的操作平台，信息分散，利用效率较低。随着信息技术的发展和调查手段的提高，建立林业自己的信息处理及管理系统，实现林业资源信息的整合与共享，依靠科技振兴发展林业已势在必行。本文提出了吉林省林业地理信息系统建设方案构想，发布出来与大家共同探讨，以形成更加完善的林业地理信息系统建设方案。

关键词： 林业地理信息系统；数据库；信息管理；信息查询；信息编辑；信息浏览

1　建设背景

"十一五"以来，特别是以国家林业局正式发布《全国林业信息化建设纲要》、《全国林业信息化建设技术指南》以及首届全国林业信息化工作会议的胜利召开为标志，我国林业信息化建设进入了统一规划、统一标准、统一管理、分工负责、全面加快发展的新阶段。进入"十二五"时期，吉林省正处在一个新的发展阶段。依靠科技振兴发展林业，尽快实现林业信息资源的整合与共享已势在必行。

2　建设框架

2.1　管理系统定位

目前的地理信息系统软件都是通用软件，不能完全满足林业的需要。这些软件虽然功能强大，但是有些功能林业上根本用不到，且体系庞大，价格昂贵，而要实现某些林业专业功能，操作又很复杂，效果并不理想。为了推动吉林省林业地理信息系统的发展与普及，加快林业现代化、数字化发展速度，必须开发林业部门自己的地理信息系统，将计算机科学、地理学、测绘遥感学、信息科学和管理科学等多学科融为一体，集成数据录入、处理、查询、图形交互显示及数据信息统计等功能。能够分析和处理物体空间（地理分布）数据及相关属性，为林业宏观和微观管理提供服务。

该系统建成后，对外可向关心林业事业的单位及个人公布信息；对内可录入、显示、统计内部数据，并逐渐加入具体的业务功能。

2.2　管理系统应包含的子系统

吉林省林业基础数据库；

吉林省林业资源数据库信息管理系统；

吉林省林业资源发布与浏览系统。

2.3 使用对象

吉林省林业厅、各地、市、县林场森林资源管理处，关心林业事业的单位及个人。

2.4 使用领域

吉林省林业基础数据库：保存吉林省林业调查规划院现有森林资源数据，作为数据库信息管理系统和资源发布与浏览系统的数据源。

吉林省林业资源数据库信息管理系统：供吉林省林业厅、各地、市、县林场森林资源管理处使用的林业资源数据的综合处理系统。

吉林省林业资源发布与浏览系统：向关心林业事业的单位及个人公开发布非保密性的林业资源的各类地图数据。

3 林业地理信息系统功能概述

3.1 林业基础数据库

林业地理信息数据库以吉林省林业调查规划院现有森林资源数据为源数据，森林防火、森林分布等各项专题业务数据由林业厅相关部门或各市、县林业局进行分级录入。

对应的数据库信息管理系统和资源发布与浏览系统两个子系统，应建立两套数据库系统。将可以公开浏览的数据及图像信息存入资源发布与浏览系统对应的数据库中，将需要保密处理的数据及图像信息存入数据库信息管理系统对应的数据库中。当有数据需要从密级数据转为公开数据时，要为用户提供数据导入导出的方法。

基础数据库中所有包含的图层结构应与吉林省森林资源规划设计调查的图层结构一致。

3.2 林业资源数据库信息管理系统

采用 C/S 架构(基于客户端和浏览器的一种程序，界面效果强大)进行部署，主要包括十七个部分：林业资源地理信息编辑、林业资源地理信息高级编辑、林业基础数据库管理、林业资源属性信息编辑、林业资源属性信息编辑、林业资源属性信息浏览与查询、信息浏览权限管理、林业高级属性信息查询、林业资源地理信息浏览与查询、林业模型加载、图层控制与查询、林区空间数据查询、地图数据操作、统计分析功能、可扩展三维模块进行空间分析、系统管理、数据输出功能、数据打印等功能。

3.2.1 信息编辑功能

能够对不同比例尺地理信息数据的编辑，支持多种数据格式，能够实现不同分辨率、不同大小数据的融合、投影变换以及数据剪裁，从而制作任意分辨率真实质感场景，构建最终的海量地形数据库。

3.2.2 高级编辑

通过 GIS 数据创建编辑引擎，通过叠加航片、卫星影像、数字高程模型以及各种矢量地理数据，迅速方便地创建海量地形数据库。通过叠加高程数据甚至能够完成真实质感三维场景的创建。

3.2.3 基础数据库管理

林业基础数据库管理主要包括对图形库和属性库的管理。图形数据库管理子系统是地理信息系统的重要组成部分。在数据获取过程中，它用于存储和管理地图信息；在数据处理过程中，它既是资料的提供者，也可以是处理结果的归宿处；在检索和输出过程中，它是形成绘图文件或各类地理数据的数据源。图形数据库中的数据经拓扑处理，可形成拓扑数据库，用于各种空间分析。图形数据库管理系统可同时管理数千幅地理底图，数据容量应达到数十千兆，主要用于创建、维护地图库，在图幅进库前建立拓扑结构，对输入的地图数据进行正确性检查，根据用户的要求及图幅的质量，实现图幅配准、图幅校正和图幅接边。

林业管理系统 GIS 应用业务范畴非常广，各个林业系统的专业属性差异较大，以至于不能用一个已知的属性集描述概括所有的应用专业属性。因此建立动态属性库是非常必要的。动态就是根据用户的要求能随时扩充和精简属性库的字段(属性项)，修改字段的名称及类型。具备动态库及动态检索的 GIS 软件，就可以利用同一软件管理不同的专业属性，也就可以生成不同应用领域的 GIS 软件。如森林防火业务库、病虫害防护业务库、林业资源业务库等。

同时，系统可根据用户的需要，方便地建立任意动态属性库，从而成为一个有力的多维属性数据库管理工具。

3.2.4 属性信息编辑功能

GIS 所编辑的数据主要是二维或三维的空间型地理数据，包括地理实体的空间位置、拓扑关系和属性三个内容。GIS 对这些数据的管理是按图层的方式进行的，既可将地理内容按其特征数据组成单独的图层，也可将不同类型的几种特征数据合并起来组成一个图层，这种管理方式对数据的修改和提取十分方便。系统针对于资源数据的管理主要包括数据采集图层的管理，采集任务的制定、分派和管理、不同比例尺地理信息数据和属性数据的编辑等。地理信息数据编辑能够通过航片、卫星影像、数字高程模型以及各种矢量地理数据的叠加实现地形和平面场景的创建。

3.2.5 详细属性信息

属性数据的编辑能够对地名、经纬坐标、林区名称、林场管理人员名称等属性进行编辑，能够建立与平面地形数据和属性数据的全方位关联。

3.2.6 属性信息浏览与查询

可以依据属性和地理信息数据，实现林业资源信息的浏览和查询，在浏览查询时可以根据用户实际业务需求动态叠加文本、图片、矢量数据、动画等，并支持平面地理信息和属性信息间的全方位关联查询。通过系统平台窗口，可以对系统中的各种电子地图进行漫游、放大、缩小、图与图的叠加及清除等逻辑运算，属性数据与空间数据联合查询等。

3.2.7 信息浏览权限管理

林业地理信息数据是国家国防建设和管理的保密数据，所以对于地理数据信息的浏览权限和安全处理是系统重要考虑的地方，在信息浏览中，对于不同权限的用户，在信息加载量、图像比例尺等方面都有详细的管理。

3.2.8 林业模型加载

通过加载林业相关的平面模型可以更加真实地展现任务区域的地理空间环境，便于指挥调度和资源安排。

3.2.9 图层控制与查询

在林业资源信息的浏览时，通过对信息图层的定向选择，可以控制模型上面显示的具体林业信息。林业信息系统中的数据非常庞大，所有数据在同一模型上显示出来势必会影响浏览效果，所以用户可以有选择性的在特定模型相关图层上显示林业数据，例如只显示树木类别、只显示道路、同时显示道路与树木类别等。

3.2.10 林业高级属性信息查询

属性信息查询可以通过多种模式进行查询，系统可根据查询信息进行林业模型的快速定位。例如地名、经纬坐标、路线、管理部门名称、管理人员名称等，方便用户快速定位某一林区的具体位置。

3.2.11 林区空间数据查询

通过林业地理信息系统数据，可以对整个林业系统按地域、按业务类别进行相关数据的空间分析，主要包括林木覆盖率、按区域林业覆盖面积对比、林业增减空间数据分析等。

3.2.12 地图数据操作

(1)地图工具：具备鹰眼功能，可进行地图平移、缩放、分层浏览以及文字标注图层开关功能；能获取选中地图中对象的信息，如火场面积、火场周长、地图上任意两点距离以及多点距离等；可进行地图基本信息显示选择：如选择显示“当前视野”、“当前坐标”、“比例尺”等；还可设定图层显示方式与图层中对象的显示方式，如“可将等高线层设为——当地图视野大于100km时便不可见”等。

(2)地图查询：具有按关键字地图查询、专业图层查询、各级单位信息查询功能；具有图形和数据的双向查询、模糊查询、定位和统计功能；能够按照查询结果显示出地图影像。

(3)地图定位：支持多种定位方法相结合，提供将地图查询结果快速定位功能，并确保定位精度。如按行政区划定位、森林覆盖面积定位、道路定位(道路名称)、常用地名定位、汉语拼音首字母定位等。

3.2.13 统计分析

能够对林业资源数据进行各种形式的统计分析，对林业资源在平面地区中的分布情况进行系统常规统计分析。

根据林业管理部门的具体业务需要和已存在的数据进行森林分布、树种分布、公益林分布等常规统计分析。

3.2.14 可扩展三维模块进行空间分析

对二维GIS中，空间分析是GIS区别于CAD的特有功能。空间份额分析三维化，也就是直接在三维空间中进行空间操作与分析，对空间对象进行三维表达与管理，使得三维GIS明显不同于二维GIS，在功能上更加强大。

3.2.15 系统管理

系统管理主要包括系统用户管理、日志管理、表单管理、权限管理、数据备份与还原等。

3.2.16 数据的输出

如何将GIS的各种业务数据变成可统计的表格数据进行输出，供各种业务用途的需要，或与其他业务系统进行数据交换，是GIS中不可缺少的一部分。GIS的输出产品是指经系统处理分析，可以直接提供给用户使用的各种地图、图表、图像、数据报表或文字报告。本系统的数据输出可以通过数据输出子系统和电子表格定义输出子系统来实现文本、图形、图像、报表等不同格式的输出。

(1)数据输出。数据输出子系统可以将编排好的图形显示到屏幕上或在指定的设备上输出。具有版面编排、矢量或栅格数据处理、不同设备输出、光栅数据生成、输出处理等功能，同时支持输出标准XML格式的数据文档功能。

(2)报表定义输出。电子表格定义输出系统是一个强有力的多用途报表应用程序。应用该系统可以方便地构造各种类型的表格与报表，并在表格内随意地编排各种文字信息，并根据需要打印出来。它可以实现动态数据联结，接收由其他应用程序输出的属性数据，并将这些数据以规定的报表格式打印出来。

(3)数据转换。数据文件交换子系统为实现本系统与其他 CAD、CAM 软件系统间架设了一道桥梁，实现了不同系统间所用数据文件的交换，从而达到数据共享的目的。输入输出交换接口提供标准的 XML 等公开格式、标准格式文件与本系统内部矢量文件结构相互转换的能力。

3.2.17 数据打印功能

能够提供数据统计分析打印的功能。

3.3 吉林省林业资源发布与浏览系统

B/S 地图数据发布系统，将吉林省林业资源的各类可公开地图数据发布在网上，终端用户可以通过浏览器对森林资源数据、各类专题图、统计报表等执行查询、统计、编辑、报表输出等操作。

4 技术性能

吉林省林业地理信息系统支持功能授权，且地理信息系统的地图和二维数据和数据在网络上传输都进行特殊加密，具有较高的安全性；系统支持多处理器并行运算，能高效处理、高速访问海量二维和三维林业数据；分布式的服务器构架，保证了大量用户正常使用系统功能；软件核心部分采用国际上先进的 ArcGIS 数字地理信息系统平台，既保证了系统的可靠性，又充分考虑了系统的二次开发，未来可通过加载三维模块提供高密级和非常复杂的特殊三维空间分析应用。

吉林省林木生物质能源开发与利用探讨

谷万祥　马晓龙

（吉林省林业勘察设计研究院，吉林 长春 130022）

生物质能源是指利用自然界的植物、粪便以及城乡有机废物转化成的能源。林木生物能源，具有可再生性，属清洁能源。发展林木生物能源，将有效引导能源开发利用，由传统的高污染石化能源开发利用走向清洁能源开发利用。对减少大气污染程度、缓解温室效应、净化空气、改善生态环境发挥重要作用。另外，生物质颗粒燃料还可以缓解林业、农村地区能源的短缺，避免造成植被破坏，生态环境不断恶化，防止“能源短缺—过渡砍伐—生态破坏”的恶性循环。开发和利用生物质能源有助于林区发展循环经济、建设资源节约型、环境友好型社会，为实现环境与林业、农业、能源与生态的可持续发展做出贡献。

1　生物质能源发展概况

目前，国内在生物质能源开发利用尚处于刚刚起步阶段，大都是试验和示范的过程，少数开始了实质性的产业化。已有不少科研院校和企业进入了林木生物质能源开发利用领域。主要有以下几方面：

(1)生物质能源发电。国能生物发电有限公司陆续在山东单县、东营、黑龙江庆安等地投资建设以林木生物质为主要燃料的发电厂。内蒙古东胜建立全木质热电联产生物质发电厂，北京国林山川生物能源有限公司正在内蒙古通辽市奈曼旗建设以灌木林资源的林木生物质热电联产项目。

(2)生物柴油。近年来，国内生物柴油年总产量估计 10 万 t。麻疯树、黄连木等油料作物加工生物柴油已具备了产业化的技术条件。

(3)成型燃料开发。全国已有一批生物质压缩成型厂。生物质经压缩成型后可直接用作燃料，也可经炭化炉炭化。获得生物炭。而技术比较成熟的林木生物质颗粒加工受生产过程中的高温高压限制、设备易磨损等，推广并广泛。

2　生物质能源发展现状

早在 20 世纪 70 年代，生物质能的开发利用研究已成为世界性的热门课题，许多国家都制定了相应的开发研究计划。美国建有 350 多座生物质发电站，在生物质利用方面处于世界领先地位。颗粒成型燃料技术在美国、加拿大、日本等国得到应用，其中美国年产量达 80 余万 t，日本年产量达 25 万 t。奥地利成功施行燃烧木质能源区域供电计划。加拿大有多个实验室和大学开展了生物质气化技术研究，并于 1998 年发布生物质循环流化床快速热解技

作者简介：谷万祥(1965～)，男，吉林农安人，高工，主要从事林业咨询、规划、设计工作。

术和设备。瑞典和丹麦正在实行利用生物质进行热电联产计划。印度开发了用流化床气化农林剩余物和木屑等技术，气体用于柴油机发电。美国建立了日处理生物质量为100t的工业化压力气化系统。美国、新西兰、日本、德国、加拿大等国先后开展了从生物质制取液化油的研究工作，欧美等发达国家在催化汽化方面也做了大量研发工作，并在工业生产中应用。目前，在全球能源消费中，生物质能源约占14%，仅次于煤炭、石油和天然气，居于世界能源消费总量的第4位。有关专家估计，生物质能极可能成为未来可持续能源系统的重要组成部分，到21世纪中叶，采用新技术生产的各种生物质替代燃料将占全球总能耗的40%以上。全球每年技术上可获取的生物质能源的资源潜力相当于65亿t标准煤，相当于2001年世界能源消费量的50%。

我国生物质能的应用技术研究自20世纪80年代以来一直受到重视，主要在气化、固化、热解和液化等方面开展研发工作。生物质气化技术研究在我国发展较快。利用农林生物质原料进行热解气化反应，产生的木煤气供居民生活用气、供热和发电。

中国林科院研发的以林业剩余物为原料的上吸式气化炉，已先后在黑龙江、福建等建成工业化装置。广州能源研究所开发的外循环流化床生物质气化技术，被应用于以木煤气为能源的干燥热源和发电系统。北京农机院、浙江大学热工所和大连环科所等也先后开展了生物质气化技术的研究工作。生物质固化技术已达工业化生产规模。

目前国内由中国林科院林化所开发完成的固化成型设备有2大类：棒状成型机和颗粒状成型机。生产的颗粒成型燃料尤其适用于家庭或暖房取暖使用。截至目前，全国已有一批生物质压缩成型厂。生物质经压缩成型后可直接用作燃料，也可经炭化炉炭化，获得生物炭，用于烧烤和冶金工业；还可生产块状饲料。这些比较成熟的技术是在高温高压条件下使林木生物质固体成型(颗粒或木质煤块)，但受其生产过程限制，高温高压造成能耗比较大、设备容易磨损等缺陷无法克服，推广并不广泛。

3 吉林省生物质能源开发利用现状

目前，吉林省已开发的项目主要以林木生物质材料的直接燃烧居多，效率极低。部分企业通过改进锅炉结构将“三剩物”用于生产供热、冬季供暖等已收到良好效果，但仍未能将这些材料的效能发挥到极致。省内开展固体成型加工的企业只是近几年有所涉及，代表企业是辉南宏日新能源有限责任公司、抚松县泉阳永财木业有限公司。

4 吉林省生物质能源开发建设存在的主要问题

4.1 生物质能源开发力度不足

(1)可开发的资源开发程度低：仅以森林生物质能源来看，木材利用率至多达到现有量的60%，尚有很大发展空间，如清林的枝丫材等未得到有效利用。

(2)产品单一：就森林生物质能源来看，目前有产品的仅限于两类：原材料直接应用；加工成质量不等的木炭、燃料块或颗粒燃料等。

4.2 已开发的产品科技含量低

生物质能源开发处于较低水平，多数为简单加工或未加工的直接利用。产品成本居高不下，难以与市场上相近的木炭、煤、柴油、汽油等竞争。

原因主要有：一是政府重视程度不够，无专门组织机构进行组织与推动，缺乏相关的扶持政策，投入少，无任何正式的官方研发规划等。二是产品开发不系统。相应配套的技术与设备缺乏，无官方统筹推动研发的源动力。技术问题是制约林木质能源利用的主要因素。多数高科技含量的技术尚不完全过关，有些技术虽然过关或能够过关，但缺乏市场竞争力。生产成本过高。三是产品的应用市场尚处于萌芽状态，生产的最终产品要得到市场认可还需要一个过程，有的仍需要国家政策的推动和相关知识的宣传、教育等。

5 吉林省生物质能源开发利用的潜在优势

吉林省可利用的森林生物质能源资源有三类，即种类资源、木材资源和油料与淀粉资源。种类资源指不具传统用材作用及其他重要经济或生态价值的灌木种类资源。木材资源主要指用材林清林产物、“三剩物”和部分薪炭林采伐物。油料与淀粉资源指野生或种植的油料与淀粉植物所产生的木本油脂与淀粉。

5.1 资源优势明显

吉林省共有木本植物430种，除主要用材树种、绿化用树种、珍贵药用树种、其他重要经济树种和具有特殊生态价值树种外，保守估计尚有200余种野生资源或人工培植资源适于作生物质能源，占吉林省总树种拥有量的46.5%，主要用材林清林产生数量可观。全省641万 hm^2 用材林5年清林一次，以每公顷清林产物干重10t计，相当于每年有1282万t的清林产物，若一半用于可再生能源生产，则每年全省有641万t可再生资源。木材生产“三剩物”是优良的可再生能源资源。以年产木材700万 m^3、木材综合利用率65%计，尚有35%即245万 m^3“三剩物”可供利用。薪炭林资源也有很大潜力。我省1.6万 hm^2 薪炭林年产薪炭材约1.3万t，如能利用高新技术对其进行加工，改变其低效消耗局面，不仅可满足居民或企业生活能源需求，同时还可有相当数量节余，支持地方经济建设。

5.2 国家政策支持

由于化石燃料的有限性，可再生能源开发得到广泛重视。2005年，国家颁行《可再生能源法》，使可再生生物质能源的开发利用有法可依。同年，国家林业局成立林木生物质能源领导小组办公室，研究出台相应推动政策，并将加大对林业生物质能源产业开始的资金扶持力度。国务院办公厅2005年底转发发改委等部门《关于加快推进木材节约和代用工作意见的通知》，鼓励充分利用枝丫材，减少生产环节浪费。扩大利用人工林、速生林，充分利用木材生产加工剩余、次小薪材等资源。财政部、国家税务总局下发通知规定，自2006年1月1日起两年内，对纳税人以“三剩物”和次小薪材为原料生产加工的综合利用产品，实行增值税即征即退办法。

5.3 林业企业转型、东北老工业基地改造等急需新项目

林业企业转型、东北老工业基地改造项目，国家投入巨资。这些资金投入多以立项形式进行。生物质能源项目是目前极具潜势的、多具有较高科技含量的环境友好型项目，国家政策支持，在选址合适、技术成熟的前提下，容易获得资助，尤其近五年，将成为林业企业转型和东北老工业基地改造的首选项目。

5.4 技术不断成熟

固体燃料加工技术已基本成熟，简便易行，投资少、见效快，需要进行改进的是固体燃料的品质、生产成本的降低和产品更高的科技附加值，通过加工设备、加工工艺、燃烧设备、成型技术的改进，完全可使这三个问题得到解决，从而使产品得到更广大用户的接受，

获得更广泛的市场。目前，已有众多研究部门在开展研究，并已得到部分解决和推广应用。木质材料的液化技术、热解决技术国内也有大量研究，部分技术已投入中试或试生产，随着我国科研工作者的不懈努力，定会得到尽快解决，并面市。由植物果实或种子生产生物柴油技术已基本成型，尚需努力的是针对具体植物种子油研制与之相配套的加工工艺。

林业生物质能源品种十分丰富，可再生、能够持续利用，发展潜力巨大。开发林业生物质能源符合国家发展生物质能源不与人争粮油、不与农争地、对环境友好的原则，适合我国的基本国情，是我国发展生物质能源的重要方面和基本特色，并越来越受到国家的重视和社会的关注。开发和利用生物质能源既解决了林木废弃物转化利用率不高、随意堆放的问题，又为各森工企业伐区生产、植树造林、减少森林火灾提供了便利条件。同时，可提供更多的就业岗位，吸纳更多的剩余劳动力就业，缓解就业压力，促进社会和谐稳定，为林农提供更多的增收渠道。同时，使用生物质颗粒燃料能减少居民因长期烧柴而造成的空气污染，尤其是避免室内烟尘对居民身体的伤害，降低呼吸道疾病的发病率，从而改善居民健康状况。另外，对森工企业调整产业结构、优化产品品种、延长产业链有着积极的促进作用。

吉林省重点国有林区森林认证与森林可持续经营的探讨

谷万祥　马晓龙

（吉林省林业勘察设计研究院，吉林 长春 130022）

保护环境，促进社会、经济协调发展，已成为举世瞩目的全球问题。为了履行可持续经营本国森林的政治承诺，许多国家和地区都在研究探讨森林可持续的含义，并倡导制定森林可持续经营的通用原则，制定定性或定量描述和定期监测森林变化的标准与指标体系，以评价不断改进的森林经营活动所产生的总体效果。20 世纪 90 年代初期，在一些非政府组织的倡导下，提出一种新的手段，试图通过市场驱动来促进世界森林的可持续经营，既森林认证机制。森林认证作为促进森林可持续经营，提高森林经营管理水平的重要手段，已经为越来越多的国家认同和接受。2005 年 4 月，森林管理委员会(FSC)对吉林省白河林业局的森林进行了认证，也是我省首次获得森林管理委员会(FSC) 认证，并颁发了证书。笔者就吉林省重点国有林区森林认证与森林可持续经营的有关问题进行探讨。

一、吉林省重点国有林区现状

吉林省重点国有林区，不仅是国家的木材及林特产品生产基地，而且是松辽平原的绿色屏障，承担着保土蓄水、维护该地区生态环境的重要职责，直接关系松花江中下游广大地区人民群众的生产生活用水和大型水利电力设施的安全有效运行。但是，由于长期以来，在林区的经营与开发建设上，重采轻育，过量采伐，加之受国家财力所限，投资不足等综合因素影响，致使森林资源遭到长期过量消耗，可供开发利用森林资源消耗殆尽。

1998 年以来，根据党中央、国务院关于要保护好天然林，将森工企业的主营方向由伐木转向营林事业的重大战略决策，在我省长白山重点国有林区的 18 个林业局、4 个森林经营局和长白山国家级自然保护区管理局范围内，启动实施了天然林资源保护工程。先后组织开展了森林分类区划、调减木材产量、公益林建设、转产项目的开发建设、分流安置下岗待业人员等项工作，使天然林资源保护工程收到了明显的实效。

吉林省天然林资源保护工程区木材减产到位，资源培育管护加强，森林经营方式发生了深刻变化。按照天然林资源保护工程方案要求，到 2003 年木材减产逐步到位，全省年木材产量调减 170.33 万 m^3，调减幅度达到 43%，7 年累计调减木材产量 861.8 万 m^3；通过造林、抚育和封山育林等公益林建设，吉林省天然林资源保护工程区森林资源总量明显增加，活立木蓄积净增长 3000 万 m^3，增长 6.1%；有林地面积达 368 万 hm^2，净增长 7.8 万 hm^2，

作者简介：谷万祥(1965～)，男，吉林农安人，高工，主要从事林业咨询、规划、设计工作。

增长2.2%，实现了活立木蓄积和有林地面积双增长，扭转了森林消耗量大于生长量的局面。森林植被、林分结构、生物多样性明显改善，生态资产增值，生态系统功能明显增强；实行木材减产、森林分类经营，引发了森林经营方式的深刻变化。

二、吉林省重点国有林区森林可持续经营存在的问题

调减木材产、妥善安置富余人员，加强森林管护是天然林保护工程的短期任务，在工程实施的几年后，这一任务已基本完成，现在必须着眼解决吉林省重点国有林区居民群众的生计、社区发展问题，减轻林区社会对森林资源的压力。从长远来看，吉林省重点国有林区必须下大力气提高森林资源质量和林地生产力。当前，影响吉林省重点国有林区森林可持续经营的主要因素主要包括天然林资源的破碎化、林区人口的膨胀、企业自我生存能力的下降，更重要的是产权制度、资源管理制度等体制性障碍，影响了林区的稳定与发展。

三、森林认证有利于吉林省重点国有林区的可持续经营

吉林省重点国有林区尽管森林采伐常常是造成森林破坏和退化的主要因素，但森林采伐本身并不意味着一定会破坏森林。如果以一种不破坏环境的方式，即模仿森林自然发育过程来采伐森林，那么采伐活动不会对森林造成不良的影响。吉林省汪清林业局金沟岭林场采育林经验告诉我们，正常的森林经营活动不会对森林造成不良的影响。森林认证强调独立性、公正性和自愿性。笔者认为从森林认证的宗旨看，是与天保工程和森林可持续经营目标相一致的，借助森林认证的机制，可以为吉林省重点国有林区天然林的保护和森林的可持续经营提供帮助。现在的关键是如何按照自然特点，制定出符合林区经营特点的认证标准和指标，建立有符合中国特色的森林认证体系。森林认证的核心是评价森林经营者经营管理森林的水平，而不是森林本身。即使有良好的森林，如果经营管理不善，或者采取掠夺式的开采，森林就会很快被破坏。相反，质量较低甚至被破坏了的森林，如果受到良好的经营管理，也能够得以恢复，实现可持续经营。当前，国际上森林认证体系有多种，但在实践中，认证必须包括全部的利益群体，符合环境、社会和经济的标准。

四、森林认证可促进森林可持续经营及森林法律法规的宣传

(一)森林认证可使森林企业获益

对于吉林省重点国有林区森林经营单位和企业来说，通过森林认证能够获得综合效益，不仅表现在直接经济利润上，而且表现在潜在的商业机遇方面 森林的可持续经营需要新技术的支撑，而森林认证提供了一套切实可行的森林可持续经营标准，供森林经营单位参考与使用；认证进程需要对公司所有的森林经营活动进行评估，对于企业来说，这本身就是向林业专家学习和提高的过程。因此，按照认证标准进行经营，从长期来看有利于增加木材总产量，提高森林生产力。

森林认证能保证森林以可持续方式经营，即采伐量不会超过生长量，从而保证森林资源的可持续供应。森林认证还可为企业引入先进的管理体系和经营体系，提高管理能力，改善经营状况，从而提高其生产效率和经济效益。当前，一些国家出于保护环境的需要，对开发森林很谨慎，而通过森林认证可以保障森林资源的可持续开发，从而有利于企业获得长期稳定的经营特许权。

开展认证工作，还可以使森林企业加强同当地社区、政府有关部门的联系和合作，改善彼此间的关系，提高企业在绿色市场中的形象和信誉。而信誉良好的企业，更容易获得银行、政府和国际组织等有关方面更多的资金和技术支持，进而提高了企业在市场上的竞争力。

（二）森林认证可以带来综合效益

森林认证的主要目的是保护环境。在不同认证体系制定的森林认证标准中，都包含有森林经营活动对环境影响的内容，由于森林认证要求有关森林经营单位制定合理的森林经营规划，防止外来有害物种的入侵，控制化学制剂的使用，减少采伐和道路建设等措施，从而有利于保护森林的生物多样性，维持森林的生态功能和生态系统的完整性，促进森林的可持续经营。

森林认证强调权益相关者共同参与森林经营标准的制定和监督森林经营的过程，从而维护了森林经营单位职工参与决策、劳动保护、福利待遇等权利：也维护了当地居民进入森林采集水果、薪材、建筑材料和药用植物等林产品的合法权利，可以使更多的人参与或关心森林可持续经营。

（三）森林认证的示范作用将推动森林法律法规的宣传，有助于提高全民的环保意识和法律意识

从目前的森林认证实践来看，认证的森林没有或极少数处于毁林或退化的状态。森林认证的主要作用是对其他森林经营者的示范效应，认证的森林提供了一个森林可持续经营的典范和模板。表明通过了森林认证的森林经营单位的森林经营良好。因为增加了真实的利益驱动，相对与单纯的法律宣传，这种榜样的示范性效果更加明显，促使森林经营者和林产品企业自觉的遵守森林法。森林认证不仅考虑了森林经营的经济效益、环境效益和社会效益，而且强调了公众广泛的参与性，森林认证活动提供了一种新的全社会办林业、全民搞绿化的途径，有助于提高全民环保意识和法律意识。

建立我国森林生态效益补偿制度的构想

曹小玉　吕　勇

（中南林业科技大学森林经理学科，长沙，410004）

摘　要：森林生态效益补偿制度的建立是保证我国生态公益林可持续发展的关键性措施。本文在对森林生态效益进行界定的基础上，分析了建立森林生态效益补偿制度的理论依据和政策、法律依据。结合我国目前森林生态效益补偿存在的问题，提出了建立我国森林生态效益补偿制度的思路。

关键词：生态效益；生态效益补偿；补偿制度

Proposal on Establishing System of Compensation for Ecological Benefit of Forest in China

CAO Xiao-yu　　LV Yong

（College of Forest of Central South University of Forestry and technology，Changsha，Hunan，410004）

Abstract：A system of compensation for ecological benefit of forest is key measures which can ensure non – industrial ecological forests sustainable development. Based on definition of ecological benefit of forest，this paper analyzes theory foundation and policy basis of compensation for ecological benefit of forest and put forward some suggestions for formulating a system of compensation for ecological benefit of forest in accordance with some existing problems in this field.

Key words：ecological benefit；compensation for ecological benefit；compensation system

目前，我国生态环境日益恶化，如何做到资源保护和经济协调、可持续发展已被提到议事日程上来。森林作为“地球之肺”其改善生态环境的作用越来越受到重视，保护森林资源，充分发挥森林生态效益，正成为时代的主旋律。然而，我国现阶段森林保护和建设缺乏资金，特别是公益林建设资金更加短缺。森林生态效益补偿制度作为解决上述问题的关键性措施，成为学者们研究的热点。

1　森林生态效益概述

1.1　森林生态效益的界定

森林生态效益是指森林系统及其影响所及范围内对人类社会有益的全部效用。其中包括森林生态系统中生命系统的效益、环境系统的效益、生命系统与环境系统相统一的整体提供的整体效益，以及由上述客体存在而产生的物质和精神方面的所有效益[1]。

1.2 森林生态效益的特点

森林具有两类产品，即木材等有形产品和生态效益等无形产品。有形产品主要表现为森林的经济效益，无形产品则主要表现为森林的生态效益。与其他产品相比，森林生态效益无形产品的特性决定了它有不可控制性、非市场交易性、公共物品性、外部经济性、复杂性和难计量性等特点[2]。

2 森林生态效益补偿的依据

2.1 理论依据

关于森林生态效益补偿的理论依据，主要有两种观点：一是劳动价值补偿理论，二是公共物品补偿理论[3]。前者认为，森林在形成过程中凝结了人类劳动，因而具有价值，即使对天然林而言，虽然它不是人类劳动的产物，但由于森林不同于一般天然矿产，它是可再生资源，用“等效替代法”来研究，可以推算出重置价，因而其生态效益也具有价值，所以应通过市场或其他方式实现森林生态效益的补偿。后者认为，森林尤其是生态公益林具有排他性、非竞争性，属于社会公共物品，具有典型的外部经济性，“当一个人从事一种影响旁观者福利而对这种影响既不付报酬又得不到报酬的活动时，而这种影响是有利的，这样就产生了外部经济性”。这使得社会成本与私人成本、社会效益与私人效益不对称，引起资源配置失误。为了达到资源的优化配置，实现森林资源的可持续发展以及生态环境的改善，需要采取适当的补偿措施对森林生态效益进行补偿，以解决森林的外部效应即市场失灵。

2.2 政策、法律依据

近十多年来，我国相继出台了有关森林生态效益补偿方面的政策、法律依据。1992 年，国务院批转国家体改委《关于一九九二年经济体制改革要点的通知》文件中明确指出：“要建立林价制度和森林生态效益补偿制度，实行森林资源有偿使用。”1993 年国务院《关于进一步加强造林绿化工作的通知》中就明确提出：“要改革造林绿化工作资金投入机制，逐步实行征收生态效益补偿费制。”1996 年中共中央、国务院《关于“九五”时期和今年农村工作的主要任务和政策措施》中又再次提出“按照林业分类经营原则，逐步建立森林生态效益补偿制度和生态公益林投入机制，加快森林植被的恢复与发展”。1998 年通过的《森林法 < 修正案 >》规定：“国家建立森林生态效益补偿基金，用于提供生态效益防护林和特种用途林的森林资源、林木的营造、抚育、保护和管理。”2000 年 1 月发布的《森林法实施条例》中明确规定：“防护林、特种用途林的经营者，有获得森林生态效益补偿的权利。”从而使森林生产经营者获取补偿权力法定化。

3 目前我国森林生态效益补偿存在的问题

2004 年，财政部和国家林业局联合出台了《中央森林生态效益补偿基金管理办法》，该办法明确规定：“中央补偿基金是对重点公益林管护者发生的营造、抚育、保护和管理支出给予一定补助的专项资金，由中央财政预算安排。”这标志着我国森林生态效益补偿工作已由试点发展到全面推开的新阶段。森林生态效益补偿基金制度的确立与全面实施，结束了我国长期无偿使用森林生态效益的历史，开始进入有偿使用森林生态效益的新时期。但目前补偿工作尚未完全到位，存在不少问题[4~5]：①补偿标准偏低，目前中央森林生态效益补偿每年每亩只有10元；②补偿标准单一，不能适应各地情况；③补偿项目不全，只补偿管护费用，未包括造林费用、抚育费用、管理费用；④补偿资金管理体系不够完善，存在补偿资金使用不合理的现象。

这些问题就其实质来讲，是由于我国的森林生态效益补偿基金制度本身是一种不成熟的制度，中央森林生态效益补偿基金对生态公益林管护者的“补助 ”算不上真正意义上的“补偿”。“补助”毕竟不是“补偿”，这是两个完全不同的概念，“补助”是政府为扶持某一特定行业而给予的优惠，这种优惠是非常有限的，“补偿”是指特定收益者因消费某一产品或服务给予生产者一定额度的支付，具有持续市场交换的意义。同时也没有达到《森林法》关于“国家设立森林生态效益补偿基金，用于提供生态效益的防护林和特种用途林的森林资源、林木的营造、抚育、保护和管理”的规定，因此，要从根本上解决上述问题，持续不断地调动公益林生产者的积极性，不断推进生态环境建设，必须建立森林生态效益补偿制度。

4 建立我国森林生态效益补偿制度的构想

4.1 明确补偿对象并搞好森林分类区划工作是建立森林生态效益补偿制度的前提

森林是经营者的经营对象，森林资源是经营对象的物质表现，森林生态效益是经营成果，无论是森林、森林资源、森林生态效益都不能自己作出投入、自己组织生产经营过程、自己提出并需要补偿，这里要补偿的只是森林经营者，而且需要外在补偿的还只是特定森林——公益林的经营者。

明确了补偿对象，就要搞好森林分类区划工作，合理界定生态公益林，首先要搞好公益林、商品林的分类规划工作。要从各地社会经济发展水平和森林资源状况出发，因地制宜、科学规划、合理布局。其次要搞好实地区划界定工作，把按照国家有关规定规划的公益林和商品林，落实到山头地块，做到权属和地类清楚、事权划分和经营主体明确、检查监督人员落实。再次，要搞好公开认定工作，把经营者的森林划定为公益林，是以取得生态效益补偿权的民事行为，必须得到经营者和当地干部群众代表、县乡人民政府的公开确认。并签字画押，登记造册，张榜公布，千万不能先行划定，侵犯经营者合法权益，伤害老百姓的积极性。

4.2 科学合理的补偿标准是建立森林生态效益补偿制度的核心问题

补偿标准是森林生态效益补偿制度的核心问题，关系到补偿的效果和补偿的承受能力。目前在理论上有两个补偿标准[6~7]：一是以森林生态价值作为森林生态效益补偿标准的依据，即森林生态效益补偿标准应是森林生态服务对全社会所具有的全部经济价值。但根据这一原则建立的补偿标准会显得过高。日本林野厅在其1978年完成并发表的《森林公益效能计量标准——绿色植物调查》研究成果中，计算了全国7种生态效益，其评价价值为910亿美元。1999年，北京市林业局和林业科学研究院对北京市森林资源和环境价值作了评估，其价值为2313.71亿元人民币，如按此标准进行补偿是国家财力目前无法承受的。二是根据马克思的劳动价值论和再生产理论作为补偿标准的根据，即森林生态效益补偿标准应是凝结在公益林中的价值，而不是使用价值(即公益林所能发挥的生态效益)。这里的价值补偿不是C+V，而是C+V+M，因为全社会的公益林不能只进行简单再生产，而要进行扩大再生产，因为人口还在急剧增长，增长的人口必然提出增长的生态需求，即使人口规模不增长，随着人类社会的发展，人们的生活水平不断提高之后也必然会有更高的生态需求水平。公益林要扩大再生产，物质基础是什么？显然单纯补偿 C + V 部分只能进行简单再生产，要进行扩大再生产还必须补偿其 M 部分，即必须保证它有增殖，有盈利。

因此，在当前情况下，科学的补偿标准应包括投入和利润两部分，其构成要素有：①营林直接投入：包括地租、造林、抚育、管护及基本建设（如林道、管护棚、防火线等）的投入，这是营造林过程中直接发生的成本费用，必须得到全额补偿。其地租反映公益林立地和地利状况，应与经营商品林时的地租等额。②间接投入：包括公益林规划设计、调查、监测、质量管理、工资及其他管理费用等间接投入部分，这也是一项成本费用，应得到补偿。③灾害损失：包括病虫害、火灾、洪灾、风灾、崩塌等自然灾害使公益林受到损失而需要恢复生态效能所需的费用，应得到补偿。④利息：使用资金只能用于经营公益林而不能改变用途，投入到赢利性更大的项目中，因此公益林投入资金的利息也应得到补偿，且应按同期商业利率计算额给予补偿。⑤非商品林经营利益损失：由于经营公益林而限制商品林经营所造成的经济损失。这种损失也应得到合理补偿，使其获得社会平均营林利润。

4.3 拓宽补偿资金来源渠道是建立森林生态效益补偿制度的关键

森林的生态效益是多方面的，除一些效益属特定对象享有（如库区周围的水源涵养林、村庄周围的风景林）外，其大多数效益都属于一个较大地域范围的全社会享有。因此，基于森林生态效益的公共物品属性，其森林生态效益补偿资金的来源也应该是多元的，可通过以下渠道筹集：一是财政投入。由国家、省拨付公益林补偿基金，以承担公益林建设与管理单位的人员经费以及基础设施建设费用。公益林的主导利用是发挥生态功能，受益的是全社会，由于社会利益的总代表只能是各级人民政府，理应由财政支付公益林的价值补偿。财政投入应是森林生态效益补偿资金的主要资金来源。二是向森林生态效益的直接收益者收取森林生态效益补偿费用。笔者认为当前可以从以下几个方面收取补偿费：①国家大中型水库、城市自来水厂，按实际供水量的营业收入的一定比例缴纳；②从水电站电费收入中，按每度电固定金额征收；③从事内河航运的单位和个人，按其营业收入的一定比例缴纳；④各类旅行社，按其营业收入的一定比例缴纳；⑤在风景名胜地、森林公园、自然保护区、旅游度假村、城市园林绿化公园、狩猎场、滑雪场内从事各种经营活动的单位和个人，按其营业收入的一定比例缴纳。三是银行给予这些生态公益林建设工程较大数额的低息长期贷款；四是向社会积极募捐。如成立生态公益林的慈善机构，设立慈善基金，接受社会各界人士和有关单位的捐赠，慈善机构通过广播、报刊、电视等媒体举办慈善晚会，筹措生态公益林生态效益补偿资金。

4.4 加强森林生态效益补偿资金使用的监督管理是建立森林生态效益补偿制度的重要条件

森林生态效益补偿资金的监督管理主要是两方面：第一是看森林生态效益补偿制度是否得到认真执行，资金运行的安全性是否得到保证，补偿金有无发生侵吞、挪用、截留、串用等违规行为的发生。森林生态效益补偿面向森林经营者的补偿，森林生态效益补资金应落实到森林经营者的头上。如果出现发放过程中层层截留等违规现象，生态效益补偿资金就不会发挥任何作用。因此，必须加强森林生态效益补偿资金发放情况的监督，把资金运作监督体系作为补偿政策设计的重点。第二是看补偿资金安排是否合理，使用的效果是否明显，是否保质保量完成公益林的建设任务，达到预期的目的。因此，各级林业主管部门应当建立生态公益林档案和森林生态效益补偿资金支出财务档案。同时对每一个生态公益林经营者建立森林生态效益补偿落实情况监督卡，并把它发到公益林经营者手中。这样，上级主管部门就可以根据补偿标准定期对生态公益林档案、森林生态效益补偿资金支出档案和森林生态效益补偿落实情况监督卡的一致性进行检查，发现问题及时纠正。

4.5 完善森林生态效益补偿的立法是建立森林生态效益补偿制度的保障。

森林生态效益补偿的法律制度是协调经营者和收益者之间的利益关系，为公益林提供稳定资金来源的重要保障。这一制度已在我国法律、部门规章和部分地方法律中得到体现，但其法律体系还很不完善，不能适应社会经济发展，从国际上看，运用强制性的法律手段，对开发利用自然资源造成的生态功能丧失和生态公益林的生产者进行经济补偿是许多国家成功的经验，如瑞典 1991 年颁布了世界上第一个生态税法案；欧盟已建议在其成员国内部推广二氧化碳税，并制定了具体措施；日本《森林法》规定："国家对划为保安林(即生态公益林)的森林所有者，国家补偿由于被划为保安林而遭受的损失"[8]。我国目前需要完善生态效益补偿的立法任务有：第一，修改《环境保护法》。目前，作为综合性基本法的《环境保护法》存在着结构性缺陷，实际上是防治污染的法律，并没有规定保护自然自然资源的基本原则、基本制度、和监督管理机制。森林是生态环境建设主体，增加保护森林等生态资源的法律规定，使保护生态和防治污染并重。应增加森林生态效益补偿原则的规定，把森林生态效益补偿与征收污染排污费制度结合起来，促进补偿工作开展。第二，修改《森林法》。首先，明确森林生态效益补偿渠道。其次，明确公益林清查、核定和评价机构，提高补偿数据的法律地位，增加补偿的严肃性。再次，明确对非公益林的经济扶持政策。第三，制定和颁布《生态效益补偿基金管理条例》。森林生态效益补偿是一项涉及多方面利益的复杂的系统工程，需要由国务院颁布的《生态效益补偿基金管理条例》，从而把生态效益补偿的目的、主体、对象、标准等，用法律的形式固定下来，取得全社会共同遵守的效力，才能使法律手段的强制作用得以充分发挥。

参考文献

[1]张帆．环境自然资源经济学[M]．上海：上海人民出版社，1999.

[2]孙德宝．浅谈森林生态效益补偿机制[J]．北京林业管理干部学院学报，2003(2)：35～39.

[3]王曼．浅析森林生态效益补偿制度的理论基础 [J]．西北林学院学报，2008(4)：32～36.

[4]孙佳音，周玉华．公益林效益补偿政策与法律问题探讨[J]．黑龙江省政法管理干部学院学报，2005(2)：105～107.

[5]雷玲，徐军宏，郝婷．我国森林生态效益补偿问题的思考[J]．西北林学院学报，2004，19(2)：138～131.

[6]宋莎，文冰，赵从娟．我国森林生态效益补偿标准研究进展 [J]．林业调查规划，2009(5)：34～37.

[7]陈爱平．公益林生态效益价值的理论依据及补偿机制实现形式[J]．贵州林业科技，2002(1)：60～64.

[8]李明阳，郑阿宝．我国公益林生态效益补偿政策与法规问题探讨[J]．南京林业大学学报，2003，(6)：57～61.

金山屯林业局野生花卉栽培技术

田德君　郑在军　彭立新　潘　宇
（金山屯林业局，黑龙江省金山屯，153026）

一、长柱金丝桃

【学名】*Hypericum ascyron* L.

【别名】中心菜、中心草、红旱莲、黄海棠、旱莲草、湖南连翘

【科属】金丝桃科金丝桃属

（一）形态特征

多年生草本，高 50～100cm。茎直立，具 4 条棱线。单叶对生，无柄，近革质，长圆状卵形至长圆状披针形，基部抱茎，全缘，下面具有黑色腺点。单花或聚散花序，顶生或腋生；花黄色，大型，径 4～8cm；萼片 5；花瓣 5，黄色，雄蕊多数，5 束；花柱 5，花柱与子房略等长或稍长。蒴果成熟时先端 5 裂。种子多数，棕色，表面具网纹，一侧具细长膜质狭翼。花期 7～8 月；果期 8～9 月。

（二）生物学特性

生于山坡林缘、草丛、向阳山坡、溪流及河岸湿草地。喜肥沃、湿润土壤。喜光，也稍耐阴。

（三）栽培技术

1. 种子采集

于自然开阔的山野、林缘灌丛、路旁草甸。9 月末采集种子，自然晾干，待果角开裂，风选清除杂质，即得到纯净种子。

2. 播　种

以床播为宜，床的规格高 25cm，宽 1.3m，长 5m，床的过缘应起土埂，以利保水，因种子细小，最好兑细河沙，宽幅条播，床面要平，直接播于床面，覆土要不见种子为宜，应浸床并用小棚覆盖，以利保温保湿。

3. 幼苗管理

4 月 20 日种子发芽，及时撤除覆盖物，在幼苗抽出 2 片叶前应尽量保持苗床较大湿度，5 月 4 日真叶出现，及时清除杂草，保证幼苗正常生长。

4. 圃地定植

（1）地块选择：应选排水良好的沙壤土及向阳通风处栽植。

（2）做床整地：栽植多以床栽为主，床的规格高 25cm，宽 1.3m，长 30m，在整地做床时用多菌灵 800 倍液土壤处理，并施入腐熟有机肥，每亩 $2m^3$。

（3）定植：于 6 月 5 日将 6～8 片真叶小苗定植于苗床，栽植深度应掌握比原根深 1～

2cm 为宜，株行距 15cm×15cm。

5. 田间管理

新植小苗，成活后应适当蹲苗，苗期后充足供水，促进生长，用专人观测，并拍照记录。及时清除杂草。

6. 物候观测

6 月 15 日开始生长，6 月 20 日生长旺盛，7 月 10 日现蕾，7 月 25 日开花，花期 50 天，株高 1m。

二、柳　兰

【学名】*Chamaenerion angustifolium*（L.）Scop.

【别名】红筷子、遍山红、糯芋

【科属】柳叶菜科柳兰属

(一)形态特征

多年生草本植物，高约 1m，直立，通常不分枝。叶互生，披针形，长 8~14(23)cm，宽 1~2.5cm，背面仅中脉被毛，近全缘，总状花序顶生，伸长，花序轴被短柔毛；苞片线形，长 1~2cm；花大，4 基数；不整齐，两性，径 1.5~2cm，红紫色或淡红色；雄蕊 8；花柱弓状弯曲，柱头 4 裂，子房下位，密被毛。蒴果略四棱形，具长柄，皆密被毛。种子多数，顶端具一簇种缨。花期 6~8 月；果期 8~9 月。

(二)生物学特性

生于森林地区火烧迹地、开阔地、林缘或山坡上。耐寒，喜凉爽、湿润气候及湿润、肥沃、排水良好的土壤。稍耐阴。畏炎热、干旱的环境。

(三)栽培技术

1. 种子采集

于森林地区火烧迹地、开阔地、林缘较湿地上，8~9 月采集蒴果，看到下面朔果开裂，种子上有白毛，即可采取，自然阴干，怕风，干透后收起即可，5~15℃贮存。

2. 播　种

3 月 31 日，夜间温度 10℃左右，将种子(带种缨)均匀平铺在床面上，使种子与土壤结实，没有覆土，盖上苇帘，浇透水，上面扣小棚，以利保湿，见土稍干时及时补水，利于种子发芽，因种子极细小，覆土不能出苗。

3. 幼苗管理

因小苗怕炎热，应遮阴，保证土壤湿润，是保苗关键，小苗期与杂草很难分辩，不能中耕除草，4 月 14 日幼芽长出，5 月 4 日真叶出现。

4. 圃地定植

(1)地块选择：选择土壤湿润不积水地块。

(2)做床整地：圃地以床栽为主，床的规格高 15cm，宽 1.3m，长 30m，床边做土埍，以利保水保湿。

(3)定植：于 6 月 7 日，将高 10cm 定植于苗床，栽植深度比原根深 1cm 为宜，株行距 15cm×20cm，柳兰栽植时不易成活。

5. 田间管理

移苗后土壤湿度大，杂草生长快，需及时清除，用专人观测，并拍照记录。

虫害发生严重，及时用敌敌畏灭杀。

6. 物候观测

6 月 17 日开始生长，6 月 26 日生长旺盛，7 月 20 日开花，花期 25 天，株高 55cm，没有野生条件长的高。

三、山马兰

【学名】*Kalimeris lautureana*（Debx.）Kitam.

【别名】山鸡儿肠、北马兰

【科属】菊科马兰属

（一）形态特征

多年生草本，高 40 ~ 80cm。茎直立，单生或 2 ~ 3 个簇生，被白色向上的糙毛，上部分枝成扫帚状。茎中部叶披针形、倒披针形或线状披针形，长 3 ~ 6（9）cm，宽 0.5 ~ 2（4）cm，顶端尖或钝，下面沿脉有毛，全缘或有疏齿；无柄。头状花序单生枝顶，排成伞房状；总苞半球形，径 10 ~ 14mm；总苞片 3 层，背部被短毛；边花舌状，淡紫色，中央花管状花，黄色。瘦果。冠毛不等长。花果期 7 ~ 9 月。

（二）生物学特性

生于山阳坡、草甸、林缘、沟边、荒地、灌丛处。

（三）栽培技术

1. 种子采集

多于低山区、平坎或丘陵的潮湿地带，9 月末采集成熟种子，自然晾干，风选清除杂质，5 ~ 15℃贮存。

2. 播　种

3 月 30 日，夜间温度 10℃左右，采用小幅条播，播幅 5cm，间距 5 ~ 8cm，直接将种子播于床面上，播后镇压一次，使种子与土壤密实，然后覆土，覆土厚度为种子 2 ~ 3 倍，浇水盖上苇帘，保持床面湿润。

3. 幼苗管理

4 月 15 日种子发芽，当幼苗达 50% 发芽后，适时撤除苇帘，一般在阴天或傍晚时为好，4 月 29 日真叶出现，及时松土，清除杂草，间除弱苗密苗。

4. 圃地定植

（1）地块选择：选择土壤肥沃，排灌方便，通风良好的地块。

（2）做床整地：栽植多以床栽植为主，床的规格高 25cm，宽 1.3m，长 30m，在整地做床时，用多菌灵 800 倍土壤处理，施入腐熟有机肥，1200 ~ 1500kg/亩。

（3）定植：于 6 月 4 日，将 4 ~ 6 片真叶的小苗定植于苗床，栽植时最好将大小苗分开，株行距 15cm × 20cm。

5. 田间管理

新植小苗，成活后应适当蹲苗，苗期后充足供水，促进生长，用专人观测，并拍照记录，及时清除杂草。

6. 物候观测

6 月 14 日开始生长，6 月 25 日生长旺盛，7 月 25 日开花，花期 70 天，株高70 ~ 100cm。

四、野火球

【学名】*Trifolium lupinaster* L.

【别名】野车轴草、也火球、野火萩

【科属】豆科车轴草属

(一)形态特征

多年生直立草本，高 30 ~ 60cm。通常数茎丛生，茎略呈四棱形，被疏毛。掌状复叶互提高，有小叶 5 枚，稀 3 ~ 7 枚；托叶膜质. 大部分抱茎呈鞘状，叶柄几全部与托叶合生；小叶披针形或狭椭圆形；边缘有细锯齿，侧脉约 50 对以上，被微毛；小叶柄极短。花序球形，腋生或顶生，花 20 ~ 35 朵；总花梗被柔毛；花冠红色或紫红色。荚果膜质，长圆形，有种子 1 ~ 2 粒。种子宽卵形。花果期 6 ~ 9 月。

(二)生物学特性

生于低湿草地、林缘灌丛或路旁草地上，以肥沃的黑钙土和黑土上居多。

(三)栽培技术

1. 种子采集

多在低湿草地、林缘灌丛或路旁草地上，9 月中旬采集发黄成熟的花朵，自然晾干，取出黑色种子，清除杂质，5 ~ 15℃贮存。

2. 播　种

3 月 30 日，夜间温度 10℃左右，采用小幅条播。播幅 5cm，间距 5 ~ 8cm，使种子与土壤密实，然后覆土，覆土厚度为种子 2 ~ 3 倍，镇压后盖上苇帘，浇透水，保持床面湿润。

3. 幼苗管理

4 月 17 日种子发芽，5 月 1 日真叶出现，及时清除杂草，加强肥水管理，间除弱苗小草。

4. 圃地定植

(1)地块选择：选择土壤肥沃，排灌方便，通风良好的地块。

(2)做床整地：栽植多以床栽为主，床的规格高 25cm，宽 1.3m，长 30m，在整地做床时，用多菌灵 800 倍液土壤处理，施入腐熟有机肥，每亩 $2m^3$。

(3)定植：于 6 月 3 日，将 4 ~ 6 片真叶小苗定植于苗床，栽植深度应掌握比原根深 1cm 为宜，株行距 15 ~ 20cm。

5. 田间管理

野火球移苗后生长缓慢，不耐杂草，应及时清除杂草，用专人观测，并拍照记录，加强肥水管理。

6. 物候观测

6 月 12 日开始生长，6 月 20 日生长旺盛，6 月 28 日开花，花期 50 天，株高 54cm。

五、黑心菊

【学名】*Rudbeckia hirta*

【别名】臭菊

【科属】菊科金光菊属

(一)形态特征

一二年生，株高60~100cm，头状花序8~9cm，重瓣花，舌状花黄色，有时有棕色黄带，管状花暗棕色。枝叶粗糙，多分枝。叶片较宽，基部叶羽状分裂，5~7裂，茎生叶3~5裂，边缘具稀锯齿。头状花序以至数个春生于长梗上。春秋播，花期夏季至秋季，耐寒耐旱，管理粗放，丛植片植，公路绿化，花坛花境，草地边植。也可作切花，露地越冬，能自播繁殖。全株被毛，近根出叶，上部叶互生，叶匙形及阔披针形，叶缘具粗齿。头状花序。舌状花单轮，金黄色；筒状花深褐色，呈半球形。花期5~9月。

(二)生物学特性

适应性很强，较耐寒，很耐旱，不择土壤，极易栽培，应选择排水良好的沙壤土及向阳处栽植，喜向阳通风的环境。

(三)栽培技术

1. 种子采集

多于路旁草地通风、向阳的地方，于9月中旬采集成熟头状花序，自然晾干，用手搓出种子，风选清除杂质，5~15℃贮存。

2. 播　种

3月30日，夜间温度10℃左右，采用小幅条播，播幅5cm，间距5~8cm，使种子与土壤结实，然后覆土，因种子细小，覆土厚度以不见种子为宜，镇压后盖苇帘，浇透水，保持面湿润。

3. 幼苗管理

黑心菊适应性强，不择土壤，播种后4月7日种子发芽，4月19日真叶出现，因全株被毛，浇水应选择晴天上午为好，除草时应避免将小苗带出苗床。

4. 圃地定植

(1)地块选择：因黑心菊适应性强，适生于砂质壤土上，一般排水良好，均能生长正常。

(2)做床整地：苗圃栽植以床栽为主，床的规格高25cm，宽1.3m，长30m，整地做床时需要深翻，深度应在25cm以上，结合整地，施足基肥，并用五氯硝基苯土壤消毒。

(3)定植：于6月4日在床上双行交错栽植，株距25cm，栽植时宜浅勿深，以根颈露于地表为准。栽植过深容易引起根颈腐烂，定植后，只在沟内灌水。

5. 田间管理

新植小苗应适当挖水蹲苗，苗期后充足供水，促进生长，黑心菊花大、叶多生长期消耗养分多，应及时追肥，在花期应提高磷钾肥的施用量，在中耕除草时，消除外层老叶，以改善光照、通风条件，有利于花芽的发育和生长。用专人观测，并拍照记录。

6. 物候观测

6月12日开始生长，6月20日生长旺盛，6月26日开花，花期70天，株高60cm。

六、月见草

【学名】*Oenothera biennis* L.

【别名】夜来香、山芝麻、绮霄草

【科属】柳叶菜科月见草属

(一)形态特征

2年生草本，第一年仅进行营养生长。具肉质多汁粗根。形成丛生莲座状叶，叶伏于地面，具长柄，倒披针形，密生白色伏毛，第二年 抽出花茎。茎高0.5～1m，疏生白色长硬毛。茎生叶披针形或倒披针形，长5～10cm，边缘微具稀疏浅牙齿或近全缘，两面疏生细毛。花单生于茎上部叶腋，淡黄色或黄色，夜间开花；花4数；雄蕊8，黄色；子房下位，4室。蒴果长圆形，稍弯，略四棱形，疏生长毛，成熟时4瓣裂。种子具棱角，紫褐色。花期6～7月；果期7～9月。

(二)生物学特性

生于山区向阳地、沙质地、荒地或河岸沙砾地。适应性强，耐瘠耐酸耐旱耐寒。对土壤要求不严，一般中性，微碱或微酸性土，排水良好，疏松的土壤上均能生长，土壤太湿，根部易得病。

(三)栽培技术

1. 种子采集

多于路边草丛中，9月中旬将植株上面未成熟果角去掉，即得纯净种子，5～15℃贮存。

2. 播 种

3月31日，采用小幅条播，播幅5cm，间距5～8cm，使种子与土壤结实，然后覆土，覆土厚度为种子2～3倍，镇压后浇水，保持土壤湿润，播种后10天左右，种子即可萌发出幼苗。

3. 幼苗管理

4月8日种子发芽，4月11日幼芽出土，幼苗在第二对真叶伸展前与杂草幼苗极相似，不能中耕除草，只有在第二对真叶展开后才能进行。

4. 圃地定植

(1)地块选择：因月见草适应性强，一般排水良好，疏松土壤均能生长。

(2)做床整地：栽植以床栽为主，床的规格高25cm，宽1.3m，长30m。

(3)定植：于6月3日将高10～15cm小苗定植于苗床，因其直根性，栽植深度以最下面叶片为准，株行距20cm×20cm。

5. 田间管理

因长势较快，不能有超出床面杂草。用专人观测，并拍照记录。

6. 物候观测

6月12日开始生长，6月22日生长旺盛，6月27日开花，花期45天，株高1.1m。

七、聚花风铃草

【学名】*Campanula glomerata* L.

【别名】灯笼花

【科属】桔梗科风铃草属

(一)形态特征

多年生草本，高50～100cm。茎直立，密被白色硬毛或绒毛。基生叶丛生，被粗毛，有长柄，卵形，茎生叶无柄，披针形至卵状披针形，基部浅心形或下延成半抱茎，两面生粗毛，边缘具细锯齿。花多数集生于茎顶端及上部叶腋，花直立；5数花，蓝紫色；柱头3裂。蒴果成熟时室背开裂。种子扁长圆形。花期7~9月；果期9~10月。

(二)生物学特性

生于山坡、路边草地、林缘或林间草地。

(三)栽培技术

1. 种子采集

于山坡林缘、湿草丛，9月中旬后，将整个植株采回，自然晾干，用布包裹，将种子搓出，风选后即得纯净种子，5~15℃贮存。

2. 播　种

播种一般春秋均可，发芽适温21~22℃，春季3月30日，采用做床条播，播幅5cm，间距5~8cm，将种子直接播于床面，因种子细小，覆土以略见种子为好，轻轻镇压后盖苇帘，浇透水，保持床面湿润。

3. 幼苗管理

4月17日幼芽出土，5月15日真叶出现，小苗生长缓慢，中耕除草应注意带起小苗，加强肥水管理，间除病弱小苗。

4. 圃地定植

(1)地块选择：选择土壤肥沃，排灌方便，通风良好的地块。

(2)做床整地：栽植以床栽为主，床的规格高25cm，宽1.3m，长30m，在整地做床时，用多菌灵800倍液土壤处理，施入腐熟含钙磷较高的有机肥1000~1200kg/亩。

(3)定植：于6月4日，将4~6片真叶小苗定植于苗床，栽植深度应掌握比原根深1~2cm为宜，株行距15cm×15cm。

5. 田间管理

移苗后土壤湿度大，杂草生长快，需及时清除，虫害发生严重，及时用敌敌畏灭杀。用专人观测，并拍照记录。

6. 物候观测

6月16日开始生长，6月27日生长旺盛，当年没有开花。

八、兴安乳菀

【学名】*Galatella dahurica* DC.

【别名】乳菀

【科属】菊科紫菀属

(一)形态特征

多年生草本，高30~100cm。全株被乳头状短毛。茎直立，单一，坚硬，黄绿色，基部紫红色，上部分枝。叶互生，无柄，中部线形或线状披针形，稀长圆状披针形，稀长圆状披针形，长4~8cm，宽3~8cm，基部渐狭，先端渐尖，全缘，表面密被腺点，背面疏生腺点，具3条明显脉；茎上部叶线形，具1条脉。头状花序半球形，排成伞房状；具1~2个线形的苞片；总苞近半球形；总苞片3~4层；边花舌状，淡蓝紫色，不扎实；中央花管状，黄色，结实。瘦果卵形。花期6月下旬~7月；果期8~9月。

(二)生物学特性

生于草原、碱地、沙质草地、灌丛、林缘。

(三)栽培技术

1. 种子采集

多于低山区平地或路边、丘陵潮湿地，9月末采集成熟种子，自然晾干，搓出种子，风选清除杂质，5~15℃贮存。

2. 播　种

3月31日采用小幅条播，播幅5cm，间距5~8cm，直接将种子播于床面上，播后镇压一次，使种子与土壤结实，然后覆土，覆土厚度为种子2~3倍，浇透水盖上苇帘，保持床面湿润。

3. 幼苗管理

4月15日幼芽出土，当幼苗达50%发芽后适时撤除苇帘，一般在阴天或傍晚为好，5月5日真叶出现，及时中耕除草，间除弱苗、密苗，以利于小苗正常生长。

4. 圃地定植

(1)地块选择：应选择排水良好的地块，以酸性肥沃、湿润土壤为宜。

(2)做床整地：床的规格高25cm，宽1.3m，长30m，在做床时对土壤进行消毒，并适当掺入腐熟的有机肥。

(3)定植：于6月4日将6~8叶小苗定植于苗床，栽植时最好将大小苗分开，栽植规格20cm×20cm，覆土应掌握比原苗根颈深1cm左右为宜。

5. 田间管理

中耕除草时将外面老叶清除。用专人观测，并拍照记录。

6. 物候观测

6月10日开始生长，6月20日生长旺盛，当年没有开花，株高30cm。

九、大花剪秋萝

【学名】*Lychnis fulgens* Fisch.

【别名】剪秋萝

【科属】石竹科大剪秋萝属

(一)形态特征

多年生草本，高50~80cm。全株被较长的柔毛。茎直立，单一，中空。叶对生，无柄，卵形或卵状披针形，两面及边缘被毛。花2~3朵或更多，顶生，形成密集的头状伞房花序，基部具2枚苞叶；花梗密生柔毛；花萼筒具10条脉，有较密的蛛丝状绵毛，花后萼的上部膨大呈筒状钟形；花茎3.5~5cm，瓣片鲜深红色，2叉状深裂，爪与鳞片之间具2枚鳞片状暗红色附属物，雄蕊10枚；花柱又丝状，子房花柱5。蒴果顶端5齿，齿片反卷。种子成熟时表面被疣状突起。花果期6~9月。

(二)生物学特性

生于草甸、林缘灌丛间及山坡阴湿地。

(三)栽培技术

1. 种子采集

多于草甸、林缘灌丛间、山坡阴湿地，8 月末采集，因野生分布较少，种子采集困难。

2. 播　种

种子繁殖春播秋播均可，春播 3 月 2 日播于温室，条播

为主，行距 10cm，播后覆土厚度 0.5 ~ 0.8cm，稍加镇压即可，当温度达到 20℃ 即可发芽，15 天左右出苗。

3. 幼苗管理

3 月 19 日幼芽出土，发芽率达 80%，4 月 20 日真叶出现，红花剪秋萝温室育苗时易得叶斑病、锈病，可用百菌清、粉锈宁等防治。

4. 温室定植

幼苗长至 7 ~ 8 对真叶时，摘心一次，5 月 3 日直接将小苗定植于温室，株行距 15 ~ 20cm，及时中耕除草，以免杂草滋生。栽植密度不宜过小，易倒株。用专人观测，并拍照记录。

5. 物候观测

5 月 13 日开始生长，6 月 1 日生长旺盛，6 月 8 日开花，花期 20 天，株高 50cm。

十、石　竹

【学名】*Dianthus chinensis* L.

【别名】石竹子

【科属】石竹科石竹属

（一）形态特征

石竹花因其茎具节，膨大似竹，故名。多年生草本，高 30 ~ 60cm。茎单一或数个，直立或稍上升，常由基部开始分枝，平滑无毛，节部膨大。叶对生，披针形或线状披针形，基部渐狭成短鞘围抱节上，叶脉 3 或 5 条。花顶生，单一或 2 ~ 3 朵簇生，花梗长，集成聚伞花序，花径 2.5 ~ 3.5cm；萼下苞 2 ~ 3 对；萼圆筒形，有时带紫色，萼齿具细睫毛；花瓣 5，鲜红色、白色、红紫色或粉紫色，上缘具不规则牙齿。蒴果长圆状筒形，比萼长或近等长。种子椭圆状倒卵形。花期 6 月下旬至 9 月；果期 7 月下旬至 10 月。

（二）生物学特性

主要生于山坡、疏林下、草甸及碱性草原。其性耐寒、耐干旱，不耐酷暑，夏季多生长不良或枯萎，栽培时应注意遮荫降温。喜阳光充足、高燥，通风及凉爽湿润气候，生长适温为 15 ~ 20℃，要求肥沃、疏松、排水良好微酸性的土壤或沙质壤土，忌水涝，好肥。粗砂土，重黏土及低洼、排水不良的土壤不宜栽种。

（三）栽培技术

1. 种子采集

多在路旁、荒地或田野中，9 月初采集，种子变黑，果角变黄，阴干开裂，去除杂物即可得到纯净种子。

2. 播　种

于 3 月 18 日将种子用冷水浸种 48 小时后控干，直接将种子播于床面上，采用宽幅条播，播幅为 20cm，间距 5cm，每平方米 4 行，播后镇压一次，使种子与床土密结，用腐殖

土覆土，厚度以超过种子 2 倍为宜，上覆盖苇帘，并浇透水，保持土壤湿润。

3. 幼苗管理

3 月 19 日种子发芽，4 月 20 日真叶出现，当苗出土 30% ~50% 适时撤除苇帘，苗木生长适温度为 10 ~20℃。

4. 温室定植

5 月 3 日小苗生长出 4 ~5 片真叶，苗高达到 6 ~7cm 时进行移植。定植株行距 15cm × 20cm，因那时室外尚不能移栽，直接定植保护地内。用专人观测，并拍照记录。

5. 物候观测

5 月 10 日开始生长，5 月 19 日生长旺盛，6 月 1 日开花，花期 60 天，8 月 16 日种子成熟，9 月份再次开花，株高 44cm。

开展中幼龄林抚育几点体会

田德君　郑在军　于春友　潘　宇
（黑龙江省伊春林管局金山屯林业局，153026）

森林抚育是实现林业发展的需要，森林抚育是推动林业发展的重要措施，对提高林地生产力、增加森林蓄积、改善林分结构培育后备资源，保障国家生态、木材安全将起到极大的推动作用。

一、提高林地生产力，改善林分结构

森林抚育是提高林分质量，培育后备资源的重要途径，我局的林地多为中幼龄林，占我局现有林地的93%。天保工程二期的启动，上级给予资金的增加为我局加强森林经营提供了有利的契机，加强森林抚育力度，特别是加强对中幼龄林的抚育力度。对提高我局林地的生产力、改善林分结构，引导森林正向演替，向顶级群落(阔叶红松林)；变纯林向针阔混交发展，以提高林地生产力和各种生态效能，达到近自然森林分布规律，具有重大意义，是功在当代利在千秋的伟大工程。

二、森林抚育的经济效益

我局对五年前进行过抚育的中幼龄林生长情况调查如下：

幼龄林抚育前后生长情况调查表

树种	林龄	全株高	郁闭度	未抚育5年平均高生长	未抚育5年全株高	抚育后5年平均高生长	抚育后5年全株高	高生长百分比
红松	7年	1.3m	0.5	23cm	2.7m	33cm	3.2m	43.5%
云杉	7年	2m	0.4	40cm	4.45m	60cm	5.45m	50%

中龄林抚育前后后生长情况调查表

树种	全株高	林龄	平均胸径	未抚育5年平均高生长	未抚育5年全株高	未抚育5年平均胸径	抚育后5年平均高生长	抚育后5年全株高	抚育后5年平均胸径	高生长百分比
落叶松	6m	15年	9cm	60cm	12.8m	10m	80cm	13.8m	12m	33.3%

通过调查数据显示我局五年前进行过生长抚育的中龄林，净生长量为12.88，蓄积为196.8m^3/hm^2，未进行透光的重点公益林的净生长量为9.76，蓄积为177.3m^3/hm^2，进行透

光的林分比未进行透光的林分单位蓄积增加了 19.5m^3，依据现有市场价格推算进行过抚育的林分比未进行的增加 2 万元/hm^2 的经济效益。我局共有 1374hm^2 的落叶松中龄林，全部抚育后可我局增加 2748 万元的经济效益；我市现有 37.3 万 hm^2 的中龄林，全部抚育完成后可为我市增加 746000 万元的经济效益。

三、森林抚育的生态效益

抚育后的林分每增加 1m^3 蓄积可以吸收 350kg 二氧化碳、并向大气输送 262kg 氧气，按照我市现有 37.3 万 hm^2 中龄林计算，全部完成抚育后，可比未抚育前多吸收 2545725t 二氧化碳、输送 1905657t 氧气，对降低大气温室效应，改善区域生态环境起到重大作用，对减少地表径流量和径流速度，使得地表水和地下水资源不断增加，对缓解本区域河流洪涝灾害及水资源有效补给起到不可忽视的作用。

四、森林抚育的社会效益

森林抚育财政补贴是天保工程二期的重要组成部分，森林抚育是安置富余职工的需要，我局木材大幅度减产，富余职工人数急剧增加，就业压力不断增大。落实好森林抚育财政补贴，能够安置我局富余职工 2000 多人、每年增加职工收入 7000 多元，能使我局职工安居乐业，确保我局社会稳定和谐。

综上所述为更好地提高我局的森林抚育质量，提出以下几点建议：

(1)随着《大小兴安岭生态保护与经济转型规划》和“天保二期”工程的实施，把生态建设和提高森林质量作为了林业的主要建设任务，大幅增加了营林工作量，凸显了营林工作的重要性。重点公益林急需抚育地块，国家未开放，除去河流两岸，局界、场界生态脆弱区的其他重点公益林应适当给予逐步放开。

(2)通过采小留大、采劣留优、间密留稀的抚育措施，清除妨碍目的树种生长的林下灌丛，伐掉所有不良木、非种质资源过熟木和“霸王”树，并对部分保留木进行整枝。抚育时对珍贵树种幼苗、幼树全部保留。

(3)对天然中、幼龄林，达到大径用材林选划改培标准的进行选划改培，采用疏伐、施肥、排水、修枝等技术措施，培育大径用材林。

(4)对透光抚育和生长抚育腾出的可更新地块，按照见缝插针、适地适树、栽针保阔、栽阔育针的原则进行林冠下更新。更新树种主要以红松、胡桃楸、水曲柳、山槐等珍贵树种为主，通过混交方式进行。

林木产品网络销售平台建设的探讨

李海波　孙守意

（吉林省林业勘察设计研究院）

随着信息技术的发展，电子商务已经成为一种新兴的产品销售模式，淘宝网等大型网络交易平台业绩的迅猛发展，也证明了网络销售也是未来销售模式的发展方向，这也为传统的林木产品的产销体系带来了新的机遇和挑战。

一、网络销售的优势

(1)将传统的商务流程电子化、数字化。大量减少人力、物力，降低成本；突破时间和空间的限制，使交易活动可以在任何时间、任何地点进行，从而大大提高了效率。

(2)利用网络销售的开放性和全球性的特点，创造更多的商务机会。

(3)充分利用网络销售，使公司快速进入全球化市场，利用广泛的信息资源，提高企业的竞争能力。

(4)减少中间环节，大幅度提高公司运营效率，降低管理成本。

二、网络销售平台建设基础

网络销售与企业信息化有着极为密切的关系。作为我国信息化战略的重要组成部分，网络销售一直得到了国家的大力支持和行业的积极推动。企业信息化是网络销售的基础；网络销售是企业信息化的历史产物。企业信息化进程孕育了网络销售，推动了网络销售的发展；而网络销售的发展又促进了企业信息化的深入进行和深层次开发。没有企业信息化，社会对网络销售不可能有强烈的追求，置身于网络销售中，人们才能感受到企业信息化的重大意义。在网络和信息化社会中，网络销售以其显著的信息优势为企业奠定了激烈竞争中的生存之源和立足之本。这些信息优势主要取决于企业的信息化程度，决定着网络销售信息优势的创造与发挥。因此，现代企业的自动化、信息化与网络销售活动必须融合在一起。

三、网络销售平台主要实现功能

(1)利用网络销售平台，宣传企业形象。

(2)通过会员注册等方式收集直接客户和终端客户信息，采用推送手段促销。

(3)提升客户和我们销售环节的交互能力，改变现有的信息传递模式。

(4)支持家具商和厨具商直接在网上对我们产品的下单并支付，实现真正的网络销售，尤其是零散客户的网上下单并电子支付业务。

(5)增加终端客户使用我们的直接客户的产品的采购心得，增加终端客户的粘合度，推动直接客户的客户忠诚度，促进潜在直接客户的购买欲望，逐渐成为环保家具和厨具采购交流网站。

(6)支持订单形成后订单审核环节的流程化处理，并可灵活修订审核发货流程。

四、网络销售平台工作流程

系统整体流程：

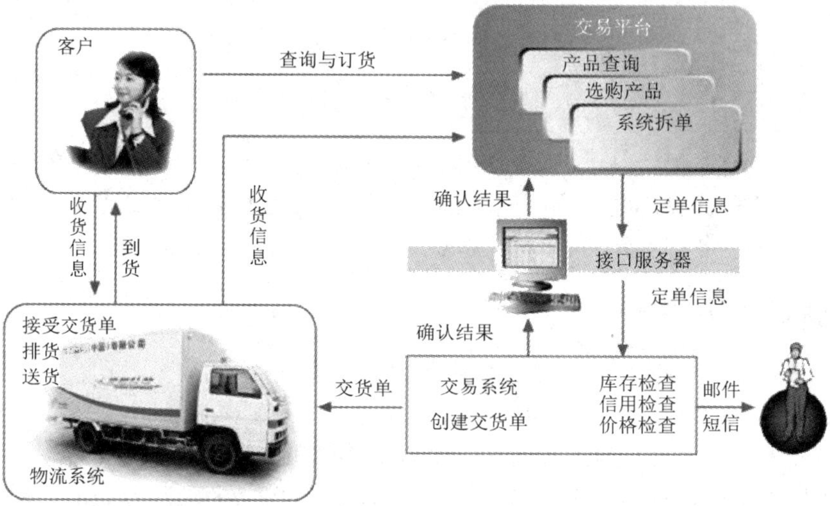

网络销售平台是一套企业级的 B2B 网上综合分销解决方案，实现公司与下游分销商、客户和其他销售途径通过网络有机结合。并形成了对客户市场活动的有机支持。

通过网络销售平台，客户从网上下订单，系统执行信用、价格、库存等检查，以及货物出库等，在这一系列过程中，客户可以及时获得交易相关的各种信息，如价格信息、库存信息、跟踪查询订单状态，发货、已发货或已收货等物流信息；并可随时查询自己的信用额度、应收账款、待开发票订单金额、可用信用额度、逾期金额、资金使用率，资金往来对账表等，从而提高各方资金使用效率及风险控制能力。这样，不但订单处理速度提高，而且由于实时交易数据可以立刻反馈在系统中，后续的商务操作也明显简化。商务人员可以随时从网上查询到所需要的各种交易数据和配送等信息，极大地简化了交易的流程，使企业销售人员从大量的程序性和重复性劳动中解放出来，使其将这部分原本被占用的时间应用到其他的工作中。从而，有效降低销售成本，提高管理效率和客户满意度。

通过网络销售平台系统，将分散的客户、销售商、代理商等信息整合在一个系统中，使得企业能及时掌握市场动态，并做出快速响应。它也促使企业经营管理理念从“以产品为中心”向“以客户为中心”转移，为客户提供真正个性化的服务。

五、平台主要技术要求

(1)支持跨平台的系统技术架构和对其他中间件的兼容性更良好。推荐使用的业务架构为 Struts2 + dbcp + MSSQL，在设计网络销售系统的时候考虑到多平台，使该系统与现有的硬软件环境有良好的兼容性，使维护系统方便，降低平台移植维护成本，同时兼顾与其他中间件产品的兼容性。

(2)使用 Struts2 + dbcp MVC 系统构建模式，降低开发技术难度和开发质量风险。计划将整体网页架构细分为视图逻辑、业务逻辑和数据访问三层，对使用浏览器的客户端采用MVC的设计模式，从而使系统的应用实施更加灵活、更加容易维护。而Struts2框架提供了视图层和控制层的MVC实现。可以更方便地控制客户的应用请求行为。应用程序通过Struts2的Controller来控制程序请求，提供动态URL跳转。同时使用dbcp连接池可以使后台访问数据库更加稳定可靠。MVC模式可以使网站对单元测试的支持更加出色，在团队开发模式下表现得更加出众。

(3)系统支持流行的常见浏览器，适应不同客户群体的使用习惯。无论是在DIV + CSS布局上，还是在Javascript与JQuery结合上，都会充分考虑到兼容现在所有主流浏览器(包括绝大部分版本)，并在开发过程中进行详细的浏览器兼容性测试，以使不同使用习惯的用户群能够正确统一的显示。通过使用针对不同浏览器的CSS Hack、兼容的Javascript语句，通用的Jquery Plugin来达到兼容现有主流浏览器的目的。我们将会测试的浏览器有Interne-tExplorer (IE6. 0/IE7. 0/IE8. 0)和基于IE Tridend核心的浏览器(例如Maxthon、The World等)、基于Geckos核心的Firefox浏览器、基于WebKit核心的Safari、Chrome浏览器和基于Presto核心的Opera浏览器。

(4)确保访问速度，优化服务器性能。对系统的产品列表与新闻公告页等大访问量的页面使用现在大型门户网站应用比较广泛的网页静态生成技术。网页静态生成省掉了服务器处理时间与调用数据库的时间，访问速度快，大大降低了服务器的压力，提升服务器的性能与稳定性。同时生成静态路径利用搜索引擎的抓取和收录，同时，静态页面从理论上讲是没有攻击漏洞的，也保障了服务器的安全。

(5)充分考虑网站推广的需要，因为一定需要网站推广方式提升网站客户访问量。在使用静态生成方案后会有利于网站搜索引擎推广，因为在搜索引擎排名中静态页面的排名权重要高于动态路径的页面。而搜索引擎也会优先检索静态的html页面。对网页做好SEO (Search Engine Optimization)，即搜索引擎优化。我们会通过关键词设置、站点设计、站点的内部链接、导出链接等方式来进行相关的优化，同时通过设置适当的友情链接方式来提高网站的PR值，以提高搜索引擎排名，从而提高网站访问量，最终提升网站的销售能力与宣传能力。

(6)灵活的网站风格变换，降低审美疲劳。通过精心设计，美观大方的页面可以令用户以一种非常愉悦的心情浏览网页，同时我们会在网页中应用Ajax，同时结合JQueryPlugin，例如FacyBox，TableShouter等，使网站显示富有动感，能够更加直观的展示产品。同时增加访客的浏览兴趣，同时在界面上会使网站更加专业美观，无形中就提升品牌形象。

(7)为系统发展预留接口和解决方案，平台切换灵活。使用更加弹性的，基于DZNT的模块化式的开发架构，使每个功能与展示都作为DZNT的一个模块出现。而模块之间都相互独立又有机结合，使各个功能模块之间达到一种低耦合高内聚的状态。单一模块开发与维护都相对容易，且某一模块出现问题的时候几乎不会影响其他模块。同时又可以根据需要添加新模块，维护简便。

总　结

在充分利用本企业的技术优势和管理优势的基础上，建立网络销售平台，可使公司的管理和生产水平上升到一个新台阶，快速和国际接轨，整合企业物流、资金流和信息流，提升企业科学决策能力，而且适应国家信息化发展战略思路，可以为社会提供丰富的信息资源。

平顶山市森林生态系统服务功能评价初探

周君璞[1]　郑小贤[1]　高　祥[2]　徐　光[2]

（1. 北京林业大学省部共建森林培育与保护教育部重点实验室，北京，100083；
2. 吉林省汪清林业局，吉林汪清，133200）

摘要：森林生态系统服务功能评价是为了评价特定区域内的森林生态系统的各种直接或间接服务功能的经济价值。本研究的目的是评估平顶山市森林生态系统服务功能的价值，为平顶山市合理规划森林资源与利用森林的生态效益提供依据。本研究采用价值量评估法，把森林生态服务功能的价值分为直接经济价值和间接经济价值，根据《森林生态系统服务功能评估规范》，对平顶山市森林的生态系统服务功能进行评估。结果表明：平顶山市森林生态系统服务功能总价值为 1007045. 01 万元/a，其中直接经济价值为 56545 万元/a，占总服务功能价值的 5. 61%；在间接经济价值中，以涵养水源功能价值所占比例最大，为 45. 15%；固碳释氧功能占总价值的比例为 36. 41%；净化大气环境功能价值占 5. 40%；固土保肥功能价值占 7. 43%。

关键词：平顶山市；森林生态系统；生态服务功能；价值；评估

Preliminary discussion of assessment of the forest ecosystem services in Pingdingshan City

ZHOU Jun-pu　ZHENG Xiao-xian

(The key Laboratory for Silviculture and Conservation of Ministry of Education,
Beijing Forestry University, Beijing, 100083)

Abstract: The assessment of the forest ecosystem services is to evaluate the direct or indirect value of the forest ecosystem service in certain areas. The purpose of this research is to evaluate the value of the forest ecosystem service in Pingdingshan city, To provide the basis for the reasonable planning for the urban forest resources and the utilization of the ecological benefits of forest. In this assessment, we use the value evaluation method, The value of the forest ecosystem service is divided into direct economic value and indirect economic value. Based on the frame of the《Specifications for assessment of forest ecosystem services in China》, the value of the forest ecosystem service in

基金项目：林业公益性行业科研专项(20100400320)。

作者简介：周君璞(1987～)，男，河南周口人，在读硕士，研究方向为森林可持续经营。
E-mail：zhoujunpu0520@163. com

通讯作者：郑小贤(1956～)，男，上海人，教授，研究方向为森林可持续经营。E-mail：zheng8355@bjfu. edu. cn

Pingdingshan city were assessed. The results show that: The total value of the forest ecosystem service in Pingdingshan city is 10070. 4501 million yuan. One of direct value accounts for 5. 61%, about 565. 45 million yuan; About the indirect value, The largest part is the economic value of water conservation function, counting for 45. 15% of the total value; fixing carbon and releasing oxygen service value accounts for 36. 41%; Purify environment function takes of the total value of 5. 40%; The economic value of the function of keeping the soil accounts for 7. 43%.

Key words: Pingdingshan City; Forest ecosystem; Ecosystem service; value; assessment

生态系统功能是生态系统结构的外在表现，是生态系统所固有的本质属性。生态系统服务功能又称生态服务，是建立在生态系统功能基础上，人类能够从中获益的生态系统功能[1]。森林生态系统作为地球上结构最复杂、功能最多和最稳定的陆地生态系统，在生态环境维持和改善方面起着不可替代的重要作用[2]。生态服务功能是指自然生态系统及其所属物种形成与维持的人类赖以生存的条件和过程，它支撑和维护了地球的生命支持系统、生命物质的地化循环与水文循环、生物多样性、大气化学成分的平衡与稳定等。随着工业文明的发展和全球变化的加剧，森林的保持水土、涵养水源、固碳释氧、净化空气、美化环境等生态服务功能日益引起人们的重视。科学、量化、客观地评价森林的生态服务功能，对加深人们的环境意识，促进和加强林业建设在国民经济中的主导地位，提高森林经营管理水平，加快将环境纳入国民经济核算体系及正确处理社会经济发展与生态环境保护之间的关系等具有重要的现实意义[3]。

1 研究区概况

1.1 自然地理

平顶山位于河南省中南部，地跨 111°14′~113°45′E, 33°08′~34°20′N 之间，属于温暖带大陆性季风气候，春季气温回升快，少雨多风；夏季高温多雨，降水量集中且不稳定，年际变化大；秋季风高地燥，昼夜温差大；冬季雨雪偏少，干冷多风。地貌类型多，山脉、丘陵、平源、河谷、盆地齐全。年平均气温在 15. 2 ~ 15. 8℃，年均降水量 612 ~ 1287mm，十分有利于植物生长。平顶山市共有 10 个土壤类型：黄棕壤、棕壤、褐土、潮土、砂姜黑土、紫色土、红黏土、水稻土、粗骨土和石质土。其中，黄棕壤、棕壤和褐土属地带性土壤、黄棕壤与褐土大致以沙河为界，沙河以南为黄棕壤，沙河以北为褐土；棕壤只在鲁山县和汝州市两域海拔 800m 以上的山区中有小面积分布。

1.2 森林资源

根据平顶山 2009 年森林资源二类调查数据，全市林业用地总面积 242952. 66 hm^2，由原始次生林和人工林两部分组成。原始次生林林区，集中在石人山一带。人工林多分布在西部山区和丘陵地带。全市有林地面积 194841. 75hm^2，占林业用地面积的 80. 2%，疏林地面积 2444. 38hm^2、灌木林地面积 4179. 32 hm^2、未成林造林地面积 8391. 33 hm^2、无林地面积 325. 89 hm^2、宜林地面积 31989. 73hm^2、苗圃地 742. 10hm^2。活立木蓄积量 873 万 m^3，其中森林蓄积量 698 万 m^3、疏林蓄积量 1. 6 万 m^3、四旁树蓄积量 173 万 m^3、散生木蓄积量 0. 1 万 m^3。森林中各林种蓄积为防护林 470. 6 万 m^3、特用林 4. 5 万 m^3、用材林 224. 2 万 m^3。森林中各优势树种蓄积为杨树 180. 5 万 m^3、栎类 351. 1 万 m^3、刺槐 25. 5 万 m^3、硬阔叶林 9. 5

万 m^3、软阔叶林 7.7 万 m^3、混交林 15.5 万 m^3、毛竹林 869.5 万根。全市森林覆盖率 24.98%。目前，该市建成区绿化覆盖面积 1638.5 hm^2，园林绿地总面积达到 1484.8hm^2，其中公共绿地 554.86hm^2。城市三绿指标分别为：绿化覆盖率 27.49%，建成区绿地率 24.91%，人均公共绿地 6.22m^2。现有国家级自然保护区 1 处，国家级森林公园 2 处，省级森林公园 3 处，省级湿地公园 1 处。

2 森林生态服务功能界定

森林生态服务功能指森林生态系统和其生态过程所形成、所维持人类赖以生存的自然生态环境条件与效用[4]。森林生态系统为人类提供食物、药品等各种生产生活原料，支撑与维持地球生命支持系统，维持生物物种与遗传多样性，维持大气的平衡与稳定，净化环境的作用，即是其生态服务功能[5~6]。长期以来对生态系统服务的评价方法主要有两类，一类是物质量评价法，另一类是价值量评价法，根据价值量的体现形式，可以把森林生态系统服务功能的价值分为直接经济价值和间接经济价值[7]。其中直接经济价值指产品及加工品年净价值，主要是指生态系统产品所产生的价值，它包括食品，医药及其他工农业生产原料，景观娱乐等带来的直接价值[8]；森林生态系统的间接经济价值主要体现在森林的生态服务功能方面，也就是森林的生态效益，间接经济价值包括很多方面，本研究根据平顶山市的实地情况和研究的需要主要从以下四个主要方面来评估森林生态系统服务功能的间接经济价值，即：①固碳释氧的价值；②净化大气环境的价值；③保育土壤的价值；④涵养水源的价值。本研究首先评估森林生态系统的直接经济价值，然后以 2008 年国家林业局发布的中华人民共和国林业行业标准——《森林生态系统服务功能评估规范》(LY/T1721—2008)为依据，来评估其间接经济价值，即上述森林的四项生态服务功能价值。

3 采用的数据及来源

本研究进行生态服务功能评估时所采用的数据来源如下：

(1)2009 年《平顶山市统计年鉴》。

(2)平顶山市 2009 年的森林资源二类调查数据。

(3)国家及平顶山市权威部门发布的公共数据。

(4)2008 年国家林业局发布的中华人民共和国林业行业标准——《森林生态系统服务功能评估规范》(LY/T1721—2008)。

(5)相关研究成果资料及公开发表的文献资料[9]。

4 评价指标

本研究采用的评价指标包括：直接经济价值，即林产品及加工品价值；间接经济价值即：固碳释氧、净化大气环境、保育土壤、涵养水源等四项功能。具体为固碳、释放氧气、吸收 SO_2、提供负离子、滞尘、减弱噪音、固土、保肥、调节水量等指标[4]。

5 评估方法

5.1 森林直接经济价值

主要包括林产品价值、种植业生产价值、草地提供的畜牧产品和药用植物、水域提供的水产品等。其经济价值均采用市场价值法来估算：

$$FP = \sum S_i \cdot V_i \cdot P_i \tag{1}$$

式中，FP 为区域森林生态系统木材或果品价值；S_i 为第 i 类林分类型或果品的分布面积；V_i 为第 i 类林分单位面积的净生长量或产量；P_i 为第 i 类林分的木材或果品价值[7]。

5.2 间接经济价值

5.2.1 固碳释氧价值

固碳释氧功能是指森林生态系统通过生物量碳库、枯落物碳库、土壤有机碳库和动物碳库固定碳素，并通过光合作用制造氧气的功能。森林生态系统是地球陆地生态系统的主体，是陆地碳的主要储存库。本文通过固碳和释氧两个指标对森林固碳释氧功能进行评估[9]。

固碳价值：森林植被和土壤固碳价值的计算公式为：

$$U_{碳} = AC_{碳}(0.4445B_{年} + F_{土壤碳}) \tag{2}$$

式中：$U_{碳}$为森林植被年固碳价值(元/a)；A 为森林面积(hm^2)；$C_{碳}$为固碳价格(元/t)；0.4445 为 1.63(林木每形成 1t 干物质，需吸收 1.63 t 二氧化碳)和 27.27%（二氧化碳的含碳率)的乘积；$B_{年}$为森林的年净生产力[$t/(hm^2 \cdot a)$]；$F_{土壤碳}$为森林土壤单位面积年固碳量[$t/(hm^2 \cdot a)$][10]。

释氧价值：森林植被每年释氧价值的计算公式为：

$$U_{氧} = 1.19C_{氧}AB_{年} \tag{3}$$

式中：$U_{氧}$为森林植被的年释氧价值(元/a)；$C_{氧}$为氧气价格(元/t)；A 为森林面积(hm^2)；$B_{年}$为森林的年净生产力[$t/(hm^2 \cdot a)$]；1.19 为林木每形成 1t 干物质，要释放 1.19t 氧气。

固碳价格和释氧价格采用《森林生态系统服务功能评估规范》推荐的价格，分别为 1200 元/t 和 1000 元/t[10]。

5.2.2 净化大气环境价值

5.2.2.1 吸收 SO_2 的价值

根据《森林生态系统服务功能评估规范》(LY/T1721—2008)。吸收二氧化硫价值计算公式为：

$$U_{二氧化硫} = K_{二氧化硫}Q_{二氧化硫}A \tag{4}$$

式中：$U_{二氧化硫}$为森林植被每年吸收二氧化硫价值(元/a)；$K_{二氧化硫}$为治理二氧化硫污染的费用(元/kg)；$Q_{二氧化硫}$为单位面积森林每年吸收二氧化硫量[$kg/(hm^2 \cdot a)$]；A 为森林面积(hm^2)。

治理二氧化硫污染的费用采用《森林生态系统服务功能评估规范》推荐的价格，即 $K_{二氧化硫} = 1.20$ 元/kg[10]。

5.2.2.2 提供负离子的价值

提供负离子价值计算公式为：

$$U_{负离子} = 5.256 \times 10^{15} \times AHK_{负离子}(Q_{负离子} - 600) / L \tag{5}$$

式中：$U_{负离子}$为森林植被每年提供的负离子价值(元/a)；$K_{负离子}$为负离子的生产费用(元/hm^2)；$Q_{负离子}$为森林中的负离子密度(个/cm^3)；A 为森林面积(hm^2)；H 为林分高度(m)；L 为负离子能存留时间(min)。其中负离子的生产费用为 5.8185×10^{-18}元/个[4]。

5.2.2.3　森林滞尘价值

滞尘价值计算公式为：

$$U_{滞尘} = K_{滞尘} Q_{滞尘} A \tag{6}$$

式中：$U_{滞尘}$为森林植被每年阻滞降尘价值(元/a)；$K_{滞尘}$为清理降尘费用(元/kg)；$Q_{滞尘}$为单位面积森林植被的年滞尘量[kg/(hm^2·a)]；A 为森林面积(hm^2)。[10]其中 $K_{滞尘}$为0.15元/kg。

5.2.2.4　减弱噪音的价值

森林减弱噪音量可以由森林生态站直接测定，减弱噪音的经济价值可的计算公式为：

$$U_{噪音} = K_{噪音} A_{噪音} \tag{7}$$

式中：$U_{噪音}$为森林年减弱噪音价值(元/a)；$K_{噪音}$为减弱噪音费用(元/km)；$A_{噪音}$为森林面积折合为隔音墙的公里数(km)。其中减弱噪音费用 $K_{噪音}$为400000元/km[4]。

5.2.3　保育土壤的价值

森林植被的存在，基本可以消除雨滴对表层土的侵蚀，可划分为森林固土和森林保肥2个指标对保育土壤功能进行评估。

森林固土价值：采用每年减少淤积泥沙和土壤损失进行计算，公式为：

$$U_{固土} = AC_{库}(X_2 - X_1)/\rho \tag{8}$$

式中：$U_{固土}$为森林的年固土价值(元/a)；A 为森林面积(hm^2)；$C_{库}$为水库库容造价；X_2为无林地的土壤年侵蚀模数[t/(hm^2·a)]；X_1为各林地土壤侵蚀模数[t/(hm^2·a)]；ρ 为泥沙的平均密度(t/m^3)。

森林保肥价值：计算公式为：

$$U_{肥} = A(X_2 - X_1)(NC_1/R_1 + PC_1/R_2 + KC_2/R_3 + MC_3)/100 \tag{9}$$

式中：$U_{肥}$为森林年保肥价值(元/a)；A 为森林面积(hm^2)；N、P、K 分别为土壤中氮、磷、钾的平均质量分数(%)；R_1和 R_2分别为磷酸二铵的含氮率(%)和含磷率(%)；R_3为氯化钾的含钾率(%)；C_1、C_2和 C_3分别为磷酸二铵、氯化钾及有机质的平均价格(元/t)；M 为土壤中有机质的平均质量分数(%)。磷酸二铵、氯化钾及有机质的价格采用《森林生态系统服务功能评估规范》推荐的价格，分别为2400、2200元/t和320元/t。

5.2.4　涵养水源的价值

涵养水源功能是指森林对大气降水的调节作用，本研究主要以森林的调节水量的功能为主要指标来评估。调节水量价值：根据水库工程的蓄水成本来确定，其计算公式为：

$$U_{调} = 10C_{库}A(P - E) \tag{10}$$

式中：$U_{调}$为森林的年调节水量价值(元/a)；C 库为水库的库容造价(元/m^3)；A 为森林面积(hm^2)；P 为林外年降水量(mm/a)；E 为森林年蒸散量(mm/a)。单位库容造价采用《森林生态系统服务功能评估规范》推荐的6.1107元/t[10]。

6　评估结果

6.1　森林直接经济价值

森林生态系统的有机物生产主要体现在木材产量上，对于一般的森林，其木材生产是最主要的直接价值。根据2009年《平顶山统计年鉴》和平顶山市2009年的森林资源二类调查数据，运用公式(1)可知：平顶山市森林生态系统服务功能的直接经济价值为56545万元/a。

6.2 间接经济价值

6.2.1 固碳释氧价值

其中固碳价值由公式(2)可知：代入平顶山市森林年净生产力和森林面积的数据，即可算出平顶山市森林年固碳价值为126300万元/a。释放氧气价值同理由公式(3)可计算出平顶山市森林年释放氧气的价值为240400万元/a。

6.2.2 净化大气环境价值

Ⅰ吸收SO_2的价值由公式(4)计算，平顶山市境内植被主要属于暖温带落叶阔叶林，阔叶林对SO_2的吸收能力值为88.65kg/(hm^2·a)[11]，代入森林面积A和治理二氧化硫污染的费用$K_{二氧化硫}$的数值可以计算出平顶山市森林生态系统吸收SO_2功能的总价值为340.15万元/a。Ⅱ提供负离子的价值由公式(5)计算，代入数据后可以算出顶山市森林生态系统年提供负离子的经济价值为24559.81万元/a。Ⅲ 滞尘价值由公式(6)计算，其中阔叶林的滞尘能力为10.10t/hm^2/a，可以算出平顶山市森林年滞尘功能价值为10980.19万元/a。Ⅳ减弱噪音的价值评估由公式(7)计算，可知平顶山市森林生态系统年减弱噪音价值为18419.86万元/a。

6.2.3 保育土壤的价值

其中固土价值由公式(8)可算出平顶山市森林年固土总价值为67865.84万元/a。

保肥功能价值评估由公式(9)计算，可算出平顶山市森林生态系统肥力保持的总价值为6934.16万元/a。

6.2.4 涵养水源的价值

由公式(10)可计算出平顶山市森林涵养水源的价值为454700万元/a。

7 结果分析与讨论

通过上述评估计算过程，可以得出平顶山市森林生态系统服务功能评价的结果汇总见表1。

表1 平顶山市森林生态服务功能价值

功能类型	总价值(万元/a)	价值构成(%)
直接产品	56545	5.61
固定CO_2	126300	12.54
释放O_2	240400	23.87
吸收SO_2	340.15	0.04
滞尘	10980.19	1.09
提供负离子	24559.81	2.44
减弱噪音	18419.86	1.83
固土	67865.84	6.74
保肥	6934.16	0.69
涵养水源	454700	45.15
总计	1007045.01	100

评估结果表明，平顶山市森林生态系统服务功能总价值为1007045.01万元/a。各项服务功能所占比例如图1，平顶山市森林生态系统服务功能的直接经济价值为56545万元/a，占总服务功能价值的5.61%；在间接经济价值中，以涵养水源功能价值所占比例最大，为45.15%，价值量为454700万元/a；固碳释氧功能占总价值的比例为36.41%；净化大气环境功能价值占5.40%；固土保肥功能价值占7.43%。

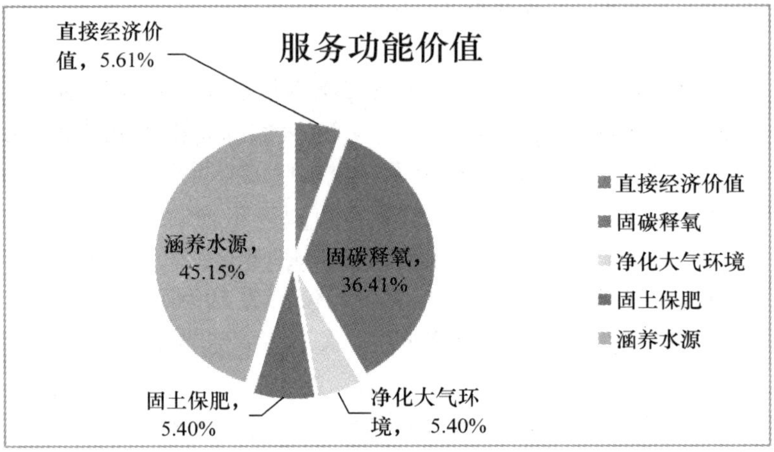

图1

综上所述，平顶山市森林生态系统服务功能有很大的经济价值，并且其间接经济价值要远远大于其直接经济价值。可以看出森林在生态服务方面具有巨大的经济潜力，森林生态系统服务功能评估是现阶段国内外研究主要热点之一，其评估方法和评估指标体系的统一是必要的，也是大势所趋[10]。本研究所采用的评估指标和方法来自于《森林生态系统服务功能评估规范》，并选用部分本标准推荐的国家权威部门发布的社会公共数据，因此本研究的评估结果具有一定的准确性和规范性，能比较真实地反映平顶山市森林生态系统服务功能的状况。森林生态系统服务功能所包含内容十分广泛，由于受到资料及研究方法的局限，本研究并未对平顶山市森林的净化水质功能、营养物质积累功能、森林防护及森林游憩等指标进行评价。因此评估方法和评估指标体系的进一步完善将是森林生态系统服务功能评估的一个重点。

参考文献

[1]李文华．生态系统服务功能价值评估的理论、方法与应用[M]．北京：中国人民大学出版社，2008.

[2]李景文．森林生态学[M]．北京：中国林业出版社，1982.

[3]田卓林，张华．大连市森林生态系统服务功能评估[J]．城市环境与城市生态，2009，22(5)：22～24.

[4]LY/T1721—2008. 森林生态系统服务功能评估规范[S].

[5]郭浩，王兵，马向前，等．中国油松林生态服务功能评估[J]．中国科学C辑，2008，38(6)：565～572.

[6]王兵，李少宁，郭浩．江西省森林生态系统服务功能及其价值评估研究[J]．江西科学，2007，25(5)：553～559.

[7]张华．城市森林生态系统服务功能价值评估初探[J]．环境保护科学，2009，35(5)：55～57

[8]欧阳志云，王如松，赵景柱．生态系统服务功能及其生态经济价值评价[J]．应用生态学报，1999，10(5)：635～640.

[9]温庆忠，魏雪峰，孔德昌，等．滇池流域森林生态服务功能价值评估[J]．云南大学学报(自然科学版)，2010，32(3)：365～372.

[10]徐成立，王雄宾，余新晓，等．北京山地森林生态服务功能评估[J]．东北林业大学学报，2010，38(7)：80～82.

[11]余新晓，鲁绍伟，靳芳，等．中国森林生态系统服务功能价值评估[J]．生态学报，2005，25(8)：2097～2100.

强强融合创新
——推进林业信息化的新理念

陈谋询
（北京林业大学）

摘要：从林业信息化发展需要出发，根据实施中的现实条件与基础，分析各有所长、各有所短的实际，提出实施强强融合创新理念，以推进林业信息化。

我国林业信息化进入了全面、快速发展的新时期。林业系统各层、各级、各领域和环节，都面临如何进行、特别是有用与有效推进信息化的问题：广大林业生产、管理、服务等部门，面临如何选择与应用信息技术，提升科学生产、管理、服务等水平问题；信息技术推广、开发部门，面临如何根据林业建设需要，技术与业务结合，实现自主创新，应用于实践的问题。一个共同的问题是：如何改变过去许多地方、许多时候和许多项目，或者技术与业务脱节、实用性差，或者为技术而技术，或者仅仅满足于手工系统计算机化等局面，实现信息技术与林业实际真正意义上的综合创新，产生新的理念、方法和技术，把林业信息化的初级阶段推向更新、更高的阶段。本文提出采取强强融合创新理念，以推动林业信息化。

1 林业信息化中“强、弱”理念

“强、弱”是一个问题的两个方面，它们都是一个相对的概念。由于林业信息化涉及各个单位的各个部门、领域和环节，有各自的运行规律与特点、方式与方法，以多种理论、方法和技术指导实践。在实施信息化过程中，需要林业业务与信息技术综合集成。从事生产、管理、服务等的业务单位及其组成部门与个人，从事信息技术的单位与个人，均在某一方面，具有自己的优势，是这方面的强者，其他方面可能是弱者。这就是“强”、“弱”的相对性，即任何单位、单位内的各部门和个人，对于林业信息化，没有全面、绝对的“强”，只有局部、相对的“强”。过去一个时期，把“强”绝对化了，一提信息技术应用，仅仅想到、依靠从事这方面研究、教学、设计单位，和相关专家、教授，轻视了具有实践经验、新技术应用的主体单位和个人，结果所开发的软件和系统，技术先进，但是可操作、实用性较差。

信息化中的“强”另一特性是：时效性。变化是林业建设、信息技术发展一个普遍规律，任何单位和个人，如果不能适应变化，不断地学习、探索，那么“强”会逐渐削弱，相反，如果能够与日俱进，那么“强”会不断增大。过去所开发的有些软件和系统，多停留林业建设传统的方式、方法上，所取得的结果，往往多有效率、少有效益。没有取得20世纪80年代科学工作者的预言：计算机的应用将引起业务各方面重大变革的结果。

信息化中的“强”又一个特性是：局限性。它主要指“强”的范围。“强”是在一定环境、条件下存在，有一定的空间范围。信息技术在一单项或者有些局部中的应用，一些单位、部门，和IT企业，通过学习与调研，均可以独立研究与实践。但是，它局限于单项或者局部应用。而当前信息化趋势向一体化、网络化、智能化、集成化、虚拟化方向发展，涉及多部门、多领域、多环节，需要多学科、多种理论、方法、技术集成，原来理念和方式、方法应以转变，赋予新的理念与发展模式。

2 强强融合创新——林业信息化整体协同提升的必由之路

我国林业信息化中，无论是基础实施信息化、生产工艺(包括生产、经营、科教等等领域)信息化，还是科学管理信息化等，都需要以新的方式、方法改造原模式，各层各级一个共同愿望是"创新"。在林业信息化中，没有全面、绝对"强"的条件下，可以采取的方针之一是：继承发展、融合创新。后者进一步具体化，可选择的是：强强融合创新。

强强融合创新，是将多种具有"强"势要素通过创造性的聚合，实现要素之间互补匹配，使它们的整体功能发生质的飞跃，形成独特的不可复制、不可超越的能力和竞争力，产生创新型成果，推动林业信息化进程。其中，创新是出发点与归宿，融合是手段，强强是对要素的选择。强强融合创新是整体的推进模式，在最近一个时期，需要通过各类的强强融合创新，促进林业系统：信息和知识意识全面提高，公众公平应用和享受信息技术，提高精神和物质水平；实现以'物'为中心向以'知识'为中心转变，以知识推动林业发展；改变林业高度分散、时空差异大、现代化程度差、稳定性和可控性低的弱点，为节省能源、提高资源利用率、提高物流速度和效率、提高林业产业的整体性、系统性和协调性；推进与实现集约化、自动化和智能化，改造传统林业生产方式，改进生产工艺过程，促进粗放经营向集约经营转变，实现在精确时间空间条件下，实现精细的生产、管理和服务；推动网络化管理，加快实现管理科学化，促进林业走向社会，社会参与林业；应用和发展林业信息技术，增加相应产值，逐步形成新的林业产业，调整林业产业结构，实现林业跨越式发展。

强强融合创新形式多种多样。最基础、最根本的是业务强强融合创新，也是主流方式。因为所有信息化项目，都关系到林业生产、管理、服务等方面业务现在与将来，关系到计算机、网络、时空数据处理等业务现状与发展，这些具有业务优势的要素，组成整体，通过的融合创新，才能不断产生新的理论、技术和方法。从这个基础出发，为了一些环节、领域需要和可能。可以扩大为环节或者领域的强强融合创新。在组织形式上，信息化需要各类业务、信息工作者完成，最广泛是组成团队进行强强融合创新，各类人为了同一信息化的研究、实践、推广、教学、服务等，协同共关。由此，不同单位和单位内各个部门，都有自己的优势，这就选择合作伙伴与合作方式，奠定了基础，产生了部门强强融合创新、单位强强融合创新等等。

分析过去信息技术在林业中应用纵横，与当前的一些信息化项目经验教训，可以发现凡是在实施中，信息技术、林业生产、管理业务结合比较好的系统、软件，先进性、可操作性、实用性都比较好。相反，或不被接受，或不能推广，或年年开发、年年修改，不能应用。国家林业局、湖南林业厅等行政单位，电子政务中的相应系统，基本覆盖日常文书事务处理，得到广泛使用，因为这些系统开发、使用中，用户与开发单位紧密沟通，使系统实用、方便；湖南、辽宁等省运行的森林资源监测、林地管理、网络森林培育、林木网上医院等，也是有关林业业务和信息技术业务有机的结合，取得较好结果。浙江农林大学与龙泉市林业业务部门，联合开发森林资源监管系统，13个子系统，完成森林资源管理、木材采伐、运输、加工等全程适时监管，林业局局长介绍说：软件开发只提供3万元资金，因为技术开发主持人——农林大学信息学院院长提出的理念是：林业局提供林业生产、管理业务分析，学校提供技术支持，两者互补互利互赢。这一方式不仅说系统全面、实用、简便，而且系统已在省内外推广应用。笔者在20世纪80年代中，曾经参与计算机在林业中应用课题，在国内没有可鉴借的条件下，研建森林资源管理信息系统，内部组织了具有林学、经济、管理、数学、自动化、计算机等专业知识的老师、研究生参与，外部联合甘肃省林勘院、小陇山林业局的业务技术人员，开展研究。并内请林业系、林经系、森工系、计算中心等部门、外请中科院地理所、标准化所、林科院、规划院相关专家指导。这一方式的结果，不仅在国内首先提出了森林资源管理信息系统在林业中的地位、作用、整体框架，开发了包括利用野外数据采集器，可以运用常用的森林资源调查方法，收集数据，室内点对点通讯，自动建立数据库；创建了包括资源、植被数据库、方法库、模型库等数据库群；具有分析、评价、数据更新、预测、决策和林木资产管理功能的软件系统。而且，通过研究与实践，学校、林业局和林勘院都培养了一批技术人才。这一项目在当时起到了示范作用，而今，由于计算机硬件和系统软件的发展，这个成果不能直接推广，但是数据更新、预测、决策等子系统思路和计算方法，仍可借鉴。例如数据更新、预测系统利用系统的数据与方法，多种途径与方法的自动建模、自动或者自选模型、时间与空间上的自定范围和项目、各林分因子变化的匹配以及误差分析等方面的计算方法与功能，按现标准衡量，也不失其先进性。与以上情况相反，也可以发现，现在一些地方或者项目，受思维方式、管理机制、运行环境和利益驱动等多种影响，实质性的联合或者综合开发在减少，单兵团甚至单兵作战，有所发展，影响着信息化进程。

就其要素之间的紧密程度而言，融合是比结合、联合等更高一层次的互补方式，互联网消除了时间与空间距离，可以每时每刻进行零距离的沟通，使各种融合成为可能。

3 推动强强融合创新基础

实施各种强强融合创新需要有一定基础与条件，需要在思想、机制、技术等方面进行准备强强融合创，在当前，在理念上，首要解决的是共同认识、共同意愿、共同责权利、共同行动等基础准备。

共同认识，是强强融合创新的思想基础。共同认清林业信息化是为林业发展进行不断创新，从这一某种意义上分析，实质是建设“创新型林业”的过程，当前大趋势是“开放、集成、高效”，主要方向是“一体化、网络化、智能化、集成化、虚拟化、精细化”。林业信息化任重而道远，需要多学科、多专业的知识与实践经验。林业系统各组成单位和个人，各有所长、各有所短，可以选择的重要途径是强强融合创新，促使林业信息化全面、协调、可持续发展。

共同意愿，是强强融合创新的组织基础。在强强融合创新实施中，具体选择合作要素时最重要的是共同的意愿，包括共同的目标、共同的合作意向、共同的相互了解与选择，以及在这些基础上，共同的优势互补匹配方式、方法、共同的协同与协调等等，只有这样强强才能真正意义上的融合，从而实现真正的创新。

共同责权利，是强强融合创新保证。任何人只要进入相关的林业信息化团队伍，应该承担起融合创新的责任，并享受有知情、参与、语言、监督以及共享成果等权利。任何人特别是主持人，应该学会纳万水千山之意，容千语万言之情的胸怀，保证融合创新顺利实施。

共同行动，是实施强强融合创新的必需条件，决策层与上层管理部门应该逐渐构建适应强强融合创新需要的环境和平台，逐步建立相应的运行机制；广大业务单位与信息技术单位或者部门，着力于总结、宣传自身的优势，了解和分析相关单位或者部门的优势；对于每位致力于信息化事业的个人，应该清楚自己所“强”、所“弱”，建立良好的心智，以吸取人之所长，实现互补。

总之，当今的林业信息化需要新的理念、新的模式，强强融合创新是可选模式之一，不仿深入研究，进一步探索，逐步推广实施。

人工红松林镶嵌自然带天然更新阔叶树营造技术

倪柏春[1] 倪　薇[2] 郑在军[3] 田德君[3] 于春友[3] 刘立华[3]

（1. 伊春林业科学院，黑龙江伊春，153000；2. 中科院沈阳生态所，辽宁沈阳，110016；3. 金山屯林业局，黑龙江金山屯，153026）

摘要：在中共中央、国务院作出《关于加快林业发展的决定》后，国家林业局又作出了《加强林业科技成果推广的决定》。本文是在承担“中央财政林业科技推广示范资金跨区域重点推广示范项目——红松次生林高效经营与人工林丰产综合技术推广示范”过程中，应用推广“人工红松林镶嵌自然带天然更新阔叶树营造技术”的阶段性成果，现总结如下，以供同行参考。

关键词：人工红松林；镶嵌自然带；天然更新；阔叶树

Natural Regeneration hardwood construction techniques of artificial Korean pine forest mosaic natural Zones

NI Bai-chun[1] NI Wei[2] ZHENG Zai-jun[3] TIAN De-jun[3] YU Chun-you[3] LIU Li-hua[3]

(1 Yichun Academy of Forestry sciences, Yichun Heilongjiang Province, 153000; 2. Institute of applied ecology. Chinese academy of sciences Shenyang Liaoning Province, 110016; 3. Jinshantun Forestry, Jinshantun Heilongjaing Province, 153026)

Abstract: After the Central Committee made the “decision” of Accelerate the development of forestry, State Forestry Administration has made “to strengthen the decision of forestry science and Technology Achievements”。I am in the process of research topics “Demonstration of central government funds to promote forestry science and technology focus of promotion of demonstration projects across regions—Efficient Management of the Korean pine secondary forest and High - yield plantations integrate Technology promotion demonstration”, Promote the application of Initial results by “Natural regeneration hardwood construction techniques of artificial Korean pine forest mosaic natural zones”, now be summarized as follows, reference for the peer.

Key words: artificial Korean pine forest; mosaic natural; zones; natura regeneration; hardwood

---

作者简介：倪柏春(1962 ~)，男，林学高级工程师，从事森林培育经营，黑龙江省伊春市伊春区临山路10号　邮编：153000　电话：13845877462

前　言

从上世纪后期开始，人们认识到环境质量对可持续发展的重要，因此，对保护环境，保护森林的呼声日趋高涨。森林的生态价值远远高于生产木材，充分发挥森林的生态效益，已成为今后造林和森林经营的主要目的。

以红松为主的阔叶红松混交林，是东北三省东部山地林区的顶极群落，是历经数百万年自然选择而形成的，其生态稳定，土壤肥沃，物种丰富，能量循环、水分循环功能高，具有很高的生产力和生态功能。当原始的阔叶红松林被采伐以后，如何恢复这里的森林，是当代林业工作者长期的、历史的任务。

1　技术指导原则

(1)充分利用现有的科学技术成果，开发阔叶红松林区的自然潜力，从造林设计开始，把理论与生产实践结合起来，培育高质量的针阔叶红松林，提高生态效益和林地生产力。

(2)充分利用本林区阔叶树种天然更新的优势，把天然更新潜力与人工更新造林结合起来，实现人工天然混合更新，培育人工天然混交林，为营造生态公益林，培育生态与用材兼容林，提高生态效益与经济效益，提供新的实用技术。

(3)充分利用好本林区育苗生产高标准的优势，在提高苗木质量的前提下，降低人工植苗株数，减少苗木和人力消耗，扩大更新造林成果，减少育林投资，实现少投入，多造林，造好林。

(4)提高林地早期的生产力，缩短利用周期，增加林地的早期收益。

(5)有利于实现人工林物种多样性，有利于林特产品繁衍，有利于森林可持续经营和林业可持续发展。

(6)选择适宜的造林地，为速生丰产打下坚实的基础。

2　造林设计

2.1　人工植苗

树种：红松(S_{2-2})、红皮云杉(S_{2-2})。

天然更新树种：阔叶树乡土种。

2.1.1　设计的理论依据

(1)黑龙江省东部林区的阔叶树，尤其是山杨、白桦、枫桦、柞树，有极强的天然更新能力。采伐迹地、火烧迹地、退耕地，在1~5年内阔叶树天然更新的幼苗幼树可达5000~10000株/hm^2。

(2)天然更新的杨桦树，初期生长快，成林易，是迹地森林更新的先锋树种，是保护红松，红皮云杉幼林生长的优良生境。

(3)天然更新杨桦林早期速生，20年左右的林分高可达12m，不仅可形成侧方庇护效应，发挥明显的生态功能，而且林分有较大立木蓄积。而红松和红皮云杉在1~10龄间生长缓慢，适度的上方庇护或侧方庇护有利于幼树生长和减轻自然灾害。

(4)红松和红皮云杉是我省东部林区两种人工更新主要树种，其生长速度、生态习性有许多相似之处，在天然林内多有伴生，人工混交造林，在伊春林区近年有所应用。

(5)天然更新阔叶树有很好的生态功能和经济意义，应当作目的树种与人工更新幼树同等对待，同样经营。

2.2 密度设计

2.2.1 理论依据

(1)黑龙江省东部林区的原始阔叶红松林组成，红松占4~6成并混有少量云冷杉等针叶树。

(2)按黑龙江省国有林区更新造林技术规程（2003）。如每公顷天然更新的乔木幼苗、幼树达1500株以上，再人工栽植红松、云杉等幼苗500~2000株，或500~800丛植生组，即达到人工天然混合更新标准。

2.2.2 密度设计

本项目的设计密度为：用林地的2/3面积，即每公顷6600m^2，人工植苗2500~3000株，其中红松1300~1500株，红皮云杉1200~1500株。平均株行距1.5m×1.8m~1.5m×1.5m。

2.3 配置方式

采取人工栽植红松和云杉镶嵌自然带，天然更新阔叶树形成针阔混交林方法。

2.3.1 配置图示

A. 镶嵌自然带6m，留待天然更新；人工植苗12m。

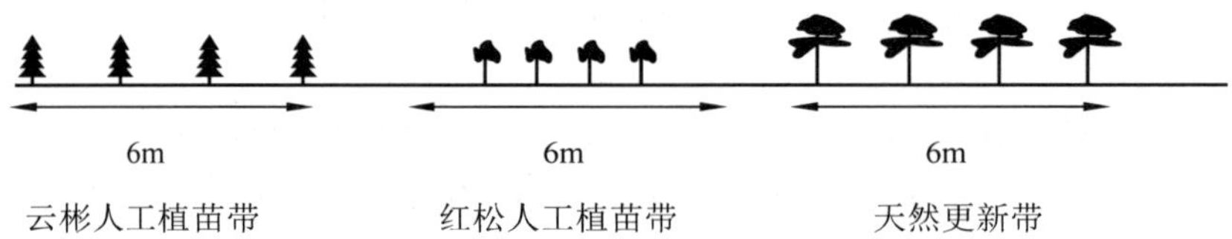

B镶嵌自然带10m，留待天然更新，人工植苗20m。

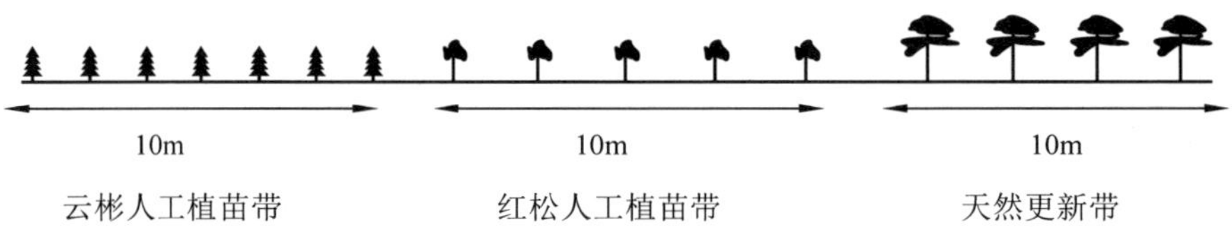

2.3.2 理论依据

(1)红松、红皮云杉1~10龄有较强的耐荫性，可在适度庇荫的杨桦柞等阔叶林冠下生长，而10年后，最迟14年以后需较多光照，尤其是阔叶林带的侧方庇护更为有利。

(2)方便操作，易于实施。尤其是幼林时的透光抚育，克服以往砍去上层阔叶树，大批砸伤下层红松和云杉的弊端。

2.4 整地造林

2.4.1 整 地

采取细致整地，造林前一年秋季带状或全部清理灌丛、杂草后进行整地。植苗带宽12m或20m，镶嵌自然带宽6m或10m。整地方式为穴状整地，规格为穴径50cm，深25cm，先清除草皮，打碎土块，拣出杂物。横山堆放林地清理物，顺山宽带造林。

2.4.2 造 林

造林采用二种密度，即人工植苗2500~3000株/km^2，平均株行距1.5m×1.8m ~1.5m×

1.5m。造林时选择壮苗栽植，保证成活率。

3 应用效果

3.1 人工与天然混合更新效果

3.1.1 红松、红皮云杉人工造林的效果

红松、红皮云杉镶嵌自然带内天然更新频率达74%，天然更新阔叶树株数占全部天更阔叶树的52.69%，不仅比例已超过人工更新，而且幼树生长十分繁茂，超过人工更新幼树，预先保留的天然更新带内，阔叶树过密，人工更新带内也有过多的阔叶树，应人工调节，保证人工更新幼树正常生长。

3.1.2 红松人工成林内天然更新效果

过去红松曾大密度造林，造林密度4400株/hm^2，20年以上的林分中红松只保存2000株/hm^2左右，而由于阔叶树的存在，林分总密度仍达到4000株/hm^2左右，多者达5800株/hm^2。

3.2 人工与天然混交林分生长量

人工与天然混交所形成的新一代阔叶红松林与人工纯林相比，其林分生长量是有差异的，不同比例的人天混交林对全林及红松径生长的绝对值相差甚微，但增长率影响较明显。就全林蓄积生长而言7红3阔人天混交林更接近于纯林，7红3阔的比例使全林和红松都有最大的胸径。

3.3 人天混交林的生态效益

3.3.1 不同比例的人工天然混交林对森林生态系统内部生态平衡的影响

一个生态系统内，物种越单纯，其生态越脆弱，功能越小，维持生态平衡所需投入的能量就越多。对于数百万年来一直与多种阔叶树伴生而形成稳定的生态群落的红松而言，更是如此。

(1)人天混阔叶红松林能有效抑制病虫害的发生：近年来，红松流脂溃疡病较为猖獗，尤其是红松人工纯林，主要危害15~30年生的活立木主干。在病部起松脂泡、流脂、扁干或细缢环截树干后导致整株死亡(病原菌为混杂芽盘菌 Tympanis Confusa Ny 1)。保留阔叶树，少栽红松，形成的人天混交林可有效地抑制此病发生。

(2)人天混形成的阔叶红松混交林对松梢象虫甲有很强的抑制功能，因而，对防止红松早期分叉，也有极好的作用。松梢象虫甲种群大小的变动与空气湿度、光照、温度有直接关系。阔叶树比重大，尤其是构成上层林冠后，减少下层光照。增大了空气湿度，降低了温度，从而抑制松梢象虫甲种群扩大，同时下木和灌木多的林分也能抑制它的种群扩大。

(3)人天混阔叶红松林对林地肥力的影响：落叶、阔叶树的丰富凋落物，以及较高的养分元素含量，有利于森林实现自养循环，从而也有利于保持和提高林地土壤肥力，使林木生长后期有较高的生产力。凋落物层及土壤非毛管孔隙，又有较高的水分涵养功能，发挥较大的生态效益。

据取样分析(伊春林科院土壤化验室)，与红松混交的阔叶树其落叶养分含量普遍也高于红松，以它们的平均值计，N是红松的1.39倍，P是1.85倍，K是1.51倍，Ca是3.03倍，Mg相当于红松的72%，而干物质含量比红松略多。

综上所述，红松人工纯林虽有较高的生长率，但生态脆弱，病虫灾害发病率高，土壤质

量降低，养分循环能力小。7 红 3 阔的人工天然混合更新的阔叶红松林生长率高，生态也较为稳定。是今后培育人天混阔叶红松林的合理模式。

3.3.2　人天混阔叶红松林的生态功能

不同类型的森林持水力。据研究资料分析，白桦、山杨、柞木、杂木和硬阔叶林等阔叶林及红松人工纯林持水能力有较大的差异，阔叶林为 584.67t/hm^2，红松人工纯林为 423.47t/hm^2，相差 161.20 t/hm^2(38.06%)。

红松人工纯林的持水量是天然阔叶次生林的 72%，二者差 161.20t/hm^2，主要原因是红松人工纯林土壤板结，土壤昆虫及小动物孔穴也少，土壤有效持水减少所致。只有引进天然更新阔叶树，保留林下灌丛等植被，形成针阔混交林才能解决这一不足。

3.4　营造人天混交阔叶红松林的经济效益

培育人天混交阔叶红松林，比红松人工纯林有较大的经济效益，其中直接效益是减少人工造林的成本；减少森林病虫防治经费；培育多树种多材种，适应未来市场需要。间接效益有提高林分持水力，水源涵养功能；增加 N、P、K、Ca 等养分元素回归量，保持土壤肥力，提高林地后期生产力；增加林下物种多样性，提高林地综合价值。

3.4.1　直接经济效益

(1)降低造林成本 1/3。

(2)减少病虫防治费 60%。

(3)培育多树种混交林　满足未来市场对木材多品种的需求。

(4)提高林地早期生产力，增加中间收益，25 年间伐，收回造林成本。

3.4.2　间接效益

(1)提高水源涵养能力。据上述计算，营造人天混阔叶红松林成林后，1000 万亩涵养水源比人工纯林多 1 亿 t。

(2)提供大量非木材产品。

(3)提高森林防火和抗虫害能力。

4　结　论

人工红松林镶嵌自然带天然更新阔叶树营造技术已较成熟，在林区营林生产中进行了大面积推广应用，取得了明显的生态效益、经济效益和社会效益。建议在我省东部林区推广应用，并逐步完善该技术，为提高我省造林质量，提高森工职工林业经营水平，增加职工及地方财政收入，提供科技支撑。

参考文献

[1]周玉新，唐罗忠日本企业的海外造林状况[J]. 世界林业研究，2005，18(4)：79～80.

[2] 张昌顺，李昆. 人工林养分循环研究现状与进展[J]世界林业研究，2005，18(5)h35～39.

[3] Reinhard Mosndlf，彭鸿，候琳. 中欧地区的森林培育及其启示[J]世界林业研究，2005，18(3)：70～72.

[4] 张昌顺，李昆. 人工林地力衰退与维护研究综述[J]世界林业研究，2005，18(1)：17～22.

[5] 陈东立，余新晓，廖邦洪. 中国森林生态系统水源涵养功能分析[J]世界林业研究，2005，18(1)：49～54.

三种枸杞快速繁殖技术研究

刘 思　蔡 超　安文娟

（吉林省林业勘察设计研究院，长春，130022）

摘要： 本文以枸杞、新疆枸杞、宁夏枸杞三种枸杞的种子为外植体，进行了组培快繁的研究，并筛选枸杞组织培养最佳外植体的方法、培养程序及培养基配方。结果表明，通过组织培养方法获得的外植体染菌率低，而水培方法获得的外植体染菌率很高，采用种子作为外植体比较适合；在初代培养中，枸杞最适合的培养基为 MS＋1.5 6BA＋0.2IBA，宁夏枸杞和新疆枸杞最适合的培养基为 MS＋2.5 6BA＋0.2IBA；继代培养三种枸杞最佳培养基均为 MS＋0.5 6BA＋1.0IBA；在壮苗培养中，三种枸杞最佳培养基均为 MS＋0.5 6BA＋0.1IBA；在生根培养中，培养基以 1/2MS＋0.1IBA 最好。在炼苗移栽过程中，基质以腐质土：蛭石：河沙＝1：1：1 对炼苗最好。

关键词： 枸杞；组织培养；繁殖

Study on rapid propagation techniques for three kinds of Lycium barbarum

LIU Si　CAI Chao　AN Wen-juan

（Jilin Academy of Forestry Reconnaissance and Design，Changchun，130022）

Abstract：Seeds of Lycium chinense，Lycium barbarum L. and Lycium barbarum Pojark were cultured in tube. The results were as follows：Pollute rate of explant from tissue culture is lower than water culture. Seeds are the better explant. MS＋1.5mg/L6－BA＋0.2mg/L IBA was the better medium for Lycium chinense. And MS＋2.5mg/L6－BA＋0.2mg/L IBA was he better medium for Lycium barbarum Pojark. and Lycium barbarum L.；MS＋0.5mg/L6BA＋1.0mg/LIBA was the better medium of propagation of three species . Plus 6－BA0.5mg/L and IBA0.5mg/L in MS was better stronger medium. And plus IBA0.1mg/L in 1/2MS medium will get higher rooting rate. the better transplanting medium was rotten quality soil，vermiculite and river sandy 1：1：1.

Key words：Lycium L.；tissue culture；propagation

作者简介：刘思（1976～），男，吉林省镇赉县人，工程师，2000 年毕业于北华大学，同年工作于吉林省林业勘察设计研究院，多年从事森林资源调查工作。

1 前 言

枸杞(*Lycium chinense*)为茄科植物，又名枸杞菜、狗牙子、枸杞子。枸杞是茄科多年生落叶灌木，全世界约有80种，广泛分布在北温带欧亚大陆。我国约有7个种3个变种。目前，我国通过人工栽培形成的枸杞林，主要为宁夏枸杞，通称“茨圆”或“红果子”，主产地为宁夏。枸杞萌发力强，生长旺盛。枸杞种子的生活力很强，在适宜的条件下一般经过7~10d可发芽出土，种子保存4年后发芽率仍达91%，5年后下降到47%。枸杞树的经济寿命很长，一般树体寿命能达60~70年，好的栽培条件下，有的树100年之久仍能结果。一般枸杞树大约在35年开始衰老，产量剧减，果实小、质量差、骨干枝和主枝大量死亡，结果枝很少，树冠残缺不全，冠幅大大减少，根、茎腐烂严重，失去经济栽培价值，应进行全园更新[1]。

枸杞营养成分丰富，鲜果可溶性固形物含量15%~20%，总糖8%~12%，有机酸0.45%~0.55%，粗脂肪1.87%，粗蛋白3.13%，粗纤维1.62%，氨基酸0.3%~0.7%，灰分0.95%，VC含量14.5~42.1mg/100g·FW[2]。传统医学对枸杞的药理功效多有详细记载，本草纲目记载，“春采叶，名天精草；夏采花，名长生草；秋采果，名枸杞子；冬采根，名地骨皮”。现代医学对枸杞的药理成分进行了深入广泛的研究，发现多种高含量的功效成分，胡萝卜素19.61mg/100g·FW，生物碱(甜菜碱)1.17%~1.55%，枸杞多糖1.0%~1.5%，以及黄酮542.5mg/100g·DW，SOD、芸香甙、萜类、肽类、甾类、牛磺酸等[3]。

枸杞子对特异性、非特异性免疫功能均有增强作用，还有免疫调节作用；有抗肿瘤作用、有抗氧化、抗衰老作用；有保肝及抗脂肪肝的作用；能刺激机体的生长，对某些遗传毒物所诱发的遗传损伤具有明显的保护作用；对造血功能有促进作用；能影响下丘-垂体-性腺轴功能，并有较好降血糖作用；可增强生殖系统功能，加强离体子宫的收缩频率、张力及强度；可增加小鼠皮肤羟脯氨的含量，显著增强小鼠的耐缺氧能力，延长其游泳时间，抗疲劳；并且有一定降压作用[4,5]。因此，科学界越来越重视对枸杞子的研究。

2 材料与方法

2.1 材 料

枸杞(*Lycium chinense*)、新疆枸杞(*Lycium barbarum Pojark*)、宁夏枸杞(*Lycium barbarum L*)三种枸杞的种子。

2.2 培养基

实验所用培养基为MS培养基，成分及含量列于表1。

2.3 培养基的制备

(1)称取规定数量的琼脂和蔗糖，加入一定量的蒸馏水，加热使其溶解。

(2)在烧杯中加入规定量的各种母液，包括生长调节物质和其他的特殊补加物。

(3)将母液混合物加入融化的琼脂中，再加入糖类物质，定容至所需体积，搅匀。

(4)用1mol/L的氢氧化钠和盐酸调节pH值为5.8。

(5)趁热将培养基分装到容量为150ml的三角瓶中，各装入20ml。

(6)用锡纸盖住瓶口。

(7)在121~126℃灭菌15min。

表 1 MS 培养基成分及含量

Tab. 1 MS culture composition and content

（单位：mg/L）

大量元素		微量元素		有机物质母液		其 他	
成分	含量	成分	含量	成分	含量	成分	含量
NH_4NO_3	16500	KI	166	甘氨酸	400	琼脂	8000
KNO_3	19000	$Na_2MoO_4 \cdot 2H_2O$	50	盐酸硫胺素	80	蔗糖	30000
$CaCl_2 \cdot 2H_2O$	4400	$CuSO_4 \cdot 5H_2O$	5	盐酸吡哆素	100	$FeSO_4 \cdot 7H_2O$	5.56
$MgSO_4 \cdot 7H_2O$	3700	$CoCl_2 \cdot 6H_2O$	5	烟酸	100	$Na_2EDTA \cdot 2H_2O$	7.44
KH_2PO_4	1700	$MnSO_4 \cdot 4H_2O$	4460	肌醇	10		
		$ZnSO_4 \cdot 7H_2O$	1720				
		H_3BO_4	1240				

(8)灭菌后，待压力归零后将培养基取出让其凝固。

2.4 接种方式

采用两种方法获得外植体，即水培和组织培养的方法。

(1)将枸杞种子放置于培养皿中，在23℃进行催芽处理。待种子发芽长至 2 ~ 3cm 时，将胚轴剪下作为外植体接种到初代培养基中。

(2)将种子接种到培养基中，待种子萌发，苗高约 1 ~ 2cm 时取出，将胚轴剪下作为外植体接种到初代培养基中。比较二者优缺点，确定具体用哪种方法获取外植体。

将饱满的种子接种到培养基中，待种子萌发，苗高约 1 ~ 2cm 时取出，将剪掉胚根的外植体接种到增殖培养基中。初代培养选择 MS 为基本培养基，6 种不同激素浓度配比。继代培养选择 MS 为基本培养基，6 种不同激素浓度配比。壮苗培养选择 MS 为基本培养基，3 种不同激素浓度配比。生根培养选择 1/2MS 为基本培养基，5 种不同激素浓度配比。比较枸杞在不同的培养基中的生长情况，根据其生长情况确定最适的培养基。

2.5 培养条件

将接种后的培养材料放在培养室内进行培养。培养条件为，温度在 22 ~ 28℃，光照时数 10 ~ 12h/d，光照强度 2000 ~ 3000Lx。

2.6 培养程序

2.6.1 外植体筛选

外植体植入后每天观察并记录水培和组织培养两种方法获得的外植体染菌率、获得外植体天数和产生愈伤组织天数。

2.6.2 初代培养

初代培养选择 MS 为基本培养基，6 种不同激素浓度配比见表 2。外植体植入后每天观察一次，记录愈伤组织生长状况和不定芽的个数。

表 2　诱导不定芽的培养基配方

Tab. 2　Medium with different hormone to induce adventitious buds　(单位：mg/L)

序号	基本培养基	6 - BA	IBA	NAA
1	MS	2.5	0.2	1
2	MS	2.0	0.2	
3	MS	1.5	0.2	
4	MS	1.5	0.2	0.1
5	MS	1.0	0.1	
6	MS	0.5	0.1	

2.6.3　继代培养

继代培养选择 MS 为基本培养基，6 种不同激素浓度配比见表 3。继代培养每天观察并纪录长出幼苗时间和幼苗数量。

2.6.4　壮苗培养

壮苗培养选择 MS 为基本培养基，3 种不同激素浓度配比见表 4。壮苗培养每 5 天观察一次，记录苗生长粗壮程度。

2.6.5　生根培养

生根培养选择 1/2MS 为基本培养基，5 种不同激素浓度配比见表 5。生根培养每天观察一次，记录产生不定根时间和不定根数量。

表 3　继代培养生长调节剂配比方案

Tab. 3　Medium with different hormone to subculture　(单位：mg/L)

序号	基本培养基	6 - BA	IBA
7	MS	0.5	0.5
8	MS	0.5	1.0
9	MS	0.5	1.5
10	MS	0.5	2.0
11	MS	1.0	0.5
12	MS	1.0	1.0

表 4　壮苗培养培养基配方

Tab. 4　Medium with different hormone to good seedling　(单位：mg/L)

序号	基本培养基	6 - BA	IBA
13	MS	0.5	0.2
14	MS	0.5	0.1
15	MS	0.5	

表 5　生根培养培养基配方

Tab. 5　Medium with different hormone to induce roots　(单位：mg/L)

序号	基本培养基	IBA	NAA
16	MS	1.0	

（续）

序号(№)	基本培养基	IBA	NAA
17	MS	0.5	
18	MS	0.1	
19	MS	1.0	0.1
20	MS		1.0

2.6.6 炼苗移栽

移栽基质：沙，田园土，腐质土：蛭石：河沙 =1:1:1。

移栽基质处理：用0.1%高锰酸钾溶液对各种基质消毒。

将生了根的枸杞苗，先在室温内除去扣膜锻炼3d，然后取出单苗洗净根上的培养基，把根部浸入1000倍的多菌灵溶液消毒3min，晾干后栽入基质中。

3 结果与分析

3.1 外植体筛选

通过组织培养方法获得的外植体染菌率低，而水培方法获得的外植体染菌率很高。见表6，这主要是因为组织培养方法是通过接种种子然后获得的外植体，接种种子时，种子在用$HgCl_2$消毒时有种皮包被，消毒时间稍长也不会对种子造成太大的伤害；而水培方法采用的外植体是水培后的小苗，组织幼嫩，本身带有杂菌，在用$HgCl_2$杀菌的过程中，对$HgCl_2$比较敏感，时间过长会将植物组织杀死，时间短则灭菌不彻底，污染率会升高。本试验的结果为采用种子作为外植体。

3.2 初代培养

为了更好的比较三种枸杞的差异，我们对三种枸杞所适最佳培养基进行了初步筛选。由表7可见，在初代培养时，对于宁夏枸杞和新疆枸杞来说，1号培养基优于其他不同浓度激素配比的培养基，它可以更快地诱导外植体脱分化产生愈伤组织，诱导植株伤口薄壁细胞脱分化的能力强；而且愈伤组织再分化产生不定芽的数量多。在1、2培养基中，初期枸杞外植体没有反应，既不产生愈伤组织，也不生长出不定芽，过一段时间后，切口处变成褐色，明显表现出缺乏生长素的症状。3号和4号对于诱导枸杞外植体脱分化、再分化的能力大小相近。在5、6培养基中，枸杞外植体均能脱分化产生愈伤组织，再分化形成不定芽，但5、6号诱导外植体脱分化能力较差，表现为产生的愈伤组织时间较长而且量少。因此对于枸杞初代培养，选用3号作为培养基。

表6 获得外植体两种不同方法

Tab.6 Two methods to gain explant

处理	$HgCl_2$消毒时间(min)	接种瓶数(瓶)	染菌瓶数(瓶)	染菌率(%)	获得外植体天数(d)	产伤愈伤组织(d)
水培催芽	6~7	50	35	70	7	8~10
组织培养	8~9	50	5	10	30	8~10

注：表中数字为接种后30d观察值。

表7 不同的激素种类及含量对不定芽发生的影响

Tab. 7 Effect to induce adventitious buds in MS with different hormone

序号	Z 愈伤组织(个)			不定芽数量(个)		
	枸杞	新疆枸杞	宁夏枸杞	枸杞	新疆枸杞	宁夏枸杞
1	无	较多	较多	0	18	19
2	无	一般	一般	0	13	15
3	较多	一般	一般	18	12	12
4	较多	较少	较少	16	7	9
5	一般	少	少	14	4	5
6	较少	少	少	9	2	3

注：表中数字及结果为接种后25d 观察值。

3.3 继代培养

表8 不同的激素种类及含量对继代培养的影响

Tab. 8 Effect to subculture in MS with different hormone

序号	长出幼苗时间(d)			幼苗数量(个)		
	枸杞	新疆枸杞	宁夏枸杞	枸杞	新疆枸杞	宁夏枸杞
7	35	35	30	10	11	13
8	8	30	30	30	20	22
9	9	31	33	35	9	8
10	10	34	33	32	12	13
11	11	32	31	36	17	18
12	12	37	35	34	17	19

注：表中数字为接种后40d 观察值

由表8 可以看出，在继代培养时，8 号培养基中激素浓度配比比较适合三种枸杞幼苗的形成。因为在10 号培养基中，长出幼苗的时间早，而且在一定的时间内幼苗数量的数量多。继代培养的周期为5 ~7 周。

3.4 壮苗培养

由表9 可以看出，在壮苗培养时，对于三种枸杞来说14 号优于其他两种激素浓度配比的培养基。在14 号培养基中的幼苗生长的粗壮。

表9 不同的激素种类及含量对壮苗培养的影响

Tab. 9 Effect to good seedling in MS with different hormone

序号	幼苗生长的粗壮程度		
	枸杞	新疆枸杞	宁夏枸杞
13	一般	较粗	一般
14	较粗	较粗	一般
15	较细	一般	较粗

注：表中结果为接种后40d 观察值。

3.5 生根培养

三种枸杞在不同激素浓度配比的培养基中诱导产生不定芽、不定根情况见表10。

由表10可以看出，在生根培养时，16号培养基中激素浓度配比比较适合三种枸杞的不定根发生和生长。因为在16号培养基中，不定根发生的时间早，而且在一定的时间内不定根产生的数量多。

表10 不同的激素种类及含量对不定根发生的影响

Tab. 10 Effect to induce adventitious roots in MS with different hormone

序号	产生不定根时间(d)			不定根数量(个)		
	枸杞	新疆枸杞	宁夏枸杞	枸杞	新疆枸杞	宁夏枸杞
16	5	5	5	15	14	16
17	7	7	7	10	9	11
18	11	12	12	4	4	4
19	6	6	6	12	11	12
20	7	7	7	11	9	10

注：表中不定根数量为接种后12d观察值。

3.6 移栽

移栽初期，苗木幼嫩，光线强易死苗，因此必须遮荫，使光强为全光的30%左右。等苗木成活后逐渐拆除遮荫，由散射光逐渐转到直射光。在整个移栽过程中，要作好喷水工作，使空气相对湿度保持在70% ~85%。在炼苗移栽过程中，基质以腐质土:蛭石:河沙 =1:1:1 对炼苗最好。

4 小结与讨论

(1)选取外植体的方法，通过组织培养方法获得的外植体染菌率低，而水培方法获 得的外植体染菌率很高。

(2)初代培养枸杞最佳培养基为 MS +1.5 6BA +0.2IBA，宁夏枸杞和新疆枸杞最佳培养基为 MS +2.5 6BA +0.2IBA。

(3)继代培养三种枸杞最佳培养基均为 MS +0.5 6BA +1.0IBA。

(4)壮苗培养三种枸杞最佳培养基均为 MS +0.5 6BA +0.1IBA。

(5)生根培养时三种枸杞培养基以 1/2MS +0.1IBA 为最佳。

(6)在炼苗移栽过程中，基质以腐质土:蛭石:河沙 =1:1:1 对炼苗最好。

参考文献

[1]袁宝财，达海莉，李晓瑞．宁夏枸杞的生物学特性及开发利用前景[J]．河北林果研究，2001.
[2]姚健，李建强，燕新洪，等．枸杞的用途及栽培[J]．现代化农业，2000.
[3]崔爱萍，王年锁．枸杞的价值及栽培技术[J]．山西林业技术，2000.
[4]陆钦尧，黎明．益寿中草药选解[M]．北京：人民卫生出版社，1987.
[5]中等卫生学校试用教材《中草药学》编写组．中草药学[M]．广州：广东人民出版社，1980.

浅析森林认证机制及其与森林可持续经营的关系

陶立超

（北京林业大学林学院）

摘要：在森林可持续经营研究加深的背景下，森林认证机制也陆续建立起来，并在世界范围内得到认可和实施。本文浅析了森林认证的概念、目的、过程、标准与指标，以及森林认证与森林可持续经营的关系。

关键词：森林认证；森林可持续经营；认证机制

The Brief Analysis of Relationship between Forest Certification and Forest Sustainable Management

TAO li-chao

（Department of Forest Sciences, Beijing Forestry University）

Abstract: Under the background of deepening of sustainable forest management, forest certification mechanism has been built one by one and accepted and implemented worldwide. This paper introduces the concept, purpose, process, criteria and index of forest certification, and indicated the relationship between forest certification and forest sustainable management.

Key words: forest certification; sustainable forest management; certification system

20 世纪 90 年代初，联合国环境与发展大会以后，为了促进森林可持续经营的发展和确保其能够得到彻底落实，森林认证成为配合森林可持续经营的一种相应机制，得到许多国家政府和森林工作部门的关注和认可，在全世界许多国家建立并迅速得到发展[1]，其中以美国和澳大利亚为代表[2]。相对于其他林业发达国家来说，中国的森林认证起步较晚，目前已经建立了森林认证体系，但不够完善。国内对森林认证的潜在影响和作用作了一些研究，并集中在对森林可持续经营的影响方面，如陆文明[3]研究了森林认证对森林可持续经营和林产品贸易的影响，徐斌[4]的森林可持续经营的认证机制和中国森林认证可行性研究，但这些研究都未明晰地阐述森林认证与森林可持续经营的关系。因此，探讨一下森林认证与森林可持续经营的关系对深入理解森林认证机制及更好地促进森林可持续经营有一定的意义。

1 森林认证机制

1.1 森林认证的概念

森林认证通常包括森林经营的认证和林产品产销监管链的认证，森林经营的认证，也叫做森林可持续经营认证，通常所说的森林认证就是森林可持续经营认证的简称。森林认证是由独立的第三方对某个森林区域的经营活动是否是可持续森林经营进行认定的过程[5]，这就涉及3个组成要素，即申请认证的森林区域及其所有者、预先确定的标准和指标、开展认证活动的独立的第三方机构[5]。森林认证也就是针对森林经营单位，由独立第三方认证机构根据所制定的森林经营的标准，按照规定的和公认的程序对特定森林区域的森林经营绩效进行审核，以证明其达到可持续经营或负责任经营要求的过程。产销监管链认证是对林产品生产加工企业的各个生产环节，包括从原木的运输、加工到流通整个链条进行跟踪，以确保最终产品源自于经过认证的经营良好的森林或其他合乎要求的来源[6]。

1.2 森林认证的目的

森林认证是配合森林可持续森林经营而建立的一种促进机制，用来保护森林资源，保护生物多样性，维护生态系统的稳定性，同时也为了让人们能够放心的买到并使用可持续经营的森林生产出的产品，使人们在这种机制中对森林的可持续经营起到监督的作用，以市场需求促进森林的可持续经营。由于人们环境意识的增强，要求使用生态的林产品及林副产品，因而森林消费性产品逐渐被冠以“生态标签”。澳大利亚的森林认证为了保护森林资源，将20%的天然林保护起来禁止采伐，还提出了一些林纸产品的强制性指标和措施[7]。森林认证可以使无形的森林服务商品化，全球化，被越来越多的人认可，也使有形的林产品及林副产品向高标准高质量方向发展，提高森林经营水平，最终使整个林业可持续发展走向正规化、制度化。

1.3 森林认证的过程

森林认证依不同的认证体系，步骤也有所不同，但其主要步骤还是大同小异，一般包括申请、检查(或审计)、确定和颁发征书。目前，森林认证体系中最可依赖、最有影响力并受各国和市场广泛认可的是森林管理委员会(FSC)认证，它是审批独立的第三方认证机构的森林认证标准并监督其实施的认证管理机构。一个营林单位首先要考虑认证的必要性及带来的竞争优势，在熟悉了解森林认证的相关知识之后向森林认证机构提出书面申请，认证机构会根据此营林单位的经营历史、状况和林业政策粗略地判断是否有进行马上认证的必要，如果有必要，双方约定时间后认证机构派相关专业工作人员到实地进行考察，考察过后就进行审核，审核内容主要包括营林单位的环境政策、林业经营规划和经营程序等重要文件和相关批准手续文件，审核须经过专家评定小组复查，复查合格后就可以给营林单位颁发证书。认证过后森林认证机构将对森林认证证书持有者进行定期复查，一般以1年为标准进行年审，以确定其是否符合森林认证标准的要求。

1.4 森林认证的标准与指标

森林认证的标准与指标体系在世界范围内最具影响力和被最广泛认可的就是FSC的标准，它可用于任何国家的森林认证[8]，属于全球性的认证体系。FSC通过了森林管理委员会原则和标准，这些原则和标准为优质森林经营认证提供了框架和一般标准，在这些标准与指标的大前提下，国家根据自身的森林资源特点和经营条件，制定出符合自己国情的一套相应的标准与指标体系，以促进本国森林认证体系的建立和满足自身发展的需要。

目前，在国际上还有一些通过 FSC 认证授权的应用于区域和国家比较知名的森林认证标准与指标体系，如泛欧森林认证体系 PEEC、运用于美国和加拿大的工业林认证的可持续林业倡议体系 SFI、应用于美国私有林和非工业林的认证的 ATFS 以及加拿大的标准化协会体系 CSA 等[8]。除此之外，还有一些独立的第三方认证机构等。关于森林可持续经营研究，全球共有 9 大不同的区域组织，被称为“九大进程”，即国际热带木材组织进程、蒙特利尔进程、泛欧赫尔辛基进程、非洲干旱地区进程、塔拉波托进程、非洲木材组织进程、近东进程、中美洲进程、亚洲干旱地区进程。这些区域性的国家与经营单位级别的森林可持续性指标体系，有着共同的特点，标准数一般为 6 个左右，指标数大约为 27 个，标准的主要内容也大致相同，包括生物多样性保护、森林生态系统生产能力的维护、森林生态系统健康与活力维护、水土资源保持、森林在碳循环中的作用、森林的多种社会经济效益、相关法规政策体制[9]。

2 森林认证与森林可持续经营的关系

2.1 森林可持续经营是森林认证的前提和保证

森林可持续经营是在一定作业手段等技术条件下，通过对人的经营行为的规范，以人与人、人与环境的和谐为宗旨，建立起包括体制与法规、公众参与、标准与指标等内容的人类经营森林的行为规范。森林可持续经营的标准与指标为森林认证各项规范和标准的建立提供了思路，也就为发展认证机制提供了一个有用的框架和出发点。因此，森林可持续经营标准与指标对森林认证起到了一种指导作用。

森林可持续经营与森林认证的目的都是为了提高森林经营水平，促进林业的可持续发展。森林可持续经营标准与指标是用来评定国家层次的森林的经营水平是否符合可持续经营原则，而森林认证标准是评估森林经营单位层次的森林是否达到良好经营。森林可持续经营规范制约着森林经营者的行为，能够使森林得到良好经营，生产出更多更好的森林产品，这就产生了森林认证的需要。因而，森林可持续经营是森林认证的前提，没有森林可持续经营，森林认证就没有意义。

森林可持续经营是一个长期的过程，经营产生的业绩和效益需运用森林认证进行评估，在此过程中森林可持续经营会使森林认证的理念得到广泛传播。同时森林经营是一个不断提高，不断深化的过程，这也会促进森林认证体制机制的完善，使森林认证由主要针对用材林向针对所有林种转变，由主要针对木材产品向其他非木材产品转变。森林认证依赖于森林经营的可持续性，森林可持续经营标准与指标可以促进森林良好经营，因而为森林产品认证提供了可靠保证。

2.2 森林认证对森林可持续经营的鞭策和引导

森林认证是一种运用市场机制来促进森林可持续经营并实现生态、社会和经济目标的工具。由于森林认证是建立在国家水平甚至是国际水平上的基础上来实现的，必须经过严格的森林认证程序，其中森林认证与森林可持续经营紧密相关，前者的标准与指标就体现了一系列森林经营的可持续性原则。

森林认证虽然建立在自愿原则的基础上，但是随着林业的现代化、国际化发展，森林认证成为国际林业的一种发展趋势，人们对森林的可持续经营目标的要求越来越高。这就如同为森林经营者设置了一道道坎，森林经营者为了提高自己森林资产的价值及其在林业中的竞争力，就会想方设法地改善经营手段和方法，完善森林结构，促进森林生态服务功能的发挥，这就促使森林经营者提高经营水平，使木材生产标准化，逐步提高林产品、林副产品及森林服务的质量。实际上，森林认证的产品要求是来自经营优良的森林，这有利于保护森林的生物多样性、各种生态过程，防止水土流失和环境恶化，这将促进森林经营的可持续性。开展森林认证，落实森林可持续经营标准与指标，可以为森林可持续经营提供范例和模板，这也将促进森林可持续经营，森林认证产品的销售与消费以一种市场机制促进着森林的可持续经营。森林认证是对森林可持续经营的一种鞭策。

同时，森林认证有利于促进国家与国家、地区与地区之间甚至国家与地区之间的森林经营经验交流。在森林经营的过程中，森林认证作为一种衡量森林经营是否达到符合可持续经营原则和目标的工具，可以对森林进行监测和评价，达到监管的作用，森林认证逐渐引导森林经营向真正的可持续方向发展，使其不偏正轨。因此，森林认证在森林可持续经营中起到了引导作用，从而实现林业的可持续发展。

2.3 相互促进，共同发展

森林认证源于日益突出的森林面积锐减、森林退化加剧等环境问题，它是由环境非政府组织与民间爱护环境自发形成的组织逐步发展起来的，以探讨解决森林经营中存在的各种弊端，通过对森林经营活动进行评估，将森林绿色产品的生产商与具有高要求高标准的生态消费者联系起来的一种市场机制。森林认证与可持续经营有着密切的关系。首先，森林可持续经营能带动森林认证体系的完善与发展。从森林认证的起源与形成过程可以看出，森林可持续经营能够生产出人们所需要的高标准生态产品，产生了森林认证的需要，随着经营手段和技术地不断提高，森林认证的标准也会增加和得到丰富，认证体系会逐步完善。其次，森林可持续经营的成果需要森林认证来检验和核实，森林认证也可以不断促进森林可持续经营。森林认证能够弥补并解决森林可持续经营宏观政策中的不足，认证的市场机制对森林可持续经营提出了更高的要求和标准，这就促进经营手段和技术的改革与创新，推动森林可持续经营机制的发展。因此，森林认证与森林可持续经营相互依靠，相互促进，共同发展。

3 对森林认证的展望

各国虽然已经形成森林认证机制和相应认证单位，但森林认证体系还处于发展的低级阶段，认证的森林资源不全面，主要只针对用材林和有形的木材产品，认证的内容涵盖的范围不够广，这限制了对森林可持续经营的促进作用，另外，森林认证的总面积很小，占全世界森林面积也很小[4,8]，森林认证的影响力和作用在不同方面或地区差别很大。在中国，森林认证的理念还未深入人心，认证的市场需求动力不足[6]，张新欣[10]的研究调查中显示，中国有相当一部分比例的森林经营单位在经营规划、监测评估、环境影响方面与 FSC 的要求差距较大，是森林经营单位比较普遍的薄弱环节。世界的森林认证体系有待进一步完善，需要向针对包括其他林种和非木材林副产品在内的森林资源认证方向发展。总之，对森林认证的研究还不够多，不够深入，要实现全球的森林认证还有很长的路要走。

参考文献

[1]徐斌，赵劫．中国产销监管链认证现状[J]．森林认证通讯，2002，01.

[2]朱春全，董珂．各权益相关者在推动森林认证中的作用[J]．森林认证通讯，2001，1.
[3]陆文明．森林认证对森林经营和林产品贸易的影响[J]．林业科技管理，2001(4)：16～20.
[4]徐斌．森林可持续经营的认证机制及中国森林认证可行性研究[D]．北京：中国林业科学研究院，2000.7.
[5]刘娟．论森林可持续经营及森林认证[J]．林业调查规划，2005，30(3)：62～67.
[6]徐斌．森林认证对森林可持续经营的影响研究[D]．北京：中国林业科学研究院，2010，7.
[7]孟令义，陆洪．澳大利亚森林可持续经营与森林认证对我国的启示[J]．中国林副特产，20085.
[8]黄雪菊．森林可持续经营的认证机制与中国森林认证对策研究[D]．北京：北京林业大学，2005.
[9]亢新刚．森林资源经营管理[M]．北京：中国林业出版社，2001，9～13.
[10]张新欣．我国FSC森林认证结果及其影响分析[D]．北京：北京林业大学，2007.

完善生态补偿制度与强化森林科学经营之技术和政策研究

何美成　易正树　闫顺利　李建军　席明星　等
（国家林业局驻武汉森林资源监督专员办事处，武汉，430079）

摘要：本研究在回顾国内外森林生态补偿与森林科学经营研究与实践的基础上，以湖北省马尾松林分为实例，针对我国公益林应该补偿多少、怎样补偿的问题，提出了确定公益林补偿标准的新方法——“机会成本－生态区位调节法”，据此测算了生态补偿额度，提出了实施对策与建议；同时研究制订了商品用材林科学经营的优化模式，全面分析了其投入、产出和效益，提出了强化森林科学经营的主要措施。整项研究旨在从技术与政策两个层面，为国家宏观决策并制定政策法规提供依据，促进集体林权制度改革主要目标早日实现。

关键词：森林；林权制度改革；生态效益；补偿；经营

1　前　言

“生态受保护、农民得实惠”是集体林权制度改革的主要目标，如何更好地解决集体林产权明晰之后的收益权和处置权与生态环境保护之间的矛盾，是当前迫切需要研究解决的重大问题。这一问题既关系到集体林权制度改革工作的成败，也关系到广大林农的切身利益和“双增”目标能否如期实现，更关系到我国的生态安全和资源能源安全。研究和破解这一难题，是森林资源监督机构的应尽义务。初步研究表明，只有建立健全生态补偿制度，加大国家和受益群体对生态公益林的投入和回馈，同时积极引导和帮助林农加大科学经营森林的力度，充分发挥森林生产潜力，才能更好地解决保护与发展的矛盾，进而真正实现集体林改的主要目标。因此，本研究具有重要的现实意义和广泛的社会影响。

2　国内外研究概况

2.1　森林生态补偿研究进展

森林是陆地上最大的生态系统，对于维护自然生态系统的平衡和改善生态环境以及保障国土生态安全具有重要意义（蒋发进等，2008）。随着森林资源的破坏，尤其是全球环境状况的进一步恶化，森林所提供的生态价值日益受到更多的关注（刘际建等，2001；赖晓华等，2004）。生态公益林是以发挥森林的生态功能，提供生态效益如水源涵养、水土保持、动植物基因保存、游憩保健、净化空气、调节气候、防风固沙等为主要任务的森林。建设生态公益林成为改善生态环境的重要组成部分，是一项服务于社会、受益于全民的非盈利性社会公益事业（韦美玲，2001）。然而，由于森林的生态效益外部性和公共物品的特性，较大部分难以通过传统的市场实现其经济价值(李文华等，2006)，要使公益林保护政策彻底贯彻落实，就必须对公益林经营者进行相应的补偿(张眉等，2010)。而如何给森林生态服务提供者实施补偿以调动人们保护生态的积极性，实现社会公平和可持续发展，借鉴国际经验构建符合我国实际的森林生态补偿机制是目前亟需解决的重大课题(何勇等，2009)。实践表明，森林生态补偿标准合理与否影响到经营主体对公益林的有效管护，关系到国土生态安全。正因为如此，科学地确定生态补偿标准成为社会与众多学者关注的热点与焦点，也是生态补偿研究的难点(张志云等，2010)。

国外关于森林生态效益的研究始于19世纪末。第二次世界大战后，德国相继出现“林业政策效益论”、“和谐理论”、“林业服务于国家和社会”、“森林多功能理论”等。直到20世纪末，森林生态服务补偿的研究才逐渐发展起来，特别是以Daily(1997)主编的《自然服务功能：人类社会对自然生态系统的依赖性》为代表。随后，森林生态补偿逐渐成为林学、生态学与生态经济学的研究热点。森林趋势组织和卡通巴工作组对森林生态效益的市场化交易潜力方面进行了大量的研究，在澳大利亚、加拿大、巴西、英国及日本等地召开了多次关于森林生态服务的国际研讨会，内容包括森林的碳储存服务、水文服务、生物多样性服务以及森林景观服务等，同时对森林生态服务市场开发与建立所需的法律与制度环境、开发这一市场面临的关键问题与步骤等也进行了深入探讨(李文华等，2006；崔一梅，2008)，为森林生态补偿机制研究提供了大量的理论支持。同时，许多国家及区域也采取了不同方式对森林生态效益补偿进行尝试。例如，哥斯达黎加1995年就开始进行环境服务支付项目(PES)，该项目由国家森林商业基金支持，对土地使用者进行的林木重新栽植、可持续采伐、天然林保护行为进行土地利用特别补助(何勇等，2009)；芬兰为了保护珍贵的森林资源，国家采用购买的方式对生物多样性价值给予经济补偿；美国对其西部11个州范围内的国有林区征收放牧税，并将其中一部分用于牧场的更新、保护和改良(雷玲，2005)；英国伦敦的国际环境与发展研究所(IIED)、美国的森林趋势组织分别就环境服务市场及其补偿机制在世界范围内对自发或政府组织推动的案例进行研究和诊断，作为理论的探讨和市场开发的依据(何勇等，2009)。通过对主要林业发达国家森林生态效益补偿模式和方法的统计可以发现，主要的方法包括政府购买林业生态效益作为森林所有者的经济补偿；对森林生态效益直接受益部门征收补偿费，对造林营林者减免森林资产税收；森林生态效益补偿市场化。以上都为我国森林生态补偿研究提供了很好的借鉴。

我国森林生态效益补偿机制启动较晚。直到2001年国家森林生态效益补助政策才正式出台，将森林生态效益补助资金纳入国家公共财政预算并正式付诸实施，标志着我国开始步入一个有偿使用森林资源生态价值的新阶段(赖晓华等，2004)。2001年11月，国家财政部在全国开展森林生态效益补助资金试点工作，试点范围包括河北、辽宁、黑龙江、山东、浙江、安徽、江西、福建、湖南、广西及新疆11省(自治区)的685个县(单位)和24个国家级自然保护区，涉及重点防护林和特种用途林2亿亩，为建立森林生态效益补偿基金制度奠定了基础。2004年12月，财政部、国家林业局共同颁布《中央森林生态效益补偿基金管理办法》，标志着我国森林生态效益补偿基金制度正式建立(张眉等，2010)。2006年发布的《中华人民共和国国民经济和社会发展第十一个五年规划纲要》明确提出了在天然林保护区、重要水源涵养区等限制开发区域建立重要生态功能区，促进自然生态恢复。按照谁开发谁保护、谁受益谁补偿的原则，建立生态补偿机制。

目前国内森林生态效益补偿研究主要集中在生态补偿的基础理论、必要性、模式和标准等几个方面，大量的研究使得我国森林生态效益补偿取得了许多宝贵的经验。尤其在补偿标准的确定上，采用森林生态系统服务功能及其价值评估为依据。郑礼法等(2001)、韦美玲(2001)、葛亲红(2005)、张家来等(2007)分别从不同角度进行了深入探讨。他们的研究表明，我国目前的补偿标准明显偏低，而且生态公益林的经营管理容易受自然、经济因素等影响，所以各地补偿标准差异较大，加之现有的研究都是探索性的，许多研究往往是简单的定量化，尤其是在生态补偿标准实施程度方面考虑相对较少。迄今研究生态系统服务价值的方法主要有：市场价值法、非市场价值法(替代成本法、旅行费用法、享乐价值法)、条件价值法、集体价值法等等。这些方法各有千秋，目前尚无统一且公认的方法，加之其目的不是直接为建立生态补偿制度服务，因此难以满足实际需要，用作生态补偿的标准也难以令人信服(吴水荣，2001)。

总之，尽管目前国内在森林生态效益补偿研究方面取得了一定的成果，但生态补偿的指标和定量化方法的研究还处于起步阶段，各地补偿标准研究多停留在理论层面，国家和地方政府真正进行公益林补偿时并没有参照任何一种标准，导致许多科学问题仍然存在模糊和不确定性，生态补偿实践工作仍处于探索阶段(冯艳芬等，2009)。

2.2 森林科学经营研究与实践动态

森林科学经营是一个相对古老而又永恒的课题，但其内涵却在不断地丰富和发展，理论、技术和方法也在日臻成熟与完善。早在公元前300年间，我国就出现了森林科学经营的原始思想，可考证的如《孟子》所曰："斧斤以时入山林，树木不可胜用也；……，树木不可胜用，是使民养生丧死无憾也；五亩之宅，树之以桑，五十者可以衣帛矣"(引自《孟子：寡人之于国也》)。这段话道出了"近自然"和"可持续"林业的基本内涵。公元6世纪《齐民要术》(贾思勰，北魏)对杨树经营提出"岁种三十亩，三年九十亩，一年卖三十亩，……周而复始，永世无穷"。这一论述较《孟子》单纯从采伐自然资源视角的论述有明显进展，体现了造林经营的思想。从18世纪中期开始，德国人就提出了森林永续利用的概念，并逐步进行了实践与完善。近2个世纪以来，随着工业文明在欧洲的兴起，发达国家在森林经营方面也占据了领先地位。当今社会对林业的经济需求和生态需求处于双重高涨时期，传统的森林经营方法和手段，既不能满足林业健康发展的要求，也不能使其充分发挥生态功能，严重制约着林业的快速发展。如何保持森林的健康、充分发挥森林的多样功能，导致森林经营已经从以木材或其他林产品的生产为主、向以培育健康稳定的森林为主的森林可持续经营转变。实施森林科学经营，完善相应的理论、技术和政策法规，成为当前重要而紧迫的世界课题。

从1980年起，已有一些国际组织，如热带林业行动计划(TEAP)、国际热带木材协议(ITTA)、濒危野生动植物种国际贸易公约(CITES)、巴西热带雨林保护行动计划等，开始致力于调整林业政策，保持热带林可持续经营(蒋有绪，2000)。1992年联合国环发大会以后，森林可持续经营的概念已在全球获得了普遍承认。发达国家采取和发展中国家结对子的双边磋商以及研讨会等形式讨论涉及森林的各种问题，包括森林可持续经营的标准和指标体系，与此同时，关于可持续森林经营的标准和指标体系的讨论得到大多数国家的响应(周国林，1999)。截至1998年，国际上有关森林可持续经营标准与指标的主要区域性进程有蒙特利尔进程、赫尔辛基进程、塔拉波托(Tarapoto)倡议、非洲干旱区进程、中美洲进程、近东进程、国际热带木材组织(ITTO)进程、非洲木材组织(ATO)进程和亚洲干旱区进程等9个进程(雷静品等，2004)。近年来，国外许多国家和组织开展了森林可持续经营问题的理论、标准、方法、示范等方面的研究，并形成了森林永续利用理论、森林多功能经营理论、森林多效益主导利用理论、森林可持续发展理论等诸多森林经营理论。目前可归纳为三个有代表性的森林经营体系：一是以德国为代表的近自然森林经营理论和技术体系，二是美国首倡的森林生态系统经营思想和方法，三是加拿大的模式森林经营计划和管理体系。总的趋势是由最初的单一的木材永续利用向经济效益、生态效益和社会效益综合利用的森林可持续经营方向发展(张蕾，2007)。

我国自20世纪50年代起，许多科研工作者对森林可持续经营的理论、模式、评价方法、指标体系和标准的构建等进行了大量的实践研究和探索，目前已分别在江西分宜县(代表我国亚热带地区)和甘肃张掖市、黑龙江丽江自然保护区(代表我国温带地区)设立了试验基地，以制定和验证中国地区水平的标准和指标。同时，许多研究者积极倡导和研究森林科学经营，取得了大量可喜的成果。刘于鹤、林进等(2008)在对我国大小兴安岭、长白山林区，福建、江西、辽宁、广东、甘肃和内蒙古等省(区)30多个县(局)进行林业改革和森林经营专题调研后，提出了加强森林经营、提高森林质量的基本构思和十点建议。唐守正等(2006)在总结国内外森林生态采伐研究成果的基础上，结合东北天然林区的生态采伐实践活动，提出了“天然林生态采伐更新技术体系”，认为依照森林生态理论指导森林采伐作业，可使采伐和更新达到既利用森林又促进森林生态系统健康与稳定，实现森林可持续利用之目的。张守攻等(2001)对森林可持续经营的理论及标准与指标体系进行了系统的论述。王洪波(1995)针对吉林省国有林区的特点，建立了由资源承载指标、环境承载力、生活质量、经济发展、技术管理和社会发展指标在内的6个二级指标和15个三级指标构成的国有林业局可持续林业评价指标体系，并在松江河林业局进行了验证。

森林可持续经营研究作为我国森林科学经营研究的一个方面和方向取得不错的成绩，但也存在许多问题。比如许多关于森林可持续经营的研究大多都是宏观和定性的分析，至今为止还没有制定出一套能用于我国森林可持续经营定量评价的指标和指标体系。生态林业被认为是我国林业发展的必由之路，其概念可简述为：优化的森林结构和功能，永续充分利用森林自然力，以实现多目标总体效益最佳的产业。如何在保持森林的生态效益和社会效益长期稳定的前提下满足人们对木材和其他林产品的利用需求，也是世界林业发展的基本问题。目前，在集体林权制度改革完成了明晰产权的主体工程之后，如何引导和带动广大林农开展森林集约经营、规模经营、科学经营，着重针对森林经营周期长、风险大、科技含量较高等特点和要求，积极探索高投入、高产出、高效益的科学经营模式，已经成为我国广大务林人特别是林业科技工作者的主攻目标。

3 研究目标、内容与技术路线

本研究以全国集体林权制度改革为背景，以集体林为主要对象，以湖北省主要森林类型—马尾松林分为范例，提出不同立地条件、不同生态区位的公益林补偿标准、以及完善我国森林生态补偿制度的对策和办法；同时研究制订商品用材林科学经营的技术与措施，为林农增收提供强有力的科技支撑，进而巩固和扩大林改成果。整项研究着力从技术与政策两个层面为国家宏观决策并出台相关文件、法规等提供理论和实践依据，促进集体林权制度改革主要目标早日实现。

主要研究内容包括公益林补偿标准的确定、森林科学经营方法与效益分析、以及相关政策措施研究。

研究的技术路线是：针对不同生态区位、森林立地条件、林分质量状况、林地权属及经营状况，采用“充分借鉴、突出重点、点面结合、系统工程、全面合作”等攻坚策略，将三项研究内容划分为三个既相互联系、又相对独立的专题，全面开展并完成相关研究。其中，对于公益林的生态服务功能价值仅仅依据一般的（常规的）经营管理水平予以评价；而对于商品用材林则重点研究森林科学经营的模式及其前景和效应。

4 湖北省森林资源状况与集体林权制度改革进展

4.1 森林资源状况

4.1.1 基本情况

湖北省位于我国中部、长江中游，是三峡、葛洲坝、丹江口等大型水利枢纽的所在地，战略地位十分重要。全省土地总面积 1859.0 万 hm^2，其中林地面积 849.85 万 hm^2，占 45.72%；森林面积 713.86 万 hm^2，森林覆盖率 38.4%。活立木总蓄积 31324.69 万 m^3，森林蓄积 28652.97 万 m^3，占活立木总蓄积的 91.47%；平均每公顷蓄积 50.06m^3，天然林为 51.32m^3，人工林为 45.80m^3；平均每公顷年生长量 4.40m^3，天然林为 4.04m^3，人工林为 5.59m^3。全省森林面积以防护林所占比例为最大（43.79%），其次是用材林（40.61%）。主要优势树种为马尾松，全省马尾松林面积占森林面积的 35.6%。这是本研究选择马尾松为范例的重要原因。

4.1.2 森林分类经营状况

湖北省认定的国家级公益林为 3317.65 万亩。按权属分，国有 589.06 万亩，集体 877.34 万亩，个人 1833.1 万亩，其他 18.15 万亩。省级公益林 1000 万亩，市县级公益林 395.87 万亩。全省森林分类经营工作从 2001 年 1 月正式启动，已经深入人心并取得了显著成效。

4.1.3 森林资源的主要特点

湖北省森林资源呈现以下主要特点：

（1）林龄结构不尽合理。全省乔木林资源中，以中幼龄林占绝对优势，面积所占比例为 87.31%，蓄积比例为 75.94%。表明加强中幼林培育、开展森林科学经营的任务和潜力较大。

（2）天然林资源比较丰富。全省天然林面积 519.01 万 hm^2，蓄积 22645.90 万 m^3，分别占全省森林面积和蓄积的 72.70% 和 79.04%。说明天然林保护工程任务繁重、近期可以采伐利用的森林资源较少。

（3）森林资源质量较差。全省森林平均每公顷蓄积仅 50.06m^3，相当于全国平均值的 58.29%；平均每公顷年生长量 4.40m^3。可见通过森林科学经营，提高林地生产力的空间较大。

（4）公益林中集体权属所占比例较大。全省国家级公益林中集体权属占 26.5%，省级公益林中集体权属占 33.52%。

（5）公益林保护等级较高。湖北省划定的国家级、省级、市县级公益林中，保护等级在一、二级的公益林比例超过 95%。

4.2 集体林权制度改革进展

4.2.1 林改动态

自2006年底，湖北省委、省政府出台《关于深化集体林权制度改革的试行意见》后，湖北省集体林权制度改革开始实施。据国家林业局《林业改革动态》发布，湖北省在2009年度集体林地确权情况、家庭承包经营落实情况和确权林地发证情况等三项衡量主体改革的指标排名中，均位居全国前列。截至2010年底，全省已完成林改确权面积11805.9万亩，发证面积11699.11万亩，分别占总任务11865.2万亩的99.5%和98.6%。在抓好主体改革的同时，各地积极推进各项配套改革措施。林权抵押贷款工作有了进展，森林资源流转市场开始发育，林业要素市场体系初步建立，林权交易日益增多，森林资源资产评估体系初具雏形。

4.2.2 主要成效

通过4年的探索和实践，湖北省集体林权制度改革工作成效显著，森林资源持续增长，生态状况明显改善，林业经济不断壮大，林农收入稳步增加，林区社会更加和谐。

一是调动了农民发展林业的积极性。林改后，部分农村富余劳动力不再外出打工，转而上山投资发展林业。特别是有的地方政府还专门出台了鼓励社会各界投资林业的政策规定，群众都争着要山林的经营权。二是农民经营林业得到了实惠。由于林改而出现的林地、林木资源升值，给农民带来了不少实惠。同时林改中出台的一系列减轻农民涉林负担、增加林农补贴的政策，也促进了农民收入的增加，使农民真正得到了实惠。三是加强了生态保护和建设。林改后，明确了林权70年承包期不变，农民植树造林的积极性普遍高涨。农民对林地的经营和开发有了长远的规划，有利于护林、防火、防病虫害等，有利于生态的长远保护。四是促进了林业产业的发展。五是促进了林区社会的和谐稳定。林改中大量山林权属纠纷的调处，不仅妥善解决了一批历史遗留问题，营造了林业发展环境，而且改善了邻里关系，促进了农村和谐稳定。

4.2.3 当前存在的突出问题

(1)公益林补偿标准太低。在实行补偿的国家重点公益林和省级重点公益林中，每年每亩补助标准为10元，而建成1亩生态公益林，需成本2000元左右，此外还要负责森林防火、森林病虫害防治等日常管护工作。国家和省里的补偿仅是杯水车薪，林农的切身利益和保护生态公益林的热情受到严重伤害。

(2)森林经营技术匮乏。林改之后集体林权过于分散，加之林业社会化服务组织不健全，科技推广、市场营销、农民培训等服务工作不能很好开展。一些林农不知道应该种什么、如何种、种了怎么办。林改之后如何科学地经营森林成为制约林农增收致富的首要问题。

5 公益林生态补偿标准的确定

5.1 确定公益林生态补偿标准的影响因素

补偿标准的确定是公益林生态补偿机制的核心要素与难点。合理确定补偿标准可以起到激励引导作用，平衡生态公益林的供给与需求。根据公平、合理的补偿原则，经营者不能加重受益者的补偿量；反之，受益者也不能随意降低补偿量，经营者与受益者的经济交换应当公平、合理。合理的补偿标准应该既能使补偿主体能够承受，又能使补偿对象愿意接受。补偿标准的制定实施受多种因素影响，对一些重要因素阐述如下：

(1)国家及地方经济发展水平：对生态林进行补偿的关键问题是资金。一般而言，国家经济发展整体水平制约着公益林的发展，补偿标准的确定要与国家经济发展水平相适应，而且不同的地区经济发展水平也具有差异性，制定森林生态效益补偿标准应结合地区经济发展水平，因地制宜地制定合理的补偿标准。

(2)森林生态系统质量：生态质量的高低是由多样性、自然度、脆弱性和人类威胁、面积适宜性和美学上的舒适感等共同决定的。因此，对于生态质量较高的林分适当降低管护费用，而生态质量相对较差的则提高管护标准，避免大面积平均使用财力和按面积固化补偿标准。

(3)生态区位：在制定森林生态效益补偿标准时应考虑地域生态系统的重要性及生态系统服务功能的差异性，生态区位重要、生态脆弱地带的公益林，一般分布在条件比较恶劣的环境中，其生长受到环境的抑制，生长状况相对较差，营造、管护、抚育需要更多的资金投入。

(4)林种：《森林法》将防护林和特种用途林划归为生态公益林。防护林相当一部分可以产生直接经济效益，如农田牧场防护林为某一特定经济主体占有经营，既可以从择伐木获得经济收益又可从提高农牧产品产量获得经济收益；特种用途林的情况较复杂，如森林公园可以从门票中获得一定的收入，自然保护区内的禁伐林没有任何经济收益。因此，确定公益林补偿标准时应该考虑不同林种的收益状况区别对待。

(5)林分质量：生态公益林的林分质量直接关系到补偿资金的分配比例，不同的林种、树种具有不同的造林成本，其发挥的生态效益也不同。同一树种，不同的林龄、林分质量所发挥的生态效益也不同。因此，应综合考虑林种、树种、林龄、林分质量，科学地确定森林生态效益补偿的标准。

(6)林地权属：国有生态公益林不需要支付经济损失补偿只需要落实管护补助资金，集体所有、企业所有和林农个人所有的生态公益林在落实管护补助资金的基础上，还要补偿其因禁止商业经营所造成的经济损失。

5.2 确定公益林生态补偿标准的主要方法

5.2.1 现有方法及其特点

(1)生态系统服务功能价值法：运用市场价值法、机会成本法、基本成本法、人力资本法、生产成本法和置换成本法等方法估算出生态系统服务功能的价值，并且利用估算出的价值进一步确定出生态补偿的标准(张家来，2007a；2007b)，更加接近自然真实生态效益，一般为生态补偿的理论标准，成为生态补偿的上限。缺点是数据需求量大，计算繁琐，生态服务功能结果往往非常大，超出人类社会生产的价值；研究人员采用不同的指标及不同的计算方法，所计算的结果不一样。

(2)生态效益等价分析法：定量化生态功能损失的一种方法，并且可以计算出弥补生态功能破坏所需要的补偿比例。优点是能够很好地度量生态环境被损害的价值。缺点是由于有很多假设，在假设条件没有被满足时，得到的结果是不准确的；很多时候，得到的结果并不能充分反映当前的情况；由于参数因子很多，需要专业人员进行认证，在这个过程中可能会出现由于因子选择差异造成的评价结果不同(Richard *et al*，2004；Brian *et al*，2006)。

(3)市场价值法：把生态系统服务功能看成一种商品，围绕着商品建立一个市场，市场的买卖双方分别是生态补偿的补偿者和受偿者。优点是能够兼顾生态补偿的补偿者和受偿者两方面的利益，在双方都能达到满意的条件下开展生态补偿，这是其他方法所不具备的。缺点是生态系统服务功能的市场不容易建立，存在某些技术性的局限，其使用范围小(Robles *et al*，1997；Bishop *et al*，2002)。

(4)意愿调查法：通过询问被调查者对于改善或者保护环境的支付意愿，从而确立补偿标准。优点是可以把生态补偿利益相关方的收入、直接成本和预期等因素整合为简单的意愿，避免了大量的基础数据调查，而且根据意愿调查获得的数据能够得出生态系统服务提供者自主提供优质生态系统服务的成本，也可以得到补偿提供者所愿意支付的最大值，直接针对利益相关者进行调查，故其应用范围很广。缺点是风险比较大，调查得出的结论可能会与真正的意愿不相符合(James，2003；Walter *et al*，2008)。

(5)机会成本法：该法主要考量生态系统服务功能的提供者为了保护生态环境所放弃的经济收入、发展机会等。优点是直接补偿生态系统服务功能的提供者保护环境所遭受的经济损失，可以准确的计算出区域保护环境的成本，避免了对复杂的生态系统服务功能价值的估算。缺点是所考虑的机会成本不全面，数据的真实性决定机会成本法的准确度，大部分社会调查得出的数据都带有偏差(陈钦，2006；Stefano *et al*，2007)。

(6)微观经济学模型法：主要的原理是关于生态系统服务功能提供者和享受者的微观决策，也就是经济学中生产者和消费者的生产或消费决策过程。优点是通过严格的经济学推导，得出理论上的结果，属于客观的推理过程，具有逻辑严谨等特点，可以作为生态补偿标准方法研究的理论依据。缺点是大量的探讨理论上的数值关系并没有被实证研究所证实，其应用价值还处于探索阶段。利用微观经济学模型法来确定生态补偿的标准还没有形成一个较为统一的体系(Sven *et al*，2008)。

5.2.2 确定补偿标准的新方法

综上所述，生态服务功能法虽然客观地考虑了公益林的生态价值，在我国研究也比较广泛，但该方法所计算的结果较大，部分评价指标及其评价方法公众难以认可，也超出政府对生态效益补偿的承受能力，所以往往成为生态效益补偿的理论标准；市场价值法在操作上比较简单而支付意愿法相对成熟，在国外已经得到很好的应用，而国内暂时没有形成较为规范的交易市场，现阶段在我国无法推广；生态效益等价分析法和微观经济学模型都还处于理论研究阶段，在实际操作中还没有形成成熟的案例；意愿调查法主要取决于被调查者的素质，很难形成可靠地依据，使政府部门制定补偿标准存在很大的差异。

众所周知，对于同一林分，在其被区划为公益林或商品林前后，其森林生物量和森林生态效益是一定的。于是得出两点推论：一是立地条件、林龄和林分结构基本相同的两块林分，在其被区划为公益林和商品林前后，两者的森林生物量和森林生态效益是基本相等的；二是被区划为公益林的经营者或所有者，在公益林因保护需要不能被采伐利用期间，每年应当获得与同质商品林常规经营收益等额甚至更高的补偿。这可以看作提出机会成本法的基础理论。

机会成本法是指在无市场价格的情况下，资源使用的成本可以用所牺牲的替代用途的收入来估算。在公益林生态补偿中，不是直接用保护森林的收益来测量，而是用为了保护森林资源而牺牲的最大的替代选择的价值去测量。在具体计算中，以林农为保护森林资源而放弃的木材经营价值来衡量。

因此，相对其他方法而言，我们认为机会成本法更为简捷直观，更能被广大林农和社会各界认同，具有更强的可操作性。在实际应用中，有可能忽略或遗漏某些机会成本，但其评价结果与我国经济发展现状以及林业整体水平较为适应，可以直接计算生态系统服务功能提供者因保护环境所遭受的经济损失，并可以准确计量各地区保护环境的成本。根据机会成本确定的生态补偿额度能达到促使补偿者自觉保护环境的目的，而且机会成本法避免了对生态系统服务功能价值的复杂估算，得到简单的保护成本，既维护了保护者的基本利益，也为补偿者预留了尽力提高补偿标准的余地。

然而，均一的补偿标准往往会使生态补偿存在较大的缺陷，应当考虑不同生态区位公益林的生态价值差异。本研究着力提出"可操作性较强、政府可以接受、林农比较满意、公众觉得公平、将来还可增加"的公益林补偿标准确定方法，提出在机会成本法的基础上，增加生态区位重要度这个调节系数，综合确定其补偿标准，对于特别重要生态区位的公益林给予更多补偿，一般生态区位的公益林给予较少补偿，以使生态补偿标准既体现对公益林拥有者的利益保护，也体现不同生态区位下公益林生态服务功能的差异。我们将这种新方法暂且命名为"机会成本－生态区位调节法"。

5.3 实例研究结果

5.3.1 马尾松林分类型划分

我国生态公益林按照主导功能可以划分为防护林、特种用途林；按照建设等级可以分为国家级、省级、市县级公益林；按照权属可以分为国家公益林和集体公益林；按照保护程度又分为重点公益林、一般公益林。但在特定时空条件下，社会经济发展对生态公益林服务功能主导需求是不同的，所以对生态补偿范围尽量遵循 2 个原则：一是生态优先、确保重点，因地制宜、因害设防，集中连片、合理布局，实现生态效益和经济社会效益的和谐统一；二是尊重林权所有者和经营者的自主权，维护林权的稳定性，保证已确立承包关系的连续性。据此将我国公益林生态效益补偿森林类型、划分标准、补偿原则等列表 1。

根据国家"七五"林业攻关课题"马尾松人工林速生丰产技术研究"的结果，本研究按立地指数将湖北省马尾松林分划分为好（Ⅰ）、中（Ⅱ）、差（Ⅲ）3 个立地等级。其中Ⅰ级马尾松林分立地指数在 18 以上，Ⅱ级的立地指数 14～16，Ⅲ级的立地指数低于 12。

5.3.2 马尾松公益林补偿标准

（1）生态补偿标准测算的设定条件：

①依据湖北省马尾松产区及自然条件，确定其种源为南带良种；

②轮伐期内不考虑间伐，收入主要为第 20 年木材销售收入；

③依据当下银行利率等因此，参考相关文献，林业行业贴现率确定为 5%；

④以轮伐期 20 年计算，种植密度均为 2500 株/hm^2；

⑤不考虑地租；

⑥经营模式为常规（一般）经营水平：第一年造林，抚育三年，以后各年成本仅为固定管护费，第 20 年采伐销售。

表1 公益林生态效益补偿森林类型表

类型组	类型	划分标准	补偿原则
防护林	水源涵养林	以涵养水源、改善水文状况、调节水的小循环和防止河流、湖泊、水库淤塞以及保护居民点饮水水源为主要目的的森林	水源涵养林主要提供生态环境服务，保护水资源。按照目前的财力，采取不充分补偿的原则，调整水资源价格，成为一种有效的外部成本内部化的经济补偿形式
	水土保持林	以减缓地表径流、减少冲刷、防止水土流失，保持和恢复土壤肥力为主要用途的森林	除了水土保持林的造林、抚育、管护费用外，从事生产建设等活动损坏水土保持设施，使其水土保持功能降低或丧失的，应根据其生态环境破坏的估算价值缴纳水土保持林补偿费
	防风固沙林	以降低风速、防止风蚀、固定沙地、保护农田、果园、经济作物、牧场免受风沙侵袭为主要用途的森林	对于符合条件的防风固沙林，根据其保护的效果，给予相应的资金补助和经济补偿
	护岸林	以防止岸坡被水冲刷崩塌、固定河床为主要目的的森林	政府应支付征用或占用林地的土地补偿费和安置补助费等
特种用途林	国防林	为军事需要而划定的森林。如沿海边疆或要塞、基地等有利于我方军事隐蔽的森林	具有特殊的用途，不以经济收益为目的，根据造林、抚育及管护的成本由国家进行补偿
	自然保护林	指专门划定的，用以保护珍奇动植物资源、典型的生物群落和自然景观等的森林	补偿主体是中央地方财政、受益地区以及保护区内依托森林资源的相关产业

(2)林分投入产出的测算方法与结果：

①营林成本：营造林地所投入的资金及人力即为营林成本，分为不变成本和可变成本。不变成本包括种苗、整地、栽植、抚育、管护等费用，其标准参照《防护林造林工程投资估算指标(试行)》(2009，北京)；可变成本为采运成本，包括木材采伐、加工及运输等费用，与产量成正比。各年度成本内容及额度见表2，其中工价为当地当前平均工价，采用长江中上游平均工价60元/工日。

②生长与收获预测：根据国家八五科技攻关项目的研究结果，集成马尾松林优势高生长模型、胸径生长模型、直径分布模型和树高曲线方程等(王鹏程等，2000a；王鹏程等，2000b)，预测马尾松人工林生长过程；在此基础上，利用建立的削度方程与出材率表材积方程预测林分木材产量(王鹏程等，2001；王鹏程等，2000b)。各级立地公顷出材量见表3。

③营林收入：因不考虑间伐，也不采取其他经营措施，则轮伐期内前19年没有收入，20年时采伐销售，不营林，没有投入成本。每公顷森林木材销售利润按下式计算：

$$P = (V \times r \times n \times s - C' \times V) \times (1 - q)$$

式中：V—— 单株材积；

r—— 出材率；

n—— 每公顷株数；

s—— 每立方米木材价格，依据当下市场平均价格取600元/m^3。

C'—— 每立方米采运成本；

q—— 税率，采用3%。

表 2　各年度营林成本统计表

年份	不变成本					可变成本			总计(元/hm^2)
	种苗(元/株)	整地(工日/hm^2)	栽植(工日/hm^2)	抚育(工日/hm^2)	管护[元/(hm^2·年)]	采伐(元/m^3)	加工(元/m^3)	装载运输(元/m^3)	
第 1 年	0.2	58	23	18	50				6490
第 2 年				18	50				1130
第 3 年				18	50				1130
第 4 年					50				50
第 5 年					50				50
……					……				……
第 19 年					50				50
第 20 年						80	50	200	330 × V

表 3　各级立地公顷出材量

指数级	D(cm)	H(m)	出材率	单株出材(m^3)	公顷株数	公顷出材(m^3)
10	11.8	10.0	0.82	0.046801	2500	117.0024
12	11.9	12.0	0.83	0.057455	2500	143.6372
14	12.5	13.7	0.85	0.073378	2500	183.4457
16	13.0	16.3	0.86	0.094594	2500	236.4861
18	14.9	17.6	0.88	0.134621	2500	336.5535

(3)补偿标准的测算与确定：

采用机会成本法，根据各技术经济指标和生长预测结果，采用贴现方法，计算净利润和净现值(NPV)，确定补偿价值。在计算过程中，按照分类补偿的原则，先分别计算立地指数为 10、12、14、16、18 的生态补偿标准，再分别计算不同生态区位的调节系数。

①净现值 NPV 计算：

以 20 年净现值 NPV 作为标准，采用贴现方法进行计算：

$$\mathrm{NPV} = \sum_{t=1}^{20} \frac{Ct}{(1+i)^{t-1}}$$

式中，i——贴现率；

Ct——第 t 年净资金流量。

②内部收益率 IRR 计算：

$$\mathrm{IRR} = i\text{低} + \frac{(i\text{高} - i\text{低}) \times \mathrm{NPV}_i\text{低}}{\mathrm{NPV}_i\text{低} + \mathrm{NPV}_i\text{高}}$$

③补偿额度计算：

据上，测算不同立地指数级公益林的净现值和净利润列于表 4，并得出各级立地每年每亩补偿金额见表 5。

净现值计算方法是动态的经济评价方法，可以较好反映项目的盈利状况，但针对生态公益林补偿存在一定缺陷：一是公益林生态补偿是对现有林进行补偿，不存在现阶段造林项目实施，因此，其补偿是对前期造林与管护、近期管护工作的补偿，无需贴现；二是公益林补偿标准不可能年年变动，不可能随经济增长灵敏波动。因此，建议按净利润法确定补偿标准。将上述计算结果按立地等级进行算术平均得出，Ⅰ立地等级马尾松公益林平均补偿标准为 196.7 元/(亩·年)，Ⅱ级为 114.6 元/(亩·年)，Ⅲ级为 62.9 元/(亩·年)。

表 4 不同立地指数级马尾松公益林投入产出表

指数级	公顷出材(m^3)	投入(元/hm^2)	产出(元/hm^2)	NPV(元/hm^2)	IRR	净利润(元/hm^2)	净现值[元/(亩·年)]	净利润[(元/(亩·年)]
10	117.00	48481	70202	3419	6.9	21721	11.4	54.3
12	143.64	57550	86183	6265	8.1	28633	20.9	71.6
14	183.46	71109	110067	10518	9.5	38958	35.1	97.4
16	236.49	89172	141891	16185	11.0	52719	54.0	131.8
18	336.55	123251	201932	26877	13.2	78681	89.6	196.7

*注：表中投入与产出为未折现实际值。

表 5 不同立地指数马尾松林机会成本法补偿金额计算值

指数级	10	12	14	16	18	备注
补偿金额[元/(亩·年)]	11.4	20.9	35.1	54.0	89.6	净现值法
	54.3	71.6	97.4	131.8	196.7	纯利润法

④生态区位调节系数：为了便于统计分析和生态补偿资金的发放与管理，我们采用与森林分类和公益林区划完全一致的标准，根据公益林所处生态区位的重要度分别标定为国家级、省级、市县级，依次用极重(Ⅰ)区、较重(Ⅱ)区、一般(Ⅲ)区表示。并将各级自然保护区全部划归极重区。根据相关研究成果(张家来等，2008)，湖北省Ⅰ区、Ⅱ区、Ⅲ区的生态区位价值比为 21.15: 15.42: 12.86，为此确定湖北省马尾松公益林的生态区位调节系数(C)分别为Ⅰ区 137%、Ⅱ区 100%、Ⅲ区 83%。

根据某一具体小班马尾松公益林所处的立地等级、生态区位与小班面积，用对应的单位面积补偿标准、调节系数(C)和小班面积三者相乘，即可得出该小班每年应得生态补偿金额。

按照湖北省国家级、省级、市县级公益林的面积加权估计，其马尾松公益林的生态区位综合调节系数为 1.246，各立地等级的平均补偿标准应分别调节为Ⅰ级 245.1 元/(亩·年)，Ⅱ级 142.8 元/(亩·年)，Ⅲ级 78.4 元/(亩·年)。假定中央财政承担生态补偿标准全额的 20%，剩下的由地方财政和其他渠道分担，则中央财政补偿马尾松公益林的标准为：Ⅰ级 49.0 元/(亩·年)、Ⅱ级 28.6 元/(亩·年)、Ⅲ级 15.7 元/(亩·年)。

5.3.3 全省马尾松公益林生态补偿额度测算

根据湖北省森林资源二类调查成果(1999)，全省马尾松公益林共 1028.0 万亩，其中集体权属约为 522.2 万亩。Ⅰ级、Ⅱ级、Ⅲ级的马尾松林分别为 712.9 万亩、237.9 万亩、77.2 万亩，其中集体权属马尾松林分别为 362.2 万亩、120.9 万亩、39.1 万亩。据此并考虑生态区位调节系数，估测湖北省马尾松公益林生态补偿的总额度为 214743.9 万元/年，其中集体权属的马尾松公益林为 109098.9 万元/年；平均每亩 208.9 元/年。

假设中央财政按总额度的20%予以补偿，则可估算出全省马尾松公益林生态补偿额度42948.8万元/年，其中集体权属的马尾松公益林为21819.8万元/年；平均每亩41.8元/年。测算结果详见表6。

表6 全省马尾松公益林生态补偿额度测算一览表

立地等级	面积(万亩)		补偿标准	补偿额度(万元/年)		区位综合系数	全额补偿(万元/年)	
	合计	集体		合计	集体		合计	集体
总计	1028.0	522.2		172346.65	87559.27		214743.93	109098.85
Ⅰ	712.9	362.2	196.70	140227.43	71244.74	1.25	174723.38	88770.95
Ⅱ	237.9	120.9	114.60	27263.34	13855.14	1.25	33970.12	17263.50
Ⅲ	77.2	39.1	62.90	4855.88	2459.39	1.25	6050.43	3064.40

6 强化森林科学经营的途径与效益分析

马尾松是我国松属中分布最广、数量最多的主要用材树种，在南方各省区森林蓄积中约占半数。马尾松因其较高的综合利用程度和良好的木材特性，已成为重要的建筑及纸浆用材树种。

6.1 典型经营模式

根据已有研究成果和实践经验，对于马尾松人工林，必须针对不同种源、立地条件和初植密度，结合当地社会经济条件来确定最佳主伐年龄，才能够充分有效地利用林地生产力，为社会生产出更多合格的林产品，并提高森林经营者的收益。因此，本研究侧重从经济角度出发，探讨湖北省马尾松建筑用材林和纸浆林的典型经营模式。

6.1.1 立地选择

立地质量对林木生长影响很大，故立地选择在人工林培育中占有十分重要的地位。结合湖北省实际，选择12、14、16、18共4个立地指数级进行分析。

6.1.2 种源选择

研究表明，不同种源的种苗对马尾松的平均胸径、平均高、平均优势高等变量都有显著影响，南带良种在林分胸径、树高生长等方面有明显优势(丁贵杰，1997)，因此选择南带良种进行经营模式设计。

6.1.3 整地方式

整地与林木生长的关系十分复杂，它与立地条件、土壤理化性质等因素有密切的关系。鉴于块状整地灵活性大，省工，成本较低，并结合湖北省自然条件及生产实际，均选用块状整地的方式。

6.1.4 密度效应

不同的造林密度对于林分的胸径生长等有显著影响，进而影响林分的蓄积及出材量。而且根据培育目标不同，造林密度也有差异。对于建筑用材林和纸浆林，采用不同的密植措施，对于其经济效益将会产生不同的影响。

6.1.5 采伐年龄的确定

过大的采伐年龄并不一定能够带来更高的经济效益，确定人工林主伐年龄的依据是林分成熟龄，即数量成熟龄、工艺成熟龄和经济成熟龄。具体原则是：“以工艺成熟为基限，重点考虑经济成熟，适当兼顾数量成熟。”

根据所选用的一整套生长与收获相容性模型，以林分材积平均生长量最大时的年龄为数量成熟龄；根据各技术经济指标和生长预测结果，采用贴现方法，以净现值(NPV)最大为标准，适当兼顾内部收益率(IRR)的方法确定经济成熟龄；工艺成熟龄一般按材种平均生长量最大确定。

综合考虑3个成熟龄，根据权重法来确定主伐年龄。当经济成熟龄大于(或等于)工艺成熟龄时，主伐年龄的计算表达式为：主伐年龄 = 经济成熟龄 ×0.7 + 数量成熟龄 ×0.3；当经济成熟龄小于工艺成熟龄时，主伐年龄即为工艺成熟龄。

6.1.6 湖北省马尾松用材林的优化经营模式

研究表明，在适宜地区和立地上，选用马尾松南带优良种源可显著提高经济效益，故在经营措施优化过程中，确定选用南带优良种源。根据培育目标的不同，对栽培过程中其他主要经营措施，如密度、间伐次数、间伐时间、间伐强度、整地方式和施肥进行合理组合，形成众多可供选择的马尾松人工林经营模式。用所建经营模型系统，先对各种培育方案的生长效应、收获量、主伐年龄、经济效益等进行综合评价和分析，确定出各种成熟龄和主伐年龄，然后对各经营模式采用搜索对比法进行优化比较，最后结合不同培育目标，分别从不同指数级选出建筑用材林和纸浆林的1～2种优化经营模式(表7)，并采用相应的造林、抚育、经营管理、采伐等具体的经营措施(表8)。

6.2 林分收获预测及投入产出效益分析

利用相关研究结果，组装马尾松人工林不同种源生长效应增长百分比预测模型、不同整地方式的生长效应预估模型、立地指数预测模型(优势高生长模型)、疏伐模型系统、间伐木平均胸径预测模型、伐后直径生长模型、胸径生长模型、直径分布模型、树高曲线方程、湖北省马尾松二元材积公式及材种出材率表等进行林分生长收获的预测(丁贵杰，1997；王鹏程等 2000b)。

为进行经济分析，调查收集马尾松人工林营林生产投入、采伐及木材加工成本、装车、销售、运费、木材价格和各种间接费用等技术经济指标，详见表9。

表7 不同立地马尾松人工林优化经营模式

林分类型	SI	培育目标	树种配置	造林密度	整地	间伐(时间、强度)	保留密度	主伐年龄
建筑用材林	14	小径材	纯林	2500	块状	2(11a，30%；15a，25%)	1312	23
	16	中径材	纯林	1667	块状	2(13a，20%；17a，20%)	1067	22
	18	中径材	纯林	1667	块状	2(12a，20%；16a，20%)	1067	20
		大径材	纯林	1667	块状	2(12a，25%；16a，25%)	939	26
纸浆林	12	小径材	纯林	4444	块状	1(11a，30%)	3110	20
	14	小径材	纯林	3900	块状	1(11a，25%)	2925	19
	16	小径材	纯林	3333	块状	1(11a，25%)	2378	18
	18	小径材	纯林	2500	块状	1(10a，25%)	1812	17

表 8　马尾松用材林主要经营措施表

经营措施	关键环节	建筑用材林	纸浆林
A. 造林技术	树种配置	纯林	纯林
	整地方式	块状，40cm×40cm×30cm。	块状，40cm×40cm×30cm。
	种苗要求	Ⅰ级、Ⅱ级实生苗木。	Ⅰ级、Ⅱ级实生苗木。
	造林方法	人工造林	人工造林
	造林密度	幼苗 1600～2500 株/hm^2，分布均匀。	幼苗 2500～4400 株/hm^2，分布均匀。
B. 幼林抚育		连续抚育 3 年，松土、除草、除萌、培土。	连续抚育 3 年，松土、除草、除萌、培土。
C. 成林抚育		间伐两次，分别在 12 年、16 年左右，强度为 20%～30%。	在 10 年左右，强度为 25%～30%。
D. 采伐利用		皆伐或小片择伐	皆伐或小片择伐
E. 培育目标		主要为中径材或大径材。	主要培育小径材。
F. 经营周期		20 年或以上	20 年或以内

表 9　马尾松用材林经营主要技术经济指标

费用	建筑材			纸浆材			
	14	16	18	12	14	16	18
林地清理费(元/hm^2)	600	600	600	600	600	600	600
整地费(元/ hm^2)	2880	1920	1920	4493	4493	3840	2880
栽植费(元/ hm^2)	1380	920	920	2453	2153	1840	1380
种苗费(元/株)	500	320	320	889	780	667	500
抚育间伐费(元/ hm^2)	8590	9639	10400	6856	7549	8430	9154
间接费(元/ hm^2)	50	50	50	50	50	50	50
采伐费(元/m^3)	80	80	80	80	80	80	80
木材加工(元/m^3)	50	50	50	30	30	30	30
装车销售(元/m^3)	50	50	50	50	50	50	50
运输费(元/m^3)	150	150	150	150	150	150	150

采用以上方法，预测林分主伐年龄及采伐时的平均树高、平均胸径以及公顷出材量结果见表 10。根据各技术经济指标和生长预测结果，采用贴现方法，计算净现值和内部收益率，结果也列于表 10。

由表 10 可以看出，不同立地条件马尾松生长情况差别较大，应根据实际立地情况选择经营类型。建筑用材林对立地要求更高，立地指数低于 12 则不适宜经营纸浆林，低于 14 不适于经营建筑用材林。而且林分密度应适当。由于建筑用材对材径要求较高，主要培育中径材到大径材，造林密度相对较低，其间伐次数及强度均大于纸浆林；而纸浆林对材径要求不高，可以适当密植，以充分发挥林地生产力，创造更高的经济效益。

表10 马尾松用材林科学经营的生长收获与效益预测表

经营类型	SI	培育目标	主伐年龄	H	D	出材量(m^3)	NPV	IRR(%)
建筑用材林	14	小径材	23	16.3	20.3	334.349	13416.0	11.6
	16	中径材	22	17.9	23.8	399.953	21059.7	15.3
	18	中径材	20	18.6	24.8	447.499	25449.7	17.9
		大径材	26	22.0	29.0	622.665	41622.8	14.3
纸浆林	12	小径材	20	11.0	12.7	226.000	2209.1	9.1
	14	小径材	19	12.3	13.6	269.297	6971.0	11.0
	16	小径材	18	14.0	15.7	324.353	13473.8	13.9
	18	小径材	17	15.8	18.3	369.641	19600.1	17.3

6.3 马尾松不同经营模式的收获效益比较

按常规技术生产和经营马尾松用材林，不同立地等级的马尾松林的生长收获及经济技术指标见表11。常规技术生产和经营马尾松林年木材生产量分别为：Ⅲ级为0.4934m^3/(亩·年)、Ⅱ级为0.8405m^3/(亩·年)、Ⅰ级为1.1218m^3/(亩·年)；年净利润分别为99.24元/(亩·年)、189.29元/(亩·年)、262.27元/(亩·年)。

选择科学经营技术，培育马尾松林建筑材和纸浆材生长收获及经济技术指标也列于表11。按湖北省马尾松林培育建筑材和纸浆材的面积分别为70%和30%估算，采用森林科学经营模式，优化经营马尾松林年木材生产量分别为：Ⅲ级为0.7913m^3/(亩·年)、Ⅱ级1.2166m^3/(亩·年)、Ⅰ级为1.4790m^3元/(亩·年)，年净利润分别为174.6元/(亩·年)、281.53元/(亩·年)、349.054元/(亩·年)。

与同等立地条件下常规经营的产量和效益相比，科学经营模式的Ⅲ、Ⅱ、Ⅰ立地等级马尾松林分年木材生产量分别提高了60.4%、44.7%和31.8%，年净利润分别提高了76.0%、48.7%、33.1%。

6.4 全省马尾松林科学经营效益总体估计

根据湖北省森林资源二类调查成果(1999)，全省商品用材林中马尾松约为2258.2万亩，其中Ⅰ、Ⅱ、Ⅲ立地等级的马尾松林分别为1566.02万亩、522.59万亩、169.59万亩。按上述单位面积产量和效益以及全省马尾松林培育建筑材和纸浆材的面积比例为70%和30%估算，常规经营模式的总体年木材产量为2279.67万m^3，单位面积平均年木材产量为1.01m^3/(亩·年)；总体年净利润为526471.24万元，单位面积平均年净利润为233.14元/(亩·年)。采用科学经营模式，总体的年木材产量将达到3086.12万m^3，单位面积平均年木材产量为1.37m^3/(亩·年)；总体的年净利润为723354.46万元，单位面积平均年净利润增长到320.32元/(亩·年)。两种经营模式对比分析，采取科学经营方式和技术，全省马尾松用材林年木材产量将增加806.45万m^3，增产35.4%；年净利润增加196883.22万元，增收37.4%，说明森林科学经营的效益十分明显。马尾松用材林不同经营模式的产量与效益比较列于表12。

表 11　不同经营模式技术指标与效益比较表

经营类型/模式	SI	技术指标				生长与收获						效益比较				
		种源	初植密度(株/hm^2)	幼林抚育	间伐(时间、强度)	主伐年龄(a)	保留密度(株/hm^2)	平均胸径(cm)	平均树高(m)	单株材积(m^3)	公顷出材(m^3)	投入(元/hm^2)	产出(元/hm^2)	净利润(元/hm^2)	NPV(元/hm^2)	IRR(%)
常规经营	10	南带	2500	3a	不间伐	20	2500	11.8	10.0	0.04680	117.00	48481	70202	21721	3419	6.9
	12	南带	2500	3a	不间伐	20	2500	11.9	12.0	0.05746	143.64	57550	86183	28633	6265	8.1
	14	南带	2500	3a	不间伐	20	2500	12.5	13.7	0.07338	183.45	71109	110067	38958	10518	9.5
	16	南带	2500	3a	不间伐	20	2500	13.0	16.3	0.09459	236.49	89172	141891	52719	16185	11.0
	18	南带	2500	3a	不间伐	20	2500	14.9	17.6	0.13462	336.55	123251	201932	78681	26877	13.2
科学经营:建筑用材林	14	南带	2500	3a	2(11a,30%;15a,25%)	23	1312	20.3	16.3	0.25484	334.35	124335	200609	76274	13416	11.6
	16	南带	1667	3a	2(13a,20%;17a,20%)	22	1067	23.8	17.9	0.37484	399.95	145433	239972	94539	21060	15.3
	18	南带	1667	3a	2(12a,20%;16a,20%)	20	1067	24.8	18.6	0.41940	447.50	161885	268499	106614	25450	17.9
	18	南带	1667	3a	2(12a,25%;16a,25%)	26	939	29.0	22.0	0.66312	622.67	219689	373599	153910	41623	14.3
科学经营:纸浆林	12	南带	4444	3a	1(11a,30%)	20	3110	12.7	11.0	0.07267	226.00	89921	135600	45679	2209	9.1
	14	南带	3900	3a	1(11a,25%)	19	2925	13.6	12.3	0.09207	269.30	104493	161578	57085	6971	11.0
	16	南带	3333	3a	1(11a,25%)	18	2378	15.7	14.0	0.13640	324.35	122463	194612	72149	13474	13.9
	18	南带	2500	3a	1(10a,25%)	17	1812	18.3	15.8	0.20400	369.64	136546	221785	85239	19600	17.3

*注:表口投入与产出为未折现实际值。

表 12 马尾松用材林不同经营模式产量与效益比较表

立地等级	单位面积对比						面积(万亩)	总体估计			
	年产量			年净利润				年产量		年净利润	
	常规经营(元/亩)	科学经营(元/亩)	比增(%)	常规经营(元/亩)	科学经营(元/亩)	比增(%)		常规经营(万 m^3)	科学经营(万 m^3)	常规经营(万元)	科学经营(万元)
总计							2258.20	2279.67	3086.12	526471.24	723354.46
Ⅰ	1.1218	1.479	31.84	262.27	349.05	33.09	1566.02	1756.76	2316.14	410720.07	546619.28
Ⅱ	0.8405	1.2166	44.75	189.29	281.53	48.73	522.59	439.24	635.78	98921.06	147124.76
Ⅲ	0.4934	0.7913	60.38	99.24	174.60	75.94	169.59	83.68	134.20	16830.11	29610.41

7 相关政策措施与建议

完善森林生态补偿制度和强化森林科学经营是一项刻不容缓、任务繁多、结构复杂、影响深远的社会系统工程，仅仅研究和提出相关的理论、方法和技术，不能从根本上解决当前存在的主要问题。只有及时研究和出台推广、落实和保障各项技术方法的配套政策和法律法规，才能收到事半功倍、一劳永逸的成效。为此，提出如下政策措施与建议：

7.1 关于森林生态补偿的政策建议

7.1.1 尽快确立森林生态补偿标准的形成机制

公益林的价值包括森林自身的商品价值和生态价值，对公益林的补偿主要考虑其生态价值。由于生态公益林禁止商品性采伐，其所有者或经营者投入的营造林成本无法正常回收。随着社会经济的发展，生态公益林保护越来越多地受到价值规律的冲击。对于公益林的所有者和经营者给予合理经济补偿，是完善森林生态效益补偿机制、保证公益林持续发挥生态效益的客观需要。当前国家和省级确定的森林生态补偿标准较低，且缺乏科学的测算依据，群众普遍反映这一补偿标准不能体现森林的自有价值，因而一些地区生态公益林管护的效果并不理想。为此，建议国家研究出台公益林生态补偿标准的测算方法，尽快明确全国各地公益林的生态补偿标准，进而确立森林生态补偿标准的形成机制。例如，本研究提出的生态林补偿标准是以当前商品木材市场价格为基数测算的，是一个不完全的较低补偿标准，今后应随着木材市场价格的变化以及物价指数的变动适当进行相应调整。

本研究提出的测算公益林生态补偿标准的新方法——“机会成本—生态区位调节法”，是以森林的木材商品价值为补偿基点，兼顾了确定生态补偿标准的主要影响因素，具有“可操作性较强、政府可以接受、林农比较满意、社会觉得公平，将来还可增加”等特点和优势，其科学性、前瞻性、灵活性和可操作性十分明显，建议国家林业局组织有关方面充分论证后推广实施，为尽快科学确立公益林生态补偿标准的形成机制奠定坚实基础。

7.1.2 积极建立多渠道生态补偿机制

鉴于森林生态效益是为社会公众服务的，所以其生态补偿费用理应由各级人民政府代表社会公民利用公共财政资金率先买单，并合理确定中央和地方各级财政的分摊比例。要逐步建立政府主导、市场运作、社会参与的生态补偿和生态建设投融资机制，积极引导国内外资金投向生态建设和环境保护。既要坚持政府主导，努力增加公共财政对生态补偿的投入，又要积极引导社会各方参与，拓宽生态补偿市场化、社会化运作的路子，形成多方并举、合力推进森林生态效益补偿的有效途径。以中央财政森林生态效益补偿基金为导向，将利益的提供者和获得者的权利、义务、责任综合起来，重新配置市场资源。同时应按照谁开发谁保护、谁受益谁补偿的基本原则，建立健全森林生态补偿体制。如，通过建立生态价值评估体系，完善区际生态补偿政策，或者通过征收生态税等形式，建立诸如流域下游对上游、工业区对林业区的反哺协调机制；对于依托森林资源开发并对植被保护和恢复负有责任的石油、矿产、水利、电力、旅游、野生动物表演等行业，应当在其经营收入中核定一定比例的森林生态补偿基金。

7.1.3 探索建立多元化补偿制度

将资金补偿作为森林生态效益补偿的一种基本方式，探索建立多元化补偿方式并存的制度。重点公益林的生态区位非常重要，而大多数地方经济欠发展，农民群众世代靠山吃山，林木既是主要经济来源，也是主要能源。只有很好地解决了农民吃饭和烧材问题，才能从根本上保护好重点公益林。因此，建议国家在农村能源建设、基本农田建设和退耕还林等惠农政策上，在森林防火、林业有害生物防治等管护能力建设上，向重点公益林区域适当倾斜照顾。对于自然条件恶劣、生存条件较差的地区，国家应加大生态移民力度。对非国有的重点公益林试行国家收购政策，实行一次性或分步骤买断，可大幅度降低生态补偿成本。对于自然保护区内非国有的森林，在核心区内的，由国家进行赎买，转变其所有制形式；在实验区内的，应完善林下资源开发政策，允许林农通过林下资源利用开发获得部分收益。对于风景名胜区内的公益林资源，应通过资产评估进行资本运营，采取与直接利益者利益分成的方式解决公益林补偿问题。对生态公益林的经营者和管护者可以给予粮食、油料、燃料等实物补偿，还应适当减免公益林经营者和保护者的税收。

7.1.4 全面推进补偿立法工作

森林生态效益补偿制度是我国《森林法》确定的重要森林资源保护管理制度，对于加强森林资源保护，维护生态安全具有重大而深远的作用。当前，我国森林生态效益补偿制度的法律体系尚不完备，亟待加快立法进程，以法律明确以下重要内容，为森林生态补偿工作提供法律保障：一是明确生态补偿的必要性和强制性。应明文规定凡国家和地方政府纳入生态公益林范围的森林，必须对权益人进行补偿，并由政府负责强制执行。二是明确补偿标准的形成机制。在确定科学实用的公益林生态补偿标准测算办法的基础上，规定补偿金额与木材市场价格和物价指数挂钩的调节机制，以保障森林生态效益提供者的合法权益。三是明确建立补偿基金制度的方法、措施，明确补偿基金的筹措渠道、补偿范围、补偿对象等内容。四是制定补偿基金管理办法。明确管理部门、管理与使用制度，规范资金运行，防止资金的滥用。五是明确森林生态补偿制度有关法律约束的各个方面的权利、义务和法律责任。对不按有关规定执行生态补偿制度相关法律的单位和个人，制定相应的行政和刑事处罚条款。

7.1.5 切实强化补偿资金管理

生态公益林补偿资金管理中的违规行为严重影响资金的使用效率，恶化了干群关系，败坏了社会风气，甚至给地方社会稳定带来了现实的威胁。为此，建议采取以下措施，保证生态公益林补偿资金的安全运行，并遏制职务犯罪：一是加强以报账制管理为核心的资金管理工作，防止资金被挤占、挪用、截留。二是补偿资金实行专户储存、专账管理、专款专用、封闭运行，任何单位和个人不得挤占、挪用、截留、借用。三是建立健全补偿资金管理责任制，要层层签订责任状，明确各级政府“一把手”为第一责任人，对资金管理工作负全责。

四是建立健全监督网。建立由纪检监察机关牵头，林业、审计、检察等部门参加的补偿资金监督网，采取定期召开联席办公会议、信息资料交换和联合检查等方式，共同开展资金监管工作。五是强化合同的约束功能。要严格执行管护合同，严格质量检查验收程序，防止虚报假冒或者以次充好。

7.2 关于森林科学经营的政策建议

7.2.1 全面实施森林分类经营

森林分类经营是实现森林科学经营的重要基础，也是开展森林科学经营的关键举措。我国实施森林分类经营多年，取得了巨大成效，积累了丰富经验，也暴露了一些问题，出现了新的矛盾。为此建议：一是各地认真总结分析以往实施森林分类经营的成绩和问题，对分类区划明显不合理的地段及时进行调整；二是切实做好宣传和解释工作，化解群众的不良情绪，及时处理公益林生态补偿资金发放不及时不到位等问题；三是对于森林分类经营工作开展迟缓的地方，要加强引导和指导，为森林科学经营提供基本保障。

7.2.2 强力推进集体林权制度改革

当前，集体林权制度改革工作正在全国各地蓬勃开展，为商品林科学经营创造了有利条件。但是，林改之后，南方集体林区林权分散、林块分散的现状，导致林权主体利益的多元化、营林行为方式的多元化，给森林科学经营造成了较大困难。为此，在主体改革基本完成后，应大力推进林木采伐管理以及森林资源评估、流转、抵押等领域的配套改革，积极整合林业资源，引导和帮助林农通过租赁、股份合作、成立林农合作组织、建立林业要素市场等多种方式，努力实现集体林区商品林的规模经营、集约经营乃至科学经营。

7.2.3 不断加大政策激励和资金投入

影响森林科学经营的因素较多，其中良种壮苗、技术指导、科技示范、资金扶持、人才培养是比较突出的因素。为此建议国家出台以下激励政策：一是将国家目前实行的部分农业补贴政策延伸到林业领域，建立营林补助机制，对林木良种繁育、营林机械设备、森林科学经营必需的基础设施建设等给予补贴和扶持；二是选派专业技术人员深入林区，对林农和其他森林经营者无偿进行科技指导，科技人员的劳务费由政府列专项经费统一支付；三是选择条件成熟的林场和其他森林经营者开展科技推广与示范活动，将科技成果迅速转化为生产力，并带动周边群众走科学经营森林的道路；四是对实施森林科学经营的林农和其他森林经营者给予资金补贴和扶持，以提高全社会实行森林科学经营的积极性；五是加强森林科学经营的人才培养，鼓励农林院校大力培养森林科学经营人才，并提高这些人才的政治和经济待遇。同时，进一步加大再教育和科技培训力度，壮大森林科学经营的人才队伍。

7.2.4 积极推行森林经营方案制度

推进森林经营方案制度，是解决南方集体林区森林粗放经营的重要途径。为此，建议国家积极探索和推进南方集体林区实施森林经营方案制度，明确编案程序、办法、措施和审批机制，同时在森林采伐政策上明确对通过编案审批的森林经营者具有按方案优先采伐利用的政策便利，以此引导和推进森林经营方案制度的施行，保障森林科学经营技术与措施落到实处。

7.2.5 认真开展保护与发展森林资源目标责任制监督检查

实施森林科学经营是保护和发展森林资源的重要措施和基本要求。建立和执行保护与发展森林资源的目标责任制是《森林法》及其实施条例对地方各级人民政府的法律规定。为此，建议国家林业局各派驻森林资源监督机构在相关监督检查中，应强化对森林科学经营方面的检查和指导，督促县级以上地方人民政府积极采用森林科学经营方法和措施，建立健全保护与发展森林资源的任期目标责任制，切实做好森林资源保护和利用工作，实现青山常在、永续利用、越采越多、越采越好。

8 研究结论与讨论

在集体林权制度改革这个伟大壮举中，“生态受保护，农民得实惠”不仅是两句响亮的口号，而且必须采用坚实的理论技术和可行的政策法规予以推广落实。因此，本研究力图从理论和技术与政策和法规两个层面、一揽子解决公益林补偿和商品林科学经营的突出问题。得出的主要结论与建议如下：

(1)研究提出了确定公益林生态补偿标准的新方法——“机会成本 - 生态区位调节法”。该法以机会成本法为基础，以生态区位的重要度为调节系数，充分考虑了影响森林生态补偿标准的主要因素，进而能够比较直观、公平地评价公益林的生态价值，合理确定公益林生态补偿标准。

(2)研究表明，不同树种、不同立地条件、不同生态区位的森林生态价值存在显著差异。因此，公益林生态补偿标准应分别树种、立地等级和生态区位而确定。本研究初步确定了湖北省马尾松公益林生态补偿标准为：Ⅰ立地等级 196.7 元/(亩·年)、Ⅱ立地等级 114.6 元/(亩·年)、Ⅲ立地等级 62.9 元/(亩·年)；并提出采用与公益林区划完全一致的标准(便于生态区位的认定和补偿资金的发放)，将国家级、省级、市县级公益林依次用极重(Ⅰ)区、较重(Ⅱ)区、一般(Ⅲ)区表示，同时确定湖北省马尾松公益林的生态区位调节系数分别为Ⅰ区 137%、Ⅱ区 100%、Ⅲ区 83%。

(3)宏观测算了湖北省马尾松公益林生态补偿总额度。根据湖北省森林资源二类调查成果(1999)，测算出该省马尾松公益林生态补偿总额为 214743.9 万元/年，其中集体权属的额度 109098.9 万元/年，平均每亩 208.9 元/年。这些数据为国家和地方政府宏观决策与财政预算提供了可靠依据。

(4)研究提出了马尾松用材林的科学经营模式。就立地选择、种源选择、整地方式、密度效应、采伐年龄确定等关键技术措施，系统阐述了马尾松用材林的典型经营模式，并筛选推荐了优化经营模式，便于全面指导林农科学经营，大力提高森林生产力。

(5)全面分析了科学经营马尾松用材林的投入、产出和经济效益。采用森林科学经营模式，优化经营马尾松林年木材生产量分别为：Ⅲ级 0.7913m^3/(亩·年)、Ⅱ级 1.2166m^3/(亩·年)、Ⅰ级 1.4790m^3元/(亩·年)，年净利润分别为 174.60 元/(亩·年)、281.53 元/(亩·年)、349.05 元/(亩·年)；与同等立地条件下常规经营的产量和效益相比，其年木材生产量分别提高了 60.4%、44.7% 和 31.8%，年净利润分别提高了 76.0%、48.7%、33.1%。

(6)森林科学经营的效益十分明显。就湖北省马尾松用材林 2258.20 万亩这个总体而言，采用科学经营模式，总体的年木材产量将达到 3086.12 万 m^3，平均 1.37m^3/(亩·年)；总体的年净利润为 723354.46 万元，平均 320.32 元/(亩·年)。相对于常规经营模式，全省马尾松用材林年木材产量将增加 806.45 万 m^3，增产 35.4%；年净利润增加 196883.22 万元，增收 37.4%。不言而喻，全国商品用材林科学经营的潜力和效益是巨大的。

(7)为完善森林生态补偿制度，应积极推广科学实用的森林生态补偿标准测算方法，尽快确立生态补偿标准的形成机制；逐步建立政府主导、市场运作、社会参与的森林生态补偿体制，实行多渠道生态补偿机制；将资金补偿作为森林生态效益补偿的一种基本方式，探索建立多元化补偿方式并存的制度；全面推进森林生态效益补偿的立法工作，为生态补偿制度提供坚实的法律保障；切实强化生态公益林补偿资金管理，确保补偿资金的安全运行，并遏制职务犯罪。

在具体操作上，建议参照本研究测算的马尾松公益林生态补偿额度、结合我国社会经济发展水平，实行中央财政承担20%[平均41.8元/(亩·年)]、省级财政承担20%、其他渠道分担20%(例如出台流域下游对上游、工业区对林业区反哺等政策)的多元化、多渠道补偿机制，先行提高森林生态补偿标准，并随着国家财力的增强逐步提高中央政府的承担比例，其余差额部分则允许森林经营者从最终采伐木材的收益中弥补。同时，用法律条款对上述内容作出明确规定，以利各方按章办事，使得以林农为代表的公益林经营和保护者吃下定心丸。

(8)为强化森林科学经营，应全面实施森林分类经营，为森林科学经营提供基本保障；强力推进集体林权制度改革特别是配套改革工作，努力实现集体林区商品林的规模经营、集约经营乃至科学经营；不断加大森林科学经营的政策激励和资金投入，重点在种苗繁育、技术指导、科技示范、资金扶持、人才培养等方面由国家出台激励政策；积极推行森林经营方案制度，保障森林科学经营技术和措施落到实处；认真开展保护与发展森林资源目标责任制监督检查，督促县级以上地方人民政府积极采用森林科学经营方法和措施，大力发展森林资源。

参考文献

[1]陈钦．公益林生态补偿研究．北京：中国林业出版社，2006. 115～129.

[2]崔一梅．北京市生态公益林补偿机制的理论与实践研究．北京林业大学博士毕业论文，2008.

[3]丁贵杰．马尾松人工林生长收获模型系统的研究．林业科学，1997，23(1)：57～66.

[4]冯艳芬，刘毅华，王芳，等．国内生态补偿实践进展．生态经济，2009，8：85～89.

[5]何勇，张健，陈秀兰．森林生态补偿研究进展及关键问题分析．林业经济，2009，3：76～79.

[6]胡艳波．基于结构森林经营的天然异龄林空间优化经营模型研究．中国林业科学研究院博士毕业论文，2010.

[7]蒋发进，许彦红，刘思慧．中国森林生态效益补偿研究进展．内蒙古林业调查设计，2008，31(5)：4～6.

[8]蒋有绪．国际森林可持续经营问题的进展．资源科学，2000，22(6)：77～82.

[9]赖晓华，陈平留，谢德新．生态公益林补偿资金补偿标准的探讨．林业经济问题，2004，24(2)：105～107.

[10]雷静品，肖文发，黄选瑞，等．森林可持续经营标准与指标体系研究的最新进展．世界林业研究，2004，17(6)：1～5.

[11]雷玲．森林生态效益补偿机制研究．西北农林科技大学，2005.

[12]李文华，李芬，李世东，等．森林生态效益补偿的研究现状与展望．自然资源学报，2006，21(5)：677～688.

[13]李晓光，苗鸿，郑华，等．生态补偿标准确定的主要方法及其应用．生态学报，2009，29(8)：4431～4440.

[14]刘际建，王德善，李圣春，等．生态公益林补偿机制的初探．水土保持学报，2002，16(6)：145～147.

[15]刘于鹤，林进．加强森林经营、提高森林质量．中国绿色时报，2008年12月30日．

[16]唐守正．东北天然林生态采伐更新技术指南．北京：中国科学技术出版社，2006.

[17]王洪波，孟宪宇．区域实践可持续林业的条件．林业资源管理，1995(特刊)：24～30.

[18]王鹏程，庄尔奇，周志翔，等．湖北省马尾松人工林生长收获模型初探．湖北林业科技．2000，(3)：1～4.

[19]王鹏程，周志翔，涂炳坤，等．湖北省马尾松纸浆林主伐年龄的确定．华中农业大学学报．2000，19(2)：168～172.

[20]王鹏程，庄尔奇，涂炳坤等．湖北省马尾松人工林削度方程及材种出材率表的研究．华中农业大学学报，2001，20(1)：67～72.

[21]韦美玲．广西金秀县大瑶山生态公益林的补偿标准探讨．广西林业科学，2001，30(3)：152～154.

[22]吴水荣，马天乐，赵伟．森林生态效益补偿政策进展与经济分析．林业经济，2001，4：20～24.

[23]叶兴庆，汪绚等．完善森林生态效益补偿制度的政策建议．林业工作研究，2008(1)7～9.

[24]张家来，王鹏程，薛家翠，等．基于GIS界定湖北森林生态效益区的研究．林业科学，2007b，43(5)：130～134.

[25]张家来，章建斌，戴均华，等．湖北森林生态资源价值的补偿标准．林业科学，2007a，43(8)：127～133.

[26]张蕾．中国林业分类经营改革研究．北京林业大学博士毕业论文，2007.

[27]张眉，刘伟平．我国生态公益林补偿标准问题探讨．世界林业研究，2010，23(3)：69～72.

[28]张守攻，朱春金，肖文发，等．森林可持续经营导论．北京：中国林业出报社，2001，120～130.

[29]张志云，郭正福．生态公益林补偿标准的确定．亚热带资源与环境学报，2010，5(3)：19～25.

[30]周国林．国际森林可持续经营的新进展．世界林业研究，1999，12(5)：1～5.

[31]Bishop J. Pro－poorMarkets for Environmental Services：A New Source of Finance for Sustainable Development? Presentation made at the World Summit on Sustainable Development，Johannesburg，2002.

[32] Brian R，William W W. Policy evaluation of natural resource injuries using habitat equivalency analysis. Ecological Economics，2006，58(2)：421～437.

[33]Daily G C，Soderquiant T，Aniyar 5，*et al.* The value of nature and the nature of value. Science，2000，289：395～396.

[34]James B，Lisa W. Measuring Ecosystem Service Benefits：The Use of Landscape Analysis of Evaluate Environmental Trades and Compensation. 2003.

[35]Richard W D，Thomas C G，William H D. The use of habitat equivalency analysis in natural resource damage assessments. Ecological Economics，2004，48 (1)：49～70.

[36]Robles D，Kangas，Lassioe J P，*et al.* Evaluation of Potential Gross Income from Non2timber Products in a Riparian Forest for the Chesapeake Bay Watershed. Agroforestry Systems，1997，44 (223)：215～225.

[37] Stefano P，Elias R，*et al.* Paying for the environmental services of silvopastoral practices in Nicaragua. Ecological Economics，2007，64 (2)：374～385.

[38]Sven W，Montserrat A. Decentralized payments for environmental services：The cases of Pimampiro and FROFAFOR in Ecuador. Ecological Economics，2008，65 (4)：685～698.

[39]Walter I，Jetse S，*et al.* Can payments for ecosystem services secure the water tower of Tibet? Agricultural Systems，2008，96 (123)：52～63.

小陇山林区油松中幼林龄抚育效果评价

潘德乾[1]　赵文杰[1]　刘文桢[2*]　张宋智[2]　郭小龙[2]

（1. 甘肃省小陇山林业实验局，天水，741020；
2. 甘肃省小陇山林业实验局林业科学研究所，天水，741022）

摘要：运用重要值、角尺度、混交度、大小比数和优势度、开敞度、生长率、天然更新等对油松人工林中幼林龄抚育间伐前后林分状态变化进行分析。结果表明：抚育前后林木的分布格局由均匀分布靠近随机分布。平均混交度略有上升，幅度不大。但顶级树种油松的混交度呈明显上升趋势。油松人工林直径大小比数变化不大，保持了顶级树种在群落中的优势地位。开敞度则由于抚育间伐后林木间距的增大而得以提高，达到了优化目的，林分的胸径平均生长率提高了47.7%，蓄积生长率提高了51.7%，充分说明适宜的抚育间伐可提高林分各树种生长率，从而使林分逐步达到健康稳定的林分结构。抚育间伐样地天然更新增加了11.1%。对照样地天然更新减少了9.8%，林分经过抚育后，林隙空间的增大，随着光照、温度、水肥等条件的改善，从而促使土壤中的天然种子萌发，加快了天然更新。

关键词：小陇山；油松；人工林；抚育间伐；效果评价

The evaluating of*Pinus tabulaeformis* at the west side of Qin-ling mountain by stand spatial structure

PAN De-qian[1], ZHAO Wen-jie, LIU Wen-zhen[2], ZHAN Song-zhi[2], GUO Xiao-long[2]

（1. Xiaolongshan Forest Experiment Bureau of Gansu Province Tianshui, 741020;
2. Xiaolongshan Research Institute of Forestry of Gansu Province, Tianshui, 741020）

Abstract: The researcher analyses the changes of state on young and middle - aged planted Chinese pine before and after tending it with intermediate cutting, by the indexes of important value, angle scale, mingling degree, neighborhood comparison, dominance, opening degree, growth rate, and natural regeneration and so on. The results show that the stand distribution pattern before and after tending changes from uniform distribution to random distribution. The mingling degree slightly rises, but not in a wide range. The mingling degree of climax species Chinese pine appeared obvious increasing trend. The neighborhood comparison of diameter of planted Chinese pine changed little,

---

基金项目：秦岭西段典型森林生态系统健康维护与经营技术示范（200804022G）。

作者简介：潘德乾（1964～），男，甘肃天水人，高级工程师，主要从事森林经营、森林培育研究。

and that maintained the dominant position of the species in community. The opening degree increased owing to expanded stand distance after intermediate cutting, the stand DBH average growth rate increased by 47.7%, the accumulation growth rate increased by 51.7%, and those speak volume for appropriate intermediate cutting could improve growth rate of all stand tree species, thus the stand will reach a healthy and steady structure gradually. The natural regeneration increased by 11.1% in intermediate cutting sample plot, but the control plot decreased by 9.8%, with the improved conditions of light, temperature, water and fertilizer by tending stand with intermediate cutting, the natural seeds are apt to sprout and the natural regeneration is accelerated.

Key words: Xiaolongshan; Chinese pine; planted forest; tending with intermediate cutting; effect evaluation

林业生产周期长、见效慢的特点决定了运用功能评价的方法对森林经营活动结果进行评价必然具有一定的滞后性，不能掌握经营活动对森林各项指标的影响，从而不能在经营过程中及时调整经营措施，如果在经营过程中采取的措施不当，往往会造成事与愿违的结果。新的结构建模思想的出现使得传统的功能建模思想受到了很大的冲击，传统的功能评价已转向情景状态的评价[1]。小陇山林区是我国北方典型的天然次生林区，是嘉陵江、渭河的发源地，属重要的水源涵养区，对渭河下游陕西关中平原、嘉陵江下游汉中平原和四川嘉陵江流的生态安全有着直接和间接的关系。在维护黄土高原西部以及黄河、长江流域地区生态平衡、生物多样性保护、改善生态环境、维护区域生态系统的平衡、保障社会经济的可持续发展方面发挥着极其重要的作用[2]。小陇山林区总面积 83.02 万 hm^2，林地面积 81.4 万 hm^2，其中，中幼龄林面积 41.2 万 hm^2，有天然林中幼龄林 31 万 hm^2，人工中幼龄林面积 10.2 万 hm^2。林区森林覆盖率 63.6%，活立木总蓄积 3451 万 m^3。2009 年作为国家级森林抚育试点林区，开展中幼龄林抚育工程。为了准确评价中幼龄林抚育效果，以小陇山百花林场中幼林抚育区具有代表性的油松人工林分，运用结构化森林经营理论与方法，通过对林木水平分布格局、竞争关系及林分树种组成等的分析确定经营方向及目标，并对油松人工林抚育间伐前后林分的树种组成、树种多样性、空间利用程度和竞争态势等状态变化进行分析，研究小陇山林区中幼林龄抚育措施效果，以期为实现小陇山林区森林可持续经营提供依据。

1 实验区概况

实验区设在小陇山林业实验局百花林场仙坪营林区 87 林班 1 号小班，地理坐标为 34°16′22.6″N，106°26′43.4″E，坡度 31°，海拔 1685m，年均降雨量 510mm，无霜期 185 天。土壤以褐色森林土为主。林分为 1978 年低质低产林分改造进行人工造林，造林密度为 5000/hm^2(株行距为 1.3m×1.3m)经营前林分郁闭度 0.9，林龄 29 年。乔木层主要树种为油松、辽东栎、锐齿栎(*Quercus aliena* var. *acutiserrata*)、青榨槭、白桦(*Betula platyphylla*)、鄂椴(*Tilia oliveri*)、漆树、华山松(*Pinus armandii*)、茶条槭、红桦、五角枫、黄榆、梾木、大叶椋子、杜梨、秦岭白蜡、黄花柳、毛梾(*Swida walteri*)、桦叶四蕊槭。平均胸径 11.7cm，平均高 11.2m，每公顷蓄积 156.57m^3。

灌木以白檀(*Symplocos paniculata*)、平榛(*Corylus heterophylla*)、葱皮忍冬(*Lonicera ferdinandii*)为主，平均高 0.42m，平均盖度 12%，团块状分布。草本以垂穗苔草(*Carex dimor-*

pholepis)、茖韭(*Allium victorialis*)、心叶淫羊霍(*Epimedium brevicornu*)为主，平均高0.26m，平均盖度5%。

2 研究方法

2.1 样地调查

2007年6月，分抚育间伐和不抚育间伐(对照)测设面积为0.36hm^2(60m×60m)样地，在抚育间伐样地采取强度34%的间伐作业。采用T72型GPS对实验区进行定位确定地理坐标、海拔，并在样地内，对乔木树种胸径大于5cm的个体进行每木检尺，记录树种、株数、年龄、树高、枝下高、胸径、冠幅；并在样地内的四角和中心设置5m×5m的样方5个，进行灌木和草本的调查，记录灌木和草本的种类、高度、盖度、株数。采用罗盘仪测定坡向、坡度，坡位。同时用罗盘仪和超声波测距仪对样地内胸径大于5cm的林进行每木定位，以结构化森林经营理论为基础，将全部林木划分为保留木和采伐木进行标记。利用SVMS软件分析试验区林分的角尺度、物种多样性指数、混交度、大小比数和优势度、开敞度，确定林木间的相互关系。2011年7月进行了复查。

2.2 结构参数指标

运用林分空间结构分析方法，分别计算抚育间伐前后林分的重要值、角尺度[4~6]、混交度[7,8]、大小比数[9]和优势度[1]、开敞度参数[11]等指标，分析评价抚育间伐前后的林分结构变化。

2.2.1 物种多样性指数

物种多样性是指一个群落中物种数目和各物种的个体数目分配的均匀度，反映了群落组成中物种的丰富程度及不同自然地理条件与群落的相互关系，以及群落的稳定性与动态，是群落组织结构的重要特征[1]。

Shannon—Wiener多样性指数

$$H' = -\sum_{i=1}^{s} p_i ln p_i$$

式中：H'为Shannon—Wiener多样性指数；p_i为为第i个树种株数在林分树木总株数中所占百分比；s为为林分中树种的数目

2.2.2 角尺度

角尺度W_i被定义为a角小于标准角a_0(72°)的个数占最近4株相邻木的比例[4,5,12]用公式表示为：

$$W_i = \frac{1}{4}\sum_{j=1}^{4} Z_{ij}$$

其中：$Z_i\begin{cases}1，当第j个\alpha角小于标准角\alpha_0\\0，否则\end{cases}$

样地内林木角尺度在[0，0.475]之间，表明林分处于均匀分布，角尺度在[0.475，0.517]之间，表明林分处于随机分布，角尺度在[0.517，1]之间，表明林分处于团状分布。

2.2.3 混交度

混交度(M_i)用来说明混交林中树种空间的隔离程度[8,10]。定义为参照树i的4株最近相邻木中与参照树不属同种的个体所占的比例[1,7,12]，用公式表示为：

$$M_i = \frac{1}{4}\sum_{j=1}^{4} v_{ij}$$

式中：$v_{ij}\begin{cases}1 & 当参照树 i 与第 j 株相邻木非同种时\\0 & 否则\end{cases}$

2.2.4 大小比数和优势度

大小比数(U_i)是指胸径大于参照树的相邻木占4株最近相邻木的比例[1,9,12]，用公式表示为：

$$U_i = \frac{1}{4}\sum_{j=1}^{n} k_{ij}$$

其中：$k_{ij}\begin{cases}0 & 如果相邻木 j 比参照树 i 小\\1 & 否则\end{cases}$

即：4株相邻木胸径都大于参照树时，参照树的大小比数为1.0，表明参照树处于绝对劣势；都小于参照树时，参照树为绝对优势(0)；其他依次类推为：亚优势(0.25)、中庸(0.5)、劣态(0.75)。树种的优势度用相对显著度和树种大小比数的结合[1]来表达，公式为：

$$D_{sp} = \sqrt{D_{sp} \times (1 - U)}$$

式中：D_{SP} 为树种优势度；D_g 为相对显著度；U_{sp} 为树种大小比数。

树种优势度的值0～1之间。接近1表示非常优势，接近0表示几乎没有优势。

2.2.5 开敞度

开敞度参数表示的是林木发展的可能性和经营空间的大小。在此定义为：林内任意一株林木到最近的4株相邻木水平距离与它们各自高度比值之和[11,13]。可用下式表示：

$$k_i = \sum_{j=1}^{4} (d_{ij}/h_{ij})$$

式中：k_i 为第 i 株树木的开敞度；d_{ij} 为样点到第 j 株数的距离；h_{ij} 为第 j 株树的高度。

3 结果与分析

3.1 林分组成

表1为林分中林木分类标记后主要树种测树因子及按重要值排序后结果。从表1表明：保留木为林分中的优势木，同时是具有较高经济价值的优势树种，抚育间伐前后优势树种的平均胸径和平均树高略有上升，群落保持着相对稳定的优势。伐掉了处于相对劣势小径级材，为中径级长势良好的林木个体创造了良好的生存空间，并保留了阔叶伴生树种，使林分混交度有所上升，树种隔离程度提高，使林分结构进一步稳定。

表1 抚育间伐前后主要树种测树因子

Tab.1 The main tree species measurement factor pre-and post intermediate cutting

树种	采伐前					采伐后				
	株数 (N/hm^2)	$\overline{D}$(cm)	$\overline{H}$(m)	胸高断面积 (m^2/hm^2)	蓄积 (m^3/hm^2)	株数 (N/hm^2)	$\overline{D}$(cm)	$\overline{H}$(m)	胸高断面积 (m^2/hm^2)	蓄积 (m^3/hm^2)
油松	2025	12.5	11.5	24.79	135.48	1013	13.3	11.9	14.04	77.83
辽东栎	225	7.3	9.4	0.94	4.85	175	7.7	9.7	0.82	4.31

(续)

树种	采伐前					采伐后				
	株数(N/hm^2)	$\overline{D}$(cm)	$\overline{H}$(m)	胸高断面积(m^2/hm^2)	蓄积(m^3/hm^2)	株数(N/hm^2)	$\overline{D}$(cm)	$\overline{H}$(m)	胸高断面积(m^2/hm^2)	蓄积(m^3/hm^2)
锐齿栎	163	7.4	9.1	0.69	3.54	163	7.4	9.1	0.69	3.54
青榨槭	150	6.5	10	0.5	2.66	125	6.3	10.1	0.39	2.12
白桦	63	8.6	9.1	0.36	1.75					
鄂椴	75	7.5	9.8	0.33	1.83	63	6.2	9.3	0.19	0.99
漆树	113	6.1	8.7	0.33	1.57	88	6.4	8.9	0.28	1.36
华山松	25	11.7	9.5	0.27	1.41	25	11.7	9.5	0.27	1.41
茶条槭	38	6.2	7.9	0.11	0.48	13	6.1	7.5	0.04	0.15
红桦	38	6.2	7.9	0.11	0.46	38	6.2	7.9	0.11	0.46
五角枫	38	5.5	10.4	0.09	0.51	38	5.5	10.4	0.09	0.51
黄榆	25	6.6	9.3	0.09	0.4	25	6.6	9.3	0.09	0.4
楝木	38	5.4	8.5	0.09	0.39	38	5.4	8.5	0.09	0.39
大叶椋子	38	5.3	10.3	0.08	0.46	38	5.3	10.3	0.08	0.46
杜梨	13	7.7	6.5	0.06	0.2					
秦岭白蜡	13	6.2	9.8	0.04	0.2	13	6.2	9.8	0.04	0.2
黄花柳	13	6	8.4	0.04	0.16	13	6	8.4	0.04	0.16
毛楝	13	5.5	10.3	0.03	0.17	13	5.5	10.3	0.03	0.17
桦叶四蕊槭	13	4.5	6.7	0.02	0.07					

图1为林分经过抚育间伐后直径分布变化情况，由于抚育间伐主要针对中径级和一些小径级中无培育前途的受挤压木以及角尺度0.25和0.75的进行采伐调整，各树种径级频率分布随林分结构调整有所增长，但林分直径分布结构变化不大。

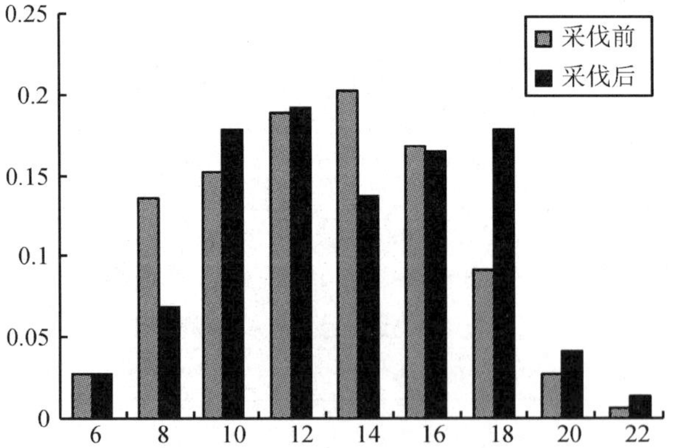

图1 经营前后直径分布的变化

Fig. 1 The variation of diameter distribution before and after management

3.2 空间利用程度

3.2.1 抚育间伐强度分析及对林分郁闭度影响

试验区样地抚育间伐前林分共有林木3119株(胸径≥5.0cm)，总胸高断面积为29.0m^2。抚育间伐后样地林分共有林木1881株(胸径≥5.0cm)，总胸高断面积17.3m^2，按林木株数和胸高断面积计算，间伐强度分别为39.7%和34%，明显高于15%。由于林分初植密度较大，每亩达208株，未及时进行林分生长抚育，抚育间伐前林分郁闭度为1，间伐强度偏大有助于林分生长及其他树种的更新。抚育间伐后郁闭度保持在0.7，有利于林分植被的快速恢复，保持了林分植被的多样性，增大单株生存空间。

3.2.2 林木分布格局

图2为林分抚育间伐前后林分平均角尺度的变化。图2表明，抚育间伐前林分有平均角尺度为0.431，左侧高于右侧，为均匀分布。为了促使林木分布格局向随机分布转变，将林分中的保留木中的油松和主要伴生树种的中、大径木角尺度为0和0.25单木与其最近4株相邻木构成的结构单元作为调整对象，采用“首遇先调”的原则，调整林木的分布格局。如图2，初次抚育间伐后，结构单元角尺度在0、0.75和1的分布变化不大，由抚育间伐前的0%、8.73%和0.79%增加到抚育间伐后的1.42%、10.85%和2.83%；结构单元角尺度为0.25的结构单元由抚育间伐前的38.1%减少到抚育间伐后的27.36%，角尺度为0.5的结构单元由抚育间伐前的52.38%增加到抚育间伐后的57.55%。总体而言，调整后林分平均角尺度为0.466，林分林木分布格局发生了由均匀分布向随机分布转化的趋势。

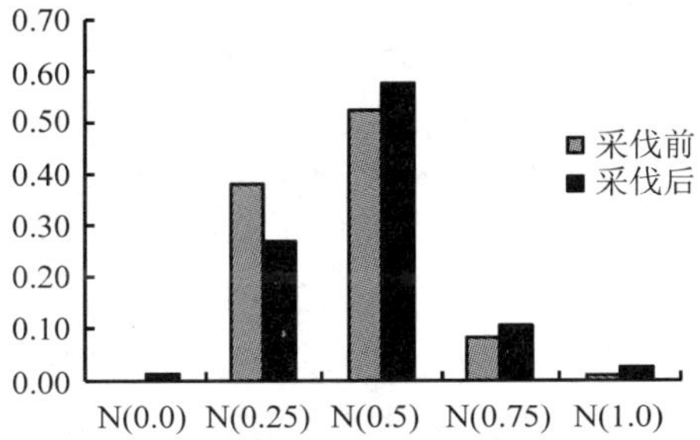

图2 经营前后林分角尺度变化

ig. 2 The change of angle index pre - and post intermediate cutting

3.3 物种多样性

3.3.1 物种多样性指数

通过间伐调整，实验区抚育间伐前乔木树种Shannon-Wiener多样性指数为1.88，进行抚育间伐后，林分的乔木树种的Shannon-Wiener多样性指数为1.86，基本保持不变；林分内灌木和草本物种由10种降为9种，发生了轻微变化，人为干扰对灌木层和草本层产生了一定的影响。在经营5年后灌木和草本物种由经营前10种增加到15种，说明抚育间伐使林木间空隙的增大，为乡土树种的侵入和林下植物创造了有利条件和适生环境。

3.3.2 混交度

图3为林分中林木与其最近4株相邻木构成的结构单元混交分布图。由图3可看出，样地内抚育间伐前后林木个体与其最近4株相邻木构成的结构单元的混交度变化较大，抚育间伐前处于零度混交的比例最高，为27.36%，其次为极强度混交，比例为25%，处于弱度混

交、中度混交和强度混交的比例相对较低；抚育间伐后，处于弱度混交的的比例明显下降，处于极强度混交的比例由抚育间伐前的25%上升到了37%。

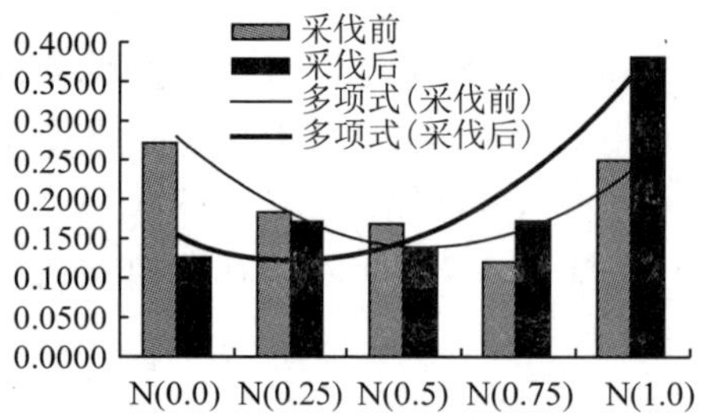

图3 经营前后林分混交度变化

Fig. 3 The variation of stand mingling degree before and after management

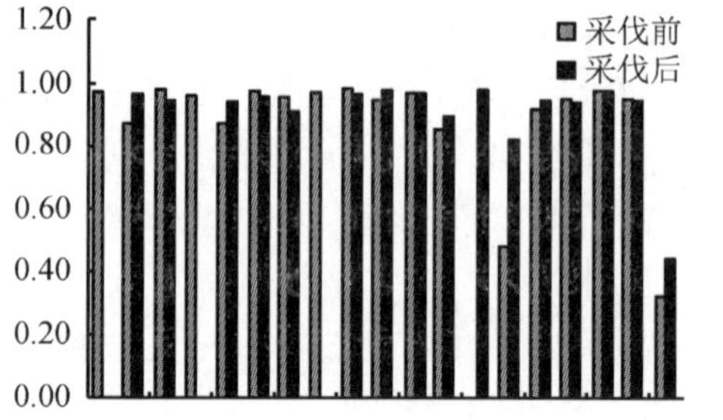

图4 经营前后各种混交度变化

Fig. 4 The variation of all tree species mingling degree before and after management

图3是林分中主要树种经营前后混交度变化情况。图4表明，抚育间伐后，油松的混交度由经营前的弱度混交变为中度混交，毛栜由抚育前的极弱度混交转变为极强度混交，这是由于毛栜原来处于丛生，经过抚育，将丛生的弱株、病株等去除掉，从而使得其周围与不同树种相邻，混交度急剧上升。抚育伐除了相邻漆树的不良个体，使漆树的混交度上升较大。白桦、杜梨和桦叶四蕊槭由于在林分中处于劣势树种，被压严重，在抚育中伐除，混交度归零。其余树种混交度变化不大，阔叶树的整体混交度都有所很高。林分抚育后零度混交的比例降到最低为12.7%，弱度混交、中度混交的比例略有下降，强度混交和极强度混交的比例都有所增加。林分的平均混交度由经营前的0.473提高到0.627。经营后 M_i 从0到1取值的比例从下降的趋势转变为上升趋势，说明林分整体混交程度有所增加，有利于林分由单层纯林向复层异龄针阔混交林结构发展。

3.4 竞争态势

大小比数是用来分析林木个体大小分化程度的有效参数[1,11,12]，见表2，抚育间伐前毛栜大小比数为0.03，黄榆为0.41，油松为0.43，这几个树种在结构单元中的大小比数较小，在结构单元中较其他树种更具优势。结合相对显著度来看，油松总体上较其他树种具有明显优势，其次为锐齿栎和辽东栎。抚育间伐后大小比数油松为0.34，黄榆为0.41，华山松为0.53，这几个树种在结构单元中的大小比数较小，在结构单元中相对于其他树种更具优势，华山松的优势度明显提高。

3.4.1 林分生长

林分经过抚育间伐后各树种的年均生长率都有不同的变化，详见表3。抚育间伐后林分中光热条件得到较大改善，水肥等营养条件得到极大改善。抚育间伐样地林木的胸径年均生长率和立木材积生长率都高于对照样地，油松胸径生长率提高了48.2%、立木材积生长率提高了54.4%，华山松胸径生长率提高了46.9%、立木材积生长率提高了49.1%，栎类胸径生长率提高了48.2%、立木材积生长率提高了66.8%，林分的胸径平均生长率提高了47.7%，蓄积生长率提高了51.7%，充分说明适宜的抚育间伐可提高林分各树种生长率，从而使林分逐步达到健康稳定的林分结构。

表 2　抚育间伐作业前后林分和主要树种角尺度、混交度、大小比数、相对多度和相对显著度变化

Tab. 2　the change of the angle index, mingling, neighborhood comparison and opening degree of the stand and main tree species pro – and post intermediate cutting

树种	采伐前					采伐后				
	角尺度	大小比数	混交度	相对多度(%)	相对显著度(%)	角尺度	大小比数	混交度	相对多度(%)	相对显著度(%)
白桦	0.58	0.68	0.96	2.02	1.25					
茶条槭	0.62	0.78	0.87	1.22	0.39	0.53	0.94	0.96	0.69	0.21
大叶椋子	0.53	0.95	0.97	1.22	0.28	0.36	0.95	0.95	2.02	0.48
杜梨	0.53	0.53	0.95	0.42	0.20					
鄂椴	0.53	0.66	0.87	2.40	1.15	0.53	0.73	0.93	3.35	1.10
红桦	0.37	0.87	0.97	1.22	0.39	0.61	0.86	0.95	2.02	0.65
华山松	0.66	0.66	0.95	0.80	0.92	0.41	0.53	0.91	1.33	1.54
桦叶四蕊槭	0.53	0.97	0.97	0.42	0.07					
黄花柳	0.53	0.78	0.97	0.42	0.12	0.53	0.78	0.96	0.69	0.20
黄榆	0.78	0.41	0.94	0.80	0.30	0.78	0.41	0.97	1.33	0.50
楝木	0.62	0.98	0.97	1.22	0.30	0.45	0.93	0.96	2.02	0.50
辽东栎	0.52	0.74	0.85	7.21	3.24	0.50	0.71	0.89	9.30	4.77
毛楝	0.87	0.03	0.03	0.42	0.10	0.28	0.94	0.97	0.69	0.17
漆树	0.64	0.62	0.48	3.62	1.14	0.53	0.71	0.82	4.68	1.62
秦岭白蜡	0.28	0.78	0.91	0.42	0.13	0.28	0.78	0.95	0.69	0.22
青榨槭	0.49	0.80	0.94	4.81	1.74	0.48	0.68	0.93	6.65	2.28
锐齿栎	0.53	0.73	0.99	5.23	2.39	0.53	0.70	0.97	8.67	4.00
五角枫	0.45	0.87	0.95	1.22	0.31	0.45	0.78	0.94	2.02	0.52
油松	0.51	0.43	0.32	64.92	85.58	0.48	0.34	0.44	53.85	81.23

表 3　采伐及其对照样地主要树种年生长率表

Tab. 3　The annual growth rate of main tree species in cutting plot and control plot

树种	采伐样地			对照样地		
	树高年均生长率(%)	胸径年均生长率(%)	材积年均生长率(%)	树高年均生长率(%)	胸径年均生长率(%)	材积年均生长率(%)
油松	4.95	6.94	6.98	4.93	4.68	4.52
华山松	5.08	6.98	7.03	5.06	4.75	4.93
栎类	4.56	7.17	8.96	4.51	4.81	5.37
其他阔叶树	5.07	4.98	5.04	5.03	4.72	4.45
平均	4.96	6.96	7.01	4.94	4.71	4.620

3.4.2　天然更新

由表 4 可见抚育间伐样地天然更新由 2007 年的 3186 株/hm^2，2011 年增加到 3541 株/

hm^2，增加了11.1%。对照样地天然更新由2007年的3730株/hm^2，2011年减少到3365株/hm^2，减少了9.8%，林分经过抚育后，林隙空间的增大，随着光照、温度、水肥等条件的改善，从而促使土壤中的天然种子萌发，加快了天然更新，为林分逐步向针阔混交林演替创造了有利条件。

表4 样地林下天然更新

Tab. 4 The natural regeneration under sample plot

树种	采伐样地				对照样地			
	2007年		2011年		2007年		2011年	
	平均树高(m)	株数(株/hm^2)	平均树高(m)	株数(株/hm^2)	平均树高(m)	株数(株/hm^2)	平均树高(m)	株数(株/hm^2)
白桦	0.5	19	2.60	50	0.50	25	1.12	38
茶条槭			1.10	38	0.80	263	3.96	225
大叶椋子	0.82	250	1.52	225	0.65	625	1.45	575
椴树	0.11	88	1.41	113	0.74	88	0.94	61
多毛樱桃	2.77	313	3.37	325	0.78	113	0.85	92
甘肃山楂			0.61	25	0.20	138	1.70	125
湖北花楸	1.70	13	2.30	13	0.20	13	1.22	7
华山松			0.38	63	0.60	25	0.64	21
黄榆	1.34	188	1.94	213	0.47	225	2.77	213
辽东栎	2.45	425	2.95	575	0.62	575	3.64	488
漆树	1.75	100	1.32	88	0.00	38	1.86	50
青麸杨	2.00	13	2.94	11	0.69	200	1.94	175
青榨槭	1.00	113	1.32	100	1.00	75	1.38	62
锐齿栎	0.78	863	1.96	913	0.47	875	2.72	763
水榆花楸	1.00	13	1.21	13	0.50	13	1.53	11
唐棣					1.00	13	2.68	9
小叶白蜡	1.86	475	1.96	463	1.50	88	1.53	100
小叶钓樟	2.50	313	2.98	313	1.22	338	1.87	350
总计		3186		3541		3730		3365

4 结论与讨论

(1)百花林场具有代表性的人工油松林中幼龄林抚育实验区，通过抚育间伐调整，Shannon—Wiener多样性指数基本保持不变，保持了原群落物种的稳定性和丰富度。人为干扰对林下植被产生了一定的影响，但随着林分郁闭度的降低，林间空隙的增大，为乡土树种和林下植物创造了有利条件和适生环境。

(2)通过林分空间结构分析，林分水平分布格局由轻微均匀分布转变为轻微随机分布，但在人工中幼林抚育过程中只抚育一次是达不到理想稳定的林分结构，随着几次抚育措施的实施，结构的调整，需逐步人工促使向复层异龄针阔混交林发展，达到健康稳定的林分结构。

(3)水肥等营养条件得到极大改善，抚育间伐，使树木个体间的距离加大，林木的平均开敞度都有明显的增长，间伐后林木光照条件、资源空间得到极大改善，抚育间伐样地林木的胸径年均生长率和立木材积生长率都高于对照样地，油松胸径生长率提高了48.2%、立木材积生长率提高了54.4%，华山松胸径生长率提高了46.9%、立木材积生长率提高了49.1%，栎类胸径生长率提高了48.2%、立木材积生长率提高了66.8%，充分说明适宜的抚育间伐可提高林分各树种生长率。林分通过5年，抚育间伐样地天然更新增加了11.1%，对照样地天然更新减少了9.8%，林分经过抚育后，林隙空间的增大，随着光照、温度、水肥等条件的改善，从而促使土壤中的天然种子萌发，加快了天然更新。

(4)研究区的人工油松林林龄较小，抚育间伐后空间结构并非最优，要促使现有的油松人工林向最优的林分结构转变，需要经过对林分不同生长时期结构分析，确定合理的结构调整方向和目标，来实现真正意义上的林分空间结构上的优化。

参考文献

[1]惠刚盈，Klaus von Gadow，胡艳波，等. 结构化森林经营[M]. 北京：中国林业出版社，2007.

[2] 马建伟，张宋智，郭小龙，等. 小陇山森林生态系统服务功能价值评估[J]. 生态与农村环境学报，2007，23(3)：27 ~30，35.

[3]Pretzsch H. Structural diversity as a result of silvicultural operations. In：Olsthoorn A FM，Bartelink HH，Gardiner J J，*et al*. (eds). Management of mixed_ species forest：silviculture and economics. Dlo Institute for Forestry and Nature Research(IBN_ DLO)，Wageningen，1999，158 ~172

[4]贾秀红，郑小贤. 长白山过伐林区云冷杉针阔混交林空间结构分析[J]. 华中农业大学学报，2006，25(4)：436 ~440.

[5]安慧君，惠刚盈，郑小贤，等. 不同发育阶段阔叶红松林空间结构的初步研究[J]. 内蒙古大学学报，2005，36(6)：714 ~718.

[6]Hui G Y，Gadow K. Das Winkelmass – Theoretische Überlegungen zum optimalen Standard winkel[J]. *Allgemeine Forst u. Jagdzeitung*，2002，173(9)：173 ~176.

[7]郑丽凤，周新年，等. 松阔混交林林分空间结构分析[J]. 热带亚热带植物学报，2006，14(4)：275 ~280.

[8]Gadow K，Zur Bestandesbeschreibung in der Foresteinrichtung[J]. *Forst und Holz*，1993，48(21)：602 ~606.

[9]惠刚盈，Gadow K，Albert M. 一个新的林分空间结构参数——大小比数[J]. 林业科学研究，1999，12(1)：1 –6.

[10]Gadow K，Füldner K. Zur Methodik der Bestandesbeschreibung[R]. Klieken：Vortrag anlaesslich der Jahrestagungder A G Forsteinrichtung，1992

[11]郝云庆，王金锡，王启，等. 柳杉纯林改造后林分空间结构变化预测[J]. 林业科学，2006，42(8)：8 ~13.

[12]惠刚盈，克劳斯·冯佳多. 森林空间结构量化分析方法[M]. 北京：中国科学技术出版社，2003.

[13]胡艳波，惠刚盈. 优化林分空间结构的森林经营方法探讨[J]. 林业科学研究. 2006，19(1)：1 ~8.

小叶锦鸡儿人工林黄土高原丘陵区土壤改善过程的研究

温晓林　何振仲
（吉林省林业勘察设计研究院，130022）

摘要：本文以晋西北黄土高原丘陵区不同龄级的小叶锦鸡儿人工林为研究对象，选择了6、14、20、27a小叶锦鸡儿人工林和撂荒地进行了对比研究。结果表明，随着林龄的增长，土壤理化性质均得到较好的改善，土壤容重降低，孔隙度增加，土壤持水能力也得到较大提高，土壤pH值下降，土壤有机质、全N、有效P含量均比撂荒地有不同程度的提高，同时速效K含量明显低于撂荒地，总体上表明：20a小叶锦鸡儿人工林对土壤理化性质的改良作用是相对最明显的。

关键词：晋西北黄土高原丘陵区；小叶锦鸡儿；人工林；土壤理化性质；

1　研究的目的意义

我国黄土高原地区地跨山西、内蒙古、河南、陕西、甘肃、宁夏和青海等7省(自治区)，共287个县(旗)，总土地面积为62.68万km^2。高原丘陵区生态系统是一个结构简单、十分脆弱的系统。而植物使周围土壤性质发生变异所需时间与环境条件、基质中养分含量有关，越是贫瘠的土壤，越是容易受到灌丛化效应的影响[1]。小叶锦鸡儿是豆科具刺灌木，广泛分布于我国“三北”地区，它具有耐寒、抗旱、耐贫瘠和耐高温等特点，同时小叶锦鸡儿根系庞大，生长快，4~5年时间即可达到保持水土的目的[2]。不同龄级的小叶锦鸡儿人工林，对其周围环境的影响的差异是明显的。本研究以晋西北黄土高原丘陵区地上不同龄级的小叶锦鸡儿人工林为对象，分析了不同龄级小叶锦鸡儿的生长状况及对土壤改良、土壤含水量、林下植被恢复等方面影响的差异。为黄土高原丘陵地区水土流失防治生产实践提出理论支持，探讨了小叶锦鸡儿人工林群落的演变规律，因此本文有着一定的理论意义和实践意义。

2　研究结果及其分析

2.1　不同龄级小叶锦鸡儿人工林土壤养分空间差异分析

2.1.1　不同龄级小叶锦鸡儿人工林土壤有机质空间差异

不同龄级小叶锦鸡儿人工林在0~20cm的土层中有机质含量表现为：20a ＞27a＞6a＞14a＞撂荒地；在20~40cm的土层中有机质含量总体变现为：27a＞20a＞14a＞撂荒地＞6a；在40~60cm的土层中有机质含量总体变现为：14a＞20a＞6a＞27a＞撂荒地。

20a各土层中平均有机质含量均很高；27a在0~40cm土层中有机质含量很高，而40~

60cm 土层中有机质含量急剧减少，在 60cm 土层中有机质含量远远少于 6a、14a、20a；14a 在 0～20cm 土层中有机质含量很少，但在 20～40cm 土层中有机质含量急剧增加；6a 土壤有机质含量在 0～60cm 土层中的垂直变化趋势呈折线变化，0～20cm 土层变化不大，20～40cm 随着土层深度的增加而减小，40～60cm 随着土层的增加而增大；而撂荒地土壤有机质含量在 0～20cm 随着土层的增加而增大，在 20～60cm 随着土层深度的增加而减小。不同龄级小叶锦鸡儿人工林有机质含量总体表现为：20a＞27a＞14a＞6a＞撂荒地。

2.1.2 不同龄级小叶锦鸡儿人工林土壤 pH 空间差异

不同龄级小叶锦鸡儿人工林在 0～40cm 的土层中土壤 pH 值总体表现为：20a＜27a＜6a＜14a＜撂荒地；而 40～60cm 土层中土壤 pH 表现为：27a＜20a＜14a＜6a＜撂荒地，撂荒地各土层中土壤 pH 值均最高。

不同龄级小叶锦鸡儿人工林土壤 pH 值在 0～60cm 土层中的垂直变化趋势均呈折线变化。20a 土壤 pH 值在 0～20cm 土层中随着土层深度的增加而减小，在 20～40cm 土层中随着土层的增加而增大，在 40～60cm 土层中又随土层的增加而减小；27a 与 6a 的土壤 pH 值随土层深度的增加其变化一致，都是在 0～40cm 土层中随土层深度的增加而减小，在 40～60cm 土层中随深度的增加而增大；14a 土壤 pH 值在 0～20cm 土层中随着土层深度的增加而增大，在 20～60cm 土层中随土层深度的增加而减小；撂荒地土壤 pH 值在 40～60cm 土层中随土层深度的增加而增大，而在 0～40cm 土层深度中变化不大。总体上可以看出不同龄级小叶锦鸡儿人工林土壤 pH 值总体表现为：20a＜27a＜6a＜14a＜撂荒地。

2.1.3 不同龄级小叶锦鸡儿人工林土壤全 N 空间差异

不同龄级小叶锦鸡儿人工林在 0～20cm 土层中土壤全 N 含量表现为：20a ＞14a＞27a＞6a＞撂荒地；20～40cm 的土层中土壤全 N 含量表现为：20a ＞27a＞14a ＞6a＞撂荒地；而 40～60cm 的土层中土壤全 N 含量大体表现为：14a＞27a ＞20a＞6a＞撂荒地。20a 各土层中平均全 N 含量均较高，而 6a、14a 和 27a 土壤全 N 含量交替变化，撂荒地各土层中全 N 含量均较少。撂荒地和 20a 土壤全 N 含量最大值出现在 20cm 土层中；14a 和 27a 土壤全 N 含量最大值出现在 0cm 土层中；6a 土壤全 N 含量最大值出现在 40cm 土层中。

不同龄级小叶锦鸡儿人工林土壤全 N 含量在 0～60cm 土层中的垂直变化趋势均呈折线变化。20a 和撂荒地土壤全 N 含量在 0～20cm 土层中随土层深度增加而增大，在 20～60cm 土层中随土层深度增加而减小；14a 土壤全 N 含量在 0～20cm 土层中随土层深度增加而减小，在 20～60cm 土层中随土层深度增加而增大；6a 和 27a 土壤全 N 含量在 0～20cm 土层中随土层深度增加而减小，在 20～40cm 土层中随土层深度增加而增大，而在 40～60cm 土层中随土层深度增加又减小。总体上可以看出不同龄级小叶锦鸡儿人工林土壤全 N 含量总体表现为：20a＞14a＞27 a＞6a＞撂荒地。

2.1.4 不同龄级小叶锦鸡儿人工林土壤有效 P 空间差异

不同龄级小叶锦鸡儿人工林在 0～40cm 土层中土壤有效 P 含量大体表现为：27a＞20a＞14a＞6a＞撂荒地；在 40～60cm 土层中土壤有效 P 含量大体表现为：27a＞20a＞6a ＞14a＞撂荒地。27a 土壤有效 P 含量很高最大值出现在 40cm 土层处，在 0～40cm 土层中随土层深度增加而增大，在 40～60cm 土层中随深度的增加而减小；20a 和 6a 土壤有效 P 含量在 0～20cm 土层中随深度的增加而减小，在 20～40cm 土层中随深度的增加而增大，在 40～60cm 土层中随深度的增加又减小；14a 土壤有效 P 含量在 0～40cm 土层中随深度的增加而减少，在40~60cm土层中随深度的增加而增大；撂荒地土壤有效P含量在0~20cm土层中随深度的增加而增大，在20~60cm土层中随深度的增加而减小。由图可知不同龄级小叶锦鸡儿人工林在各土层中有效P含量总体趋势表现为：27a>20a>14a>6a>撂荒地。

2.1.5 不同龄级小叶锦鸡儿人工林土壤速效K空间差异

不同龄级小叶锦鸡儿土壤中速效K含量总体趋势表现基本一致，0~60cm各土层中均表现为：撂荒地>6a>14a>27a>20a。撂荒地速效K含量最高，主要是由于撂荒地地表植被稀少，对土壤中交换性钾和水解性K利用得少，导致速效K含量较高；而20a小叶锦鸡儿林地上植被最多，对土壤中速效养分含量影响是最大的，这与本研究进行的不同龄级小叶锦鸡儿人工林样地状况调查结果是吻合的，但是与贺山峰，蒋德明等人的"随着植被生长发育年限的增加，土壤中速效钾含量逐年增加"这一结论是矛盾的。

不同龄级小叶锦鸡儿人工林土壤速效K含量在0~60cm土层中的垂直变化呈折线波动。6a与撂荒地在0~20cm土层中随土层深度的增加而增大，在20~60cm土层中随土层深度的增加而减小，最大值出现在20cm土层中；14a、20a、27a的变化趋势相同，在0~20cm土层中随土层深度的增加而增大，在20~40cm土层中随土层深度的增加而减小，在40~60cm土层中又随土层深度的增加而增大，其最小值出现在40cm土层中。

2.1.6 不同龄级小叶锦鸡儿人工林土壤水解N空间差异

不同龄级小叶锦鸡儿人工林土壤水解N含量总体表现为：20a>27a>撂荒地>14a>6a。20a水解N各土层含量都很高，这是由于土壤中近期能够被植物吸收的无机态氮和部分有机质中易分解的、比较简单的有机态氮总量多，这能够反映出20a小叶锦鸡儿人工林土壤氮素供应与释放状况良好。撂荒地植被稀少，水解N含量剩余较多。另外，各龄级小叶锦鸡儿人工林土壤水解N最大值均出现在40cm土层中，最小值出现在0~20cm土层中，而撂荒地水解N含量最大值出现在20cm土层中，最小值出现在60cm土层中。

20a和6a土壤水解N含量在0~60cm土层中的垂直变化是先增大后减小；27a和14a土壤水解N含量在0~60cm土层中的垂直变化是先减小后增大再减小；撂荒地土壤水解N含量在0~60cm土层中的垂直变化是0~20cm土层中随深度增加而增大，在20~60cm土层中随深度增加而减小。

2.2 小叶锦鸡儿对立地质量改善作用

2.2.1 土壤含水量动态变化

小叶锦鸡儿人工林含水量由于生长龄级不同而呈现出明显的差异。土壤深度为0cm~30cm时，不同龄级小叶锦鸡儿人工林随着土壤深度的增加含水量均出现先增加后减少，而作为对照的撂荒地则随着土壤深度的增加含水量先减少后增加；这是因为地表枯枝落叶物较少所致，在土壤深度40~60cm范围内，不同龄级小叶锦鸡儿人工林随着土壤深度的增加含水量均出现先降低后增加，而撂荒地则在该土层范围内出现先增加后降低趋势；这主要是因为不同龄级小叶锦鸡儿群落中有一部分地表植被根系分布在此土层中，导致含水量出现波动式变化，而且趋势相近，而撂荒地含有植被较少，所以在此土层中含水量变化趋势正好与小叶锦鸡儿相反；而在土壤深度70~100cm范围内，不同龄级小叶锦鸡儿人工林随着土壤深度的增加含水量出现波动式变化，总体上出现先减小后增加趋势，这是由于，小叶锦鸡儿大部分根系生长在该土层中，导致含水量有所下降，而后随着土壤深度的增加14a生小叶锦鸡儿和撂荒地的土壤含水量有所增加，其他龄级土壤含水量均有所降低。

2.2.2 对土壤物理性质的改良作用

(1)不同龄级小叶锦鸡儿土壤容重和孔隙度的变化：随土壤土层深度的增加，土壤容重变大，也就是说随着土层深度的加深土壤变的紧实结构性变差。随小叶锦鸡儿龄级的增加土壤容重增大，同时各龄级土壤容重均比撂荒地大，总体表现为：20a > 27a > 6a > 14a > 撂荒地。不同龄级小叶锦鸡儿人工林的土壤容重在 1.459 ~ 1.674g/cm^{3}之间。最小值出现在撂荒地 0 ~ 20cm 处，最大值在 6a 小叶锦鸡儿 40 ~ 60cm 处。最大值出现在 6a 小叶锦鸡儿 40 ~ 60cm 处，可能是由于 6a 在 40 ~ 60cm 土层中根系分布较少，土壤容重比其他龄级大。

(2)不同龄级小叶锦鸡儿土壤饱和持水量与田间持水量的变化：饱和持水量是指土壤中的孔隙全部被水充满时所能保持的最大水分量。根据对不同样地的测定，饱和持水量在 19.39 ~ 22.55% 之间。最小值出现在撂荒地 0 ~ 20cm 处，最大值出现在 20a 小叶锦鸡儿人工林 40 ~ 60cm 处。各样地均表现为随土层深度的增加，土壤饱和含水量不断增大。不同龄级小叶锦鸡儿人工林与撂荒地土壤饱和含水量表现为：20a > 27a > 14a > 6a > 撂荒地。

田间持水量是当大量的水分浸透土壤后，过多的重力水流出，而留下来的水分处于一定的平衡状态时土壤所保持的水分含量。根据对不同样地的测定，田间持水量与土壤饱和持水量变化规律相同。

3 结 论

(1)通过对小叶锦鸡儿人工林种群结构的研究，表明小叶锦鸡儿种群随着年龄的增长，大径级的个体数增多，幼苗的数量减少，群落天然更新能力较弱，由于黄土高原丘陵地区温度、水分条件限制，幼苗难以长成成熟个体，这就需要人为的抚育措施帮助其更新。

(2)植物不仅对水土起到了保护和固定的作用，还可使土壤母质向着土壤形成的方向逐步演化。植被恢复与土壤肥力恢复是相互促进的，并且随着植被恢复而不断增强。黄土高原丘陵地区种植小叶锦鸡儿人工林后，土壤物理性质得到很大改善，具体表现在：土壤容重降低，孔隙度增加，土壤持水能力也得到较大提高，尤其是 20a 小叶锦鸡儿人工林改良效果最为明显。

(3)土壤化学性质也得到很好的改善。随着小叶锦鸡儿人工林的不断发育，群落土壤中腐殖酸不断积累，土壤的 pH 值降低，土壤中的有机质、全 N、有效 P 含量均比撂荒地有不同程度的提高，但速效 K 含量较撂荒地下降。总体来说，20a 小叶锦鸡儿人工林对土壤化学性质的改良作用是相对最明显的。

(5)综上，不同龄级的小叶锦鸡儿人工林在 20a 时基本上达到顶峰，而 27a 小叶锦鸡儿人工林已经开始出现了衰退的迹象，所以应该在小叶锦鸡儿人工林生长达 20a 后开始逐步进行人工更新，以保证小叶锦鸡儿人工林的生态效益。

参考文献

[1] Perez F L. The influence of organic matter addition by caulescent Andean rosettes on surficial soil properties[J]. Geoderma, 1992, 54: 151 ~ 171.

[2] 曹成有，朱丽辉，蒋德明，等. 科尔沁沙地不同人工植物群落对土壤养分和生物活性的影响. 水土保持学报，2007，21(1)：168 ~ 171.

新形势下平原绿化由“线”到“面”的思考

刘安兴　徐　军　杜　群

（浙江省森林资源监测中心，杭州，310020）

摘要：当前，全国各地大力建设现代林业，高度重视森林资源的保护和发展，成效显著。但随着山地造林的日趋成熟，平原地区森林面积相对不足的矛盾日益突显，在许多省份，林业绿化工作的重点已逐步从山区扩展至平原。本文从平原绿化的角度，以浙江省为例，分析了平原地区发展森林的重要性，提出了在新形势下发展平原片林的新思路，并指出要将通道绿化、农田林网等林带拓宽成片林，以这样的发展方式来达到森林与城市(城镇)相融合的发展要求。

关键词：平原绿化；发展；平原片林

The Plains Greening Projects Develop from Line to the Surface under the New Situation

LIU An-xing, XU Jun, DU Qun

(Center for Forest Resource Monitoring of Zhejiang Province, Hangzhou, 310020)

Abstract: Currently, all parts of the country are making great efforts to modem forestry construction and thinking highly of the conservation and development of forest resources. However, with the increasing maturity of the mountain afforestation, the contradiction that forest area of plain region is relatively insufficient has been increasing. In many provinces, the focus of the forestry virescence work has been gradually extended from mountain area to plain area. From the point of view of the plains greening, the writer takes Zhejiang province as an example, analyzes the importance of developing the forest on plain area and puts forward the the new ideas of developing plain woods in the new situation. Also, the writer indicates that the farmland and green corridors can be broaden to woods, in order to achieve the development of the fusion of forestry and cities (towns).

Key words: the plains greening; development; plain woods

近年来，我国林业建设得到了前所未有的重视，森林资源的保护和发展成效显著。随着林业绿化工作的不断深化和扩展，平原地区发展森林，改善环境，增强固碳，已成为现代林业建设新的发展重点和目标。以浙江省为例，目前全省林业绿化工作的重点逐步从山区扩展至平原，但从成效上来看，通过道路绿化、山体绿化、农田林网、城镇村庄绿化等措施进行的平原造林，多为“点”、“线”结构上的增绿扩量，难以在“面”上有实质性的发展和提升，产生的生态与社会效益也有所局限。如何在平原绿化上寻求新的突破点，全面增大片林面积，充分发挥平原森林的生态效能，已成为最新课题。本文从平原绿化的角度，以浙江省为例，提出了要颠覆以往“带”的概念，全面发展平原片林，并将着力点放在通道绿化、农田林网等林带拓宽成片林的建设上，将“线”逐步转换成“面”的发展思路。

一、平原绿化的发展重点应放在平原片林的发展上

（一）平原片林是当前社会可持续发展的需要

改革开放以来，浙江省经济飞速发展，城市化步伐逐步加快，人类破坏自然所带来的影响也日益突显。同时，随着城市污染逐步加重，空气质量下降严重，人类社会对城市森林的生态需求达到了前所未有的高峰。从全省的生态状况来看，城市生态建设用地比例失调、污染程度加剧、污染种类增多、人居环境欠佳、生物多样性丧失等一系列生态环境问题接踵而至，严重制约了人类社会的发展。从人类活动分析，平原地区正是城镇的所在地，是人类活动最为频繁和密集的集聚地，同时也是生态环境日益恶劣最为严重的区域。人类对平原地区发展森林的愿望也最为强烈。从森林分布来看，目前全省森林覆盖率已达高位，并呈现出山地森林面积已近饱和，而平原地区绿量不足，片林面积相对过少的局面。

我们应充分意识到，现在开展的平原片林建设，并不同于传统意义上的林业建设，其功能不再以生产木材等林产品为主导，而是主要用于改善城市生态环境，净化改善城市视觉景观形象，增加城市生物多样性，提供人们游憩活动条件，促使人们身心健康，提升土地利用价值，使城市与森林和谐共存，人与自然和谐发展等。可以说，它是用于缓和人类社会快速发展与环境恶化之间矛盾的一大措施，并且是受益面最广、最为有效、最为方便、最为持续、最为体现民生的措施。所以，平原地区发展片林，是新时期，新形势下社会发展中自身的需求，它直接影响到人类社会发展的可持续性。

（二）从“线”到“面”是新形势下对林业发展的新要求

新世纪以来，森林生态建设得到前所未有的重视，浙江林业得到了迅速的发展，并适时提出了建设“森林浙江”的最新目标。近年来，全省营造林工作成效显著，山地造林日趋成熟，许多山区县甚至已无林可造，但平原造林困难重重，平原绿化相对薄弱。浙江省森林资源清查数据显示，2009 年全省森林面积 601.36 万 hm^2，森林覆盖率 59.07%[1]。综合 2004～2009 年浙江省森林资源年度监测数据，5 年来全省森林面积及森林覆盖率一直处在高位徘徊状态，并已很难再有所提升。然而，由于农村种植结构调整、基本建设征占用林地等因素的影响，全省林地面积 5 年内，减少了 7.23 万 hm^2，森林的增长空间正在紧缩。此外，由于经济社会高速的发展，对土地的需求日益“旺盛”，农地等非林地转为林地的来源日趋减少，通过外延式扩张增加森林面积难度甚大，扩展森林面积已经成为林业发展的“瓶颈”。

在浙江省的“十二五”发展规划中明确提出，要加快“森林浙江”建设，推进森林扩面提质。浙江省林业厅将森林“扩面”的重点放在了平原绿化上，并提出了在“十二五”期间，全省平原力争新增林木面积 180 万亩以上；到 2015 年全省平原林木覆盖率提高到 18% 以上的“1818”平原绿化行动。但平原地区的土地资源十分宝贵，要在城镇中另辟蹊径营造森林，几乎是不可能完成的任务，如再以传统“点”、“线”造林的方式开展平原绿化工作，也难以满足当前社会需要以及“1818”行动的要求。所以，综合各方面因素，在当前林带的基础上，以从“线”拓展到“面”的形式在平原地区营造片林，是最切合实际，最能取得实效的方法。

二、平原片林的发展重点应放在拓展农田防护林带与通道绿化上

(一)拓展农田防护林带，为农业发展服务

从平原地区拓宽林带的可行性以及迫切性上分析，当前拓宽的重点应首先放在农田的防护林带上，包括高速公路两边的农田防护林。农田防护林是农田生态系统的保障，进一步加宽后能有效的缓解当前农业生产中存在的诸多突出问题。

(1)可大大减轻灾害对农作物的侵害。近年来旱灾的加剧已经成为浙江省最大的农业灾害。尤其是今年以来，平均降水量比常年同期偏少五成，直至6月份全省农业受旱面积已达18万亩。单纯依靠发展农田水利事业克服农田干旱难度较大，且不能从根本上解除旱灾对农业生产的威胁。而大力推广营造农田防护林，特别是营造林田相间的片林，形成适宜农作物生长的环境，可大大降低农业旱灾。实践表明，农地在防护林带的保护下，一般可增加空气湿度10% ~20%，土壤蒸发减少30% ~40%[2]。此外，由于树冠对雨雪水有截留作用，因而能延缓地表水径流速度，增加降水的渗透性，减少泥土的流失和河渠泥沙的淤积，从而改变干旱性质。农田防护林还能减轻洪涝灾害、水灾、冻害等自然灾害对农作物的侵害。

(2)可改良土壤，提高土壤肥力。①农田防护林带建成后对降低土壤表层及耕作层的全盐量效果极为明显，可防止次生盐渍化。实验表明，农田防护林对农田土壤有明显的脱盐作用，有减少土壤中CO_2和$HC0_3^-$的效果，使土壤碱性减弱，pH值降低。农田防护林带还有改善盐碱土水溶性组成成分的作用。受林带庇护的土壤，Ca^{2+}比例增大，Na^+减少，从而改善了土壤的通透性和可耕性。②农田防护林能改良土壤结构，增加土壤有机质含量，提高土壤肥力。据监测，7 ~8年林地土壤有机质含量比农地土壤增加近一倍，土壤氮、磷养分含量显著提高，土壤容重降低，非毛管孔隙度增加，通气透水性能提高。同时，林木大量的枯枝落叶促进了整个农田生态系统的物质循环。③农田防护林还能增加土壤微生物种群数量和提高酶的活性，有效地提高土壤肥力水平。研究表明，林带根系活动能明显提高土壤酶活性，在林带四周土壤酶活性较高，随着林带距离的增加酶活性变小，根际土壤酶活性明显高于非根际土壤[3]。

(3)可改善农区环境，形成农田小气候。农田防护林对农区环境的影响是多方面的，随着农田林网布局的合理化，宽度的增大，对农区环境的影响加大，可形成适宜农作物生长的农田小气候。①可产生防风效应。据大量研究表明，农田防护林有明显降低风速的作用，一般可降低风速30% ~40%，大面积林网还能使风速发生递减作用。②可产生温、湿度调节效应。农田防护林在一定范围内对太阳辐射、空气温度、土壤温度等气象要素产生影响。从对林带的监测来看，其对空气温度的影响表现出季节性变化，春秋季增温，夏季降温，冬季升温。同时，由于防护林降低风速，减少农田水分蒸发量，会产生明显的增湿效应。③可产生水文效应。多年的观测表明，林带对蒸发蒸腾、空气湿度、积雪分布、土壤含水量、地下水位、大气降水等，均有一定有益的影响[4]。④可产生污染物的防护效应。当前，由于农药、杀虫剂、化肥的过量使用，农田面源污染严重；在污水灌溉集中的地区，农田受重金属污染的土地比例十分高。相对而言，树木因病虫害少、保土能力强，很少使用化肥、农药等；树木具有增强土壤肥力，减轻农业面源污染的作用；树木能吸收重金属元素，对重金属污染也具有较强的防护能力。

（二）拓展平原通道绿化，为改善城市环境服务

随着城市化、现代化进程的加快，汽车数量急剧增加，汽车污染愈演愈烈，并已成为大中城市的主要污染源，原来所实施的公路绿化已难以平衡当前环境污染源的快速增加，城市市民已经成为城市快速发展后环境污染加剧的直接受害者。所以，进一步拓展和建设通道绿化已经迫在眉睫，它不仅能很好地净化公路空气、防止尘污、减缓噪声危害，还是治理污染、改善区域环境的重要手段。

（1）具有固碳增氧功能，是改善区域小气候的重要措施。在城市中，由于二氧化碳排放量增多，同时由于它的比重较大，多下沉于近地面气层中，导致空气质量下降，并产生温室效应。一般大城市空气中的二氧化碳可达 0.05% ~0.07%，局部地区甚至可达到 0.2%[5]。森林不仅是二氧化碳的消耗者，而且还是氧气的天然加工厂。树木通过光合作用吸收二氧化碳放出氧气，又通过呼吸作用在氧的参与下产生二氧化碳，但总的来说，增加的氧气量大于消耗的二氧化碳量。研究表明，树木每生长 $1m^3$ 蓄积，约需吸收 1.83t 二氧化碳当量[6]。所以地势相对较低的平原地区，片林的大面积发展，能很好地促进空气中氧气含量的提升，减轻二氧化碳含量，减缓温室效应。同时，森林还具有保持水土、涵养水源、净化水体、防洪防风、抗污染等生态功能。总之，在平原地区大力拓展通道绿化，发挥森林的多种生态效能，是缓解城市污染，治理生态环境恶化，改善区域小气候重要途径之一。

（2）具有强大的“净化”、“美化”城市环境功能。城市公路营运对大气环境的影响主要来自道路车辆的尾气排放。而绿色植物如同空气过滤器一样，它能吸收大量的有害气体，对空气起到净化作用；有些树木本身还能分泌杀菌素一类的挥发性物质，能杀死空气中的原生动物、细菌、真菌以及有害微生物，对人类有一定保健作用；绿化带还能通过降低近地面流场风速，可使空气中弥漫的颗粒物发生沉积。研究表明，绿化带对固态和气态的大气污染物均有较强的防护效果，但绿化带的宽度不同、结构不同，防护效果也不同[7]。所以，拓展通道绿化，是缓解当前道路污染不断加重的有效选择。此外，通道绿化作为平原绿化的一部分，它的发展还可大大促进城市的环境美化，增加景观多样性，并能够为人们提供休闲和娱乐的场所，使人消除疲劳、身心愉悦。

（3）对重金属污染及噪音都具有较强的防护作用。公路路域重金属污染主要包括铅（Pb）、锌（Zn）、铜（Cu）、镉（Cd）等。树木根系在吸收矿质营养元素的同时，也会将土壤中的重金属元素吸收进入体内，通过自身的吸收和循环，从而降低土壤的重金属污染。多项研究表明，绿化带可有效降低铅污染程度，且双行绿化带的防护作用优于单行绿化带；复层结构林地重金属污染主要集中在公路两旁 20 m 的范围内，少林地、无林地重金属的污染范围有一定扩大；公路两侧污染区的宽度与路侧林带的高度、密度密切相关，林带高、树木密度大，则可以更好地阻挡污染物的扩散，使其在较近距离累积。此外，植物的茎和叶能在一定程度上吸收和减弱噪音。研究表明，绿化林带宽度与噪音衰减呈正比，与能见度成反比的关系；灌木和乔木同时利用，可使林带产生最好的降噪效果[7]。所以，在公路两旁，特别是高速公路两旁，大力拓展通道绿化，合理调整林分结构，可有效的防护重金属污染以及降低车辆的噪音。

三、拓展农田防护林带与通道绿化应着重做好以下四个方面的工作

(一)加强宣传，转变观念，推行合理的发展政策

当前，群众生态意识虽有提高，但对拓展平原片林的深远意义认识不足，特别是在拓展农田防护林带上，大部分农户看到的是只眼前的利益受到损害，难以辩证地看待造林和农业的互补关系，更难以用发展的眼光去看待农田造林工作。在这个方面，首先应该加强宣传，要让农户清楚地意识到，发展农田防护林其实就是为了加强农业抗灾抗污染能力，为了保证农作物的增产提质，为了确保食品安全等系列生态问题。同时，政府部门应研究及制定相关的发展政策，如：对按规定在农地上造林的农户给予适当的补偿，并确定将今后的相关收益都归于农户；对一些不愿意植树的农户，或以肥换瘦，或以多换少的形式，进行土地调整；在农田外围或高速公路边拓展防护林，各级政府应积极与村户签订有关协议，对涉及集体的地块，积极采取租赁、承包、股份合作等多种形式开展造林工作，以取得农民群众的支持等。总之，在拓展农田防护林带的造林过程中，首先应协调好造林中的责、权、利三者之间的关系，最大限度地调动广大群众造林护林的积极性，以保证该项工作的顺利开展。

(二)加强研究，开展试点，建立科学的发展模式

在我国，农田防护林、通道绿化等工作的相关研究已有所开展，但大部分研究都只局限于“带”的概念，对拓展成片林的研究甚少。在浙江省，平原绿化工作目前正在起步阶段，拓展平原防护林带的设想在全省并无前例。该项工作涉及面广，涉及的部门较多，眼前的效益并不十分明显，建设格局和拓展宽度难以统一，所以开展的难度很大，在起步阶段会有一个长期的摸索过程。特别是对于农田防护林和通道绿化的拓展，从当前的情况来看，并不是涉及的所有对象都要拓展，也不是全省各地都能统一性的进行拓展。应该是在充分分析各方面的因素，科学评价拓展后综合效益的基础上进行可行性的研究，有选择性开展由“带”到“面”的拓展工作。所以，要全面的推动这项工作，首先应该开展相关的研究以及试点工作，对拓展的建设标准、技术方法、效益评价体系、同步监测体系等进行深入的调研，形成理论体系和相关技术规定，努力建立科学、高效、多方位的发展模式。

(三)因地制宜，合理规划，形成生态为先的可持续发展思路

无论是农田防护林，还是通道绿化的拓展，都不是盲目、无序、无限量的拓展。而是要根据当地的实际情况，在充分调研的基础上，按生态经济学原理，进行合理的规划布局，从而确立科学的发展战略，形成可持续性的发展思路，逐步的推进。从长远的发展来看，对于农田防护林，应更加注重防护林建设对农业可持续发展的意义，同时要充分考虑当地农业状况，社会经济状况等各方面的因素，因地制宜地进行合理布局，着力做到因害设防，宜网则网，宜带则带，宜片则片。如：在人均耕地较多或灌溉渠系网络化地区要多建林带林网，在适宜发展单一走向的地区可用宽林带取代林网；在地势不规则的丘陵，大片农田的最外层，灾害性、污染性较强的农地等区域，则应注重长期的防护效益，将林带拓展成片林或随地势发展片林。对于通道绿化，应更加注重拓展后对当地环境污染所产生的生态效益。特别是对于高速公路、一级公路等大路两边的通道绿化，从长远的生态效益来看，可以拓展的都应进行大面积的拓展。特别是对于公路与农田较近的区域，只要有条件，都应努力将防护林带拓展成片林。

（四）创新理念，借鉴经验，实现多方位的发展格局

平原地区是人类活动的密集地，也是人为污染最为严重的区域，要在平原地区发展片林，需要考虑的因素较多，难度较大，以山地造林的发展方式难以实现。平原地区从“带”到“面”的拓展是一项新的工作，同样也是针对当前城市环境污染，发展平原片林的初步构思。所以，在开展该项工作过程中，理念的创新、技术的革新、成功经验的总结及借鉴等都显得十分重要。同时，平原片林的发展要特别注重与城市发展的衔接问题，要多方位的，多渠道的与城市建设相结合，将其科学合理的融入到城市建设中，促进城市的综合发展。在此，特提出以下几点设想，以供参考。一是在通道绿化的拓展上，可以与城市居民的休闲相结合，如可将片林的拓展与城市的慢行系统、游步道等相结合，可将林带拓展成城市中的休闲片林等。二是在农田防护林的拓展上，有条件的地方可借鉴国外农庄的经营理念，如法国法律将不同产区的葡萄酒分为4个等级，不同级别的产区，对当地森林所形成的环境有着不同的要求。此外，他们还凭借葡萄酒的名气和当地森林的特有环境大力发展旅游业。三是要多方位结合，注重解决当前突出、敏感的问题，如针对食品安全问题的农田外围防护林建设；制定与绿色食品达标要求相关的农田防护林标准等。

参考文献

[1]第八次全国森林资源清查浙江省森林资源清查成果报告[R]. 国家林业局华东森林资源监测中心、浙江省林业厅，2009.

[2]李慧颖. 农田防护林带对农作物及土壤的防护作用探析[J]. 中国科技财富，2010(16)：305~305.

[3]王洪锋，刘德凯. 浅谈农田防护林的土壤改良效益与胁地现象的克服[J]. 黑龙江科技信息，2009(26)：154~154.

[4]赵顺财，张桂香，范玉琴. 浅谈农田防护林的环境效益[J]. 青海农林科技，2010(1)：77~78.

[5]刘宪明，王志君. 森林对大气污染的净化功能介绍[J]. 林业勘查设计，2003(2)：32~32.

[6]贾治邦. 发展林业：应对气候变化的战略选择[J]. 求是，2010(7)：54~56.

[7]王慧，郭晋平. 通道绿化带生态效益研究进展[J]. 山西林业科技，2010(3)：37~40.

樱草蔷薇种实性状的观察与测定

王　云
（吉林省林业勘察设计研究院，长春，130022）

樱草蔷薇（*Rosa primula* Boulenger.），别名大马茄子（甘肃），蔷薇科（Rosaceae）蔷薇属（*Rosa*）落叶木本植物，为直立落叶小灌木，高 1 ~ 2m。分布于我国河北、河南、山西、甘肃、陕西、四川等地。樱草蔷薇生于阳坡、林下或灌丛中。耐寒耐旱，对土壤要求不严，在微碱性土壤上也能生长，在富含腐殖质、排水良好的中性或微酸性轻壤上生长和开花最好。极喜光，在庇荫下生长不良，枝叶较疏散，萌条较多，开花少，亦较晚。不耐积水，受涝则下部叶片变黄脱落，甚至全株死亡。萌蘖性较好，生长迅速。

樱草蔷薇在园林应用上与同科属的黄刺玫极为相似，经常作为第二层绿化树种，是北方春末夏初的重要观赏花木。开花时一片黄色，鲜艳夺目，一名黄蔷薇，指的就是这种植物的花。适合庭园丛植、孤植或作花篱。樱草蔷薇在长春市及吉林省园林应用不多，但其花期较重瓣黄刺玫提前 5 ~ 7 d，可弥补北方春季观花植物少的缺陷，增加景观效果。作者以樱草蔷薇为材料，观察并测定有关种实性状变异和花期物候特征，旨在为北方城市绿化花木的选择和培育提供参考。

1　材料与方法

1.1　材料与来源

以长春大学西区校园内的 2 株樱草蔷薇的果实与种子进行观察与测定，并与相同栽培环境下的单瓣黄刺玫有关性状进行比较。

1.2　方　法

对樱草蔷薇的种实性状及有关形态性状进行室外观察与测定，并进行描述。果实采摘后置于实验室阴凉、通风处自然晾干，剥去果皮，分别收集 1 号树和 2 号树的种子。并依据国家标准《林木种子检验规程》（GB2772—1999），对不同植株的种子重量进行抽样检测。

2　结果与分析

2.1　研究材料为樱草蔷薇

樱草蔷薇初花花色淡黄，与单瓣黄刺玫极为相似，两者极易混淆。对樱草蔷薇的花期、单花花期、花色、复叶的小叶数、腺点、小叶的锯齿进行观察，并与单瓣黄刺玫进行比较，结果见表 1。

表 1　樱草蔷薇与单瓣黄刺玫性状比

树种	花期(d)	花色	叶背腺点	复叶的小叶数(枚)	小叶锯齿	单花花期(d)
樱草蔷薇	13～15	淡黄色	浅黄色、密被	7～15，希 17	重锯齿	5～6
单瓣黄刺玫	14～16	深黄色	无	5～11，希 13	单锯齿	5～6

从表 1 可以看出，樱草蔷薇和单瓣黄刺玫除花期、单花花期基本相同外，花色等其他性状均有显著差别，最重要的特征是叶背面的腺点。樱草蔷薇的叶背面密被浅黄色腺点，以叶脉处分布集中，而单瓣黄刺玫则不被腺点。此外，复叶的小叶数差异亦较大，樱草蔷薇为 7～15 枚，希 17 枚，而单瓣黄刺玫为 5～11 枚，希 13 枚。因此，观察研究的材料为樱草蔷薇。

2.2　樱草蔷薇株间的性状变异

将两株樱草蔷薇株间的性状观测结果记入表 2。

表 2　樱草蔷薇株间性状变异

株号	花期(d)	单花花期(d)	花径(cm)	果实成熟期	果实颜色	果实脱落期	备注
1	15	5～6	5.3	8 月 3 日至 8 月 20 日	蓝黑色	8 月 20 日至 11 月 15 日	果实宿存至 11 月中旬
2	13	5～6	4.6	8 月 4 日至 8 月 15 日	紫红色	8 月 15 日至 8 月 30 日	

从表 2 可以看出，樱草蔷薇株间性状差异显著，尤其是花径、果实成熟期、果实颜色、果实脱落期。1 号树花径较 2 号树大 0.7cm，果实成熟期相差 6 d，果实脱落期相差可达 3 个月(1 号树果实宿存)；最显著的特征是果实颜色，1 号树为蓝黑色，2 号树为紫红色，具有不同的果实观赏效应。上述性状的差异是遗传基础不同造成的，并可稳定地遗传给后代。

2.3　樱草蔷薇株间种实性状的变异

2.3.1　形态性状

从表 3 可以看出，1 号树果实中含有种子的粒数较 2 号树平均多出 5.4 粒，种子亦较小，种皮颜色紫红色，而 2 号树则为黄褐色略带紫红色成分，差异显著。

表 3　株间种实性状的变异

株号	果实含种子粒数(粒)	种子大小(长 cm×宽 cm)	种皮颜色	种皮特征
1	19.2	4.3×3.1	紫红	极其坚硬，不易吸水，通透性极差。
2	13.8	4.7×3.5	黄褐色略带紫红	

2.3.2　种子重量

按“四分法”抽取种子重量测定检验样品，每株树重复抽取 8 组，每组 100 粒，用分析天平分别称重(称量精度 1 / 1000)，记录读数。然后计算平均值，结果见表4。经计算，樱草蔷薇 1 号树的千粒重为 22.2g，2 号树的千粒重为 26.1g，前者显著小于后者。

表 4　樱草蔷薇重量测定

重复号	1	2	3	4	5	6	7	8	均值
1 号树重量(g)	2.290	2.279	2.230	2.240	2.213	2.160	2.193	2.189	2.224
2 号树重量(g)	2.698	2.566	2.663	2.574	2.645	2.517	2.643	2.558	2.608

3 小 结

通过对观测材料形态性状与单瓣黄刺玫的形态性状的比较分析，表明长春大学西校区开单瓣黄色花的植株为樱草蔷薇，而非单瓣黄刺玫，最重要的特征是叶背面密被浅黄色腺点，以叶脉处分布最为集中。樱草蔷薇株间种实性状存在显著差异，最显著的特征是：果实颜色，1 号树为蓝黑色，2 号树为紫红色；种皮颜色，1 号树为紫红色，而 2 号树则为黄褐色略带紫红色成分；种子重量，1 号树为 22.4 g，2 号树为 26.1 g。此外，1 号树的果实具有较长的宿存期，与 2 号树有显著差异。上述性状的差异是遗传基础不同造成的，并可稳定地遗传给后代。可根据需要选择不同类型应用于园林。

参考文献

[1]郑万钧．中国树木志(第二卷)[M]．北京：中国林业出版社，1985.
[2]喻方圆，周景莉，洑香香．林木种苗质量检验技术[M]．中国林业出版社，2007.
[3]GB 2772—1999，林木种子检验规程[S].

二、文献综述

我国森林经营的有关问题探讨

张会儒
（中国林业科学研究院资源信息研究所，北京，100091）

摘要：从森林经营概念的解析入手，剖析了我国在森林资源的数量和质量及功能、森林经营方面存在的问题；论述了森林经营的必要性和紧迫性，重点论述了在我国开展幼中龄林抚育经营的紧迫性；介绍了吉林省汪清林业局、哈尔滨市林业局、中国林科院热林中心3个单位在森林经营方面的成功案例。最后，提出了加强我国森林经营工作的措施和建议。

1 森林经营的概念

森林经营的概念有广义和狭义之分。联合国粮农组织于1997年给出了一个广义的森林经营的定义：森林经营是一种包括行政、经济、法律、社会、技术以及科技等手段的行为，涉及天然林和人工林，它是有计划的各种人为干预措施，目的是保护和维持森林生态系统各种功能，同时通过发展具有社会、环境和经济价值的物种，来长期满足人类日益增长的物质和环境的需要。关于狭义的森林经营的概念，我国早在1985年《森林法》颁布实施时，当时的林业部编写的《森林法讲座》中就给森林经营以科学的界定。“以营林为基础是我国林业建设的基本方针，其基点是放在森林资源的培育和管护上，围绕培育与管护这一基本点所采取的一系列科学经营森林的措施，称之为森林经营。从林学观点来看，森林经营是森林培育以及管护现有森林所进行的各种生产经营活动的总称。”“森林经营管理是指对森林经营活动依法进行的决策、规划、组织、指挥、调节和监督”[1]。本文讨论的既是这种狭义的森林经营。

2 我国森林资源和森林经营存在的问题

2.1 森林资源的数量、质量及功能问题

根据第七次全国森林资源清查，我国在森林资源的数量、质量及功能方面主要存在以下问题[2]：

（1）森林资源总量严重不足，而且由于人多地少的尖锐矛盾，难以持久大量增加森林面积；据第七次全国森林资源清查，我国现有4404万 hm^2 的宜林地中质量好的仅占13%，质量差的占52%，而且全国宜林地60%分布在内蒙古和西北地区，今后全国森林覆盖率每提

基金项目：林业公益性行业专项“我国典型森林类型健康经营关键技术研究（201004002）”。

作者简介：张会儒（1964～），男，研究员，博导，主要从事森林资源可持续经营研究。Email：：huiru@caf.ac.cn

高1个百分点都需付出更高代价。

(2)森林质量和生产力低下。我国森林中乔木林质量好的仅占16.66%，中等和差的占83.34%；乔木林质量指数为0.57，质量整体上处于中等水平；森林平均胸径仅为13.3cm，平均蓄积量仅为85.88m^3/hm^2，只有世界平均水平的78%，仅为欧洲的40%；我国人工乔木林的蓄积量更是低至49.01 m^3/hm^2，不到世界的50%。

(3)生态服务功能不强。我国乔木林中生态功能好的仅占11.31%，中等和差的占88.69%；全国乔木林生态功能指数平均为0.54，生态功能总体上处于中等水平。

2.2 森林经营问题

(1)长期重造、轻抚育经营。虽然很早我国就提出了以营林为基础的林业方针，但由于各方面的原因，没有在实践中很好的贯彻执行，虽然提倡大力营造人工林，投入大量的财力和人力营造了大面积的人工林，但森林生产力并没有明显提高，还带来了森林结构不合理、地力衰退等新的问题。

(2)大木头挂帅，永续利用的思想没有很好落实。虽然我国多年来也倡导森林资源的永续利用，但由于林区社会庞大，经济落后，还是以大木头挂帅，这一思想在实践中没有得到很好的落实，出现了森林资源趋于枯竭、生态服务功能非常低下的严重局面。

(3)干部考核机制不完善。森林培育的是一个长期的过程，森林经营的效果很难在短期内见效。而目前干部的任期很短，缺乏对其任期内的森林经营工作进行评价考核办法，因此，其主要精力放在了森林资源保护和提供职工的生活水平上，而这些需要大量的资金来解决，主要来源还是木材收入。造成了森林经营工作不是以促进森林生长为目标，而是以获取经济收入为目标，"让森林休养生息"成了一句空话。

(4)法律法规不健全。我国《森林法》第二章第十六条规定了"各级人民政府应当制订林业长远规划。国有林业企事业单位和自然保护区，应当根据林业长远规划、编制森林经营方案，报上级主管部门批准后实行"，"林业主管部门应当指导农村集体经济组织和国有农场、牧场、工矿企业等单位编制森林经营方案"[3]。由于过于原则，缺乏森林经营的可操作性，致使在森林经营管理过程中没有真正体现森林经营方案的法律地位和作用，经营单位不编制森林经营方案或编制了经营方案也不按方案执行的现象十分普遍，没有发挥森林经营方案的真正作用。本次《森林法》修订征求意见稿中还是对这一问题采取了模糊的表述。

(5)政策不完善。1998年开始实行的天然林保护工程，对我国的森林资源的保护和恢复起到了重要作用，成绩非常显著，使天然林区的森林资源休养生息，得到了恢复性的增长，林区的社会负担有所减轻。但由于投入不足，林区依靠木材收入支撑经济社会运转的局面依然没有改变。同时由于天保工程把"减产、分流"作为重点，在森林培育方面，尤其是森林栽培、森林抚育和低价林改造扶持政策缺位，措施不力，林区"资源危困、经济危机"的局面并没有得到扭转。2009年底，为落实中央林业工作会议精神和"双增"目标，转变林业发展方式，提高森林质量和林地生产力，促进林区富余职工就业和林农增收，国家林业局和财政部开始了森林抚育补贴试点项目，目前投资已达50亿元。但实际操作中，部分单位由于经济危困，没有按照森林抚育的技术规程操作，"采大留小、采好留坏"的现象仍然存在。

(6)分类经营体系不完善。1999年，我国开始实行新的分类经营体系，即将森林分为公益林和商品林。这种分类是根据林业资金的管理方式分类的，实际上为分类管理而非分类经营。同时，由于各地在分类区划界定时，以多争取国家投资和保留可采资源为出发点，没有严格按照要求来进行，造成了区划不合理和公益林区划面积过大等问题。现在由于对公益林实行了严格的保护政策，限制了正常森林经营活动的开展。

(7)对森林采伐与森林培育的关系的认识有误区。从本义上讲，森林采伐不但是森林利用的途径，更主要的是调节森林结构、促进林木生长的重要经营措施。森林主伐利用、森林抚育采伐和林分改造采伐等都是森林培育的重要环节。无论是商品林，还是公益林，都必须通过森林抚育经营提高森林质量。因此，采伐与培育不是对立，而是和谐的关系，但这一关系没有得到很好的认识，“一说保护，就禁止砍树”。全面禁伐和把抚育采伐的木材也纳入采伐限额的做法，不符合森林经营的自然规律。

3 森林经营的必要性和紧迫性

3.1 森林经营的必要性

关于森林经营的必要性，总的来看，主要是提高森林质量、缩短森林的培育周期，更好地发挥森林的多种功能，具体来讲，有以下几方面：

(1)调整森林结构，突出主导林木。通过森林抚育间伐和改造措施进行森林结构和类型的调整，突出森林中主导林木，明确森林经营方向，经营措施，经营重点。如生态林可形成以林为主，乔、灌、草结合的立体混交结构，提高林分质量和林分生产力，使森林质量得以改善，实现生态功能最大化；商品林通过抚育间伐促进林木生长，培育大径材。

(2)降低林分密度，改善林木生长环境，促进森林更新。经过抚育间伐，林分内株数减少，林冠郁闭度下降，使林内光照强度增加，林内空气、土壤的湿度、温度、理化性质也相应地发生了变化，有利于死地被物的分解，提高了土壤的肥力。由于林内环境更有利于树木的生长，林木的管饱和导管长度增加，木材纤维长度加大，秋材所占百分率提高，年轮宽度较间伐前增大，木材的质量也相应得到提高。同时，环境条件的改善，促进了林下天然更新，也给人工栽植珍贵树种创造了有利条件。

(3)增加林分的稳定性。部分中幼林因自然稀疏，枯死木增多，为森林病虫害的发生和蔓延提供了场所，为森林火灾、雪压、风倒等自然灾害孳生了条件。森林抚育间伐不但能改善林分结构，提高森林质量，而且有利于改善林分的卫生状况，增强抗御自然灾害的能力。

(4)实现早期利用。中幼林通过抚育间伐后，可以获得间伐材，使经营者获得早期收益。同时，通过抚育间伐，可以有效地促进保留木的生长，缩短了林木培育周期，实现提早利用木材的目的。

(5)成过熟林的择伐和更新既可及时地利用木材，同时保证在林地上仍能继续有林木生长，实现林地的连续覆盖，不断的发挥森林各种有益效能，避免因自然灾害造成资源的损失和生态服务功能的下降。

3.2 森林经营的紧迫性

目前森林经营的紧迫性主要体现在幼中龄林的抚育经营方面。

据第七次全国森林资源清查，我国现有乔木林中幼龄林面积为5261.86万hm^2，占33.82%，中龄林面积为5201.47万hm^2，占33.43%，二者合计占67.25%[2]。虽然近年来采取了一些抚育经营措施，但欠账仍然很大。据调查，黑龙江省急需抚育经营的幼中龄林面积达300多万hm^2，且以每年5万～10万hm^2的速度增加；黑龙江森工急需抚育经营的幼中龄林面积达400多万hm^2，约占全局幼中龄林面积的50%；吉林省急需抚育经营的幼中龄林面积达200多万 hm^2，约占全省幼中龄林面积的40%；辽宁省急需抚育经营的幼中龄林面积达110多万 hm^2，约占全省幼中龄林面积的30%。这些幼中龄林由于未能采取切实有效的抚育经营和改造等措施，致使林分密度过大，林木分化明显，生长不良，甚至出现了自然稀疏的现象，造成了资源的浪费，亟待进行抚育。如果森林抚育及时，就能促进林木健康生长，增加林下物种多样性，促进林下更新，增强森林抵御自然灾害和抵抗病虫危害的能力，减少林业的经济损失。同时，通过及时抚育经营，科学控制林分密度，林农就能够充分地利用林地发展林地经济，在促进林农增收致富的同时，解决了农民工就业和林区社会稳定的问题，森林的社会效益更加显著。森林抚育经营的实践证明，及时进行森林抚育经营，林业就能够获得显著的生态、经济和社会效益。反之，林业乃至全社会的损失将是巨大的。因此，进一步加强森林抚育经营工作是当前和今后一段时期一项十分迫切的任务。

4 我国森林经营的成功案例

尽管存在以上困难和问题，还是有一些森林经营单位在坚持不懈地进行森林经营的尝试，积累了成功经验，为全国的森林经营树立了榜样。

4.1 案例一：吉林省汪清林业局

“3个3000万”：建局时森林蓄积3200万 m^3，迄今为止共消耗3880万 m^3，目前仍有森林蓄积4018万 m^3。森林生产力和生态服务功能都得到了良好发挥。主要做法：

(1)确立了“育林为主、采育结合”的森林经营指导思想。

(2)长期坚持并认真实行了采育兼顾的森林经营方式。

(3)积极寻求并坚定不移地走以科技为支撑的森林经营之路。

(4)努力强化并严格实施了一系列有效的配套管理办法。适应采育结合的需要，汪清林业局在生产中确定了节制主伐、加大抚育的经营对策。

4.2 案例二：哈尔滨市林业局

仅十余年时间，三个实验林场就扭转了资源颓势，走上了资源与经济的良性循环。1998年至今，已培育出优质森林20万亩，平均公顷蓄积量达到了130.8 m^3，超过了全国平均水平(84.7m^3/hm^2)，也超过了世界平均水平(114m^3/hm^2)。10年间每公顷平均净增蓄积26.2m^3。主要做法：

(1)以近自然经营的理论为指导，采用目标树培育方法。

(2)采取适当的抚育强度。

(3)培育异龄复层混交林，即多世代的不同树种的混交林。

(4)看重更新，采取措施人工促进天然更新。

4.3 案例三：中国林科院热林中心

经过30年的经营与培育，中心森林资源质量明显提高。森林蓄积量从86万 m^3 增加到目前的139万 m^3，森林成过熟林每公顷蓄积量达到178.05 m^3，森林年生长量9.2万 m^3，年消耗量6.9万 m^3，森林资源已进入越采越多，越采越好的良性发展阶段。主要做法：

(1)针叶林近自然改造——目标树作业体系。

(2)大力发展珍贵优良阔叶用材树种：丛植培育技术、“针阔同龄混交”、“针阔异龄混交”、“阔叶异龄混交”、“阔叶同龄混交”、“阔叶纯林”、“四旁种植”6种森林培育模式。

5 加强我国森林经营工作的措施和建议

根据森林经营的必要性和我国存在的问题，提出如下建议[4,5]：

(1)加强宣传，提高对森林经营重要性、必要性和紧迫性的认识。积极宣传加强森林经营的重要性，是各级林业主管部门的重要任务。森林经营的内涵很丰富，这里的“经营”概念，包含了林地、林木等全部森林资源的筹划营谋，按照自然规律和经济规律进行人为治理，达到森林生态，森林收获和经济效益既定的目标。通过宣传，提高社会对森林经营的认知程度，澄清与纠正在森林经营工作中存在的种种误区，转变一些以为林业就是简单的“挖坑种树，动斧砍树”、“一说保护，禁止砍树”以及把培育与采伐对立等模糊认识。

(2)加快国有林区改革进度。总体来看，经过几次改革，我国国有林区的情况有了很大改善。特别是天然林保护工程实施以来，成绩非常显著，使森林资源得到了恢复性的增长，林区的社会负担有所减轻。但由于投入不足，林区依靠木材收入支撑经济社会运转的局面依然没有改变，“资源危困、经济危机”的局面并没有得到扭转。建议进一步加大国有林区改革力度，在进一步“减产、分流”及基础上，将国有森林经营单位列入事业单位，专门从事森林资源的保护、经营和培育，定员定岗；同时，经济上采取“收支两条线”的管理政策，即对于来源于木材采伐的收入全额上缴国家，所需行政和人员经费由国家财政差额拨款，不足部分由森林经营单位通过发展林下经济和多种经营弥补。森林经营活动(如育苗、造林、抚育采伐等)经费由国家根据任务情况专项下达。采取这种措施，将从根本上切断以木材收入作为经济来源的渠道。同时，完善制定配套的干部政绩考核体系，突出对森林资源保护、经营和培育的考核要求。完善森林资源的监督体制，加大森林资源的监管力度。通过以上措施，解决森林经营动力不足的问题。

(3)完善森林分类经营体系。从森林的自然属性上来看，每片森林都具有多功能的属性。为了协调解决严格保护和经营利用的矛盾，可以以主导功能来分类，每一类采取不同的政策措施，这就是分类经营。但目前的划分为两类，不足以解决严格保护和经营利用的矛盾。建议对此分类体系进行完善，划分为三类，即森林分类的“飞机模型”：一翼：严格保护林；一翼：商品林；机身：多功能森林(或多用途林)。严格保护林是指重要生态区位的森林，以生态保护和生物多样性保育为主导功能，如江河源头及两侧一定范围、自然保护区和森林公园等的森林，采取严格的保护措施；商品林是指以生产商品材为主导功能的森林，如速生丰产林、工业原料林和经济林等，以经济效益为最大化开展森林经营。以上两种的划分比例应严格控制。多功能森林(或多用途林)是指用于木材产品的生产、水土保持、生物多样性保存和提供社会文化服务的任何一种组合的森林，这是森林经营的主体对象，按照森林经营规程和经营方案开展多功能经营。

(4)抓紧森林采伐管理等制度的改革。森林抚育、林分改造的森林采伐限额管理，不应成为森林抚育和低价林改造的瓶颈，要从有利于森林培育、有利于经营主体、有利于森林资源保护“三个有利”的原则进行完善。凡是按规范要求编制森林经营方案，按方案中确认的合理年采伐量，纳入森林采伐限额的管理。另外，现行各项规程、标准以及管理办法，凡不利于加强森林经营工作，脱离实际的，应清理、修改和完善。

(5)建议国家启动森林经营工程。2010 年中央 1 号文件《中共中央　国务院关于加大统筹城乡发展力度 进一步夯实农业农村发展基础的若干意见》中，明确提出了启动森林经营工程，但目前还没有具体的行动。建议尽快启动相关工作。主要是抓紧编制全国森林经营工程规划，重点突出森林抚育措施。森林经营工程可以分解为森林抚育工程、大径材培育工程、珍贵树种培育工程、低价林改造工程等等。当前要抓紧试行示范工程，建立示范区，以县(局、场)为尺度，建立森林经营工程管理体系，以县(局、场)为单位编制森林经营类型，各森林经营主体编制森林经营方案，按方案实施。经过试点，总结经验，示范推广。

(6)健全森林经营的法律法规。我国现行的林业法律体系中，森林经营有关法律法规方面还很不健全。《森林法》对森林经营的规定过于原则，缺乏可操作性，建议本次修订中进一步明确表述，少用“应当”，多用“必须”。同时，借鉴美国、日本、芬兰等许多国家都制定了《国有林经营法》、《私有林经营法》的经验，着手制定我国《森林经营法》。通过法律规定森林经营的各种形式，包括森林经营的主体与客体，经营权取得和限制，森林经营的基本准则，森林经营规划与森林经营方案的编制执行，森林经营与各方面的关系，森林经营效果的保障，森林经营风险管理等等。立法有一个过程，可先以法规或部门规章形式，予以明确。对过去不切实际，不利于加强森林经营的规章制度和规程规范，进行清理修订。只有森林经营有法可依，有章可循，林业生产力的解放和发展才能得到切实保障。

(7)加大林区基础设施建设力度。当前林区的道路以及公共基础设施与现代林业极不相称，与其他基础工业行业相比，落后甚多。林区道路密度过低，不利于森林防火，也不利于森林经营活动。林区职工生产、生活基础设施，几十年没有多大进步，不利于“安居才能乐业”。建设社会主义新农村与新林区都是时代的要求，体现社会进步，也是加强森林经营工作的不可忽视部分。建议国家按工业基地和新农村建设的标准，支持林区和林场的道路以及公共基础设施的建设，为森林科学经营提供保障。

参考文献

[1]张建国．林业建设的当务之急——森林经营[J]．林业经济问题，2003，23(3)：125～127.

[2]贾治邦．中国森林资源报告——第七次全国森林资源清查．中国林业出版社，2009.

[3]国家林业局．中华人民共和国森林法．北京：中国林业出版社，1998.

[4]张会儒．森林经理：问题与对策．林业经济，2009，(6)：39～43.

[5]中国老科协林业分会．加强森林经营，提高森林质量调查研究报告．2009.

森林蓄积量遥感估测研究进展

涂云燕　彭道黎

（北京林业大学，北京，100083）

摘要：本文在光学遥感和微波遥感范围内对国内外森林蓄积量遥感估测的研究进展进行了论述，介绍了森林蓄积量遥感估测已经取得的进展。从论述中知道了森林蓄积量遥感估测的方法经历了传统的地面估测到遥感多元线性回归估测与非线性的 KNN 法与人工神经网络估测，其主要研究集中在遥感数据源选择、优化估测模型、估测范围变化上。并针对目前遥感蓄积量估测存在的问题，提出了一些对策。对于近年出现的新的蓄积量遥感估测方法，预测了森林蓄积量遥感估测的发展趋势。

关键词：光学遥感；微波遥感；森林蓄积量；多元线性回归；神经网络模型

Research Summary of forest Volume Estimation based on Remote Sensing

TU Yun-Yan，PENG Dao-Li

（Beijing Forestry University，Beijing，100083 ）

Abstract：The research progress in the remote sensing estimation of the forest stock volume within the scope of the optical and the microwave remote sensing both at home and abroad was summarize, describes the progress made by the remote sensing estimation of the forest stock volume. Know from the discussion the method of remote sensing of forest volume estimation through the traditional ground research to multiple linear regression estimation of remote sensing and nonlinear KNN method and artificial neural network estimation, and its main study focused on remote sensing data selection, optimization estimation model to estimate changes in the scope. And for the current problems in the remote sensing estimation of the forest stock volume, put forword some strategy. For recent years, the appearance of new remote sensing estimation method, estimating the trend of remote sensing estimate of forest stock volume.

Key word：optical remote sensing；microwave remote sensing；the forest stock volume；multiple linear regression；neural network model

引　言

森林蓄积量估测工作一直以来都是林业科学研究者的重点与难点。传统的一、二类调查存在劳动强度大、调查周期长、投入大等问题。为了提高质量和效率，近年来新方法和手段不断出现，从传统数量化方法到线性多元回归分析，从地面手工测量到航空遥感，再到人工神经网络的应用，一系列的新方法、新手段使森林蓄积估测比传统方法省时、省力，节约经费。但仍存在一些问题，不断探索新方法使森林蓄积量定量估测更精确、更省时省力成为今后主要的发展方向。

1 国外研究进展

20 世纪 60 年代后，美国摄影测量学会提出了非成图方法，既在航空相片上抽取直接估测各类土地面积，为森林蓄积量测定奠定了基础。随后的十几年，国内外着手研究直接用卫星资料估测蓄积量[1~2]。

1984 年，Nelson 等开始应用 Airborn Laser 数据估测森林树冠郁闭度[3]，为森林蓄积量遥感估测奠定了基础。森林郁闭度作为影响森林蓄积量估测的必不可少的因子，不仅对蓄积量估测模型建立、自变量选择有重要影响，对预测模型影响也很大。1988 年他用 Laser 数据获得美国佐治亚州南部部松林的林冠高度数据，然后建立生物量和蓄积量回归方程以估测森林蓄积量，结果显示，蓄积量的估算精度与用人工方法估测的结果偏差平均在 2.6%[4]。1989 年美国 LARSON&MCGOWIN 公司利用卫星影像测量 18 种不同土地和森林类型的面积，然后再利用获得的立木材积抽样数据测算各种类型松树、阔叶树立木材积平均值，结果比传统方法精确省力[2]。Breidenbach 等基于贝叶斯方法用 Airborne Laser 数据对 Forbach 森林蓄积量进行估测发现非参数 KNN 方法的精度通常优于线性回归模型[5]。

Gemmell 用 TM 数据，探讨了影响森林蓄积量估测的各变量影响度。结果表明，TM4 波段、TM5 波段和蓄积量相关度较大，同时蓄积量和林分高、林龄、树种组成、坡向、坡度相关性都很大。其中郁闭度和蓄积量的相关系数最大[6]，这一理论为蓄积量估测定性因子与定量因子选取奠定了基础。Fazakas 等应用 TM 数据结合国家资源清查数据，用最近邻近法(KNN)对瑞典中部森林的蓄积量进行估测[7]，结果显示，当对单个像元蓄积量进行估测时，精度很低，当把像元合到一起时，精度大大提高。Tomppo 等应用 TM 数据、IRS - 1C WIFS 数据结合样地数据，用非参数最近邻近法建立的非线性回归估测模型对大面积区域的森林蓄积量进行了估测，所得数据与实测相差很小[8]。Makela 等应用 TM 数据的像元平均值作为估测的自变量，用 KNN 算法分树种地估测了林分蓄积量，但和实测数据相比，分树种蓄积量估测精度很低[9]。

2 国内研究进展

森林蓄积量遥感估测[2,10]在 1982 年提出航天遥感数据的多元估测方法，形成方法锥形，1986 年样本形状、组织方法，分流域建立方程地面估测，后来与航空资料以及航天与航空资料相结合的像片材积表方法。1989 年三种方法估计精度的进一步比较，成本初步分析，样本数量研究，比值项作用的进一步验证。遥感波段非线性比值项的提出和参与估计，为提高蓄积量估测精度及充分利用遥感信息提供了保障；建立了以遥感、GIS 和 GPS 为基础的森林蓄积量定量估测理论体系。在理论研究的基础上，成功开发国内第一套功能相对完备、可操作性强的蓄积量估测软件系统。这期间数理统计进展也推动了国内外从航空相片、卫星图像上进行判读，估测的发展。目前，我国森林蓄积量遥感估测主要集中在光学遥感数据和微波遥感数据进行森林蓄积量估测的研究。

2.1 光学遥感数据的森林蓄积量估测进展

袁凯先等利用 TM 数据，用多元回归和编制林分数量化材积表两种方法进行蓄积估测的精度和效益分析，结果表明用该方法完全可用于二类调查，经费比传统至少节约了 1/2 左右，效率至少提高了 50%，同时大大减小了劳动强度[11]。侯长谋等人以 TM 数据波段灰度值及 GIS 因子为自变量，对定性因子定量化，对林分进行逐步聚类以类似分层抽样方法抽取样地，逐步回归选择最优变量建立马尾松林分蓄积量判读模型，并用不同时相的遥感数据及其同期外业调查数据进行验证。结果表明，所建立的马尾松蓄积量判读模型线性关系显著，估算精度达到广东省森林资源连续清查规程的要求。之后，他们用相同方法建立的杉木林分蓄积量判读模型也可应用于森林连续清查间隔期内广东省杉木林分蓄积量的估算[12~13]。陈楚等以 RS、GIS 可提取的因子为自变量，运用偏最小二乘(PLS)估计的数学模型建立森林蓄积量估测模型，克服了传统的基于最小二乘(OLS)估计模型无法克服样地少、各自变量之间相关性强及对蓄积量的解释性不强等问题[14]。张彦林以 TM 数据基础，结合地面 542 个样地调查数据，建立蓄积量与遥感信息之间的回归方程，对森林蓄积量进行估测。通过对参与建模变量进行了 Box - Cox 变换，建立森林蓄积量反演模型，提高了模型的估测精度，解决了在大尺度范围内利用 TM 数据对森林蓄积量估测问题[15]。黄伟平等，运用残差平方和法，对湖南省新化县曹家镇 20 个一类调查样地对应的 SPOT5 影像的 9 个遥感因子组合进行了多重相关性研究。结果表明：除遥感因子 SP_2外，其余因子对森林蓄积量的估测都有重要作用。通过方差扩大因子对各遥感因子的多重相关性诊断表明：剔除 SP_2后，各遥感因子间的多重相关性大幅减小[16]。

2.2 微波遥感森林蓄积量估测进展

微波遥感是 20 世纪 90 年代引进应用的一种遥感技术，它是从遥感平台向地面目标发射微波，传感器接收地面目标回波的一种探测方法，波长从 0.1 ~ 100cm，是目前遥感传感器接收波长最长的一段波谱。能全天候全天时工作，且穿透力强，使其在区域的蓄积量估测方面有其他光学遥感数据不可替代的作用。但其缺点光谱分辨率低，在山区容易产生盲区、阴影大、地类影像特征不如光学遥感[17]。

王臣立等人利用雷达示波器后向散射系数与森林蓄积量、树高、胸径的关系，进行对数模型模拟，估测森林蓄积量，其精度基本符合林场大面积总体估测的精度要求，但小班水平应用效果不理想[18]。冯仲科等利用 LIDAR 测量树高，用其与抽样木的材积之间进行回归分析，建立起两者之间的回归模型，用这一模型测出的蓄积量与标准样地的相对误差为 4.25%，符合林业要求[19]。朱海珍等分别选取 HH、HV 及 HV/HH 值分析森林蓄积量与 SAR 后向散射系数之间的关系，根据其散点图形状进行方程拟合及优选，完成蓄积量的估测。利用独立的检验样本对结果的评价结果是 RMSE 为 16.526 m^3/hm^2，与实际情况相符合[20]。杨永恬等，基于 ALOS PALSAR，利用非线性回归方法对吉林省汪清林业局建立了固定样地蓄积量与所对应的 PALSAR 像元后向散射系数之间的关系，结果表明，除杨树等树种组外，PALSAR 的 HV 后向散射系数与蓄积量呈良好的正相关关系，对多数树种而言，交叉极化方式(HV)后向散射系数与蓄积量的决定系数比同极化方式(HH)的略高。若以林场为单位统计，采用回归方法得到的估测结果与直接利用固定样地估测的结果相差很小[21]。范凤云[22]基于机载 LiDAR 和 ALOS PALSAR 全极化 SAR 数据利用改进的树冠识别算法，提取了林分平均高，估测了森林蓄积量，发现低密度激光雷达估测大面积山区森林参数是可行的。杨永恬将光学数据的光谱反射率与植被指数结合队 PALSAR 的交叉极化后向散射系数作为自变量，地面实测数据作为因变量，通过建一立多元回归模型进行回归分析。结果表明对各树种组，其模型的相关系数均较基于单一数据建立的回归模型相关系数高，均方根误差也降低[23]。

3 基于人工神经网络森林蓄积量的估测

在影响森林蓄积量及郁闭度的主要遥感和 GIS 因子与蓄积量及郁闭度间是否存在确定的数学关系，数学模型是线性还是非线性的，具体表达如何，很难确定。为避免假设模型不正确造成不利影响。人工神经网络被引用到了森林蓄积量的估测中，它是一种新型的估测蓄积量的方法，是一种非线性的系统，它采用黑箱式操作，通过少量的样本数据(可包括遥感数据和 GIS 数据)，经过适当的学习算法，对网络进行训练，训练结束后的网络就可以进行森林蓄积量的估测。目前，广泛应用于森林蓄积量估测的神经网络模型是 BP 网络和 RBF 网络[24]。

李际平等利用 BP 模型预测了森林蓄积量和各龄组蓄积量精度很高，并指出 BP 模型难以求得数据做统计检验的缺点[25]。邓斌等采用人工神经网络方法拟合杉木林分蓄积量与林地质量、林龄、林分密度之间的非线性关系，建立了杉木可变密度蓄积量收获预估 BP 网络模型，并对所建立的模型进行精度检验。结果表明，所建模型预测精度高。该模型不仅适用于湖南省杉木林分蓄积量收获预估，还可推广应用于其他树种蓄积量以及生长量的收获预估[26]。张志等采用人工神经网络方法对金沟岭林场的混交林建立了可变密度蓄积量 BP 网络模型，采用回归方程适应性检验法分别对模型的拟合效果进行适应性检验。检验结果表明所有模型是实用的，不存在系统偏差[27]。琚存勇等用主成分变换和经规则化调整法进行泛化改进的 BP 神经网络在森林蓄积量建模估测，并与普通 BP 神经网络进行了比较。结果表明，泛化改进的 BP 神经网络比普通 BP 神经网络具有更高的预报精度达到了 99%，且利用主成分得分作为仿真模型的变量比直接用观测值作变量具有更快的速度[28]。王臣立等通过分析南方地区的尾叶桉和加勒比松不同植被指数与蓄积量的关系，选择合适的植被指数，建立了多元回归与神经网络模型。结果表明，单波段 TM 数据和大多数植被指数与蓄积量相关性并不好，神经网络比回归分析模拟效果好，但预测效果并不比多元回归好[29]。李崇贵将 BP 网络和径向基网络结合“3S”技术运用到了地段的森林蓄积量定量估计上，实现了对林班或小班蓄积的估测。精度完全满 足调查精度要求。同时他还应用 MATLAB 技术开发出了森林蓄积量定量估测软件[30]。

综上所述，森林蓄积量遥感估测主要难点在以下几方面：一是怎样选取合适波段数、比值项及定性因子，因遥感波段及比值波段间可能存在一定程度的多重相关性，这种相关性将对森林蓄积量估测模型待定参数求解带来较大危害。利用方差扩大因子可有效诊断所设置的遥感波段间是否存在多重相关性。采用平均残差平方和准则可有效选择对蓄积量估测有重要解释作用的遥感波段，且所选波段间的多重相关性相对较小[31]。二是如何确定森林蓄积量估测模型及解算方法。在森林蓄积量多元回归估测中求取参数常用的方法线性的最小二乘法(LS)、岭估计法、逐步回归法和偏最小二乘估计法到非线性的人工神经网络法估测法。当各遥感和 GIS 因子间存在多重相关性事，需用岭估计或偏最小二乘估计建立估测方程。三是最优变量选择方法。根据已有研究文献，森林蓄积量估测中最优变量选择主要有岭迹分析法、平均残差平方和准则、C_p准则、AIC 准则。李崇贵等利用 matlab 编程，对可能影响蓄积量估测的自变量因子组合，采用岭迹分析法、平均残差平方和准则、C_p准则、AIC 准则进行筛选，并构造了四种方法的评价函数，得到了平均残差平方和选择的最优变量，实现了对自变量自动筛选的仿真技术[32~34]。

4 结论与展望

(1)森林蓄积量遥感估测数据主要是光学遥感和微波遥感。在设置蓄积量的遥感和 GIS 因子时，没有考虑从遥感图像上难以有效获取的重要测树因子，如树高、胸径等。而这些因子对蓄积量估测起非常重要的作用。伴随高空间分辨率遥感技术的发展及国家对林业投入的增加，在结合地面调查、高空间分辨率遥感图像能有效识别上诉因子条件下，可考虑将上述因子作为影响蓄积量估测的 GIS 信息参与分析，从而实现林班、小班蓄积量的估测。因此，先进测绘仪器和更高分辨率、更广泛的遥感数据将引入林业应用中。

(2)森林蓄积量估测的方法经历了传统的地面估测到遥感多元线性回归估测与人工神经网络估测。多元线性估测是主流，其研究方向主要集中在使用优良回归模型、自变量自动筛选仿真技术上。

(3)人工神经网络估测森林蓄积量是一个研究热点，但由于其操作是暗箱操作，无法表达和分析被预测系统的输入和输出间关系，因而也难于对求得的数据做统计检验，随机性是其应用的一大障碍，一个地区的训练结果对于另一个地区可能并不适用。且将其应用于基于林斑和小斑单元上的蓄积量定量估测研究深度还有待进一步提高。

(4)人工神经网络知识的表达还需要模型化和形式化，改进型神经网络模型估测将是未来的研究热点。

参考文献

[1]程武学，杨存建，周介铭，等．森林蓄积量遥感定量估测研究综述[J]．安徽农业科学，2009，37（16）：7746~7750.

[2]赵宪文．林业遥感定量估测．北京：中国林业出版社，1996.

[3]NELSON R，KRABILL W，MACLEAN G. Determining forest canopy characteristics using airborne laser data [J]．Remote Sensing of Environment，1984，15(3)：201~212.

[4]NELSON R，KRABILL W，TONELLI J. Estimating forest biomass and volume using airborne laser data[J]. Remote Sensing of Environment，1988，24(2)：247~267.

[5]BREIDENBACH J，KUBLIN E. Estimating timber volume using airborne laser scanning data based on bayesian methods[J]. IUFRO division 4 meeting：extending forest inventory and monitoring over space and time. 2009 (5)：19~22.

[6]GEMMELLFM. Effects of forest cover，terrain，and scale on timber volume estimation with Thematic Mapper data in a rocky mountain site[J]．Remote Sensing of Environment，1995，51(2)：291~305.

[7]FAZAKAS Z，NILSSON M，OLSSON H. Regional forest biomass and wood volume estimation using satellite data and ancillary data[J]. Agri－cultural and Forest eteorology，1999，99：417~425.

[8]TOMPPO E，NILSSON M，ROSENGREN M，et al. Simultaneous use of Landsat－TM and IRS－1CWiFS data in estimating large area tree stem volume and aboveground biomass[J]. Remote Sensing of Environment，2002，82(1)：156~171.

[9]MAKELA H, PEKKARINEN A. Estimation of forest stand volumes by Land sat TM imagery and stand. level field inventory data[J]. Forest Ecology and Management, 2004, 196 (2/3): 245 ~ 255.
[10]赵宪文，李崇贵，斯林，等．森林资源遥感估测的重要进展[J]．中国工程科学，2001，3(8)：15 ~ 24.
[11]袁凯先，陈玉山，包盈智，等．森林蓄积量的遥感估测[J]．林业资源管理．1996 (3)：13 ~ 17.
[12]侯长谋，杨燕琼，黄平，等．基于 RS_ GIS 的马尾松林分蓄积量判读模型研究[J]．林业资源管理，2002，(5)：55 ~ 57.
[13]黄平，杨燕琼，侯长谋．基于 RS、GIS 的杉木林分蓄积量判读模型研究[J]．中南林业调查规划，2003，22(1)：25 ~ 27.
[14]陈楚，关泽群，张鹏林，等．利用 RS 和 GIS 的森林蓄积量偏最小二乘估测研究[J]．湖北林业科技，2004(4)：25 ~ 28.
[15]张彦林．BOX – COX 变换在遥感数据建模中的应用[J]．东北林业大学学报，2010，8(38)：120 ~ 122.
[16]黄伟平，谭三清，张贵，等．估测森林蓄积量的遥感因子选择研究[J]．中南林业科技大学学报，2010，4(30)：112 ~ 115.
[17]游先祥，遥感原理及在资源环境中的应用．北京：中国林业出版社，2003，9.
[18]王臣立，牛铮，郭治兴，等．RadarsatSAR 的森林生物物理参数信号响应及其蓄积量估测[J]．国土资源遥感，2005，(2)：24 ~ 28.
[19]冯仲科，杨伯钢，罗旭，等．应用 LIDAR 技术预测林分蓄积量[J]．北京林业大学学报，2007 (S2)：45 ~ 50.
[20]朱海珍，庞勇，杨飞，等．基于 ENVISAT ASTAR 数据的森林蓄积量估测研究[J]．地理与地理信息科学，2007，23(2)：51 ~ 55.
[21]杨永恬，李增元，陈尔学，等．基于 ALOS PALSAR 数据的森林蓄积量估测技术研究[J]．林业资源管理，2010(2)：113 ~ 117.
[22]范凤云．基于机载 LiDAR 和 ALOS PALSAR 全极化 SAR 数据的山区森林蓄积量估测方法研究．硕士论文，2010.
[23]杨永恬．基于多源遥感数据的森林蓄积量估测方法研究．博士论文，2010.
[24]程武学，杨存建，周介铭，等．森林蓄积量遥感定量估测研究综述．安徽农业科学，2009，37(16)：7746 ~ 7750.
[25]李际平，邓立斌，何建华．基于人工神经网络的森林资源预测研究[J]．中南林学院学报，2001，21 (4)：19 ~ 22.
[26]邓立斌，李际平．基于人工神经网络的杉木可变密度蓄积量收获预估模型[J]．西北林学院学报，2002，17 (4)：87 ~ 89.
[27]张志，杨海周，孙玉军．可变密度蓄积量的 BP 网络模型[J]．河南林业科技，2005，25 (1)：1 ~ 3.
[28] 琚存勇，蔡体久．用泛化改进的 BP 神经网络估测森林蓄积量[J]．林业科学，2006，42 (12)：59 ~ 61.
[29]王臣立，牛铮，郭治兴．基于植被指数和神经网络的热带人工林地上蓄积量遥感估测[J]．生态环境学报，2009，18 (5)：1830 ~ 1834.
[30]李崇贵，石强，赵宪文，等．用岭估计研究以 RS 和 GIS 为基础的森林郁闭度估测[J]．林业科学，2001，37 (5)：24 ~ 30.
[31]李崇贵，赵宪文，李春干．森林蓄积量遥感估测理论与实现[J]．北京：科学出版社，2006.
[32]李崇贵．用非线性理论研究以“3S”为基础的森林蓄积量估测．博士学位论文，2001.
[33]王松桂，陈敏，陈立萍．线性统计模型线性回归于方差分析．北京：高等教育出版社，1999.
[34]李崇贵，赵宪文．以遥感和地理信息系统为基础的森林蓄积量 LS 估计自变量选择研究[J]．遥感学报，2001，5，(4).

森林植被遥感分类技术及方法概述

孙 翀

（北京林业大学）

摘要：森林资源的调查、规划、管理、监测、评价、预测预报、决策等各个环节都离不开现实的、客观的、准确的信息，但是林业资源分布广、经营面积辽阔，属于再生性生物资源，而且对于森林资源清查的主要技术手段大多是居于传统的森林资源监测及调查方法，调查和成图周期长，数据过时严重、更新困难，实时性、现实性差并且劳动强度大，体力消耗大，成本高，还受自然因素如地形、水文、气候等条件限制，尤其对一些高、寒、热等人迹罕至的调查困难地区常存在数据信息的空白。因此国家需要投入较多的人力、物力、财力和时间，并且很难满足森林资源监测和林业可持续发展的需要。

遥感技术的出现及遥感影像分类技术的发展为传统的林业资源勘测调查等提供了一个崭新有效的新途径。遥感影像的分类是对研究地区进行信息提取的重要手段。但是随着遥感技术的发展，传统的分类方法在技术层面和分类精度上显示出了明显的不足。为了更多地获得有效信息，提高分类的精度，人们进行了很多的研究。

关键词：植被遥感；研究进展；分类方法；发展趋势

1 引 言

森林资源是林业和生态环境建设的基础，是陆地生态系统的主体，对于经济、社会和环境的可持续发展有不可替代的作用。森林资源的调查、规划、管理、监测、评价、预测预报、决策等各个环节都离不开现实的、客观的、准确的信息，因此，人们迫切希望能快速、准确、高效地获取森林资源信息，及时监测其变化情况，以实现森林资源的科学管理和有效利用。但是林业资源分布广、经营面积辽阔，属于再生性生物资源，而且对于森林资源清查的主要技术手段大多是居于传统的森林资源监测及调查方法，包括：国家每隔 5 年所进行固定样地的一类调查，每隔 10 年的二类调查，还有三类调查、伐区设计等方法，以此实现对各个时期的森林资源状况作调查。5 年一次的全国森林资源连续清查样地全国有 23 万个固定样地，依靠传统地面调查方法，调查和成图周期长，数据过时严重、更新困难，实时性、现实性差并且劳动强度大，体力消耗大，成本高，还受自然因素如地形、水文、气候等条件限制，尤其对一些高、寒、热等人迹罕至的调查困难地区常存在数据信息的空白。因此国家需要投入较多的人力、物力、财力和时间，并且很难满足森林资源监测和林业可持续发展的需要。

遥感技术的出现及遥感影像分类技术的发展为传统的林业资源勘测调查等提供了一个崭新有效的新途径。遥感影像的分类是对研究地区进行信息提取的重要手段。但是随着遥感技术的发展，传统的分类方法在技术层面和分类精度上显示出了明显的不足。为了更多地获得有效信息，提高分类的精度，人们进行了很多的研究，归纳起来主要有两方面：一是寻求新的、更有效的分类方法；二是加入新的数据源，进行多源数据参与分类的研究。传统分类采用参数化统计分类方法，前提是假设图像数据的特征空间符合某种参数化密度分布规律。近些年，地理信息系统应用和普及，使我们可以较容易地获得所需要的与图像分类有关的地理辅助信息，如数字高程模型、坡度数据、土壤类型数据、森林植被现状数据等，这些信息应用在目视判读上可以帮助我们改善判读精度，在一定程度上削弱了"同谱异物"和"同物异谱"的影响。

2 森林植被遥感分类技术的国内外研究

2.1 国内研究进展

20世纪80年代以来，我国应用植被指数变化、植被指数的动态聚类及经验正交函数等方法对大范围植被分类进行了研究[1]。例如，袁金国[2]提出采用植被指数进行植被分类，用PVI区分针叶林和阔叶林，用RVI区分各针叶林树种。还有一些学者对传统的分类方法加以改进，也收到了很好的效果。如朱建华等[3]提出一种适用于多光谱遥感图像分类的自适应最小距离算法，这一算法通过对样本集合的自适应精细划分来调整最小距离分类器的参数，他对TM遥感图分类的实验结果表明，该方法对16类地物(包括若干典型植被)进行监督分类，精度可达92.9%。随着遥感技术发展，许多新的分类技术不断地涌现，姜青香，刘慧平等[4]以北京市丰台区为试验区，将灰度共生矩阵的纹理分析方法应用于图像分类中，试验结果表明：光谱与纹理特征结合得到的分类精度明显高于单纯光谱分类精度以及单纯纹理特征分类精度。在这些新的技术方法中，基于人工神经网络的分类方法在实际研究中应用较多。例如，刘旭升，张晓丽[5]使用Landsat7 ETM+遥感数据和森林资源分布图等地理辅助数据，应用BP神经网络方法对森林植被进行了分类，对针阔林的分类精度分别达到了80.47%和89.48%；郭明新选择神经网络BP模型作为分类器对单一时相TM数据进行土地利用自动分类，其分类精度达94.8%，能满足实际需要。在各种新的技术和方法发展的同时，GIS正作为一种辅助手段参与到遥感分类中，它被引入到了许多的分类方法中。例如，刁淑娟[6]根据遥感图像的光谱信息和空间信息特征及不同植被的分布规律，并利用地形辅助信息对四川省攀枝花地区的植被进行了分类研究，分类精度达到90%，与最大似然分类方法分类结果相比，分类精度提高了10%；刘纪远等[7]利用GIS技术对中国东北的植被进行了综合分类研究，结果表明，与传统的应用最大似然分类方法对单一遥感图像分类相比，该综合分类方法分类精度提高了18.3%；黄建文，陈永富[8]等人通过对海南霸王岭林区三个时期(1986、1991和1996年)的TM影像的监督分类研究，得到了该地区三个时期森林面积统计数据，为森林植被的变化分析提供了依据；陈艳华，张万昌[9]利用一种决策树生成算法(C 4.5算法)自动提取知识，基于知识建立决策树用于山区影像分类，并结合研究区土地利用类型与DEM空间统计关系的先验知识，在GIS空间分析的基础上进行影像分类的后处理，该方法极大地改善了山区地表覆被分类的精度，得到了试验区较为可靠的遥感分类结果。

2.2 国外研究进展

20世纪90年代以来，国外学者在遥感分类及其应用方面做了大量的工作。Gail. A.

Carpenter 等人在最大似然法、线性混合模型、ARTMAP 神经网络三种方法的基础上提出了一种新的数据模型——ARTMAP 混合分类方法，并利用该方法制作了加利福尼亚州的玛县国家公园的森林植被分布图，通过结果的评价与分析得出结论，基于 ARTMAP 混合模型的分类方法精度较高，能很好地区分硬叶林和针叶林；Sulong 等[11]在 GIS 支持下利用 1: 5000 的航空照片和 TM 影像，将马来西亚 Kemaman 红树林划分为 14 个植被类型，分类精度分别达到 91.2% 和 87.8%；Volker Walter 介绍了一种建立在最大似然法基础上的基于对象的遥感分类方法；R. Huguenin，M. Kraska，D. Van Blaricom 和 J. Jensen 利用子象元分类在 TM 影像上区分柏树和蓝果树，其中柏树的总精度为 89%，蓝果树的总精度为 91%，并且通过地面调查得出结论，当柏树和蓝果树处在纯象元中或与其他树种或水混合时可以成功地区分。

3 森林植被遥感分类方法分析

3.1 传统遥感分类方法

遥感图像的计算机自动识别分类，就是根据遥感图像数据特征的差异和变化，通过计算机处理，自动输出地物目标的识别分类结果。它是计算机模式识别技术在遥感领域的具体应用，是遥感图像应用处理的重要内容和关键技术之一。传统的计算机自动识别技术按有无样本可以分为监督分类和非监督分类。

3.1.1 监督分类方法

监督分类就是根据已知的样本和类别的先验知识，确定判别函数和相应的判别准则，其中利用一定数量的已知类别的样本的观测值求解待定参数的过程称之为学习或训练，然后将未知类别的样本的观测值代入判别函数，再依据判别准则对该样本的所属类别做出判定[14]。它主要包括最小距离法、费歇尔线行判别方法以及最大似然比分类法。监督分类需要对所要分类的地物有先验，即先要在研究区中选择出包括所有要区分的各类地物的训练区样本。监督分类方法虽然是在训练区的基础上进行的，在一定程度上也提高了分类的精度，但对于具有复杂地理环境和生物分布特征的林区，其分类结果的精度达不到人们的要求。

3.1.2 非监督分类方法

非监督分类是指人们事先对分类过程不施加任何的先验知识，而仅凭数据遥感影像地物的光谱特征的分布规律，即自然聚类的特征进行“盲目”的分类。其分类结果只是对不同类别达到了区分，但并不能确定类别的属性。非监督分类主要包括分级集群法波谱特征曲线图形识别法、平行管道分类以及动态聚类法。这种分类的特点是分类效率高，只需设定几个参数，剩下的全部由计算机完成，但是分类精度不高，一般只用在预分类中。

3.2 目前常用的森林植被分类技术

由于传统计算机自动分类识别技术的分类精度不能有效满足人们对遥感图像的要求，研究者开发了许多新的分类识别方法，使遥感图像分类识别朝着精确、快速的方向发展，取得了一些好的效果。总结近年来新技术发展的具体应用，主要有以下几种方法：人工神经网络分类法、模糊分类法、基于分形理论的分类法、基于多时相、多源遥感数据的分类法、纹理分类法、分层分类法、基于决策树技术的分类法、基于小波理论的分类法、基于混合像元模型的分类法、基于光谱特征的分类法等。下面对常用的几种森林植被自动分类新技术做简要地介绍。

3.2.1 植被指数分类方法

植被指数是度量植被信息的一个重要参数，它是红光和红外波段的不同组合。植被指数已作为一种遥感手段广泛应用于土地利用覆盖探测、植被覆盖密度评价、作物识别和作物预报等方面，并在专题制图方面增强了分类能力。

植被指数按发展阶段可分为三类：第一类植被指数基于波段的线性组合(差或和)或原始波段的比值，由经验方法发展的，没有考虑大气影响、土壤亮度和土壤颜色，也没有考虑土壤、植被间的相互作用。第二类植被指数大都基于物理知识，将电磁波辐射、大气、植被覆盖和土壤背景的相互作用结合在一起考虑，并通过数学和物理及逻辑经验以及通过模拟将原植被指数不断改进而发展的。第三类植被指数是针对高光谱遥感及热红外遥感而发展的植被指数。这些植被指数是近几年来基于遥感技术的发展和应用的深入而产生的新的表现形式。

3.2.2 基于多时相、多源遥感数据的分类方法

基于多时相、多源遥感数据的分类方法大致可以分为三类：第一类是利用不同时相的同一平台的遥感数据上各种植被信息差异或者随时间的变化规律不同而进行分类；第二类是通过多光谱数据和高空间分辨率数据的融合对植被分类，已达到提高分类精度的目的，这种方法中融合的多光谱数据和高空间分辨率可以是同一平台的也可以是不同平台的；第三类是借助遥感数据和非遥感数据(例如专题数据、地形数据等)的复合或者利用非遥感数据辅助遥感数据的方法对植被进行分类。这三种方法通常体现在遥感数据分类的前期数据准备阶段，具体分类过程中可以采用不同的分类原理和方法，而第三类方法有的时候也体现在数据分类的过程中，如在海拔高度复杂的山区，利用影响植被分布的地理数据(海拔、土壤类型、降水量等)与植被类型之间的对应关系辅助分类。

3.2.3 基于纹理的分类方法

通常遥感影像分类多数都是基于光谱特征的，随着遥感影像空间分辨率的提高，会使纯像元的数目增加，混合的数目减少，从而提高分类的精度，但从另一方面来看，会使影像分类的类别增加，不同种类之间的光谱差异增大，在一定程度上增大了遥感分类的难度，使分类的精度降低。因此，针对有些问题仅仅依靠光谱信息分类是很难达到要求的。纹理是遥感影像重要的特征之一，纹理信息的分析在遥感分类识别中呈现了日益重要的作用，尤其在高分辨率的遥感数据中应用越来越多。

目前常用的纹理分析方法有灰度共生矩阵、灰度游程长度法、自相关模型、Marko 随机场模型、分形模型以及小波变换法等。陆关祥[16]利用一种基于小波变换的纹理分析，提取叠加褶被信息的图像处理方法，通过对南天山东段铜花山—硫磺山地区的多次反复实践和验证，取得了野外难以获取的良好效果。姜青香，刘慧平等以北京市丰台区为试验区，将灰度共生矩阵的纹理分析方法应用于图像分类中。试验结果表明光谱与纹理特征结合得到的分类精度明显高于单纯光谱分类精度以及单纯纹理特征分类精度。

3.2.4 人工神经网络分类方法

人工神经网络是由大量的处理单元(神经元)广泛互连而形成的网络。它是在现代神经科学研究成果的基础上提出的，反映了人脑功能的基本特征，是人脑的某种抽象、简化与模拟[17]。近些年来，人工神经网络识别技术已经引起了广泛的关注，并发展和提出了多种生理模型的具体方法，应用于遥感影像分类专题信息提取、特征分析等认知问题，其中常用的

有多层感知器模型、基于知识的多层感知器的前向神经网络模型自组织竞争神经网络模型、基于径向基函数的前向神经网络模型模糊自组织共振理论的映射模型等。

刘旭升，张晓丽[5]使用 Landsat7 ETM + 遥感数据和森林资源分布图等地理辅助数据用 BP 神经网络方法对森林植被进行了分类，对针阔林的分类精度分别达到了 80.47% 和 89.48%。李朝锋等人通过分析概率神经网络的基本结构及其训练算法，建立了卫星图像分类的概率神经网络模型，并通过实例对比分析了概率神经网络与 BP 网络分类模型的分类效果。郭明新选择神经网络 BP 模型作为分类器对单一时相 TM 数据进行土地利用自动分类，其分类精度达 94.8%，能满足实际需要。

4 发展趋势及展望

尽管经过多年努力人们已经在地面植被的判识中做了许多工作、制作了全国 NOAA AVHRR 地面植被分布图，及地面气候带的划分，这种大面积种植划分，利用 NOAA 卫星混合像元问题不是很突出，采取简单的混合像元分解技术精度可达到要求，而对于地形复杂、耕作制度多样、作物混种严重的地区，AVHRR 资料的“同谱异物”、“同物异谱”现象严重，给不同作物的识别带来了一定的难度。为此人们已作了努力：与高空间分辨率遥感资料结合，如陆地卫星资料、航片等；与微波遥感资料结合，如机载或星载的微波辐射计和合成孔径雷达等，利用微波遥感全天时全天候，能穿透云雾及植被的特点，提高 NOAA 卫星解译精度；综合应用“3S”技术，进一步实现“3S”一体化。

近 20 年来，森林植被遥感分类研究取得了很大进步，但分类精度的提高一直是一个难以解决的问题。随着人工智能技术和理论的日益发展，当前森林植被分类的研究和应用也在向更高层次的智能化方向发展。基于知识的人工智能技术、数据挖掘和知识发现技术及高光谱技术是森林植被遥感分类的发展趋势，但在知识的获取、量化及综合不确定性知识等方面是较难处理的问题，需要做进一步的研究和探索。同时随之而来的是更多的信息要处理，因此也需要快速发展更新的信息处理技术。

参考文献

[1]李星敏，郑有飞，刘安麟．遥感植被分类方法的概述及发展[J]．陕西气象，2002(3)：20～23.

[2]袁金国．森林植被遥感分类研究[J]．河北师范大学学报．1999，23(2)：274～277.

[3]朱建华，刘政凯，俞能海．一种多光谱遥感图像的自适应最小距离分类方法[J]．中国图象图形学报，2000，5(1)：21～24.

[4]姜青香，刘慧平．纹理分析方法在 TM 图像信息提取中的应用[J]．遥感信息应用技术．2003(4)：24～27.

[5]刘旭升，张晓丽．基于 BP 神经网络的森林植被遥感分类研究[J]．林业资源管理，2005(1)：51～54.

[6]刁淑娟，孙星和，袁崇桓．山区植被类型信息提取方法研究[J]．国土资源遥感，1995(3)：34～39.

[7]刘纪远，庄大方，凌扬荣．基于 GIS 的中国东北植被综合分类研究[J]．遥感学报，1998，2(4)：285～291.

[8]黄建文，陈永富．山区林地多季相 TM 影像综合分类研究[J]．福建林学院学报，2004，24(2)：136～139.

[9]陈艳华，张万昌．地理信息系统支持下的山区遥感影像决策树分类[J]．国土资源遥感，2006(1)：69～73.

[10]Carpente. A，Sucharita. G，Macomber. S，Siegfricd. M，and Curtis. W. A Neural Network Method for Mixture Estimation for Vegetation Mapping[J]. Remote Sensing of Environment，1999，70：138～152.

[11]Sulong I，Mohd－Lokman H，Mohd－Tarmizi K. Mangrove Mapping Using Landsat Imagery and Aerial Photographs：Kemaman District，Terengganu，Malayisa. Environment [J]. Development and sustainability，

2002，4：135～152.

[12]Walte V. Object－based classification of remote sensing datafor change detection[J]. ISPRS Journal of Photogram metry&Remote Sensing，2004(58)：225～238.

[13]Huguenin R，Kraska M，Van Blaricom D，et al. Subpixel application for vegetation classification using TM [J]. ISPRS Journal of Photogrammetry&Remote Sensing，1997(63)：717～725.

[14]孙家炳. 遥感原理与应用[M]. 武汉：武汉大学出版社，2003.

[15]张远，杨彬，殷鸣放，等. 山区森林资源遥感动态监测的研究[J]. 福建林业科技，2005，32(1)：30～33.

[16]陆关祥，周鼎武，王居里. TM图像叠加褶皱信息提取——基于小波变换的纹理分析[J]. 中国地质. 2002，9(4)：435～439.

[17]徐建华. 现代地理学中的数学方法[M]. 北京：高等教育出版社，2006.

[18]赵宪文. 面向21世纪的中国林业遥感[J]. 中国工程科学，1999，1(3)：16～21.

森林资源动态监测研究综述

莫　可

（北京林业大学信息学院）

摘要：开展森林资源动态监测工作是实现“可持续发展林业”的基础和必要手段，具有十分重要的意义。本文从介绍森林资源动态监测的发展背景开始，综合讨论了森林资源动态监测体系中使用的技术，包括：3S集成技术、计算机网络技术、通讯技术、抽样调查与数学模型、数据库技术及其他方法与技术。然后介绍了国内外森林资源动态监测体系的现状，通过分析总结得出了森林资源动态监测体系未来的发展趋势，即：监测综合化、监测周期化、高新技术集成化。

关键词：森林资源；动态监测；综述

1　森林资源动态监测背景介绍

1.1　社会背景

为了充分发挥森林的经济、社会、生态三大效益，掌握森林资源的动态变化规律是基础，对森林资源实施监测是必要的手段。森林资源监测的目的在于查清森林资源的数量和质量，包括森林、林木、林地以及依托森林、林木、林地生存的野生动植物和微生物的现状及其消长变化情况[1]。森林资源动态监测是将森林资源的数量和质量作为时间函数的调查，森林资源动态监测体系则是组织、建立、实施森林资源动态监测的一整套方法，是行政与技术的综合体[2]。

随着人类社会的发展，对资源的消耗呈现爆炸式增长，对森林资源的需求首当其冲。由于森林面积的全球性减缩，生态环境不断恶化，保护森林和发展森林已日益引起人们的广泛重视。1987年，世界环境与发展委员会（WCED）在报告《我们共同的未来》（our common future）中提出了可持续发展的概念。在1992年巴西首都里约热内卢的联合国环境与发展大会上又签署了包括《关于森林问题的原则声明》在内的5个文件，此后世界许多国家、国际组织积极响应[3]。

1.2　行业背景

我国林业领域内关于森林资源动态监测领域的工作，早在1983年就在福建进行了相关的试点，提出利用遥感技术、电子计算机、数学方法进行，力求掌握以省级为单位的森林资源消长动态变化。1984年，汪兆忠在福建省的试点工作中，结合地面实测数据，开展了遥感技术的应用试验[4]。1993年，随着遥感技术等高新技术的逐渐发展，寇文正、周昌祥、徐茂松[2]等人针对我国森林资源监测体系发展中的不足（尤其是以各省为控制总体进行森林资源连续清查的国家级森林资源监测体系），较早地提出了应用3S手段和数学模型手段发展森林资源监测体系的思想。2003 年，王允寿、陈景和、张金良[5]等人进行了关于山东省森林资源动态监测体系框架的探讨，认为当前监测体系中无论是国家森林资源连续清查(又称一类调查)还是森林经理调查(又称二类调查或森林资源规划设计调查)，都不能及时准确地监测森林资源的变化动态(前者只能反映宏观状况，县以下的数据无法精确掌握，后者耗费人力、物力巨大且调查间隔长，所得数据反映的是过去 5 年间的综合水平)。此后，黄力平[6]、刘安兴[7]、王文生[8]等人分别对新疆、浙江、内蒙古等省(自治区)的森林资源动态监测体系进行了研究和探讨。在此期间，以 3S 技术为代表的高新技术被逐渐深入应用到森林资源动态监测中，国家森林资源连续清查工作中也开始综合使用样地调查与遥感判读的调查方法。

2 建设森林资源动态监测体系的重要技术

当前被应用到森林资源动态监测体系中的重要技术包括以下几个方面：

2.1 3S 集成技术

3S 是遥感(RS)、地理信息系统(GIS)、全球定位系统(GPS)这 3 项相互独立而在应用上又密切关联的高新技术的总称。遥感(RS)可以快速、廉价地得到地面物体的空间位置和属性数据。在林业中，遥感技术被用于土地利用和植被分类、森林面积和蓄积估计、土地沙化和侵蚀监测、森林病虫害和火灾监测等方面。地理信息系统(GIS)是以地理坐标为控制点，对空间数据和属性数据进行管理和分析的技术工具。它是森林调查监测、统计分析、规划设计和经营管理的工具。全球定位系统(GPS)能够利用地球通信卫星发射的信息进行空中或地面的导航与定位。在林业领域，全球定位系统可用于遥感地面控制、伐区边界量测、森林调查样点的导航和定位、森林灾害的评估等诸多方面[9]。正是因为 3S 技术具有上述功能和特性，将其应用在森林资源动态监测工作中，可以详细掌握森林资源现状及其消长规律，提高森林资源管理水平，为各级林业主管部门提供正确的决策依据。作为森林资源动态监测中最重要的技术之一，3S 技术是目前被探索和研究最多的领域。侯长谋[10]、焦一之[11]、袁占良[12]等学者和专家均对 3S 技术如何在林业资源管理及森林资源动态监测领域内开展应用进行过研究。此外，施拥军[13]等人还针对 3S 技术在实际应用中面临的困难提出，应积极发展我国自己的对地观测小卫星技术和机载遥感集成平台技术，为推动 3S 技术的发展提供保障。

2.2 计算机网络技术

计算机网络技术在森林资源监测中的应用是进行林业信息化管理的必要手段[14]。计算机网络是一种数据通信系统，在结构上是将在不同地理位置上的许多分立的计算机(系统)通过数据通信链路互联起来使其成为一个集合体，其目的是使网络中的计算机硬件、软件和数据资源可以共享，更加有效地提高计算机系统的使用效率。在森林资源监测领域中，应用计算机网络技术有 3 方面优点：①实现资源共享。利用计算机网络，可形成一个覆盖管理区域的自动监测系统，与上级自动监控中心联网，方便与其他林业信息系统进行林业数据的联网共享。②可节约大量资金，信息化、自动化的工作手段将解决大量的人力物力的浪费，从而节约资金。③增强信息系统的可扩展性。以计算机网络为信息发布载体，通过分布式数据库管理系统、WebGIS、虚拟现实技术等的应用以及专用信息发布平台和空间数据搜索引擎的开发应用，向社会提供高质量的信息服务。利用网络技术还可实现空间数据的在线处理和制图，如测量平差、专业制图等。

2.3 数据库技术

数据库技术是计算机科学技术中发展最快，应用最广泛的重要分支之一。从开始的层次数据库、网状数据库到关系数据库，以至目前的分布式数据库，数据库技术不断地取得突破性进展，已成为一门相对成熟的技术。由于林业行业数据存在数量巨大、分布范围广泛的特点，因此应用分布式数据库等最新数据库技术，能够很好地满足林业数据的管理需求。在森林资源监测方面，世界各国已利用数据库技术研建了各种各样的林业数据库管理系统。随着操纵和管理数据库的大型软件以及用户需求的发展变化，将使得新一代数据库系统的发展呈现百花齐放的局面，其特点是：一是渗入面向对象的方法和技术；二是与多学科技术的有机结合；三是面向应用领域[15]。

2.4 抽样技术与数学模型

数学方法是以数学为工具进行科学研究的方法，具有定量性、抽象性、预测性、精确性和适用性的特点。森林资源动态监测中很多问题的解决是离不开数学方法的，如数理统计与多元分析、概率分布与随机过程、线性代数、集合论、模糊数学等方法在森林资源动态监测中的数据提取、数据统计分析以及信息预测、信息分析评价和定量化等方面都有应用[14]。在动态监测体系中，除3S技术外，传统的抽样技术不可缺少。基本的抽样方法，如简单随机抽样、分层抽样、整群抽样、二阶与多阶抽样、系统抽样等，在林业资源调查及监测中都有所应用。应用抽样技术与3S技术相互协作进行调查和监测，可以充分展示现代科技赋予现代林业的高效率、低成本、高精度的特点。我国在林业抽样方面也进行了一些深入的研究：全志杰[16]等在森林资源清查中应用2期抽样方法进行了动态监测的研究，朱维凡[17]等进行了PR抽样技术的研究，汪丽[18]等进行了角规抽样方法的研究，此后肖银松[19]则结合遥感数据进行了二阶抽样和三阶抽样的研究。

2.5 通讯技术

在森林资源动态监测过程中，通讯是不可或缺的环节，它为动态监测实现实时信息获取与处理提供了技术保证[14]。在这里通讯技术特指无线移动通讯技术。大多数的动态监测系统应用，包括森林资源动态监测系统在内(又如灾害应急系统、智能交通系统等)，均要求通讯交换的空间数据是大数据量、实时的、双向的，即现场数据(图像、地理信息等空间数据)与指挥中心(服务器端)的决策要保持双向实时无线通讯。在森林资源动态监测体系之下，与以3S技术为基础进行森林资源面积与蓄积的监测不同的是，以通讯技术为基础的森林资源动态监测系统能够基于实时传输的数据进行更为精确的监控。近几年随着信息和网络技术的发展，通讯技术已取得了令人鼓舞的成就，特别是宽带网络技术、IP技术、2G及3G通信技术、数据微波技术以及卫星数据中继技术和调频副载波技术等的发展为森林资源动态监测系统的建立创造了必要的技术条件。通讯技术与其他技术的联合应用，往往为森林资源的监控工作，提供了新的方法和思路[20]。

2.6 其他方法与技术

除上述森林资源动态监测技术与方法外，刘安兴在《浙江省森林资源动态监测体系方案》一文中还提出，应提高经营档案技术。经营管理活动应该有规范的档案记载。这些档案材料对于小班数据更新十分重要。森林火灾、病虫害档案对于省级汇总也是必不可少的[7]。基于经营档案技术，季碧勇[21]提出以县级森林资源地理管理信息系统和动态数据库作为数据更新平台，以森林资源档案台账更新为主体，辅以补充调查、小班复位调查，同时结合生长模型及其他数学方法，对县级森林资源数据进行动态更新。

3　国内外森林资源监测体系现状

3.1　国外森林资源动态监测体系发展现状

德国和瑞士有上百年的森林经理调查和编制执行森林经营方案传统，到 20 世纪 80 年代，两国建立了以大面积抽样设置固定样地为特点的全国森林资源清查体系。德国国家级森林清查主要有 3 种，一是全国森林资源清查，二是全国森林损害调查，三是全国森林土壤调查，并正在研究将 3 种周期不同、内容不同的调查合起来。瑞士早在 1956 年就形成了全国森林资源清查概念(NFI)，1981 年瑞士联邦政府决定每 10 年进行一次全国森林资源清查，包括 4 项长期目标：①提供全瑞士森林总体情况和森林功能及长期变化的信息；②进行森林损害调，每年报告树冠生命力测定情况；③实施长期监测计划，研究各种森林生态系统的健康、分布和发展状况；④逐月主管机关报告有关虫和真菌危害情况，提供植物卫生服务。瑞典在 1923～1929 年建立了覆盖全国的 NFI。1953～1962 年开展第 3 次清查时，抽样设计引入了方阵法(Tractsystem)，每年进行一次全国调查。近 10 多年来，瑞典林业调查部门将注意力转向森林生态环境和生物多样性方面，有关这些方面的内容已步加入到清查系统中。

美国的森林资源清查与分析(Forest Inventory and Analysis，FIA)以州为单位逐开展资源清查，利用 GIS 系统等进行全国性汇总。从 20 世纪 90 年代开始，美国开展了森林健康监测(Forest Health Monitoring，FHM)，监测森林健康状况和森林发展的可持续性。FIA 与 FHM 开始时相互独立，1998 年提出了设计一个综合 FIA 与 FHM、全国采用统一的核心监测指标、统一标准、定义，每 5 年提交一次监测报告的年度资源测系统(Annu - alInventories)的要求，2003 年开始采用新的森林资源清查与监测体系。新的森林资源清查体系的计特点是采用全国统一的系统抽样的三阶抽样设计，每个州每年都调查 20% 的固定样地取代原来每年调查若干州的固定样地，综合了 FIA 和 FHM 的野外调查部分，每 1 年产出一次资源清查报告。

日本于 1953 年第一次进行了以全国为对象的森林抽样调查，此后以抽样调查为主的民有林森林调查规范和利用航空像片进行抽样调查的国有林森林调查规范逐步得到了完善。

3.2　我国森林资源动态监测体系发展现状

我国最早的森林资源调查的雏形，可追溯到若干世纪之前，竹农采用油漆标号隔年逐株连查的方法对新竹进行标记。新中国成立后，我国就开始了系统的森林调查工作。自 1975 年以来，我国已建立了以省为总体以固定样地为基础的国家森林资源连续清查的动态监测体系，该监测体系的成果在我国林业的发展与决策中起到了重要作用。然而，随着人们对森林多种效益的认识不断深入，保护森林资源意识的不断提高，该体系逐渐体现不足。1994 年，杨存健分析了当时的森林资源动态监测体系，提出了以下几点不足[22]：①以省为总体的国家森林资源连续清查，其成果难以反映地区及地区以下范围的森林资源动态变化情况。②监测体系难以反映森林资源动态变化的空间分布，也不能落实到山头地块。③监测体系缺乏重点性和针对性，对所有地区均采用同样的技术手段。④监测内容不够丰富，还应增加监测内容和指标。⑤该体系需要大量固定样地，增加了工作量，还会因为固定样地可能受特殊对待，引起系统监测成果偏估。针对我国森林资源监测体系发展中的不足，林业行业的学者和专家们应用包括 3S 技术在内的方法和技术手段，在这一领域进行了许多研究和探索。2003

年，王允寿在研究山东省森林资源动态监测体系框架时[5]，提出建立以3S技术为基础的县市省三级监测体系，并对应建立相应的管理体系和质量监督体系，以解决现行体系数据无法反映到地区及地区以下级别的问题。2005年，刘安兴在研究浙江省森林资源动态监测体系方案时，提出利用一类调查和二类调查及三类调查的现行体系[7]，从提高时间分辨率（从5年提高到1年）、空间分辨率（汇总三级数据，即得到地区及地区以下级别森林资源数据）和扩充监测内容三个方面改善现有体系。佟立君[23]讨论了黑龙江省国有林区森林资源动态监测管理系统利用3S技术在获取与处理森林资源数据方面开展的工作。2009年，李春干[24]以广西为研究区域，以高空间分辨率卫星遥感数据为源数据，辅以相关调查资料，在GIS支持下，采用空中抽样的方法，在遥感图像上布设样地，通过目视判读方法确定样地的土地类型、优势树种（组）等，据此计算了森林面积和构造土地类型转移矩阵。同时根据历史调查资料分析得到森林类型单位面积蓄积量，并以此来计算各类林木蓄积量，从而实现了研究区域森林面积、蓄积的动态监测。2011年，叶根华[25]等以松阳县2009年度森林动态监测为例，通过应用“3S”技术、数据库技术、数学模型等技术，实施了森林动态监测，为开展县域森林资源动态监测、体系建设提供了一定的参考。

4 森林资源动态监测技术发展趋势

当前森林资源监测技术发展主要特征，大体上表现在3个方面：即森林资源监测体系的综合化、森林资源监测周期的年度化和高新技术的大量应用。

森林资源监测体系的综合化[7]，表现为监测内容的日益丰富、跨部门的协同合作和信息共享。传统的森林资源监测重点主要在森林的蓄积、面积上。而目前监测内容已经扩展到森林生态系统的各个方面，如森林健康、森林生物量、生物多样性、野生动植物、湿地资源等。我国的森林资源连续清查一直注重于森林面积和蓄积数据，近年来随着对森林健康和环境情况的重视程度的提高，也增加了一些这方面的内容，如森林健康等级、湿地类型、荒漠化类型、森林群落结构、自然等。但从总体设计来看，以及从数据的处理、分析和利用看，重点依然在森林的面积和蓄积上。

森林资源监测周期的年度化[7]，表现为各国逐步将监测周期由多年缩短到1年。进入20世纪80～90年代以后，美国林业及会各界对森林多资源及生态环境的信息需求迅速增长，并要求提高数据的一致性，以便进行不同地区或同时间之间数据的比较。旧的美国FIA系统平均监测周期为10年，美国从20世纪90年代开始讨论年度监测的问题，1998年通过的法案在要求将FIA与FHM合并成新的FIA。同时，要求新的FIA将监测周期缩短为1年，即进行年度监测。其他如欧洲的森林健康监测、瑞典的森林资源监测也都是按年度进行的。我国浙江省研建的森林资源动态监测体系的框架技术方案显示，其体系建设的目标就是实施全省与县级森林资源年度公报制度。

现代化森林资源监测技术是包括3S集成技术、计算机网络技术、数据库技术等多种技术乃至多种学科的综合和集成[26]。随着3S一体化技术及网络技术的迅速发展，以其为技术手段的森林资源综合管理的可操作性越来越明显，展示了广阔的发展前景，将在森林资源监测方面带来巨大的变革和深远的影响。建立区域性森林资源地理信息系统，能够以高时空分辨率，多层次、动态描述森林资源的时空分布特征，描绘森林资源的动态变化规律，研究和探索森林资源在区域内的空间分布状况以及相应的时空演替规律，为科学合理地经营管理，实现森林资源的持续发展和分类经营提供准确的依据。

参考文献

[1]于政中. 森林经理学[M]. 北京: 中国林业出版社, 1993.
[2]寇文正, 周昌祥, 徐茂松. 森林资源动态监测体系及其建立技术[J]. 林业资源管理, 1992(03): 26~30.
[3]亢新刚. 森林资源经营管理[M]. 北京: 中国林业出版社, 2001.
[4]汪兆忠, 森林资源动态监测试验工作步骤[J]. 林业资源管理, 1984(04): 64.
[5]王允寿, 陈景和, 张金良. 关于山东省森林资源动态监测体系框架的探讨[J]. 山东林业科技, 2003(04): 44~45.
[6]黄力平, 张小平, 赵直. 新疆森林资源动态监测体系的构想[J]. 新疆师范大学学报(自然科学版), 2005(03): 136~140.
[7]刘安兴. 浙江省森林资源动态监测体系方案[J]. 浙江林学院学报, 2005(04): 449~453.
[8]王文生. 关于内蒙古大兴安岭林区森林资源实施动态监测方法的探讨[J]. 内蒙古林业调查设计, 2006(03): 23~24.
[9]王雪, 卫发兴, 崔志新. 3S技术在林业中的应用[J]. 世界林业研究, 2005(02): 44~47.
[10]侯长谋. 3S技术在广东省森林资源动态监测中的应用[J]. 中南林业调查规划, 2002(02): 44~45.
[11]焦一之. "3S"技术在森林资源调查中的应用[J]. 河北林果研究, 2007(04): 360~362.
[12]袁占良, 李强, 牛军庆. 3S技术在森林资源动态监测中的应用研究[J]. 森林工程, 2008(05): 29~31.
[13]施拥军, 王珂. 3S技术在林业中的应用[J]. 浙江林业科技, 2002(06): 46~50.
[14]徐萍, 徐天蜀. 森林资源动态监测技术综述[J]. 云南大学学报(自然科学版), 2007(S1): 251~254.
[15]康文智, 李媛, 崔建. 森林资源动态监测技术探讨[J]. 内蒙古林业调查设计, 2010(01): 65~66+83.
[16]全志杰. 淳化县森林资源动态遥感监测及演变趋势预估[J]. 林业资源管理, 1996(03): 17~21.
[17]朱维凡, 韦希勤. PR抽样在森林蓄积量调查中的应用[J]. 内蒙古林业调查设计, 1999(01): 26~27.
[18]汪丽, 崔彤. 角规点抽样在林分蓄积量调查中的应用[J]. 内蒙古林业调查设计, 1997(04): 130~132.
[19]肖银松. "3S"及抽样技术在森林资源动态监测中的应用[J]. 西南林学院学报, 2004(02): 60~64.
[20]张莉莉, 王军强, 陈磊. 基于WSN与GIS技术的森林火灾监测预警研究[J]. 农业技术与装备, 2010(06): 8~10.
[21]季碧勇. 基于固定样地的县级森林资源动态监测技术方法[J]. 林业资源管理, 2009(05): 50~53.
[22]杨存健. 浅析森林资源动态监测体系[J]. 云南林业调查规划, 1994(01): 29~31.
[23]佟立君. 黑龙江省国有林区森林资源动态监测管理系统的研究[J]. 中国林副特产, 2005(03): 74~75.
[24]李春干, 陈琦, 谭必增. 基于卫星遥感数据空中抽样的大尺度森林资源动态监测[J]. 林业资源管理, 2009(02): 106~110+127.
[25]叶根华, 王文武, 刘建宇. 县级森林资源动态监测方法研究与实践[J]. 华东森林经理, 2011(01): 27~31.
[26]刘晓辉, 唐树金. 森林资源动态监测在大兴安岭东部林区中的应用[J]. 内蒙古林业调查设计, 2008(02): 58~60.

森林景观分类方法研究进展及发展趋势

岳　刚

（北京林业大学林学院，北京，100083）

摘要： 森林景观分类是森林景观结构、功能和动态研究的基础，同时也是森林类型划分、林相图绘制、森林资源清查、森林景观规划等的依据。本文回顾了国内外森林景观分类方法的发展历程，指出其中存在的问题，并简要分析未来森林景观分类方法的发展方向。

关键词： 森林景观分类；研究进展；发展趋势

Abstract: Forest landscape classification is the basis of researches on forest landscape structure, function and dynamics, which is the basis for the division of forest types, forest mapping, forest inventory, forest landscape planning etc. This paper briefly review the development history of forest landscape classification methods, pointed out the problems of them and analyse the future development directions of forest landscape classification methods.

Key words: forest landscape classification; research progress; development trend

1 引　言

景观分类既是景观结构、过程和功能研究的基础，又是开展景观评价、规划、保护和管理的前提条件，是景观生态学理论与实践相结合的纽带，其实质是将具有显著异质性的部分确定为不同的景观类型，而将相对均质的部分确定为相同的景观类型[1]。景观的定义有多种表述，但大多是反映内陆地形、地貌或景色的(诸如草原、森林、山脉及湖泊等)，或是反映某一地理区域的综合特征[2]。而作为森林景观，可以将其理解为在一个区域内森林中，一种森林类型仅是景观要素之一，由于地理环境因素长期演变协调，或者局部地貌条件影响，一个区域内存在若干天然森林类型，并且呈彼此镶嵌现象，共存共荣，相对稳定，因此从理论上就有必要从生态系统生态学上升到景观生态学高度，将每一森林类型(或是其中的植被类型)视为景观要素，研究它们的空间分布格局，系统间生态关系及相互作用机制[3]。森林景观要素类型的划分是开展森林景观生态研究、分析景观格局结构、进行景观规划设计的基础[4]。遥感技术为森林景观研究提供了从局部具体林分的生态研究跨越到景观层计划和经营的桥梁[5]。将地面样地调查数据和遥感数据结合起来作为森林景观生态学研究中的基础数据，以及时获得大范围，多时相、多波段的地表状况信息，为不同时序上从局部到整体的景观综合分析创造了条件[6]。早期的森林景观分类研究主要是基于人工目视解译，解译的精度主要依赖于解译者的经验，且费工费时不能满足信息时效性的需要。随着航空、航天遥感技术的发展，各种资源环境卫星的相继升空，为开展高时效、多尺度景观分类研究提供了契机，计算机自动分类技术的发展也使得分类的效率和精度得到大幅度提高。当前，伴随着人工神经网络技术、专家系统等智能分类技术的发展，以及高空间分辨率、高光谱分辨率、高时间分辨率卫星的应用，为森林景观分类研究提供了更为广阔的空间。

2 国内外森林景观分类研究进展

随着景观生态学理论和应用研究的发展，遥感技术以及计算机技术的进步，森林景观分类的传统方法不断改进，而新的、智能的分类方法也不断涌现，景观分类研究取得了前所未有的进步。下面就国内外森林景观分类方法发展进程作简要介绍。

2.1 目视解译分类方法

遥感数据的波谱、极化、时间和空间特征反映了自然界中物体的相应特征，由遥感影像获得地学专题信息，传统的方法是通过目视解译。目视解译就是作业人员根据样本的影像特征(色调或色彩，即波谱特征)和空间特征(形状、大小、阴影、纹理、图形、位置和布局)，与多种非遥感信息资料相结合，用生物地学相关规律，进行由此及彼、由表及里、去伪存真的综合分析和逻辑推理的思维过程[7]，并以此识别图像上的目标，定性定量地提取目标的形态、构造功能、性质等信息。陈述彭先生曾肯定了目视解译方法，认为“目视解译不是遥感应用的初级阶段，或者是可有可无的，相反，它是遥感应用中无可替代的组成部分，它将与地学分析方法长期共存、相辅相成”[8]。目视解译分类方法的应用主要有两种形式，人工判读和人机交互式目视解译。

2.1.1 人工判读分类

人工判读分类通过航片、卫片或多种遥感图像资料的结合，进行人为判读之后，经手工编汇土地利用图或数字化处理，得到土地利用分类信息。这种形式从开始采用遥感手段进行土地利用调查，一直到现在，仍然被广泛使用着。比如俞纯绅、张妙玲等以1:10万TM卫星影像图为基本信息源，采用了目视解译与野外调查相结合的方法进行长江三角洲地区耕地变化的遥感调查[9]。

2.1.2 人机交互式目视解译

从20世纪70年代起，随着计算机技术和遥感图像处理技术的发展，人们就开始利用计算机进行卫星遥感图像的解译研究，所以人机交互式目视解译分类方法逐渐形成。人机交互式解译就是人机交互影像判读，以遥感数字影像为基本信息源，在相应软硬件工作环境下，利用计算机高速的数据处理和图像处理软件对图像提取和编辑处理，帮助解译人员进行遥感影像解译的一种方法[10]。一般步骤是首先利用数字图像处理软件对遥感数字图像进行几何纠正与位置配准，然后采用人机交互方式从遥感影像中获取有关地学信息。如陈宁强和戴锦芳运用CorelDRAW6软件对人机交互式土地资源遥感解译的条件、过程及主要特点做了探索性研究[11]；张松岭、杨邦杰等人提出了基于GIS的耕地遥感监测人机交互式图像解译系统[12]；刘常富以2006年QuickBird卫星影像为数据源，在ArcGIS的支持下进行目视解释和数字化，对沈阳市景观格局进行分析[13]；王原等以2003年QuickBird遥感影像和同时期的TM影像，采用人机交互解译的方法对马鞍山城市森林景观进行分类[14]。

但是目视解译存在一定的局限性：①目视解译方法要求解译人员具有各种丰富的知识，要求解译者在心理上和生理上对解译工作有一定的灵性和经验；②费时费力，工作效率较低；③主观因素作用大，容易产生误判；④无法与遥感和地理信息系统相结合。因此，遥感图像的自动解译就成为迫切的需求。

2.2 传统计算机自动分类的统计模式分类方法

随着遥感应用研究的深入和计算机技术的发展，利用计算机技术实现卫星数字图像地学专题信息的自动提取技术就应运而生。遥感影像的计算机自动分类是对地球表面及其环境在遥感影像上的信息进行属性识别和分类，把具有相同属性的地物划分为同一类，并进而达到识别图像信息所对应的实际地物，提取所需地物信息的目的。遥感影像分类是模式分类(Pattern Classification)在影像处理中的应用，它将影像数据从二维灰度空间转换到目标模式空间。模式分类一般分为统计分类和结构分类，统计分类着重于定量的统计方法，而结构分类则基于描述影像的结构信息、结构特征，利用形式语言中的规则进行分类。目前遥感分类中应用较多的是传统的统计模式识别方法(监督分类方法中的最大似然分类法，最小距离法等和非监督分类中的等距离混合法，循环集群法等)。

2.2.1 监督分类

地物的光谱特征通常是以地物在多光谱影像上的亮度来体现，不同的地物在同一波段上的亮度值不同，同时不同的地物在各个波段影像上呈现的亮度规律也不同，因此，可以通过亮度特征的提取，利用决策理论实现对特征空间的划分，达到区分不同地物的目的。监督分类方法一般首先根据地物的光谱特性和遥感影像上的光谱分布选取一定数量的训练样本，根据样本提取出每一待分类地物的统计特征参数，并计算每类地物分布的先验概率，然后根据这些求解出的统计特征参数和类别先验概率并使用一定的分类判别准则判定其所属类别[15]。

监督分类方法可以分为与分布无关方法和与分布有关的统计分类。与分布无关方法无需任何有关于观测目标先验概率分布的知识，是一种启发式的学习分类过程，又称无参数的分类。与分布无关的统计分类方法则基于一定的先验概率分布模型，这种分类方法假定数据的概率分布参数待定，一般概率分布模型多采用多变量 Gaussian 分布[16]。常用的与分布无关的分类方法有 K 近邻法(K – Nearest Neighbor)和决策树法(Decision Tree Classifier)。K 近邻法要求有较大的训练集以保证算法的收敛性。而当分类数较大时，决策树方法性能比较优越，且不论特征空间是否线性可分，决策树算法均能保证收敛。与分布有关的统计分类方法主要有贝叶斯分类器(Bayesian Classifier)、最大似然度分类。在目前应用的分类算法中用的较多的是最小距离法、平行六面体法和最大似然法等。最小距离法和平行六面体法所产生的分类结果往往有较多的错分和漏分情况，因此分类精度不高，而最大似然法有着严密的理论基础，对于呈正态分布的数据判别函数容易建立，分类精度较高。Olker Walter 介绍了一种建立在最大似然法基础上的基于对象的遥感分类方法[17]；Martin M E，Nevman S D 等用高光谱数据采用最大似然法把森林分为 11 类，其总体精度达到 75%[18]。在国内，朱建华等提出了一种适用于多光谱遥感图像分类的自适应最小距离算法，这一算法通过对样本集合的自适应精细划分来调整最小距离分类器的参数，他对 TM 遥感图分类的实验结果表明，该方法对 16 类地物进行监督分类，精度可达 92.9%[19]；郭泺结合林相图和地形图，用 ERDAS 软件对 TM 遥感影像进行监督分类，并进一步采用人机综合解译对监督分类结果纠正，将泰山景观划分为 12 个基本类型[20]；刘常富采用监督分类对 2001 年和 2006 年两期的 QuickBird 遥感影像进行沈阳城市森林景观类型划分及其景观动态研究[21]。

但是由于“同物异谱”现象的存在，计算机自动分类远远不能达到要求。监督分类可以有效开发数据内容，但需要分类类别的先验知识和大量的训练样本，实际应用中有时无法满足条件，得不到足够的校准信息，因此这种方法不容易应用。另外监督分类方法通常采用高斯分布模型描述样本的概率分布，对实际上并非高斯分布的样本进行分析时就会产生较高的误识率。

2.2.2 非监督分类

在遥感图像处理中非监督分类(unsupervised classification)是一种常用的方法，又称聚类分析或空间集群，是按照象元灰度值向量或波谱样式在特征空间聚集的情况划分类别，通过对各类的光谱响应曲线进行分析，与实际调查数据比较后确定最终地物类别[22~24]。

非监督分类方法主要有：①ISOMIX(等混合距离)分类法。根据地物光谱特性的不同，由计算机对方差大的"光谱集群"自动进行不断分裂，直至对地物获得合理分类为止，此法又称分裂法。②K均值聚类。通过迭代，逐次移动各类的中心，直至得到最好的聚类结果为止[25,26]。③ISODATA聚类(迭代自组织数据分析)算法的基本准则是距离度量，评价聚类结果的准则主要是类内的最大标准差和类间的最小距离，如果类内最大标准差超过给定的闭值，则对该类进行分裂处理；如果类间的最小距离小于给定的闭值，则对相应的两类进行合并处理。非监督分类是基于整个区域特征进行，不需要先验概率，无须事先确定输入样本的类别，简单易行，并具操作独立，但常常可能丢失特定的却是相关的细节信息，进而限制了分类的客观性。采用非监督分类可以更好地获得目标数据内在的分布规律，但分类结果不一定最佳。这些算法所产生的分类结果往往有较多的错分和漏分情况。④分层聚类方法(SSHC)。骆剑承[27]等提出基于尺度空间的SSHC，它是一种以热力学非线性动力机制为理论基础的新型聚类算法，是视觉松弛化过程的模拟。与传统基于统计方法的聚类算法相比较，SSHC具有样本空间可服从自由分布、通过规则可获取最优聚类中心点及类别、可在聚类过程中融合后验知识等优点。

2.3 目前常用的森林景观自动分类新技术

由于传统遥感影像计算机分类采用的统计方法只是对各波段灰度值的统计特征进行的，并且卫星遥感光谱数据的空间分辨率比较低，导致计算机分类面临很多模糊对象，分类结果精度不高，不能有效满足人们对遥感图像的要求，研究者开发了许多新的分类识别方法，使遥感图像分类识别朝着精确、快速的方向发展，并取得了较好的分类效果。总结近年发展起来的自动分类新技术，有以下几种主要的方法：植被指数分类法、人工神经网络分类法、专家系统分类法、基于知识的分类方法、决策树分类法、基于多时相、多源遥感数据的分类法、基于纹理的分类法、模糊模式分类等。下面对常用的几种森林景观自动分类新技术作简要介绍。

2.3.1 植被指数分类方法

植被指数是度量植被信息的一个重要参数，它是红光和红外波段的不同组合。植被指数已作为一种遥感手段广泛应用于土地利用覆盖探测、植被覆盖密度评价、作物识别和作物预报等方面，并在专题制图方面增强了分类能力。植被指数按发展阶段可分为三类：第一类植被指数是基于波段的线性组合(差或和)或原始波段的比值，由经验方法发展的，没有考虑大气影响、土壤亮度和土壤颜色，也没有考虑土壤、植被间的相互作用(如RVI等)。它们表现了严重的应用限制性，这是由于它们是针对特定的遥感器(LANDSATMSS)并为明确特定应用而设计的。第二类植被指数大都基于物理知识，将电磁波辐射、大气、植被覆盖和土壤背景的相互作用结合在一起考虑，并通过数学和物理及逻辑经验以及通过模拟将原植被指数不断改进而发展的(如 PVI，SAVI，MSAVI，TSAVI，ARVI，GEMI，AVI，NDVI 等)。它们普遍基于反射率值、遥感器定标和大气影响并形成理论方法，解决与植被指数相关的但仍未解决的一系列问题。第三类植被指数是针对高光谱遥感及热红外遥感而发展的植被指数(如 DVI，TS - VI，PRI 等)。这些植被指数是近几年来基于遥感技术的发展和应用的深入而产生的新的表现形式。尽管许多新的植被指数考虑了土壤、大气等多种因素并得到发展，但是应用最广的还是 NDVI，并经常用 NDVI 作参考来评价基于遥感影像和地面测量或模拟的新的植被指数，NDVI 在植被指数中仍占有重要的位置。近些年来，有很多学者通过计算植被指数对森林植被进行分类研究。

对于第一、二类植被指数，只需要使用多光谱数据的红色波段和近红外数据即可，但是在应用时有一定的使用条件。例如，NDVI 在农作物生长的初始季节，将过高估计植被覆盖的百分比；在农作物生长的结束季节，将产生估计低值；RVI 对大气影响敏感，而且当植被覆盖不够浓度时(小于 50%)，它的分辨能力也很弱，只有在高植被覆盖密度的情况下效果较好；对于第二类植被指数，它们在一定程度上消除了环境因子的影响，尤其是土壤背景对于植被光谱的干扰，但是在计算过程中需要借助野外光谱仪实测植被冠层反射率数据。第三种植被指数是在高光谱和热红外数据发展的基础上产生的，因此对于研究数据只是适用于高光谱数据和热红外数据。国内外有许多学者对植被指数的改进和应用进行了深入探究。比如 Running 等根据不同植被指数及通过卫星遥感监测到的植被结构特点，提出了简单的逻辑判识方法[28]；McDonald，verstraete 等采用 N0AA，TM 数据根据光谱植被指数 NDVI、PVI、SAVI 进行森林分类，精度接近 70%[29,30]；袁金国提出采用植被指数进行植被分类，用 PVI 区分针叶林和阔叶林，用 RVI 区分各针叶林树种[31]。

2.3.2 人工神经网络分类

人工神经网络(Artificial Neural Network，ANN)是由大量的处理单元(神经元)广泛互连而形成的网络。它是在现代神经科学研究成果的基础上提出的，反映了人脑功能的基本特征，是人脑的某种抽象、简化与模拟[32]。包括 BP 神经网络、Kohonen 神经网络、径向基神经网络、模糊神经网络、小波神经网络等各种神经网络方法。它企图模拟人脑神经元网络的信息反馈方式，进行数据分析[33]。结合遥感影像分类的目的和要求，遥感影像数据分析一般采用 BP 算法。利用 BP 网络对遥感影像的分类通过两个阶段实现，一是根据选取的样本数据，网络先进行学习；二是利用学习结果对整幅遥感影像进行分类，它虽然比一般统计方法要好，但是却存在学习速度慢，不易收敛，效率不高等缺点。采用动量法和学习率自适应调整的策略，可以提高学习效率并增加算法的可靠性。有研究验证在不能精确描述图像概率分布模型的情况下，神经网络方法分类性能优于最大似然度方法[34]，但神经网络方法计算复杂度大，尤其是其训练过程，因此它更适于观测数据缓慢变化的情况。Gail A. Carpenter 等人在最大似然法、线性混合模型、ARTMAP 神经网络三种方法的基础上提出了一种新的数据模型—ARTMAP 混合分类方法，并利用该方法制作了加利福尼亚州的玛县国家公园的森林植被分布图，通过结果的评价与分析得出结论，发现 ARTMAP 混合模型的分类方法精度较高，能很好地区分硬叶林和针叶林[35]；Foody G M，Lucas R M 等利用 ANN 方法对巴西 Mato Grosso 地区的热带森林类型进行了分类，结果表明这种方法划分结果与实际接近，优于其传统分类方法[36]；胡希军等应用神经网络进行遥感图像自动分类，获得了较高的分类精度[37]；李朝锋等人通过分析概率神经网络的基本结构及其训练算法，建立了卫星图像分类的概率神经网络模型，并通过实例对比分析了概率神经网络与BP网络分类模型的分类效果[38]；刘旭升，张晓丽使用Landsat7 ETM+遥感数据和森林资源分布图等地理辅助数据，应用BP神经网络方法对森林植被进行了分类，对针阔林的分类精度分别达到了80.47%和89.48%[39]。

2.3.3 专家系统分类方法

专家系统方法是人工智能的一个分支，它利用人工智能语言如C、LISP、PROLOG语言以及某一领域的专家分析方法或经验，对目标的多种属性进行分析、判断，确定其归属。在国外，Steven A. Sader，Douglas Ahl等人选择了两个研究区，利用四种分类方法对研究区内的湿地进行分类研究，研究发现，基于GIS专家规则的遥感分类方法精度最高[40]；而Skidmore等基于数字高程数据建立专家系统并对桉树类型进行分类[41]。近年来国内学者对专家系统也进行了深入研究，比如陈永富等介绍了一种以TM遥感图像光谱分类为基础，专家知识为依据，应用地理信息系统提取各种辅助信息的分类方法。以山西省限县为案例进行了研究。该方法以图斑作为基本分类单元，按照一定的专家系统推理机制，对光谱分类中精度低的地类作进一步判别，提高了分类精度[42]；王立海等对DEM、坡向等地理因子和土壤类型等环境因子与森林植被分布之间的内在规律进行了定量分析，并结合对遥感图像预分类的定性分析，形成分类知识库，建立了适用于针阔混交林的自动分类识别专家系统[43]。

2.3.4 基于知识的分类方法

基于知识的分类方法是模拟人的目视判读过程，它通常是把一个分类的问题分解成一个树状的层次结构。一旦层次结构建立，接着就要为每一类别建立知识规则。该方法以光谱数据为基础的统计模式识别方法给出的结果作为初始数据，使用辅助数据和知识库中的规则，进行不精确推理，最后确定出像元点所属的类别。国外学者Middelkoop[44]等、Bolstad[45]等、Kontoes[46]等对充分利用影像信息和辅助数据进行分类，特别是使用基于知识的方法进行分类做了大量研究。

2.3.5 决策树分类法

决策树算法一般分为3类：单变量决策树(Univariate Decision Tree，UDT)、多变量决策树(Multivariate Decision Tree，MDT)和复合决策树(Hybrid Decision Tree，HDT)。决策树算法用于遥感数据分类的优势在于对数字图像数据特征空间的分割上，其分类结构简单明了，尤其是UDT结构，十分容易解释[47]。Aikison，Friedl等引入人工神经网络和决策树算法使分类精度得以进一步提高[48]。陈艳华，张万昌利用一种决策树生成算法(C 4.5算法)自动提取知识，基于知识建立决策树用于山区影像分类，并结合研究区土地利用类型与DEM空间统计关系的先验知识，在GIS空间分析的基础上进行影像分类的后处理，该方法极大地改善了山区地表覆被分类的精度，得到了试验区较为可靠的遥感分类结果[49]。陈君颖以IKONOS遥感影像和Quickbird遥感影像，采用决策树分类算法和高分辨率光谱特性，提出结合纹理信息的高分辨率遥感植被分类方法，精度达到91.89%和91.94%[50]。

2.3.6 基于多时相、多源遥感数据的分类方法

基于多时相、多源遥感数据的分类方法大致可以分为三类：第一类是利用不同时相的同一平台的遥感数据上各种植被信息差异或者随时间的变化规律不同而进行分类；第二类是通过多光谱数据和高空间分辨率数据的融合对植被分类，已达到提高分类精度的目的，这种方

法中融合的多光谱数据和高空间分辨率可以是同一平台的也可以是不同平台的；第三类是借助遥感数据和非遥感数据(例如专题数据、地形数据等)的复合或者利用非遥感数据辅助遥感数据的方法对植被进行分类。这三种方法通常体现在遥感数据分类的前期数据准备阶段，具体分类过程中可以采用不同的分类原理和方法，而第三类方法有的时候也体现在数据分类的过程中，如在海拔高度复杂的山区，利用影响植被分布的地理数据(海拔、土壤类型、降水量等)与植被类型之间的对应关系辅助分类。

以上这些方法没有自己统一的理论基础，只是某一种具体分类思想的基础，渗透在其他分类方法之中，但是弥补了单一数据类型的不足，增加了地物的信息量，也提高了数据分类的精度，是目前植被遥感分类的常用方法。Eric C. Brown de Colstoun 等将多时相的 ETM + 影像用于国家公园的植被制图，地物的总体分类精度为 82%，kappa 系数为 0.8[51]；Franklin[52]、Peddle[53]先用线性分类器对光谱、纹理、DEM 进行分类，后来提出多种数据源的证据推理分类方法，结果明显优于用传统的统计模式识别方法；Srinivasan 使用多源遥感数据，按照各类别的波谱模型对多源遥感数据进行了分类[54]；Townsend 等提出了一种等级分类方法，应用多时段多光谱卫星数据将美国卡罗莱纳州东北部的 Roanoke 河漫滩森林湿地群落分为 21 个森林群落类型和 7 个其他生态重要群落，用模糊集合理论评价精度达到 96.6%[55]；Mayaux，Gianfraneo 等综合利用 AvHRR、ATSR、ERS-1 以及 SAR 四种卫星数据，结合地面辅助资料对中非刚果地区进行森林植被制图，精度达到 74.6%[56]；黄建文，陈永富等人通过对海南霸王岭林区三个时期(1986、1991 和 1996 年)的 TM 影像的监督分类研究，得到了该地区三个时期森林面积统计数据，为森林植被的变化分析提供了依据[57]。

2.3.7 基于纹理的分类方法

通常遥感影像分类多数都是基于光谱特征的，随着遥感影像空间分辨率的提高，会使纯像元的数目增加，混合的数目减少，从而提高分类的精度，但从另一方面来看，会使影像分类的类别增加，不同种类之间的光谱差异增大，在一定程度上增大了遥感分类的难度，使分类的精度降低。因此，针对有些问题仅仅依靠光谱信息分类是很难达到要求的。纹理是遥感影像重要的特征之一，纹理信息的分析在遥感分类识别中呈现了日益重要的作用，尤其在高分辨率的遥感数据中应用越来越多。

目前常用的纹理分析方法有灰度共生矩阵、灰度游程长度法、自相关模型、Markov 随机场模型、分形模型以及小波变换法等。姜青香和刘慧平等(2003)以北京市丰台区为试验区，将灰度共生矩阵的纹理分析方法应用于图像分类中，试验结果表明：光谱与纹理特征结合得到的分类精度明显高于单纯光谱分类精度以及单纯纹理特征分类精度[58]；颜梅春以南京市钟山景区为例，利用 IKONOS 影像数据的纹理信息进行植被分类，并将结果与用光谱信息、植被指数信息的分类结果比较，发现信息分类的精度最高，可作为最佳方法用于植被分类[59]。

2.3.8 模糊模式分类

由于现实世界中众多的自然或半自然现象很难明确划分种类，反映在遥感影像上，也存在一些混合像素问题，并有大量的“同谱异物”或者“同物异谱”现象发生，使得像元的类别难以明确确定。因此，针对不确定性的数学方法成为遥感影像分析人员所瞩目的方法。模糊模式分类是依据隶属原则进行判别。这种方法的关键是确定适当的隶属度函数。在实际的模式分类问题中，要分类的对象往往不是论域中的某个确定元素，而是论域中的模糊子集，此时研究的不是某元素对集合的隶属程度，而是两个模糊子集之间的贴近程度。D. Wu，Linders. J利用SAR数据分别采用模糊聚类、逐步回归和主成分分析法进行特征提取和森林分类，结论是模糊聚类法具有较高精度，达到71.11%[60]。

3 森林景观分类研究发展趋势

目前内外关于森林景观分类方法的研究已经取得了很大发展，而且越来越向多源遥感数据的融合、多种方法的复合、多种知识的综合等方面发展，森林类型分类的精度也在不断提高。通过深入分析国内外森林景观分类方法的历史和现状，未来森林景观分类方法的研究应该注意以下几方面。

3.1 多时相、多源信息融合发展

单时相、单源遥感分类越来越不适应森林景观分类的研究，特别在面对复杂生境中对植被进行分类时，其精度远远达不到人们的要求。因此多时相、多源信息融合能充分利用多源遥感数据的光谱信息、纹理信息、角度信息、时相信息和非遥感辅助信息的多层次融合，可以很好地提高分类的精度。

3.2 多方法互补分类

使用单一分类方法进行植被分类，往往存在许多缺陷，不能对所有类别进行有效识别，而多方法互补分类通过不同分类方法的有效组合，可实现优势互补，显著提高分类的数目和精度。

3.3 多图像特征遥感智能解译

过去都是基于单一图像特征信息进行植被分类，常常会出现误判或漏判的情况，所以基于多图像特征的遥感智能解译将是实现遥感智能解译的关键。它主要集中在对遥感影像中的信息进行分类、抽取遥感图像多种特征，建立遥感图解的模型，对影像中的专题信息进行数学描述，使计算机能够模拟人对遥感图像特征包括图像色调、颜色、形状、大小、纹理、图形、阴影、位置和相关布局进行理解。

3.4 发展高光谱技术

高光谱技术的出现和发展，为解决森林植被分类的一些特殊问题提供了可能，如树种区分等，因此对于提高森林植被分类精度，开展高光谱技术应用和智能化分类软件研制也是一个途径。但是由于高光谱遥感数据费用昂贵等原因，在应用方面还有很长的路需要我们不断地探索，这些是值得我们深思的问题。

3.5 应用数据挖掘和知识发现技术

数据挖掘(Data Mining，DM)是从大量的、不完全的、有噪声的、模糊的、随机的数据中提取隐含在其中的、人们事先不知道的但又是潜在有用的信息和知识的过程。知识发现(Knowledge Discovery in Data，KDD)是从大量数据中提取出可信的、新颖、有用的并能被人理解的模式的高级处理过程。DM和KDD技术为遥感图像分类的知识获取开辟了一条新途径，它在遥感和GIS领域的主要应用是GIS智能化分析和知识驱动的遥感图像解译。采用这种技术可以发现GIS植被空间数据库中隐含的关于多数据层空间模式及其相互联系的有关知识，从数据中提炼出有用的信息，经过归纳转变成知识，知识比数据更概括、精练、可靠和容易理解。因此，利用GIS数据中的知识比直接利用GIS数据本身可能对提高遥感图像分类的精度和可靠性更有效。数据挖掘中的归纳学习与传统图像分类方法的结合方式，是值得进

一步研究的问题[61]。

3.6 发展智能化森林景观分类方法

应用多源遥感影像作为主要数据源，以人工神经网络(ANN)为核心，以影响分类的地理信息和地学知识作为辅助数据进行分类。地学知识的获取可以从专家咨询和数据库的知识发现技术两个途径获取，结构化地理信息从GIS空间数据库中获得并以栅格格式与遥感影像进行严格配准。将多源植被遥感数据融合于神经元网络中，把专家知识和来自于GIS空间数据库的启发性知识融合于分类中，模拟专家视觉活动和逻辑判断过程，实现智能化的森林植被遥感分类和信息提取。智能化分类可以为解决森林植被分类中"同物异谱"和"同谱异物"问题提供新的有效途径，同时有利于突出小区域特征，解决混合像元的识别问题。

4 小 结

在森林植被分类的研究历程中，除了目视解译、传统的监督分类和非监督分类方法，还有植被指数法、模糊模式分类、基于分形的纹理方法、人工神经网络分类、专家系统分类方、决策树分类法等方法不断涌现。近几十年来，许多前人提出了各种基于图像的分类算法与理论，但是遥感图像分类判别的准确度并不理想。为了进一步提高遥感图像分类的准确率，国内外许多研究人员将多种地理数据、专家知识加入到计算机遥感图像解译的过程中来[62]。遥感影像分类和识别的发展方向始终是向着判别结果无限近似于目视判读的方向发展，大量的新技术新方法的不断发现和应用，将使从万米以外的高空所获取的数据经过加工处理，向人们展示无限接近于其自然视力极限范围内的森林景观面貌。

参考文献

[1]梁发超，刘黎明．景观分类的研究进展与发展趋势[J]. 应用生态学报，2011，(06)：1632~1638.

[2]邬建国．景观生态学——格局、过程、尺度与等级[M]. 北京：高等教育出版社，2007

[3]陈敬忠．东北天然林区森林景观分类及规划的研究 [D]. 北京林业大学，2004

[4]陆元昌，陈敬忠，洪玲霞，雷相东．遥感影像分类技术在森林景观分类评价中的应用研究[J]. 林业科学研究，2005，(01)：31~35.

[5] Quattrochi D A , Pelletier R E. The Analysis and Interpretation of Landscape Heterogeneity[M] . *New York* : *Springer Verlag* , 1991 : 52~76

[6] 李书娟，曾辉．遥感技术在景观生态学研究中的应用[J] . 遥感学报，2002 , 6 (3) : 233~239.

[7]濮静娟．遥感图像目视解译原理与方法[M]. 北京：科学技术出版社，1992.

[8]陈述彭．遥感地学分析的时空维数[J]. 遥感学报，1997，1(3)：161~171.

[9]张银辉，赵庚星．土地利用/土地覆盖遥感分类方法的研究综述[J]，2002，23(3)，21~25.

[10]李建利．人机交互式多波段数字图像解译技术方法研究[J]. 测绘标准，1999 , 15 (2) : 13~15.

[11]陈宁强，戴锦芳．人机交互式土地资源遥感解译方法研究[J]，遥感技术与应用，1998，13(2)：15~20.

[12]张松岭，杨邦杰，王飞，等．基于GIS的耕地遥感监测人机交互式图像解译系统[J]，农业工程学报，1999，15(2)：185~188.

[13]刘常富，吕东梅，李小马．基于QuickBird卫星影像的沈阳城市森林景观格局[J]. 东北林业大学学报，2009，(07)：52~54.

[14]王原，吴泽民，张浩，等．基于RS和GIS的马鞍山市分区城市森林景观格局综合评价[J]. 北京林业大学学报，2008，(04)：46~52.

[15]游代安，蒋定华，余旭初．2001. GIS 辅助下的 Bayes 法遥感影像分类[J]. 测绘学院学报，18(2)：113 ~ 117.

[16]李四海．提高遥感数据分类应用性的有效途径．国土资源遥感[J]，1995，4：1 ~ 13.

[17] Volker W. Object – based classification of remote sensing datafor change detection [J] . *ISPRS Journal of Photogrammetry&Remote Sensing*，2004(58)：225 ~ 238.

[18]Martin，M E，Nevman S D. Determining Forest Species Composition Using High Spectral Resolution Remote Sensing Data[J]. *Remote Sensing of Environment*，1998，65(3)：249 ~ 254.

[19]朱建华，刘政凯，俞能海．一种多光谱遥感图像的自适应最小距离分类方法[J]. 中国图象图形学报，2000，5(1)：21 ~ 24

[20]郭泺，夏北成，余世孝．森林景观格局研究中的尺度效应[J]. 应用与环境生物学报，2006，(03)：304 ~ 307.

[21]刘常富，孙冉，李小马，等．基于 RS 与 GIS 的沈阳城市森林景观格局动态变化[J]. 东北林业大学学报，2009，(04)：13 ~ 15.

[22]刘文敬．内蒙古草地沙化遥感监测图像自动分类方法研究[M]. 北京：北京林业大学，2005，5.

[23]赛晓勇，闫永平，徐德忠，等．遥感图像非监督分类在退田还湖区钉螺孳生地监测的初步应用[J]. 中华流行病学杂志，2005，26(2)：85 ~ 91.

[24]张治英，徐德忠，周晓农，等．遥感图像非监督分类分析江宁县江滩钉螺孳生地植被特征[J]. 中华流行病学杂志，2003，24(4)：261 ~ 265.

[25]吴文．长三角遥感水质分类技术研究[D]. 江苏省南京市：南京理工大学，2006，6.

[26]耿修瑞．高光谱遥感图像目标探测与分类技术研究[J]. 北京：中国科学院研究生院，2005，1.

[27]骆剑承，梁怡，周成虎．基于尺度空间的分层聚类方法及其在遥感影像分类中的应用[J]. 测绘学报，1999，28(4)：319 ~ 324.

[28] Steven W，Tomas R A. Remote sensing based vegetation classification logic for global land cover analysis[J]. *Remote sensing of Environment*，1995，51(1)：39 ~ 48.

[29]McDonald A J，Gemmell F M and Lewis P E. Investigation of the utility of spectral vegetation indices for determining information on coniferous forests[J]. *Remote Sensing of Environment.* 1998，66(2)：250 ~ 272.

[30]Verstraete M and Pinty B. Designing optimal spectral indexes for remote sensing applications [J] . *Remote Sens.* 1996：1254 ~ 1265.

[31]袁金国．森林植被遥感分类研究[J]. 河北师范大学学报．1999，23(2)：274 ~ 277.

[32]徐建华．现代地理学中的数学方法[M]. 北京：高等教育出版社，2006.

[33]罗丹．基于 RS 和 GIS 的北京山区森林植被空间结构分析和预测[D]. 北京：北京林业大学，2007，6.

[34]王耀南．星遥感图像的神经网络自动识别分类[J]. 湖南大学学报，1998，25(4)：61 ~ 66.

[35]Gail A，Gopal S，Macomber S，Curtis E. A Neural Network Method for Mixture Estimation for Vegetation Mapping[J]. *Remote Sensing of Environment.* 1999，70：138 ~ 152.

[36]Foody G M，Lucas R M，Curran P J，Honzak M. Mapping tropical forest fractional cover from coarse spatial resolution remote sensing imagery. *Plant Ecology.* 1997：143 ~ 153.

[37]胡希军，瞿有甜．神经网络在遥感图像自动分类中的应用研究[J]. 浙江师范大学学报(自然科学版，1996. 19(4)：82 ~ 85.

[38]李朝锋，杨茂龙，许磊，等．概率神经网络与 BP 网络模型在遥感图像分类中的对比研究[J]. 国土资源遥感，2004(4)：11 ~ 18.

[39]刘旭升，张晓丽．基于 BP 神经网络的森林植被遥感分类研究[J]. 林业资源管理，2005(1)：51 ~ 54.

[40]Steven A. Accuracy of Landsat – TM and GIS Rule – Based Methods for Forest Wetland Classification in Maine [J]. *REMOTE SENS. ENVIRON*，1995(53)：133 ~ 144.

[41]Skidmore A K. An expert system classifies Eucalyptus forest types using Thematic Mapper data and a digital ter-

rain model. *Photogramm Eng Remote Sens* , 1989, 55 : 1449 ~ 1469.

[42]陈永富，王振琴，张玉贵，等．专家系统在 TM 遥感图像分类中的应用研究[J]．林业科学研究，1995，4：344 ~ 347.

[43]王立海，赵正勇，杨旗．利用 GIS 对吉林针阔混交林 TM 遥感图像分类方法的初探[J]．应用生态学报，2006，(04)：4577 ~ 4582.

[44]Middelkoop H, Lucas L F. Implementation of Temprol Relationships in Knowledge Based Classification of Satellite Images[J]. *Photogrametric Engineering&Remote Sensing*, 1991, 57(7): 937 ~ 945.

[45]Bolstad V and Lillesand T M. Rule – based Classification Models[J]. *Flexible Engineering&Remote Sensing*, 1992, 58(7): 965 ~ 971.

[46]Kontoes C, Wilkinson G, Burrill A, Goffredo S and Megier J. An Experimental System for the Integration of GIS Data in Knowledge – based Analysis for Remote Sensing of Agriculture[J]. *International Journal of Geographic Information System*, 1993, 7(3): 247 ~ 262.

[47]吴非权，马海州，沙占江，等．基于决策树与监督、非监督分类方法相结合模型的遥感应用研究[J]．盐湖研究，2005，13(4)：9 ~ 13.

[48]Atkinson R M and Tatnal L. Neural networks in remote sensing, [J]*Remote sensing*, 1997, 18(4): 699 ~ 709.

[49]陈艳华，张万昌．地理信息系统支持下的山区遥感影像决策树分类[J]．国土资源遥感，2006(1)：69 ~ 73.

[50]陈君颖，田庆久．高分辨率遥感植被分类研究[J]．遥感学报，2007，(02)：221 ~ 227

[51]Eric C, Michael H, Thompson C, Commisso K, Timothy G. National Park vegetation mapping using multi – temporal Landsat7 data and a decision tree classifier[J]. *Remote Sensing of Environment*, 2003(85): 316 ~ 327.

[52]Franklin S E, Peddle D R. Classification of SPOT HRV Imagery and Texture Features[J]. *International Journal of Remote Sensing*, 1990, 11(3): 551 ~ 556.

[53]Peddle D R. An Empirical Comparison of Evidential Reasoning, Linear Discriminate Analysis, and Maximum Likelihood Algorithms for Alpine Land Cover Classification[J]. *Canadian Journal of Remote Sensing*, 1993, 19 (1): 13 ~ 44.

[54]Srinivasan A. Knowledge – based Techniques for Multi – source Classification[J]. *International Journal of Remote Sensing*, 1990, 11(3): 505 ~ 522.

[55]Townsend P A, Walsh S J. Remote sensing of forested wetlands: application of multitemporal and multispectral satellite imagery to determine Plant community composition and structure in southeastern USA[J]. *Plant Ecology*, 2001, 157: 129 ~ 149.

[56]Philippe M, Gianfranco G. Central African Forest Cover Revisited[J]. *Remote Sensing Of Environment*. 2000, 71(2): 183 ~ 196

[57]黄建文，陈永富．山区林地多季相 TM 影像综合分类研究[J]．福建林学院学报，2004，24(2)：136 ~ 139.

[58]姜青香，刘慧平．纹理分析方法在 TM 图像信息提取中的应用[J]．遥感信息应用技术．2003 (4)：24 ~ 27.

[59]颜梅春．高分辨率影像的植被分类方法对比研究[J]．遥感学报，2007，(02)：235 ~ 240.

[60]Wu D and Linders J. Comparison of three methods to select feature for discriminating Forest cover types using SAR imagery[J]. *Remote Sens*. 2000, 21(10): 2089 ~ 2099.

[61]刘涛．基于人工神经网络的森林植被遥感分类研究[D]．河北农业大学，2009

[62]程昌秀，严泰来，朱德海，等．GIS 与 RS 集成的高分辨率遥感影像分类技术在地类识别中的应用[J]．中国农业大学学报，2001，6(3)：50 ~ 54.

遥感影像在林业二类调查中应用的几点建议

栾忠平
（吉林省林业勘察设计研究院）

摘要：本文根据目前的遥感影像具有高分辨率，多光谱等特征，对二类调查工作提出一些建议。
关键词：二类调查；遥感影像

二类调查是以国有林业局（场）、自然保护区、森林公园等森林经营单位或县级行政区域为调查单位，以满足森林经营方案、总体设计、林业区划与规划设计需要而进行的森林资源调查。其主要任务是查清森林和林木资源的种类、数量和分布，客观反映调查区域自然、社会经济条件，综合分析与评价森林资源与经营管理现状，提出对森林资源培育、保护与利用意见。二类调查成果是建立或更新森林资源档案，制定森林采伐限额，进行林业工程规划设计和森林资源管理的基础，也是制定区域国民经济发展规划和林业发展规划，实行森林生态效益补偿和森林资源资产化管理，指导和规范森林科学经营的重要依据。

二类调查工作艰苦，时间紧，任务重，技术质量要求高。特别是森林经营区划是否标准，卫星影像图的判读正确与否关系到整个二类调查工作能否保质保量按期完成。只有正确掌握遥感影像图的判读技术并按《森林资源规划设计调查技术操作细则》的区划条件要求认真区划，才能顺利完成二类调查工作。为了提高森林经营区划的精度和速度，在开展二类调查工作时必须认真分析和掌握遥感影像图的图像特征及成像特征。然而，现在我们所能够获得的遥感影像，均是具有较高分辨率，而且具有多波段影像信息，可以大大提高我们进行野外调绘的效率。

一、二类调查的现状

目前吉林省森林资源规划设计调查采用 3S + PDA 相结合的方式进行野外调绘工作，即将遥感（RS）影像、数字高程模型（DEM）、移动 GIS、GPS 集成到掌上电脑中。利用 RS 影像和 DEM 进行野外小班界线、林分、储量等信息的核实、判读，并在移动 GIS 中进行数据的录入及小班界线的编辑与修改；GPS 可以实时的将工作人员的位置信息显示在 RS 影像和移动 GIS 中。大大提高了工作人员的工作效率，减小了劳动强度，又不会因为地形图的误判而走错道路。但是，目前在林业调查中所应用的遥感影像，只是进行了较为简单的辐射校正和几何校正，而没有更进一步的对遥感影像进行处理，如图像增强，空间滤波，卷积等。

二、遥感影像的优点

（一）记录地面真实景观

遥感影像能够完整的记录所覆盖区域内各要素的反射光谱信息，并生成可见影像，其影像特征包括地物的形状，大小，色调，阴影，纹理，质感和位置布局等多方面的特征及规律。

(二)遥感影像的高分辨率特征

目前用于商业用途的遥感卫星数据已经达到了较高的空间分辨率。如 SPOT5 遥感卫星影像的空间分辨率达 2.5m，快鸟(QUICK BIRD)遥感卫星空间分辨率为 0.61m，WORLD VIEW 遥感卫星的空间分辨率为 0.5m。同时也具有较高的时间分辨率，现在在轨运行的卫星一般的回访周期为 7～10d，我国的风云气象卫星平均两小时左右就可获得一张卫星云图。

(三)遥感影像的多光谱特征

目前的遥感卫星多具有多个多光谱波段和一个全色波段。多光谱波段可以记录我们肉眼所不能识别的地物光谱信息，利用多光谱信息我们可以将具有特殊光谱特征的地物很精确有划分出来。不同波段的影像叠加可以提高我们对地物的分辨能力，将多光谱影像与全色波段影像进行融合，获得的影像即具有高分辨率又具有多光谱特征，对地物信息的提取有很大的帮助。

三、在二类调查中应用遥感影像数据的建议

目前在林业二类调查中应用的遥感影像只是进行了相对比较简单的辐射较正和几何校正，多数影像都没有进行正射校正和影像分类。这样在实际调绘的工作过程中就会给调绘工作带来一定的困难，降低调绘的精度。

因此，针对遥感影像应用提两点建议：

(一)对遥感影像进行正射校正处理

遥感影像能够完整的记录所覆盖区域内各要素的反射光谱信息，并生成可见影像，有利于我们方便的获取宏观区域的地物信息。然而，由于地形起伏和遥感设备成像原理的不同，我们所获得的影像存在一定程度的地理位置偏移的现象。采用正射校正的方法对遥感影像进行校正可以很大程度地纠正这种偏移。可以提高调绘工作的准确度，减轻工作强度。因为在各个林业调绘单位都有所调绘地区的 DEM，所以对所调查地区的遥感影像是可行的。

(二)对遥感影像进行地物分类处理

传统方式的野外调绘工作都是依照遥感影像上的一些颜色，形状，大小，色调，阴影，纹理等特征对物进行识别，要求工作人员有熟练的经验才能够提高分类的精确度，花费的时间也较长；另外，由于遥感影像中存在“同物异谱和异物同谱”现象，对工作人员划分小班也是十分不利的，很容易落掉重要的地物信息。

目前我们获得的遥感影像都具有高分辨率，多光谱特征。如果只对影像进行辐射校正和几何校正，很显然不能将手中的遥感影像充分的利用。利用遥感影像处理软件对影像进行图像增强，不同波段叠加，影像融合，监督分类和非监督分类等处理。然后，与原有的数字林相图相对比，对小班进行内业的划分。对地物信息可以容易确认部分直接勾绘出小班边界线，对不能确定的区域进行标注。进行野外实地调查时，针对已经确定的区域进行再次实地确认后便可直接进行其他工作的测量，对不能确定的区域进行实地划分。这样可以大大减轻外业工作的工作量，而且能够提高外业工作的准确程度。

综上所述，如果我们能够充分地利用遥感影像的高分辨率，多光谱的特征来对影像进行处理分析，可以很大程度地提高二类调查的野外工作部分的效率与精度。

这类遥感影像仅仅依靠目视判读是无法达到预期的效果的。

参考文献

[1]胡增林.Spot5 遥感影像照片在森林资源二类调查上的应用[J].环境科学与管理，2009，2：42～43.

[2]全红瑞，侯瑞霞，等.森林资源二类调查中 3S 技术的应用[J].中国林业产业，2006，4 42～44.

[3]姚乃有.卫片在森林二类调查中应用的一些体会[J].广西林业，2009，2 17～18.

[4]罗刚，崔岩.正射影像图在森林资源二类调查中的应用[J].内蒙古林业调查设计，2000，2 22～24.

[5]姚荣江，何丙辉."3S"技术在森林资源二类调查中的应用前景[J].林业调查规划，2004，3 22～26.

[6]李玉江，杨东，周文成.森林分类经营和二类调查中存在的问题与建议[J].林业勘查设计，2009，3：27～28.

[7]朱玉琴.卫星影像图在二类调查中的应用浅析[J].林业科技情报，2008，3 ：24～25.

[8]张春峰，管钢诗.对二类调查中小班区划技术要求的探讨[J].林业勘查设计，2009，3：19～20.

[9]侯瑞霞，全红瑞，于凌霄."3S"技术在森林资源二类调查中的应用[J].林业调查规划，2006(3)：11～13.

澳大利亚森林可持续森林经营现状及启示①

邓 广 张 旭 陈 艳

（中国林业科学研究院资源信息研究所，北京颐和园后东小府1号

中国林科院33号信箱，100091）

摘要：本文依据《2008年澳大利亚国家森林报告》描述澳大利亚森林可持续森林经营取得的成果以及这些功能实现的情况。澳大利亚森林可持续森林经营已经是一个非常完整先进的体系，而且目的、作用、实践与效果具体、可落实、可评估，有机地整合在一起。本文在此基础上，结合中国的实际情况，对中国当前森林多功能经营和可持续森林经营提出了一些启示性的建议。

1 多功能经营评估的框架

澳大利亚占世界大约4%的森林面积，是世界第六大森林大国，森林的自然保护区面积占世界第四。澳大利亚林业工作者认为，森林是提供广泛而动态环境和社会生态效益和服务的复杂生态系统。在澳大利亚林业的语境下，多功能经营与可持续森林经营的意义是一样的。可持续森林经营的基本目标就是永恒地维持广泛的森林价值，但是评估达到目标的进展是困难的。可持续森林经营标准和指标用来简化评估的任务。澳大利亚可持续森林经营标准有七项，分别如下：

（1）保护生物多样性；

（2）维持森林生态系统的生产能力；

（3）维持生态系统的健康和活力；

（4）保护和维持土壤和水资源；

（5）维持森林对全球碳循环的贡献；

（6）维持并增强满足社会长期多元社会经济利益；

（7）森林保护和可持续经营的法律、机制和经济框架。（MIG）

这些标准与蒙特利尔进程工作组1994发布的《国际温带与北方森林保护和可持续经营标准与指标研究进程》，即《蒙特利尔进程》是一致的。蒙特利尔进程工作组包括12个国家，它们是阿根廷、澳大利亚、加拿大、智利、中国、日本、韩国、墨西哥、新西兰、俄罗斯、美国和乌拉圭，上述成员国的领土遍及全球七大洲中的五个洲，合在一起涵盖了世界温带和北方森林面积的大约90%，同时包括一些热带森林地带，共占世界森林总面积的60%。成员国通过负责制订政策的工作组以及技术顾问委员会，共同推动各自国家制订和实施国际认同的温带和北方森林（除欧洲以外）保护和可持续经营的标准和指标。（MIG）

---

① 本文得到中央级公益性科研院所基本科研业务费专项资金项目IFRIT200905和国家科技支撑计划课题2006BAK01A27资助。

澳大利亚真正把这些标准应用到本国独特的森林经营和森林评估活动当中，取得了很好的效果。1992 年，澳大利亚联邦政府、州和地区制定了“国家林业政策声明”，确定了林业发展的十大目标(吴伟光)，同时准备每五年发布一次《澳大利亚国家森林报告》。《2008 年澳大利亚国家森林报告》是第 3 个报告，其目的是让社会公众和世界了解澳大利亚森林的现状及其变化的趋势。在这个报告中使用了上述 7 项森林保护和可持续经营标准及其 44 个指标来描述和评估澳大利亚国家层面上森林可持续发展的情况。在这个报告发布之前，聘请了大量的代表各种利益团体的澳大利亚林业专家、管理者来评估报告涉及的标准和数据，其成果是《2008 年澳大利亚可持续森林经营标准和指标框架》。

2 澳大利亚森林现状

澳大利亚森林面积 14937 万 hm^2，其中原始林 14740 万 hm^2，约占 98.7% ，人工林 197 万 hm^2，约占 1.3%，森林覆盖率为 19%，人均森林拥有量为 7hm^2。澳大利亚原始林主要是常绿阔叶林，原始林树种以桉树为主，大约占 78%，相思占 7%，人工林树种 52% 为辐射松等针叶树。陈健波等(2010)比较 2003 年的数据发现其森林面积有大幅减少[3]，2003 年澳大利亚森林面积 16400 万 hm^2，森林面积减少的主要原因是这次森林调查采用高分辨率遥感数据和新的方法来估计森林覆盖率，减少的面积中只有很小的部分来源于森林真正的减少。70% 的森林产业由私人经营，其中包括私人所有、私人租赁和本地经营的土地。在这五年中，正式的自然保护区中的原始林由 13% 增加到 16%，增加了 150 万 hm^2，达到 2300 万 hm^2。多用途公共原始林面积从 1140 万 hm^2 减少到 940 万 hm^2，这部分森林以木材生产是主要目标。(MIG)

根据优势树种定义的森林类型主要有 8 类，即金合欢林、柏树林、木麻黄林、桉树林(下分 11 个子类)、红树林、白千层灌木林、雨林和其他。昆士兰州的森林面积最大，占总森林面积的 35%，其中 50% 左右是中等桉树疏林。(MIG)

3 自然保护区

大约 16% 的澳大利亚森林分布在正式的自然保护区中，其中包括近四分之三的老龄林。目前，澳大利亚为了农业生产和城市扩张砍伐森林在减少，森林居住物种在增加。从 1997 年到 2007 年，澳大利亚的多用途公共原始林持续减少，而正式的自然保护区面积持续增加，而且这是一个长期的趋势。在主要的原始林木材生产领域，澳大利亚人和一些州政府达成了区域森林协议，制定了 20 年保护和可持续经营原始林的计划。其中规定要建立全面的、足够的、有代表性的保护区体系(CAR)。从 2000 ~2006 年，雨林类型的保护区面积从原来的 33% 增加到 55%，红树林类型的面积从 13% 增加到 18%。澳大利亚人认为，正式的自然保护区网络是非正式自然保护区的补充。非正式自然保护区除了森林保护的目的还为了木材和其他林产品的生产，也有的是私人经营为了保护的目的。非正式自然保护区的面积近年来也是增加的，虽然没有国家层面上的数据。老龄林有着非常重要的生态学意义，老龄林甚少经过木材收获、道路通达或者大面积砍伐。老龄林通常包括巨大的上层木，生长良好的其他树种的下层木和灌木，具有许多生态学特征，如枯立木、林地上巨大的倒木和许多空心筑巢。相当数量的野生物种依靠老龄林维持其长期生存。估计澳大利亚有 503 万 hm^2 高湿森林是老龄林。从 2000 ~2006 年，老龄林减少了 20 万 hm^2，主要原因是森林大火引起的。73% 的老龄林在正式的自然保护区内。根据澳大利亚 Greenhouse 办公室估计，2000 ~ 2004 年每年木本植被减少 26 万 hm^2(0.25%)，原因是为了农业生产和城市扩张砍伐森林。昆士兰州的两类森林，即半郁闭金合欢林和中等桉树疏林是主要的砍伐对象。自然保护区及老龄林的重要性在于有许多物种生活在森林里，据《1999 年环境保护与生物多样性保护公约》有 1287 种森林居住物种受到攻击或处于危险之中。(MIG)

4 森林的固碳作用

澳大利亚是世界上人均温室气体排放大国，主要原因在于大量依赖化石燃料能源。商品林(原始林中的商品林和人工林)及其产品 2005 年净吸收 5650 万 tCO_2，可以平衡大约 10% 的澳大利亚温室气体排放，其中原始林中的商品林占 5.5%，人工林占 3.5%，木制品和木房屋结构及家具占 1%。森林既吸收温室气体也释放出温室气体，澳大利亚森林总体上是碳汇。澳大利亚原始林中的树在其生物量(干、枝、叶和根)中固定了 65.6 亿 t 碳，桉树疏林和半郁闭桉树林固碳最多，分别占到总固碳量的 37% 和 33%。这个固碳量相当于把 2400 万 tCO_2 从大气中取走，或者相当于澳大利亚 2005 年净排放量的 46 倍。这个固碳量也相当于 1800 年以来由于人类活动造成碳排放的 3.3%。澳大利亚的森林土壤是另一个重要碳汇源，它固定了 55.1 亿 t 碳，相当于澳大利亚 2005 年净排放量的 39 倍，木麻黄和柏树疏林中保有的土壤碳比例最高，热带桉树疏林中保有的土壤碳比例最低。森林中固碳量随着时间变化，受到温度、降雨、树种组成、经营管理方式、林火、收获、病虫害等自然和人为扰动等因素的影响。虽然变化量对于总的固碳量来说比例很小，但是它对于每年的碳计量来说还是影响很大。(MIG)

5 森林的涵养水源作用

澳大利亚大部分高品质水源都在森林的集水处，因此林业工作者在向社区和环境提供干净水方面扮演了重要角色。所有的多用途公有林要遵循多功能经营的规范，其中的要求就有要降低土壤侵蚀，许多被经营措施都有造成土壤侵蚀的可能，比如木材装车场、运木材的道路等，所以根据规范在收获后要恢复环境。大多数私有林也遵循相似的经营规范。林火可能是对来自森林高品质水源最大的威胁。2003 年在澳大利亚首都区主要集水地发生了一场林区大火，烧了 840km^2 的保护区森林。接着又遇到相当于 27 年总量的强暴风雨，河岸和山坡上的沉积物、烧后的树、矿物质大量冲入河流中。首都区主要水源供应地的 Corin 、Bendora 和 Cotter 水库受到污染，以至于政府暂时关闭了它们。(MIG)

6 可持续木材生产

可持续木材生产是指从森林中收获一定数量的木材和其他林产品，同时在整体上保证森林生态系统的功能并且使产品流永远是连续的。澳大利亚原始林的木材收获主要发生在公有林中，这类林有个名称叫做多用途公有林。从整个澳大利亚范围来看，多用途公有林的面积在减少而转为自然保护区。从多用途公有林获得的木材蓄积量也在减少，而从人工林中获得的木材蓄积量在增加。重要的原始林的木材收获主要发生在新南威尔士州、昆士兰州、塔斯马尼亚州、维多利亚州和西澳大利亚州。这些州都依据森林经营的法律和规范，通过正式的程序计算多用途公有林中可持续收获高质量锯木原材和胶合板产品的数量。数据计算要考虑很多参数，包括森林类型、龄级、立木蓄积、地形、可达性、木材生长以及多功能森林经营规范和其他规章的约束，主要是要确保休闲用途、水源以及自然保护等。(MIG)

人工林产出的木材占据了澳大利亚近三分之二的原木供应，这个比例还会增加，因为原始林木材采伐在减少，而人工林木材采伐在增加。根据2010年人工林调查的更新数据，2009年澳大利亚人工林面积增加2.4%，从197万hm^2增加到202万hm^2，其中99万hm^2(49%)是硬木树种，102万hm^2(51%)是软木树种和小面积混交林。其中49 658hm^2新种人工林是2009年报告的，31%是2008年报告的。新种人工林中包括43231hm^2硬木和6427hm^2软木。过去10年中，人工林面积增加了51%，主要增加的是硬木，其面积增加了超过150%，而软木面积增加了8%。软木锯材原木和纸浆材供应到2010年达到上升后的稳定水平，而硬木(主要是桉树)纸浆材供应到2010年后还会上升，可用于出口和纸张工业。(MIG，NFI)

7 对中国的启示

澳大利亚森林可持续森林经营或多功能经营已经是一个非常完整先进的体系，而且目的、作用、实践与效果具体、可落实、可评估，有机地整合在一起。相比之下，中国在森林多功能经营或可持续经营方面存在着较大的差距，而且处于一个无法突破的困境。我国南方多省引进了澳大利亚桉树，发展纸浆林多年，其木材产量既无法满足需求，落后的经营方式导致地力退化、不可持续发展，由此更加加剧人地矛盾。希望澳大利亚森林可持续森林经营能够给我们带来一些有益的启示：

(1)按照可持续森林经营或多功能森林经营的原则制定森林经营方案在林区层次上进行长时间的实践，使得可持续经营标准与指标的研究不与实际的经营活动脱节，需要在一些林场建立几十年有法律约束力的实验基地。在先期研究方面，首先需要有一个合理可行，可以不断丰富充实的研究框架。要把软件研制、生长模型研究与实际的多功能森林经营活动结合起来，使之成为一个相互促进的循环，而不是成为无法结合的脱离的领域。澳大利亚以1%人工林的面积解决了50%的木材产量，由此我们需要解决可持续木材生产的问题。从森林培育的角度来说，如何选择大径阶的桉树品种，发展优质桉树，提高桉树的经营水平是南方桉树发展较快省份不得不面对的问题，利用较少的土地资源大幅度提高桉树木材蓄积。

(2)按照可持续森林经营或多功能森林经营的原则定期进行森林资源及其功能的评估，使得森林资源清查、调查与多功能森林经营评估的工作有机地结合在一起，其结果作为有效反馈可以指导下一阶段的多功能森林经营活动。森林资源报告应该更加通俗易懂，面向社会公众；社会大众通过网络可以很便捷地获得权威可靠有实用价值的森林资源信息。

(3)需要在教学层面上开展对于学生多功能森林经营实际经验和技能的培养，包括对于正在工作的林场员工多功能森林经营能力的训练。多年前，徐国祯先生在他的澳大利亚高等林业教育考察报告中就指出，澳大利亚高等林业教育具有务实精神，教育的方方面面都“面向生产，注意培养有实际工作能力的林业工作者”，“在教学计划中，体现了以森林资源管理为重点，核心是计划—决策—管理，培养出来的学生能负责大片区或无林地的计划和规划，有组织管理的能力”。

(4)把信息技术、空间技术、统计技术、人工智能等现代工具作为可持续森林经营的辅助工具运用到实际的工作中，使得现代林业经营活动更有效率，产出的信息能够持续丰富。

(5)从林业政策层面来讲，一个稳定的政策导向非常重要，政策不能经常反复波动。多功能森林经营的原则实际上就是可持续森林经营的落实，我们需要在立法层面更加明确。单纯地把公益林以多功能经营或多目标经营的口号变成可以采伐的商品林在目前的制度框架下是违反多功能森林经营原则或者说可持续森林经营原则的。澳大利亚除禁止采伐的森林外，采伐森林无需办理许可证，原始林也可以采伐，而且原始林的采伐量也要满足另外50%的木材需求，但是这些行为都有很严格的各种法律限制和多功能经营的技术要求，由此可见林业政策的有效实施非常重要。

参考文献

[1]MIG. Australia's State of the Forests Report 2008, Montreal Process Implementation Group for Australia, Canberra, 2008.

[2]NFI. Australia's Forests at a Glance, National Forest Inventory, Bureau of Rural Sciences, Canberra, 2011.

[3]陈健波，周卫玲，黄开勇，等．澳大利亚的森林经营、林业研究及启示．广西林业科学，2010，39(2)：112～116.

[4]徐国祯．澳大利亚高等林业教育一瞥．世界林业研究，1989，1：84～90.

[5]黄东，谢晨，赵金成，等．澳大利亚多功能林业经营及其对我国的启示．林业经济，2010，2：117～121.

[6]武来成，杨馥宁，郑小贤，等．澳大利亚森林经营方案编制及借鉴．世界林业研究，2007，20(6)：62～66.

[7]吴伟光．澳大利亚林业概况及其启示．世界林业研究，2002，15(4)：62～68.

森林生态系统稳定性分析、问题和建议

孙丽萍　牛　纯

（吉林省林业勘察设计研究院，长春，130022）

摘要：本文一方面用生态环境特征、敏感性，物种特征、植被类型、结构、适应性、抗逆性等，对主要天然林、人工林进行了稳定性分析；另一方面采用各龄组面积、蓄积、株数 3 项指标对主要天然林、人工林、各旅游景点分区块进行了生态系统稳定性分析评价、找出问题，提出建议。

Analysis of Ecosystem Stability of Jingyuetan National Forest Park and proposal of the problems

SUN Li-ping　NIU Chun

（Forestry Survey and Design Institute of Jilin Province，Changchun，130022）

Abstract：The Thesis has an analysis of stability on natural forests and plantation with the factors of environmental character，sensitivity，species character，vegetation type，structure，adaptability，stress resistance etc，in addition，evaluates and analyzes the ecosystem stability of natural forests，plantation，and all scenic spots in blocks through three main factors of area，individual number and reserves，above all，to raise the problems and proposals.

1　公园概况

1.1　自然概况

长春净月潭国家森林公园，地处长春市东南部，距市区 9km，位于东经 125°20′13″～125°34′08″，北纬 43°41′56″～43°51′99″，总面积 12271.1hm^2，森林覆盖率 59.8%。气候处于温带半干旱半湿润气候区。其主要特点：春季干燥，少雨多风；夏季炎热，降雨集中；秋季凉爽，气候宜人；冬季少雪，气候寒冷。年平均气温 4.7℃，年均降水量为 593.8mm，年均风速为 4.3m/s，无霜期 145d。地貌有低山丘陵、阶地、洪积台地和河漫滩，海拔在220～406.5m。土壤以白浆化暗棕壤为主。现有净月潭水库一座，设计容量为 2574 万 m^3。植被比较丰富，现有高等植物 550 多种。主要乔木、灌木达到 30 多种。交通方便，距长春龙嘉国际机场 29.0km，距长春火车站 16km，长营、长青两条省级公路贯穿南北。从市区开往公园有轻轨，多路旅游专线公交车。

1.2　旅游资源概况

公园的森林游憩资源具有独特的景观和地理优势。园内有连绵峻秀的群山，浩瀚的人工林海，碧波荡漾的潭水。林景、山景、水景等自然景观及人为景观错落有致，形成了山水相依、绿树掩映的生态景观。春观花，夏避暑，秋赏叶，冬观雪，构成了净月潭四季变幻的风情画卷。

近几年来，由于深入贯彻有效保护、合理开发景区资源的方针，到目前为止，已建成景区、景点 18 处。其中：有森林浴场、游船娱乐等面状景区 11 处；高山滑雪、越野滑雪等线状景区 3 处；山地自行车等游乐设施 4 处。为国内外，尤其是长春居民提供了旅游观光、度假休闲、文化教育的综合性游憩场所，公园已成为名副其实的森林旅游胜地。近两年，年游客人数已突破 150 万人次。

1.3 森林资源概况

总土地面积 12271.1hm^2，其中，林业用地面积为 9950.9hm^2，占总面积 80.79%，有林地面积 7315.9hm^2，占林业用地面积 73.52%，有林地蓄积 881124m^3。天然林面积 2011.7hm^2、蓄积 226141m^3，人工林面积 5304.2、蓄积 654983m^3。公园有林地林分平均蓄积为 120.4m^3/hm^2，林分平均株数为 964 株/hm^2。近成过熟林面积占 63.56%，针叶林面积占 63.0%，阔叶林面积占 37.0%，纯林面积占 86.05%。

2 影响森林生态系统稳定性的主要因子

森林生态系统的稳定性取决于生态环境的特征、生态环境的敏感性、抗干扰能力以及构成森林生态系统的物种生物学特性、植被类型特征和结构等因素。稳定的森林物种应具有较强的适应性、抗逆性、弹性、持久性。根据上述条件对公园森林生态系统进行稳定性分析。

公园的森林生态系统属于天然和人工混合的复合型森林生态系统。园内除了净月潭水库这个水体外，主要为天然和人工的森林环境，是森林生态系统最重要的载体，因此，其主导作用是无可替代的。并且林分结构是生态功能的基础，生态功能是林分结构的表现。林分结构决定生态功能，因此本评价拟采用园内的植被林分结构及优势树种的年龄来评价生态系统的稳定性。采取 3 项指标来分析：面积、蓄积、个体数(株数)。

3 森林生态系统稳定性分析、评价

3.1 人工林生态系统稳定性分析、评价

3.1.1 主要人工树种稳定性分析

公园人工林面积为 5304.2hm^2，占公园森林总面积的确 72.5%。人工造林各树种面积、蓄积及结构详见表 1。

表 1 人工林各树种面积、蓄积结构统计表

优势树种	面积(hm^2)	比例(%)	蓄积量(m^3)	比例(%)
红松林	173.6	3.27	29435	4.49
云杉林	22.5	0.42	1316	0.20
樟子松林	2055.4	38.75	245657	37.51
落叶松林	1807.4	34.07	251571	38.41
黑松林	518.1	9.77	81894	12.5
其他松类	0.7	0.01		0.00

(续)

优势树种	面积(hm^2)	比例(%)	蓄积量(m^3)	比例(%)
水曲柳林	29.9	0.56	2437	0.37
胡桃楸林	8.7	0.16	27	0.00
柞树林	3.1	0.06	372	0.06
榆树林	8.8	0.17	998	0.15
白桦林	6.0	0.11	20	0.00
杨树林	180.3	3.40	9217	1.41
柳树林	44.1	0.83	1734	0.26
杂木林	89.7	1.69	137	0.02
针叶混交林	227.0	4.28	23641	3.61
阔叶混交林	58.7	1.11	475	0.07
针阔混交林	70.2	1.32	6052	0.92

(1)樟子松人工林稳定性分析:

樟子松(*Pinus sylvestris* L. var. *mongolica* Litv.)原产地在大兴安岭北部的寒温带,耐寒性强,能耐-40℃以下的低温。根系发达、抗旱性强、不苛求土壤水分,是喜光、早期生长快的树种。净月潭引种樟子松有60多年的历史,是由寒温带移植到中温带,其光照、温度、水分及土壤条件都有很大变化。在正常年份,樟子松林分生长良好,表现稳定。20a时立地指数可达8~10m,生产力较高,说明对公园的生态环境较为适应。但是,对公园来说,樟子松属于“北树南移”,成林后,当遇到早春土壤未化冻、但气温较高时,树冠即开始打破休眠、发生蒸腾,而根系此时不能有效吸收水分,从而造成生理干旱。这种现象在吉林省通化、吉林、长春、辽源地区均有发生。严重时,可造成樟子松林分大面积枯死(如东丰县、梅河口市等)。2005年在公园樟子松林分普遍出现过一次生理干旱现象,造成樟子松春、夏之际树冠针叶一片枯黄。同时,幼林阶段鼠害较严重。由于多为纯林,对森林防火,病虫害预防十分不利。樟子松对空气中SO_2等有毒气体抵抗性中等。

(2)长白落叶松人工林稳定性分析:

长白落叶松(*Larix olgensis* Henry)原产长白山山地,分布于海拔500~1600m的混交林中,分布区内寒冷、湿润多雨,降水量最大地段可达1000mm,大黑山脉是天然林分布的外缘,该树种是公园造林面积仅次于樟子松的树种。长白落叶松耐寒、喜光、对土壤肥力要求不高,pH值适应范围6~8,有一定的耐水湿能力,浅根性、抗风能力较差。在公园营造的人工林13年生立地指数为10~12m,生产力较高。正常年份林分生长较为稳定,总体适应性较强。但是长白落叶松的特点是不耐干旱。这在2000~2004年之间体现的特别突出,由于春季干旱,公园内已经生长几十年的长白落叶松大面积生长衰弱,引发次期性害虫落叶松八齿小蠹暴发成灾,最终导致长白落叶松林分大面积枯死。同时长白落叶松林分还易发生早落病和松毛虫;对SO_2的污染抵抗能力也较弱;因多为纯林,对森林防火及病虫害防治不利;又由于其浅根性,易发生风倒灾害。

(3)黑松人工林稳定性分析:

黑松(*Pinus thunbergii*)自然分布在华北、西北地区,最北界在辽宁省千山山脉北段,是温带树种。适生于华北西北地区的干冷气候，抗旱能力较强，可耐 -25℃的低温，耐干旱，在年降水量300mm 的内蒙古大青山也能正常生长。喜光，在郁闭度0.3~0.4 林冠下更新良好。对土壤肥力要求不高，耐瘠薄，喜生于微酸性土壤上，不耐盐碱，pH 值7.5 以上生长不良。该树种属于深根性，侧根发达植物，是可以在自然裂缝的岩石砬子上生长的长寿树种。净月潭的黑松引种栽培近70 年历史，造林后可以成活成林，但生产力较低。因从自然分布向北移植距离较大，抗寒性较差，属于“南树北移”，因此，常常遭受冬季低温冻害，导致干型弯曲，早春针叶枯黄。油松虽耐干旱瘠薄与人为活动干扰，但受外来入侵有害生物日本松干蚧以及微红松梢螟、纵坑切梢小蠹的危害较为严重。该树种虽生长较慢，但树形美观，是城市绿化的优良树种。

(4)红松人工林稳定性分析：

红松(*Pirnus koraiensis* Sieb. et Zucc.)自然分布于长白山区及小兴安岭，适生于温凉湿润的气候：年平均气温0~6℃，年降水700~1200mm。能耐 -50℃最低气温，在积温2200~3200℃时生长正常。喜深厚肥沃的pH 值在5.5~6.5 微酸性土壤，在干旱瘠薄的土壤及低温地带生长不良。该树种属浅根性、侧根发达的“长寿树种”，树龄可达500 年。公园因空气较干燥，降水不够丰富，湿润度0.5，土壤较瘠薄，其生长速度仅是温度0.7~1.0 的适宜地区60%~70%。净月潭红松引种造林有70 多年的历史，可以成活成林，丰富公园的物种，但对生态环境要求较高。同樟子松类似，个别年份早春气候不正常情况下易发生生理干旱，造成树冠针叶枯黄甚至枯死。如2008 年公园中的针阔混交林中就发生了红松早春生理干旱现象。所以对森林公园旅游区内的红松林分要严格控制人为活动的干扰，以保证林下植被、土壤不被破坏，枯枝落叶得到很好的分解、增加土壤肥力，提高蓄水能力，为红松生长创造良好的环境。红松是珍贵的用材林、经济林和观赏树种，应防止人为干扰，保证其林分健康、稳定生长。

3.1.2 主要人工树种稳定性评价

樟子松、落叶松、黑松这3 种树的面积、蓄积量、株数3 方面的都园内人工林中的最高的3 种树，其优势程度明显。因此，对这3 种树的3 个指标(面积、蓄积量、株数)按照树龄来详细统计，结果表明：樟子松不同龄树的面积分布：成熟林>中龄林>近熟林>幼龄林>过熟林；蓄积量：成熟林>近熟林>中龄林>过熟林>幼龄林；株数：中龄林>近熟林>成熟林>幼龄林>过熟林。落叶松不同龄树的面积分布：成熟林>近熟林>过熟林>中龄林>幼龄林；蓄积量：成熟林>近熟林>过熟林>中龄林>幼龄林；株数：成熟林>近熟林>中龄林>过熟林>幼龄林；黑松不同龄树的面积分布：过熟林>成熟林>近熟林>幼龄林>中龄林；蓄积量：过熟林>成熟林>近熟林>中龄林>幼龄林；株数：成熟林>过熟林>幼龄林>近熟林>中龄林。

樟子松面积和蓄积量均为成熟林占首位，株数却以中龄林为主，说明这个种群非常稳定。落叶松成熟林和近熟林为主；说明这个种群稳定性相对较高；而黑松以成熟林和过熟林为主，可以看出这个种群稳定性一般。

3.2 主要天然林生态系统稳定性分析、评价

3.2.1 天然林生态系统稳定性分析

公园天然林面积为2011.7hm^2，占公园森林总面积的27.5%。天然林各树种面积、蓄积及结构详见表2。

表 2 公园天然林各树种面积、蓄积结构统计表

树种	面积(hm^2)	比例(%)	蓄积量(m^3)	比例(%)
椴树林	9.5	0.47	1218	0.54
柞树林	1277.9	63.52	142545	63.03
榆树林	38.9	1.93	3386	1.50
杨树林	0.6	0.03	67	0.03
柳树林	11.4	0.57	667	0.29
杂木林	7.3	0.36	310	0.14
阔叶混交林	645.2	32.07	76417	33.79
针阔混交林	19.5	0.97	1489	0.66
胡桃楸	1.4	0.07	42	0.02

(1)以柞树为主天然次生林群落稳定性分析:

公园中天然次生林2011.7hm^2,占森林面积27.5%。在天然次生林中,以柞树为主的林分占天然林面积的63.7%。柞树是公园天然林中的绝对优势树种,因此重点对柞树的生物学特性,生态习性与稳定性进行分析。

柞树(*Quercus mongolica*)是落叶阔叶林主要建群种,广泛分布于东北、华北、西北各省区。具有喜光、耐干旱瘠薄、耐寒性强、深根性、寿命长的特点。在-40℃低温地带不受冻害。在干燥、瘠薄的阳面陡坡,其他树种不易生长的立地条件下都可以正常生长。柞树树皮较厚、抗火性强、根系萌发能力强,火灾或砍伐后易恢复自然更新。对环境因子波动、人为干扰都有极强的抗御能力。从林龄结构分析,林分面积:近熟林>中龄林>成熟林>幼龄林;林分蓄积:近熟林>中龄林>成熟林>幼龄林;林分株数:近熟林>中龄林>成熟林>幼龄林。因此,以柞树为主的天然林是构成公园森林生态系统稳定性最强的群落。

(2)其他阔叶树林分稳定性分析:

杨、柳、榆、椴、胡桃楸等阔叶树种占天然林面积的26.3%,且均是乡土树种,其组成的混交林适应性强,生长健壮,并且种源丰富,天然更新良好。从林龄结构分析,林分面积:近熟林>中龄林>幼龄林>成熟林;林分蓄积:近熟林>中龄林>幼龄林>成熟林;林分株数:近熟林>中龄林>幼龄林>成熟林。因此可见,该林分也是稳定的森林植物群落。

3.2.2 天然林生态系统稳定性评价

根据天然林各树种面积、蓄积结构统计表,结果表明,面积分布:柞树占园内林地总面积的63.7%,其次为阔叶(其他)树,占园内总面积的30.91%,几种优树种的面积次序为:柞树>阔叶(其他)树>榆树>针阔混>椴树>柳树>杂木>杨树;蓄积分布:柞树占林木总蓄积量的63.16%,其次为阔叶(其他)树,占总蓄积量的32.83%,它们的次序为:柞树>阔叶(其他)树>榆树>针阔混>椴树>柳树>杂木>杨树,与面积排序一致。株树分布:柞树占林木株数的比例为63.69%,其次为阔叶(其他)树,占32.02%,它们的次序为:柞树>阔叶(其他)树>针阔混>榆树>椴树>杂木>柳树>杨树。

通过上述指标说明柞树和其他阔叶树的面积、蓄积、株数都是近熟林和中龄林占主体,并处于生长旺盛期。表明由上述林分构成的森林生态系统较为稳定。

4 各旅游景点分区块进行稳定性分析评价

从表 3 表明，用不同龄组所占的面积比例来判断相应地区的生态稳定性，数据统计结果如下：

表 3 不同旅游点(区)不同各龄组所占面积的比例(%)

树龄	过熟林	中龄林	成熟林	近熟林	幼龄林
垂柳园、普陀寺、塔楼	0. 088123	0. 149425	0. 51341	0. 249042	
鹿苑	0. 260391	0. 195599	0. 062347	0. 227384	0. 254279
森林浴场		0. 083878	0. 216776	0. 680828	0. 018519
滑雪场和冰雪游乐园	0. 319506	0. 161518	0. 186231	0. 308032	0. 024713
小森林浴场		0. 056851	0. 845481	0. 078717	0. 01895
沙滩浴场	0. 052174	0. 023188	0. 35942	0. 42029	0. 144928

(1)荷花垂柳园、普陀寺、碧松净月塔楼：由于几个景点距离非常近，故合并三个区分析。本区判定结果为成熟林 > 近熟林 > 中龄林 > 过熟林。各龄组成为稳态群落状况，因此本区稳定非常强。

(2)鹿苑：本区分析结果为：过熟林 > 幼龄林 > 近熟林 > 中龄林 > 成熟林。各龄组成以过熟林和幼龄林为主，因此本区稳定性较差。

(3)森林浴场：本区分析结果为成熟林 > 近熟林 > 中龄林 > 幼龄林。各龄组成以成熟林和近熟林为主，因此本区稳定性较强。

(4)滑雪场和冰雪游乐园：合并起来进行稳定性分析，结果表明：过熟林 > 近熟林 > 成熟林 > 中龄林 > 幼龄林。各龄组成以过熟林为主，因此本区稳定性较差。

(5)小森林浴场：本区分析结果为：成熟林 > 近熟林 > 中龄林 > 幼龄林。各龄组成以成熟林和近熟林为主，因此本区稳定性较强。

(6)沙滩浴场：本区分析结果为：近熟林 > 成熟林 > 幼龄林 > 过熟林 > 中龄林。各龄组成以近熟林和成熟林为主，因此本区稳定性较强。

5 存在问题和建议

5.1 存在问题

(1)该园已有 60 多年的林业建设基础，形成以针叶树种为主体的有 30 多个树种组成的森林生态系统。人工林以樟子松、长白落叶松、黑松和红松为主；次生林中柞树优势，其次为白桦、黑桦、紫椴、糠椴、春榆和槐树等。总的表现为：针叶林面积占 63. 0%、阔叶林面积占 37. 0%、单纯单层林面积占 86. 05%、混交林面积占 13. 95%，乔木树种多、灌木和地被植物少。上述群落类型，生态位空缺，抵御森林病虫害能力差，林火等级较高，景观单调，需要在原有的基础上进行改造，提高风景名胜区的森林景观质量，为人们提供更高层次的旅游、游憩、观赏的群落环境。

(2)单位面积株数明显偏高：

表4 有林地各龄组面积、蓄积与株数统计表

	起源	平均值	幼龄林	中龄林	近熟林	成熟林	过熟林
面积(hm^2)			787.6	1333.6	2357.0	2285.8	703.5
蓄积量(m^3)		120.4	41.5	94.8	117.9	144.6	170.5
株数	人工	1053	1614	1311	1136	816	657
	天然	724	1551	824	688	476	655

从表4可以看出，公园森林特别是人工林，单位面积株数明显偏密，导致林木生长分化。枯死木、濒死木、被压木增多。林内卫生状况不好，因而影响森林整体健康质量和森林生态系统的稳定性。

(3)公园是长春市及周边地区主要的森林游憩景区，随着人民生活水平的提高，公园游人数不断增加。大量游人的涌入，人为活动增加必将对公园森林生态系统稳定造成影响。

5.2 建 议

通过生态系统稳定的研究结果显示，目前公园稳定性较差的林份为鹿苑、滑雪场和冰雪游乐园所处林地。鹿苑所处的林地以过熟林和幼龄林为主；滑雪场和冰雪游乐园所处林地以过熟林为主，抓紧时间恢复、改造林分。

森林浴场是公园管理重要的旅游景点与主要的旅游项目。随着人民生活水平的提高和对自然环境的热爱，现有的两处森林浴场接待能力明显不足，另外森林浴场自身也需要恢复。建议规划开发新的森林浴场，与原有森林浴场交替使用，使森林的健康得以维护。

公园按照保护优先、持续发展的原则，积极而慎重地对人工针叶林、疏林、次生灌丛，因林制宜地采用“阔缝栽针”、“栽针补阔”和生态择伐、生态疏伐、降低密度等人工诱导针阔混交林方法，开展林木组成和结构调整与改造工作，加强森林病虫害防治和防火工作，不断提高森林和群落环境质量，使其在维护本区的生态环境中发挥积极作用。

为充分发挥系统的自我恢复能力对天然林郁闭度达到0.6以上的天然次生林和现有的人工幼、中龄林中，在单位面积上达到合理株数，进行封山育林。在天然次生阔叶林中，有部分郁闭度在0.2~0.5之间的林分用耐阴针叶树进行林冠下造林。

通过建议的实施，进一步优化森林结构，全面提高森林资源、森林生态景观质量和森林生态系统的整体功能，森林健康和生物多样性得到全面维护和促进，使森林生态系统的抗干扰能力更强，稳定性更高。

参考文献

[1]牛纯，刘毅．长春净月潭国家森林公园森林经营方案．

[2]吉林省林业勘察设计研究院，2008年6月．

可持续发展的森林资源综合管理

涂云燕　彭道黎
（北京林业大学，北京，100083）

摘要：随着人们对森林效用追求的不断上升、森林经营理论的转变，可持续森林资源综合管理的技术支撑外延也在不断扩大。为此，本文首先简单回顾了从传统森林永续利用到可持续经营理念的历史演变，探讨了可持续发展的森林资源综合管理技术，并结合现代的形势和科技发展水平，分析了森林经理学在未来的发展动向。

关键词：森林经营理论；综合管理；技术

Abstract: With the increasing pursuit of effectiveness for forest, and the change of forest management theory, technical support extension of integrated management of sustainable forest development is also expanding. This article reviewed the historical evolution of forest resources management theory from the traditional concept of sustainable forest management to the sustainable development of forest resources management, combined with the modern situation and the level of technological development, analysis of the trends of the forest management discipline in the future .

Key words: forest management theory; integrated management; technology

自 1992 年环保大会以来，可持续发展战略在全世界得到了认可，人类—资源—环境的相互依存与协调发展已成为世界各国关注的焦点之一。森林对地球上的生物特别是人类生存所具有的重要性也日益被人们所接受。森林从最初的维持生命支持系统的木材利用到现在超出其作为直接资源的林产品的价值的可持续利用思想转变与森林经营理论密切相关的。经营理论作为森林经理重要的一部分，是制定林业发展战略的灵魂，是森林经理学科发展的最短板，它直接关系到林业的兴衰成败，正确的经营思想对合理进行经营和管理森林具有极大的指导意义。任何一种森林经营理论的发展，一是取决于社会的发展和需要，二是取决于人们对森林效用的追求，并与林业发展息息相关。因此无论哪种经营理论，都是时代的产物，都有一定的特定背景。在形势不断发生变化的同时，其呈现出了与时代相适应的特点。作为可持续发展技术支撑的森林资源综合管理也与林业发展遥相呼应。

1. 演变过程

森林经营历来都是林业生产的主体内容。虽然人类从很早就自觉和不自觉地进行着森林经营（孟子就曾经说过，“斧斤以时入山林”），但现代意义上的森林经营理论出现在 18 世纪。从 1713 年德国卡洛维茨提出“森林永续利用理论”开始，林学家们提出了形形色色的森林经营理论。先后产生了诸如森林永续论、“法正林”理论、木材培育论、森林多效益永续经营理论、船迹理论、协同论、林业分工论、新林业理论、近自然林业及可持续发展理论等等[1]。虽然这些理论在时间、观点上有些重叠，但大体上仍可按认识的深度(时间演变序列)归结为“永续利用理论”、“森林多功能理论”和“森林可持续经营理论”。

1.1 永续利用理论

始于1618年捷克反哈布斯堡王朝统治起义的三十年战争，使德国出现一片荒凉景象，百废待兴，到17世纪中期，重建家园与发展(制盐、矿冶、玻璃、造船业等工业)需求，使德国对木材的需求量猛增，开始大规模采伐森林。这种对经济利益的追求，给森林带来了前所未有的灾难性破坏，从而导致了18世纪初的震动全国的“木材危机”。由于危机的出现，促使林业工作者对过去的森林经营理念和林业发展的自然规律进行了反思和探索。1713年，德国森林永续利用理论的创始人汉里希·冯·卡洛维茨首先提出了森林永续利用原则[2]，提出了人工造林思想。这一理论的出现也为近代林业的兴起与发展拉开了序幕。为实现永续利用的目标，1826年，德国林学家J·C·洪德斯哈根在总结前人经验的基础上，创立了“法正林(Normal Frost)”理论[3]。其经营核心以年龄结构、林地纯收益最大为目标。

1.2 森林多功能理论

传统森林经理学以用材林永续经营为中心指导思想，森林经理学家对森林多效益的研究不够深入随着生产的不断发展，森林资源的多效益性逐步得到重视，森林经理学家对森林的多效益性有了较深刻的认识。在林业经营活动中除了森林直接提供各种林产品的物质生产功能外，森林的各种间接生态效益也成为规划决策活动的重要依据之一[4,5]。

森林永续利用理论的缺点之一是只考虑木材生产，在该理论指导下大面积种植人工纯林的不良后果很快就引起林学家的关注。

1867年，德国林学家奥拓·冯·哈根认识到木材不是森林经营目标的全部，提出了“森林多效益永续经营理论”，认为林业经营应兼顾持久满足木材和其他林产品的需求，以及森林在其他方面的服务目标。简单地说，他认为“永续利用”的思想没有错，但永续利用的不仅是木材而是“多效益”。1933年，德国的《森林法》中明确规定：永续地、有计划地经营森林，既要最大量地生产木材，又必须保持和提高森林的生产能力；经营森林应尽可能地考虑森林的美观、景观特点和保护野生动物；必须划定休憩林和防护林[6]。

森林多功能理论是林学家们对林业认识上的第二次突破。它的最大贡献，就是承认森林的“间接效益”(包括生态效益和社会效益)，认识到随着社会需求的变化，森林的非木材功能对于人类的价值会日益增加并上升到主导地位。森林多功能理论强调三大效益一体化经营，强调生产、生物、景观和人文的多样性；在技术上主张长伐期和择伐作业；人工林天然化经营[7]。

1.3 森林可持续经营理论

到了20世纪90年代初，随着全球范围内环境质量的下降，生物圈面临严重的威胁，以及人们对森林效用追求，一系列的经营理论被各国提出来了。如美国的森林生态系统健康经营、新林业理论等。其实各种“森林可持续经营理论”与上述“森林多功能理论”并无大的差别。同森林多功能理论相比，可持续经营理论在下列观点上进一步深化了认识。一是强化了林业“可持续发展”的理念。二是强化了生态系统的观念。任一地块的森林不是孤立的，而是一个生态系统，且与其他地块的森林和临近的陆地、水面等构成更大的生态系统。用林学家 Plochmann(1982)的话说:“永续利用的出发点不应该是各种林产品和间接效用，而是作为能发挥多种效用的森林生态系统。”[8]

从森林与人类的原始和谐相处、森林的过度利用、森林的保护恢复到森林的可持续发展的历史演变过程表明，人类对森林的认识是一个实践、认识、再实践、再认识的逐步深化过程。森林经营理念也走过了单纯追求木材生产经济效益、永续利用森林、森林多功能经营到森林可持续经营的历程。但各理论并不是独立的，或者说各理论有其特点的时代意义。从传统森林经理到可持续发展经营是继承与发展的关系。可持续经营本身就有永续的思想，法正林的理论用于指导今天木材生产与采伐，仍然是可行的，并且是可持续的要求。

2 我国可持续发展的森林资源综合经营管理技术

森林资源综合管理技术体系与森林经理理论发展遥相呼应。当森林经理理论发生变化，就会促使人们寻找与森林经理理论相适应的技术体系，二者都受经济、技术条件，及人们对森林认识的影响，与林业发展历程息息相关，是历史与社会发展的产物。从世界林业发展的进程看，一般经过森林原始利用、木材过度利用、森林恢复发展、多功能利用和可持续发展五个阶段。相应的技术体系由森林面积和木材蓄积监测，到多资源或多功能监测的过渡，并逐渐向与林业可持续发展相适应的森林资源综合经营管理方向发展。

2.1 森林资源综合管理的技术探讨

目前，我国森林资源综合监测还处于理论阶段，对涉及生物多样性、森林生态系统、水土保持、碳循环、社会和经济效益等的定量模型研究还处于研究阶段。怎样运用定量方法构建森林资源综合监测评价指标体系，成为森林资源综合监测研究的热点也是拟解决的问题。

2.1.1 3S 一体化技术在森林资源综合监测中的应用

利用 GPS、GIS、RS 的有机结合为森林资源全方位多层次的综合监测提供有力的技术支持。运用 GPS 双向通讯，把样地的数据实时地传递到处理中心(RS、GIS)进行实时处理、实时绘制森林资源分布图、林相图，准确反映森林资源各项监测指标的变化。并采用定量化处理对定性数据进行处理，从而在空间的角度定量地对森林资源进行描述，在获取充分数据的基础上为决策者提供大量的信息，为可持续森林经营决策的制定提供参考。

2.1.2 系统控制论在林分结构调整中的应用[9]

把森林资源作为一个大系统，它与其他资源不同，其主要特点是：空间分布广，生长周期长；影响因素众多；结构复杂；功能综合；可再生行强；未来发展趋势具有不确定性；自然规律与经济规律交织在一起，不可分割。对其林分结构调整引入系统控制论(即预测的反问题)。如对一片林分生长状况：

设定 $y = ax_1 + bx_2 + cx_3 + \cdots\cdots$

y：既定目标效果(如森林资源系统某一指标)；

a、b、c：调整系数

X_i：可控变量各林分因子(可以为定量的，也可以是定性的)；

如何控制自变量 X_i 的取值，使 y 达到既定目标。

2.1.3 计算机仿真技术森林资源综合监测中的应用

森林资源数据众多、复杂，计算量庞大，是森林资源定量计算、监测、管理等难点之一。引入计算机仿真技术实现了对林分密度、森林生长和收获预估、控制以及森林资源动态预测等森林资源综合实时管理。可以预见，森林经营方案编制及实施效果评价的微机辅助系统、林业专题自动化制图系统等是今后的研究方向。目前利用 matlab 实现计算机仿真成为热点，如李崇贵应用 MATLAB 技术开发出了森林蓄积量定量估测软件，克服了传统蓄积量估测自变量与样地选取的不足，实现了蓄积量估测最优自变量、样地自动选择。可以预见，利用 matlab 软件实现人工智能关于多资源多目标的综合管理将成为研究的趋势与热点。

2.1.4 网络技术在多层次森林资源综合管理中的应用[10]

通过网络技术发布森林资源数据，在发布平台上可以得到发布的森林资源的主要指标，把森林资源的属性数据和图像数据同时呈现出来，使管理实现数据一体化。对各类森林利用的社会、经济、政治及生物物理等进行有机的综合探究，从而在地方、国家到全球的多个层次和规模上实现森林资源综合管理。如 ArcGIS Server 提供了 . NET 和 JAVA 两种软件二次开发的接口，可以采用 . NET 作为二次开发的平台，采用 C#语言作为开发语言。结合 WebGIS 技术、计算机技术、空间数据库技术，构建基于 WebGIS 的数字林业管理的基本框架创建数据发布平台，实现发布地图服务，实现对森林资源数据的共享。

3 森林经理的理论与技术变革

可持续发展作为新时代森林经理的基础理论，继承与发展了永续利用理论，是今后森林经理的指导思想、目标。转型期的森林经理学科主要工作就是突破传统森林经理的理论、技术和模式；将传统木材永续经营改造为森林可持续经营。当然这里的突破与改造并不是摒弃永续利用理论与模式，而是在其基础上取其精华，去其糟粕。

森林资源管理的复杂性、区域性、综合继承性特点，决定了森林资源经营管理需要采取差异性手段。如美国的森林生态系统模式，并不是说全国都实行这一模式，在商品林地方仍然实行大砍大造。永续利用、多功能经营其实质都是可持续发展的一种表现。只是不同地区，自然、经济条件的不同采取不同的经营模式。目前，我国的国情、林情决定了我国森林经理还处在多功能经营阶段。

对未来的可持续森林经理理论与技术变革主要在：

（1）建立可持续森林经理的理论体系——应用基础理论、原理、原则、模式、多学科的综合理论体系，同时森林认证与森林文化作为可持续森林经营的内容将得到更好的完善；

（2）建立可持续森林资源经理的技术体系——构建适合我国国情与林情的森林可持续经营体系，引入集成化、网络化、智能化可操作的技术解决各种具体区域管理的技术系统，同时开放式、个性化、适时动态条件下的集成化森林资源管理信息系统也是研究的热点。

参考文献

[1]陈柳钦．林业经营理论的历史演变[J]．中国地质大学学报(社会科学版)，2007，7(2)：50～56.
[2]于政中．森林永续利用与持续林业经营[J]．北京林业大学学报，1994，7，1(16)：95～100.
[3]詹昭宁．中国森林经理探讨[J]．林业经济问题，2007，027(no.1)：89～96，S751～S757.
[4]张会儒．森林经理：问题与对策[J]．林业经济，2009(06).
[5]陈谋询．我国 21 世纪森林经理发展趋势分析[J]．华东森林经理，2001(02).
[6]周生贤．中国林业的历史性转变[M]．北京：中国林业出版社，2002.
[7]解厚忠．森林经理学科面临的形势和几个热点问题[J]．安徽林业科技，1997(03).
[8]张继义．浅谈森林经营理念的发展过程[N]．林海日报，2005，12，24(3)．

[9]朱明德，佘光辉．统计预测与控制[M]．北京：中国林业出版社．
[10]王阿川，李 丹，王霓虹．基于 J2EE 和 ArcGIS 平台的森林资源信息管理系统的应用[J]．东北林业大学学报，2007，35(10)：92～96.

我国森林公园的规划设计、现状及发展趋势

陈 英 杨 华
（北京林业大学省部共建森林培育与保护教育部重点实验室，北京，100083）

摘要：本文阐述了森林公园的概念，同时通过对国内外森林公园的研究，指出了我国森林公园的总体规划设计理念和原则、对我国森林公园的现状进行了评价，并对其发展趋势进行了预测。森林公园的总体规划设计应根据旅游的需求，对森林公园景观资源的开发和保护制定出科学的方案，最大限度的发挥森林公园的经济效益、社会效益及生态效益；我国森林旅游资源极其丰富，有待加快开发；同时要注重培养人才、加强管理。

关键词：森林公园；规划设计；现状；发展趋势

The Planning Design, Present Situation and Development Trend of Forest Park in China

CHEN Ying YANG Hua
(Key Laboratory for Silviculture and Conservation, Ministry of Education of Beijing Forestry University Beijing Haidian, 100083)

Abstract: This paper expounds the concept of forest park, and points out the idea and principle of forest park planning design, evaluates the present situation and forecasts the future development trend of forest park in china through doing some research on the forest park at home and abroad. The overall plan of the forest park design should be based on the needs of tourism, and we should make a scientific plan for the forest park landscape resources exploitation and protection, then express maximumly forest park economic benefits and social benefits and ecological benefit; forest tourism resources are very abundant in china, so they are needed to speed up the development; and the same time, we should Pay attention to training talents and strengthening the management.

Key words: forest park; planning design; present situation; development trend

自 1872 年世界上第一个国家公园——美国黄石公园诞生以来，到目前为止，已有 100 多个国家和地区建立起各种类型的森林公园和自然保护区 3000 多个，总面积达 4 亿多 hm^2，

基金项目：林业公益性行业科研专项(20080427)(201104051)。

作者简介：陈英，硕士。主要研究方向：森林资源监测与评价。电话：15201436756 Email：chenying2005052@163.com

占世界总面积的3.5%[1]。随着改革开放的深入，国民经济的持续发展，人民生活水平逐步提高，旅游已成为现代社会的一项重要生活内容。返璞归真，进行生态旅游，回归大自然已逐步成为一种新的消费时尚。随着森林旅游的发展，森林公园的建设逐渐兴起，并在全国范围内广为发展。我国的森林公园和自然保护区虽然起步较晚，但是发展较快。

1 前 言

1.1 森林公园的概念

1999年发布的《中国森林公园风景资源质量等级评定》国家标准，对"森林公园"作了科学的定义，并得到了学术界的认可，指出森林公园是"具有一定规模和质量的森林风景资源和环境条件，可以开展森林旅游，并按法定程序申报批准的森林地域"[2]。它明确了森林公园必须具备以下条件：

第一，是具有一定面积和界线的区域范围。

第二，以森林景观为背景或依托，是这一区域的特点。

第三，该区域必须具有旅游开发价值，要有一定数量和质量的自然景观或人文景观，区域内可为人们提供游憩、健身、科学研究和文化教育等活动。

第四，必须经由法定程序申报和批准。

凡达不到上述要求的，都不能称为森林公园。森林公园既不同于风景名胜区，也有异于城市公园[3]，可按旅游半径大小分为城市型、近郊(乡村)型、郊野(自然)型和山野(原野)型森林公园[4~5]。

1.2 森林公园开发的必要性

森林公园具有丰富的动植物资源，气候条件良好，是一个天然的"氧吧和绿肺"，这样的优越条件为旅游的开展提供了极佳的基础。因此，通过对森林公园的旅游开发，将森林公园与旅游结合起来，具有重大的意义。首先，可促进区域经济的发展。旅游业是一个跨行业、跨地区的产业，发展的联动性与带动性强，对于区域经济的发展有着很大的促进带动作用。其次，可增进国际交流。通过森林公园的旅游开发在吸引入境游客的同时，可增加当地与国外的交流，促进旅游目的地的国际发展水平。再者，转变了林业的经营思想，扩展了林业部门的经营手段，使林业行业从比较单一的木材经营及销售加工转向第三产业，创造出更佳的经济效益及社会效益。最后，森林公园的旅游开发可唤起人们对生态环境和自然资源的保护意识[6]。

2 国内外森林公园规划建设

2.1 国外森林公园发展概况

许多发达国家为满足广大城市居民对大自然野外娱乐游览的需要，都很重视对城郊森林的保护和利用，100多年前便开始了对森林资源有系统有组织的开发和建设，开展了森林旅游业。

美国的国家公园1872年美国建立了世界上第一个国家公园—黄石公园。到目前为止，已建立了337处国家公园，分布于49个州，占地32万km^2的国家公园体系，设有统一的经营管理机构，有一套完整的理论体系和明确的指导思想，其中的国家娱乐资源保护区和城郊的国家游乐胜地类似我国的森林公园。此外，美国还有2433.33万hm^2"森林"，其内树木主要起环境保护作用，除进行必要的林分改造和抚育间伐外是不允许大面积集中砍伐的。在美国为保护森林，在国家公园内，商业性、娱乐性建筑受到严格的限制，服务性建筑也规定分散布置，且每组建筑规模部不大，造型朴素、自然，与环境融为一体。

日本的国立公园　日本对自然景观、森林资源极为爱惜。20 年代便在全国掀起了兴建国立公园的运动，1931 年出现了“国立公园法”。1957 年又制定“自然公园法”。从法律上加以保障。日本在木材大量进口的情况下，也极力保护好本国的森林资源，而不乱采伐。现日本有国立公园 27 处，国定公园 51 处，都、道、府、县立自然公园 291 处，三者总面积达 521 万 hm^2，占国土面积的 13.77%，目前仅在国立公园和国定公园参加各种活动的便多达 5 亿多人次，效益十分可观。

前苏联的森林公园　森林公园这一名称较早见于前苏联，他们对森林公园的规划建设、管理等制订了一整套系统的理论和傲法。大城市周围森林公园常占地 300 ~ 500hm^2，平均每个游客占地 500 ~ 1000m^2。为使森林不遭破坏，森林公园的规划和建设都严格控制建筑物，甚至限制游览路线，以较完整地保护自然风景。

根据 1971 年批准的莫斯科总体规划，平均每个居民将有 22m^2公共绿地，加上森林公园平均每人将达到 33m^2，规模相当可观。

波兰的森林公园　波兰对森林公园的建设有许多成功的经验，并有系统的理论和明确规定。如限制游人量(风景公园平均每百米平方允许人活动，森林公园每百米平方最多容纳 33 人)等[7]。

2.2　国外森林公园的规划建设

2.2.1　美国森林公园规划指导思想

美国森林公园规划指导思想的演变经历了总体规划、综合行动规划和行动决策构架三个阶段。规划工作的重点，由以经济和美学价值为导向的旅游设施建设和视觉景观规划，转向为以“如何更好地保护资源为导向”的资源管理规划。国家公园功能重心由景观欣赏利用向生态资源保护转移。

2.2.2　美国国家公园设立标准

美国国家公园设立标准包括：①资源特征方面具有国家意义；②开发建设层面具有适宜性和可行性；③行政管理上要求由国家公园管理局直辖，并拥有详细的管理方案或手段[3]。

2.2.3　美国国家公园规划工作层次、程序及内容要点

美国国家公园的规划与决策强调规划工作内容的层次性；规划过程全面引入公众参与和中期管理机制；注重多方案的比较和多学科背景规划决策队伍的组织。美国国家公园现阶段规划的主要内容，包括软性规划和硬性规划两个方面。软性规划主要指解说、游客服务、教育、资源管理、监督以及基础研究方面的规划；硬性规划主要指对物质设施方面的规划，包括道路、建筑物、基础设施等；规划重点偏向于软性规划的内容，突出资源管理的目标。

2.3　国内森林公园总体规划建设

2.3.1　规划设计思路

森林公园是大自然的一个凝缩，它能为人们提供一个良好的生态环境。森林公园总体规划设计是森林公园建设中一项极为重要的工作，规划设计是对未来的一种设想和计划。而这种设想是建立在科学的基础上，经过努力，一定能实现。为此，森林公园的总体规划设计应根据旅游的需求，对森林公园景观资源的开发和保护制定出科学的方案，最大限度的发挥森

林公园的经济效益、社会效益及生态效益[8]。

针对森林公园的开发建设形势，应不断提高森林公园规划设计水平，最大限度为用户服好务。

2.3.2 规划设计指导思想

森林公园是以森林及其生态环境等自然景观为主体的郊野型公园，规划设计应突出其自然野趣，充分发挥游憩保健、休闲度假、科普科考、运动娱乐等多种功能。不同类型的森林公园具有不同的景色，游人参与的形式也各有侧重，且每一个森林公园的景观资源都有其独特的方面。规划设计时必须突出重点，发挥优势，归纳形成自身的风格和特性，将这些风格和特点以文字加以浓缩凝练，形成规划设计的指导思想[9]。

具体地说，对于自然景观类型的森林公园，规划设计应尽量做到保持原始的自然面貌，满足游客按照自己的意愿和兴趣观赏未经开发的自然环境；对于历史名胜类型的森林公园，应重点保护好园内的历史遗迹、名胜建筑，维护其自身的风格特点，以观赏学习历史文化或革命传统教育为主，不能凭空发展；对于综合性的森林公园，主要满足游客的游憩需求，如旅游度假、运动休闲等，并要为游客提供更多的游乐项目[10~11]。

2.3.3 森林公园的规划设计原则

第一：重点原则，重点原则就是要求因地制宜，突出旅游资源中最有特色的部分，强化公园的主体。森林景观是森林公园的主体。森林公园的规划与开发，应坚持以森林资源为依托，充分发挥林区潜在的能力，保持森林野趣，使森林景观资源来于自然美而胜于自然美。

第二：多元原则，多元原则就是要求从多方面不同程度地展示旅游资源的价值，体现公园的综合功能。在加强森林、自然、人文景观建设的同时，还要从发展旅游的角度，按风景区所拥有的性质和特色，配套建设与之相适应的旅游设施，讲究食、住、行、游、购、娱一条龙服务，多元化发展。

第三：可行原则，可行原则就是要求在符合技术、经济条件和社会、生态要求的前提下进行公园开发建设。公园规划建设必须符合国家基本建设管理程序，在总体规划设计的基础上做好小区扩初(施工)设计，并严格按批准的设计实施，不得随意变更。

第四：生态原则，生态原则就是要求注重景观资源保护和自然生态平衡，以保护为基础，以开发促保护。在保护森林生态环境的前提下，实现资源保护与公园开发相结合，以保护促旅游，以旅游养保护。公园建设必须有利于风景资源的保护，有利于环境质量的提高。

第五：协调原则，协调原则就是要求建设内容相互补充，景区意境相互融合，建设环境相互协调。森林公园规划和开发项目本身应相互协调，综合平衡。建筑物、构筑物应自然天成，注意与自然景观资源的协调和共生，讲求和谐的建筑风格和浓郁的地方气息[12~13]。

3 森林公园的总体规划

森林公园总体规划即有类同于风景名胜区的总体规划，结构安排与国营林场的森林经营方案相协调，尤其在附属工程建设等方面，其内容基本一致。总体规划的主要部分与特点及其处理方法归纳如下[14~16]：

3.1 基础资料

按照主管部门对森林公园总体规划的要求，多森林公园建设和总体规划有关的内容进行调查、收集、分析、整理成完整的基础资料。基础资料共包括5个部分：

第一，基本情况：即将总体规划中的基本情况纳入基础资料中，详细介绍森林公园的自然地理条件和社会经济状况。

第二，森林资源：概要介绍森林资源的统计数据、结构特征和发展趋势，以及森林动物资源。

第三，汇总与描述：根据风景资源的调查，进行全面的汇总，并按景区分类予以描述性介绍。

第四，介绍旅游状况：包括旅游设施和附近地去我的旅游景点，当地的旅游产品。

第五，题咏或文字选辑存：摘录古今中外知名人士对风景资源的赞颂和有关记载。

3.2 依托城镇

为了避免风景名胜建造旅游城镇的"破坏性建设"问题，我们在总体规划中提出森林公园开展森林旅游的依托城镇，既避免了"破坏性建设"，也可节约大量的基本建设投资。

3.3 功能区划

森林公园的功能区划应以国营林场的经营区划为基础，在实践上森林公园的保护区划与国营林场的林种区划相协调，以保证国营林场的正常经营活动。具体地讲，森林公园的建设在总体上不能影响国营林原有的林业生产的经营布局。

3.4 绿化美化

在绿化规划上注意运用林学、生态学和没美学理论，在保证绿化的基础上，美化森林环境，创造森林植物景观。保证绿化是绿化规划的基础，对于荒山我们应采取两种规划措施，在立地条件较差的地方，以保证绿化为重点，首先保证绿化起来；在立地条件允许的地方，绿化与美化相结合，绿化时根据景观要求，直接营造适合于景观要求的造林树种。

3.5 全面规划，重点突破

森林公园的风景资源是人类的宝贵财富，我们只有把它保护好，在保护的基础上合理开发利用。因此，我们必须对森林公园作详尽调查，细致分析，全面规划。

3.6 调查区划，反复推敲

风景资源的调查与景区区划方法必须反复调查和仔细地推敲，细心品味，道道技术与艺术的统一。

4 森林公园的管理

森林公园的建设管理更重要，自确定建园开始就涉及管理问题，科学地管理才能使人们在休息游览获得收益，达到陶冶情操、消除疲劳、提高学习工作效率的目的。也只有认真细致地加强管理，保护城市生态环境，满足人们日益增长的文化生活需要才有可能[17]。

(1)加强宣传，严格执行有关法规，有效地防止和制止各种破坏性活动和违章建设。

(2)培养一支有技术懂管理的干部队伍。森林公园经营管理工作是一项复杂而繁重的任务，培养好人才是搞好公园建设的关键。

(3)统一领导，分区包干，责任到人，发现问题，及时解决。

(4)开展科学研究，不断总结经验，促进管理，进一步提高管理水平。

(5)理顺管理体制，协调部门关系，健全管理机构。

5 我国森林公园现状评价

5.1 资源丰富

我国地域辽阔，历史悠久，旅游资源，特别是森林旅游资源十分丰富。森林本身不仅是一种重要的自然旅游资源，而且为其他自然、人文和社会旅游资源提供了良好的生态环境条件。在全国4200个国营林场中，拥有森论风景资源、具备旅游开发价值的就有600多处。自1982年由国家批准建立了我国第一个国家森林公园——张家界国家森林公园以来，到1992年底，国家已批准建立了森林公园255处，总面积达182.5万hm^2，分布在24个省(自治区、直辖市)。

5.2 发展迅速

我国森林公园经过20世纪80年代平均约以每年3个的速度稳步发展后，90年代进入了迅速发展阶段，森林公园数成倍增长。到1992年底，已发展到255个，其中近两年建立的森林公园，约是80年代建立森林公园总数的9倍，近年来的发展几乎呈直线上升的态势。

5.3 分布不均

我国现有的255个森林公园分布在全国24个省(自治区、直辖市)，河北、河南2省，分别只有1个森林公园。而安徽、浙江、湖北3省分别达到23、30和36个。森林公园的分布存在着东南多、西北少的趋势。这与我国的气候分布、经济分布、人口分布以及森林分布规律是基本一致的。

5.4 类型多样

由于我国森林公园的建设工作起步较晚，还没有统一的分类方法，但就其总体来讲可分为三类：第一类是自然景观类型的森林公园，公园主要是 以森林、山脉、湖泊、瀑布、冰川自然景观为主，如湖南省张家界森林公园、四川省九寨森林公园等；第二类是历史名胜类型的森林公园，公园以森林景观为衬托，以历史遗迹、名胜建筑、革命历史等人文景观为主，如陕西省楼观台森林公园、四川省剑门关森林公园；第三类为综合性的森林公园，这类森林公园集自然景观、人文景观和游乐设施于一体，公园多位于大、中城市的近郊，如四川省龙池森林公园等[18]。

5.5 效益不一

我国森林公园的建立才刚刚起步，缺乏相应的配套旅游设施、建设资金和管理经验等。因此，目前许多森林公园的效益还不高，有些甚至还没有真正开展森林旅游。

5.6 人才缺乏

目前，在我国森林公园的开发和管理方面，主要存在两个问题：一是缺乏专业人才；二是现有人员素质过低。森林公园的管理人员，大都是原来的林场职工，缺乏必要的专业只是和经营管理经验，经营水平低，管理方法落后，这是目前我国森林公园效益不高的主要原因之一[19]。

6 我国森林公园的发展预测

6.1 旅游人数将迅速增加

进入20世纪以来，由于全球经济的迅速发展和交通现代化进程的加快，大大推进了国际间的交往，旅游业以其独有的特点异军突起、迅猛发展。近几年来，随着旅游业的发展和旅游规模的不断扩大，国际旅游业也正在经历着一场新的革命。旅游者由贵族化走向平民化，旅游已成为越来越多居民物质文化生活的一部分旅游动机由单一性向多元化方向发展，内涵越来越丰富；旅游目的地由集中向分散方向发展，旅游者开始走向世界各个角落旅游流的结构由单向流动向双向流动变化，发展中国家的旅游者正在加入国际旅游者的队伍，给旅游业带来了巨大的发展潜力。同时，随着现代文明的发展，到本世纪年代，西方出现了“生态觉醒”，人们产生了“回归大自然”的强烈愿望。而森林旅游是一项独具特色的旅游业，能满足人们这种及其他多方面的需要。森林旅游作为一种绿色产业，已深入到世界各个角落，在国民经济中的地位日益突出。

根据国家旅游发展规划，到2000年，我国接待海外游人将达850万~900万人次，国内旅游人数将达到4.5亿~5亿人次。根据我国旅游业的现状和森林旅游的发展趋势，预计到2011年，我国每年进行森林旅游的将达到23亿人次以上。

6.2 森林公园将稳步发展

近年来，旅游点游人大幅度增长，大有人满为患的趋势，给我国旅游业带来了巨大的压力。为尽快改变我国旅游景点过于集中，旅游热点拥挤的被动局面，适应国内外旅游业迅速发展的需要，加快森林公园的建设步伐，大力发展森林旅游业已是大势所趋。为此，林业部召开森林旅游工作会议，要求凡是森林环境优美，生物资源丰富，自然景观和人文景观比较集中，具有观赏、文化、科研价值和一定规模，经过保护管理、合理经营和适度开发后，可供人们游览、观光、休息、疗养、科研、教育的国营林场，都要逐步建立森林公园。

6.3 经营管理将逐步规范

进入90年代以来，我国森林公园的数量急剧增加。为适应形势发展的需要，在全国森林公园工作会议前后，林业部筹备成立了森林公园管理办公室，从而结束了森林公园无专门机构管理的历史。随着管理机构、规章制度的建立和健全，随着建设资金的不断增加和专业人才的大量培养，我国的森林公园和森林旅游业，将逐步走上制度化、规范化的轨道[20]。

参考文献

[1]刘建立．浅谈森林公园规划设计．河北林业科技．2008，12(6)：63~65.
[2]谢莉，李梅．城市森林公园概念的界定．四川林勘设计，2010，6(2)
[3]高翅．森林公园刍议[J]．中国园林，1997，13(6)：7~8.
[4]兰思仁．国家森林公园理论和实践[M]．北京：中国林业出版社，2004.
[5]杨会娟，李春友，刘金川．中国森林公园游憩机会谱系(CFROS)构建初探[J]．中国农学报，2010，26(15)：407~410.
[6]森林公园专题研究．北京山合水易规划设计院[J]．2010，4.
[7]古新仁，刘苑秋．森林公园规划建设建议[J]．江西林业科技，1995，2：40~43.
[8]林业部调查规划设计院．中华人民共和国国家标准[S]．国家森林公园设计规范．2005.
[9]唐正良，刘安兴．森林公园总体规划技术与理论探讨[J]．浙江林业科技．1994，14(3)：43~49.
[10]李文胜．森林公园规划设计探讨[J]．现代农业科技．2009，12：28~32.
[11]韩业全．森林公园规划设计的探讨[J]．林业科技情报．2003，35(4)：64~66.
[12]章礼拐．森林公园开发规划的基本原则[J]．华东森林经理．1997，11(2)：38~41.
[13]中华人民共和国林业行业标准．森林公园总体设计规范[S]．LY/T5132—95
[14]熊志平．我国森林旅游与森林公园规划若干问题的探讨[J]．中南林业调查规划，1995，(4)：39~40.

[15]李沁，张剑英．谈国家森林公园总体规划及其完善问题[J]．山西林业科技，1994，(3)：41～43.
[16]吕忠义．森林公园总体规划理论与技术的探讨[J]．华东森林经理，2000，(1)：1～9.
[17]王长安．论我国森林公园建设和森林旅游业在林业及国民经济中的地位与作用[J]．林业资源管理，1997，(5)：61～63.
[18]杨保国．浅谈森林公园规划设计[J]．四川林勘设计．1999.2：38～40.
[19]黄尚绎．浙江森林公园现状与发展的探索．华东森林经理．1993，1(7)：45～48.
[20]李世东．我国森林公园的现状及发展趋势．中南林学院学报．1994，14(2)：163～167.

三、学科建设

森林经理：森林的可持续经营与适应性管理

徐国祯
（中南林业科技大学）

摘要：研究森林经理学科的发展，包括对我国森林经理工作实践的总结，是关系到加强我国森林经营工作极其重要的一个方面。由于对森林经理的性质、概念、名称以及对建国以来森林经理工作实践的评价存在着认识上的不一致。这就更加需要学术界不同见解的交流、质疑、综合，尤其需要利用跨学科研究的优势对森林经理的过去和未来进行剖析。本文就这方面的问题发表一些看法，目的是抛砖引玉，求真务实。

关键词：森林经理；可持续森林经营；适应性管理

Abstract：Research the development on the course of the forest management sum up the experience of the practice forest management in china is very important , how to develop forest management. Due to the difference views on the characters、ideas、names and its practices in new china of this course, so it is necessary the academic exchange and through consultation different views , especially using the superiority of multi – disciplinary、interdisciplinary and its integrated approach , to counter the past and feature of the forest management carry on system analysis . In this paper author issue an opinion and so that others may follow suit and seek common ground while reserving difference.

Keywords：forest management；sustainable forest management；adaptive forest management

一、森林经理形成与发展的回顾

森林经理作为一门学科形成于 18 世纪，背景是当时工业革命的兴起和科学技术的发展。一门学科发展总是有时代的背景，它离不开社会的发展、科学技术的进步以及生产的需求。学科的发展既有相对稳定的一面，又必须与时俱进。所以它有一定的阶段性，相对稳定性和连续性。因此重要的不仅是名称上，同时也在于对概念、性质和内涵的界定上。

概念是人们在反复实践中将事物共同的本质特点抽提出来加以概括，从感性上升到理性认识的过程与成果，并经得起实践检验。概念反映了对象本质的一种思维方式。所以概念也总是一个时代的哲学思想和人们思考问题、解决问题思想方法的反映。而理论体系则是通过某个概念范畴出发，能合乎逻辑地展示全部框架内容，并由相关知识构成一定的知识体系。

森林经理是从公元 14 世纪到 18 世纪由德奥等国创立而形成一门学科的。初期森林经理是以确定森林采伐量和进行林木估价为主要任务。因此曾命名“森林评价”（Forest taxation，1788）“森林估价”（Forstabsch · tzung，1926），进而更加重视森林的永恒保续，所以有“森林收获调整”(Waldertragsregulierung，1841)的涵义。再进而为了森林如何能保持永续收获，必须研究森林内部构成，即着眼于生产组织，因之名为“森林作业统制”(Forst betriebsegulierung，1865)，最后采用森林经理(Forst einrichtung)这个名称，德文“einrichtung”一词具有组织、安排、调节、建立秩序的意思。其实质是：“以最高货币回报选择树种，以给定立地的最高内部收益率确定经济轮伐期”。“森林经理在德国萌芽，曾把森林分为蓄积、利用、保持三个主要部分。”并在生长量、蓄积量、采伐量之间形成一种时间空间和时空相结合的结构和秩序，实现森林永续利用。也只有这样，“林业才有作为‘业’而存在的条件，以此为对象，形成了森林经理学体系。”[1~2]所以它是既有理论研究，即森林永续利用理论和法正林(Normal Forest)学说作为基本理论，又以编制森林施业计划作为实践任务而发展起来的一门学科。早期森林经理的概念中十分强调木材的“经济与永续”，它是建立在地租理论基础上，并形成了它们的数学表达式。从而形成了当时以森林经营的经济合理性和生产持续性为主要特征的知识体系与技术体系，并以取得经济活动收益最大化为目标，形成一整套森林永续经营利用理论。其内涵包括：组织森林经营，建立生产秩序，编制施业方案，为实现永续而不断调整。这也和早年美国林学家 Filbet Roch 给森林经理下的定义有相似之处，即“建立并维持一个有秩序的企业”(“Setting up，putting in order，and keeping in order a forest business”1925)[3]既然，这个企业是以能永续作业的，是“蒙受经济上尽可能小的风险获取尽可能的最大收益”这一概念上的地租理论。应该说当时这门学科涉及的领域是宽泛的，包括了生物的、技术的、经济的、社会的、管理的诸多方面。但当时的主要领域是技术与经济。所以美国森林经理学家 K·P·戴维斯曾认为：“森林经理学是综合性显著，对技术经济问题进行分析和抉择的管理学科。”(1966)早期德国著名森林经理学家瓦格尔(C. Wanger)提出森林经理的三个实践任务是：①确定林业企业经营目标，选择合理利用立地的途径与确定生产周期的生产成果；②制定造林、保护、收益的组织和技术措施；③提出确保森林永续利用的收获调整法。“他以为森林经理非自成为一科学，而系采撷数种独立科学范围之立意而成为一实用科学。”[4]用今天的话讲，它是一门综合性的应用学科。同时，由于它符合当时商品林经营的要求，所以才 具有一定发展的生命力延续至今。

处在21世纪的今天，随着资源和环境等的生态问题的严峻形势，森林经理不仅是只追求经济的合理性，同时也要追求生态的合理性。从长期考虑经济发展与环境的关系出发，更应该是在寻求生态系统稳定的基础上追求经济的稳定与合理。所以，“森林这一主题涉及环境与发展的整个范围的问题和机会，包括在持续发展的基础上进行社会发展的权利在内。”(《关于森林问题原则声明》世界环发大会，1992)。因而“森林是人类的前途、是维护地球生态平衡的保障，从生态的、经济的、社会的意义上讲，面积足够大的、健康的和谨慎经营的森林生态系统存在，对于我们人类之生存是必不可少的”(联合国粮农组织前总干事 萨乌马，1991)。由此可见，森林问题是一个涉及自然、经济、社会、文化等诸多方面的问题，是一类由极其复杂因素相互作用的复杂性问题。森林和林业的问题已远远超出它们自身的范围，是一个带有系统性，全面性，即社会性的问题。所以人类从来没有像今天这样认识到森林除了它的经济意义外，更重要的是它的生态意义和社会意义。

所谓综合学科是指研究社会现象、自然现象中多个领域的一门科学，因而它往往涵盖多个学科领域。这也正是由于近代科学发展中出现了许多与自然、经济、社会密切相关的重大问题，需要多学科交叉、综合研究，因而形成了一批交叉学科、综合学科。例如空间科学、环境科学、生命科学、生态科学等等。科学本身是人为划分的，而科学问题是客观存在的，所以当代科学在高度分化基础上高度综合也是一种发展的必然趋势。显然，随着对森林认识的深入森林经理也越来越发展成为一门研究森林经营复杂问题的综合学科。

这里特别值得提出的是，20 世纪中叶，系统科学与生态科学的崛起和发展对整个时代发展起着不可估量的意义。两门科学都是把世界作为一个完整的不可分割的整体看待，系统科学的认识论和方法论，生态科学的整体观和发展观，它们的重大意义在于重新认识世界是不可分割的整体，特别是把人类引回了自然界。人是自然界的一个重要组成部分，人类又能主观能动地影响自然界，包括积极的和消极的方面，建设的和破坏的方面。人类社会每时刻都在和自然界进行着物质、能量、信息的交换。“这种关系一旦被打乱或停止下来，人类就无法继续生存了。”[5]这两门科学极大地改变了人们的思维方式和对生产方式的认识，同时也对资源和环境管理方式产生了极其深刻的影响。当 20 世纪下半叶，全球生态与环境处在十分严峻的形势下，它们的意义尤其重大。正像未来学家阿尔温·托夫勒在《第三次浪潮》一书中所指出：“生态论者与系统论者观点一致，对综合性及知识完整性，进行着共同的斗争。”为此，我们必须从认识论和方法论上解决“全面而不是片断地观察问题”（西蒙·拉莫 Simon. Ramo）。当威胁到人类生存与发展的资源与环境问题，特别需要强调“全面、协调与可持续发展”时，人们认识到世界文明的发展只能走可持续发展这条路。

生态科学和系统科学对林业发展的影响是巨大的，体现在：①对森林和林业的重新定位，森林是一类开放的复杂的巨系统，林业也是一类与社会、经济、自然紧密结合的复合生态系统，它们都具有复杂的层次结构和功能关系；②对森林资源和环境管理的好坏，相对于自然生态环境和社会经济环境变化来说，它们存在着严重的滞后效应，一般有 20～30 年时差。所谓“认识既晚，改正也难”；③和森林有关的资源与环境的变化，充满着“变化－复杂性－不确定性－冲突”，即存在着动态的非线性和不确定性关系。从上述几点出发，在哲学思想上提出要把整体论和还原论相结合。这正和迅猛发展的生态科学为寻求生态系统的整体性，合理性，为可持续性的森林经营理论与实践奠定了科学发展的基础。系统科学及其体系不仅具有理论价值，还有重要的实践意义。对于林业的实践，森林经营的实践来说，它们都是社会实践，森林经理作为组织森林经营的社会实践特别要求有整体性、目的性和组织性。如何把不同的科学技术，不同层次的知识综合集成起来，形成指导林业与森林经营社会实践的理论、方法和技术，以解决社会实践中的问题，不论从系统科学，生态科学，乃至森林经理学都存在一个认识论、方法论和价值观转变的问题。

这里还值得提出的另一门科学技术，就是当代信息科学的发展，以致有人把 21 世纪作为信息化的信息时代和生态化的生态时代相提并论。当代科学与技术的发展需要现代信息技术、空间分析技术和计算机技术，以带动森林经营技术实现数字化和信息化的跨越。而以现代生态科学为基础的空间优化技术紧密依赖现代空间分析技术、信息技术、计算机技术和数值分析技术。所有这些，无疑给森林经理在组织森林经营以及资源与环境的管理上，提高到经理在解决不确定性和动态性的资源和环境管理的技术方法上起到不可估量的作用。

二、森林经理内涵中的两个重要方面——森林可持续经营与森林适应性管理

森林经理从它的内涵来看，包括了两个重要的方面：一是合理组织森林经营，朝着可持续的森林经营（森林可持续经营 Sustainable Forest Management）方面发展；二是科学管理森林

资源，使得和森林相关的资源和环境朝着适应性管理(adaptive management)方向发展。

(一)"组织"的概念和内涵

"组织"是人类最普遍的社会现象，它是一个有目标的人群活动和一定的技术系统有机的结合，并按照特定关系组成一定模式工作的统一体。所以要了解系统内部例如：森林经理内部格各个要素间的相互关系。以及与系统外部，即环境各要素间的相互关系，以及系统内外要素间的互动关系。林业经营的对象—森林，正是一个对外开放的，并且与外部环境不断发生着物质、能量，信息交换的动态的、开放的系统。传统森林经理研究的是森林内部木材生长量、蓄积量、利用量之间的关系。它的外部环境主要是市场和经济价值。现代森林经理正随着森林价值观念的转变，森林多资源，多功能效益的合理经营和永续利用，它的社会化程度越来越高。森林的多少，经营的好坏将影响到国民经济许多部门。所以，过去那种只从林业内部，只从经济效益着眼的森林经营显然不能适应现今森林经营管理的要求。当代林业发展是建立在林业生态建设发展战略的基础上，这就是说要适应生态建设、循环经济与和谐社会的三者统一要求，也就是把林业的生态效益，经济效益和社会效益紧密地结合起来。所以，这是项复杂的组织管理(经营)的工作，也就是过去常说的："森林经理是一系列复杂工作的综合。"从林业部门整体来讲，这是一项组织管理工作；从作为一个企业来讲，则既包含组织经营(森林可持续经营)又包含组织管理(森林适应性管理)这两方面的工作内容。

所以"组织"当做名词来理解，是指某种事物的有序存在方式，既事物由一定的组成要素结合成一定层次结构、功能存在的形式和运作关系。例如作为林业最基层的单位，一个企业，一个林场，一个经营单位就是一类组织。而组织作为一类活动，既动态过程的理解，包括：①在一个组织中有一定的共同目标，共同的愿景；②包含有若干组成要素，形成一种稳定的结构关系；③在森林经营中组织又是一种社会现象，就是说资源与环境的社会管理，涉及"人管"和"管人"；④组织经常要从实际情况出发，做出规划和决定决策的实施，例如编制森林经营方针。所以"组织"当动词来理解是一种活动，经营与管理的活动与过程。森林经营正是通过一系列的造林、营林技术来实现经营目的，包括从采种、育苗、造林、抚育、保护、采伐、更新。这一系列造林营林过程是围绕着一定目标"组织之，经营之。"它们是不可以孤立肢解的、杂乱无章的，它们靠的是通过森林经理工作从森林区划，组织森林经营类型(作业级)、确定森林经营周期(森林成熟)，制定森林经营技术体系(作业法)，最后，通过一定的经营方式，形成在可持续森林经营的理论指导下，组织成为一种可持续经营，即永续经营的有序的技术体系。

(二)管理的概念和内涵

而"管理"就是这用组织、计划、协调、指导、控制、调整等基本活动，以便充分利用人力、资金、设备、资源、市场等要素，使其相互组合，达成某个经营单位(林场)的目标和任务。即以它必然要通过上述一系列管理职能来实现的，例如，通过定期的森林调查去反映，掌握管理对象的全部森林资源、森林经营信息；通过规划的职能对森林经营的未来做出谋划与憧憬；通过区别的职能以建立起一定区域内林业上生态、经济、社会环境相适应的互动关系；通过组织职能使得森林资源在长期动态变化的经营过程中，使管理对象的结构不断调整以适应发展的目标与功能，而且能够在整体指导下，区别对待，分类指导。最后通过控制调整这个职能，使森林经营对象能整合成为一个有序的时空结构，按照已定目标使管理对象从一种状态向另一种比较理想的状态转移，形成一种系统化、有序化、生态化、产业化，社会化管理的过程。

（三）森林的可持续经营与适应性管理

从早期的森林永续利用到今天的森林可持续经营，尽管“森林永续作业”的精神没有过时，但它的内涵和实现途径已经有了很大的发展与改变，从单目标到多目标、多途径、多方案选优，这就体现在第十一届世界林业大会安塔利亚宣言中所指出的那样：“森林可持续经营是一种包括政治，经济，法律，社会，以及科学与技术等手段的行为，涉及天然林和人工林。它是长期的有计划的通过各种人为干预措施，目的是保护和维持森林生态系统及其各种功能。”[6]所以它完整地体现了森林经营在目标、结构、功能、过程与环境之间的动态统一。所以它既是一个组织森林可持续经营的过程，又是一个组织森林适应性管理的过程。

今天，包括森林经营在内的资源与环境管理，正发展成为的一种适应性管理的过程。这正是由于在人类经营下的森林资源充满着变化、不确定性、动态性和复杂性，充满着矛盾、冲突与管理。所谓适应性管理是指“规划和管理标准对于正在改变的生物物理学科和人类目标必须要有充分灵活性”。[7]它是对资源和环境管理不确定性的一种对策，它包括下列内容：①只有不断学习，建立学习型组织才能适应今天这个社会出现的变化和复杂性；②不断获取信息对信息管理，才能与时俱进；③尊重历史，尊重经验，特别是需要把信息、知识、智慧和经验结合起来；④资源与环境管理需要社会的广泛参与和社区共管。总之，森林资源的适应性管理是指在森林生态系统功能和社会对林业的需求两个方面建立起可测定目标，通过控制、科学管理、监测和调整等活动（手段）以满足森林（生态系统）可能达到的经济目标，社会目标和生态目标。

适应性管理也是针对传统管理中存在的问题：①单一目标和对目标、政策完整性的肢解；②单一关注的尺度和标准，即缺少综合与整合；③没有注意到所有政策都带有一定程度的试验性质，包括成功与失败，需要不断调整；④以往的管理者缺乏弹性，往往是一锤定音；⑤不能进一步量化，缺少量化的依据，或者说是缺乏一种非线性动态管理。

所有这些，对于森林经理来说，它的重要意义在于综合，利用跨学科研究的综合；在政策执行上采用弹性政策，例如在限额采伐与采伐限额的管理上；要采用适应性政策代替僵化了的政策；要充分利用计算机信息管理的优势，不断监控，及时调整改变着的森林资源态势。所以森林经理工作两大重要任务是：森林可持续经营与适应性管理，体现为：“可行在技术，成效在管理。”

三、中国森林经理学科建设与森林经理工作发展的回顾

新中国成立前，从晚清到民国初，基本上没有进行过系统的森林经理工作，只对部分林区作过勘察。日本帝国主义侵占我国台湾和东北时期，为了掠夺森林资源曾进行过调查和规划，其目的只是为了掠夺我国森林资源，谈不上按规划执行。至于抗日战争时期农林部先后曾在西北、西南地区设立九个国有林区管理处，还在西北、华中、华南地区设立水源林区，这些机构都勘查管辖范围内的森林，大都是根据生产需要进行的。当时的解放区陕甘宁边区也分区考察了所在地的森林资源。[8]真正开展全国性森林资源调查是从建国初期在林垦部成立了“四司一室”（即林政司、森林经理司、造林司、森林利用司和办公室）之后，在前苏联专家的指导下，组成了森林经理、土壤、制表、更新、林型、病虫害、航测、航调等专业队伍。从1950～1962年间在全国2.95亿hm^2林区面积上，进行了不同方法，不同精度森林资

源清查。而第一次全国资源清查是1973~1976年运用数理统计理论为基础的抽样调查方法进行的，一直延续至今已进行了七次。至于说到森林经营方案的编制、审查，也曾进行过多次。特别是20世纪50年代中，在东北配合森林经理调查编制了森林施业案，成立了森林经营所，甚至派出了一批高等学校的林学专业毕业生担任森林经营所所长(1955)，由于种种原因，大都没有坚持下去。应当说这一阶段为全国森林经理的工作奠定了物质、技术、人才基础，成绩是巨大的，特别是1958年出版了中国第一部《森林经理规程》，以及编制了相关的各种技术规定，这就为以后的森林经理和森林经营奠定了基础。尽管它在很多方面还存在着照搬了前苏联森林经营管理模式的弊病，但毕竟在我国从无到有，而且为国民经济第一个五年计划提供森林资源数据，也为克服建国初的三年经济国难作出了贡献。

这个时期高等学校的森林经理学科从1952年起开始翻译前苏联莫托维洛夫著的《森林经理学》[9]作为高等学校教材。1955年由苏联专家B·B·巴姆菲洛夫在北京林学院培养了一批森林经理研究生，连同进修教师和干部近百人，讲授了森林经理学和航空在林业上应用二门课，以及编写了从教学实习，生产实习，毕业实习，课程设计，教学方法指导书等，从而为中国森林经理学科建设、人才培养、科学研究奠定了一定的基础。此后在1959~1960年期间，在林业高等院校华北协作区、华东协作区先后又结合中国国情编著了《森林经理学》和《森林经营规划学》。[10]

早在20世纪50年代初，也曾暴露出森林经营和森林经理工作中学习前苏联存在的一定问题，特别是东北林区采伐方式和更新方式上的争论以及森林经理调查方法上存在的问题。集中起来讲，就是前苏联计划经济体制和粗放的森林经营方式，如对东北原始森林采取的大面积集中皆伐和人工更新方针，曾引起学术界关于东北森林经营方式的学术争论，这种粗放的经营方式结果也是导致了东北林区过伐的重要原因之一，典型的如伊春林区原始林的消失。尽管当时也有形势的需要，但学术分歧也是客观存在。

此后的年代，由于中国处在连续不断的政治运动中，政策多变，体制不稳，可以说每一次大的政治运动总是带来一次次森林资源的大破坏。特别是1958年调查队层层下放，到1960年虽有所恢复，但是在1966年"文化大革命"全国林业调查规划设计队伍第二次下放或撤销。在此期间提出了许多有悖于科学森林经营的口号，例如："大砍大造"、"造多于伐"。"造是永续"把整个森林经营简单归纳为：两个方面，即"造与伐"；两项指标，即"森林覆盖率与森林蓄积量"，而对森林资源结构组成，森林的生产率的低下，森林多种功能效益的发挥没有得到应有重视，真正事关全局的"以营林为基础"和森林经营这个根本，始终没有落在实处。总之，我国森林经营管理的问题是带有系统性，全面性，整体性的问题。但是也不可否认在此期间我们做了许多基础性研究工作，例如，全国森林主地条件类型划分，中国林业区划，中国生态林业理论与实践的研究，林业系统工程研究，中国社区林业发展的研究以及在此期间编制了各种森林经营技术数表和技术规定。同时在东北吉林省汪清林业局对东北原始林采伐方式经营方式的研究；甘肃小陇山天然次生林改造的研究。广东省雷州林业局桉树人工林经营模式研究，以及南方集体林区杉木人工林永续经营方式的研究等，都取得了十分宝贵的经验。至于改革开放的年代，我们在林业和森林经营各个方面更跨上了一个新台阶。

中国林业发展虽然取得一定的成绩，但走过了一条曲折艰难的道路。总体上来讲，一是缺乏一种明确的指导思想；二是没有坚实的理论基础作指导，特别是结合中国的国情、林情、民情的内容；三是经济体制的和经营机制上的问题严重束缚了林业的发展；四是在森林经营管理方法上的严重滞后，缺乏全面协调，综合集成。出路是认真学习“科学发展观”，从思想、理论、方法、手段上，从林业与社会、经济、生态、文化的相互关系上落实“以人为本，全面、协调与可持续发展”的科学发展观，通过综合集成的方法一体化地解决问题。

四、学科建设的若干设想和做法

(1)森林经理研究的对象是一类开放的复杂巨系统，森林经理研究的问题必然是一类复杂性问题，所以对它采取的方法必然是从整体出发、区别对待、分类指导、从定性到定量综合集成的方法。

(2)学科建设必须本着继承与发展，改革与创新的原则，重要的是在研究学科体系是如何形成和发展的基础上，研究森林经理学科交叉、综合的科学性，使学科交叉综合符合森林经理固有的规律，而不能任意肢解、拼凑。

(3)森林经理学科与森林经理工作是两个既相区别又紧密联系的概念。“学也者，观察事物而发明其真理者也；术也者，取其发明之真理而致诸用者也。”“学主理，术主用”(梁启超)是一种理论与实践的关系。当前，中国森林经理缺乏的正是能结合国情、林情、民情的科学理论指导，迫切需要总结自己的，借鉴国外的理论与实践。

(4)用系统论的整体思维把以木材生产为中心的永续利用理论，转向以森林生态系统的可持续发展为内涵，通过保持生物多样性和生态系统的完整性、稳定性来维持产品和服务永续收获的目标。再通过林业区划和区域规划以及森林经营区划，研究森林经营“整体上统筹兼顾，局部上分而治之”的区别对待、分类指导、分类经营的具体途径。

(5)总结研究中国行之有效的不同森林经营模式，并上升到理论高度。例如有上千年历史的杉木人工林农林间作复合经营模式。楠竹林笋竹两用择伐永续作业模式。桐树，桉树人工林短轮伐期可持续经营模式，天然次生林工程封山育林模式，东北天然林“采育兼顾伐”模式，北方山区小流域综合治理生态经济沟模式等等。此外还必须高度重视集体林区社区共管、社会广泛参与的社区林业模式(Community Forestry)。

(6)在研究不同类型森林经营模式时，研究并修订森林经营的各项技术经济指标、各种数表以及各项技术规定和规程，最终形成以各类森林作业法为核心的森林经营技术体系。

(7)认真总结新中国成立以来森林经营方案从编制到执行过程中的问题。为何绝大多数不能执行，要从经营机制、管理体制上，从技术、资金、人才等外部环境配套上，从森林经营方案形式内容上认真总结。然后通过不同地区、不同类型试点、研究、总结后，再加以铺开，不要一哄而上，千篇一律。

(8)森林经营人才培养是当务之急。全国29778个林业站，16万余职工，在调研1429个林业站中，具有本科学历的仅735人占职工总数3.85%，具有高级职称的职工占1.6%，中级职称的占21%。更重要的是“分布下，留不住”、“不能适应基层需要”。[11]这是一个亟待解决的重大问题。

五、几点结论

(1)森林经理是实现林业目标和任务不可或缺的重要手段。它的主要任务是：通过组织森林经营，合理利用人类干预自然和充分发挥自然力作用，制定出的一种中长期林业发展战略决策和规划(森林经营方针),并通过不断实践、调整,以便充分发挥森林的整体效益、多种效益和综合效益。

(2)森林经理的对象—森林生态系统是一类开放的、复杂的巨系统。它的影响和作用已远远超出森林自身的范围,所以林业是一类与社会、经济、自然紧密结合的复合生态系统,即复杂系统。这就决定了森林经理所要研究解决的问题是复杂性问题。它必须依靠多学科,跨学科,综合研究的方法研究森林经营的复杂性。

(3)森林经理研究对象的主体是人,是各类产权主体;而它研究的客体是各类森林(生态系统)。所以作为资源与环境管理的森林必须是包含“人管”和“管人”。正像生态问题不能从社会问题中分割出来一样,人和自然的关系实际上是人和人之间关系的反映。所以森林经理必须采取自然科学和社会科学一体化综合研究的方法。

(4)作为一项工作,森林经理是一系列复杂工作的结合;作为一门学科,它体现为多学科的交叉综合,是一门综合学科。但仅仅定性为综合学科是不够的,它所涉及的知识正在不断扩大,不仅在生物学、生态学、经济学领域,而且在社会学领域,包括对人在资源与环境管理中的地位给予正确的评价。这就是在广泛的社会领域中看到越来越多的管理问题。因而它是组织森林可持续经营和对森林适应性管理的一门综合性的管理学科(Management Science)是作为一级学科的林学和同是一级学科的管理学科的交叉学科下二级学科,再往下则是三级学科,包括像林木测算,森林资源信息管理,林业系统工程等等。显然,森林经理作为林学一级学科下的二级学科位置是比较合适。

(5)正是由于森林经理研究的对象是开放的复杂巨系统,是一类复杂性问题。所以对它的研究应当体现在思想、理论、方法、手段上的“四统一”。即把森林作为开放的复杂巨系统对待,形成一种系统思想。研究它们的组成要素、结构、功能、过程和外部环境;同时把森林可持续经营作为基本理论,研究组织可持续经营理论;用广义的生态系统方法和途径,以及组织管理的技术手段—系统工程,运用钱学森教授提出的,“开放的复杂巨系统理论和从定性到定量综合集成的方法”[12],把它作为一门综合性的管理(含经营)学科来对待。

(6)中国有五千年悠久的农林业历史文化。它具有极其丰富的林业遗产。正像有的学者所指出的那样,中国传统文化中有“术”而无“学”。这一点正需要我们从十分丰富的祖国农林业文化遗产和结合当代林业发展丰富的实践中。加上借鉴国外先进的森林经理理论与实践,通过继承、发展、改革、创新,研究并走出一条富有中国特色的森林经理之路。

参考文献

[1]周桢. 森林经理学[M]. 台北:国立编译馆,1967.

[2]井上由扶. 森林经理学[M]. 陆苏兆等,译. 北京:中国林业出版社,1980.

[3]Charles Hstoodard, essentials of foresty practical——3edition 1978 by John & Sons inc p142.

[4]周桢. 森林经理学[M]. 台北:国立编译馆,1967.

[5]陈敏豪. 生态文化 无影灯 森林经理. 中南林业调查规划,2001(增刊):15~18.

[6]森林可持续经营的标准和指标[G]//森林可持续经营1998(北京)学术研讨会论文集. 林业资源管理(特刊),1998.

[7](加拿大)布鲁斯. 米切尔,资源与环境管理[M]. 北京:商务印书馆,2004.

[8]熊大桐等. 中国近代林业史[M]. 北京:中国林业出版社,1989.

[9]北京林学院森林经理教研组. 森林经理学[M]. 北京:农业出版社,1961.

[10]华东华中区高等林学院(校)教学用书，森林经营规划学[M]. 北京：中国林业出版社，1959.
[11]刘于鹤等. 人才问题已成为制约森林经营的瓶颈，中国老科学技术工作者协会林业分会，2010 年 12 月(内部材料).
[12]钱学森. 一个科学新领域——开放的复杂巨系统及其方法论//钱学森. 论地理科学，杭州：浙江教育出版社，1994.

中国森林经理再探讨
——森林经理学科滑坡诊断

詹昭宁
（国家林业局资源司）

摘要：本文分析森林经理学科滑坡的内因和外因，以期从反思中求得森林经理的振兴。
关键词：森林经营；森林经理；永恒主题

前　言

本文所指的“森林经理”，狭义是指森林经理学科，广义则指包含：森林经理工作、森林经理学科、森林经理学等。自从20世纪70年代开展“森林资源连续清查”以后，“森林经理”在林业高等院校，普遍受重视，有的被列为省、部甚至国家重点学科。20世纪80年代北京林业大学的森林经理学科进入国家重点学科，90年代末国家重点学科资格被否定（后来又重新定为重点学科）。这个马鞍形的变化，影响了全国林业院校森林经理学科，也影响了全国的森林经理工作。其标志是引发了森林经理大滑坡。近10年来，情况并没有好转。本文目的是为了振兴中国的森林经理，包括学科建设及在生产中的应用。为避免诊断结果“以偏概全”，请同行学者不吝赐教。

1　造成森林经理学科滑坡的内部原因

俗语说：“良药苦口利于病，忠言逆耳利于行。”一个事件的发生，总是由外因通过内因起作用造成的。

1.1　“森林经理”名称之争是对森林经理事业的伤害

1962年后，对“森林经理”的名称争论不休。由于“森林经理”一词直译自日文，有人认为令人费解。因此，建议译为“森林调查规划”、“森林调查设计”、“森林经营规划”或“森林经营管理”等等。有人说在日本“森林经营方案”也叫“森林计划”。以上种种，各有各的看法和理由，莫衷一是，难于统一。结果至今仍维持使用原有的“森林经理”名称。其实，名称，尤其是学科的名称，因其不是普通用语，所以没有必要一定要让“全民”都能理解，只要业内人士明白就行了。比如20世纪50年代林业业内人士都清楚“森林经理”是干什么的。再如“拓扑”一词则非专家不能窥其奥。

1.2　森林经理学科建设没有与时俱进

从广义来说，森林经理学科包括森林经理学本身，还包括外围支撑学科：测树学和遥感在林业中的应用，组成森林经理大学科。反思在这三方面，虽有进步，但进步不大，创新不多。

1.2.1 森林经理的内涵

森林经理原来是研究森林经营的，主要研究用材林实现永续作业、永续利用。森林经理工作的范畴原来包括：森林资源清查、森林经理调查和作业设计等三类。（森林经理调查又根据森林经营强度，调查的细致程度分三个等级，如森林公园调查属于经营强度最高的三级调查。）我们的森林经理（包括森林经理工作和教科书）从苏联引进后，由于没有和我国的森林经营实际情况很好结合，更谈不上有针对性地对不同林区的经营有创新的方法。教学上只能是从概念到概念。有的大专院校虽有实习林场，但也没有总结出多少实践经验来指导周边的林场实施科学营林。在理论上也没有突出的创新。有人说森林经理是一门技术学科，有的说是经济技术学科，争论也是概念、内涵的范畴，很少结合生产。几十年来开了无数研讨会，讨论的内容总也挣不脱这个怪圈

商品林（主要是用材林）为达到永续作业、永续利用的目的，要求编“森林经营方案”。对公益（生态）林、特用林和薪炭林等林种，要不要编森林经营方案？据《森林法》第十六条规定：“各级人民政府应当制定林业长远规划。国有林业企业事业单位和自然保护区，应当根据林业长远规划，编制森林经营方案，报上级主管部门批准后实行。林业主管部门应当指导农村集体经济组织和国有的农场、牧场、工矿企业等单位编制森林经营方案。”这说明编森林经营方案是针对所有林种的。而我们的教材，过去偏重于用材林，如计算轮伐期、回归年等等内容。对其他林种如何经营缺乏系统的研究与理论提升，因此，反映在教科书上就是一片空白。

笔者认为森林经理的核心，简言之，是叙述不同森林类型的作业理论与操作方法。如最近特别推崇的德国“近自然森林”（原称为“近自然林业”。侯元兆订正为“近自然森林”。）。有人称它为“经营模式”，笔者认为把它看作“作业方法”更为贴切。“培育近自然森林的林学体系是‘近自然育林’。近自然森林是一种森林类型。近自然育林是一种育林理念。它的核心作业体系或作业法，是‘目标树作业体系’”（侯元兆）。在德国和法国“目标树作业体系”普遍用于培育耐阴性乡土阔叶树种，营造复层、混交、异龄林。“目标树”多选那些珍贵的、市场上需求量大的、价格高的阔叶树培育大径材。基本特点是依靠天然更新的自然力生长，通过人工选择培育“目标树”，实行科学疏伐。疏伐时对不同生长期的林木，采取保持不同生长空间来保证“目标树”的营养需要。对比之下，不管是“作业法”也好，是“经营模式”也好，总之我们的教材缺乏类似的实验资料。再说，过去《森林经理学》教材中不讲“作业法”，而是在《森林生态学》中讲，后来在《森林培育学》中讲。但是讲的多是幼林抚育范畴，不包括成林后的培育技术。从这方面来说，我们的林学教材连接也没有形成系统。

1.2.2 60年一贯制

我们的森林经理学教材和森林经理工作，都是20世纪50年代从苏联全面引进的。对这些技术，有的我们有所改动。比如苏联采用方格调查法区划林班，我们改为综合区划法。从大的方面看没有太多的改动。1957年在广东怀集县做集体林森林经理，套用的是国有林森林经理的指导思想。几年工夫，把怀集县的林子全砍光了。直到1982年在全国造林设计工作会上，他们才对此做法不满。因为砍光了怀集的丰富森林，使其沦落为穷县。又如，由于十分复杂的原因造成东北国有林区无林可采时，出现了资源危机，这时有的学者认为是实行了错误的“大木头挂帅”指导思想造成的。于是呼吁要实行“多功能经营”。但是对“多功能经

营”我们也只是停留在概念上。回想1985年资源司林业区划办公室将河南省西峡县创造的，通过培训万名农民规划员，引导农民脱贫致富的经验，总结为“集体林区森林经理的西峡模式”的事实，我们森林经理的一些学者对此并不认同。认为西峡县的农民在林地种龙须草、山茱萸、猕猴桃不属于森林经理的内容。再如，囿于固有的森林经理概念，对待南方种杉的丰富经验缺乏勇气去总结，对广东珠江三角洲的“桑基鱼塘模式”、江苏北部里下河地区的“农林复合经营模式”，也都没有引起森林经理学者的关注，认为和传统的森林经理概念合不上，没能在理论上加以总结，更谈不上推广。实际上这反映一个矛盾，一方面期望除了纯粹的用材林森林经理之外，期盼森林经理能在“多功能经营”上有所建树，但是对“多功能经营”应该包括些什么内容并没有明确的见解。问题是“多功能经营”是否仅限于生态效益？对于林地的林下种植业、养殖业是否属于“多种经营”的范畴？是否属于森林经理规划的范围？也缺乏统一的认识。具体的林情是集体林区的经营主体——林农在经营山地时，极其关心林下的种植业、养殖业和副业经营。农民在脱贫上的这些需求，是否应该纳入规划内容？“西峡模式”之所以成功，是因为农民通过规划，对山地的综合利用，对以林业带动各业发展，对脱贫致富，对恢复生态环境有明确的目标和期望。

再说，20世纪80年代在全国开展的《中国林业区划》，它在“全国农业区划”大背景下，根据全国发展林业的自然条件、经济条件和各地域对发展林业的需求状况，作科学的区划[1]，林业区划制定全国各地域的林业生产布局，规定森林经营的发展方向。有的森林经理学者认为，这是森林经理向宏观规划层次的发展，属于宏观战略谋划。然而，对此有些森林经理学者并不认同，认为不属于“经典的”森林经理范畴。当然，在学术上对一些问题有不同的看法，是很正常的事。但也说明如果对出现的新事物囿于固有的观念，客观上必然阻碍学科的发展。当然，我们也关心外国的林业新理论、新动向，以期从中吸收有益的经验。比如，如果用“中国林业区划”和现代在美国出现的“新林业”理论做比较，“新林业”理论的最大特点是在林业用地上强调保持和改善林分质量与景观结构的多样性……是新林业思想的核心。[2]“新林业”理论主要框架是由“林分”和“景观”两个层次组成。“林分”是较低的层次，主要是生产木材，同时也发挥森林生态的多种效益。对“景观”层次则强调在“景观”层次中的“林分”要合理分布。强调木材生产的经济效益和森林生态效益的分布、构成要达到最优化。按笔者理解“新林业”理论类似于“中国林业区划”的含义，但“新林业”理论只停留在理论阶段，而我们的“中国林业区划”，是在近百名与林业有关学科的学者参与协作下完成的，不但在构架上完成区划的理论体系，而且在实际上取得了区划成果，可供林业决策时参照。在这一点上，笔者认为“中国林业区划”胜于“新林业”理论。说明我们的学者在林业理论建设上是有创造力的，无需妄自菲薄。

1.2.3 夸大卫星相片在森林经理的作用

30年来在森林经理调查中存在夸大卫星相片作用的现象。卫片在调查中用于区划经营区边界时或者优于航片。但在小班调查中，有许多调查项目连航空相片目前还没办法解决，如林分树高、平均直径、林分年龄、出材等级等。在森林资源清查中利用卫片，曾把玉米地判读成有林地。[3]值得探讨的是卫片“判读”的方法，一旦使用错误的方法必然导致错误的“判读”结果。如果说，坚持强调目前卫片完全可以替代航片在森林经理调查中应用的话，那么，最好拿出个有说服力的样板来。如果说要跨越“航片”去发展“卫片”，这样就会夸大卫片的作用去误导森林调查使用工具的方向，延误发展航片应用的效益。

1.2.4 学科学时减少

现在林业院校的《测树学》课时基本上都是48学时，比在“文革”期间复课闹革命时的课时少了40%。全国又没有一个统一的教学大纲，这样造成了不少学校连“树干解析”都不讲，大学生基本不能通过“树干解析”来研究林木的生长规律，又怎能强求我们的经营决策更加科学合理？从中可以看出“泛森林经理”学科滑坡的严重程度与不良后果。

1.3 学科建设没有和生产应用结合

如上所述，森林经理学科对林业生产第一线的事物缺少关注。如南方种杉的经验、“桑基鱼塘模式”、江苏北部里下河地区的“农林复合经营模式”、“ 西峡模式”、黄河河岸沙地泡桐林经营等缺乏总结，并提升到理论来探讨。近年来，哈尔滨市郊三个市直属林场(山河、转山和丹清河林场)，效法德国的“近自然森林”进行作业试验，并总结出很好的经验。从笔者了解的信息来看，哈尔滨市林业局的同志们在这方面做的工作是很出色的。从结果来看，他们在某些环节甚至超过德国。原因是我国劳动力成本低，所以做了德国人没有做的人工促进更新和清除林下的杂草和灌木，从而促进了林木的生长。总的看来，我们的实验才开始，还有待在理论上总结。比如，德国总结了在疏伐时林木间的距离：25×D(目标树当前的胸高直径)。这个结论是否适合我们，还有待摸索。以上例子说明，由于学科建设没有和生产应用相结合，致使我国森林经理理论成为无根之末。当然，形成这样的局面原因很多，也很复杂。但是外因归外因，内因最终还得通过反思解决，解铃还需系铃人。

1.4 缺乏有权威的学科带头人

现在各个林业院校的森林经理处于各自为战的局面，就连学科名称认识也不统一。原因之一是，缺乏一个有权威的学科带头人。比如，前年出现的讨论“林木市场成熟”理论，森林经理分会自始至终都处于失声状态，更不要说组织会员开展讨论了。虽然在福建农林大学的《林业经济问题》、老教协林业专业委员会的《通讯》以及《科技日报》和《森林生态服务网》上发表了一些文章，但那都是自发的行为。“林木市场成熟”的讨论，是一场各抒己见的学术争论。但是这场争论还不普遍、不深入。其实，真理是越辩越明，能够在理论上探讨和加深对森林经营的认识，促进林业理论的发展，是件好事。而且，崇尚“不惟上，不惟书，只惟实”的理念，是当今我们建立学习型社会所倡导的。

1.5 森林经理逐渐失去吸引力

林业院校无论学生入学时选专业、或教师选科研课题，森林经理都不是很受欢迎的。一个原因是林木生长期长，短期内难出成果。所以多倾向于选测树学、计算机或遥感在林业中的应用一类的专业和课题，造成森林经理逐渐被边缘化。另一方面，学生考虑毕业后森林经理到基层林场工作的机会多，生活、工作条件较城市辛苦。还有一个原因，自从森林经理被取消了重点学科以后，一些教师感到迷茫，在定位上无所适从，甚至找不到学科的发展方向。

2 造成森林经理学科滑坡的外部原因

其原因既多又复杂，本文只能探讨其主要方面。

2.1 领导者的思维也是生产力

梁希部长是新中国林业的开拓者，十分重视森林经理。建国初期的林垦部设有森林经理司[1]，在1951年，林垦部就组建多个森林经理调查队。1953年组建航测队在东北大海林林区进行航测试点。李范五副部长来林垦部前，是东北抗日联军领导者之一，到林垦部任第一副部长。他对林业有深刻的了解和领导林业生产的高超艺术，令我辈初出校门的学生佩服得五体投地。他在作报告时，谈到“林学概论”所涉及的有关问题，甚至能整段背诵出来。在解释“森林经理”有关经营区区划的施业区和林管区时，还能说出俄文原名。在林业工作中，李部长从外行成为内行，掌握了森林生长和林业生产的规律。为了摸清森林的家底，狠抓森林调查。同时从苏联引进成套先进的航空摄影测量调查技术，培养了一大批掌握先进技术的人才，为我国日后的林业发展奠定了人才基础。

改革开放以来，林业有了极大的发展。其间，也出现了一些不符合林业发展规律的失误。比如，有的领导上任伊始，不调查，不听取意见，高歌“林业就是改善生态环境”。[4]结果把林业产业部门抛弃了，把林业部也撤了，降格为国家林业局，任期8个月就调走了。给林业生产和发展留下许多遗憾和后患。前几年，有一位厅长刚上任，就要求全省在一年之内编完各县、市林场的“森林经营方案”，而且还要求编制全省性的“森林经营方案”(省的林业发展规划)，由于违反了客观规律，最终根本未能完成。这成为林业界的一则笑话。这些例子说明，他们和李部长相比，差距何其远。所以说长官意志要有科学基础。有的人认为林业就是造林和砍树，没什么高深学问。领导林业用“触类旁通”一般规律的思维，忽略森林和林业的特殊规律和特点。没有区别林业和农业的不同，忽视了林业生产的长程性，林木要求长期培育的特点。也没有区别森林采伐业和采掘工业的不同，忽略了森林的可再生性，森林是可以永续作业、永续利用并维持可持续发展的特点。林业的优势一方面是依靠长期的森林培育，一方面是通过培育千方百计获取高质量(高产出)木材的可持续利用；同时，也能够最大限度地发挥森林生态效益，造福社会。

谈到森林生态效益，在涉及全球气候变化的中国林业时，侯元兆最近(2011年5月)提出，“森林资产承载着民族实力和民族安全，……是石油和矿产枯竭后的发展依靠，要建立一个动态稳定的全国森林生态大系统，……强调追求‘生态’必须通过增加立木资产的这个环节。‘生态’不是空穴来风，是体现在森林立木蓄积的增长上的，要通过多功能森林的近自然培育(来实现)。”按笔者理解，增加造林面积只是获取“碳汇”的第一步，更重要的是加强森林培育，最大限度增加森林蓄积量，是获取“碳汇”的根本。它体现吸收大气中二氧化碳转换的结果，是看得见摸得着的。

上面的列举仅是浅显的例子，说明领导人的思维多么重要。至于那些涉及林业或林学深层次理论的以及涉及林业方针、政策的，关系到全局性的决策错误或失误，并非没有，只是在这里三言两语说不清。

2.2 管理体制

关于森林经理外业调查和内业编制森林经营方案的管理，最早由林垦部的森林经理司管理，后由林业部森林调查设计局管理，最后由森林资源和林政管理司的森林调查处履行森林经营方案编制的职能。2002年以后，就没部门管了。[5]近年编制森林经营方案的管理职能，由资源和林政管理司与绿化造林司分头管理。没有机构统一专管森林经理事业，也是导致森林经理衰弱的重要原因。

2.3 缺乏资金投入

俗话说“巧妇难为无米之炊”。1987年大兴安林区大火后，大兴安林区停止了上交育林基金，因此，林业部无力每年向各省、区提供森林经理调查经费补助，而各省、区森林经理的调查经费投入也变得力不从心。在一次会议上，一位同志的发言值得深思。“去年我检查了一个乡镇的林业项目的财务账。我发现：全国是‘六大工程’，到省是‘六大工程’，到县还是‘六大工程’，可到乡镇这一级就没有戏了，所有的工程资金在乡镇一级根本没有单独立账，有什么钱花什么钱，没有不敢花的钱。应该给老百姓的钱，到不了老百姓手里，所以老百姓对‘六大工程’没有积极性。”[3]又据报导：“辽宁提出‘十二五’全省林业站建设目标：林业职工工资纳入县财政预算。重点林区实现乡镇林业站由县林业主管部门垂直管理，从体制管理、经费投入、人员配备上加大力度”(白雪松，《中国绿色时报》2011－01－07，头版)。报道表明，2011 年前，辽宁省乡镇林业站职工工资是没有纳入县财政预算的，除辽宁省外，其他省的情况又如何？没有人头费，职工靠什么生活？连人头费都没有，只好吃作业费。有什么作业项目就吃什么项目的经费。看来，国家的经费投入制度要改。客观上营林经费是需要长期稳定投入，然而现行财政体制是没有项目就没有经费。正因为这样，新造人工林和天然更新的中幼林，由于没有抚育经费，耽误了“林时”，导致林木长期得不到及时抚育，导致浪费了林地和林木的生产潜力。

还有一个问题，现在无论是国家层面，还是省的层面，无论是自然基金，还是科技支撑等项目基本没有森林经理的课题，现有的科研导向基本上都是短、平、快，能立竿见影的，如林木育种、森林培育、森林保护、森林生态等方面的为多。说明主管部门相关人员对森林经营——森林经理的不认识。误导着林业科研的方向。对林业建设是一个严重的缺失。

2.4 缺乏森林经理的人才

20 世纪 50 年代中央和各省都有森林经理调查队。[1]那时，林业部每年向各省、区下达森林经理任务，每年召开森林经理工作会。70 年代后，这项工作逐渐放松了。原因是一方面缺少资金支持，另一方面林业部在森林调查上，重点抓“全国森林资源连续清查”。当然，这和对森林经营认识的深刻程度有关，也和森林经营的指导思想所确立的指导方针有关。正如最近几年林学界探讨的结论指出的：在林业生产上，只抓两头，一头抓造林，一头抓采伐。没有抓漫长的森林生长期中的培育工作。具体表现为没有机构、没有人员、没有经费。在这种大背景下，森林经理人才流失。各级林业机构对森林经理不重视，自然会影响森林经理学科的滑坡。现在全国的农林高等院校中就没有森林经理专业，学科被边缘化，人才缺失，尤其基层森林经理人才的缺失，成为森林经理滑坡恶性循环必然结果。

3 如何振兴森林经理

3.1 提高对森林经营的认识

《森林法》规定要编“森林经营方案”，领导发出号召指出：“森林经营是林业发展的永恒主题”。目前的状况是没下大力气狠抓落实。事实上，一切好的方针、政策不落实就会落空。所有各级领导和他们的参谋团队，都需要提高对森林经营的认识。林业的宏观大方向要抓，更重要的是抓微观落实。要充分认识目前我国木材安全正处在一个关键的时刻。近五年来，关于我国木材的年消耗量曾有如下报道：①王志宝(2006)指出：我国木材供需缺口已由 2000 年的 4115 万 m^3 上升到到 2004 年的 6962 万 m^3，年均长 17.92%。预计到 2015 年，我国生产建设用材需求量约为 3.3 亿至 3.4 亿 m^3，而国内(仅)可提供 1.95 亿 m^3。[6]②贾治邦(2007)指出：目前我国每年森林蓄积消耗量已达 5.5 亿 m^3，每年缺口 2 亿 m^3，到“十一五”期末缺口达到 3 亿 m^3。[7]据“第 7 次全国森林资源清查”报告，现在年采伐消耗量为 3.79

亿 m^3。而天然林采伐量为1.89亿 m^3，人工林采伐量为1.23亿 m^3，合计为3.12亿 m^3。这和年采伐消耗量为3.79亿 m^3 相比，还存在6700万 m^3 的消耗量差额，这个差额是从哪个林种里采伐的？应该好好探源。有这样的一种言论，最好取消“轮伐期”，愿意怎么采就怎么采。那不就成了赤裸裸的乱砍滥伐了吗!？还谈什么森林经营！在狠抓落实“森林经营是林业发展的永恒主题”上，笔者希望：以“十二五”规划为契机，通过改革，狠抓“森林经营”，从此走上科学营林之路；不然：对致力森林经营缺乏足够的推力和动力，勉强维持目前的状况；从而，由此继续发展，等待下一个更为深重的森林资源危机的到来，那时的处境将比现在的状况更为艰难。[1]

3.2 要健全机构

实话实说，撤销林业部以后，林业局的职权有限，林业的社会地位急剧下降。在林业问题日益成为全球共同关注的政治话题的今天，林业被边缘化的趋势已引起了许多政协委员的关注，建议恢复林业部，建立一个有效率的科学林业行政管理体系[8~26]。

致谢：对在成文中提出意见的朋友们，笔者表示衷心感谢!

参考文献

[1]詹昭宁. 中国森林经理探讨[J]，林业经济问题，2007，27(1)：93~94.

[2]詹昭宁. 探讨落实“永恒主题”的时代意义——兼议生态经济林业理论//中国老教授协会林业专业委员会. 通讯，2011年3月30日：6、10页。

[3]吕树英. 森林经理与林业发展//森林经理与林业发展座谈会文集，[C]中国林学会森林经理分会中国老教授协会林业专业委员会森林经理学组北京林业大学资源与环境学院，北京，2002年10月19日：24页。

[4]詹昭宁. 现代林业集约化森林经营的思考[J]，林业经济问题，2007，27(5)：474.。

[5]翁宜民. 森林经理与林业发展//森林经理与林业发展座谈会文集，[C]中国林学会森林经理分会 中国老教授协会林业专业委员会森林经理学组 北京林业大学资源与环境学院，北京，2002年10月19日：25页。

[6]齐联等. 加快推进商品林建设 缓解木材供需矛盾，[N]，中国绿色时报，2006-03-09：A1版.

[7]贾治邦. 坚持科学发展 建设现代林业 为构建社会主义和谐社会做贡献[N]，中国绿色时报，2007-02-09：1~2版.

[8]刘慎元，齐联，贾达明. 国家生态安全需要林业部[N]，中国绿色时报，2007-03-07：1-2版。

[9]詹昭宁. 西峡模式——南方集体林区森林经理理论与实践[M]. 1992年.

[10]詹昭宁. 建立林地林木资源评价系统的设想[J]. 林业资源管理，1993，6.

[11]詹昭宁. 从划分林种谈起——兼谈森林分类经营的衍化[J]. 林业工作研究，1996，11.

[12]詹昭宁. 中国林业发展战略有关几个问题的探讨[A]//林业系统工程学会. 林业发展战略与林业系统工程学术研讨会论文集，1999.

[13]詹昭宁. 慎待中龄林——议东北林区森林资源的恢复//中国老教授协会林业专业委员会. 通讯，2005，2.

[14]詹昭宁. 读林沉思录——用科学发展观看林业[J]. 林业经济问题，2006，26(3).

[15]詹昭宁. 国有林区改革风险防范与对策[J]. 林业经济问题，2006，26(5).

[16]詹昭宁，现代林业与生态经济林业理论和实践[J]. 林业经济问题，2007，27(6).

[17]詹昭宁，颜文希. 建立森林分类经营示范点的刍议——走出森林经理困境[J]. 林业经济问题，2008，28(3).

[18]詹昭宁．转换机制 科学经营——探索河南省西峡县科技兴林之路[J]. 林业经济，2008，6.
[19]詹昭宁，颜文希，高兆蔚．中国林业建设的理性思考——学习与实践科学发展观笔记[J]. 林业经济问题，2009，29(1).
[20]詹昭宁．落实森林经营方案的几点建议//中国老教授协会林业专业委员会．通讯，2009，2.
[21]詹昭宁．寻找国有林区森林经营突破口//中国老教授协会林业专业委员会．通讯，2009，4 期。
[22]詹昭宁，张莉莉．中国国有用材林该如何经营——兼议“林木市场成熟论”的缺陷[J]. 林业经济问题，2010，30(1).
[23]詹昭宁．落实森林分类经营的几个问题//中国老教授协会林业专业委员会．通讯，2010，2.
[24]詹昭宁．碳汇交易与实施森林经理的重要性//中国老教授协会林业专业委员会．通讯，2010，3.
[25]詹昭宁．国有林区改革终极目的不是实行私有化[J]. 林业经济问题，2010，30(4).
[26]詹昭宁．对当前森林经营的思考[J]. 林业资源管理，国家林业局调查规划设计院，2010，6.

教材建设、科学研究、人才培养
——谈森林经理学科建设

李明阳　刘　敏　刘米兰
（南京林业大学森林资源与环境学院，南京，210037）

摘　要：论文首先回顾了新中国成立60年来森林经理学教材建设的曲折历程，指出现有森林经理学教材存在着目的任务不实、基础理论不稳、调整方法贫乏、研究内容单一的缺陷。其次，以2005～2011年国家自然科学基金森林经理学科资助项目为例，分析了当前森林经理学科研究技术重于方法、方法重于理论、科学研究与生产实践脱节的倾向。在此基础上，论文分析了我国现有22个森林经理学硕士授予单位的研究方向、2011年全国森林经理学硕士需求情况、2008～2011年南京林业大学森林经理学硕士就业情况，指出在研究生培养上存在着研究方向杂乱、内在逻辑不清、培养目标与就业市场脱离的趋势。文章最后从教材建设、科学研究、人才培养3个方面对森林经理学科提出了合理化建议。

关键词：森林经理学科；教材建设；科学研究；人才培养

作为林学学科的三大支柱（林木培育、森林利用、森林经理）之一的森林经理学，形成于18世纪的德国。160多年来，随着时代的进步和社会经济的发展，森林经理学科是在不断变革和发展的。但与其他学科相比，其发展变革表现得比较迟缓。进入21世纪以来，随着国家林业建设重心的转移、市场经济体制改革的深入、城市化步伐的加速，短周期工业原料林基地建设、野生动物调查、分类经营、森林认证、湿地保护、荒漠化监测、森林旅游、城市森林规划等各种林业调查规划实践活动蓬勃开展，对以用材林永续利用为目标、以收获调整理论为核心的传统森林经理学提出严峻的挑战。在新的形势下，如何从教材建设、科学研究、人才培养等方面对森林经理学科的发展现状进行分析，剖析存在的问题，探讨未来发展方向，是森林经理理论工作者和森林经理实践人员共同面临的问题。

1　森林经理学教材建设的历史回顾

学科建设，教材先行，因而教材建设成为衡量森林经理学科发展水平高低的一个重要标志。如何客观评价现存的森林经理学教材，未来的森林经理学教材如何构建，是摆在高等农林院校森林经理教育工作者面前的首要课题。

新中国成立以来，我国高等农林院校的森林经理学教材先后经历了1951年苏联林学家Т·И·莫洛维洛夫的翻译版、1983年北京林学院主编的试用版、1991年北京林业大学于政

作者简介 李明阳（1967～），男，河南三门峡人，博士，教授；主要研究方向：风景林调查规划、森林资源监测、3S应用研究。E-mail：lmy196727@ 126. com；Tel：18951086732

中主编的修订版、2001 年北京林业大学亢新刚主编的新版的长达 50 年的漫长发展历程。然而，纵观新中国成立以来森林经理学教材建设历程可以看出，虽然教材版本不同，表述方式各异，研究内容单一、目的与任务不实、基础理论不稳、调整方法贫乏的问题没有发生根本的改变。

进入 21 世纪以来，随着国家林业建设重心的转移、市场经济体制改革的深入、城市化步伐的加速，野生动物调查、分类经营、森林认证、湿地保护、荒漠化监测、森林旅游、城市森林规划等各种林业调查规划实践活动蓬勃开展，对以用材林永续利用为目标、以收获调整理论为核心的传统森林经理学提出严峻的挑战。随着高校扩招和毕业生就业重心的不断下移，向造纸原料林基地、乡村林业、城市林业、风景区和森林公园、园林绿化行业转移已成为林学本科专业、森林经理学研究生就业的主要渠道。在这种背景下，传统的森林经理学教材已经失去了修订的基础，采用全新的教材——森林规划设计已成为必然。

2010 年，在新的全国农林院校《森林经理学》统编教材迟迟未能出版的背景下，南京林业大学规划教研组主编的学校第三批精品教材《森林规划设计》出版。在编写教材的过程中，编者对以往历次版本的森林经理学教材进行了重大的变动，调整的主要内容有：完善了森林规划设计的理论体系，增加了森林生态系统经营、林业分类经营、景观生态学内容；充实了规划内容，介绍了空间直观模型、多情境规划方法，加大了生态公益林规划的比重；更新调查规程，增加了森林资源监测、森林评价、森林认证内容；首次建立主要的三级林种的森林作业设计方法；增加了 3S 技术在森林规划设计应用的内容；通过课后复习思考题、规划案例探讨、森林作业法实践分析加强了实践环节比重；在森林规划各论、组织经营单位、森林资源监测等有关章节，吸收了科学研究的最新成果。

2 森林经理学科研究现状分析

科学研究现状体现了当代科学技术与生产力的发展水平，也体现为理论与实践的研究导向。依据“着力营造有利于创新的研究环境，着力推动源头创新”的工作定位和“依靠专家，发扬民主，择优支持，公正合理”的评审原则，国家自然科学基金择优支持有重要科学意义或重要应用前景的基础性研究，尤其是符合国际科学发展趋势，具有战略性、前瞻性、基础性和开拓新兴科学技术领域的研究项目。因此，国家自然科学基金资助项目的数量多少、类型分布，反映了一个学科的研究重点和发展趋势。登录国家自然科学基金委员会网站，通过项目检索的方式，进行 2005 ~ 2011 年森林经理学科国家自然科学基金资助项目的分类比较和量化分析（表 1），剖析研究热点、存在的问题，从而为森林经理学科未来科研发展方向，提供数据支撑。

表 1 2005 ~ 2011 年国家自然科学基金面上资助项目类别分析

资助方向	资助项数	百分比（%）	最多类别（项数）	备　注
高新技术应用	14	27	林业遥感（7）	涉及林业遥感、森林可视化、计算机模拟仿真 3 个方向
森林培育与经营	12	23.1	天然次生林经营（4）	涉及风景林、水土保持林、毛竹林多个林种，热点不明显。
森林资源监测	11	21	抽样理论与方法（5）	涉及森林抽样理论与方法、年轮形成机制与木材密度、森林结构 - 功能研究、林木干形与树冠形状 4 个方面

（续）

资助方向	资助项数	百分比(%)	最多类别(项数)	备　注
热点研究	7	13.5	碳储量、碳汇(5)	涉及气候变化及其响应机制、碳储量与碳汇2个方向
森林基础研究	4	7.7	森林土壤(2)、植物生理(2)	涉及森林土壤、植物生理2个方向
森林规划	3	5.8	风景林评价规划(2)	涉及风景林调查规划、用材林规划2个方向
管理模式	1	1.9	管理模式(1)	涉及管理模式1个方向

2005～2011年国家自然科学基金项目资助课题总计(不含重点项目)52项，从表1可以看出，近年来森林经理学科科学研究呈现出以下特点：①高新技术立项课题(27%)＞森林培育与经营(23.1%)＞森林资源监测(21.0%)＞森林规划；②风景林、自然保护区林、城市森林等公益林规划理论与方法的立项课题数量较少；③热点研究集中于碳汇和碳储量，气候变化、生物入侵立项课题较少；④缺少不同研究方向之间的综合研究，森林资源监测、森林可持续经营、森林规划之间协同研究的立项课题尚未见到；⑤传统森林经理研究领域测树制表、森林成熟方面的立项课题呈现萎缩趋势。

3　森林经理学科研究生培养现状分析

3.1　森林经理硕士研究生招生单位研究方向分析

据不完全统计，2011年，全国森林经理硕士研究生培养单位共22家，其中博士培养单位8家。在22个森林经理硕士培养单位中，除中国林科院外，依托院校为985的高校1所，211高校2所，其他普通院校18所。按院校类型分，林业科研单位1所，林业综合院校5所，教育部直属农林院校1所，地方农林院校15所。按空间分布上看，东北地区2所，华北地区4所，西北地区4所，西南地区2所，华东地区4所，华中地区5所，华南地区1所(表2)。从全国森林经理硕士研究生培养单位的院校类型及空间分布看，森林经理硕士培养单位呈现出层次类型多、空间分布比较均匀、地方院校农林院校所占比重大、总体招生规模较大的特点。

表2　森林经理学硕士招生单位一览表

地区分布	数量	招生单位名称	备　注
东北地区	2	东北林业大学，沈阳农业大学	东北林业大学为博士授予点，黑龙江省、国家林业局重点学科，依托单位为211高校。
华北地区	4	中国林科院，北京林业大学林学院、北京林业大学信息学院，河北农业大学	除河北农业大学外，均为博士授予点，其中北京林业大学为国家重点学科，依托单位为211高校。
西北地区	4	西北农林科技大学，甘肃农业大学，新疆农业大学，内蒙古农业大学	西北农林科技大学为博士授予单位，依托单位为985高校。
西南地区	2	西南林业大学，四川农业大学	西南林业大学为国家林业局、云南省重点学科。
华东地区	4	南京林业大学，福建农林大学，浙江农林大学，山东农业大学	南京林业大学、福建农林科技大学为博士授予点，浙江农林科技大学为浙江省重点学科。
华中地区	5	中南林业科技大学，华中农业大学，江西农业大学，安徽农业大学，河南农业大学	中南林业科技大学、江西农业大学为博士授予点，省重点学科。
华南地区	1	华南农业大学	

通过 Google、百度等搜索引擎，收集 2011 年 22 个森林经理硕士研究生招生单位招生简章中的研究方向，分门别类地加以统计分析(表 3)。从表 3 可以看出，我国森林经理硕士授予单位研究方向呈现出以下特点：①各个森林经理硕士授予点在开展森林可持续经营、森林资源监测等传统森林经理研究领域研究的同时，普遍重视 3S 技术、森林可视化、计算机模拟仿真等高新技术应用；②在开展自然科学研究的同时，森林经理授予单位逐渐展开森林资产评估、旅游文化、森林文化等社会科学的交叉研究；③从全国尺度上，22 家培养单位共有 9 个研究方向，内容涉及基础理论、应用基础、高新技术、政策法规，研究方向偏多、研究内容偏广、研究力量过于分散，导致森林经理学科难以集中优势力量围绕国家对林业的重大需求展开科研攻关；④学科性质不明，研究方向与行业奋斗目标逻辑不清、研究手段与研究内容混淆的现象比较明显(见表 3 的评价)。

表 3　森林经理硕士招生单位研究方向分析

方　向	院校数量	包 含 内 容	评　价
1. 森林可持续经营	17	包含森林可持续经营理论与技术、森林资源可持续发展、森林可持续经营评价、森林生态系统经营	应作为林业行业的奋斗目标，作为二级学科的研究方向缺乏技术支撑，改为主要林种作业法设计
2. 3S 技术应用	14	包含遥感与地理信息系统、3S 技术与资源信息管理、数字林业	技术手段，服务森林监测、森林规划，不宜单独作为研究方向
3. 森林资源监测	8	包含景观资源监测与评价、林分生长模型、森林资源监测技术、森林测计、森林生态系统监测技术、森林结构与功能	监测重心转向生态系统结构与功能监测，作为规划主业的预业，适宜作为一个研究方向
4. 森林规划	5	包含森林可持续经营规划、森林及其环境评价与规划设计、景观评价	应该作为学科的主业，适宜作为主要的研究方向
5. 可视化与计算机模拟	4	包含森林可视化、林业信息技术、森林生长计算机模拟、林业信息技术	技术手段，服务森林监测、森林规划，不宜单独作为研究方向
6. 统计预测与控制	5	包含数量森林森林经理学、林分生长模拟、数学模型理论与方法	技术手段，服务森林监测、森林规划，不宜单独作为研究方向
7. 森林资产评估	3	包含林业经济、林业资源评估、森林资产评估	属于社会科学研究内容，为森林规划服务
8. 森林培育	2	包括林木遗传改良与生物技术、人工林培育与利用、林木抚育栽培	严格意义上不属于森林经理研究内容，应并入森林作业法设计
9. 旅游与文化	6	森林文化、森林美学、生态旅游、森林旅游、社会林业、城市林业、乡村林业	属于社会科学研究内容，为森林规划服务

3.2　森林经理硕士研究生供需分析

为了了解全国林业行业对森林经理硕士研究生的需求情况，以便为森林经理研究生专业方向设置和招生规模制定提供数据支持，通过 Google、百度等搜索引擎，收集 2011 年全国森林经理研究生需求情况(表 4)。用人需求单位合计 11 个，研究生需求人数 20 人，平均每家不足 2 人，呈现出需求单位数量少、总量偏低、进入门槛高、重心下移的趋势。考虑搜集信息不完全情况，将现有需求人数放大 1 倍，全国人才需求总量约 40 人，其中，林业行政事业单位 30%，林业勘察设计部门 20%，林业科研院所 35%，相关企业 15%。全国 22 家森林经理研究生培养单位，每年招生数量大小不一(4 ~ 12 人)，按照平均每家 8 人计算，每年毕业生约176人，毕业生中从事专业有关的工作比例约为22.7%。最近几年，全国硕士研究生毕业后从事专业相关岗位的比例大约为16.7%(源自《研究生与学位研究》，2011)，略高于全国比例。随着研究生扩招的进行、行政事业单位改革启动，林业科研院所进人的门槛会逐渐提高，而林业勘察设计部门的岗位需求将会保持平稳下降的趋势，林业基层事业单位、GIS研发企业、园林绿化公司，将会成为森林经理研究生就业的主要渠道。

表4　全国森林经理硕士生需求情况2011年不完全统计表

单位性质	需求人数	备　注
林业勘察设计	4	福建、贵州林勘院，黑龙江森工集团、海南省林业局
林业行政事业	6	三明市林业局，上海林业站，广东、广西林业局直属事业单位，黑龙江森工集团直属事业单位
林业科研院所	7	福建三明学院，赣州职业技术学院，林科院亚林所，山东林科院
相关企业	3	北京地伟信息技术公司，广东森科园林公司

3.3　南京林业大学森林经理硕士研究生去向分析

在进行全国森林经理硕士研究生供需分析的同时，笔者收集了南京林业大学森林经理硕士研究生2008~2011年就业去向不完全统计一览表(表5)。从表5可以看出，在2008~2011年53名毕业研究生中，以在科研院所、勘察设计、行政事业单位就业的居多，共计32人，合占60.38%，其中从事与专业有关的岗位24人，占45.28%，选择攻读博士学位、到企业去工作的学生占有一定比例，分别占毕业生人数的11.32%、13.2%，出国、未落实就业岗位的现象开始出现，分别占就业人数的3.8%、11.32%。作为一个主要从事野外工作的艰苦行业，森林经理女硕士研究生的就业去向值得关注。从表5可以看出，女生攻读博士的比例较低、从事科研院所教辅岗位的比重较大，反映了女生求稳、急功近利的职业选择倾向，而到林业勘察设计部门、企业就业的女生数量增多，则反映了女生职业选择趋向现实的变化趋势。岗位未落实的女生所占比重较高，则是森林经理的行业特点、研究生就业期望、女生生理特征之间种种矛盾冲突作用的结果。

表5　南京林业大学2008~2011森林经理硕士研究生就业去向不完全统计一览表

岗位性质	人数	说　明	备　注
行政事业	9	计生委、规划局、林业局、农委、统计局	大部分需参加“事参公”考试
勘察设计	11	广西、广东、浙江林勘院，南京测绘院	女生5人
科研院所	12	南京林大，南京环科所，森林公安专科学校，南京师大	女生比重较大，以教辅岗位居多(8人)
读　博	6	南京大学，南京林大，中国林科院，南京土壤所	女生1人
企　业	7	GIS开发、数据处理、软件销售、中介咨询	女生4人
出　国	2	中粮集团森林可持续经营计划，非洲援外	均为男生
岗位未落实	6	与就业岗位发布信息时间滞后、回家乡就业失去联系有关	女生比重较大

4　森林经理学科发展建议

4.1　教材建设

为了与林业调查规划实践接轨、为了拓展森林经理学科对外交流合作的生长空间、为了迎接日趋严峻的研究生就业市场的挑战，建议将学科名称改为社会能够理解并普遍接受的名称，如森林规划设计、森林资源调查规划，并编写能够反映最新林业科研成果、林业调查规划实践、社会对林业人才需求的统编教材。鉴于目前森林经理学界在教材名称、学科基础理论、研究方法、教材内容等重大问题上短期内难以达成一致意见的背景下，可以考虑根据地方院校的森林资源状况、生源构成、社会对当地生态环境需求，编写具有地方特色的森林经理学教材。

4.2 科学研究

在主要林种可持续经营方法研究基础上，迎合国家对林业在绿化环境、减缓气候变化的重大需求，开展风景林、珍稀用材林、自然保护区特用林、环境保护林的可持续经营技术体系配套方法(森林作业法)研究。在森林资源监测领域，除继续加强森林抽样调查理论方法研究外，将强气候变化情境下测数制表、生长模型研究。在森林规划领域，加强风景林、湿地、乡村观光林业、城市森林、自然保护区特用林规划的理论与方法研究。在热点追踪方面，强化气候变化情境下主要树种分布及应对机制研究。在高新技术领域，加强森林可视化与森林经营规划，遥感与气候变化、生物入侵、人类干扰的综合研究。

4.3 人才培养

鉴于研究生培养目标与人才市场的需求越来越远、研究生就业重心不断下移、从事非专业工作比例越来越大的现实考虑，在森林经理硕士研究生培养模式上，必须坚持科研素养、专业技能、生存技能并举的培养方案。在科研素养上，着力培养研究生热点把握能力、文献检索能力、论文写作能力、学术报告展示能力、科研项目申报书撰写能力。在专业技能培养方面，强化森林经理硕士研究生森林资源信息采集与获取能力、3S 应用能力、数据统计分析能力、专题图制作能力。为了应对日益严峻的就业形势，在培养研究生科研素养、专业技能的同时，必须根据研究生培养单位的学科优势、所在区域的产业结构导向，进行必要生存技能的培养。对于南京林业大学来说，针对学校在园林规划、风景林调查、3S 应用开发能力较强的比较优势，面对江苏省经济发达、对环境绿化人才需求量巨大、南京市软件产业蓬勃兴起的产业结构特征，结合应用科研和横向合作课题，努力培养森林经理研究生园林制图、GIS 系统开发技能，同时在课程设置上增加经济管理、市场营销相关知识的学习。

针对在读的森林经理硕士研究生中，数学、计算机、地理信息系统、城市规划专业毕业的本科生比例较大的现实考虑，在条件成熟前提下，森林经理学科可依托于学科较强的 3S 技术应用、数字林业、计算机模拟仿真优势，积极申报地图学与地理信息系统等新的学科硕士授予点，同时尝试进行与城市规划、园林规划等学科进行研究生联合培养试点。

参考文献

[1]丁思统，李霞．森林经理学的定位与发展[J]．林业资源管理，2005，82~84.

[2] 陈平留，郑德祥．南方森林经理必须适应市场经济的发展[J]．中南林业调查规划，2001，20(增刊)：108~113.

[3]北京林学院．森林经理学[M]．北京：中国林业出版社，1983，52-55.

[4]徐国祯．再谈森林经理学科建设和发展[J]．林业资源管理，1997，(特刊)：5~10.

[5]亢新刚．森林资源经营管理[M]．北京：中国林业出版社，2001.

[6] 于政中．森林经理学[M]．北京：中国林业出版社，1993.

[7] 李明阳．森林规划设计[M]．北京：中国林业出版社，2010.

[8] 李明阳．从教材演变谈森林经理学科建设[J]．林业调查规划，2006，31 (6)：1 ~ 5.
[9] 李明阳．南方森林经理的困境和出路[J]．中南林业调查规划，2001，20(增刊)：122 ~ 126.
[10]金大刚．面向现代林业的森林经理理论与实践[J]．中南林业调查规划，2001，20(增刊)：48 ~ 53.
[11] 陆兆苏．对森林经理学若干问题的检讨[J]．林业资源管理，2001，(增刊)：61 ~ 69.

森林经营方案实施不力的主要原因及解决的对策

苏世河

（黑龙江省第一森林调查规划设计院，牡丹江，157009）

摘要：阐述了森林经营方案实施现状，分析了森林经营方案实施不力的主要原因，提出了解决森林经营方案实施不力的对策。

关键词：森林经营方案；实施不力原因；解决对策

Main Cause and Solutions for Lacking of Implementation of Forestry Operation Programs

SU Shi-he

（Heilongjiang province first forest survey plans and designing institute，Mudanjiang，157009）

Abstract：The author illustrates the current status of implementation of forestry operation programs，and analyzes main cause and Solutions for lacking of implementation of forestry operation program and puts forward the solution methods for lacking of implementation of forestry operation programs.

Key words：forestry operation programs；cause of lacking of Implementation；solution methods

森林经营方案是森林经营主体为了科学、合理、有序地经营森林，充分发挥森林的生态、经济和社会效益，根据森林资源状况和社会、经济、自然条件，编制的森林培育、保护和利用的中长期规划，以及对生产顺序和经营利用措施的规划设计。

《中华人民共和国森林法》明确规定了要编制森林经营方案，所以编制和实施森林经营方案是一项法定性工作。森林经营方案是森林经营管理重要的科学基础和依据。科学编制森林经营方案，是加强森林的科学经营管理，实现森林可持续发展的重要手段；是森林经营主体制定年度计划、组织经营活动、安排林业生产和林业主管部门实施森林资源管理、监督的重要依据；是建立高效、透明、科学、有序的森林资源经营管理体系的重要载体。所以，实施执行森林经营方案十分重要，也十分必要。

作者简介：苏世河（1960～），男，黑龙江省桦南人，高级工程师，从事森林森林资源调查规划设计工作。

但是在实践中，森林经营方案实施执行的并不理想，就是连编制森林经营方案较早的森工企业也实施得并不好，我们必须着力解决森林经营方案实施不力的现状，充分发挥森林经营方案功能，促进林业可持续发展。现根据森工企业实施森林经营方案情况谈一下森林经营方案实施不力的主要原因及解决的对策。

1 森林经营方案实施现状

在现实中，森林经营方案实施情况很不理想。编制森林经营方案从调研开始，直至专家评审，这么一步一步地认认真真地做下来，投入了很多的人力物力，结果却是多数编完了，也就完成了它使命，被束之高阁，再也没有了用处。个别幸运的森林经营方案，还可能被掸掉尘土，被有些写材料的人拿出来做一下参考而已。这就出现了一方面认真去编写，一方面又用途不大，或没有用处的十分尴尬的局面。这就是现实当中森林经营方案的结局。森林经营方案没有得到实施，没有发挥作用，这就是森林经营方案应用现状，可以说森林经营方案实施极为不力。

2 森林经营方案实施不力的主要原因

编制森林经营方案不是为了编制而编制，而是为了实施。现实中森林经营方案没有达到实施的目的。森林经营方案实施形成如此局面，可以说因素很多，但是主要原因是森林经营单位认识模糊、林业管理部门重视不够、制约机制有所缺失以及林业企业实施森林经营方案条件不具备。

2.1 森林经营主体认识模糊

森林经营主体对于森林经营方案重要性及实施森林经营方案的重要意义认识模糊。森林经营主体，特别是森工企业，在林业“两危”时期，企业负担重，问题较多，生存都成了问题，更无暇顾及森林经营方案实施情况，森林经营方案没有得到实施。在实施天然林保护工程以后，林业企业的局面得到了扭转，企业经济、社会得到了大发展，但有的企业仍然对森林经营方案重要性及实施森林经营方案的重要意义认识模糊。有的认为森林经营方案可有可无，用途不大，没有森林经营方案，森林经营的也很不错，有了森林经营方案，也未必就有多大用途；有的担心实施森林经营方案可能会束缚森林的经营与发展；有的认为编制森林经营方案，上级反复强调下我们编了，实施没有过多要求，我们也就没有落实……这些错误的认识，都对森林经营方案的应用在一定程度上产生了抑制作用。

2.2 林业管理部门重视不够

林业管理部门对于编制森林经营方案重视有加，对于森林经营方案实施重视不够。往往是对编制森林经营方案要求很严格，并组织专家对于森林经营方案进行评审论证。当森林经营方案通过后，该实施时林业管理部门作为就是另一番天地了。有的林业管理部门只是例行公事，在会上只是简单谈一谈，说一说而已，对实施要求不多了；有的林业管理部门在森林经营方案编制完成后，就没有了下文，好像就完成了任务，实施就好像与他们没有多大关系了，什么实施要求没有，检查实施情况就根本谈不上，可以说对于森林经营方案实施一概不管不问。林业管理部门这些行为直接影响着森林经营方案实施。

2.3 制约机制有所缺失

《中华人民共和国森林法》、《中华人民共和国森林法实施条例》对于森林经营方案编制与实施有所要求，但是对于实施要求还不够，对于不执行森林经营方案没有作以约束。《森林经营方案编制与实施纲要》也是粗线条的，也是远远不够的，所以，这些林业法律法规是不足的，也是有所欠缺的，这对执行森林经营方案在一定程度上缺乏了制约机制。

2.4 林业经营主体实施条件不具备

由于长期以来，对于林业企业，尤其对是森工林业企业的政策、资金等方面投入不够、扶持不到位，上级下达的采伐限额不尽合理等因素，虽说第一期天然林保护工程使得森工企业经济社会状况得到一定扭转，但还是不够的。等等这些外部因素都限制了森林经营方案实施，森工企业还不具备森林经营方案实施的条件。

3 解决森林经营方案实施不力的主要对策

随着第二期天然林保护工程和林业发展"十二五"规划的逐步实施，林业政策、扶持资金等逐步到位，林业企业经济将逐步得到大发展，为森工企业彻底实施森林经营方案提供了良好条件，使得森工企业彻底实施森林经营方案提供了可能。在实施森林经营方案条件趋近成熟的条件下，采取以下几个方面的主要对策。

3.1 补充立法，确立权威

在《中华人民共和国森林法》第二章第十六条中提到"国有林业企业事业单位和自然保护区，应当根据林业长远规划，编制森林经营方案，报上级主管部门批准后实行。"在《中华人民共和国森林法实施条例》第二章第十一条中提到了编制森林经营方案。也就确立了森林经营方案的法律地位和权威性。

但是这还不够，只有在《中华人民共和国森林法》和《中华人民共和国森林法实施条例》当中增加不实施与违反森林经营方案的处罚条款，才能更具有法律地位和权威性、强制性，这也才能更利于森林经营方案实施，促进林业科学永续的发展。只有这样，才能使凡是不实施森林经营方案或不按森林经营方案实施，依法追究其责，予以处置。这是很需要解决的一个问题。

3.2 制定"办法"，健全机制

为贯彻落实《中共中央 国务院关于加快林业发展的决定》的有关精神，全面推进我国的森林可持续经营工作，规范和引导森林经营主体科学编制和实施森林经营方案，根据《森林法》和《森林法实施条例》的有关规定，制定了《森林经营方案编制与实施纲要》。但这还远远不够的，还应该制定一个"森林经营方案实施管理办法"。来进一步完善执行森林经营方案管理制度，健全必要机制，保证森林经营方案的实施。

3.3 政策调控，促进应用

《森林经营方案编制与实施纲要》规定"森林经营主体要依据经营方案制定年度计划，组织经营活动，安排林业生产"。也就是要在森林经营中，严格落实森林经营方案各项规划要求，努力实现各项指标，一切要围绕森林经营方案进行工作，合理组织经营森林资源，严格按照森林经营方案规划设计的各项任务和年度安排制定年度计划，编制作业设计，组织并开展各项经营活动。

要依法落实好森林经营方案，要有支持鼓励政策，同时又要有调控手段。凡是按经营方案确定的经营项目，予以优惠措施；凡是依据森林经营方案进行的各项经营活动，予以鼓励政策。以此来促进森林经营方案进行应用，发挥森林经营方案的作用。

3.4 考评领导，作为依据

在森林经理期到期时，要对森林经营方案实施情况进行评价与考核，把森林经营方案的实施效果作为评价林业经营管理水平的重要依据。对于实施不力的，应给予处罚；对于实施好的，应予以奖励。

要将森林经营方案作为重要依据，对于森林经营主体的主要领导、主管领导在离职时，对于任期内落实森林经营方案情况进行评价与考核。将落实森林经营方案情况作为领导干部考核的重要指标之一。

要将森林经营方案作为重要依据，考核各级林业主管部门领导保护发展森林资源目标责任制的重要依据。

3.5 检查核查，密切结合

林业主管部门要依据森林经营方案实施管理，监督检查森林经营活动。要把森林资源经营管理的各项检查、核查、验收与森林经营方案的执行情况紧密结合起来。并使之制度化、经常化以及规范化。

3.6 项目立项，充分考虑

编制各种林业设计、计划、规划，以及与森林经营有关或对森林资源有影响的工程项目和投资计划应把森林经营方案作为依据，应充分考虑森林经营方案中规划的森林经营目标和主要规划内容等，不应该违背。项目审查部门对项目审查也应该充分考虑森林经营方案，对于违背森林经营方案的项目，不予以审批。

林业发展“十二五”规划中讲到：“深化森林采伐管理改革，指导森林经营者编制与实施森林经营方案，建立以森林经营方案为基础的森林采伐限额管理。”我们应该借此契机，认认真真地编制出科学合理的森林经营方案，扎扎实实地推进森林经营方案的实施。

参考文献

[1]《森林经营方案编制与实施纲要》

[2]《中华人民共和国森林法》

[3]《中华人民共和国森林法实施条例》

[4]刘于鹤，林进．编好实施好森林经营方案是加强森林经营提高森林质量的关键

森林经营方案编制与实施探讨

段　河

（内蒙古林业监测规划院，内蒙古察右后旗，010020）

摘要：论述了森林经营方案的特点和实施效果，结合现代林业的发展需求，针对存在的问题提出相关建议。

关键词：国营林业局；森林经营方案；编制；实施

引　言

随着现代林业的发展与国营林业局森林经营方案编制工作即将深入展开，针对国营林业局在上一个经理期森林经营方案编制和实施过程中出现的问题，总结经验和教训，以完善编制方法，是十分必要的。

为了贯彻执行国家林业局下发的“国营林业局编制森林经营方案原则规定”。规定中明确指出：森林经营方案是国营林业局科学地经营森林，实现永续利用，编制中长期和年度计划，进行作业设计，组织、安排生产经营活动的法定文件，是上级主管部门检查、监督、考核其工作的主要依据之一。

大兴安岭地区的国营林业局已普遍开展森林经营方案的编制工作，由于涉及面广、工作量大，所完成的森林经营方案大多采用设计单位与生产单位互相配合、共同编制的方法。实践证明，由此编制出来的经营方案不但技术上满足要求，且更加符合生产实践，易为生产单位执行实施。

1　森林经营方案实施的特点

总的来看，大多数森林经营方案质量较高，内容齐全，指导思想明确，组织机构健全，执行程序正确。从经营方针的确定、经营单位的组织、造林树种的选择、合理采伐量的计算以及基建、多种经营项目的安排都经过科学的计算，仔细的筹划。在“以营林为基础，普遍护林，采育结合，永续利用”的林业建设方针指导下，结合国营林业局综合考虑，执行起来也较为顺利。

各地区营林业局森林经营方案所定的 10 年经理期起算不一，多数已执行过 2 个经理期以上。由于社会、自然、经济等诸方面因素的制约，经营方案的实施不可能与实际情况完全一致，特别是上述因素发生了变化，例如：自然灾害的发生，人为因素对资源的破坏，国民经济计划的需要等，都会影响森林经营方案的按计划实施，这就需要对经营方案的前期执行效果进行反馈，总结经验，吸取教训，以完善编制方法，使其趋于合理。

林业局有了森林经营方案，它的经营就不是盲目的，而是一种有导向的经营。依照森林经营方案所组织的一切森林经营活动，都是有目的的行为，必须通过反馈来纠正偏差，保证目标的实现。具体的做法是按照森林经营方案的内容，分解年度目标，实行目标管理，建立目标制订——目标落实——目标结果评价——信息反馈的管理体制，尤其是针对前三年的森林和采伐目标。

2 森林经营方案实施的效果

编制森林经营方案是林业生产由粗放经营转向集约经营的重大措施。从大兴安岭地区来看，各个国营林业局森林经营方案在一个经理期的实施过程中，取得了较明显的效果。总结如下：

2.1 林政管理有法可依，对采伐限额进行了全方位论证

方案实施以后，各林业局的林业生产有章可循，森林经营方案为指挥林业生产和资源管理提供了科学依据，森林资源数量和经济效益都跨上了新台阶。

对采伐限额进行了定性、定量、定时、定位的论证。所谓定量即指确定采伐数量的大小，定性就是指确定林种、树种和龄组，定位就是指安排采伐计划到山头地块的小班，定时就是对采伐年度做出安排。因此，森林经营方案是采伐限额的具体化，是对采伐限额进行的定量、定性、定位、定时的多维论证。

2.2 为森林永续利用创造了有利条件，为科学营林提供了保证

森林经营方案实施后，林业局对本单位在经理期内各年度采伐计划心中有数，尽早作出了长期规划和年度计划。有采伐指标的年度及时安排更新。同时，可调整林业局森林资源的林种、树种和龄组结构，为今后林业局的生产经营活动创造了条件，使得森林资源实现越采越多，越采越好，青山常在，永续利用。

经营方案中确定的经营方针，以及在此基础上得到的经营类型表、小班活动安排表、立地类型表与经营措施类型表，构成了科学营林生产的规范和指南，全局的每个小班都可以对号入座，因地制宜地安排树种选择、整地造林、抚育间伐、等作业，从而建立规范化营林生产体系，使营林生产由粗放经营转向集约化经营。

3 森林经营方案实施中存在的问题

森林经营方案在个别国营林业局的实施过程中，也陆续暴露了一些问题：

(1)影响森林经营方案实施的因素多，例如投资渠道不畅，资金不足，行政干预过多，市场价格影响，与地方用地的纠纷，林地被征用，自然灾害频繁等等，而原方案内容过于具体，应变能力不强，造林更新、抚育管理、林木采伐既分解到年度又落实到小班地块。同时，又没有对前期方案的实施效果及时进行反馈来调整计划，从而“牵一发而动全身”，使森林经营方案的后期规划成为一纸空文。

(2)部分林业局对森林经营方案应有的法定地位重视程度不够，一些领导对森林经营方案的地位和作用认识到位，把它当做一项任务完成以后就束之高阁，依然按照个人意图安排生产经营项目。由于上级林业主管部门对所编森林经营方案采取了严格而慎重的审定、审批制度，按照经营方案所定的年采伐量和投资概算批给年度采伐限额及贷款、投资，因此造成了林业局工作上的被动。

(3)由于编案任务集中，因而速度较慢，方案提交过迟，没有彻底掌握好森林资源数量上动态变化，或者二类资源调查数据不准确，林业局又没有对资源数据适时进行修正，造成经营方案部分失效。加上实施单位技术力量薄弱，职工素质还需进一步加强。技术人员严重不足，文化程度、政治素质和业务素质都偏低。这种情况下，方案很难被接受、理解，更谈不上变为现实。

4 建 议

4.1 形成完善的方案编制、执行检查、审计管理制度

进一步确定森林经营方案的法定地位。运用行政手段把森林经营方案的地位与作用，编制与审批，执行与检查，执行效果的验收与审计等过程用行规的形式肯定下来，用法律、法规约束经营方案的编制和实施。方案实施的关键在于领导，为保证经营方案实施的连续性，领导成员可以换届、下岗，但经营方案不能变，要把方案的实施作为上级主管部门考核其成绩的指标之一。

健全森林经营方案编制和实施的管理制度在现行有关的各项规章制度基础下，形成一套较完善的森林经营方案编制、执行和检查、审计的管理制度是保障经营方案顺利实施的重要措施。编案中要强调决策者、规划人员和执行人员的有机结合，正确把握理论与实践的关系，增强方案的弹性。在实施过程中还要不断调整和完善，使方案更趋于合理，保证下一步计划的实施。

提高职工对森林经营方案的认识，林业局职工在上岗前要有计划、有组织的进行技术培训，对经营方案的作用、内容和意义作适当的宣传，使广大基层干部、群众对经营方案有一个大致的了解，从而调动对执行方案的积极性，把实施方案作为他们的自觉行动。

4.2 加强森林资源的档案管理，加快森林分类经营改革工作

小班要长期固定，坚持地籍管理。在加强资源档案建设的同时，逐步建立、健全各种经营数表和调查数表，监测资源消长的动态变化，正确估测资源数据，为森林经营方案的顺利实施提供保证。

森林经营方案要符合当前国家关于林业发展的思路。大兴安岭地区现有的国营林业局普遍存在着资源危机和经济危困，发展受到了极大的限制。目前，国家林业局要求全国加快国有林场森林分类经营改革工作，已取得了很好的成绩，积累了经验。森林经营方案的编制要适应这一形势，对不同类型的国有林场要按其资源培育方式，根据生态公益林和商品用材林的不同特点和经营规律来编制经营方案，建立与其相适应的管理体制和组织经营形式，确定符合标准和规范的森林经营类型和经营措施类型，实施分类指导，使经营方案既符合国家环境、生态建设的需要，又可使大多数国营林业局摆脱困境，走上可持续发展的道路。

中国林业信息化方略
——内涵与发展、战略重点与规划方法①

浙江省林业信息化规划组

我国林业信息化进入一个新阶段。面对全面启动信息化之时，急需解决的问题是：明晰其内涵、了解其发展、选定战略重点、运用适宜的规划方法，推进林业信息化。本文将就这些问题进行讨论。

1 林业信息化概要

1.1 林业信息化概念

林业信息化是在世界和国家信息化大环境下，根据林业需要，孕育、发生和发展。其核心思想是"化"，是与现代化同步、引领林业现代化的过程。是林业发展中的一次历史性变革，林业现代化的一个重要标志。是一个技术支撑、一个复杂的系统工程。

林业信息化至今仍然是一个尚在不断完善、发展、未统一的概念，可以从不同角度理解。笔者认为简明的含义是：根据林业特点和需要，用信息技术装备林业的过程。在当前科技发展趋势下，林业信息化应该是：在国家、区域信息化指导和约束下，进行统一规划与协调，在林业生产、管理、服务等领域的各个环节，信息技术与林业科学技术融合，采取一体化、集成化、网络化、智能化、虚拟化、精细化等主要方式，生产、分配、使用知识，以获取更大、更合理的社会、经济和生态效益。

因此，林业信息化的目的，是为促进林业现代化和林业可持续发展；目标是在林业管理、生产、服务等领域的各个环节，不断应用信息技术，开发和利用信息资源，支持林业生产和管理活动；出发点和基础是：根据林业生产和管理规律，选择和应用信息技术，信息技术与林业业务融合，不断产生新的理念、方法和技术，开发信息资源，促进林业可持续发展。

林业信息化主要作用在于：全面提高信息和知识意识，着力于公众公平应用和享受信息技术，提高精神和物质水平，实现以"物"为中心向以"知识"为中心转变，以知识推动林业发展；它将改变林业高度分散、时空差异大、现代化程度差、稳定性和可控性低的弱点，为节省能源、提高资源利用率、提高物流速度和效率、提高林业产业的整体性、系统性和协调性；它在机械化的基础上，实现集约化、自动化和智能化，改造传统林业生产方式，改进生

---

① 本文是近年实践总结。特别是参加浙江省林业信息化规划、国家林业局信息办的信息化战略研究等活动，促进系统思考与归纳。陈谋询、崔赛华、武刚、张莉莉、李昀、陈钊等老师，武帅、宋亚军、王琳、董桂学、吴艺辉等研究生，和浙江林业规划院的陈春雷、翁卫松参与了林业信息化规划研究，陈谋询、陈钊、张摹博、张莉莉、李昀、吴保国参与了林业信息化战略研究，国家林业局信息化办公室李世东主任、温战强处长、浙江林业规划院的刘安兴院长、李土生原副院长等进行指导。

产工艺过程，促进粗放经营向集约经营转变，实现在精确时间空间条件下，实现精细的生产、管理和服务；它推进网络化管理，加快实现管理科学化，促进林业走向社会，社会参与林业；它应用和发展林业信息技术，增加相应产值，逐步形成新的林业产业，调整林业产业结构，实现林业跨越式发展。

1.2 林业信息化构成

开发和利用信息资源，服务林业建设，涉及林业各个部门、领域的各个环节，需要有一个全面进行信息化建设的思路。可以从多个角度考察林业信息化构成。

从林业单位和部门角度考察。按部门或单位划分，应该包括林业事业单位和部门：林业行政管理、林业业务管理、林业企事业、林业科技部门科技、林业教育等单位和部门、农村林区等等，都需要推进信息化。各个单位和部门，按所承担的职能与领域，进行信息化建设。例如：林业政务信息化、林业业务管理信息化、林业项目管理信息化、林业生产信息化、林业科学技术信息化、林业教育信息化、林业市场流通信息化、林业职工与林农生活的信息化等。只有全面推进才能促进林业整体提升。

从技术角度考察。它由核心层、支撑层、应用层组成。把它和林业生产、管理结合起来考虑，其基本组成是：基础设施信息化、生产（业务、工艺）过程信息化和管理信息化。基础实施信息化，主要包括以互联网、物联网、计算机为核心的硬件平台建设、以林业基本公共数据库、知识、方法、模型为核心的平台建设、以规范化与标准化为核心的环境平台建设、以及林业生产中常用的数字化工具。生产（业务、工艺）过程信息化，指管理、生产和教育、科技各个部门，在经营、生产、科研、教学中的业务信息化，它主要是以智能化为核心的自动控制系统的开发。在各种信息技术支持下，自动取获、处理数据，辅助科学决策与控制。它将信息技术与业务紧密结合，改造旧工艺，为基层生产单位和生产者建立采用新工艺、方法、技术和手段的环境。是直接应用于基层生产，服务于广大林业工作者与林农，实现科学、集约经营和管理的技术支持系统。管理信息化，主要指以林业网络化管理为核心系统建设，在当前，它一方面以电子政务推动，另一方面以森林资源网络化管理为主体，实施管理网络化工程。它将对传统管理思想和模式进行变革，突破传统管理时间、空间的限制，信息充分共享，不仅可以在系统内实现全时空、广信息、多媒体、快速度、零距离和交互虚拟管理，而且能够使林业走向社会，社会参与林业。

1.3 林业信息化特点

林业信息化具有整体性、差异性、多样性、复杂性、动态性、离散性等特点。需要精心的规划和设计、统一基础上的灵活协调，实行适应性管理。

林业信息化整体性。林业的整体性，决定了林业信息化在时空两个方面的整体性。它既是国家和区域信息化的组成，又由林业内部各个部门、领域信息化有机综合；它要考虑信息化过去和现在，更需要注重它的未来。因此，应该采取统筹规划基础上、有计划、全面、积极、稳步地推进的策略。

林业信息化的差异性。主要表现在社会、经济、人文环境，认识、素质、组织、技术等条件，价值观与发展水平等方面，形成了区域间的差异，以及同区域各单位、领域、环节信息化发展基础和水平的差异。数字鸿沟客观存在，缩小数字鸿沟，促进均衡发展，是信息化中需要解决的问题。

林业信息化的多样性，林业的多效益、多功能、多结构、多学科、多技术、多层次，以及差异的存在，决定了林业信息化在需求、数据、形式、信息处理方式、方法和发展道路等方面的多元化，它是选择信息技术和设计实施信息化工程的基础。

林业信息化的复杂性。林业信息化的差异性，造成了林业信息化的多样性，也就决定了林业信息化的复杂性，多因子、非线性、随机决定了它是一个复杂的系统工程。

林业信息化的动态性。林业主要经营对象是再生资源，并在一定社会、经济、自然环境之中，信息技术发展又日新月异，两者随着时间的变化而变化。林业信息化必须采取动对动的策略，一方面建设动态模型、方式，适应动态变化，另一方面不断完善和发展，进行建设。

林业信息化的离散性。林业事业分布在广大地区，几乎所有的国土都有林业经营、管理、服务对象，多种网络技术的应用，与多种媒体网络化系统的开发，是林业信息化中需要解决的技术课题，只有这样才能发挥林业信息化的整体效果。

以上各点决定了林业信息化是一个长期发展的过程，根据需要和科技发展，不断创新是林业信息化的最基本、最重要的任务。

2 林业信息化发展

2.1 国外林业信息化发展概述

随着信息技术的发展与应用，自20世纪中叶开始，世界各国虽然没有统称林业信息化，但均根据自身的基础与条件，进行着各种形式建设。普遍注重是根据林业发展需求和特点，选择适用的信息技术，开发、利用信息资源，推动林业生产力的发展。大致经历了50~60年代的科学计算；70年代数据库的开发和数据的处理；80年代以来的利用互联网，进行信息管理、知识处理阶段；现在已进入智能、集成、虚拟时期。

根据国外林业信息化发展过程，以下几方面对于我国林业信息化具有借鉴意义：

(1)世界林业信息化稳步发展的轨迹。世界林业信息化发展经历了：产生、发展、快速发展、全面提升等阶段，从单机、联机到网络，从科学计算到数据、信息、知识管理，从管理到生产、服务，从单项到综合、系统、集成，从自动化到智能化等过程，在发展理念、组织实施、应用创新、推广应用等方面积累了许多经验与教训，为我国林业信息化提供了启示。

(2)夯实基础是实施信息化的基础。国外林业信息化经验证明：夯实基础是实施信息化的关键。只有信息化认识的提高，信息意识的增强，信息使用能力的加强，才能有实施信息化的共同目标与意愿，才能有序的行动。只有建立了公共数据库、方法库、模型库、知识库、统一的规范和标准，才能节约成本，资源共享，有效的建设各种应用系统。

(3)信息技术与林业业务结合，是林业信息化的根本。国外成功之处，在于执行了一条坚持根据林业发展需要，立足林业实践，重在实用，选用信息技术，两者紧密综合，产生新的理念、方法与技术，服务林业的技术路线。

(4)适应时代发展，不断提升和发展是林业化的关键。可持续林业是一个动态过程，信息技术发展更是日新月异，因此密切注视它们的变化、需求、发展，不断推进信息化进程，是发达国家不断提升与发展成功经验。

2.2 我国林业信息化发展道路简评

2.2.1 中国林业信息化发展进程

林业信息化与信息技术在林业中应用息息相关，信息技术应用可以追溯到20世纪50年代初，即航空相片在森林资源调查中的应用，但是，那时应用内容与范围极其有限。直到20世纪70年代末，随着国家的复兴，科技的进步，我国林业系统，通过信息技术的引进、消化、应用创新、自主创新，开始了真正意义的林业信息化里程。根据林业信息化的发展过程和状态，已经经过了起步探索阶段、拓展应用阶段，而今进入到加快发展阶段。

(1)起步探索阶段(20世纪80年代初至90年代初)。

这一阶段信息技术在林业中的应用，从森林资源调查、规划、管理、教学、科研部门开始，引进计算机单机应用为主，以森林资源调查数据统计、储存、管理为主要应用领域，学习、推广、应用计算机技术，中国林业信息化在研究与实践中起步。

组织上，成立了部级林业信息中心，开办了一系列计算机应用和遥感技术培训，推广信息技术应用。并于80年代中，成立了我国第一个面向自然资源信息管理的林业信息管理专业，培养复合型的林业信息管理人才。

信息技术应用上，本阶段初期，主要用以森林资源调查中的科学计算和数据统计汇总，从林分、林木生长预估、制表到调查数据统计汇总，逐步在森林资源调查规划部门使用，开发了全国连续清查程序。在单项科学计算和统计分析基础上，产生了林业常用统计分析软件包。同时，在80年代初，林业系统利用70年代完成的全国清查数据，建立了我国第一个自然资源数据库，开始了林业数据计算机管理领域。以后又陆续开发了单机的一、二、三类森林调查和其他专业调查数据库，开始了计算机林业数据管理领域。

在单项数据管理基础上，本阶段中开始，逐步从单项数据向综合数据管理、信息管理方向发展，研建了如：1987年的《森林资源管理信息系统》、1988年的《森林资源和灾害管理信息系统》，1990年的《县级资源与环境信息系统》，以及1988年的《林火管理信息系统》等等。

在航空遥感应用基础上，本阶段开始引进航天遥感和图像处理技术。林业系统其他领域应用计算机技术，略晚于森林资源管理部门。

(2)拓展应用阶段(20世纪90年代初至21世纪初)。

本阶段的特点是：计算机技术应用从森林资源管理领域向其他领域扩展，从研究向生产、管理实践发展，从上层应用向基层地方普及，从单项应用向综合、系统方向转变。在引进了空间信息处理、多媒体、互联网等技术以后，林业信息管理水平更有进一步提升，进入了新的拓展阶段。

在组织和人力资源开发上：国家和一些省、地建立了相应的管理机构，一些林业院校开办了相关专业，科研单位和高等院校着力于新理念、新技术的研究和实践，并形成了从本科到研究生的多层次信息管理与技术的培养体系。

这个阶段信息技术在林业中应用范围不断扩大，林业统计部门，进一步完善、优化林业数据统计系统；种苗系统于90年代初完成了林业行业中的第一个领域的信息化规划，开发了面向全行业的统计分析等软件；森林资源、湿地、荒漠、生物多样性保护、林业工程等重点业务领域，开发了纵向管理信息系统，此外还研建了森林资源和灾害信息管理系统、森林病虫害防治管理信息系统、林业政策法规管理信息系统、国家林业局人事管理信息系统等多个管理信息系统；森林资源调查规划领域，在原有基础上，进一步引进空间信息管理、多媒体、网络、模型、模拟技术，正在向综合集成方向发展。林业生产、事业单位，也开展了计算机应用研究和实践，研建了面向本单位需要的系统或者软件。

这个时期，林业信息化基础实施有了较大发展，林业基本属性数据库继续完善，国家级和部分省级航天遥感数据库在建设和发展、一些标准和法规开始制订、计算机、网络等硬件已进入了林业系统所有领域与大部分单位；国家和许多省研建了森林资源清查数据库、森林资源规划设计调查成果数据库、林业统计数据库、森林资源火灾数据库等应用性数据库。特别是网络设施的建设，为网络化管理奠定了坚实的基础，2000 年，国家林业局局域网建成，实现了对内提供信息浏览、邮件下载与发送、数据交换等信息服务，对外宣传林业、展示林业发展成就、使社会公众广泛了解林业、关注林业、为林业发展建言献策的网络平台。一些省、地、县以本地的信息化实施和林业专网为依托，开发了本地林业信息化网络平台，服务于管理、生产和对外业务。

根据国家信息化电子政务为龙头的部署，林业系统进行了内外网、专网建设。经过这一阶段的建设，林业信息化逐步扩大与发展，为下一阶段创造了条件和环境。

(3)加快发展阶段(自 21 世纪开始至今)。

林业信息化经过以上两个阶段，在国家信息化进一步加速和提升的环境下，林业信息化也进入了加快发展阶段。

这个阶段林业信息化在组织上进一步加强，明确提出“加速林业信息化，带动林业现代化”的部署，完善了国家级林业信息化组织机构，建立或者健全了地方相应机构，制定了林业信息化发展规划和技术方案，召开了林业信息化工作会议，统一了林业信息化目标、任务和要求。

这个阶段的发展，首先体现在网络建设和基础设施方面，它们的建设大大推动了电子办公、在线服务等应用的发展。林业信息化的标准规范也得到了重视和制定，国家林业局积极进行林业信息化标准指南、林业信息化术语、林业信息资源目录体系框架等 8 个急需的公共性、基础性标准建设，同时梳理现行的国际标准、国家标准、行业标准及地方标准。福建、云南、辽宁、湖南等省都积极开展标准规范方面的工作。

其次，在应用方面，重在实际，面向应用。一方面在国家级继续完善、优化纵向的如森林、湿地、荒漠和生物多样性保护等重点业务领域系统基础上，进行审评并整合。另一方面，正在从管理向生产、服务方向开拓。营造林管理系统、林业灾害监控与应急系统、有害生物防治管理系统、野生动物疫源疫病监测管理系统、沙尘暴灾害应急和监测管理系统、森林公安信息化平台等正在积极研建和推进。森林病虫害防治在相关专家系统、信息系统研究与实践基础上，研建了网上森林医务系统，将森林病虫害防治推动向了新的阶段。

在林业行业纵向推进的同时，各地利用自身的优势和条件，整体推动着林业信息化建设，产生了一些先进典型。湖南省采取了大集中式的数据存放方式，将全省各地的林业数据集中存放在省厅数据中心，构建起一个比较完备的数据专用存储区域网络系统。全省空间数据库、营造林管理数据库、森林公安、森林防火专题数据库以及各种文档型数据库等公共数据库已初步建成。厅机关、14 个市州林业局、71 个县市区林业局，实现无纸化网络办公。政务信息发布及查询、公文处理和档案管理一体化、电子邮件、视频会议、视频点播和短信群发等日常办公自动化，已在全系统普遍应用。先后组织开发了全省林业电子办证、森林公安、森林防火信息管理及森林防火辅助决策系统、营造林信息化管理系统、育林基金信息管理系统、固定资产管理等应用系统，并全部投入实际应用，取得了很好的效果。浙江省龙泉市，自2004年以来，采取高起点、广应用，面向实际，应用为先策略，以电子政务为龙头，森林资源管理为重点，共享信息，服务大众，推进信息化建设。市内林业局以及相关总站、林业办证中心、17个林业工作站、10个木材检查站等网络化管理环境；建立了统一的数据库，和部分应用系统的知识库，；开发应用了“森林资源信息监管系统”，13个系统基本覆盖了森林资源生产、管理和服务职能，对森林经营和管理进行全方位、全过程、实时监控和服务。

经过多年的研究与实践，在行政与业务主管部门推动下，由规划设计、科学研究、高等院校等单位为主体，一些面向林业信息技术应用开发公司的参与，有自主产权的林业应用软件或者系统诞生，应用于全国或者地区的行政管理与服务、森林资源监管、森林培育与保护等领域，促进了林业信息化进程，孕育了林业新兴产业，产业产业结构，丰富其内容。

2.2.2 我国林业信息化业绩总结与问题分析

经过三十多年的发展，尤其是“十一五”以来，在各级林业部门的共同努力下，我国林业信息化建设已经取得了明显进展，在组织机构、基础设施、应用领域、电子政务和服务，以及标准规范等方面都取得了长足进步，为进一步加快发展奠定了坚实基础。主要表现在：

(1)组织管理体系初步建立，林业信息化保障能力逐步增强。

(2)网络建设等基础设施稳步推进，林业信息化发展构架初步形成。

(3)应用领域不断拓展，林业重点业务工作能力明显提高。

(4)电子政务快速发展，电子政务网络框架正在形成，林业系统内部办公、交流，社会服务能力日益增强。

(5)林业信息化的实践，培养了一批信息化技术骨干队伍，积累了实施信息化的经验。

(6)林业信息产业正在孕育与发展。

我国林业信息化虽然取得了一定成效，但是与时代发展、国家要求与林业发展需求，存在一些问题，主要是：

(1)信息化素质和信息化整体水平有待提高。信息技术的应用、信息化建设，决定于决策层、管理层和广大执行层的信息素养，即信息意识、信息知识、信息能力和信息道德等4个要素，信息意识是先导，信息知识是基础，信息能力是核心，信息道德是保证。它们共同构成一个不可分割的统一整体。林业系统对信息技术应用、信息化建设比相关行业，例如虽然起步较农业、水利行业不晚，但是发展缓慢，决策与管理层没有适时地进行提升或者深入部署，没有像农业、水利那样进入国家“金字”工程；没有像农业系统那样从管理、生产、服务领域全面实施信息化工程；没有像水利系统那样，自上而下地进行规划和协调实施。虽然成立了我国第一个面向行业的信息管理专业，但是没有像农业教育系统适时的建立农业信息化专业。如此等等，致使林业信息化整体上，不仅与世界发达国家、而且与国内行业信息化存在差距，改进的途径是：提高各级、各层信息素养，促进决策层准确决策、管理层有效调控、执行层努力实施，提高信息化整体水平。

(2)发展不均衡，影响协调、可持续发展。信息化中的差异性是客观存在的基本特点，但是各个地区、领域的均衡、协调发展，消除数字鸿沟是不能忽视的问题。过去一个时期，林业信息化存在片面性是一个突出的问题：一度重上层忽视下层、重管理领域忽视生产与服务、重技术轻业务，忽视信息技术与自身业务综合、重引进忽视有用的自主创新、重硬件忽视应用软件的开发、重数据管理的初级阶段忽视向信息、知识管理方向提升等等。更有时把重点当成唯一，忽略了应该且可以实施的项目。有的把信息化当成少数单位争项目、扩投入的一个途径，一个内容覆盖多个项目，有的研究初步或者中间结果，被夸大应用，有的生产项目以研究方式运行。

(3)宏观缺少规划与调控，微观上各自同水平的开发应用。林业系统自20世纪80年代成立信息中心以后，缺少一个能指导全面建设、可行的长期规划，也没有实施宏观协调管理，忙于项目开发，多年项目不能投入使用。各地为了应用，各自重复开发，虽实用，但是不能共享。近年来，随着机构的完善，制定了规划、规范，但是仍然存在着重管理轻生产等领域、重上层轻基层、重技术轻结合业务有用创新等不够全面、协调发展的弊病。

(4)有限的投入，不均衡使用，经济、社会效益较低。较长时间，林业系统信息化没有列入发展计划，投资渠道不顺，有限的投入，往往重硬件轻软件、重购买轻实质性的引进、消化、创新、重局部项目轻整体推动，投入往往倾向上层单位等等，造成有限资源的不均衡使用，不能发挥应有的作用。效果和效益较低。

(5)信息化人力资源不足。信息化人力资源、特别是既懂林业又懂信息技术的复合型人才和具有战略眼光能够进行方向性的指导的人才奇缺，已严重影响林业信息化进程。当前从事信息化建设多是(信息)技术型人才，致使一些项目走向为技术而技术的道路。

2.2.3 我国林业信息化发展对策

根据形势发展、林业需求和存在问题，应采取以下对策：

(1)执行国家工业化与信息化融合，促进现代化的新的战略部署，进行林业信息化的战略转移。在指导思想、方针、任务进行调整，信息化与林业发展有机融合，每个领域和环节全面应用信息技术；实现局部建设，向全面推进方向转移。根据融合的需要进行职能重组；生产上，融入信息技术，组织一体化、自动化、智能化系统；组织上，在提高认识基础上，转变观念，健全组织机构，完善运行机制；管理上，打破部门界线，以信息流组织各种职能，实现集成化网络化管理；技术上在优化原技术基础上，向更新技术应用转移，引进云计算等技术。实现信息资源充分共享，数据管理向信息管理、知识管理转变。

(2)全面规划，精心设计，有序实施，协调持续发展。林业信息化涉及林业系统各个部门、领域和环节，各级规划必须考虑整体安排，明确目标、任务、分类、分期实施的目标和任务，既要立足当前又要着眼长远，既要突出重点又要兼顾全局，既要考虑上层也要重视地方基层，实现协调、持续发展。在规划基础上，对启动项目精心设计，特别是关系全局的顶层项目，必须有一个科学、可靠、可行的设计，保证质量、效益，解决“数字鸿沟”和“信息孤岛”问题。在实施中，加强监督、审议和协调工作，保证林业信息化整体效益。

(3)立足林业，应用为先，信息技术与林业有机综合，自主创新。应用信息技术，提升林业发展水平和速度，是林业信息化永恒的主题。需要改变过去为技术而技术、技术与实际应用脱节、引进与自主创新脱离的倾向，走根据林业需求，选择信息技术，通过业务重组，林业与信息技术综合创新，服务林业的道路。

(4)夯实林业信息化基础实施。在充分利用国家和地方公共信息化基础实施基础上，根据林业特点统一规划、统一标准进行基础设施建设，特别要重视知识库、方法库、物联网、林业数字化工具建设，研究与实践云计算，实现信息资源，共享支持各类应用系统的开发。

(5)加强信林业信息化教育和应用基础研究、技术推广、发展信息产业。科技、教育是林业信息化的最基础的保证，建立知识、技术创新机制，在学历教育的同时大力发展网络教育，建立技术推广、发展林业产业，为信息化创造条件和环境，应作为信息化重要内容。

3 林业信息化战略重点及其优先项目(简要，如需要详细内容可联系)

3.1 战略重点项目及其优先项目的抉择

3.1.1 战略重点项目及其优先项目必要性

林业信息化涉及各地、各部门、各领域和每个环节。它们又息息相关，相互影响和制约。由于各地、各部门、各领域和环节，在林业发展中的地位、作用不同，而且在基础、环境、条件、水平等方面存在着差异。这种“不同”和“差异”，造成了林业信息化建设的多样和复杂性，如何有计划的均衡全面发展，成为林业信息化中必须解决的问题。一个有效的策略是在时间上分阶段，空间上分别类型和重点，按内容分项目、分期推进，需要采取以重点项目引路，优先项目突破，全面推进林业信息化进程对策。即在全面规划，稳步推进的思路指导下，分别战略内容确定重点项目，从中选择优先项目，逐步实现信息管理标准化、基础实施数字化、工艺过程智能化、经营管理精准化、林业服务网络化，开发和利用信息资源，推动林业可持续发展。

3.1.2 重点项目及其优先项目选择与实施原则

林业信息化任务重、内容多，空间上涉及各个部门和每一环节，时间上是一个长期运行的过程，选择和安排重点项目和优先项目，遵循的总的准则是全面、协调、可持续发展，具体是：

(1)全面规划、统筹安排下的分期、分层和分类、分级，稳步推进的原则。林业信息化既要保证林业信息化发展的整体性，又要根据不同条件与需求的有一定的灵活性，所以必须遵循统筹安排下的分类、分层、分级、分期，稳步推进的原则。即在国家信息化战略指导下，对林业信息化战略设计和内容进行分解：在时间上，可以按按2015年、2020年、2030年等阶段分期；层次上，纵向分国家、省、县、基层等层，横向，按决策、管理、执行等上、中、下分层；根据林业信息化战略内容，按林业生产、管理、服务等职能，进行重组和林业信息化项目分类；在每一类中，分别生产和管理等领域需要，和林业信息化基础条件，确定重点项目，在重点项目中，按优先级确定优先项目。形成一个既有面又有点，既有上层又有基层，既有生产又有管理、既有基础又有应用的信息化建设策略，积极稳步地推进信息化进程。

(2)内外兼顾，各层、各级、各项协调发展的原则。各级、各层林业信息化。既要解决与环境相适应，相互协调，又要在系统内协同发展等问题，这就需要执行内外兼顾，各层各级各项之间的协调发展的原则。林业系统一个地区和领域的信息化，必须接受区域信息化和行业信息化双重约束与指导，实现信息资源共享，符合相关的标准、规范、建设目标和原则；林业内部，各层各级子系统之间，通过精心设计，组成有机整体，实施协调管理，充分信息资源共享，发挥整体效益。

(3)夯实基础、应用为先、安全可靠、持续发展的原则。林业信息化是林业发展战略的重要举措，它应该立足未来，面向实际，重在应用，所有项目应该科学、可靠、可行、可持续。因此，需要遵循夯实基础、应用为先、安全可靠、持续发展的原则。应用开发需要环境和条件。只有夯实基础，才能开发和运行应用系统，才能满足林业发展需要的一切服务。这是信息化最根本，是建设初期的首要任务，后期也需要不断完善和优化。

(4)继承与整合、综合与创新的原则。林业信息化经历了从起步，到发展、提升，进入了全面推进的阶段，各阶段都是在原有基础上，完善、优化、发展的过程。因此，也必须遵循继承与整合、综合与创新的原则。林业信息化，经过前一阶段的努力，许多地区和领域，已有一定基础，开发了一批项目。但是，林业系统对信息化的需求，已经从数据发展到信息需求，进一步提出了知识需求，从单项目、局部需要发展到全面、整体需要，要求信息化向一体化、集成化、综合化、网络化、智能化、虚拟化等方向发展，这就需要不断引进新技术，通过自主创新，特别是新颖、实用、可行、可操作的有用自主创新，建设符合我国国情、林情的各种系统。

(5)职能决定需求，需求决定功能，功能选择技术，技术服务业务的原则。在确立重点和优先项目以后，进行结构功能设计时，应该遵循的原则是：职能决定需求，需求决定功能，功能选择技术，技术服务业务。基本的技术路线是：面对各类项目的选择、开发、实施，应该从分析生产、管理职能、过程出发，进行生产、管理和服务需求分析，在此基础上，确定信息化项目的基本功能，再根据功能选择相应的信息技术，一方面从使用信息技术出发，进行林业相关职能、规范、方法等的重组，另一方面将信息技术和林业方法、技术综合创新，两者融合，发展新技术和系统，服务于林业事业。

3.1.3 重点项目及其优先项目选择与实施的依据

林业信息化作为推动林业可持续发展的动力，是林业现代化重要支柱，是国家信息化组成，它的状态和运动过程，反映了林业现代化水平，因此，林业信息化重点和优先项目确定，需要遵循下列依据：

(1)国家赋予林业的地位、部署和林业发展战略，是林业信息化重点项目的战略依据。在国家实施可持续发展战略、生态建设、西部开发、应对全球气候变化中，多次赋予林业相当高的地位，并对林业发展目标、任务、政策等进行了一系列部署，林业系统根据国家的部署，提出了林业发展战略的目标、方针、任务。在执行可持续发展战略、生态建设、西部开发、应对全球气候变化中，全面应用信息技术，在质量、数量上促进林业发展，是林业信息化的首要任务。林业信息化重点项目和优先项目的选择，应该在林业发展战略整体把握下，根据各地区、各个领域和环节的需求，和条件、基础，选择、安排重点项目和优先项目。

(2)国家信息化发展战略和林业系统的总体部署，是确定林业信息化重点和优先项目的专业依据。确定林业信息化重点和优先项目，专业基础是：根据国家确立的信息化与工业化、现代化融合的道路，以改革开放和科技创新为动力，大力推进信息化，充分发挥信息化，在促进经济、政治、文化、社会和军事等领域发展的重要作用等指导思想，和到2020年综合信息基础设施基本普及，信息技术自主创新能力显著增强，信息产业结构全面优化，国家信息安全保障水平大幅提高，国民经济和社会信息化取得明显成效，新型工业化发展模式初步确立的任务。以及林业系统确立的“加快林业信息化，带动林业现代化”的总体部署，和到是2020年林业信息化总体目标：建立起覆盖全国林业系统的信息化体系，建成国内领先的信息化平台，基础设施明显改善，信息安全保障能力大幅增强，林业信息化发展制度、标准体系基本形成，资源共享和应用水平全面提升，实现林业决策科学化、办公电子化、服务便捷化，为建设现代林业提供强大支撑。

(3)林业生产、管理、服务需求和流程，是林业信息化重点和优先项目的业务依据。当前，林业生产经营、管理模式正在变革之中，特别是信息等高新技术的应用，林业将面临一次重大变革。所以在安排项目和优先项目时，必须注意到，林业信息化不是现行系统简单的信息技术应用，更不是手工系统计算机化，需要从实现林业现代化出发，在林业生产、管理、服务领域进行全方位的变革，把现代化的生产、管理、服务模式，需求和流程，作为重点项目与优先项目的选择和安排的业务基础。以进行具有先进性、科学性、实用性、可行性的项目的实施。

(4)国内外信息技术和信息化的发展趋势，是确定林业信息化重点和优先项目技术依据。林业信息化在长期目标上，必须根据世界信息化发展趋势，确定信息化的项目与目标，项目覆盖林业各个部门与领域，以便逐步赶上世界信息化水平。在今后一定时间内部，应该根据当前世界信息化发展的一体化、网络化、智能化、综合化、集成化、虚拟化等的趋势，从生产、管理、服务等方面，安排优先项目。信息化讲究实效，应该有较高的性价比。关键在根据需要和可能，面向实际，突出应用。这就需要，不断选择可靠、可行、有效等成熟的技术，应用到林业信息化之中。需要不断引进、消化、自主创新，特别是有用的创新，产生适合林业信息化的新的方法和技术，通过验证，积极、稳妥地，将这些新技术应用到信息化建设中。避免不加选择的应用，或者是边研究边应用，避免失败或者增加成本。

(5)条件和基础，是确定林业信息化重点和优先项目的环境依据。信息化是生产力、科技发展的一个阶段，信息技术的应用需要有一定的社会、经济、科技、人力资源等条件，和已具备的信息技术应用基础。信息技术等高新技术的应用，可以取得高效益，但是需要有一定投入，并存在较大的风险。在选择和安排项目时，无论在空间和时间上都应该考虑当地当时的条件和基础。本研究提出的采取的分阶段、分期实施是在发展中时间上差异的考虑，分级实施和典型示范等措施，是根据空间上的差异，采取的必需的策略。

3.1.4 林业信息化战略项目总论（概述，如需要详细内容可联系）

根据以上原则和依据，林业信息化主要按林业业务、生产等职能，归纳为有7类，各类中按需要与可能，选择20个重点项目，又选择42个优先项目，见表1。

项目各类包括生产、管理与服务等方面，所选择的重点项目是该类的当前重点所在，发展方向是一体化、综合集成，而其中优先项目，既考虑现有系统的优化，也考虑新系统的建设，为逐步综合，成为按重点项目集成系统的组成部分。

4 林业信息化战略重点项目各论(概要，如需要详细内容可联系)

4.1 林业信息化基础设施建设

林业信息化基础设施建设，主要指为了适应林业发展及其信息化需要，符合信息科技发展形势，对于林业信息化的应用系统，具有整体意义和公共作用的设备、数据和相应的软件系统。在一定时期内，可以有两方面构想。

第一，通过对现有设施进行系统诊断，挖掘信息资源，优化结构，逐步将以数据管理为主，向信息、知识管理过渡；充分利用第二代网络，扩大网络计算功能，逐步将以数据网络为主，向信息网络、知识网络过渡，实现真正的信息资源整合、共享，提升，满足林业发展的需求。在测评基础上，选择可用、可行的项目，推广应用，广大覆盖面，发挥它们的效益，并为进一步使用信息新技术做准备。

表 1 林业信息化类和重点、优先项目

类	重点项目	优先项目个数
1 林业信息化基础设施建设	林业信息化硬软件平台建设	3
	林业公共数据中心建设	3
	林业信息化制度、规范与标准建设	2
	林业生产装备与工具数字化建设	2
2. 林业政务信息化	林业综合办公信息系统建设	2
	林业政务对外服务系统的建设	3
	适应新形势阶段型系统开发	1
3. 森林经营与森林资源监管信息化	一体化型森林经营信息系统建设	2
	森林资源监管系统优化与集成	2
4. 人工林生产与监管信息化	智能化人工林培育系统的开发	3
	集体林地区采运与林产品加工自动化系统开发	2
	林业工程与生产综合监管系统建设	2
5. 企业信息化与电子商务	林业企业信息化建设	3
	电子商务工程建设	3
6. 森林保护与应急管理信息化	森林资源安全监控集成系统控集成系统	1
	森林资源突发破坏性事件监控系统	2
7. 知识、技术创新与传播的	知识、技术应用推广与重点科研方向	3
	信息化示范基地建设	1
	林业网络教育建设	1
	林区网络文化建设	1

第二，主要方面是，积极稳妥地引进第三代通讯、物联网、云计算等技术，为建立和运行更新的技术系统，促进林业信息化。立足用户，面向应用，融合多种技术，通过互联网，进行信息节点的大协作，实现信息系统之间的互操作和利用，作为林业信息化基础建设的思路或者指导思想；把利用云计算，研建综合化、一体化、集成化、智能化、网络化的信息平台作为主要模型；把实现实时、全面、综合共享信息资源作为重要目标；将现在的单项、单环节发展为综合、集成，以数据处理为主发展为知识处理为主，以网页联通方式发展为信息平台联通方式；研究体现一体化、集成化、智能化的林业综合办公系统、森林资源及其环境管理、监测、预警、应急系统、森林培育系统、电子商务、科技与教学信息系统等重点项目的解决方案，开发新的应用程序和系统，作为主要任务。

基础设施重点和优先项目实施、使用级见表 2。

4.2 林业政务信息化

电子政务自 20 世纪 90 年代产生以来，作为电子信息技术与政务的有机结合，成为当代信息化的最重要的领域之一。林业电子政务就是应用现代信息和通信技术，将林业政务和服务，通过信息技术特别是网络技术进行集成，在互联网上实现组织结构和工作流程的优化重组，超越时间和空间及部门之间的分隔限制，在系统内外进行交流，提供全方位、规范、透明、可靠、科学的优质政务和服务。它不是网络技术的简单的应用，不是现有管理和服务流程的网络化，不仅仅是为了取得效率的提高，也不是部门的独立应用，而重在“集成”、“优化重组”、超越“分隔限制”、内外的“优质管理和服务”。

表 2　林业政务信息化重点项目及优先项目

重点项目	优先项目	建设级	使用级
林业信息化硬软件平台建设	现有公用硬软件的优化、整合与共享	各级各层	各级各层
	基于物联网的硬软件建设	各级各层	各级各层
	基于林业云计算硬软件基础设施建设	各级各层	各级各层
林业公共数据中心建设	现有数据库系统的优化	各级各层	各级各层
	林业信息集的构建	各级各层	各级各层
	林木基因图谱数据库系统的构建	省、县	县及以下
林业信息化制度、规范与标准建设	信息化管理制度建设	国家、省	各级各层
	信息化规范、标准体系建设	国家、省	各级各层
林业生产装备与工具数字化建设	林业基本生产装备数字化建设	国家、省	各级各层
	林业基本地面资源调查工具数字化建设	国家、省	各级各层

随着现代化与信息化“两化”融合执行，与云计算、物联网、第三代通讯等新一代信息技术的应用与推进，林业电子政务必将迎来一个新阶段。在今后一个时期内，应该以“电子”与“政务”真正意义上的综合为基础，以整合提升政府公共服务和管理能力为目标，以信息共享、互联互通为重点，推进林业电子政务建设。

林业政务信息化的重点是：林业综合办公信息系统建设：急需实施的是包括现办公系统的整合、优化和提升、综合分析与决策系统建设；林业政务对外服务系统的建设：优先实施互动型林业门户网站优化与建设、整合型林业门户网站建设和公众事务服务平台建设；为适应新形势与需要阶段型系统的开发等。主要项目、研建和使用者以及阶段安排见表 3。

表 3　林业政务信息化重点项目及优先项目

重点项目	优先项目	建设级	使用级
林业综合办公信息系统	现系统的整合、优化、提升	各级各层	各级各层
	综合分析与决策系统建设	各级各层	各级各层
林业政务对外服务系统	互动型林业门户网站优化	各级各层	各级各层
	整合型林业门户网站建设	各级各层	各级各层
	公众事务服务平台建设	省、县	县及以下
适应新形势阶段型系统开发的对策	适应新形势阶段型系统开发的对策	国家、省	各级各层

4.3　森林经营与森林资源监管信息化

森林资源是林业基本组成，森林资源经营与管理，是林业生产与管理的基础。它们的状态与运动方式，决定了林业生产与管理状态与运动方式。也因此，森林经营与森林资源监管信息化，是林业信息化的重要组成。

森林经营与森林资源监管信息化，指以信息技术装备森林经营与森林资源监管各环节，实现科学化、精细化经营与管理的过程。它们的目的与目标，是通过信息化，不断提高经营与管理水平，促进林业现代化进程。森林资源生产与管理发展趋势是智能化与精细化，智能化要求应用新技术，以知识推动生产力发展，精细化要求在精确的时空状态与运动方式下，实行精细的生产与管理。它们均需要根据森林资源生产与管理的特点与规律，采用现代生产与管理思想、方式、方法和技术。如果说，森林经营是林业发展的永恒主题，那么森林经营和管理的信息化，是林业发展的关键技术支撑。一体化、综合化、智能化、网络化、集成化——森林经营与森林资源监管信息化的主要方向。

今后一个时期内，可持续森林资源经营与管理，将成为我国森林经营与管理的主流模式，各个区域必须实现可持续管理，对一些林分，在它可持续思想指导下，采取不同的模式。联合国粮农组织对于可持续森林资源经营、管理提出的概念是："是一种包括行政、经济、法律、社会、技术以及科技等手段的行为，涉及天然林与人工林。它是有计划的各种人为干预措施，目的是保护和维持森林生态系统及其各种功能"。从这个概念出发，森林经营与森林资源监管信息化，分别对国有与集体林区利用信息技术装备森林经营的各个环节，实现一体化、智能化、网络化经营；从基层到县、省、国家等各级各层的各个环节采用信息技术，实现一体化、综合化、网络化的管理。以一体化森林经营系统建设与森林资源管理系统建设为重点项目，分别国有林区一体化森林经营系统建设、集体林区一体化森林经营系统建设，和现有森林资源监管系统优化、森林资源监管集成系统建设为优先项目，进行建设。它们的研建与使用单位、建设时间见表4。

表4 森林经营与森林资源监管信息化重点项目及优先项目

重点项目	优先项目	建设级	使用级
一体化森林经营系统建设	国有林区一体化森林经营系统	省、国有集团	国有集团
	集体林区一体化森林经营系统	省、县	县、基层
森林资源管理系统建设	现有森林资源监管系统优化	国家、省、县	各级各层
	森林资源监管集成系统	国家、省、县	各级各层

4.4 人工林培育、利用与监管信息化

为了调整森林分布结构、增加森林面积，提高林分质量，科学造林、管护是关键举措之一，人工林培育、利用与监管信息化是重要支撑技术。它是指以信息技术，装备人工林培育、利用等生产活动，与工程管理的过程。它的目的与任务，是根据重点人工林培育、利用与监管需要，按它们的流程，在各个阶段和环节，组织集约化生产与管理，促进人工林生产力发展。

人工林培育、利用与监管信息化建设过程中，有许多信息技术应用问题，需要建设相应系统，由于许多方面的其他项目，例如：企业信息化建设、森林资源监管系统、森林保护与应急管理信息化等项目之中，另一方面，人工林规模巨大，一些系统不可能在短期内普遍实施，需要重点突破，逐步推进。所以确定在生产领域，选择的重点和优先项目：人工林培育信息化：包括微观的主要造林树种基因图谱信息系统、中间的苗木培育系统、和智能化森林培育系统的开发，以及采运与林产品加工自动化系统：采伐运输数字化装备与过程信息化、林产品生产自动化控制系统；在管理领域建设：生产与工程监管系统：基于物联网的林业生产监管系统、林业工程项目监管系统。它们的建设和使用者、建设时期见表5。

表 5 森林经营与森林资源监管信息化重点项目及优先项目

重点项目	优先项目	建设级	使用级
智能化森林培育系统的开发	主要树种基因图谱数据库与模式识别	国家与省	县林业局、林业企业
	特殊苗木、花卉设施培育系统建设	省、县与林业企业	林业企业
	重点林木智能化人工用材林培育系统开发	国家与省	国家、省林业厅(局)、县等林业局、林业企业
集体林区采运与林产品加工自动化系统	采伐运输数字化装备与过程信息化系统	省与县、企业	省 、县林业局与企业
	林产品生产自动化控制系统	省与县、企业	省与县、林业企业
林业工程与生产监管系统建设	现有林业工程项目监管系统优化	国家与省、县	各级林业管理部门局与企业
	林业生产综合监管系统建设	国家与省、县	省 、县林业局与企业

4.5 企业信息化与电子商务

信息化是企业建设的重要组成部分，它促进企业集中统一、共享、协同，支撑着企业、优化，全面提升企业经营管理水平。林业企业信息化，指在林业系统从事林业生产或者经营林产品活动的企业单位中，根据其生产或经营活动的各个层次和环节，采用现代信息技术，将信息流、资金流、物流重组、整合和集成，充分开发和广泛利用企业单位的内外部信息资源，伴随现代企业管理制度的形成，建成现代化管理的企业的过程。

根据各单位业务重点，可以把林业企业分为两类：一类是通过森林培养，为利用林木和非林木资源，取得经济效益，从事生产和经营活动的单位，例如各类林场、苗圃、林产品加工厂以及森林公园、自然保护区等。它们不仅需要实现内外部网络化管理，以支持开展内外部的各种经营管理活动，而且需要实现生产过程的自动化、智能化，以降低成本、提高质量、增加数量；另一类是不直接从事生产活动，仅开展林产品经营的单位，例如各类苗木、花卉、林产品销售单位，它们主要是实现内外部网络化管理，支持内外部的各种经营管理活动。

生产、经营单位信息化建设可分为生产、经营单位的内部的信息化建设和外部的信息化建设。前者是生产、经营单位在内网的平台的支撑下建立的信息管理；后者是基于外网平台的信息管理。

从内容上分析，企业信息化主要在生产、经营和管理三方面进行信息化建设。包括企业单位的业务运作过程信息化、产品营销的信息化、财务管理信息化以及人力资源管理的信息化等。

根据需要与现有基础与条件企业信息化与电子商务的重点项目与优先项目(表 6)主要有：林业企业信息化建设：包括生产过程自动化控制系统建设和一体化管理系统建设；电子商务建设：包括：林业企业电子商务系统、企业 B2C 电子商务系统、区域 B2B 电子商务系统等建设。

表6　企业信息化与电子商务重点项目及优先项目

重点项目	优先项目	建设级	使用级
企业信息化建设	生产过程自动化控制系统	企业	企业
	一体化管理系统	企业	企业
	林业企业一体化——知识——效益型模型	企业	企业
电子商务工程	林业企业电子商务工程	企业	企业
	区域行业电子商务工程	行业	行业
	个体经营者电子商务通用平台	IT 企业	经营者

4.6 森林保护与应急管理信息化

森林资源稳定健康发展，是保障社会、经济发展、国土安全、生态平衡、控制气候变化等关键因素之一。森林资源保护与应急管理信息化指：为了保证森林资源稳定健康发展，根据它的规律与特点，利用信息技术装备森林资源保护的过程。它的目的是保证森林资源稳定健康发展，它的目标对森林资源发展进行有效的监测，控制影响森林资源发生与发展；它的主要任务是通过相应的方法与技术，开展对威胁森林资源健康的因素采取监测、预警、应急处置与救援、事后恢复与重建等应对活动；它的主要管理对象是：森林自然灾害，它的重点是：森林自然灾害突发性事件。

对于森林资源自然灾害的了解与控制，需要对它们进行监测、预测、预警和应急，这些发生在不同时空条件下的不同举措，是既有联系，又有区别的概念。监测是对森林资源自然灾害的状态与运动方式，进行描述、分析；预测是根据森林资源自然灾害的变量，与另外一些变量之间的关系，对森林资源自然灾害变化趋势做出量的估计；预警则侧重于区域森林资源变动过程和发展方向的险情预报，旨在预报区域森林资源变动过程中的各种不正常现象，是未来发展趋势的科学推断；而应急是对自然灾害发生以后采取的各种应急措施，进行处置与救援、恢复与重建的过程。

森林资源自然灾害的预测、监测、预警、应急等关系密切，可以组成一个有机整体，在信息化中可以按一个工程项目考虑，为了便于实施，把它分解成几部分。预测与监测不仅关系紧密，而且实质上也是一种分析，可以把它们合并成一个过程进行处理。森林资源保护与应急管理信息化的重点与优先项目可以选择为：森林资源安全监控集成系统、森林资源突发破坏性事件监控系统的森林资源突发破坏性事件预警系统与森林资源突发破坏性事件监控系统。它们的建设主持、使用单位，见表7。

表7　森林经营与森林资源监管信息化重点项目及优先项目

重点项目	优先项目	建设级	使用级
森林资源安全监控集成系统控集成系统	森林资源安全监控集成系统控集成系统	国家、省	林业系统各级
森林资源突发破坏性事件监控系统	森林资源突发破坏性事件预警系统	国家、省	林业系统各级
	森林资源突发破坏性事件应急系统	国家、省	林业系统各级

4.7 知识创新、技术创新、推广应用与林区网络文化

世界正在进入知识经济或者称信息时代。从发展生产力的基本动力分析，农业时代依靠的是劳力与土地，工业时代依靠的是资本与资源，而知识经济发展生产力的基本动力是知识

与信息。其基本过程是通过知识创新产生知识，通过技术创新，把知识转化为技术，通过推广把技术转化为生产力。林业信息化是一个过程，从以上角度出发它是一个通过不断的知识创新、技术创新、应用推广的过程。

林业信息化的知识、技术创新与应用推广，网络文化建设，应该纳入国家创新工程、林业创新工程，和新农村、新林区建设之中，不另立体系。需要研究与实施的项目，也应该纳入国家、林业科学、教育、新林区规划之中。关键是准确处理内外关系，共建项目，协调发展；其次是根据林业信息化需要，建设应用推广平台。因此，有关科研、教育项目主要由科技、教育信息化安排；林区信息化基础与社区信息化，与建设新农村、三位一体等工程协同实施。本研究选择的重点项目主要是建设应用推广与教育平台，主要有：知识、技术应用推广与重点科研方向、信息化示范基地建设、林业网络教育建设、森林健康、生态文明、绿色环境服务与传播。它们的建设主持、使用单位，见表8。

表8　知识创新、技术创新、推广应用与林区网络文化的研究重点项目及优先项目

重点项目	优先项目	建设级	使用级
知识、技术应用推广与重点科研方向	林业信息技术应用测评、中介与推广	各级各层	各级各层
	重点科研方向确立	国家、省	国家、省
	信息产业的发展	各级各层次	
信息化示范基地建设		国家、省	省及其以下
林业网络教育建设		国家、省	各级各层
林区网络文化建设		省及其以下	省及其以下

5　林业信息化规划

规划把理想变成现实的安排，是规划主体的预先承诺。是具有制约力的指导性文件，是一切管理工作的核心环节。由于林业信息化涉及面广、离数、差异等特点，更需要一个科学、可靠、可行的规划。包括具有前瞻性、战略性的全国林业信息化建设规划，提出长期和短期目标、总体结构与功能、开发顺序与优先级、资源配置；在它的指导下，制定地区、部门、领域等信息化建设规划。

5.1　林业信息化规划概要

过去，在林业信息化中：有些时候和地区，处理信息化和现代化发展战略关系不够协调；一些地方，没有把信息化提到应有的地位；有的地方在概念不清、方向不明的前提下，开展信息化建设；有的在建设中，不够全面与协调；应当时间空间分割，形成了信息孤岛。造成这些原因是多方面的，其中之一，是缺少一个全面、可行的规划。在了解规划基本含义基础上，选择合适的规划方式、方法，并实施，十分必要。

林业信息化规划，是对未来林业信息化行动的战略统筹安排。它是领导决策的依据、控制协调的基础、具体实施的方向指导性文件。

信息化规划主要反映是什么、为什么和做什么的问题。应能体现：先进性——适应形势发展，符合时代要求、科学性——依据国情林情，反映客观规律、实用性——立足业务应用，满足多元需求、可行性——符合时空条件与基础、可操作性——虚实结合，便于实施。

不同的时间、空间、不同的人、不同的基础、不同的项目，可以有不同的规划理念、指导思想、内容、方法。但是其基本的理念是：规划融入整个管理活动之中、不断修正的动态过程；长中短计划的结合，反映全面、协调、合作、和谐、创新；创新来自打破常规。规划需要：有创新精神：以新思想、新方法、新思维、新高度面对规划；正确的指导思想：科学发展观；协调时空关系：面向未来，适度超前，适应需求，立足现实；合理的技术路线，严格、科学的方式、方法：适应信息化特点的方式、方法和全面规划，突出重点的对策。

林业信息化规划的基本依据是，林业发展战略、目标、内容和需求、区域信息化的战略与要求、林业化环境、状态、基础和条件、林业生产与管理、服务信息及其流程；规划的主要内容是：目标、信息和功能需求、任务、结构与功能、多方案制定、优先级、资源分配、保障措施、时间安排等。

5.2 林业信息化规划方式、方法的选择

环境与条件决定着规划方式、方法。如果是简单的环境：可以采取等待的方式，进行尝试，可能成功也可能失败，然后再尝试；如果是相对稳定的环境：那么可以以“工艺知识”应用的方式，相对机械的进行安排，是单项、静态的方式；如果是变化的环境，可采取科学方法，进行必要的模型、模拟，进一步认识环境。开展总体规划或者综合规划。林业信息化不仅具有变化的特点，而且由于各个方面的差异，带来多样，造成复杂、不确定、冲突，事实上的不可预见性、不可完全认识性等特点，在方法上要求：综合的、整体的，试图掌握完型的系统联系——客观基本环境，并强调不断持续，强调整体、强调综合、强调协作、强调过程和结果一样重视，强调对结果达成共识 。它处在一个紊乱的环境，管理主体一方面不能完全了解和把握现在和未来，另一方面独立运作，各自为政。在这样紊乱环境下，为未来进行规划，探索一个新的规划方式，对信息管理来说，应该实行动态管理，随着环境的变化，不断进行调整，也因此，必须采取适应性规划的理念和方式。

适应性规划要求各个利益团体相互协作，界定所分享的价值，不断地学习，不断的评估和修订，这是一个无限滚动的过程。规划虽然不能保证各主体利益，但应该尽可能地满足各个方面的协调和合作关系；虽然对结果不能进行正确预测，但是，尽可能能够对可能产生的危机，进行预防；虽然不能完全适应环境变化的速度，但是尽可能的可以进行适时的调整。它利用系统方法，采取为未来作准备的方式，进行综合的、整体的，试图掌握系统内外联系的规划，它应该强调综合，强调协作，强调持续，强调过程和结果同样重视，强调对结果形成共识。

适应性规划关键在根据变化，进行无限滚动的规划的过程。对每一次规划，可以按下列方法进行：

林业信息化规划十步法：

第一步：准备→第二步：数据收集→第三步：分析和评估→第四步：构建整体概念模型→第五步：构建子系统概念模型→第六步：构建物理模型框架→第七步：重点建设项目设计→第八步：财务投入分析→第九步：效果、风险分析与对策→第十步：规划的抉择、确定，如图 1。

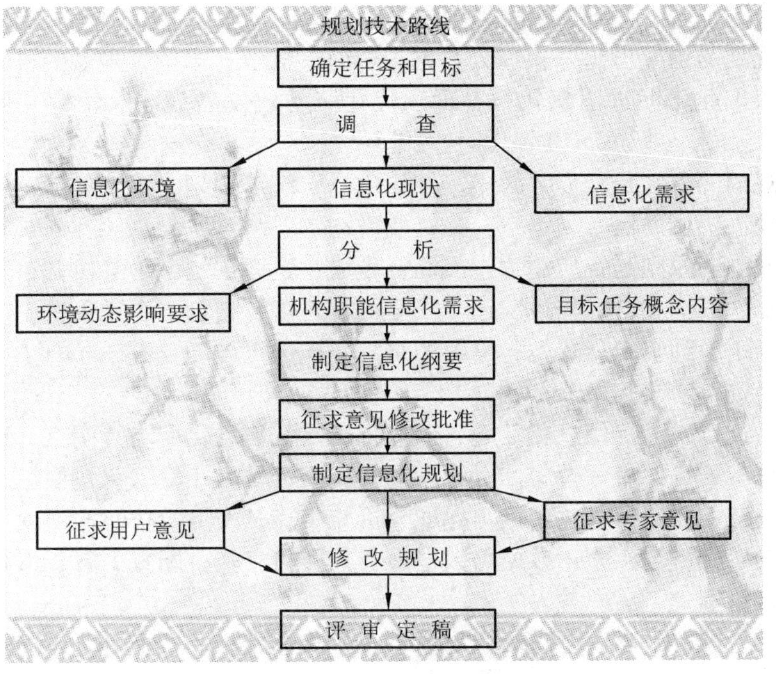

图1　林业信息化规划十步法

5.3　林业信息化规划案例

近年来湖南等省陆续进行了林业信息化规划，在形成规划的同时，积累了经验，其他各地可有选择的借鉴。

根据浙江省加快实现现代化和信息化总体战略，由北京林业大学信息学院信息管理系和浙江省林业调查规划设计院共同组成了规划小组，于2004～2005年进行浙江林业信息化规划，主要过程与结果是：

5.3.1　规划目标与任务的确定

浙江省林业信息化建设目的是：贯彻执行信息化带动工业化，工业化促进信息化，实现跨越式发展战略，根据"建设生态省、打造绿色浙江"、率先实现现代化战略目标，用新的知识理念，重组林业管理机制和生产模式；在林业系统各个领域与环节，全面应用信息技术，进行全方位的变革，促进发展林业的综合能力，从劳动密集型、资本密集型的传统林业，向技术密集型进而向知识密集型的现代林业转变；树立林业工作者对信息技术的信心、提高林业工作者应用信息技术的能力、促进信息技术的发展和普及，全面提升林业工作和经营者的精神和物质生活水平；在率先实现林业现代化，建设生态省和现代化省中，发挥作用，推进林业和林业与社会、经济全面、协调、可持续发展。

信息化建设依据是：以中央和省关于全面建设小康社会，率先实现现代化省的战略目标，作为信息化战略目标，以"建设生态省、打造绿色浙江"，实施"五大工程"、打造"五大基地"、深化"五大改革"、建设"五大体系"等作为林业信息化建设服务的对象，以国家和省有关信息化建设决定、部署和规划为指导，根据国内外信息化发展趋势、有关林业和林业信息化建设政策、法律、法规、规范、标准、浙江省和林业经济、技术基础、浙江林业信息技术应用与基础、浙江林业信息化需求与条件等为依据，制定林业信息化规划，组织实施林业信息化建设。

信息化与规划的指导思想是：以人为本；全面、科学、可持续发展的科学发展观；信息化带动工业化，工业化促进信息化，实现现代化跨越式发展战略；转型、整合、重组、创新 。

信息化与规划的方针是：以人为本，知识主导；统筹规划，综合创新；资源共享，分类实施；精心管理，协调发展。

信息化与规划的原则是：应用为先、综合集成；全面规划、统筹协调；分期实施、逐步推进；优势互补、资源共享；先进实用、安全可靠；统专结合，引进创新。

信息化规划小组到组织形式是：学习型组织形式进行规划。

5.3.2 调查与分析

规划组以通过形式进行信息化环境、信息化现状、信息化需求等调查，形成单项与综合的调查报告，汇集了有关参考资料。以光盘形式提供：国内外信息化发展综述；国内地区与行业信息化规划与发展；信息化规范与标准分析与实施；网络为核心的硬软件平台分析与实施；电子政务发展分析与实施；数据与数据整合分析与实施；国家、省、市有关信息化、林业发展和状态资料等。

在此基础上，进行了环境动态影响与要求、机构职能流程与需求、信息化目标、任务、概念与内容等分析，为了进一步规划奠定基础。重点分析项目有：

(1)环境分析。国外信息化发展动态、国外信息化发展动态、中国和国内地区信息化建设动态、国内行业和林业信息化建设动态。对浙江省林业信息技术应用现状与国内林业信息化发展系统诊断：①基本条件是：领导重视；基础设施建设已有一定基础；信息技术已经进入各个领域的应用；应用系统建设正在迅速发展。②问题是：认识上的差距、行动上的差距、具体结果差距。结论是：机会与挑战共存。

(2)概念分析。提出的概念是：在国家和省有关信息化建设指导下，进行统一规划与组织实施，在林业生产、经营、管理、科技、教育等各个部门的各个环节，应用信息技术，与林业业务、科学技术有机融合，创建林业发展新模式、方法和技术，以智能化、网络化、集成化、虚拟化等方式，生产、分配、完善、使用信息与知识，将信息和知识转化为技术，技术转化为生产力，促进林业发展实现林业现代化的过程。

主要内涵是：林业信息化主体是全体林业成员，包括林业行政和业务部门、企业、事业、团体和个人；信息化意在重组和转型，为了发挥知识的作用，为了林业发展综合能力、林业工作和经营者的素质、精神、物质生活质量的提高，核心是信息和知识；信息化时间上是一个长期过程，空间上是涉及林业管理、经营、科技、教育等各个领域的各个环节；信息化需要是基于信息技术的现代工具，智能化、网络化、集成化、虚拟化等方式；途径是统一规划和组织协调，创建符合信息时代社会生产力发展，推动林业改革的环境。

信息化地位与作用是：全面提高信息和知识意识，实现用“物”为中心向以“知识”为中心转变，以知识发展林业，公众能够公平应用和享受信息技术，提高精神和物质水平；促进林业生产力发展，实现林业跨越式发展；应用信息技术，发展林业信息技术，增加相应产值，逐步形成新的林业产业，调整林业产业结构；改变林业高度分散、时空差异大、现代化程度差、稳定性和可控性低的弱点；节省能源、提高资源利用率、提高物流速度和效率、提高林业产业的整体性、系统性和协调性；在机械化的基础上实现集约化、自动化和智能化，改造传统林业生产方式，改进生产工艺过程，促进粗放经营向集约经营转变，实现在精确时间空间条件下，实现精细的管理和经营；推进网络化管理，加快实现管理科学化，实现全时空、广信息、多媒体、快速度、零距离和交互虚拟管理，使林业走向社会，社会参与林。

(3)需求分析。对信息化提出的需求是：人力资源的培养和利用；规划和实施方法与技术；实施中的组织协调，资金来源和投入；各级信息化基础设施建设；电子政务与单位办公自动化；事务和业务网络化管理；综合、集成的信息系统；专家系统和决策支持系统；生产过程的自动化、智能化；基本林业科技数据、方法、知识、模型库的研究。

5.3.3 多方案的制订、修改和选定

规划组在规划过程中，提出了多种方案，几经多方征求意见、修改、从中确定了最终规划。规划组提供了规划过程中的中间结果。多种方案。以光盘和书面形式提供：初步规划与修改稿：包括初稿、2004 年 8 月 20 日、23 日、28 日、29 日修改稿；2004 年规划方案：包括预方案与方案 1 ~5，和规划纲要；2005 年规划修改稿：包括 4 月、8 月、11 月修改稿和说明。经过比较分析，确定的结果是：以光盘和书面形式提供：主题规划：浙江省林业信息化规划(2006 ~2010 年)；示范区规划：浙江省省级资源、林政管理信息化规划，浙江省森林资源监测中心信息化建设规划，浙江省临安市林业局信息化规划等。

确定了林业信息化建设战略目标：坚持信息化带动工业化，工业化促进信息化，实现跨越式发展战略，加快浙江省林业信息化建设，到 2006 年完成基本基础建设，实现政务网络化管理，重点系统在全省运行，在国内林业系统处领先水平；到 2010 年初步建成全省林业信息化体系，进入国内行业信息化先进行列；再用十年时间，建成比较完善的浙江林业信息化体系，接近、力争达到发达国家林业信息化水平。

所谓初步建成全省林业信息化体系，指到 2010 年，浙江省林业系统信息化基础设施完备，管理领域的应用系统框架初步建成并运行，基本实现了网络化管理，生产领域主要森林培养、经营和林产品生产自动化、智能化程度进入试运行，林业管理、生产、经营工作者可以公平享受信息服务，大部分掌握了本职范围内的信息技术和工具的使用。林业信息技术向规模化方向发展，有一定产值。林业信息产业开始形成。信息化水平总体上达到国内林业系统领先水平，进入国内各行业的信息化先进行列。

所谓比较完善的浙江林业信息化体系，指到 2020 年，在以上各个领域继续发展基础上，各个部门和领域特别是生产和经营领域在集成化、智能化、虚拟化方面有新的发展，根据世界发展动态，依靠自身能力，形成持续的自主的林业信息技术的创新形态，林业信息产业形成，产值占一定比例。信息化水平进入世界林业发达国家的信息化水平。

确定的 2005 ~2010 年目标与任务是：利用两年时间，基本建成全省林业信息基础实施和重点应用系统主体框架，林业信息化综合指标达到国内林业领先水平：在以上基础上，再用三年时间，全面完成林业信息公用平台的建设，建成全省信息网络，全面完成网络基础平台、公共数据平台、完成重要方法、模型与知识库建设、林业各类重要应用系统、公众服务系统、企事业单位信息化建设，产生一批智能化生产、管理、经营系统。

确定的具体目是：基本建成覆盖全省林业系统的林业信息网络硬件平台；开发省级和地区、县的公共基本数据管理系统，基本建成林业信息公用平台；以电子政务推动、建成林业系统电子政务的主体框架；整合各主要业务应用系统，建立森林资源信息管理为核心的林业信息管理框架；加快重点地区和企事业信息化建设，建成林业信息化典型示范区；完善林业

产业信息网，建成信息服务体系框架；建立与健全信息化管理体制，形成法规、标准规范和安全体系框架；开展信息技术研究和推广开展机制，建成信息技术研究和推广体系框架；培养和造就一批林业信息化技术和管理人才，建成林业信息化教育培训体系。

确定的林业信息化建设具体任务是：在国家、省和本规划指导下，开展各地市、县等各部门、单位的信息化规划；按省和本规划要求健全各级信息化领导和实施组织，根据不同情况，设管理机构，和信息主管；多方面筹集相关资源，增加投入力度；以电子政务推动，森林资源信息管理为核心，启动浙江省信息化工程，进行重点信息化建设：

信息技术应用人力资源培养工程；

以网络为核心的信息化基础硬软件平台建设工程；

信息化公共基本数据平台建设工程；

信息化规范与标准化工程；

重点业务应用系统(生产、管理)系统工程；

林业政务信息化建设工程；

企、事业单位信息化工程；

信息化典型示范工程；

林业信息技术科学研究与技术推广工程；

林业信息化服务体系建设工程；

信息化规划体现了：全面规划，逐步推进；整体筹划，协调发展；深入分析，概念驱动；转型重组，推动变革；结合实际，整合创新。

林业信息化在发展中，无论是理念还是方法、技术，目标、任务还是措施，都在变化之中，本文讨论的内涵、发展、战略重点与规划，只是在特定环境和条件下的论述，需要不断地补充、修正，以便为林业信息化提供更有效的依据。

四、缅怀董乃钧先生

我国森林资源监测工作的回顾与展望

——缅怀董乃钧教授

周昌祥

去年我国公布了第七次（2004～2008年）全国森林资源连续清查成果，与5年前相比，我国森林覆盖率由18.21%提高到20.36%；森林面积由1.75亿hm^2增加到1.95亿hm^2；森林蓄积由124.5亿m^3增加到137.2亿m^3；人工林保存面积0.62亿hm^2列世界第一，在国际上引起很好的反响。同时，我国也是世界上能系统定时准确公布全国森林资源数据的少数国家之一，这都归功于全国森林资源连续清查体系的建立。在这体系研建中，包含着董乃钧教授等一批教学科研生产相结合积极推进者的重要贡献。

一、回顾

新中国成立后我国开展了大规模森林调查工作，主要是学习苏联小班目测调查，把小班－林班－分区－林场－林业局－县－省汇总成全国森林资源数据，直到1965年才汇总完成（1951～1963年）第一次全国森林资源数据并予以发布。这种办法周期长、覆盖面不全、数据精度不稳定，不适应发展的需要，必须寻找新的突破。

（一）新技术的引进试验和迅速推广

1963年北京林学院董乃钧等教师，向我们介绍了以数理统计为理论基础的抽样调查技术。1964年在湖南省汝城县大坪林场进行分层抽样试验取得很好效果，董乃钧是试验技术负责人之一。1965年进一步在云南省华坪县和大兴安岭新林林业局开展分层抽样调查技术试生产，经大面积实测验证成功。林业部决定大范围推广，1966年就完成200多万hm^2森林抽样调查任务。森林抽样调查方法在全国林业调查规划系统取得共识。

（二）“四五”清查——在规定的时间内完成全国森林资源清查

1973年农林部要求在“四五”期间内准确迅速查清我国森林资源，为制定林业方针政策和各种计划规划提供科学依据，并决定分别在大兴安岭的吉文林业局（即北方试点）和湖南会同县（即南方试点）。探寻以局县为调查单位的准确快速方法，采用设置固定样地的多种抽样技术并获得成功，试点工作有14个省（自治区）林业调查工作者和10所林业院校教师参加，董乃钧是北方试点技术负责人之一。通过这次试点找到了可行方法，1973～1976年全国开展了以县局为单位森林资源清查。调查结果，全国除台湾省外的森林面积是1.22亿hm^2，森林蓄积量是87亿m^3，森林覆盖率是12.7%。这是中国第一次在规定的时间内，基本采用了统一的调查方法完成的全国性森林资源清查。另外，林业部规定今后各地规划设计

基金项目：林业公益性行业专项“我国典型森林类型健康经营关键技术研究（201004002）”。

作者简介：张会儒（1964～），男，研究员，博导，主要从事森林资源可持续经营研究。Email：：huiru@caf.ac.cn

(森林经理)调查时，除进行小班调查外，还要采用抽样调查方法控制调查总体蓄积量，以保证小班蓄积量调查的准确性。

(三)第二次清查——初步建立了全国森林资源连续清查体系框架

为了找到能定期向国家提供准确的森林资源数量和质量数据，掌握森林资源消长变化趋势的有效途径，1977 年农林部决定在江西省举办全国森林资源连续清查试点。来自 27 个省区林业调查工作者和农林院校教师 200 人参加，董乃钧也是重要成员。试点取得成功，为建立省(区、市)级，以固定样地复查为特征的全国森林资源连续清查体系打下牢固基础。到 1981 年底在 26 个省区市(西藏、上海、天津、台湾除外)全部建成，第一次清查即“五五”清查，全国共设置 13.7 万固定样地和 2.3 万临时样地。调查工作结束后，建立了“五五”清查数据库。至此，中国的森林资源清查技术，从过去的静态清查，发展到动态监测的新阶段。

(四)“第三次清查”——全国森林资源连续清查第一次复查

从 1984 ~ 1988 年历时 5 年，完成除西藏、台湾外各省区市森林资源连续清查第一次复查，1989 年林业部公布了当时我国最新森林数据成果。这次清查全国共设 25.5 万样地，其中复查样地 14 万个，新设样地 11.1 万个。

(五)第四次清查——建立全国森林资源监测体系

林业部于 1989 年 2 月发文，要求在全国建立森林资源监测体系，以便及时掌握森林资源现状和消长动态，预测森林资源的发展趋势，规定各省、市、自治区完成外业调查、成果统计表、资源分析报告、数据库相关数据、质量检查验收报告、各类图件等一并报林业部进行汇总，每 5 年发布一次全国森林资源连续清查结果，使森林资源监测工作更加规范。1989 ~ 1993 年完成全国森林资源连续清查第二次复查，并建立了西藏自治区连清体系。不少省区进一步完善布点方案并采用遥感资料丰富清查成果。全国共调查地面样地 22.72 万个，判读卫片和航片成数样地 10.63 万个。

由于全国森林资源连续清查工作已正常运转并取得良好效果，大家共同努力近 30 年教学科研生产相结合的成果 <全国森林资源连续清查技术体系的研建>，于 1989 年获得林业部科技进步一等奖，15 名主要完成人董乃钧名列其中。1992 年该成果又获得国家科技进步二等奖，只能报 9 名主要完成人，董乃钧先生为成全年轻同志，主动让奖，这种愿为人梯，淡泊名利的崇高品质令人敬佩。

(六)每五年复查一轮的全国森林资源监测体系正常运行

在国家林业主管部门统一部署下，1994 ~ 1998 年开展第五次清查，各省市区相继进行森林资源连续复查工作，共完成 18 万个地面样地复查和卫片和航片判读样地 9 万多个；在 1999 ~ 2003 年的第六次全国森林资源清查中，首次将荒漠化、沙化和湿地调查内容纳入到清查体系中，在技术手段上将遥感(RS)、全球定位系统(GPS)、地理信息系统(GIS)和手持掌上电脑数据采集技术应用于森林资源连续清查中，布设的固定样地数量达到 41.5 万个，遥感样地数量达到 284.44 万个，实现了全国各省、自治区、直辖市(除台湾省、香港特别行政区、澳门特别行政区)的地面固定样地布设全覆盖；2004 – 2008 年又开展第七次清查，全国共实测固定样地 41.5 万个，判读遥感样地 284.44 万个，获取清查数据 1.6 亿组，数据涉及森林资源数量、质量、结构、分布的现状和动态，以及森林生态状况和功能效益等方面。依据第七次清查结果和森林生态定位监测结果评估，全国森林植被总碳储量 78.11 亿 t，森林生态服务功能年价值量超过10万亿元。此间广东、福建、内蒙古三省(自治区)对森林资源及其生态状况综合监测进行了有益尝试和探索，为全国开展森林生态状况监测积累经验、提供示范。但在第六、七次清查中虽然判读了大量遥感样地，其数据主要用于编制森林分布图，并未用于森林资源数据的计算。在此期间董乃钧教授一直关注我国森林资源监测工作，担任多项专家组成员。

通过广大林业调查人员的努力，中国七次森林资源清查成果如下：

清查间隔期	活立木蓄积(万 m^3)	森林面积(万 hm^2)	森林蓄积(万 m^3)	森林覆盖率(%)
第一次(1973～1976年)	953227.00	12186.00	865579.00	12.7
第二次(1977～1981年)	1026059.88	11527.74	902795.33	12.0
第三次(1984～1988年)	1057249.86	12465.28	914107.64	12.98
第四次(1989～1993年)	1178500.00	13370.35	1013700.00	13.92
第五次(1994～1998年)	1248786.39	15894.09	1126659.14	16.55
第六次(1999～2003年)	1361810.00	17490.92	1245584.58	18.21
第七次(2004～2008年)	1491268.19	19545.22	1372080.36	20.36

二、展　望

我国自1977年举办全国森林资源连续清查试点以来，逐步建成以省区市为总体(吉林、黑龙江、西藏、甘肃、青海、新疆含2～4个副总体)，以固定样地5年复查一次为主要内容的国家森林资源监测体系，至今已有34年并进行过5次复查，目前正在开展第八次清查即6次复查。总的看来系统比较稳定，监测数据也比较灵敏可靠。但从发展角度看还面临不少挑战。

(1)如何把森林资源连续清查由监测森林面积、蓄积变化为主，向森林生态系统动态监测发展，进而使森林生态系统、湿地生态系统、荒漠生态系统和生物多样性的监测技术有机结合起来。

(2)如何把森林资源连续清查监测的森林面积、蓄积变化，进一步与研究森林碳储量与碳汇动态变化贡献紧密结合起来，进而估算森林的碳平衡。进行碳储量和碳汇计量以及动态预测。

(3)十二五规划指标有18项，其中森林增长是约束性指标，要求森林覆盖率从20.36%增长到21.66%，5年增量为1.3%；森林蓄积从137亿 m^3 增长到143亿 m^3，5年增量为6亿 m^3。如何把5年一次监测和每年造林、采伐、征占用地等实施情况调查及蓄积生长枯损测算相结合，准确及时反映“十二五”规划指标执行情况。

(4)如何提高3S技术在全国森林资源监测体系中使用成效，目前卫片判读样地只能用于编制森林分布图，不能用于森林资源数据的计算 如何突破。

(5)固定样地多次复查后是否会产生因“特殊对待”以致造成有偏估计，是否需要添加临时样地或样线来检验和校正。

(6)数十万固定样地经多次复查，蕴藏着丰富宝贵的信息如何发掘利用。

(7)如何妥善处理好一类清查数据与二类调查数据的差异，把森林调查、档案管理更新工作与全国森林资源监测衔接好。

要解决好这些挑战问题必须创新，就要有像董乃钧教授那样一大批教学科研生产相结合的积极推进者，奉献者共同努力。这也是今天我们缅怀董乃钧教授的重要内容。

参考文献

[1]“森林资源连续清查技术体系研建”工作总结.
[2]肖兴威. 中国森林资源清查[M]. 北京：中国林业出版社，2005.
[3]雷加富. 中国森林资源[M]. 北京：中国林业出版社，2005.
[4]国家林业局调查规划设计院院史(1954～2004).

缅怀林业教育事业的勤奋耕耘人：董乃钧教授

陈谋询
（北京林业大学）

我国著名林学家、林业教育家、北京林业大学教授、国家重点学科博士生导师董乃钧教授，于2011年8月1日12时37分，永远离开了我们。作为他的学生、同事，耳闻目睹了他为我国林业事业贡献的毕生精力与智慧，体念了一个林业教育工作者一生的勤奋耕耘。在此，回顾他在林业教育事业的点滴，略表缅怀之情。

董先生自1954年在北京林学院毕业留校后，分配在当时的森林经理教研室工作，主攻方向是有关森林资源经营、管理方法和技术的研究与教学，从此开始了他在这一领域的开拓、创新。初期，他和唐宗桢先生一起，参与航空测量与调查在林业中的应用实践，并于1956年，在国内林业院校率先开设了相关课程——“林业中的飞机应用”（后正名为“航空和航测在林业中应用”）。根据国内外这一领域的发展，不失时机地，于20世纪80年代初，把它发展成“林业遥感”课，在校内教学的同时，更为全国林业大专学校、生产单位，举办遥感技术在林业中应用研讨和培训班，培养了一大批该领域的骨干队伍。·期间，与唐先生等老师一起，引进了多媒体教学手段，制作了覆盖林业遥感基础、方法、技术等全部内容的电化教材，在全国推广应用。同时，组织创建了国内林业院校第一个林业遥感实验室、计算机图像处理实验室、微机实验室、培养了首位面向林业图形图象处理的研究生。1986年后，董先生担任了院级领导和学科带头人，积极组织和支持空间信息技术在林业中应用研究与教学，推动了林业遥感、地理信息系统、全球定位系统等研究、教学和实践。与此同时，董先生积极推进和参与了抽样方法在林业中的应用生产实践，于20世纪70年代，作为主要参与人，进行以抽样为基础的全国南北方森林资源调查试点，进而与有关部门一起提出与实践了国家森林资源监测体系系统建设与运行，综合应用遥感、抽样、计算机等方法和技术，为建立国际领先并符合中国国情、林情、具有中国特色的森林资源连续清查体系，做了突出贡献。这一切，不仅反映了董先生在有关领域坚实的理论、方法、技术基础，而且得力于他的不断学习进取、研究创新、实践开拓的自我超越，和团队协作发展的精神。

国内外信息技术革命推动着社会进步与发展，计算机、网络技术的应用作为林业建设的又一重要手段，进而发展成的林业信息化象征林业事业进入了一个新的阶段。董先生在这一领域，不仅亲身投入，更主要的发挥了引导、组织和领导作用，为推进林业信息化进程，做出了重要贡献。20世纪80年代初，国内改革势态已经形成，国际新技术革命逐步深入。所在学校在恢复办学以后，也正在重新兴起。当时学校内，董先生和周沛村等老师一起，在国内农林学院率先进行了计算机应用研究和教学，为林、农业有关部门，举办了一系列计算机在自然资源调查、数据处理和管理中应用培训班；组织部分老师参与林业部、国家农委组织的森林资源调查和统计分析软件开发；经过几年的研究和实践，认识到新技术的应用有待扩大、深入，因此组织十位老师起草了一份关于成立林业部林业信息中心的建议，面呈林业部领导，参加计划司召开的由林科院、部规划院和学校有关人员参加的协调会，说明意见，促进了部信息中心的成立。校领导和老师们在实践中，体会到相关人才的奇缺，已经成为影响新技术应用的关键问题之一。在这个背景下，学校根据科学技术和现代教育的发展趋势，分析相关人才需求情况，果断决定成立一个面向新形势、新需求、新内容的新专业。1984 年秋，董先生作为新专业筹备领导小组副组长，依托林业系森林经理教研室，主持新专业日常筹建工作。经过广泛调研、深入分析，提出“林业信息管理”专业筹建方案，要求将林学、管理学、数学、信息科学等学科知识融合，培养以服务林业系统为主，又能适应其他行业需要的高级信息管理人才。经过一年的准备，经教委论证、审批，林业部于 1986 年 2 月 15 日正式下文，由在北京林业大学中试办林业信息管理专业。至此，我们国家第一个面向行业的信息管理专业诞生！在国家专业目录中，首次有了信息管理专业名录，一些院校也开始创办类似专业。

“林业信息管理”专业，是一个符合时代发展、社会需要的新型专业，需要校内外有关部门的支持。董先生起着内外联系与协调的作用。在教研室内，他鼓励和支持一些老师，结合原专业业务，学习新技术，要求横向综合，开创新专业，董乃钧、周沛村等八位老师直接投入专业筹备和教学工作；他不断向校领导汇报，取得更多的关注与支持，又联系教务处、基础部、森工系、林经系和计算中心等部门，研究、分析调查资料、审议教学计划、提出课程设置和重点内容等。在校外，他联系教育司、人事司、科技司、资源司、造林司、部信息中心、部规划院、北京市林业局等领导和专家，召开座谈会、参观教学展览，给信息专业建设具体的关爱和指导；争取资源司、信息中心、种苗总站等部门，委托本专业举办新技术应用培训班，联系国家种苗总站、北京市林业局以及河北、四川、甘肃、浙江、贵州、内蒙古等林业单位，和本专业合作，共同发展林业信息管理事业，为专业发展提供条件和基础；当时资源司把本专业作为重点培训基地，连续几年委托本专业举办全国性的高级研讨班，不仅在物质和经济上给以支持，更重要的是这些来自社会的精神支持，提高了专业办学信心，丰富了有关知识，培养和锻炼了教师执教能力。

林业信息管理涉及多学科、多专业的理论、方法和技术，林业信息管理专业培养的是复合型人才，综合创新是办好专业的关键，林业信息管理专业教学计划、课程体系与内容，以及师资队伍建设等方面体现特色。在这个过程中，董先生采取统一确定基本方向，放手发挥老师各自优势的方式，精心组织、领导了专业建设。根据林业信息管理的特点，吸收相关专业的经验和内容，制订具有林业信息管理教育特色计划：确立了以系统观点为指导，林学和林业管理等为业务基础，应用数学等为主要方法，信息技术为重要手段，强调三者有机结合，突出林业信息管理为特色，运用综合创新的方式方法制订教学计划。根据林业信息的获取、存贮、处理和使用等过程与环节，以现代信息管理理念、方法、手段组织课程体系；根据林业管理需要，以森林资源及其环境管理为重点，兼顾其他经济信息管理(含林业企业管理)和办公自动化等培养方向；注重当时系统科学应用动向，安排相关知识的课程，并且新技术应用讲座四年不断线，以适应信息科技快速发展的形势，信息技术实习实验四年不断线，把计算机处理融入每门专业课程之中，而且四年集中时间的教学实习与实践不断线，以体现获得知识是“干”出来的理念。在此基础上。组织具有林业信息管理特色的课程体系，主要特点突出了“林”与信息技术结合，按林业管理需要，以对林业状态的信息描述、林业管理过程的信息流表述以及林业信息加工、生产和使用的系统综合等为依据组织课程；不唯技术而技术、不为方法而方法，采取多学科有机横向综合，制订教学大纲。林业信息管理专业需要培养既有林学与林业管理知识，又掌握管理方法和手段的复合型人才，必须有一支复合型教师队伍。他主要组织领导了三个方面工作，一是整体上建立多学科的教师队伍结构，二是老师个体上充实调整知识结构，三是在实践中提高业务水平。这个教师队伍中，既有长期从事森林经理教学和研究以及森林资源管理实践的老先生，又有毕业于自动控制、林学、数学专业的老师，以后又增加了计算机专业、林业经济专业毕业的老师，多学科、老中青组成的教师队伍，创造了相互学习、补充和发展的环境。在教学的同时，作为课题负责人，进行了我国第一个森林资源管理信息系统、地方三级森林资源监测体系、宏观森林资源管理理论等研究，开拓了研究与教学新领域。董先生的研究生不仅有来自林学，而且有来自计算机、数学、林业经济管理和林业经济等专业的学生，体现了多学科的交叉综合，师生互动互补的教育理念。

新领域的开拓、新专业的创建需要有一个良好的环境和精神。林业信息管理专业的团队，努力做到政治上相互关心、业务上相互学习、生活上互相照顾。在这个集体中，许多事的看法不一致，时有激烈争论，甚至冲突，但是多能协调处理。这种环境得力于所有老师具有一个为创建新专业而努力的共同意愿、实现自我超越的精神、得力于团队学习的作风。董先生以身作则，实现学术和工作中民主自由风气，使老师们敢于发展意见，敢于争论，专业创建的一切成果，凝聚着他的心血和集体的智慧。

董先生在 1957 年给我们传授林业航空测量和调查开始，作为他的学生和同事，和他相识相处，处处事事铭刻在心：不能忘记在航测课上课下，他引导我走向新的领域；不能忘记 1958 年，他带领我们到小兴安岭实习和我们一起进林海，学习与实践；不能忘记实习以后，在一个小车站，自发的师生联欢，和相互挥泪水告别；不能忘记他食宿在教研室，简单的生活，夜以继日的工作；不能忘记他和我们一起上高原进林区，研究和实践；不能忘记，我们一起参加学术会议，讨论交流；不能忘记，在他刚刚出院的今年 4 月初，信息专业成立 25 周年、信息学院成立 10 周年之际，他的"时代需要我们分秒必争，为开拓无限信息资源努力，信息学院全体师生员工加油"的最后遗愿和重托！

董先生的突然离去，使他的弟子、同事、朋友万分悲痛，纷纷以各种方式进行悼念，并向亲属问候。他女儿给我短信说："父亲有您们这样的好友，真的很欣慰"，我们的回答的是：我们所做的都源于董先生的为人、为事，源于他为了事业、理想所做的一切！他无愧于新中国的林人！

不知疲倦的人
——怀念恩师董乃钧先生

赵天忠
（北京林业大学信息学院）

2011年8月1日，因一点小意外，我在京外的一家医院进行腰伤治疗，中午时分接到了办公室同事从北京友谊医院传来了恩师董乃钧先生与世长辞的讯息，使我这个本来"伤身"的人又加上了"伤心"二字，同时也使得我们几个董先生的弟子在2010年12月南方森林经理研讨会期间商讨的在今年十月份举行的"活动"无法按原定计划进行，留下了终身的遗憾。

恩师故去两个月以来，他老人家的音容笑貌在我的脑海里幕幕再现。读大学期间给董先生当学生，1982年大学毕业留校在先生组建的"林业调查规划研究室"手下当"学徒"，1986年跟随恩师创建"林业信息管理"专业做他的部下，是他老人家将我这个来自山西偏远山村的农家孩子一步步引上了大学教师这个神圣的岗位和职业。回想30多年来与他的相识和相处，不由得热血沸腾、百感交集。能够与他相识并做他的属下真是快哉、乐哉！得悉先生的谢世可谓痛哉、哀哉！

董先生20世纪50年代初毕业于北京林学院（北京林业大学的前身），属我校的前几届毕业生之一，留校工作五十多年来，在森林资源调查、林业航空测量、森林经营管理、林业信息管理、森林资源资产化经营、林业可持续发展及森林资源可持续经营等方面进行了深入的研究并做了大量的工作，无论是在本科教学、研究生培养、科学研究、进修人才培训，以及指导林业生产实践的各个方面都是功绩显赫，受到了广大学生、学员、同行、同事以及相关领导的好评，并取得了多个省部级的优秀奖励，成为早期的"有突出贡献的中青年专家"并享受"政府特殊津贴"，为我国的林业事业做出了巨大的贡献。在他的身上有许多个第一，在森林资源调查中于20世纪50年代首先引入抽样调查与航片判读技术，在80年代初期首先将微型计算机应用引入到森林资源统计的工作中，并随后建立了全国第一个林业信息管理专业，为我国的林业信息化奠定了良好的基础，在90年代就抓住时机率先进行森林资源可持续经营方面的研究工作并取得了可喜的成果。如此种种，只是他做的小部分典型工作，很难用几句话来描述他对工作的热忱、他那旺盛的精力、敏锐的思维、和蔼可亲的性格，更重要的是他对林业工作的那份执著，熟悉他的人（无论是他的老师、同事或是学生）都知道，为了工作，他不知道有多少个晚上在办公室里通宵达旦、连续有多少个日子没有回家（董先生家住天坛公园附近）。后为了方便，他干脆就把家里的行李搬来，夜里在办公桌上睡觉，早上卷起行李放在办公桌下后继续工作，类似这样的事数不胜数，所以人们送他外号是工作上的"拼命三郎"。

董先生是我"信息管理与信息系统"（1986年初创时的名字为"林业信息管理"，后教育部将各校相关专业合并统一更改为现名）专业的创始人和缔造者，虽然专业随着学校的总体改革部署不断地调整隶属于不同的学院之间（经济管理学院、资源与环境学院、基础科学与信息工程学院、信息学院等），但董先生从未间断过对此专业的发展与建设的关注，无论是在岗、退休，还是养病期间。

近年来董先生的身体状况由于劳累过度而不适，在万般无奈的状况下他老人家才住院养病，我们信息教研室的老师每个学期都会抽时间前去医院或家里慰问探望。为了能让他安心养病，大家都不愿意和他交流工作上的状况以免他受累，可是，他是个与常人不一样的人，他和我们谈论的话题总是淡化他的病情而重点谈工作上的事，比如：他的想法、打算，国家林业局的政策、国家对林业方针、我国森林资源管理的可持续发展之路，我们应该怎么办等等。今年4月16日，我们信息学院筹办了“信息学院建院10周年暨信息专业成立25周年”庆典活动，活动前夕（4月15日）受信息学院领导的委托，我和郭小平书记前去看望养病在家的董先生，那时的他已经又被新的病魔折腾的不能好好休息，但他老人家依然与我们谈笑风生，并即兴为我们的“庆典”写下了“……时代需要我们分秒必争，为开拓无限信息资源努力，信息学院全体师生员工加油”的“寄语”。对于这位年近8旬的老人——我的老师，可谓之“活到老、学到老、想到老”，永远把心放在了他挚爱的林业事业上，我作为他的学生，深深为他的这种“春蚕到死丝方尽”的精神所折服。他是一个“乐林业工作而不疲”的真正“林家铺子”的林人，是一个永不放弃事业的人，也是一个值得我们永远学习和怀念的人。

恩师您放心！我们会沿着您开创的森林可持续经营、林业信息化的道路一直走下去……

怀念董乃钧先生

宋新民
（北京林业大学）

董乃钧教授年长我四岁，是我大学的老师，也是我的同事。我们亲密相处四十多年，他不幸病逝，我感到万分悲痛，心情久久难以平静。

董先生是北林大知名教授，国家重点学科森林林经理学科的学术带头人。长期以来，他作为我们这个团队的中坚，团结带领大家为学科的建设和发展做出了重大贡献。在几十年的教学与科研工作中，董先生曾获得很多次表彰和奖项 ，但他却从不向人表白、炫耀这些。我记得 1978 年恢复职称评定，当时我校还在云南，董先生借调到资源司工作，我写信叫他回昆明来办理申请副教授事宜，他回信称，一是工作脱不开，二是自己成果不多，名额有限，让给别人吧！我知道他在“十年浩劫”中以开门办学组、教改小分队、林调生等署名写过不少报告和论文，当我代他写了简单的申报后，他说那些文章都没有我的名呀！大家知道文革中有几个用实名写文章、著说的。

他参与主持的“全国森林资源连续清查技术体系研建”项目，曾获林业部科技进步一等奖。1989 年获得国家科技进步二等奖，上报材料前他曾对我说：“干实际工作最多、最累的是资源司的同志们，我只是动动嘴，出出主意。”他提出把两位处长排名提到他前面去。1980 年代我校造林学科主持的北方苗木调查方法研究项目，获林业部科技进步奖，在上报材料时，我曾听其对项目主持人说：这个课题是造林学科的，你们教研组还有好几位年轻人呢！我就算了吧！

同样，1997 年我组申报的“森林经理学科建设与改造 30 年”课题，获国家教学成果一等奖，填报申请书时，我把董先生列首位，上报时他把我改到第一位，并诚恳地跟我说：“你是报告的主笔人，别说了，就这么定了。”后来分奖金时，我们遵照董先生提出的：排上名的少分些，要照顾到退休和未排名的同志办了。董先生一生淡泊名利，为他人着想的高尚品德广为流传。这么多年，他主持与参加的多项获奖项目中，他总是担子挑重的，荣誉不计较，我们都敬佩称“董老师是个给别人做嫁衣的人”。

董老师艰苦朴素，乐于助人，是有名的“有求必应”的好人。记得 80 年代，林大刚从云南搬回北京，大家最困难的是无住处。董老师三代人一直住在天坛他爱人分的五层楼上两间房内。后来学校看他太累，分给他一间房子。董老师看到我们院里有位新来老师无处安家，他这院长心不安，就将房子让给这位老师住。他仍然坚持从天坛到北林早出晚归，两头不见太阳来回奔波，老师们都关切的劝说：“董老师要注意呀！最近又瘦了！”他只是微微一笑说：谢谢！

1996 年深秋，我同他一道去广东韶关地区参加学术会，返京的路上，他在农贸市场买了一件棉背心，在宾馆，大家看了都说好看，当时同去参加会议的黑龙江人王哲华及夫人李女士试穿后爱不释手，时值初冬，回东北天冷了，很想买一件，但是时间来不及，董老师看出李女士的心思，就主动把背心送给她了，并挽具递过来的钱，李女士感动的说：“我与董教授初次见面，真不好意思。”

还有一次，董老师陪同德国陪兹教授参观我们的实验室，正巧我刚给研究生上完课休息，外宾从留在黑板上那些计算公式得知我是在给学生讲抽样调查技术课，在交流中，他送我一本西欧几个国家森林调查方法的小册子，董老师把我介绍给外宾时说我刚出版了一本《抽样技术》一书，佩尔兹教授说他那里有大陆和台湾去的研究生可以翻译给他看，希望得到一本。因为我手头没多余的新书，用的这本太脏了，一时我不知所措，当时董老师借故离开几分钟后拿来一本《抽样技术》书，叫我签名后赠给外宾。使我摆脱了无法言说的尴尬。原来是董老师回到他办公室，将他那本较新的书用涂改液涂改后救急的。董老师这种对人热情，善解人意，为他人着想的品德给周围的同事们留下难以忘却的怀念。

董乃钧教授的一生是教书育人的一生，是奉献多索取少的一生，是执著追求献身森林经理事业的一生。今天我们在这里集会，成立董乃钧林大奖励基金成立大会，是对他的最好纪念。

董老师！你放心走吧，后来的同事与你的弟子们会把我们的学科搞得更好！